The *Real*

UNFRIENDLY SKIES

Saga of Corruption

Rodney Stich
Air Safety Activist

Library of Congress Catalog Card Number 90-80467

Stich, Rodney
        The Unfriendly Skies—Saga of Corruption

        Includes index.

1. Aeronautics, Commercial—Accidents.
2. Airlines—Accidents.
3. Government—corruption.

Human Factors I. Title

Soft Cover ISBN: 0-932438-02-4
Hard Cover ISBN: 0-932438-03-2

Manufactured in the United States of America

Order from:
Diablo Western Press, Inc.
P.O. Box 10587, Reno, Nevada 89501

or:
Diablo Western Press, Inc.
P.O. Box 5, Alamo, California 94507

Telephone orders direct:
        (outside of California) 1-800-247-7389 (AIRSFTY)
        (inside of California) 415-831-0251

Third updated printing.

UNFRIENDLY SKIES

CONTENTS

Introduction

Dedication

PART ONE—Before Deregulation

Chapters

PART TWO—After deregulation

PART THREE—Not So Invisible Government

INTRODUCTION

This book is a saga of graft, corruption and government misconduct, juxtapositioned with the deaths of little children and others, who were no match for the government-funded tactics revealed in these pages.

The author brings the reader behind the scenes, as an insider, describing sordid activities never revealed by any other source. The book describes several decades of air safety corruption, and branches out into other segments of government misconduct that made it all possible.

Every form of government misconduct found in the savings and loan, HUD, Abscam, Congressional, Defense Department, and other scandals, exists in the aviation environment. The only difference is in the *form* of payment extracted from the public.

This saga of corruption is heavily documented. It brings together the contents of administrative proceedings, judicial actions, government documents, the author's experiences as a government air safety investigator, airline and military pilot, and his evaluation of these happenings.

The successful coverup of the outrages described within these pages is a tribute to the manipulation or coverup of the news by the news media. Without their duplicity of silence, many of the air tragedies could not have happened. Many who died would be alive today.

What happened to those described within these pages could have happened to you or someone you love or rely upon. What will happen to others in the future from this same misconduct may happen to you or those you care for.

Some of the pictures and descriptions are shocking. They are included to make the public more aware of the pain, suffering, and deaths arising from the actions described within these pages.

DEDICATION

This book is dedicated to the memory of the many who have suffered so greatly in airline tragedies that should never have happened. It is dedicated to those left behind, who suffer forever the loss of loved ones, and who undergo financial deprivation that often follows air tragedies. And its dedicated to those who have yet to pay the price for the misconduct described within these pages.

It is dedicated to Edith Armstrong, who died on May 4, 1989. Her part in helping prevent further air disasters is described under the title, *The Impostors*. Among her last words, as she supported me during the latest round of attacks, were to continue the fight.

This book is also dedicated to Stan Nicola, the associate editor of *Professional Pilot* magazine who encouraged me to continue my fight to expose the government corruption that made this book necessary. I also lost this gallant ally. His small plane crashed on May 23, 1987, into the forests within 30 miles of his Nashua, New Hampshire home.

The loss of these two friends reduced the small number of loyal friends that supported me during this long battle. I also dedicate this book to Graydon Milton of Oakland, California who, despite his age—in the eighties—came to my aid when powerful forces sought to destroy me.

PART ONE

BEFORE DEREGULATION

CHAPTER ONE

Pillar Of Fire

This saga of corruption starts with one of the world's worst air disasters that occurred during the Christmas season, December 16, 1960. In some ways it is still the most brutal air disaster ever to occur in the United States or anywhere.

United Airlines Flight 826, a DC-8, departed Chicago's O'Hare Airport on a non-stop flight to New York City's Idlewild Airport (since renamed John F. Kennedy Airport). Taking off from Cleveland Airport, and also heading for New York City, but landing at La Guardia Airport, was TWA Flight 266, a triple-tail Constellation.

One of United's two navigation receivers was inoperative, and known to be so by the crew. Good judgment dictated that the crew notify air traffic control of its inoperative receiver so as to receive extra radar assistance. United did not do this. ATC cleared Flight 826 to Preston Intersection, formed by the crossing of two radials from nearby VOR navigational radios. Normally, two receivers are used to determine the holding fix, but the position can be determined by quick changing of the single remaining receiver. In the congested New York City area it was foolhardy not to request radar assistance to determine the holding fix location. Further, a slower approach speed than normal was dictated by the loss of the second navigational receiver.

Instead of arriving at the low-altitude terminal area holding pattern at approach speeds of approximately 200 knots, United

Flight 826 approached it at almost 500 miles per hour. At this speed the aircraft could not remain within the protected airspace of its assigned holding pattern even if the crew could accurately determine their holding position.

TWA was approaching its New York City destination at approximately the same time that United 826 shot through its holding fix. Both planes were at 5,000 feet. The La Guardia air traffic controller cleared TWA for an ILS[1] instrument approach to runway 04, landing to the northeast. Drizzle and low-level clouds covered the New York City area.

Following the TWA blip on his radar screen, the La Guardia controller directed TWA toward the narrow ILS course that guided planes to the La Guardia runway. Unknown traffic suddenly appeared on the radar screen moving rapidly toward TWA, its altitude unknown. In 1960 the aircraft did not have altitude encoding transponders and the radar did not show the other aircraft's altitude. Because of the high speed of the suddenly appearing traffic, the controller assumed the traffic was at a higher cruising altitude rather than the low approach airspace. But the controller routinely alerted TWA to the converging traffic, "Traffic at two-thirty, six miles, northeast bound."

THE MISSING RADAR BLIP

TWA was in the clouds and could not see the reported traffic. Again the controller advised TWA, "That appears to be jet traffic off your right now, three o'clock at one mile, northeast bound." United, slowing down but still traveling at almost six miles per minute, covered this one-mile separation in seconds. At 10:23 a.m. the two radar blips merged, indicating to the radar controller that the flight paths crossed, presumably at different altitudes. But that was not to be.

THE SOUND OF AN OPEN MIKE

The sound of an open microphone pierced the air, as if an aircraft was trying to make a radio transmission. The La Guardia controller give TWA a heading change to intercept the final ILS approach course. TWA didn't answer. Again, the controller radioed, "Transworld 266, turn further left one zero zero." Again the call went unanswered.

The controller suddenly realized what had probably happened. He quickly contacted Idlewild approach control to determine if one of their planes was missing. It was soon obvious that the lost traffic was United's DC-8. There were

---

[1] Instrument Landing System precision approach that provides lateral direction and a glide path to the runway.

now two large airliners missing over the New York City area, with ominous signs that they had collided.

One of the passengers on United Flight 826 was Stephen Baltz, a young boy traveling by himself. As he looked down at the white mantel of snow covering New York City the plane shook with a loud thud as the collision occurred. One of United's jet engines rammed into TWA at nearly 400 miles per hour, splitting open TWA's fuselage, and scooping out of the TWA cabin a woman passenger. Slowly she was fed into the knife-like fan blades at the front of the jet engine.

The airport control tower operator at Miller Army Airfield on Staten Island watched in horror as three large sections of the TWA plane hurled through the base of the overcast, trailing flames and smoke. Just before hitting the ground, two of the engines exploded, causing the wings to rip from the fuselage, followed by the separating tail section.

As the pieces rained down upon them, two workers loading a furniture truck on Hyland Boulevard dashed inside for protection. The pieces fell like shrapnel. One later recalled, "I prayed that it would be over soon." Parts of the wreckage narrowly missed a community of homes, tall apartment buildings and public schools, containing thousands of people. It was pure luck that the death toll did not include them. The falling fuselage and wing sections hit the ground with an ominous heavy thud. The impact ejected more passengers onto the snow-covered ground, turning the snow bright red.

The open spaces of Staten Island permitted an unobstructed view of this drama, and alerted rescue vehicles who rushed toward the expected crash site. Witnesses on the ground stared in shock at TWA's spiraling descent. People watched in horror as the plane ejected helpless passengers outward.

As the rear half of the TWA fuselage plunged toward them, a fear-stricken mother grabbed her six-year-old daughter and ran for her life. The huge fuselage section struck the ground fifty feet away, splitting open like a lobster shell, and ejecting more people into the snow.

"I thought it was a bombing!"

Sitting in his third floor apartment on Staten Island, a Minister felt the earth shake as the first part of the TWA plane hit nearby. "I thought it was a bombing," he later said. "I saw the plane fall in flames and smoke, and a black object fell in front of my home. It looked as though the plane was going to fall on the housing development, but it missed."

Washing windows in her Staten Island home, one woman saw United on a collision course with TWA, and then saw the crash itself. She later exclaimed, "I saw what I believe to be the right wing of the other plane fall. It spiraled down at an angle toward Hyland Boulevard. I saw the fuselage was on fire."

"It went down in a terrible way."

"Listen to the thunder," exclaimed one woman to her niece. She later explained, "I rushed to the window and I saw this *terrible* ball of fire. It was huge, and it must have been a mile off." She continued, "I watched, and it was terrible. We could see now it was a plane. It seemed to fall a few feet and there was another huge burst of flame. And then the plane went down. It went down in a terrible way." She recalled, "One wing gone, it turned over and over very slowly. You could watch it. All the way it was always red from the flames."

Sitting in his radio car, a Staten Island dispatcher for the Transit Authority buses suddenly heard a loud noise, "like a jet breaking the sound barrier." Looking up, he saw a sight he would remember forever. He described it as "parts of bodies falling from the plane." Quickly starting his car, the dispatcher picked up a nearby foot patrolman and the two of them sped toward Miller Field where the wreckage was expected to crash. By radio they alerted the bus terminal dispatcher, who in turn notified police.

They stopped several times on their way to Miller Field, gathering bloody human remains that had fallen from the spiraling plane. At the crash scene, they placed more human remains in the radio car. Impaled on a nearby tree was a woman, still bleeding.

"I prayed that it would be over soon."

At a nearby shopping center, two brothers, Peter and Gerard Paul, threw down their purchases, and ran to the crash scene, vaulting a ten foot cyclone fence. The first to arrive, the bloodied and dismembered bodies overwhelmed their comprehension. Pulling out his knife, Peter cut the safety belts from three people—two men and a woman—who moaned in pain. Arriving soldiers from nearby Miller Field helped remove these three people who barely clung to life by a thread. They placed two of them into a Coast Guard helicopter that flew the painfully injured men to the New Dorp United States Public Health Hospital. Others drove the woman to the hospital by car. The only one of the three to reach the hospital alive died a few hours later.

"It was *very* quiet inside the aircraft," they later said, "except for occasional moaning." Peter stated, "I prayed that it would be over soon."

Fire apparatus reaching the crash scene cut through the same wire fence that the Paul brothers had earlier vaulted. They directed water hoses to the now fiercely-burning forward section where the passengers fared even worse than those in the separated rear section. Arriving rescuers reeled at the sight of dismembered and decapitated bodies.

Later, after nothing more could be done for the victims, a solemn crowd gathered on the far side of the nearby cyclone fence. They stood quiet and looked sad, shocked by the great tragedy. They had difficulty comprehending the magnitude of the horror. Yellow insulation from the doomed TWA plane interlaced the bare branches above their heads, festooned as if in celebration for Christmas.

"God brought that plane in," said Colonel E. Howan, Commander of Miller Army field, as he stood at the crash scene. He noted that the falling aircraft sections miraculously missed many homes and apartment buildings. United's jet engine, torn from the wing by the initial impact, buried itself in the frozen ground of an empty playground. Still inside the engine were the remains of the ingested passenger.

ELSEWHERE, THE HORROR CONTINUED

It was all over for the passengers and crew of TWA Flight 266. But the horror continued for those on United Flight 826. After ramming TWA, and losing one of its engines, Flight 826 proceeded for eight miles in a northeasterly direction, losing altitude as it descended toward the heavily congested Brooklyn section of New York City.

The only noise on Brooklyn's Sterling Place was the occasional sloshing sound of a car going through the snow. But this shortly changed. Thousands of people on the ground in New York City watched the DC-8 streaking toward the densely populated Park Slope residential and business section. Flight 826 swept in low, and just before impact, threatened to crash into St. Augustine parochial school, containing over a thousand children.

Two men shoveling snow at the intersection of Sterling Place and Seventh Avenue suddenly heard the whine of jet engines. They looked up and saw the DC-8 coming straight at them.

A Brooklyn teacher, James Barnes, noticed a student suddenly turn pale. Barnes looked in the direction the student was staring, and saw the cause of the fright. The DC-8, not over a thousand yards away, was descending straight for the school. Suddenly the plane banked to the right, barely missing the school.

At over 200 miles per hour United's right wing rammed into a brownstone apartment building, spinning the jet's nose section directly into the Pillar of Fire Church. The three-story building instantly disintegrated, erupting into a fiery inferno. The crumbling church buried Wallace Lewis, the caretaker, in the rubble.

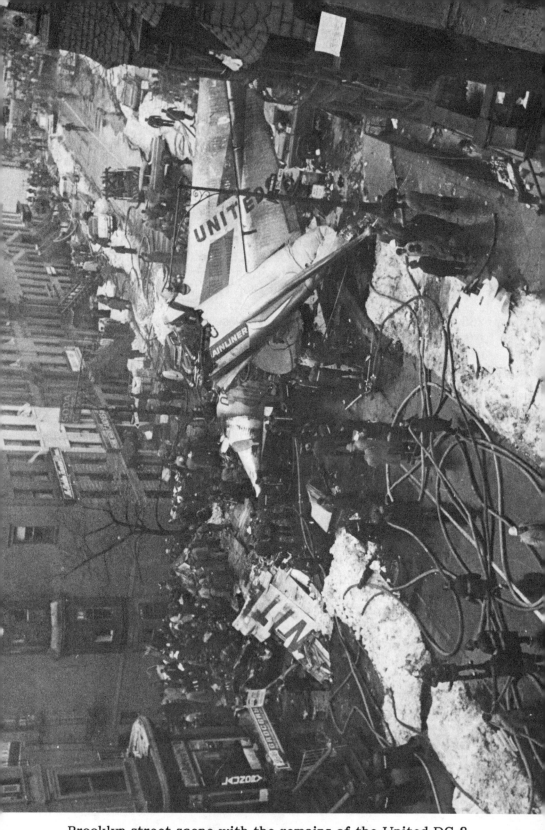

Brooklyn street scene with the remains of the United DC-8.

The DC-8 tail section crashed into the intersection in front of a small grocery store. A blazing section of the left wing thrust itself into a nearby four-story apartment building, its tip protruding grotesquely through the shattered roof.

A large section of the cabin, with passengers trapped inside, slammed against McCaddin's Funeral home. Immediately before the crash, the McCaddin's were having mid-morning coffee in their apartment over the funeral home. Suddenly, Mrs. McCaddin exclaimed, "My goodness, that plane sounds awfully low!"

Just then the entire building shook, as if hit by a bomb. Flames leaped into the air outside the broken windows. Grabbing their baby, the McCaddin family ran for their lives.

THE PITIFUL SOUND OF THE DYING

From inside the DC-8 wreckage came the pitiful, tortured screams of the dying crew and passengers. A bystander later described the cries as "the worst sound I ever heard." The first to arrive on the crash scene could see and hear the passengers screaming in pain. They could offer no help. Trapped and hopelessly beyond aid, those inside the wreckage felt the terrible heat and hopelessness of their final moments.

A young boy, injured by falling debris, ran from the crash scene, blood streaming down his face. He shouted as he ran past a flower shop, "Oh, those people are burning to death." His eyes showed the horror he had just seen. A man grabbed the boy and shook him, but the boy pulled away and ran. A woman, unaware of the tragedy that had just occurred, stated, "He must be out of his mind."

"Am I going to die?"

Not everyone perished on Flight 826. The owner of a small grocery store, stacking milk containers in the rear of the store when the crash happened, ran to the front door, pulled it open, and saw the astonishing pandemonium only a few feet away. Suddenly, he saw a little figure crawling from the burning tail section.

His clothes on fire, covered with blood, and bleeding from his nose and mouth, Stephen Baltz crawled slowly and painfully from under the flaming wreckage. Two patrolmen arrived on the scene as Stephen crawled on the ground. They quickly rolled Stephen in the snow to extinguish his burning clothes. After extinguishing the flames, a woman in a leopard coat held an umbrella over Stephen to protect him from the light rain. It was a sad scene.

"Am I going to die?" Stephen asked, looking up, and crying in pain. Stephen reached out for help. His lips quivered as he cried, "Mommy, Daddy..."

Completing his services at nearby St. John's Episcopal Church, Reverend Harry Sterling rushed outside as a police officer ran up and asked him to give absolution to Stephen. Together they rushed to the flaming wreckage, finding Stephen still conscious. The smell of burning flesh worsened the horror.

"Mother ... she's waiting for me."

The flames burned Stephen's face, hair, eyelashes, and lungs. He kept holding up his right arm, showing his bleeding hand. Rushed by police car to nearby Methodist Hospital, Stephen lay in the arms of Mrs. Dorothy Fletcher, Chief of the Brooklyn Volunteers for Civil Defense. Just before lapsing into unconsciousness Stephen sobbed, "Mother...she's waiting for me." It was only by chance that Stephen had been on this United jet. Stephen was to have flown two days earlier with his mother and younger sister, Randee.

THE FAMILIAR TELLTALE SIGNS OF TRAGEDY

At the airport terminal, families and friends, unaware of the crash, became more anxious every time the airline personnel changed the aircraft's expected arrival time. After several such delays, ticket agents removed the flight's listing from the flight board, providing the first hint of the disaster, although the public didn't recognize the omen at the time.

Finally, a United Airlines employee, holding back tears, announced that United 826 would not arrive; it had crashed. Cries and screams erupted. In the background gala Christmas music sounded through the terminal.

"What am I going to do, what am I going to do?", sobbed one young woman, waiting for her husband who would never arrive. Others tried to comfort her, saying that he was still alive. "No, no, there's only one survivor," she cried, a fact she learned from news reports of the tragedy on TV.

Throughout New York City sirens pierced the air, as over fifty pieces of emergency equipment rushed to the disaster scene. It was probably the worst disaster the nation's largest city had ever experienced.

Wallace Lewis, caretaker of the nearby Pillar of Fire Church, had not purchased a ticket for a flight in the friendly skies of United, but he was affected by United's "friendly skies." He died in the destroyed church.

"An act of God."

Fire Commissioner Cavanaugh said it was "an act of God that the major impact of the crash had been on the vacant church rather than on any of the surrounding buildings heavily occupied with tenants."

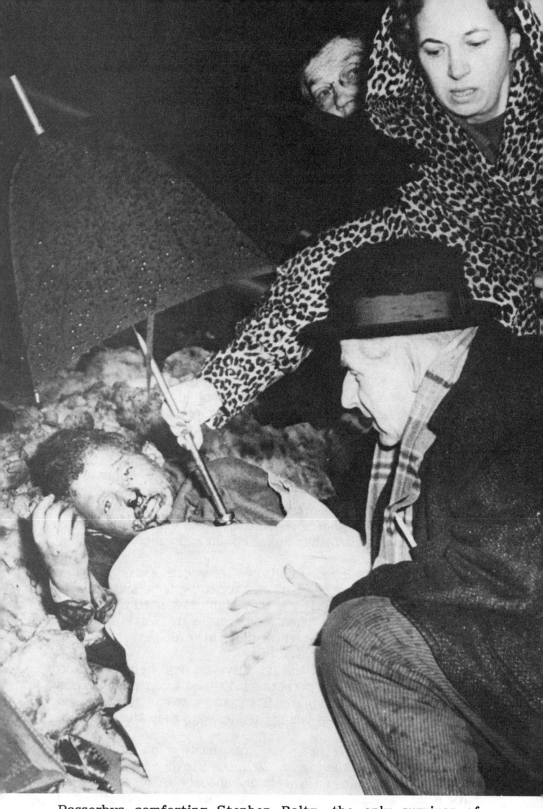

Passerbys comforting Stephen Baltz, the only survivor of United Flight 826.

THIRTEEN TONS OF HUMAN REMAINS

The crash caused dismemberment or cremation of twenty-six thousand pounds of humanity. Two hours after the initial crash, the Brooklyn fire department declared the fire under control. The gruesome task of removing and identifying the dead then began.

Lining the streets and watching from apartment windows, quiet and visibly shaken onlookers watched the grim procession of stretchers carrying away blackened, mutilated and bloodied bodies. City officials declared an unprecedented city-wide emergency by sounding the emergency disaster signal.

The only living survivor of those last desperate minutes described the experience from his hospital bed. Stephen described the beauty of the snow-covered city as the DC-8 descended. He described the fear he felt as the plane plunged toward the ground. Stephen added, "That's all I remember until I woke up here."

Stephen's father rushed from Chicago by plane to reach his badly injured son. Landing shortly after dark, a police escort rushed him to the hospital. Later, Mr. Baltz said, "My son tried to smile but could not." Medication covered Stephen's badly swollen face. The crash broke Stephen's left leg, and the ensuing fire inflicted burns on a major portion of his body. Stephen was in critical condition, and Doctors expressed fear that searing of his lung tissues had occurred.

Stephen's mother and father stayed in a room at the hospital so they could be close to their son. The morning after the tragedy, Stephen felt well enough to ask his father for a book, and permission to watch television. Chances for his survival improved. Shortly before Stephen lapsed back into unconsciousness, his father promised him a portable television set for Christmas.

Thousands of telephone calls and telegrams poured into the hospital from all over the nation, expressing hope and prayers for Stephen's recovery. It was only eight days until Christmas. It would be cruel if Stephen didn't make it. Stevie suffered terribly, but with courage, throughout his ordeal.

STEVIE JOINS THE OTHERS

The nation's prayers, the intensive medical help, could do only so much. Stephen's parents maintained a constant vigil at his bedside. Whatever plans Stephen's parents had for his future, whatever dreams young Stephen had, they all ended. He died.

A heartbroken father, his eyes misting and his voice breaking, stated to the press: "Well, our Stevie passed away at one p.m. His mother and I are tremendously saddened. But we have had so many fine people in the world send sympathy and prayers and we want to thank them. Stevie tried hard; tried awfully hard. He was a wonderful boy, not because he was my son, but because he was Stevie."

The hospital staff issued a bulletin: "All could not bring the little boy back from the effects of his severe injuries. He closed his eyes and went to sleep."

The task of identifying the horribly mutilated bodies remained. A Bellvue hospital morgue attendant said, "The bodies are so badly mangled, even worse than those from the Morro Castle.[2] It is the worst I've seen in my thirty-eight years here."

Saddened relatives and friends climbed the fourteen steps leading to Bellvue city morgue from the early morning hours and late into the night. The morgue staff avoided personal identification whenever possible. One attendant said "It's an ordeal we don't like to put people through if we don't have to." But fingerprints and dental charts did not always spare the next-of-kin the tragic ordeal of identifying a loved one.

The human suffering in the disaster, as in others, was indescribable. For some of the friends and relatives, the emotional and financial suffering continued for years afterwards. Financial settlements may wait for years after the crash, and by than the legal costs and the attorney's fees take much of the settlement. Often there is very little money for those who need it most.

THE POLITICS OF ACCIDENT INVESTIGATION

By law, the National Transportation Safety Board[3] (NTSB) investigates airline crashes. In addition to its own investigators, the NTSB is assisted by people from the FAA; aircraft, engine, and accessory manufacturers; from the airline; and from the pilot's union. They have a vested interest in protecting themselves.

Shortly after the NTSB accident investigators arrived on the Brooklyn accident scene they found the aircraft flight data recorder in the rubble of the Pillar of Fire Church. It provided information on the plane's speed, altitude, direction, and time, which was then compared with radio communications and radar information.

It was obvious that the United captain badly mishandled the flight by speeding into a low altitude holding pattern area, compounded by failure to notify air traffic control that one of his navigational radios was inoperative. This was the *direct* cause of the crash. And the NTSB reported it correctly. But

---

[2] The ship that burned off the New Jersey coast in 1934.

[3] At that time it was within the Civil Aeronautic Board and known as the Bureau of Aviation Safety. For convenience, in most cases within these pages they are referred to as the NTSB.

what the NTSB omitted from the report was a scandal that to this day has never been officially released.

The NTSB conducted an investigation of the FAA and the airline crew training records following the crash. However, the FAA records were withheld from the accident report, and for illegal reasons. If the records had been released, they would have exposed the nation's worst air safety scandal as the cause of the nation's worst air disaster.

AIR SAFETY CORRUPTION

FAA inspectors repeatedly complained, and reported before this crash, that the United Airlines training program was dangerously unsatisfactory; that many of the FAA approved company check airmen deprived the crewmembers of legally required training; that weak crewmembers were denied corrective training; that United Airlines falsified air safety records to indicate training was given, when the training was not given.

Similar to today's savings and loan and other government scandals, FAA inspectors who discovered serious fraud relating to violations of the government air safety requirements were blocked from taking corrective actions. Obstructing compliance with the air safety laws were FAA and United Airlines officials, and pressure from members of Congress.

SEQUESTERED AND SHOCKING REPORTS

By law the FAA, through its inspectors, inspects and determines whether the airline meets federal air safety requirements, and determines whether an adequate level of safety exists. The FAA approves company pilots to act in place of the FAA inspectors, and then the inspectors observe a percentage of training and competency checks conducted by these company check airmen. If they don't meet FAA standards, the company check airmen are to be removed from that function. In real life, it was the inspectors who were removed.

FAA inspectors repeatedly reported check airmen at United Airlines engaging in questionable practices, having low standards that reduced the training costs, and deprived the crewmembers of the safeguards that come with a good training program.

FALSIFIED TRAINING RECORDS

Several months before this crash FAA inspectors traveled from the Denver training center to United's maintenance base at San Francisco, to cross-check the aircraft records with the Denver training records. The intent of this unusual cross-check of records was to determine if United officials were falsifying training records and withholding training to the crew members, as the inspectors suspected.

The cross-check revealed that the legally required training and competency checks that required three to three and a half hours to complete when FAA inspectors were present, only required thirty to forty-five minutes when inspectors were not present. Obviously, United check airmen were falsifying the training records, and not providing the flight crews the legally required training. United covered up for this by falsifying the training records. This was very serious, especially now that the same program experienced the world's worst air tragedy.

On October 16, 1960 the inspectors signed an eight-page report prepared by Frank Harrell, describing these findings. That report became an official government document, and should have been the primary evidence in the NTSB investigation of the New York City air disaster. That report, and many similar reports in the FAA files, explained why the DC-8 crew mishandled the aircraft as badly as they did.

That document would have removed the blame for these many deaths from the DC-8 flight crew and placed it where it belonged; management at United Airlines and the FAA, who caused the crew to be denied the legally required training and check of their competency. The report was a block-buster.

CORRECTIVE ACTION—REMOVE THE REPORT!

After that alarming report was filed as a government document, and before the New York City crash occurred, FAA Western Region officials took action. But not what was required. Instead of forcing United Airlines officials to comply with the law, and provide the legally required training, the FAA removed Harrell from his position and transferred him to an undesirable assignment in Puerto Rico. Harrell was an outcast, in an assignment no one wanted, where his DC-8 talents were wasted. In this manner FAA officials sent a message to other FAA inspectors to look the other way, and not report illegal and unsafe practices at United Airlines.

There were many other FAA inspector reports in the FAA files showing unsatisfactory performance throughout the United training program. These other safety irregularities could be expected of any airline that stooped to falsifying training records and depriving the flight crews of this safeguard.

THE NTSB SEQUESTERED THE BLOCK-BUSTER REPORT

The NTSB was required to include the sequestered FAA report, and the many other unfavorable reports relating to United's training program, in the investigation of this crash. It is routine practice to include in NTSB accident reports FAA writings that in any way relate to the training and competency of the crewmembers. Obviously, a report indicating that the airline withheld legally required training from the crewmembers, and then falsified records to cover up, were important evidence showing the underlying cause of the crash.

As the NTSB investigation came to a close, the NTSB investigators prepared a report and gave it to the NTSB Board members, political appointees who issue the official cause of the crash. The official report withheld the scandalous findings, and constituted a falsification of the government accident report into what was at that time and for many years thereafter, the world's worst air disaster in number of people killed.

CONTINUING THE SAME AIR SAFETY FRAUD

The next step was to get rid of FAA inspectors who embarrassed the FAA and NTSB with sensitive reports. The primary FAA inspector responsible for United's DC-8 program was Frank Harrell, whose determination to correct the unlawful and dangerous training program put him in frequent confrontation with United officials who sought to reduce the training costs.

Harrell was also the FAA inspector responsible for the inspection team visit to United's San Francisco maintenance base, which led to the discovery of training record and training falsifications. United officials put pressure upon FAA management to get rid of Harrell, and this was done. The FAA Western Region transferred Harrell to an undesirable job in Puerto Rico, which inspectors associated with their version of Siberia. This move sent a warning to other inspectors not to report safety violations or safety problems at United Airlines.

The coverup continued the conditions that made the crash possible. Other crashes, and other deaths, naturally followed, making the FAA and NTSB coverup contributory causes to the tragedies. These will be explained in subsequent pages.

UNION RESPONSE

The United training program irregularities were obviously known to the pilots, and surely to the pilots' union, Air Line Pilots Association (ALPA). The union made no attempt to exonerate the crew of Flight 826, which they could have done by exposing the training program misconduct that preceded the crash. Instead, ALPA claimed that the crash was the fault of air traffic control, implying that the controllers on the ground should have been able to halt the aircraft in the sky like a traffic cop.

WARNINGS TWO DAYS BEFORE THE CRASH

Ironically, two days before this crash the head of the Federal Aviation Agency, Air Force General E.R. Quesada, testified before the House Commerce Subcommittee on airline safety. Quesada identified the obstacles and roadblocks confronting aviation safety. He identified pressure groups, and their tactics. He accused the Air Line Pilots Association (ALPA) and the Aircraft Owners and Pilots Association (AOPA) of interfering with aviation safety. *Aviation Week & Space Technology* reported his testimony:

Quesada Blasts AOPA and ALPA during FAA report to Congress—Washington—The Federal Aviation Agency Administrator E.R. Quesada accused Aircraft Owners and Pilots Assn. and Air Line Pilots Assn., last week of attempting to undermine Federal Aviation Agency's safety rules and enforcement during a farewell appearance during a House Commerce Subcommittee report on FAA's two-year existence. In his two hour, 47 page testimony, Quesada told the sub-committee that when he became Administrator of the newly created agency on Nov. 1, 1958, "I was by no means naive as to the past history of the AOPA as a self-serving group. But I must admit I was not fully prepared for the intensity of their invective or for the imaginative and sometimes devious methods they employ.

Declaring that he refused to allow the pressure groups to intimidate him or FAA inspectors, Quesada presented a case-by-case list of AOPA and ALPA attacks on government safety activities. He urged the subcommittee to insist on effective administration of the new government air safety agency.

FAA Administrators come and go, and Quesada probably did not know the bureaucratic corruption that existed deep within the FAA (which was especially bad in the FAA Western Region). Although United's executive offices were in Chicago, and the FAA office at Chicago would have been the one holding safety responsibilities for United, the certificate was held by the Los Angeles FAA Regional Office, which had a cozy relationship with United officials.

The public never learned the true cause of the crash. If it had become public knowledge, the law suits against United Airlines would have included punitive damages that were not covered by insurance. Further, the FAA would be implicated in the wrongful acts, and itself became a culpable party in this tragedy and the many deaths.

Law suits were filed against United Airlines, TWA, and the FAA, but without any of the plaintiffs knowing the truth behind the crash. The fuzzy argument for suing the FAA was that the FAA should have been able to stop the United DC-8 in flight. At the time of this crash, government air traffic services were already providing more assistance to pilots than ever before. The air traffic controller on the ground could not stop a plane ignoring its clearance limit, any more than a policeman can stop a truck running through a red light.

The total claims arising as a result of the disaster neared a third of a billion dollars. The *Journal of Air Law and Commerce* stated "371 cases amounting to 153,000,000 dollars were pending" as a result of this crash. Claims against the United States Government, defended by the Department of Justice, were close to seventy million dollars. The amount would have been much higher if the next of kin knew of the misconduct that removed the word accident from that tragedy. If the public knew what existed behind the scenes they could have sued United Airlines and the FAA for huge damages, including punitive damages. Because of the fraud, even today, United and the FAA could be sued as the statute of limitations does not start to run until evidence of the fraud is known to those with a claim.

Outspoken FAA Administrator Pete Quesada issued a statement based upon the evidence shown by the DC-8 flight recorder and other data. He either did not know of the internal FAA misconduct (could this possibly be?) or he deliberately covered up. But he did warn that unless the FAA and the airlines paid greater attention to basic safety requirements, the tragedies would continue.

United management, and the Air Line Pilots Association, each had an ax to grind against Quesada. Neither took kindly to Quesada's requirement that the crews meet the stiffer training and competency standards than Quesada initiated. Even though this air tragedy showed the importance of training, United and ALPA blamed Quesada for the crash.

Despite Quesada's warnings, the Chairman of the Senate Aviation Subcommittee, Senator Mike Monroney of Oklahoma, the recipient of campaign funds from both groups, condemned Quesada's control of the FAA, and eulogized the very groups that shared blame in the crash. The respected trade magazine, *Aviation Week*, wrote:

Monroney Increasingly Critical of FAA. Sen. A.S. Mike Monroney (D-Okla) made it clear last week that he intends to keep a closer, more critical eye on the Federal Aviation Agency as his Aviation Subcommittee continued its investigations of air safety. He made it clear that he has some misgivings about the uncritical support he gave the agency during its first two years and that he intends to keep FAA operations under close surveillance. Commending ALPA on its testimony...Sen. Monroney again raised the issue of whether FAA has exerted its full powers to promote air safety, and commented, "This is not a very good record. I don't think we're doing a good job."

POLITICAL FRIENDS
Monroney reportedly received healthy financial contributions from ALPA and other union and corporate interests. Under

the direction and insistence of Attorney General Robert
Kennedy, the United States Department of Justice acted to
relieve United of considerable financial responsibility for the
crash. This caused the public to assume a greater portion of the
financial liability arising out of the air disaster.

A *World News Digest* article stated:

> U.S. to Pay in Air Crash. It was disclosed Oct. 22 that the
> federal government [i.e., the taxpayers] had agreed to pay
> 24% of the damages of verdicts agreed on in law suits
> growing out of the Dec. 16, 1960 collision over N.Y. Harbor
> between a United Air Lines DC-8 jet and a Trans World Air
> Line Lockheed Super-Constellation. (134 people were killed.)
> United Air Lines was to pay 61% of law suit damage costs,
> Trans World 15%. The government was a co-defendant in the
> suits because the planes instrument landing approaches were
> being guided by Federal Aviation agency controllers when
> the collision occurred. A tentative government agreement to
> bear such a share of the damages had been canceled by FAA
> administrator Najeeb E. Halaby, but his decision was over-
> turned by the Justice Department. [See Vol. XXII, P. 256B-
> C3]

In the *Journal of Air Law and Commerce* appeared a description of the government's settlement of the law suits arising out
of the United DC-8 crash into New York City.

> On October 23, 1963, the United States Government,
> specifically the Department of Justice, agreed to pay
> twenty-four per cent of whatever damages are fixed as a
> result of claims and lawsuits arising from the collision of a
> United Air Lines DC-8 jet with a Trans World Airlines Super
> Constellation over Staten Island on December 16, 1960.
> United Air Lines and Trans World Airlines agreed to pay
> sixty-one and fifteen per cent respectively. ... It is interest-
> ing to note that if the case had been tried and lost, the
> Justice Department would have been responsible for paying
> the judgment out of its budget. However, since the case was
> settled, the FAA is liable out of its budget. ...

The article discussed the danger of executive department
settling of claims, benefiting industry, and added: "Would ...
political considerations cause these standards to be stretched
beyond those of even the most liberal court?"

Voicing strong disapproval of this settlement, FAA Administrator, Najeeb Halaby (who followed Pete Quesada when his

outspoken position caused his removal as head of the FAA), lambasted the settlement in an internal FAA communication:

> I opposed this settlement formula at every level in the Department of Justice up to and including the Attorney General. My opposition was based on the fact that the system (referring to the air traffic control system) cannot either then or now reach out and prevent an accident involving an airplane which flies 12 miles past a holding fix at a great rate of speed...The Air Traffic Control system is very much like the system furnished to the highway users. The government authorities furnish the stop signs, the red and green traffic lights and the rules for their use.
>
> The air traffic control system cannot physically prevent a pilot from disregarding a stop signal any more than the highway traffic control system can physically stop a vehicle whose operator disregards a red light and plunges through it. Both systems are dependent on and require responsible compliance on the part of the operator of the vehicle with the traffic rules. When a pilot is told to hold at a particular holding pattern and says he will, it is up to him. The controller on the ground cannot pilot or navigate the airplane for him ... the system in December 1960 was not capable of stopping those who did not comply with directions from the controllers. Neither does it today, despite the many advances made in the past three years. Nor will it in the future, because it is generally agreed that ultimate responsibility must reside with the pilot ... the system was not violator proof nor will it be.

THE CAUSE OF THE GREAT TRAGEDY WAS CONTINUED BY UNITED AND FAA OFFICIALS

After the New York City crash nothing changed at the FAA Denver district office and Los Angeles regional offices. Nothing changed at United Airlines. FAA inspectors continued to complain among themselves about the poor training and standards at United. FAA inspectors continued to observe United check airmen denying legally required training of its crewmembers. FAA officials continued to pressure inspectors not to report safety violations or safety problems. Harrell, the trouble maker was gone, and the other inspectors grumbled among themselves. But they rarely filed any written reports of the safety problems.

NO CHANGES IN THE CAUSES OF THE CRASH

One of the key obstacles faced by FAA inspectors in trying to make the airlines conform to the law and meet adequate safety standards was the chief of the Air Carrier Branch in Los

Angeles, Lynn Ashwell. He was reportedly looking for industry support to become the first career Administrator of the FAA. Most Administrators were political appointees. To obtain industry assistance in reaching his goal, Ashwell reportedly applied pressure to inspectors not to report unsafe or illegal practices. I encountered this problem when I joined the FAA, and got into the thick of the heat when I accepted the safety responsibilities for the United Airlines DC-8 program.

After Harrell was banished to Puerto Rico, middle-management FAA officials offered me the United DC-8 opening at Denver while I was working in Los Angeles with American Airlines, Western, and other carriers. I was already aware of some of the problems on the United assignment. But after I accepted the assignment and moved to Denver, I found the problems worse than I had been told. With the job offer I was advised that the United assignment was very difficult, but that I would get all the backing I needed. The first part of that statement was correct, and the second part was totally incorrect. There was no backing. Everyone ran scared. United was a powerful corporation that controlled the FAA through Congressional pressures. Air disasters weren't going to change management conduct at United Airlines or within the FAA.

UAL WAS CATALYST FOR FAA FORMATION

Ironically, the Federal Aviation Administration was legislated in 1958 by Congress through the Federal Aviation Act of 1958 because of an earlier United crash. Congress passed this legislation after a United DC-7 crashed into a TWA Constellation over the Grand Canyon on June 30, 1956. Both planes plunged into the Grand Canyon with the loss of all 128 people.

The former government air safety agency was the Civil Aeronautic Administration, managed by indifferent bureaucrats and responsive to political and vested interest groups. The Act granted the FAA the authority and responsibility to make and enforce air safety rules. Unfortunately, the Act brought into the new agency the same government bureaucrats from the CAA. Deeply ingrained in the CAA were government politics, favoritism, graft and corruption. These individuals, and this attitude, carried over into the FAA, preventing the conscientious inspector from functioning.

The horror of the New York City disaster faded from the public's mind. The public soon forgot. The government withheld from the public the scandal behind that great air disaster. The coverup made possible, or caused, many air disaster to follow. This book is a saga of scandals starting with the deaths of Stephen Baltz and 133 others.

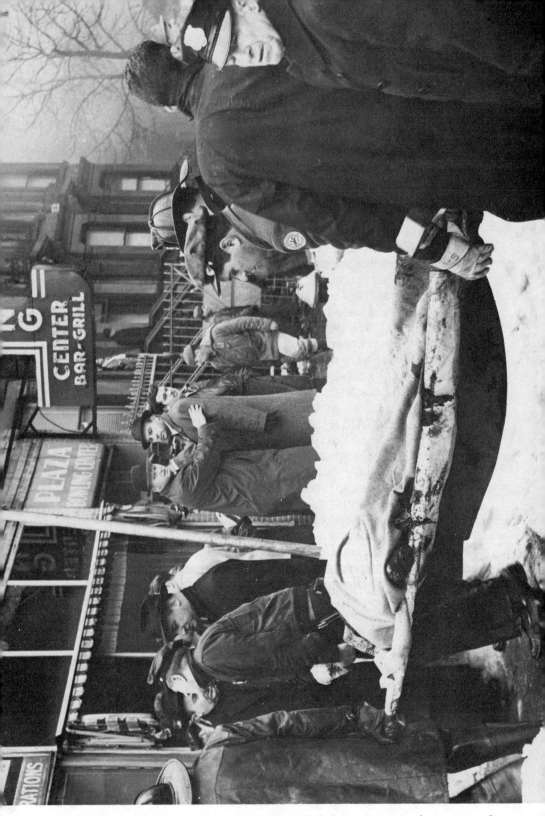

Mutilated body of one of United DC-8 occupants is removed from the New York crash scene.

CHAPTER TWO

Unsurvivable, Survivable Crash

Seven months after the New York City crash, another United Airlines crash occurred, caused by the same training program problems. This one occurred in Denver, where United had its training base that was the root cause of many United crashes. Nothing had changed since the New York City crash. If anything, the defiance by United officials to FAA safety requirements became worse with their success in escaping punishment for earlier tragedies.

The weather at Denver was beautiful. Visibility was over forty miles and the temperature a comfortable and dry 73 degrees. It was great to be alive, truly vacation time in the Rockies. Any sign of what was shortly to mar this beautiful day was not apparent to those lining the visitors platform at Denver's Stapleton airport, waiting for the arrival of United Flight 859 on this July 11, 1961.

The captain of flight 859 was a veteran pilot with thousands of flying hours. If his training had met industry standards during his long career, he should have been a sharp pilot. His copilot was a former captain who had upgraded from the older piston equipment. United Flight 859 departed Omaha, Nebraska, on what should have been a short and uneventful flight; one hour by jet, or one day by car. At 10:12 a.m. United 859 lifted off from Omaha, climbing swiftly toward its cruising altitude. The takeoff weight was almost 100 tons, but relatively light. The gross weight eventually increased to twice that weight as more powerful engines were installed.

As flight 859 climbed through twenty thousand feet and passed overhead Wolback, Nebraska, the captain, who was hand-flying the jet, suddenly felt a brief tapping in the control wheel and felt a slight yaw to the right. Something was wrong.

Simultaneously, the amber warning lights for the powered flight controls illuminated, showing loss of hydraulic pressure to the aircraft's rudder and aileron controls, and indicating hydraulic system failure. The flight controls reverted from hydraulic boost to manual. (Aerodynamic boost now provided power to move the flight controls, and the backup for loss of hydraulic pressure to the horizontal stabilizer was provided by an electric motor.)

The flight engineer moved the hydraulic pumps to the bypass position, in accordance with the hydraulic failure check list. At this point, no emergency *should* have existed. An abnormal condition existed, which any properly trained flight crew could safely handle. An emergency did exist, however; the crew didn't know the aircraft systems well enough to safely handle what started out as a relatively minor problem.

A CROSS SECTION OF AMERICA

The passengers in the cabin were a cross-section of people from all walks of life. They were unaware of the existing serious safety problems, which would shortly affect their lives.

Among the passengers were Mrs. Earl Guyer and her three daughters, eight year old Cynthia, four year old Ann, and one year old June, returning home to Fort Lyon via Denver. Dr. Earl Guyer, clinical psychologist assigned to the Veterans Hospital at Fort Lyon, waited anxiously at the United Airline's arrival gate for his family arriving on United flight 859.

ROUTINE EMERGENCY REACTION

Emergency vehicles with flashing lights sped toward the landing runway as Flight 859 approached, creating apprehension in those waiting for the flight. Dr. Guyer's entire family was on the incoming jet.

United had another problem on top of its training problems. The airline used a reverse procedure that was dangerous, that gave two crewmembers simultaneous directional control of the aircraft, and was a procedure used by no other known airline or military organization in the world.

Upon touchdown an aircraft is normally slowed by the pilot applying reverse engine thrust and brakes, ready to make differential changes in their application if directional control problems develop. Instead of a single pilot handling reverse thrust and braking (plus nose-wheel steering) United *divided* the tasks among both pilots. Directional control problems were frequent. FAA inspectors reported the procedure as unsafe, but FAA officials refused to order the procedure changed.

On that DC-8 model, the reverse system incorporated ejectors which slide out to a fully aft position by hydraulic pressure. It was important that these reverse ejectors remain fully extended and work in harmony with each other, to avoid directional control problems.

That system had a backup high-pressure air bottle to hold the reverse ejectors in the extended position, and replaced the hydraulic pressure in the event of hydraulic failure. That air bottle is activated by a lever on the pilot's pedestal. Its *only* function is in case of hydraulic system failure. But this crew didn't understand its simple function.

During the approach, the crew actuated the switches necessary to extend the reverse ejectors. Residual hydraulic pressure and the flight air loads moved the ejectors into the reverse position. However, the air loads would quickly cease to exist after touchdown, making it urgent that the air bottle be actuated before landing. If this isn't done, the reverse system could be expected to malfunction with dangerous directional control problems.

As the DC-8 continued toward the landing runway, neither the captain, the copilot, or the flight engineer, knew the reverse system well enough to realize the necessity for actuating the high pressure air supply for the reverse system, even though it was on the check list.

Flight 859 touched down on Stapleton's 26-left runway, its speed close to 140 miles per hour. Initially, the landing looked normal, and the emergency appeared to be over. The aircraft settled onto the runway, and proceeded straight ahead for the first thousand feet. But *multiple* problems were working against what should have been an uneventful landing.

Friends and relatives in the terminal watched the landing, and felt relieved as Flight 859 touched down in a seemingly normal manner. Fears subsided, but only for a few seconds.

Also watching the arrival of flight 859 were FAA personnel from the Denver office, and United Airlines training center personnel, all of whom were responsible for what would shortly occur.

Straight ahead for a thousand feet went the DC-8, until the copilot applied reverse thrust. As could be expected, the two reverse ejector systems on the left side of the aircraft slid out of the reverse position. And when they did, those two engines provided *forward thrust*, propelling that wing forward, while the two engines on the opposite wing produced *reverse thrust*, holding that wing back.

Flight 859 veered to the right, toward the terminal building. It left the smooth runway surface and encountered obstacles alongside the runway. Fortunately there wasn't other planes on the parallel taxiways. But not so fortunate was a civil engineer eating his lunch in a panel truck. He froze with fright as the

DC-8 roared toward him, crushing him and dragging him along under the sliding aircraft. He died shortly.

Flames and smoke rose from the accident scene. Less than a thousand yards away stood horrified families and friends who were unable to help.

Except for the civil engineer crushed under the aircraft, the crash was survivable. Everyone on board the aircraft was alive, and should have remained that way. But there were *other* problems repeatedly reported by the FAA inspectors that sealed the fate for many who would never leave the aircraft alive.

PASSENGER EVACUATION WAS POOR

The evacuation of the passengers went poorly. The crew left the aircraft while many passengers were still inside the cabin. In the rear cabin section, an army officer stood up and shouted for everyone to sit down. This was the worst response in any aircraft accident where survival depends on getting out of the aircraft as fast as possible.

Seated in the first class forward cabin section, an Air Force Captain rushed to the front passenger entrance door immediately behind the crew compartment, and opened it. He assisted with passenger evacuation from the forward cabin section. With his help, the evacuation from the forward first class compartment proceeded smoothly. Before long, everyone in this section was safely outside.

DON'T FORGET THOSE IN BACK!

But behind a door separating the first class from the economy section, over 60 passengers crammed into the narrow 15-inch isle, trying to evacuate from the *rear* of the aircraft. Safety was only a short distance away, behind a light swinging door at the center of the cabin. In their confused state, the passengers needed only a crew member leading them through this doorway to safety. It would have been so easy to save everyone. But no crew member provided this life-saving assistance. They were safely outside the aircraft, watching the tragedy unfold. Before long, it was too late.

Among those seated in the crowded cabin were little Jason Gale, Nancy Guyer, and her three frightened and crying daughters. Confused, and without guidance, they sat in their seat waiting for the help that never came. It was a virtual free-for-all, the weakest least likely to survive.

As the flames and smoke spread, passengers screamed, and children cried, as the heat from the flames increased. The passengers had ten minutes after the plane came to a stop to get out of the aircraft. But no one led them to safety. Finally, it was too late to save them. They were cremated alive.

Outside the burning jetliner, fight manager Lee Sloan declared, "No more planes for me, I'm riding the rails!" Lee had been escorting Jason Gale to California. He rushed back and forth shouting, "Where's Jason, where's Jason? Is Jason all right?" Lee failed to take Jason with him as he dashed from the burning jetliner.

The fierce heat caused those outside the aircraft to move away from the burning aircraft. Rescuers abandoned hope for those still inside. It was a terrible sight for Doctor Guyer. Trapped inside the burning aircraft were his wife and three children.

PROCESSION OF BLACKENED BODIES

Grief stricken families and friends watched the sad procession of blackened and charred bodies removed from the aircraft. Rescuers removed entire families in this manner. The young woman from Berkeley would never teach again. Mrs. Shepherd of Davenport would not arrive at the funeral of her friend. Mr. McDonald and his daughter Susan shared their last vacation and a common death. Little Jason was found burned to death, still in his seat, near Nancy Guyer and her three daughters, huddled together in a death embrace. Next morning a grief-stricken Dr. Guyer drove home alone, his world seemingly had come to an end.

Enmity erupted as the massive suffering and death affected people's emotions and reasoning. They directed their anger at the crew, rather than at those primarily to blame; United Airlines and FAA officials, who knew by their misconduct that crashes would continue to occur.

SHOWING OF CONCERN

The FAA Administrator and NTSB accident investigators rushed to the accident scene. Robert Murphy, heading the accident investigation, expressed sympathy for the families of persons killed or injured. I had notified Murphy and others in the NTSB of the serious safety violations and problems prior to this crash. They fraudulently wrote back that the serious crash-causing problems did not affect safety.

After the investigation, the government accident report described the obvious immediate cause of the crash, but omitted the highly sensitive behind-the-scene problems. The report described the crew's obvious lack of knowledge concerning the aircraft systems. This reflected directly upon United's training and check program, and the FAA's oversight of the program. Referring to the lack of knowledge concerning the engine reverse thrust system, the report stated: "There is an emergency provision for extending the ejectors by use of the air bottle system. That system was not used. This allowed Nos. 1 and 2 to develop forward thrust while engines Nos. 3 and 4 were producing reverse thrust during power application."

The Denver crash was directly affected by withholding legally required training that was reported in the October 16, 1960 FAA report. The accident report omitted the many other

FAA reports reporting serious safety problems in United's training program. This relationship was again covered up by the NTSB, constituting a second falsified accident report.

"United has been doing this for years; they won't change now."

Shortly before this Denver crash, an FAA inspector on the same runway sat through a harrowing landing where directional control problems arose from United's reverse procedure. Understandably upset, the inspector complained to FAA management, urging that this dangerous procedure be changed to that in use elsewhere. FAA Supervising Inspector Dave Haley replied, "United has been doing this for years; they won't change now."

The Federal Aviation Act and internal FAA directives gives the FAA the power and the duty to act on safety problems. But the desire by government officials to placate influential airlines and manufacturers, to ingratiate themselves to the companies with whom they often seek post-government employment, pressure from members of Congress, obstructs the government's air safety functions.

United Airlines had other mishaps with the reverse procedure. Before volunteering for the United assignment, I investigated one incident that occurred at a central California airport. I was new with the FAA, unaware of the other FAA reports concerning United's reverse procedure. I identified the reverse procedure as the probable cause of the incident, described it as hazardous, and recommended that the FAA order it stopped.

Eventually, the FAA *requested*, rather than ordered, United to change the reverse procedure. Although the responsibility and authority already existed, a specific Washington directive intended solely for United, known as ODCM 61-26, stated in part:

> We are of the opinion that the pilot who is physically controlling the airplane should operate reverse thrust or reverse propeller pitch thrust, as appropriate, on all landings and aborted takeoffs. This practice permits the pilot in control of the airplane to feel or sense any asymmetric conditions the instant it develops. Corrective action can then be applied by the pilot well before the asymmetrical conditions develops to the point that it is even recognizable by the pilot not in control of the aircraft...the air carrier shall be requested to revise its procedure.

United complied with this request; it didn't cost anything. Changing the training program, however, required increasing training costs, and this was not done.

I transferred to the United Airlines program shortly after the Denver crash. I discovered that the United crews *still* were not trained in the reverse system, even though ignorance of the system had already contributed to the deaths of many people. I tried to correct this lack of knowledge during flight and ground training and checks, but one inspector conveying information on a one-to-one basis could not get the job done.

Several years after the Denver crash, while walking by the crash site with United's Vice-President of flying, Gus Sommermeyer, he voiced objection to my efforts to make the crews aware of the reverse problem. Sommermeyer stated that United did not want me covering any aircraft system or procedure that United did not include in their training program.

This was a typical United attitude. By law it is the FAA's responsibility to make the determination of what flight crews must know. Here was a United Airlines official telling me what I could and could not cover on my FAA safety duties. I reminded Sommermeyer that it is the FAA's function to insure that the crews have a proper knowledge of the aircraft and procedures, and reminded him of the tragedies arising from ignorance in this same area.

Burning United DC-8 at Denver.

This Denver crash became a classic because of the senseless deaths. It was the catalyst for the most strongly worded government safety requirement ever written; a report that equated noncompliance with passenger deaths. The directive required emergency evacuation training of the crew members on a *yearly* basis, and described in detail what had to be done during this training. The intention was to prevent a repeat loss of life as occurred at Denver.

"Passenger survival in actual emergencies is directly related to the adequacy of crew training."
The recent tragic loss of life in survivable air carrier accidents has focused the attention of all responsible segments of government and industry, as well as congress and the general public, on the problems of emergency evacuation, and dramatically underscores the extreme importance of timely and aggressive actions.

It is apparent from these studies that the chance of successful evacuation and passenger survival in actual emergencies is directly related to the adequacy of crew training...The Civil Air Regulations require initial and recurrent training in emergency procedures for all crew members...to the satisfaction of the Administrator. It is necessary that immediate actions be taken to insure that such demonstration is accomplished. I am sure you recognize the urgency of the situation and the extreme importance of the procedure outlined above.

Nine months after the Denver crash, compliance with this important requirement still did not exist. The FAA Washington headquarters issued operations directive number ODCM 62-11, again stressing the need for the airlines to comply with this life-saving requirement.

A number of survivable accidents have occurred in recent years which have resulted in fatalities due to suffocation or burns. In addition, several incidents and accidents have occurred in which evacuation of passengers was impeded to such an extent that only the absence of fire, or success in controlling it, prevented serious injuries or loss of life. It is apparent from these studies and reports that passengers on all types of aircraft can be better prepared for survival by improved crew training and passenger briefing.

Despite the urgency of the training, an FAA internal directive (ODCM 63-4), dated almost a year after the two previous directives, found it again necessary to stress the importance of compliance:

> The subject of emergency crew training has been of serious
> concern to the Administrator and Flight Standards Service
> for many months. Its importance has been stressed and
> emphasized during meetings, discussions and by correspon-
> dence to the field. ...it is *evident that some carriers still
> are not complying.*

There was still another FAA report released three years after
the Denver crash, titled "Human Factors of Emergency Evacuation," it stated in part:

> ...passengers can rapidly evacuate an aircraft...if the crew
> acts efficiently ... Any delays can be fatal ... Crew knowl-
> edge and effective leadership are the most significant
> factors identified in producing successful escapes. The
> larger the number of passengers, the more important is the
> role of the crew ... All of the crew members must [have
> adequate training. Passengers] look to and expect instruc-
> tions and guidance from the professional crew... Efficiency
> of training should enhance confidence and ability to assess
> any emergency and be alert for the unexpected; which
> usually occurs, and take alternate courses of action for a
> successful emergency evacuation.

"Emergency crew training was ignored."
In one FAA report describing the findings of a Washington
inspection team, the continued noncompliance was indicated:

> Prompt corrective actions not taken [by FAA] on deficien-
> cies ... Amendments to comply with the Administrator's
> actions of March and April ... and ODCM 62-11 regarding
> emergency crew training were ignored.

A later document:

> Review of CAB accident report data showed that a large
> number of passengers involved in survivable accidents
> survived the crash impact but died as a result of asphyx-
> iation because they were unable to evacuate the airplane.
> During the period ... there were four survivable air carrier
> accidents with 106 fatalities and 137 survivors. The record
> indicated that additional people could have survived if the
> passengers had been properly briefed or directed in the
> emergency evacuation of the airplane. The Agency believes
> that the conduct of emergency procedures is a problem of

adequate crew training.

Obviously the FAA was remiss in its safety duties, as were the airlines who were not in compliance. The Air Line Pilots Association recognized the importance of emergency evacuation training, and in an *Air Line Pilot* magazine article stated:

> Emergency training for all crewmembers is important and if it were to be summarized in one word, *quality* would be the most outstanding factor which is generally lacking. If all the air carriers adopt high standards in developing their training programs in line with FAA requirements and if everyone worked on these procedures in a completely conscientious manner, there would be considerable improvement in this area.
>
> The need for passenger assistance, which is a life-saving procedure, is a most important aspect which becomes more critical as the passenger density increases. Accordingly, it is incumbent on the aviation industry to provide the air traveling public with a reasonable probability of survival recognizing that properly trained flight attendants are most important to successful evacuation and other emergencies which arise in the cabin.
>
> Throughout the history of commercial aviation are scores of accounts of persons living through the actual crash of an airliner only to die because fire spread too quickly, because they were trapped inside the cabin...and for other needless reasons ... studies of air carrier accidents ... clearly indicate that too many lives have been lost in accidents which could be categorized as survivable.

Noncompliance with the emergency evacuation training requirements by *any* airline would be serious. But noncompliance by United Airlines, who was the catalyst for the training requirement, would be irresponsible. After arriving at United's Denver training center I discovered that United was violating the emergency evacuation training requirement. I reported that instead of accomplishing the legally required training *once a year*, the training was given only every *three years*, and then only in part. I reported that United was falsifying its records to indicate that the training had been given, when in fact it had not been given. FAA officials removed my report from the files, violating federal criminal statutes.

This meant that for a two-year period many of United's crews were in noncompliance with the law in this important area, and thus were flying illegally. Although it wasn't his responsibility, I reminded one of United's instructors who taught this subject that the training did not comply with

Federal requirements, either as to frequency of training or the training covered. My reports made reference to his admission that he knew this, but that he had no choice but to do what he was told. FAA continued to ignore the matter.

CHAPTER THREE

Training

The primary direct cause of airline crashes has been blamed on pilot error, and this is correct, with an important qualifying statement almost always omitted. The pilot error is usually a result of money-saving inadequate training, the risks of which are known to the airlines responsible for the shortcoming, and to the FAA who knows of its existence. One of the easiest ways to reduce costs is to reduce the amount and quality of training, and to accept lower competency standards.

Some airlines have a good training program and high standards, although even their training could be more intensive. Reduced training costs enjoyed by those airlines with low standards become a pattern others must follow to remain price competitive. Pressure to reduce training costs usually comes from company officials who are oblivious to the needs for a safe operation, or who simply accept the calculated risk.

AIRLINE'S RESPONSIBILITIES

In theory and under law it is the air carrier's responsibility to take immediate corrective actions when safety deficiencies are obvious or reported to them by the FAA. The Federal Aviation Act states:

> "...the Administrator shall give full consideration to the duty resting upon air carriers to perform their services with the highest possible degree of safety in the public interest..."

Good training practices and high competency standards increase the probability that crew members will react properly to an abnormality or emergency, rather than just the *possibility* of their doing so.

THE FAA DETERMINES THE LEVEL OF SAFETY

By law, the FAA Washington staff sets standards for the field offices to meet, and the field office enforces them. (Or, at least, is suppose to do so.) The Federal Aviation Act requires the Federal Aviation Administration "to promote safety of flight of civil aircraft in air commerce" by the issuance of standards, rules and regulations. 49 U.S.C. § 1421 (a). Under 49 U.S.C. § 1425(b) the Administrator is also required to employ inspectors who shall *advise and cooperate* with air carriers in the inspection and maintenance of aircraft, aircraft engines, propellers, and appliances used in air transportation. To carry out these mandates the FAA developed the Systems worthiness Analysis Program (SWAP), consisting of Washington-based investigators who go into the field and conduct investigations of airlines that are already under daily inspection by the local FAA offices.

The local FAA district and regional offices approve the training program. The FAA inspectors, trained and experienced in the aircraft, determines whether the government standards are maintained. In an environment where any crewmembers' lack of knowledge can have tragic consequences, a meaningful training program with high standards is essential for adequate safety levels.

The FAA is comprised of numerous departments or fiefdoms. There is the department that establishes the safety standards, and there is the department (Flight Standards) that is suppose to enforce these standards. Just like HUD, FDA, and other government agencies, there are those employees who try to carry out the specifics and the intent of the agency, and there are those who strive to block the efforts.

In a government agency there are many reasons for the breakdown in the checks and balances; the revolving door syndrome (where government employees protect industry's violations of the law with the expectation of high-paying jobs in industry at the conclusion of their government employment); pressures blocking regulatory functions by members of the U.S. House and Senate (who apply pressure on the FAA to go easy on a particular corporation or airline); the internal FAA "pecking order," where the lower FAA personnel benefit by carrying out the wishes of higher FAA management; bribes (either outright money, gifts, or other perks).

NATIONAL TRANSPORTATION SAFETY BOARD (NTSB) RESPONSIBILITIES

The second government air safety agency is the National Transportation Safety Board (NTSB), and it has two primary functions: One is to investigate airline crashes, report the probable causes, and make recommendations to the FAA to prevent repetition. Second is to investigate any air safety problem and make recommendations to the FAA to prevent subsequent crashes.

The FAA has the authority and responsibility to put new safety rules into effect, and need not wait for the NTSB to make the recommendations. But the FAA almost *never* takes measures to correct safety problems, even though the FAA inspectors are usually the first to discover them.

Federal Aviation Regulations[4] require that the airline submit training programs to the FAA for approval:

"Each certificate holder shall establish, obtain approval of and maintain a training program" that meets the approval of the FAA Administrator, as represented by the FAA inspectors. Whenever the inspector "finds that revisions to an approved training program are necessary for the continued adequacy of the program, the certificate holder shall, after notification by the Administrator, make any changes in the program found by the Administrator to be necessary."

"Its approval should be withdrawn immediately."

Internal FAA safety directives are explicit in requiring the FAA field offices to take immediate corrective actions when an inspector discovers unsatisfactory standards. A typical directive reads: "At any time such a training course is found deficient in the quality of training provided or fails to meet the requirements of the regulations, its approval should be withdrawn immediately. Special emphasis should be placed on the continuing surveillance of air carrier training programs ..."

Federal safety directives issued under authority of the Federal Aviation Act leave no doubt that it is the FAA inspectors who investigate, evaluate and report the suitability of the carrier's training program; there are no other qualified people within the FAA. One such authority states:

[The inspector] approves or disapproves all aspects of flight crew training programs operated by air carriers after assuring full compliance with all regulatory and other safety

---

[4] FAR 121.411 and 40.290, among others.

requirements pertinent to training operations. ...assure
further training and/or initiate and implement necessary
changes in training programs. Maintain close surveillance of
ground and simulated flight training of flight crews and
initiates immediate action to correct any deficiencies in
such training ... immediately implement any training or type-
rating requirements which he deems necessary to establish
and maintain crew proficiency and meets the basic requirements of Federal Aviation Regulations.

What, then, is the problem that permitted the violations found
on the United Airlines training program? The primary problem
is with the politics in the FAA hierarchy, which favors certain
carriers or companies by looking the other way when safeguards
are violated. In carrying out this deeply ingrained practice,
FAA officials puts pressure on FAA inspectors not to report
safety violations or safety problems.

Indifferent inspectors, inspectors who gladly participate in
the practice, individually and as a group, makes this scheme a
success. FAA management exerts subtle and often not so subtle
pressures upon inspectors who don't cooperate. Its easy to keep
inspectors in line, preventing the reporting and correction of
safety violations.

If the inspectors were as aggressive and organized as the air
traffic controllers, this type of government mischief is unlikely
to occur. But the inspectors are poorly organized and simply
don't have the numbers to demand high levels of safety.
Without a powerful organization behind them, FAA officials can
single out one inspector, make life difficult for him, and teach
the other inspectors a lesson. Other inspectors then fall in line,
and cease reporting the safety problems and violations.

CHECKING CREW COMPETENCY

A key element of an adequate training program is the
periodic checks conducted to determine if a crewmember's
performance is satisfactory, or if additional training is required
to fly safely in airline operations. The FAA approved company
training manual requires that captains receive training and
competency checks twice a year, and copilots once a year.

By law, the FAA determines the acceptable level of competency, and this is described in internal FAA manuals prepared
in Washington. Because of inspector shortages, the FAA
approves company check pilots to act in place of the FAA
inspectors. The FAA inspectors periodically observe the
performance of company check airmen to determine if they are
meeting FAA standards. The *only* purpose of the FAA inspector's presence on these check flights is for that purpose. If an
FAA inspector is dissatisfied with the company check airman's

safety standards, his attitude, his cooperation, or credibility, the FAA inspector must, by internal FAA directives, report his findings, and FAA officials are required to revoke the company check airman authority.

Washington directives make it clear that the company check airman's standards have an important effect upon safety. Also, if pilots know that the check flight requires them to perform to high standards, they will usually perform to those standards, and prepare themselves ahead of time to pass the competency checks. Among the many FAA directives is the following:

> ... factual data available on several recent incidents and accidents indicates a pattern of questionable pilot instrument approach competency. In view of the extremely serious safety implications of marginal or questionable performance in this highly critical operational area, we view these indications with considerable concern. The continued competency of the pilot to skillfully execute the instrument approach is an extremely important objective of the air carrier's training and flight checking programs.

> The FAA inspector or air carrier check airman must take a highly critical view of the performance which the pilot demonstrates during type rating or proficiency flight checks. Nothing short of complete professional competency is acceptable. The attitude of the air carrier, its check pilots, are of major importance.

> Operational inspectors of this Agency will consider very carefully this training and checking phase of air carrier training programs and will be required to take prompt corrective actions where deficiencies are found.

> Assigned inspectors should constantly review and monitor the activity of company check pilots. The inspectors review and evaluation of the tests given by company check pilots will determine the adequacy and effectiveness of check pilot's performance.

> Inspectors should evaluate adequacy of standards required by check pilots on pilot proficiency checks. Inspectors should determine his technical qualifications and his ability to assure the desired high standards. The effectiveness of the air carrier's training program is based on the performance of its check pilots.

What is required by law, however, is openly violated at some favored airlines. It is almost as if FAA management is an adversary of the FAA inspectors.

INABILITY OF SAFETY INSPECTORS TO FUNCTION

One of many internal FAA reports prepared by Washington inspection teams referred to the refusal by FAA management to act on safety violations or safety problems reported by FAA inspectors, and especially as it related to the perennial safety problems at United Airlines that gave the airline the reputation of having the most crashes of any airline, most of which arose out of the safety problems that went uncorrected:

"...[the Denver FAA inspectors] are attempting to correct noted deficiencies in UAL's training program ... The reaction of UAL [to the FAA training program requirements] appears to be in the form of resistance and resentment to these policies ... United Air Line's complaints against Inspector Harrell are a manifestation of their basic disagreement and attitude with existing pilot training and certification requirements as required by the FAA."

A subsequent report, preceding the New York City and Denver crashes, showed the air safety problems still existing:

UAL's training program and their attitude toward FAA were discussed at length during discussion with the Denver ACSDO personnel. The [training] maneuver items ... are required by [law] and are presently recognized and administered as accepted procedures and standards by other air carriers ...
[the need for compliance with federal and industry accepted practices was] brought to the attention of UAL on several occasions by inspectors ...[and] when after a reasonable time, flight checks showed that corrective actions had not been taken, UAL [was again told] that the CAMS [federal safety laws] must be followed and that the flight checks be conducted according to national standards.
...[the inspectors] are attempting to correct noted deficiencies in UAL's training program.

Chuck Stacy prepared that report of safety problems, and his obstruction with corrective actions appears in later pages.

THREATS AGAINST AIR SAFETY INSPECTORS UNDERMINE AIR SAFETY

Within a month of my assignment to United Airlines I discovered the same continuing problems. In one instance United officials threatened me after I observed a serious safety problem and had tried to carry out the FAA's safety responsibilities. "We got rid of Harrell and we'll get rid of you if you continue this way," warned Bill Learned, a company check airman approved by the FAA.

I had just observed the check airman complete three pilot flight checks of other United check airmen, and had never in my entire piloting career seen such dangerous performance by pilots. The company check pilot wanted to pass all three pilots following the flight checks, despite the urgent need for corrective training and a recheck of their competency. The only reason I was present was to carry out the FAA's responsibility to insure that the company check airmen approved by the FAA met FAA standards. Learned certainly didn't meet those standards.

I tried to reason with the company check pilot, and told him that if I were their chief pilot and not an FAA inspector, my actions would be the same. I explained that United's anything-goes safety standards actually reduced the competency levels of many crew members, and that they could perform better if only the check airmen demanded better performance.

I reported that incident, and the written report recommended that the company check airman's FAA approval be rescinded, as required by FAA internal directives. Instead, the office Supervising Inspector Dave Haley, and Los Angeles regional officials, wanted to suspend *me* from the DC-8 program. That threat occurred several times thereafter, whenever I reported a serious safety problem at United Airlines. It was as if United was running the FAA, and there may be more truth to that than meets the eye.

Just how bad the pilots were was indicated by the amount of simulator time the United instructors gave them before they felt the captains were ready for a recheck. One captain had over thirty hours of simulator time, which is more than a piston pilot gets when transitioning to the jets and had never flown a jet before.

IMPORTANCE OF RECORD INSPECTIONS

Training is the most important precursor for an adequate level of safety. Government examinations of training records is a starter for insuring compliance with federal training requirements. The National Transportation Safety Board, responsible for determining the cause of airline crashes, often determines the underlying probable cause of the crash by inspecting the same airline records that must be routinely checked by FAA inspectors. Obviously, the FAA wasn't doing its job when the NTSB finds contributing causes to the crash by inspecting the same records that are routinely inspected by the FAA.

PROMPT CORRECTIVE ACTIONS

A typical FAA directive stressing the importance of record inspections stated: "Special emphasis should be placed on the continuing surveillance of air carrier training programs" by FAA inspectors, with prompt corrective actions for suspected deficiencies or irregularities.

The findings in the FAA record inspection at San Francisco, just prior to the New York City crash, where the inspection

revealed falsification of training requirements, made the importance of record inspections especially urgent. And especially at
United Airlines. Shortly after joining the FAA, and shortly after
the New York City and Denver disasters occurred, two FAA
inspectors arrived at United's Los Angeles offices to make a
mandatory record inspection. A United official ordered them off
the airline's properties, refusing to allow the inspectors to
inspect the crew records. This was a serious violation of the
government's air safety requirements, made more so by the two
recent air tragedies, and especially by the findings of record
falsification that led to the two crashes.

FAA management in the Los Angeles Western Regional
office, and primarily Lynn Ashwell, Chief of the Air Carrier
Branch, criticized the inspectors for causing problems, and
warned the inspectors not to make another try. FAA officials
knew of the record inspection scandal just prior to the New
York City and Denver crashes; they knew of the consequences
in the two recent crashes. The FAA officials knew that the
same misconduct continued, with the probability of future
tragedies.

Inspectors eventually satisfied themselves with innocuous
data inspections—such as date of birth, date of the required
checks and other minutiae—and avoided a meaningful analysis
of what the records sometimes reflected. The United and FAA
coalition was a classic case of industry controlling the regulatory agency empowered to safeguard the public's safety. And
the public paid in gory air tragedies.

Inspectors' close contact with an airline reveals problems
not shown by record inspections. The record inspections simply
augment suspicions arising from other problem areas.

ANOTHER RECORD INSPECTION REFUSAL

Just as Harrell and other inspectors suspected training
irregularities when they conducted the unexpected cross-check
of training records with aircraft logs, I also recognized the
same problems. Seeking to further support my suspicions, I
arrived at United's Denver training center to conduct a record
inspection, as required by my job duties and FAA regulations.
United officials allowed me initial access to the records. But
when I became suspicious of irregularities, and asked for
related training records, United refused to allow the inspection,
even though the records were present.

I reminded United that the law required them to produce
the records for an inspection. They persisted in their refusal.
They were hiding something. I returned to the FAA office, and
filed a report of the violation, which stated in part:

Upon analysis of the information obtained from [UAL], this inspector realized the relationship between failures and those that failed [only] when an inspector was on board. It appeared that possibly the only failures, except for possibly one or two exceptions, was [when] this inspector, or others, were on board. UAL personnel made certain records available, but refused to allow this inspector to obtain other information pertinent to, and necessary for a proper evaluation of the training center records and procedures. The information requested, available on the desk in front of this inspector, was refused.

At that time, I was unaware of the explosive record inspection findings preceding the New York City crash. But FAA management was fully aware of the earlier report and findings, and of the tragic consequences at New York City and Denver. FAA management's response to my report was predictable: they removed my report from the files, and barred me from making another record inspection. The records went uninspected.

When I discovered the inspection report missing, I entered a photostatic copy of the original report. Obviously, this wasn't appreciated.

In a Los Angeles regional office meeting with Chief of the Air Carrier Division, Al Butler, I reminded Butler of this record inspection refusal, and the FAA's negative reaction. I did not know at that time of the October 16, 1960 sequestered report. Butler knew of it; he was part of the inspection team that made the discovery. Butler didn't volunteer any information on the earlier inspection and alarming findings. Butler sympathized with me, explaining that he knew of the problems at United and that he experienced the problems himself when he was assigned to the program. But he ignored his responsibilities, and did nothing. Higher officials controlled the hands-off policy.

"United has just crashed"!

During this meeting on December 30, 1964, an inspector rushed in and said, "A United plane has just crashed near Saugus!" This was a hillside community between Los Angeles and Bakersfield on the Grapevine route along Interstate 5. The pilots mismanaged the fuel supply, causing the two engines to run out of fuel, even though fuel for several hours of flight was still on board. Fortunately no one died.

"DOCTORED" REPORTS

Doctoring of inspection reports to make favored carriers look good was another problem within the FAA. A Los Angeles-based inspector visiting the Denver FAA office complained that FAA officials ordered him to delete safety irregularities in the report following a Blue Ribbon Inspection of a Seattle air carrier. Initially included in that report, but later deleted, were important training program irregularities. Ironically, that same air carrier had just experienced a crash into the Great Salt Lake during a training flight, with the death of all on board, including an FAA inspector. There could have been a relationship between the irregularities and the crash, but this will never be known.

Removal of official reports was another problem to cover up for safety violations. Ed Jensen, Principal Operations Inspector for Los Angeles Airways, described to me the illegal removal of two reports describing serious maintenance violations at that helicopter airline. Lynn Ashwell, Chief of the Air Carrier Branch, reportedly removed the reports from the files, and gave them back to Jensen, stating, "We don't want these reports in the files."

THE CHILDREN WHO PERISHED WOULD PROBABLY BE ALIVE TODAY

Jensen said he still had the reports that Ashwell returned to him and, if the opportunity ever arose, he would gladly tell his story. I thought of this conversation after Los Angeles Airways experienced two fatal crashes near Disneyland; one on May 22, and the other on August 14, 1968, killing many children in each mishap. The NTSB blamed these accidents on faulty maintenance practices.

REMOVING OFFICIALS DOCUMENTS ARE A CRIME

Removing official government documents from government files violates several Federal criminal statutes, including section 2071 of Title 18 of the United States criminal code:

> Whoever willfully and unlawfully conceals, removes ... any record ... shall be fined not more that $2000. or imprisoned ..."

VERY FEW TO CARRY THE MESSAGE

Numerous safety articles stress the importance of good standards. But the political blocks, the covert back-room deals, the corruption, obstruct needed safety requirements from being addressed. Some airlines are not going to stress something that will raise their costs.

"The real need of civil aviation today," stated Jeremiah Dempsey, former President of the International Air Transport Association, "is not, in my opinion, supersonic transport, but the establishment of a better safety record at a cost that will still leave air travel accessible."

Speaking at a Flight Safety Foundation International Safety Seminar at Williamsburg, Virginia, Dempsey continued:

There is, I believe, among the airlines a keen awareness of the need for raising the proficiency of their own people so that the human factor, insofar as it cannot be eliminated, may be raised to a standard that will provide the best attainable safeguards against human frailties which can play so fateful a part in times of crisis ... the solution of the urgent safety problems.

THE SUFFERING THAT ACCOMPANIES AIR DISASTERS

"Civil aviation has no greater problem today," Dempsey continued, "than the problem of safety. The suffering that accompanies air disasters leaves a deep impression on people's minds ... any complacency in the effort to reduce it would not only be morally wrong and socially indefensible, it would be economically fatal to the advancement of commercial aviation." But the continued disregard of safety problems makes it obvious that such statements are only rhetoric, often ignored.

DESTROYED REPORTS

A typical example of covering up the real cause of crashes and near-crashes surfaced when FAA management (Supervising Inspector Dave Haley, Denver office) wanted me to destroy my report of an engine flameout on a United DC-8 when the engineer made an error. I prepared a report describing the incident. But instead of recommending that the engineer be punished, I placed the blame on United's flight engineer training program and the low standards. Supervising Inspector Dave Haley ordered me to withdraw the report and prepare another one, omitting reference to United's training program. He wanted me to filed a violation against the flight engineer, who was one of many victims of the training program fiasco. This required falsifying the report, omitting the causative problems. I refused to change the report, and properly so.

My report was illegally removed from the government files, and the FAA charged the engineer (George Small) with violating federal air regulations, and forced to pay a fine. FAA legal counsel accused the engineer of using poor judgment in analyzing the system abnormality, ignoring the fact that the engineer's analysis of the problem was incorrect *because* of inadequate training. By filing a violation report against the engineer, the FAA could show it took corrective actions. United crewmembers frequently confided to me that inflight emergencies or irregularities often occur, but are not reported to the FAA so as to avoid FAA license suspension or fine.

One United problem that did get reported was an unnecessarily traumatic incident involving malfunction of the pressurization system in a DC-8 cruising at 33,000 feet near Denver.

Loss of pressurization is no great problem if the manual backup system is correctly used. But in this case it wasn't, because the flight engineer and the pilots did not understand its use. This resulted in passengers threatened with a lack of oxygen, which can result in brain damage in a very short period of time. The captain made an emergency descent through altitudes assigned to other aircraft. This is a justified risk if an actual emergency had existed.

I investigated this incident and discovered that the flight engineer had been trained and checked by a company pilot who was not qualified as an engineer. Obviously a check airmen who doesn't know the systems, who isn't qualified, can't be expected to train and check another crew member for adequacy of knowledge. I recommended that the FAA require that a qualified flight engineer check the competency of the engineers, and supported my report with statements of United crewmembers who themselves admitted to the inadequacy. The recommendation was ignored.

"CREW CONCEPT," A FANCY LABEL TO REDUCE TRAINING STANDARDS AND COSTS

The poor training resulted in a serious lack of knowledge of aircraft systems, wherein very few crewmembers had the knowledge to safely handle a system abnormality or emergency. United officials cleverly got around this problem by giving it a fancy label: crew concept. Using this fancy label United conducted competency checks permitting all three crewmembers to huddle together and try to come up with the answer that all three of them should have individually known without hesitation.

The mechanics of the crew-concept procedure were asinine. During checks of the crewmembers competency a question would be asked as to what action to take for a particular abnormality or emergency. One crewmember would hesitantly come up with one guess. Another would add something to that. The third would also do so. Often the comments were wrong. Often none of the crewmembers knew the correct procedure that they each should have fully known.

The result was that when confronted with an emergency or abnormality, no one knew the correct procedure, all guessed at what should be done, and chaos occurred. This lack of knowledge repeatedly surfaced in crashes with heavy death tolls. Still, United officials stuck to their money-saving crew-concept strategy, and the crewmembers themselves bought it hook, line, and sinker. And they paid for it in occasional crashes when crewmembers were blamed for errors that resulted from the inadequate training.

At other airlines and in the military, each crewmember had to pass a test of his knowledge without asking others for the answers. It was like taking a test of one's knowledge, and taking the instructor or someone else along to answer the questions.

The knowledge by other crewmembers of the correct procedures provides greater assurance that if the captain's actions are incorrect, other crewmembers can promptly alert him to this fact. The speed with which in-flight emergencies must be solved does not permit three inadequately trained crew members to pool their knowledge, and hope that the final decision does not rest on false assumptions.

JET-UPSET

Lack of training led to other problems. High altitude jet upset was one of them. A jet upset is a loss of control at high altitude, with the aircraft falling out of control through many thousands of feet. In some cases the aircraft never recovers control. In others, as the higher density air is reached closer to the ground, the flight controls permit recovery, often under spectacularly near-fatal circumstances.

A classic jet upset which I investigated occurred on a United Boeing 720 enroute from San Francisco to Chicago on July 12, 1963. Cruising at 37,000 feet, the captain decided to climb above cloud buildups, rather than fly around them. Proper training would have shown that the aircraft could not fly at the higher altitude for the existing weight and expected turbulence conditions. United Flight 746 commenced climbing to 41,000 feet, an altitude that it never reached.

A phenomenon of high altitude operations is that the higher an aircraft flies, at a given weight, the higher becomes the stalling speed at which the aircraft literally falls out of the air. The data not made available to the flight crews showed the plane would stall before reaching 41,000 feet.

The pilots turned on the seat-belt sign, and none too soon. As the aircraft climbed it encountered turbulence, which decreased the margin above the stall. Suddenly the nose of the airplane pitched up beyond sixty degrees—seemingly straight up, and then the Boeing 720 plunged nose-down in a terrifying dive toward the ground. The rate of descent exceeded 21,000 feet per minute. The captain tried to move the flight controls, but they were locked. The crew tried to move the elevators and the horizontal stabilizer, and they too were locked in position.

The high gravity or "G" forces made it difficult for the crew to reach for various control levers. Fortunately, and life-saving, as the Boeing 720 descended to lower altitudes where the air density was greater, the plane was finally brought under control at 14,000 feet. If it hadn't been, a huge crater in the ground would have shortly occurred. The aircraft lost over twenty five thousand feet before it recovered from the high altitude jet upset.

Following this upset the FAA issued its usual order for all inspectors to insure that the air carriers provide adequate high altitude training to the crews. Inspectors hadn't been able to obtain compliance with previous FAA directives or training shortcomings and it was unlikely United would respond to a new request. Further, there wasn't much technical information available to the pilots, except the warning, don't fly too high. But "too-high" means different things under different weight, turbulence, and maneuvering conditions. There weren't any hard rules for avoiding jet upset. I was as ignorant as anyone else about the problem; my jet training was the same as other airline pilots received.

The FAA assigned to me the responsibility of investigating this mishap and making recommendations to prevent a recurrence. I studied the airline manuals, and didn't find enough for the pilots to intelligently address the problem. I obtained manufacturer manuals and examined various flight-test data. From this data I came up with a program that gave the pilots hard figures from which they could determine the maximum altitude to which they could climb (under a given weight condition, angle of bank, and estimated "G" load increase from anticipated turbulence). I prepared a chart, with examples, and a training pamphlet, which I promoted at United and elsewhere.

Encouraged by good pilot acceptance, I submitted verbal and written recommendations to United and to the FAA, including a four-page document outlining the details. United refused to change its training program, and the crew members were unable to answer questions concerning high altitude jet upsets. Being unable to answer these basic questions, the pilots were unable to comply with the latest Washington directive.

Instead of ordering United to provide the required training, FAA management avoided a confrontation by ordering me to discontinue efforts in this area and not to ask United pilots questions concerning jet upset avoidance. United continued to experience upsets. In one mishap, a jet plunged from 37,000 to 29,000 feet over central Wyoming. Although the aircraft did not crash, one passenger, George Graves of Glenview, Illinois, died of the injuries he sustained in this incident.

Jerome Lederer, Technical Director of Flight Safety foundation at that time, was quoted in *Business and Commercial Aviation* as blaming the occurrence of high altitude jet upsets on lack of training. Referring to another air safety problem, Lederer stated there was a strong need for effective check flights to detect and correct the "departure from good practice habitually and unwittingly made by pilots." Lederer identified the barrier to adequate check and training safeguards as the "very fine financial and personal arrangements between pilots and many companies [that] encourage the pilot to accept hazardous practices for fear of jeopardizing his relations with management."

When I later went to work for Flying Tigers writing their training manual for the stretched DC-8, I incorporated this technique into it. Douglas incorporated the procedure into their stretched DC-8 flight manual. They also used some of my other techniques, sometimes word for word. The jet-upset training aid slowly became adopted by other airlines.

UNSAFE SAFETY PILOT—Cost Reduction Scheme

Another cost-reduction problem in United's training program was its method of training and checking the flight engineer. All air carriers and military organizations throughout the world, except United, utilized a check pilot to train and check individual pilots, while the flight engineer was simultaneously trained and checked by a separate and qualified instructor-check engineer. In this way the engineer could be given additional advanced training, and his competency properly evaluated. Safety is greatly improved by in-depth training of the engineer.

United twisted this time-honored practice in a way that reduced the cost of training, and covered up for obviously needed corrective training. It was also fraught with dangers.

United used a single instructor-check pilot to train and check the two pilots, while simultaneously "training" and "checking" the flight engineer. Simultaneous with these multiple duties, he was also the safety pilot. The preposterous arrangement deprived crewmembers of the training to which they were entitled; eliminated the proper check of the crewmember's competency; and endangered the crews and those on the ground when the plane occasionally got out of control during training.

The instructor pilot check airman, who is also the safety pilot, normally sits at one of the pilot control seats during training and flight checks, so that he can instantly take over if an emergency flight maneuver is mishandled, as they sometimes are. He must be instantly ready to block an unsafe reaction by the pilot being trained or checked, or take life-saving corrective actions. United put the safety pilot in the observer's seat behind the captain—where there were no flight controls. In reality, the safety pilot position existed in name only. Further, the combination check and safety pilot could not see the flight engineer, let alone train and check his competency.

The check of the flight engineer consisted of evaluating whether the plane made it back without the flight engineer mishandling the systems. This didn't meet the criteria for industry accepted or FAA required training and competency check of the flight engineers. Unable to check the engineer's competency, it eliminated the need for additional training. When United changed to this bizarre arrangement their training costs went down with the elimination of the flight engineer training-check airman, and virtually eliminating the need for corrective training of the flight engineer.

Offsetting this financial saving were the many near-accidents and the repeated fatal air tragedies. This threat to air safety and lives was obviously acceptable to United and cooperating FAA officials. The conscientious inspectors expressed concern, but the FAA didn't pay attention to them.

On one of these check flights I turned to United check airman, Frank Cowles, with whom I could be candid, and get an honest response. "Frank, you know you can't possibly tell if that flight engineer you checked is competent, using United's check procedures."

"Unless he is *real* bad," Cowles replied, "I can't possibly make that determination."

Other United crewmembers admitted the problem with poorly qualified flight engineers. Captains freely admitted they couldn't trust their flight engineers because of the engineers' lack of knowledge. The former flight engineer instructors and check airmen who were transferred to class room duties, admitted the deterioration in engineer competency.

I included these admissions in my reports to show the dangerous nature of the method of training and checking and the greatly reduced competency levels that did not meet industry or FAA standards. There was no corrective actions taken.

SIMULATED ENGINE FAILURE

Before most of the training was done in simulators, and when the importance of actual flight training in simulated engine failures was recognized, a valuable training and check maneuver that was industry standard, and conducted by the military, was simulated engine failure during takeoff at the critical V1 speed. United refused to do this maneuver, and refused to allow inspectors to perform it during flight checks. An earlier FAA report addressed this problem:

Engine failure (simulated during training and check flights) while the airplane is still on the ground is against UAL policy ...

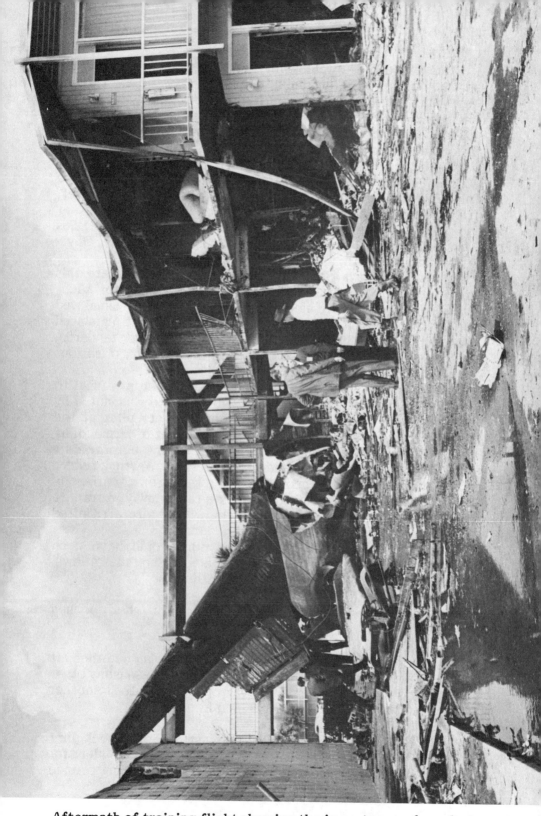

Aftermath of training flight showing the importance of an alert safety pilot at one of the pilot control seats.

The FAA decides what safety maneuvers are to be demonstrated by a pilot before being licensed to fly the aircraft. It
helps to insure the safety of flight; obviously. Many near-
crashes and actual crashes occurred following engine failure on
takeoff, and the simulated engine-failure training was very
important. A tragic example of what can result from a real
engine-failure malfunction came shortly after TWA flight 300
aborted a takeoff at Rome Airport. The captain rejected the
takeoff when an engine malfunctioned. Before it was over,
fifty-one people burned to death inside the aircraft. In another
incident a Continental Airlines DC-10 rejected takeoff at Los
Angeles Airport on March 1, 1978, resulting in loss of life. Obviously, training in this area is important.

When inspectors requested the pilots to demonstrate this
maneuver, United refused, stating "Mr. Petty [senior Vice-
President, United] will not allow an engine to be simulated
failed on the ground." But the Federal Aviation Act legislated
that the FAA will determine safety requirements and standards,
not the officials at United Airlines with their history of serious
air safety violations and air tragedies.

Actually, the inspector's protest over United's refusal to
allow simulation of engine failure on the ground was muted by
a concern for their own lives. Without a safety pilot at the
flight controls to save the aircraft in the event of mishandling
the aircraft during a simulated emergency, the inspectors didn't
push to have the required maneuver performed. A wrong rudder
application, for instance, could result in the aircraft careening
into buildings or the terminal alongside the runway, or create
a serious yaw condition with possible loss of the aircraft.United
thereby compromised safety training.

The danger of the unsafe safety pilot could have been
eliminated simply by forcing compliance with the federal laws,
one of which (FAR amendment 40-21) stated:

"In the interest of safety ... the check pilot [shall] occupy
one of the pilot positions."

This directive was intended solely for United, as no other air
carrier dared to engage in such folly. But as with so many other
federal safety requirements, it was openly violated. Another
federal directive (FS 8430.13) stated in part:

It is extremely important that the instructor or check pilot
keep both feet resting on the rudder pedals and be alert for
possible use of the wrong rudder by the pilot [being trained
or checked].

And still another federal directive stated:

> It is obvious that the preamble also recognized the safety question. It would appear, therefore, that the need for a qualified instructor or check pilot in the second seat during ground proximity and emergency maneuvers is obvious.

This last directive was issued *four years* after the one previously cited, but United continued to ignore both of them. Another federal directive—again written because of the United practice—stated:

> A check pilot who occupies the observer's seat, rather than the co-pilot position, is severely handicapped in giving a check by not being in a position to take over in an emergency. He is therefore usually disinclined to have an engine out on take-off or make 3 or 2 engine approaches, cross-wind take-off or landing, etc. This interferes with the thoroughness of the check. We feel some urgency [in] UAL's practice.

No corrective action followed this urgent memorandum. Changing this procedure, forcing United to conduct their training and check flights as other airlines throughout the world conducted them, would have eliminated the large financial savings that had accrued from these practices.

Years earlier another FAA report described the problem. The report described United's procedure of conducting flight checks in DC-8 aircraft "with two unrated applicants [students] occupying the two cockpit seats [simultaneously] during simulated emergency and instrument conditions." This practice was madness and indicated extreme poor-judgment problems at United, or contempt for basic safety requirements.

Although this was flagrantly unsafe and illegal, United officials had the audacity to complain because FAA inspectors protested the unsafe and illegal safety-pilot practice.

It wasn't at all unusual, and it was frightening, to see a United safety pilot leap out of the observer's seat and frantically grab the power levers or the control column, trying to avoid a crash, while draped over the center console between the two pilots. The people in the houses below us never realized what was going on over their heads. The danger was especially pronounced during simulated two-engine-inoperative approaches, during high-sink-rate approaches, during simulated engine failures, and especially when the pilot applied the wrong rudder.

The obvious danger was addressed in an FAA memorandum by FAA Flight Standards Chief William Krieger:

> ...there has existed a doubt concerning the safety of [this United practice] The [inspectors] in the Denver Air Carrier District Office have had several incidents in which this has created serious safety hazards ... In one case, which occurred last month during the conduct of a B-720 check, the aircraft sustained considerable damage from a landing out of such an approach ... the [safety] pilot was unable to take any direct action [because he was in the observer's seat] ... The Airman Certification Specialists [inspectors] who have submitted comments are unanimous in their opinion [that this United practice is dangerous].

The report continued: "The FAA inspector, particularly in the DC-8, occupying the second observer's seat, is unable to adequately observe the instruments during this period [to determine the performing pilot's competency]." A few days later, in response to joint inspector pressure rarely seen within the FAA, Krieger signed a document stating: "UAL certainly should not be allowed to continue [this practice]."

But the unsafe practice continued. During sworn testimony two years later at a Denver air safety hearing (yet to be described), Krieger contradicted these statements, as he sought to protect United, and excuse FAA and United refusal to comply with the internal FAA directives. He testified that the safety pilot sitting in the observer's seat was *not* a dangerous procedure.

The Denver inspectors attempted to change the practice; but that fizzled. An FAA official wrote: "At 1919 MST this date, Mr. Ashwell called and advised that he had just received an urgent call from UAL. It was my understanding that UAL was quite upset relative to the changes we had requested, making reference to the requirement that the safety pilot be seated at the flight controls." The memorandum continued: "it was our intent that a safety pilot be required on all flight proficiency-check maneuvers...." The latter reference was to United's attempt to placate the inspectors' protests by having the safety pilot at the flight controls *only* when inspectors were on board the aircraft.

I protested this attempt to placate United. The safety laws were not written to protect FAA inspectors. The danger continued to affect crew members and people on the ground. Another FAA report stated:

> [The FAA must] immediately take steps to have UAL utilize

qualified safety pilots on proficiency checks... [safety laws] did not envision safety compromise in air carrier training and checks ... It would appear, therefore, that the need for a qualified instructor or check pilot in the second control seat during ground proximity and emergency maneuvers is obvious ... in the interest of safety, for the check pilots to occupy one of the pilot positions...

"It is dangerous, and should be discontinued."
A report signed by myself and five other FAA inspectors in the Denver office stated:

[The inspectors] feel it is dangerous and should be discontinued. This was the opinion of all specialists in attendance. Stich related his observance of UAL safety pilots jumping out of the seat situated behind the Captain to take corrective action during pilot proficiency checks.

In an individual report I wrote:

The conditions whereby the United Air Lines' check pilot jumps to his feet to take corrective action is not unusual. [The procedure] requires IMMEDIATE CORRECTIVE ACTION ... With the safety pilot responsible for the [safety of the] aircraft, sitting in the jump seat which is remotely located behind the pilot, it is obvious that corrective action is limited. This practice, safety wise, is unsatisfactory. The danger is very evident when one sits through such an episode ... [This UAL practice] is fraught with hazards and could easily result in an aircraft, its crew, and an FAA inspector being lost. Add to this the occupants of the homes under the aircraft!

The warning of an impending accident was well timed. Ten days after the report was written, a United flight crew and FAA inspector rode through a harrowing incident at Cheyenne, Wyoming, that started with poor piloting technique while the safety pilot checked the captain's proficiency during simulated emergency maneuvers. Compounded by the absence of a safety pilot at the flight controls, things got out of hand fast.
"Flare it! Flare it!"
The inspector riding through the Cheyenne incident stated in his official report:

After noticing the Captain's performance in the simulator, I felt that the flight check should be observed by an FAA inspector. It became obvious that there was going to be a hard landing so I got into the second jump seat and held on to the bottom of the seat. At the same time I heard the check pilot shout, "flare it, flare it!" and then we hit the runway...

...the aircraft bounced back into the air approximately 50 feet and came down on its nose wheels and apparently blew one or both of the tires. [The captain] pulled back on the yoke and the aircraft became airborne again and it appeared to go higher and the angle of attack became more pronounced. The aircraft hit nose wheel first and bounced back into the air, higher than the preceding oscillation and back down in a steeper dive. The check pilot shouted, `stop it! stop it! pull the speed brake, reverse!

This was an exciting flight, and could easily have been a fatal one, making newspaper headlines. It didn't say too much for the training and check safeguards; the United check pilot passed the pilot being checked. That pilot may be captain on your next flight!

The report continued:

the aircraft hit hard, but with the speed brakes extended the aircraft failed to become airborne. I feel that had the aircraft made another oscillation, the aircraft would either land on its nose or back.

Many people could have been killed in their homes if this jet had crashed. This harrowing experience closely followed my written reports, and precipitated an unheard-of coordination among FAA inspectors. They refused to board any United training flight for the next few weeks, thus receiving a respite from the dangers. The FAA allowed United to continue the practice, despite the threats to the crewmembers and the people on the ground.

"We value the lives of our crews higher than that."

I discussed this practice with an Eastern Airlines official at Miami, who replied, "We value the lives of our crews higher than that."

How bad can mishandling of the flight become? *Aerospace Safety* reported a cockpit scene occurring during a flight check:

On final approach the student pilot inadvertently feathered one of the two engines. In the instant it took to analyze what had happened, the [instructor pilot] increased the power on the good engine. Thinking they were going around, the student retracted the gear. The IP immediately ordered the gear lowered and the student got the flap handle instead [which placed the aircraft near the stall speed and possibly a crash condition]. Meanwhile, the IP told the engineer to bring the engine back in. Unfortunately, the engineer hit the wrong button and feathered the remaining engine. The IP put the gear down himself and made a successful landing, despite the confusion. Then to cap this incident, the engineer moved the gear lever to 'Positive Lock' and the gear collapsed on the runway.

KEYSTONE COP ROUTINE?

Incredibly bad performance? Yes! But an inspector routinely sees various shades of this as part of his job. It isn't comforting to know what goes on in the flight station with poorly trained or improperly checked crew members.

The dangers involved in flight training doesn't mean we should eliminate such training. On the contrary, the need for *further* training under carefully controlled conditions, with the safety pilot constantly alert to the need for immediate corrective actions, is important.

A brutal tragedy at New Orleans shows what can happen if a safety pilot is not alert (or if the safety pilot was not at the flight controls) was shown by a Delta DC-8 that crashed into the Hilton Inn at New Orleans on March 30, 1967, during a late-night training flight. The New Orleans papers described the tragedy:

Nine high school girls from Juda, Wisconsin were among the 18 persons killed in the flaming crash. Eight of the dead girls were found huddled together in a charred bathroom of the motel. The body of a ninth was blown outside. The surviving students, many hysterical or in a daze, were placed under sedation ... Police Captain Marvin Leonard stated: "There were eight girls in four rooms. You could see where they took refuge in the shower stalls. They turned on the water, but it didn't do them any good." Some charred rooms were inaccessible for hours because of the heat. The charred, decapitated body of a small boy was found in the remains of one home. A woman's body was nearby.

These deaths did not result from the training as much as they resulted from two problems: One was conducting the training at midnight when alertness is greatly diminished. The second was the carelessness of the safety pilot (probably fatigue induced) who allowed an unsafe handling of the aircraft to progress far beyond normal limits. The pilot being checked had been making a simulated two-engine-out approach and had let the speed decrease below minimum control airspeed.

This tragedy also showed what can happen to those on the ground if a competent and alert safety pilot is not at the flight controls, or conducted at unsafe hours. Shortly before that crash occurred I had finished recurrent training with Pan American with most of the training conducted after midnight. My report stated that late night training flights are dangerous. The pilots are not sharp enough to cope with simulated engine failures, no-flap landings, and other simulated emergencies.

LEADING THE WEAK CREWMEMBER THROUGH THE CHECK OF HIS COMPETENCY

Another problem frequently encountered at United Airlines was the practice of company check airmen leading the crewmembers through the flight checks while the pilot's competency was being checked. Instead of checking the pilot's ability to handle the flight, we ended up checking the company check airman who literally took the check for the crewmember! It was similar to United's crew-concept where others could answer the questions or perform the maneuver, masking the possible incompetency of the crewmember being checked.

Without this help, the crewmember could not pass the test, showing the need for corrective training. This unacceptable practice continued despite inspectors' protests, and was the subject of an FAA letter years earlier: "We cannot condone the [company check pilot] instructing or leading the applicant through the check." I frequently reported the problem, as did other inspectors. But FAA management refused to force a change, making it impossible to know if the pilot's performance was satisfactory or not. I repeatedly objected to this, and repeated encountered confrontations. During one such confrontation at San Francisco with United Check Airman Dale Cavanaugh I instructed him to let the applicant being checked perform the maneuver. When he refused to do this, I notified him the check could not continue. We returned to the airport, and thereafter FAA officials suspended me from the DC-8 program.

TAKE-OFF POWER—BUT WHICH WAY?

A seemingly small but dangerous practice that has resulted in crashes and caused changes in cockpit terminology, *except at United*, had to do with power application and removal. Occasionally, especially during very turbulent conditions, the captain who may have both hands on the control wheel during heavy turbulence, may call for the power that he wants. United's procedure for ordering advancement of the thrust levers to maximum allowable thrust was to command, *"Take Off*

Power." But did he want the power taken off, or did he want maximum rated power that is normally used for takeoff?

Accident investigations have shown that under stress conditions, especially close to the ground, the sudden command, "take off power," has frequently resulted in just that—the power taken off to idle thrust. It may be that the captain wanted maximum power to execute a missed approach due to the extreme turbulence. If the power is taken off, such as when approaching the runway (and possibly over approach lights), when the captain wanted to make an emergency missed approach requiring maximum power, tragedy can result.

The term, "Take-off power," has been abandoned years ago in all known flight operations; except, of course, at United Airlines. If maximum power is wanted, instead of calling, "Take Off Power," the standard command now is to call, *"Max Power."* The consequences of the take-off power command was seen during United operations, when the crew member adjusting the power levers hesitated, not knowing whether the captain wanted the power taken off or full power added.

The *Air Line Pilot* magazine made reference to the problem, stating, "There is the critical problem of the choice of words to be used. I think all of us have been exposed to, or have experienced "Take-off" power [command] and the power is taken off, when such response was certainly not wanted."

Prior to this ALPA article I prepared an FAA letter for transmittal to United, asking to get this confusing and dangerous terminology changed. It was, of course, the FAA's responsibility to order the change because of the safety aspects. In my letter I described the problem with this confusing command, its replacement years ago by the military and other air carriers, its association with prior accidents, and the confusion seen at United by its use. I suggested changing the command to the standard, "Max Power." United's Mr. Petty refused, writing back that the command would be confusing if a pilot by the name of "Max" was in the cockpit!

I, and other inspectors, frequently reported the deficient safety standards exhibited by United Airlines check airmen. These low standards deprived crewmembers of adequate training to safely operate the aircraft. At no other major airline in the United States was this problem as bad as that which existed at United. The reason it existed, was that FAA officials were currying favor with United officials, and responding to pressures from higher ups, and from members of Congress, to relax the safety requirements.

Other airlines knew that United Airlines' officials manipulated FAA inspectors via FAA officials, and sometimes made reference to the problem. A typical example of undermining inspectors' safety functions was the experience of FAA inspector Peter Chesney of the Denver FAA office, during a confrontation with Continental Airlines. In this incident Chesney observed an unsatisfactory flight check performance by a Continental Airlines captain, who the company check airman wanted to pass as satisfactory. Chesney reported the captain's performance as unsatisfactory, requiring the captain to be taken off the schedule, given additional training, and a recheck.

Because of the company check airman's poor standards and poor attitude, the inspector recommended that the FAA remove his authority to conduct check flights—as required by internal FAA directives.

The inspector's report became an official document and could not be legally removed and destroyed. But it was removed from the official records, and the Denver air carrier district office Supervising Inspector, Dave Haley, ordered the captain reinstated, without any training or recheck to address the safety problems. The unsatisfactory report of the company check airman was also destroyed. In addition, the inspector was called back to the office on his day off, and admonished for making the report. I personally felt Haley was one of the most aviation-ignorant employees the FAA had, and that many accidents and deaths arose from his interference, and that of other FAA officials, with the lawful functions of the FAA.

Before transferring to Denver, Haley had the safety responsibilities for several airlines in the Northeast, some of which experienced a series of fatal air tragedies that were related to poor training standards. The Northeast Region addressed the problem with Haley by the government up-and-out procedure. Transfer an unwanted bureaucrat to another area, and let them worry about the problem.

Chesney testified to this incident during a Denver safety grievance hearing that will be described in later pages.

Showing the arrogant indifference to the deaths that result from this type of conduct, this Chesney incident occurred shortly after United's New York City and Denver crashes had occurred, that were obviously related to training problems that the inspectors tried to correct and which Haley obstructed.

The problem Chesney faced was far worse at United Airlines. And I had it even worse then Chesney or most of the other inspectors because the United DC-8 program contained most of the senior United pilots, and they were the most vocal in opposing the FAA role under the Federal Aviation Act. They wouldn't accept the government's safety role that came about following United's ramming of TWA over the Grand Canyon.

A similar but far worse incident occurred within a month of my arrival at United's Denver training base. As part of my official function, I witnessed the check flight performed by United check airman Clarence Pratt. This FAA-approved company check airman was conducting the six-month competency flight check on two senior United Airlines pilots, who were themselves check airmen. My report stated in part:

> The conduct of the check ride by the pilots was definitely unsatisfactory; certain maneuvers being actually unsafe. The company check pilot did not find fault with the maneuvers during the flight, and indicated satisfactory performance, despite the fact that the unsatisfactory items were repeated time and again. Upon debriefing, the check pilot informed this inspector that he considered the flight portion of both pilots satisfactory, and he did not intend to repeat any of the items. This opinion persisted even when confronted with the written notes made during the unsatisfactory portion of the flight check.

My report went into details about the dangerous flap mismanagement wherein the aircraft nearly stalled out during a missed approach at low altitude. Both pilots had poor directional control following simulated engine failures. In one instance the pilot lost 80 degrees of heading after a simulated engine failure (15 degrees was the approximate maximum allowable). The airspeed control was very poor and the deviation far exceeded tolerances. They had poor knowledge of the flight procedures. They were actually dangerous. The flight was the poorest I had ever experienced during thirty-five years of piloting, and encompassing many airlines throughout the world. I couldn't believe what I was seeing, which was the culmination of years of anything-goes competency standards, explaining why United had thirty years of crashes that should never have happened.

These three key company check airmen were responsible for setting acceptable safety standards of other pilots, and set comparable standards. These three company check airmen had a definite influence upon the standards of line pilots, and helped explain the New York City and Denver crashes, and the many others that occurred before that, and the many others that followed. I finished my report by stating:

> This inspector feels that the greatest detriments to bringing up the standards of the pilots with UAL are the laxness and low standards by certain of the flight standards check pilots. It is obvious to this inspector that many of the check pilots could increase their standards.

During the post-flight debriefing in United's offices, the United check pilot argued and insisted that the pilots should be passed, even after being confronted with the specific performance shortcomings. I tried to reason with the company check pilot, trying to convince him that additional training will correct the problems. The check pilot would hear none of this. United was on a roll, having successfully gotten rid of other inspectors who interfered with their illegal and unsafe operations. He knew FAA inspectors had no backing.

I reported the unsatisfactory company check airman performance, and recommended removal of his FAA authorization, as required by FAA internal directives. Changes were made. The next day I was advised by Supervising Inspector Dave Haley that I would probably be suspended from my job assignment on the DC-8 program. Somehow I managed to escape removal from the program. But other incidents kept occurring, preventing correction of the serious safety problems.

"You can't argue with success."

Things were never dull on the United DC-8 program. On another flight check which I observed, the pilot crossed the approach end of the runway at a dangerously high speed; forty knots too fast. If the runway had been minimum length for that particular weight, we would probably have crashed by running off the far end of the runway. And if there had been a motel or some other building at the end of the runway, our aircraft would probably have cremated some of the people in the structures.

Part of the flight check is to determine safe speed control, and forty knots too fast over the end of the runway isn't satisfactory by a long shot. Usually ten knots is the maximum acceptable excess (except during gusty wind conditions). Rather than demand that the pilot repeat the performance (and cost the airline additional money in performing the maneuver, or risk retraining), the United check airman wanted to pass the pilot.

Again I tried to reason with the United check pilot, Clarence Pratt. Rather than demanding satisfactory performance, which the pilot being checked could probably have given if he knew he had to adhere to required standards, the company check airman defended the dangerous performance. "Better fast than slow," Pratt argued. He meant it was better to crash at the far end of the runway, due to excess speed, than to crash at the approach end with insufficient speed! But the purpose of the flight check was to insure the pilot could safely fly the aircraft, and not a check of the best way to crash.

Problems were all over. Another inspector and I discussed the scheduled flight check for a United captain from Chicago the next day, who was known to be a weak pilot. I casually stated I intended to be on the flight to insure that some semblance of standards be applied. On the other side of the partition, another inspector, Ivan Behel, heard the conversation. He rushed to Dave Haley and repeated what I stated. Within an hour the Supervising Inspector ordered me not to be on the flight. No inspector—no confrontation!

This incident was common of the petty office spy system, and shows the level of maturity with which the public's lives are handled within the FAA. When I first arrived in the Denver Office, I was surprised when other inspectors motioned me outside the building to a secluded spot when we had to discuss some particular safety problem involving United Airlines. These old timers already knew the pettiness that existed, and didn't want certain inspectors eavesdropping and then running to the supervisor with gossip about inspector dissatisfaction.

It appeared that former Air Force pilots were the worst tattle-tales in this area, and I often wondered if the Air Force conducted its internal affairs in this manner.

HIGH SINK-RATE APPROACHES

Another widespread problem at United Airlines was the practice of high-sink-rate approaches, wherein the aircraft is allowed to descend at a dangerously high sink rate toward the ground. Just before making ground contact the pilot pulls back on the control column to stop the high descent rate. The danger in this type of unstabilized approach is that the aircraft may not respond, and continue its downward path, hitting the ground (or a vertical seawall) short of the runway. If the approach speed was stabilized, as required, there is very little excess speed to be traded off for halting the descent. Since United DC-8 pilots also deviated from stabilized approaches, and sometimes approached at a high speed, they got away with the high sink rate approaches. Both deviations were dangerous and unacceptable.

During an enroute check on United Airlines from Denver to Los Angeles the captain made one of the worst high-sink-rate approaches that I had yet witnessed. It was the closest flight profile to a hot-rod Navy fighter plane approach. Abeam of the downwind end of the runway, at 1500 feet, and what seemed to be less than a mile from the runway, the captain pulled the power completely off, put the plane into a bank exceeding thirty degrees, and we came down like a rock. Just prior to touching down the pilot pulled back on the control column and fortunately his extra speed saved us from ramming into the ground. It was an exciting approach, and dangerous as hell.

After the engines were shut down at the terminal I attempted to do the job the FAA paid me to do. I tactfully debriefed the flight crew, and explained the dangers of that type of approach. The captain reacted by lambasting me and implying I didn't know what I was talking about.

This attitude was made worse by the fact that the captain, Bart Stephens, was also an FAA-approved company check airman. In addition, he was one of the two captains I downgraded shortly after I arrived on the United assignment. This dangerous piloting technique and attitude required his removal from check-pilot status; he was responsible for correcting this same type of dangerous piloting performance of other pilots. Obviously he would be responsible for a continuation of the dangerous problem.

There was a funeral in Seattle several days later for an FAA inspector killed during a high-sink-rate descent during a training flight over the Great Salt Lake near Salt Lake City. Several senior ALPA members pressured the Chief of the FAA Air Carrier Operations Section, Lynn Ashwell, to remove me from the United assignment because of my comments to the United check pilot at Los Angeles. Ashwell was noted for appeasing airline and pilot union officials.

The FAA then suspended me from the DC-8 program. Ironically, relief came from a United official, Charley Skannal. While I was talking to Skannal in his Denver office on another matter, Charley picked up the phone and called Ashwell, advising that my suspension had gone on long enough, and that I should be put back on the program. Ashwell complied. I felt Skannal was more conscientious than most of United's officials. Shortly thereafter he was removed from his position.

I observed other high-sink-rate approaches at United Airlines that would have deadly consequences some months later. During an enroute check from Chicago to Denver I observed and reported that the captain, Gale Kehmeier, had a high-sink-rate approach technique. The report recommended that the receive additional training and a recheck. FAA officials refused to require the additional training. "He's always been weak," was the reply, and it seemingly ended there. But it didn't end there. In later pages 43 people were cremated alive because of the same approach technique by the same captain. The captain paid the price for the misconduct of United and FAA officials and others who knew of the problems.

The breakdown in normal relationships surfaced in many areas. On a United Airlines bulletin board in Denver I read a surly letter from a senior United captain dissatisfied with constructive criticism of his apparently unsatisfactory flight check performance. The pilot lambasted and tried to ridicule the check airman who dared to make constructive comments that would have benefited the pilot and his passengers and crew.

THE SAME PROBLEMS ON ENROUTE FLIGHT CHECKS

Inspectors conduct enroute checks on regular passenger flights, sitting behind the pilots, and evaluating their performance and their compliance with company and government requirements. Properly conducted without any harassment of the inspector, safety is improved.

One interesting enroute check that could easily have been fatal occurred around midnight during a low-visibility approach to San Francisco International Airport. As the captain maneuvered the aircraft on the Instrument Landing System (ILS) approach to the fog-shrouded runway, he drifted left of the centerline just as we approached minimum altitude. Neither the runway nor the approach lights were in sight. An immediate missed approach was required under safety and legal considerations.[5] Suddenly the captain saw the *glare* of the approach and runway lights off to the right. He tried to maneuver at less than 200 feet above the water, even though there was no horizon or any other feature to determine aircraft attitude.

"Take it around! Take it around! Take it around!"

A vertical seawall was immediately below us as the copilot shouted for the captain to execute a missed approach. The copilot was frantic. I was alarmed. I was about to shout, but the copilot beat me to it by a split second. "Take it around! Take it around! Take it around!"

A captain's authority is rarely challenged. But in this case, it was a matter of life or death. At first, the captain hesitated, but then reluctantly moved the four power levers to max rated power position, and simultaneously raised the nose to stop the descent and get a positive rate of climb. But all wasn't well. The captain suddenly experienced vertigo beyond his ability to handle it, and the copilot had to take control of the aircraft.

As we climbed out from that potentially catastrophic encounter approach control cleared the flight for another ILS approach. The captain was still unable to handle the aircraft, and the copilot then flew the approach. Fortunately, the copilot was heavy on experience and well qualified (a safeguard that cannot be counted upon today). The captain sat mute as the flight barely made it in before the fog closed down the airport behind us. The passengers never knew how close death had been. Statistically, it was a safe flight.

As the passengers left the aircraft, a problem remained. The crew was scheduled to take the plane back to Denver that night, with another load of passengers. Allowing the same crew

---

[5] Applying maximum rated power, rotating the nose upward and obtaining a positive rate of climb, and calling for the flaps to the takeoff setting.

to fly the plane would be bad judgment. It was possible the captain had an illness, or simply needed more training in low-visibility approaches. If I grounded the crew, with possible cancellation of the flight, I would surely be removed from the program, and my effectiveness would end.

I advised the crew to delay the flight until I cleared it with the Denver FAA office. I then called an FAA official at home, and explained the situation. I described the events, stated that I had no way of knowing what the captain's problem was; if it was a one-time error that could have happened to any pilot; if he needed additional training; or if he was ill. I also advised that the captain should be rechecked before scheduled for another flight. The FAA official advised to let the captain fly the trip back. Fortunately, it went uneventful, as far as I know.

TRAGEDY FROM A SIMILAR INCIDENT NEARBY

At another California airport at about the same time of night, a Flying Tiger plane crashed into a residential area during an instrument approach to Burbank Airport. Everyone on the plane perished, as well as several people on the ground. The subsequent government accident report placed the probable cause on pilot incapacitation and the inadequate training of the copilot.

The problem could have been the same as I encountered at San Francisco, and a study of both crashes might have exposed problems not previously recognized. However, the corrupted system doesn't work the way it should. Upon returning to the FAA Denver office several days later, even before I submitted the report on the San Francisco incident, FAA management criticized me. Their position was that if I had not been on the aircraft making an official enroute check, the problem would never have been known, and the FAA office tranquility would not be disturbed.

"If you don't like the way we do things here—quit!"

I expressed puzzlement at this FAA criticism from Dave Haley, the office Supervising Inspector. He responded, "If you don't like the way we do things here, quit!"

Besides putting up with Haley, who I considered a dangerous idiot, I had to contend with United. Things were never dull. A meeting between United and FAA officials occurred in United's Denver offices several days later. Frank Crismon, manager of United's flight operations at Denver, started the meeting by sarcastically challenging my right—as a FAA inspector—to question the competency of their pilots. This was the typical attitude of United officials.

United's officials never did adjust to the Federal Aviation Act following their ramming of TWA over the Grand Canyon; they resented FAA inspectors carrying out the government's air safety functions. This attitude was fostered by the collusion between FAA and United officials. If FAA officials had met their safety responsibilities, United officials probably would not have attempted many of the shenanigans they pulled.

I had the least FAA *seniority* of any of the FAA personnel present, but by far the greatest amount of aviation expertise. The others sat mute, afraid to tangle with Crismon. I stated in no uncertain terms to Crismon that "It isn't for United to question the authority of the FAA; that has been long established by law!" Crismon and I were in a heated debate until another United official motioned Chrismon to shut up.

Since Crismon raised the subject of my qualifications, I reminded Crismon that I had over 15,000 hours of pilot experience in diversified world-wide airline operations; that I held virtually every aircraft rating issued by the FAA; and that my experience probably exceeded that of most United pilots. Further, I reminded him that by law it is the inspector's responsibilities to evaluate the capabilities of airline pilots. If *I* wasn't qualified, with all this experience, the government's air safety agency might as well shut down.

Crismon's position was untenable; but mine was impossible, lacking the necessary backing. Crismon then admitted at the end of the meeting that the captain involved in the San Francisco incident had been examined by a company physician after the flight, and supposedly found to be ill. He was then removed from flight schedule. Until then, Crismon refused to admit anything was wrong, and that I and the United copilot were at fault for questioning the captain's performance. I later learned that the captain was grounded with a medical problem for over a year after that incident.

Many of United's conscientious instructors and check airmen encountered similar problems when they strived for acceptable safety standards. United training personnel told me many times that if they downgraded weak crewmembers—requiring the company to provide corrective training—company officials applied pressure to have them relax their standards. If pressure didn't succeed, they were removed from check status.

One of my reports on the dismal standards of United Airlines check airmen read: "Questionable Adequacy of Flight Standards Check Airman, Mr. Dale Cavanaugh." I described unacceptable standards that deprived crewmembers of training, the check airmen's refusal to cooperate with the inspector's participation in flight checks, and conduct destructive to the FAA's safety functions. I recommended cancelling his FAA authority.

For at least five years prior to my report other inspectors reported the same problems with Cavanaugh. Never in the many years that inspectors made these reports did FAA officials ever remove FAA approval from a United check airman. Instead, FAA and United officials harassed and threatened FAA inspectors who made the recommendations.

FAA Washington headquarters knew about the problems, and did nothing. The FAA Washington investigation teams reported the problems, but those responsible to correct them refused to do so. Shortly before my reports were made, a Washington inspection team wrote a damaging report, stating in part: "The functions and responsibilities of the Flight Standards Division, its Air Carrier Branch and the Air Carrier District Offices are not being accomplished in accordance with the functional assignments and responsibilities."

In bland language, the report stated that the FAA was not doing the safety function it was delegated to do by the Federal Aviation Act:

> FAA actions appear to be in defense of the operator rather than being conducive to achieving a high level of safety. A philosophy that allows noncompliance with regulations is not consistent with the philosophy of promoting the safety of flight ... Most supervisory levels in the air carrier programs do not indicate an awareness of their responsibility to control and evaluate their assigned programs ... Long standing deficiencies continue to exist ... the complacency of principal and supervising inspectors ...
>
> The approved training program appeared to be a document necessary to satisfy the legal requirements, but was of little practical value ... many negative comments left no doubt of substandard performance ... An air of unwillingness to "tangle" with the carrier was prevalent.
>
> Amendments to comply with the Administrator's actions of March and April ... and ODCM 62-11 regarding emergency crew training were ignored.
>
> The unwillingness to downgrade or override a company check pilot's decision ... Principal Inspectors attempted to defend the company pilot, and refused to take actions while questioning the inspector's reports ... actions taken by FAA management personnel appear to be in defense of the operator rather than being conducive to achieving a high level of safety ... known unsafe conditions have developed into highly critical situations ... An inspector recommended to the Principal Inspector that the designation of a company check pilot be rescinded had been made in numerous instances. The check pilot was found to be still in business ...

The problem is serious with respect to follow-up action on discrepancies reported by inspectors. ... A need for reevaluation of the quality and effectiveness of the FAA approved training program was evident. ... Unqualified personnel conducting flight checks and large numbers of enroute inspections. Many remarks shown on reports indicated that the company proficiency program was a farce.

Many of these remarks related to United Airlines and the FAA Denver office.

"I wouldn't allow my family to go around the field with one of them at the controls."

The problem of obtaining satisfactory safety standards existed even at the FAA training center for inspectors at Oklahoma City. A friend of mine who is now deceased, Jack Druoin, instructed in Boeing 720s at Oklahoma City. He complained to me that he and other instructors frequently protested that the inspectors were unsafe as pilots and couldn't possibly pass a flight check. "I wouldn't let my family go around the field with one of them at the controls," Druoin grumbled.

Druoin complained that FAA management pressured the flight instructors to pass unacceptable FAA inspectors on their flight checks, some of whom were actually dangerous as pilots. When the FAA instructors refused to pass the pilots, FAA management then conducted the flight checks themselves. But this quickly stopped. Within a week after initiating this change, an uncontrolled hard landing and bounce resulted in major damage to a Boeing 720 jet.

"If this was United, you wouldn't be doing this."

Other airlines were aware of the peculiar control United had over the FAA. During a government hearing in Los Angeles to revoke the operating authority for a small air carrier, Stewart Air Service, the owner protested, "If this was United, you wouldn't be doing this." He was right. I was one of the investigators who helped uncover irregularities at the small air carrier, and later found misconduct of far greater consequences at United Airlines.

DEADLY CONSEQUENCES FROM THE FAA ATTITUDE

Shortly after I joined the FAA in 1962 in Los Angeles, another inspector, Carl Whitman, found himself under attack. He had previously reported a dangerous piloting technique by an American Airlines captain during a flight check. The captain placed the 707 into a steep 45-degree bank shortly after takeoff during a low-airspeed noise-abatement climb. The captain repeated this dangerous bank during takeoff from New York City's Idlewild Airport. The plane stalled, rolled upside down, and plunged into Jamaica Bay, with thousands of people watching. Everyone on the plane perished.

FAA management was upset following this crash. But not because the FAA inspector had not done more when the dangerous pilot technique showed up on the flight check. They were upset because the inspector reported the problem on the inspection report.

FLIGHT ENGINEER COMPETENCY PLUNGED

A problem that gets no attention is the plunging level of flight engineer competency. The competency levels have declined for years, starting with the replacement of professional flight engineers with pilots who have little interest in learning the mechanics of the complex aircraft systems. In the 1950s the Air Line Pilot Association (ALPA) sought to increase their union membership by pushing for a third pilot, which would put four people in the cockpit. After considerable controversy over the matter, a presidential commission was appointed to study the matter. The Commission of aviation-ignorant members ruled in favor of the pilots' union, and the decision was made that the engineer would be a pilot. The FAA failed to maintain the engineer competency standards, and proficiency rapidly deteriorated.

The increased reliability of the jets when they entered commercial service in 1958 prevented more crashes from occurring. No longer did the crew have the serious problems of frequent engine malfunctions and failures; runaway propellers; that required *immediate* corrective actions. The greatly decreased crew competency levels were offset by the greatly increased reliability of the aircraft.

ADDRESS THE COMPETENCY PROBLEM; ELIMINATE THE ENGINEERS AND TAKE YOUR CHANCES

Compounding the decrease in engineer competency, the FAA eliminated the legal requirement for the flight engineer in the 1960s in twin-engine jets. The twin-engine jets were usually operated on the shorter flights, often into high-density airports, where fatigue and midair collision problems dictated the need for a flight engineer. In 1989, the FAA even approved the operation of the huge 747-400 without a flight engineer.

The elimination of the engineer placed added workloads upon the two pilots, many of whom already had a lower competency and experience level. During icing conditions, there is no engineer to check the deicing and anti-icing procedures. There isn't anyone to make a thorough preflight of the aircraft. There isn't anyone to monitor the numerous systems in the aircraft. Not until an emergency situation arises, and an "idiot" light illuminates, are the pilots aware there is a problem. Trouble-shooting goes out the window; they don't have the time, the experience, or competency, of professional flight engineers, to know what they are looking for.

When compound emergencies occur, as will be addressed in later pages, the two pilots are overloaded, and not capable of in-depth handling of multiple failures.

The removal of the flight engineer increased the midair collision danger. The pilots now read the long check lists that the flight engineer usually read, diverting the pilots from looking outside for other traffic. In the past, midair collisions were often avoided by the flight engineer shouting a warning. Sitting behind the pilots and often facing forward, he sees the potential collision when the pilots are busy ready check lists, approach plates, setting up radios.

Many calculated risks have been taken, knowingly sacrificing safety, and lives. The public isn't sophisticated enough to recognize the dangers, and no one cares to spell it out for them.

Body from Delta DC-8 training accident at New Orleans.

CHAPTER FOUR

FAA Kangaroo Court

The same safety chicanery continued after the New York City and Denver crashes. It continued after Harrell exposed scandalous misconduct. It continued after I replaced Harrell. United and FAA officials presented the same safety obstacles, continued the same threats to the crewmembers and passengers as they had in the past. I assumed the safety responsibilities for the United DC-8 program, and I was determined to meet these obligations, come hell or high water!

This determination obviously led to conflicts. United and FAA officials were not going to allow one government employee to either blow the whistle on their games, or eliminate the huge money-saving tactics that had been used so successfully—and tragically—for many years. Maybe it was my Austrian background. Maybe it was concern for those who would continue to suffer so badly. It was probably a combination of all these factors. A confrontation was inevitable.

My reports of safety violations and safety problems in the entire United training operations were similar to those made by my predecessors. I reported into the official FAA records that United Airline officials falsified training records, and that legally required training was withheld from the crew members. I reported that the training was inadequate to safely operate the aircraft, and that United check airmen lowered the passing grade to dangerous and illegal levels compensate for the inadequate training. I reported that United denied corrective training to crewmembers needing additional training. I reported that United refused to allow a legally required check of its training records. The FAA safety functions were made into a shambles, and FAA officials aided and abetted United in committing these outrages that had such tragic consequences.

FAA officials applied pressure, threats, and intimidation, to stop my reports, just as they did with other inspectors. The other inspectors either transferred to another airline assignment; were *forcibly* transferred; looked the other way and did not report the safety violations and problems; or joined the winning team and basked in the rewards.

I reacted in reverse. The greater the pressure, the harder I pursued the reporting and corrective actions. My actions not only threatened the status quo, but threatened to expose long standing corruption within the FAA that caused and made possible some of the nation's most brutal air tragedies. I was a threat to United Airline and to FAA officials. Something had to give.

FAA HATCHET MAN

Washington reacted to the developing crisis by sending a replacement supervising inspector to take charge of the Denver Air Carrier District office; Chuck Stacy. I thought the safety problems would improve, since Stacy knew the problems prior inspectors had with United Airlines and FAA Western Region officials. Stacy knew the consequences in the New York City and Denver crashes.

My first clue that Stacy was a hatchet man came within a few days. Before he hardly knew where his office was, let along know of the complex problems, Stacy wrote a two-page memorandum accusing me of being unable to get along with others in a work situation. He supported this charge with my reports of United's training program irregularities, reports similar to that had been reported by other inspectors for years, and which were our primary job functions. Stacy's memorandum stated in part:

I have reviewed considerable correspondence prepared by you relating to technical subjects and training requirements ... for United Air Lines. Today, during our discussion concerning the adequacy of UAL's flight engineer training and checking, the subject was again recognizable.

Stacy was referring to a morning staff meeting wherein one of the inspectors stated: "If we push this," referring to the correction of United's training program deficiencies, "United will buck us, and not do anything."

I replied, "The Agency has the authority and responsibility to take immediate corrective actions when safety irregularities are suspected. What United thinks doesn't alter these responsibilities."

Stacy's memorandum continued:

> With respect to our discussion of UAL flight engineer training ... the intent of the majority of your correspondence, although in numerous places it is inferred, or implied, is that UAL flight engineers are not meeting the CAR requirements. In view of the above, it is requested that you give careful consideration to the above subject.

The only consideration remaining for me was to discontinue my job duties, and not make any more reports of the safety violations and safety problems. During several conversations, Stacy said to me, "Your reports are a thorn in the side of the Agency. They'll get the office in trouble if an accident investigation is made."

He didn't really have to worry about that. The NTSB (at that time the CAB Bureau of Aviation Safety) had a long-standing sweetheart relationship with the FAA. They protected the FAA from blame by doctoring the accident reports, omitting reference to any highly sensitive behind-the-scene irregularities.

LONG TERM KNOWLEDGE

As Stacy's harassment continued on an almost daily basis and escalated, I called Al Butler, Chief of the Air Carrier Branch, in Los Angeles, to arrange for a meeting. During the meeting I described to Butler the multitude of safety irregularities and violations at United Airlines, the FAA blocking of corrective actions, and Stacy's obsession with blocking my corrective actions.

"I've had these problems myself..."

Butler sympathized, "I know, Rod, I've had these problems myself when I was on the United assignment." (Butler had held the primary DC-8 safety responsibilities at United *during* the New York City and Denver crashes, and knew the consequences of these same irregularities.) I later learned that he was present during the cross-check of United's training and maintenance records when the inspectors discovered that United had falsified the flight training records.

I complained about the high accident rate for Western Region air carriers, for which Butler held safety responsibilities. I described the incestuous relationship between FAA and United management.

"I'm concerned about it also," Butler replied. But his actions did not reflect concern. In Butler's possession, though unknown to me at the time, was a recently received Washington evaluation report equating the high number of airline crashes with internal FAA problems in the Western Region. Butler knew the close relationship between these crashes and FAA Western Region misconduct, which included FAA refusal to act on known safety problems.

I told Butler that Stacy's incessant attacks were forcing the continuation of the same problems that caused earlier crashes. Again, Butler sympathized. I felt higher FAA management was calling the shots: Lynn Ashwell (Chief of the Western Region Air Carrier Branch); or William Krieger (Chief of Flight Standards in the Western Region).

Since the harassment that blocked corrective actions occurred with Stacy's arrival from Washington, the probability was that the pressures were directed from Washington. That meant that the government protection of United Airlines was not confined to the Western Region, but came from Washington.

Butler was simply doing what he was told and had no initiative to buck the hierarchy. My efforts to obtain help ended in failure.

Interference with the FAA's safety functions worsened. Stacy was on a literal rampage, blocking me at every turn, and harassing me whenever he could. I requested another meeting in the Western Regional office to discuss the worsening problems, which was arranged for February 2 & 3, 1965. During this meeting I again described the serious safety problems and the FAA's bizarre blockage of corrective actions.

FAA OFFICIALS VIOLATED REGULATORY AND COMMON-SENSE SAFEGUARDS THAT RESULTED IN DEATHS

Key FAA Western Region officials were present who made key decisions adversely affecting crew competency, aircraft design safeguards, operations, and maintenance. These decisions, violating regulatory safeguards, caused or permitted to occur some of the nation's worst air tragedies in the years ahead. The FAA Western Region was the birthplace for some of the nation's, and the world's, worst air tragedies.

Among those present were Chief of the air carrier division, Al Butler; head of the Denver Air Carrier District Office, Chuck Stacy; Chief of the Flight Standards Division, William Krieger.

During this hearing I related hard-core serious safety violations at United Airlines and the hard-core obstruction with the FAA's air safety functions by the FAA itself. They ignored what I had to say, and ignored my warnings of more crashes to come. Krieger told me to "get on the team or get out."

"I won't be a party to these activities!" I said. "If I have to request a Congressional investigation, I'll do it." I also stated I would file an employee grievance protesting the safety irregularities and coverup.

"An investigation of the entire FAA Flight Standards is necessary."

The conference ended. Before leaving the building, one of the FAA officials guardedly wished me luck. He sympathized, knowing the gravity of what I was trying to expose, but smart enough to realize nothing would be done to correct the deeply ingrained corruption. Before leaving the FAA area I visited the legal counsel to discuss the problems with an attorney friend, Rick Street. He knew the FAA problems, and the inability to get the FAA to investigate itself. He candidly stated, "An investigation of the entire FAA Flight Standards is necessary."

A parallel to my intention to file an employee grievance protesting the coverup and misconduct was similar to an FBI agent using the FBI employee grievance procedure to expose, for example, FBI ties to the Mafia. (Recent revelations doesn't make this sound implausible any more.)

The FAA management group commenced actions to discredit me, and to dilute the impact of my exposures by falsely accusing me of personal misdeeds. The FAA could respond to congressional or other inquiries by claiming the grievance hearing was a personnel problem.

Before my assumption of the United assignment, and while working with American and Western Airlines in the Los Angeles area, the FAA had several times given me letters praising my technical ability and expressing appreciation for my attitude and hard work. This suddenly changed.

THE PSYCHIATRIC TACTIC

Among the petty stunts these FAA officials pulled included charging me with psychiatric problems for reporting the safety irregularities. Stacy gave me a written memorandum and order:

It is requested that a medical examination be made of Inspector Stich to determine his fitness for duty. It is believed the above request is warranted [because] I have found his performance to be marginal in the following areas: ... use of snap judgment ... I have found in his conversation and correspondence, contradiction in some cases of facts; his method of communication [referring to the government reports required by my position] frequently involve distortion, insinuations and innuendos ... has frequently expressed quivering of lips, flushed face and inability to speak normally. This usually occurs during conversation wherein he has become argumentative, or is in the process of expressing his dislike of certain procedures, policy, et., pertaining to the Agency.

Stacy would later testified at the employee grievance hearing that my reports of violations and safety problems at United Airlines supported his allegations. Apparently any inspector reporting the tragedy-related safety violations was guilty of psychiatric problems, according to the mentality prevalent in the FAA Western Region. But my reports were similar to what other inspectors had reported for years. Presumably, they too, had psychiatric problems!

Krieger sent an FAA physician from Los Angeles to conduct a psychiatric examination of me. The entire FAA office, as well as United, knew what was going on. It was quite a spectacle.

The physician, Dr. Fleming and I, met at his motel for breakfast, during which we chatted for several hours. I told Dr. Fleming what was going on, showing him the FAA Western Region hierarchy was using him in their scheme to silence me. He agreed. Upon finishing breakfast he returned to Los Angeles.

NOVEL USE OF EMPLOYEE GRIEVANCE PROCEDURE

I filed the employee grievance. It was unlike any grievance ever filed within the Federal Aviation Administration. Instead of complaining about personal problems, the grievance accused the FAA of graft and corruption associated with a series of specific air disasters.

The entire top hierarchy of the Western Region became involved in the series of petty attacks upon me. The use of the top guns in this petty manner to discredit the exposure of hard-core air safety corruption that had already been implicated in major air tragedies must have been acts of desperation. I knew the misconduct was serious, but having lived with it as long as I had, and recognizing that it had gone on for many years, I may not have recognized that it was far more serious, and had far more implications.

Stacy, who was turning into a literal government-funded goon squad, began another series of petty harassments. Stacy gave me eight sets of conflicting work assignments in writing to complete within a time span where they could not physically be completed. (I had never had written work assignments during my entire employment with the FAA.) I sought to protect myself from the inevitable by submitting a memorandum: "Request for Realistic Work Scheduling."

Due to the heavy frequency of correspondence and instructions from you, with requirements for immediate accomplishment, I find difficulty in meeting the various directives immediately. I therefore request that I be allowed to complete the numerous assignments as soon as practicable. This request is submitted to avoid receiving unnecessary reprimand-type memorandums and allow WE-260 [Chief, Air

Carrier Branch] to go untroubled with unnecessary correspondence.

WE-260 was the routing symbol for Al Butler, who received copies of all reprimands and charges made against me to Stacy. The last sentence of my request was facetious; an attempt to maintain sanity among these perverts.

I worked evenings on my own time, complying with the multiple work assignments. It was in vain. Krieger and Stacy had a good reason for this set-up. On March 17th, Krieger rushed to Denver from the Los Angeles regional office, his arrival preceded by several calls from FAA regional attorney Ned Zartman, in collaboration with the FAA regional personnel officer. Upon Krieger's arrival, I received a formal charge of insubordination for alleged failure to complete one of the many written assignments.

I looked at the charge: "I've completed this assignment and have already turned it into the office files. Stacy even looked at it this morning." Stacy, sitting nearby and overhearing my comment, didn't deny this. Regardless, Krieger refused to retract the proposed suspension. If a person didn't have psychiatric problems earlier, this gang provided them.

Civil Service Commission rules require giving ten days notice to answer this type of charge. But Krieger gave me only 24 hours to answer. The trumped-up charge appeared to be an attempt to get me out of the office until the start of the grievance hearing.

My immediate verbal reply to the charge showed there was no basis to Krieger's allegations. But to have retracted the charge, or allow me the required ten days to reply, would have defeated its intent. From the end of the next working day, when the proposed suspension would begin until the start of the grievance hearing was ten working days. This was the exact length of the suspension for the fabricated charge of insubordination.

During the next ten days the FAA Denver office was busy with management personnel from the Los Angeles Western Region headquarters, accompanied by the FAA legal staff, preparing their case against my exposures of air safety irregularities. My removal would also serve to quiet any inspector who might have dared to speak up during the hearing.

This conspiracy, using top officials of the FAA Western Region whose responsibilities included all aspects of air safety in the important FAA region had one purpose: cover up for the corruption at United Airlines and within the FAA. The major production made out of it suggests I hit a sensitive nerve. I wondered, was the scandal bigger than I realized (and I thought it was serious), and were higher government officials involved?

Krieger gave me only several hours to answer the charge that Civil Service Commission regulations require to be given ten days; I answered: "Your letter is not in compliance with Agency directives as specified in Adverse Actions, Appeals and Grievance manual OAP 3770.2; Paragraph 25 of Chapter Three does not appear to be followed..." Upon receipt of my reply Krieger telephoned regional legal counsel, Ned Zartman, who advised Krieger to proceed anyhow. Krieger then suspended me from duty.

Krieger testified during the hearing that I had advised him of the compliance with Stacy's work request, which eliminated the basis for the charge. He justified proceeding with the emergency suspension because I did not notify him in *writing* of this fact. That hollow excuse didn't make sense. Further, government regulations permit a verbal reply to such a charge.

Krieger's testimony also conflicted with a key statement in his March 19th suspension letter which stated: "After careful consideration of these charges and your reply thereto [indicating I did give a proper reply], it has been decided that the charge of insubordination is supported by substantial evidence and warrants your suspension for 10 working days."

The FAA Western Region hierarchy didn't hesitate using the FAA safety personnel in their scheme. Inspector Chesney filed the following memorandum:

> At your request the following true statement is recorded. On the evening of March 17, 1965, in the company of Inspector W.B. Perry, who was in my car, I noticed Inspector R.F. Stich entering into the Stapleton International Airport, Denver, Colorado parking lot in a government car at a time between 1645 and 1650.

I was returning from one of the multiple assignments Stacy had given to me in preparation for the insubordination charge. Chesney prepared that report, and then the next day conducted a type rating check of a United Airlines captain (Kehmeier) to determine his competency to fly the Boeing 727, and indirectly, rendering a decision on United's training program. The inspector would indeed have been courageous if he had failed the captain. A failing grade for the captain implied a failing grade for United's training program which the FAA legal and management staff sought to portray as excellent. That inspector was dissatisfied with the adequacy of the training given to Kehmeier, and dissatisfied with Kehmeier's performance, but rendered a passing grade anyhow. As will be shown in later pages, 43 persons were cremated alive in a related mishap.

Krieger responded to my earlier request for an investigation of the Denver office, and of the misconduct that I described in detail. Krieger replied:

> I have no intention at this time of conducting an inspection or requesting our Washington office to participate in an investigation as a result of your statements. I find no evidence of deficiencies in the operational phases to cause me to call for such an investigation.

United Airlines had the nation's worst record for the number of air tragedies. It had recently experienced the Denver and New York City tragedies. Washington reports blamed FAA Western Region management for the high number of airline crashes experienced by airlines which had their safety determined by the Western Region. Despite the brutal consequences that thousands would suffer if my charges were true, Krieger sacrificed lives to protect the deeply ingrained corruption.

Any person can demand an investigation, and surely I qualified as any person.[6]

EVERYONE WAS IN ON THE ACTION

The FAA Western Region hierarchy used the Denver inspectors, the Western Region medical director, the legal counsel, the personnel director, and now, the FAA security branch, in their efforts to cover up the causes of the prior air tragedies. Joe Tippets, Director of the FAA Western Region, was a key participant in the activities. Working in close liaison with Tippets and Krieger was James Neilson, Chief of the Western Region Security and Compliance staff and a former FBI agent. Neilson was aware of the safety irregularities I uncovered; we had discussed them previously when we worked on cases together. As a result of these previous investigative activities with Neilson, I received a letter of appreciation from the FAA.

But things were now different. I was identifying hard-core misconduct by FAA officials that was far more serious than any I had ever investigated outside the agency. Neilson had the lawful responsibility to uncover FAA misconduct. But his advancement and salary increases relied upon pleasing the people committing the corruption.

---

[6] The Federal Aviation Act, Public Law 85-726. Section 1001 states:

Any person may file with the Administrator or the Board, as to matters within their respective jurisdictions, a complaint in writing with respect to anything done or omitted to be done by any person in contravention of any provisions of this Act, or of any requirement established pursuant thereto ... it shall be the duty of the Administrator or the Board to investigate the matters complained of.

Feigning a safety interest, Tippets asked me in a memorandum sent through Neilson to submit a report of my allegations. However, Tippets had free access to my many reports
already in the official records. Nevertheless, I prepared a
memorandum dated March 5, 1965, preceded by a general
statement, and referred to the specifics in earlier reports:

> An actual investigation of these alleged conditions discloses
> startling findings that affect aviation safety with past
> catastrophic effects. An impartial hearing officer will
> discover conditions of grave concern to the Federal Aviation
> Agency during the investigation of this grievance ... unsafe
> operating practices, standards and procedures ... low
> standards of [certain United check airmen] ... marginal and
> in some cases deplorable piloting ability on the part of
> certain senior pilots including check pilots themselves ...
> refusal of FAA personnel, primarily management, to correct
> or allow inspectors to correct obvious safety shortcomings
> and non-compliance with Washington directives... The past
> record of fatal and catastrophic accidents of the air carrier,
> along with obvious serious conditions, required immediate
> corrective actions. These were not accomplished.

> An investigation of certain FAA management [and the part
> they played in certain] accidents may reveal startling
> implications affecting the structure of the Federal Aviation
> Agency, and the relationship of the crashes to their atti-
> tudes and actions involving safety activities.

> [referring partly to destruction of official government
> reports] refusal to take corrective actions when inspectors
> disclose safety shortcomings or noncompliance with Agency
> directives, when such action is not only authorized but
> demanded by job directives.

> Numerous safety deficiencies exist today due to failure of
> FAA management to function as their job requires. The
> authority and responsibility ... to take corrective actions
> were ignored.

> Many safety shortcomings exist. There is probably no other
> office in the United States with the massive and serious
> shortcomings that create newspaper headlines [in air
> tragedies]

Unknowingly, I stated problems similar to an earlier internal
FAA investigation in 1964 by a Washington inspection team, but

my statements were more blunt. A few days later, Tippets visited the Denver office and sarcastically admonished me, "You are imagining these things. You're making them up to defend your actions." He then warned me that if I continued I might end up being subpoenaed to Los Angeles. This warning didn't make any sense at all; I would have been glad to be subpoenaed anywhere to expose this mess. I had repeatedly *requested* an investigation.

FBI AND JUSTICE DEPARTMENT COVERUP

Prior to the start of the FAA hearing I made formal complaints of criminal misconduct to the Federal Bureau of Investigation and the U.S. Department of Justice. I offered hard evidence. I described the relationship of the criminal acts to specific air tragedies. Even though I had government authority to make this comparison in my capacity as FAA inspector, neither agency contacted me. They apparently already knew the problems and decided to cover up. This Department of Justice coverup continued for the next 25 years. Never in all that time did the Justice Department examine my evidence or contact me to obtain further information. During this entire time frame, over 3,000 people died in crashes that had their roots in the FAA Western Region misconduct.

SAYING THE RIGHT THINGS

FAA Administrator Najeebe Halaby knew of my allegations. Executive Director of the FAA, William Jennings, presided over the grievance hearing, and kept Halaby informed of my charges and evidence. But Jennings held his job only so long as his decisions satisfied the FAA Administrator. Jennings didn't hold Civil Service tenure, and had no protection against removal. His employer, the FAA, was now on trial and charged with corruption related to a series of brutal air tragedies. Halaby had the power to fire Jennings. Similarly, Halaby held his job only so long as he satisfied Washington politics.

While the FAA Western Region hierarch rampaged through the FAA offices, Halaby stated to the New England Aero Club:

> In my view, FAA was created to serve the public. It has no other reason for existence. A standard against which every decision, every activity in the Agency must be measured is whether it is in the best interest of the public, the people, the nation.

The FAA conducted the grievance hearing in a building at Denver's Stapleton Airport where some of United's activities took place. From the windows, we could look out and see where the earlier Denver crash occurred, caused by the same corruption I was now identifying.

GETTING RID OF MY ATTORNEY

I paid Denver attorney J.E. Kuttler to represent me at this hearing. But his performance during the first hour of the hearing was so grossly unsatisfactory that I dismissed him before the hour was out. It appeared he was either deliberately sabotaging me, or was incompetent. As Kuttler gathered his folders from the conference table to turn over to me, he accidentally picked up one of many folders belonging to FAA attorney Donald Boberick, and gave it to me. He thought it was part of the papers I had previously given him.

FORTUITOUS FINDING SHOWING THE COVERT CAUSE OF WORLD'S WORST AIR DISASTER

When the first day's proceeding was over, I took home my three suitcases containing evidence introduced during the hearing. As I worked late into the night preparing for the next day's presentation, I discovered the folder Kuttler accidentally picked up. Inside was a sequestered government document that was dynamite. It explained why the world's worst air tragedy had occurred (United's DC-8 crash into New York City, and many of its other crashes).

The October 16, 1960 FAA document described United's falsification of flight training and falsification of training records. The unexpected cross-check of records showed the United officials withheld training and competency checks from pilots and engineers. United then doctored up the records to indicate the full training had been given.

If this report was known to the public and its importance emphasized, United Airlines financial liabilities to the next-of-kin would skyrocket, and invoke punitive damages that had rarely been awarded prior to that time. United Airlines stock could plummet, and cause huge losses to corporations holding the stock. An exposure would show the nation's primary air safety agency was engaging in rampant corruption, and by its misconduct caused—rather than prevented—some of the past air tragedies.

The gist of the report didn't expose anything that the inspectors didn't already knew in the environment of air safety corruption. But it was hard evidence to enable others to recognize the gravity of the crash-causing corruption.

THE HIDDEN REPORT WAS A BLOCKBUSTER

The sequestered government report did more than anything else to explain why the New York City and Denver crashes occurred, and why earlier crashes occurred. If drastic changes were not made, it would explain why some of United's subsequent crashes occurred. It was a blockbuster.

The report stated in part:

> Mr. Butler said, "following an inspection and cross-check of United's training and maintenance records," what had disappointed him was that when he or Harrell were on board, the check takes 3 to 3 1/2 hours, but on inspection of the [aircraft] log book to see how long they were taking when we were NOT on board, it had been taking 1 hour 15 minutes to 1 hour 30 minutes, and we just could not understand how they could do all the required [training-check] maneuvers in that time when the second in command was also being checked.

That memorandum was undoubtedly preceded or accompanied by reports on standard FAA forms. I did not have the subpoena power to get the other reports, which FAA attorney Boberick probably had in one of the other envelopes.

The same night that I discovered the report, FAA legal counsel Boberick discovered it missing. He must surely have panicked. Before returning the report, I of course made copies for entry into the hearing record.

INTRODUCING THE EXPLOSIVE REPORT

I tried to introduce the sequestered FAA report that would have had devastating consequences revealing criminal misconduct relating to the world's worst air disaster. But Hearing Officer Jennings protected the FAA by refusing to accept it. This was highly irregular. Hundreds perished because of what was exposed in the report; hundreds and eventually, thousands, would perish over the years if the hard-core misconduct revealed by that report was not exposed and corrected. Jennings did admit its significance.

ADVERSARY PROCEEDINGS

Early in the hearing I protested the FAA legal counsel's frequent twisting of known and already established facts pertaining to air safety problems, and his interference with my submission of documents and testimony. I argued that the FAA's responsibilities were to promote safety, and not to cover up for corruption in the safety arena. There followed this seemingly prearranged rhetoric, Boberick stated: "I would ask the Hearing Officer to instruct him as to my role in this proceeding." Dutifully, FAA Hearing Officer Jennings stated: "This is an adversary proceeding..."

It most certainly should not have been an adversary hearing. FAA internal directives clearly state that grievance hearings are not to be adversary hearings.[7] FAA grievance hearing directives state that the "Grievance Inquiry is a fact-gathering process ... the purpose of the grievance inquiry is to obtain all relevant facts ... so that ... a fair and equitable decision" can be made. An adversary hearing, especially pitting the legal staff against a non-attorney employee, destroys the fact-finding process. Civil Service Commission directives state the grievance hearing must be non-adversary. Safety hearings are always non-adversary so as to bring out any matter that might lead to the cause of the crash or the existence of safety problems.

Safety requirements prohibit adversary proceedings to determine safety problems. The NTSB forbids adversary proceedings at accident investigations, so as not to impede the search for the cause of the crashes.[8] An adversary hearing pits one side against the other.

Jennings admonished me for daring to question the conduct of the FAA's legal counsel. The hearing proceeded under strict courtroom procedures. I was quickly rapped if I varied in the slightest from the legal jargon or sophisticated legal procedures. During the several weeks of hearings, the FAA attorneys continually used legal deception to deny the existence of serious safety problems I identified.

The FAA counsel objected to virtually every document or testimony I introduced into the hearing records that showed air safety irregularities. It was obvious that the FAA legal counsel's position was to totally cover up for any existing safety problem, a tactic that would have brutal consequences for several thousand people over the next few years.

At one point the FAA legal counsel sarcastically insinuated that since I had less piloting time in a particular jet than the airline pilot I was checking, I wasn't qualified to judge his competency. I had more piloting experience and flight time than most FAA inspectors. Using legal counsel's argument, none of the FAA inspectors were competent to carry out the FAA's safety responsibilities. Today, the average FAA inspector has

---

[7] The responsibility of the FAA legal counsel at this safety hearing is stated in the General Counsel handbook, GC P 2150.3: "The question the attorney must ask—what are the true facts and what does the public interest require ... the role of the FAA attorney ... has one basic objective, the promotion of aviation safety through compliance with the Federal Air regulations."

[8] Governmental procedural regulations, part 303, pertaining to Civil Aeronautic Board accident hearings seeking to determine the existence of safety irregularities, state: "there are no adverse parties ... [and] during the course of this hearing, no objections to any matter will be entertained from any party to the investigation or any other person."

far less experience. Using attorney Boberick's argument,[9] none of the FAA inspectors are qualified.

Airline pilots accumulate flight time faster than the inspectors. Most inspectors would be unqualified in their jobs if this criteria prevailed. And the NTSB investigators, most of whom have very little flight time, would be unqualified to make accident reports.

WHO IS BEING PROTECTED?

During recess, outside the hearing room, I brought this ludicrous reasoning to Jennings' attention. He replied: "This is a normal defense action." I replied, "Whose defense, certainly not the passengers!" [or crew.]

In another instance the FAA counsel implied I was not legally licensed as a flight engineer, and as such, was unqualified to judge the quality of United's training program. But I had more experience as a flight engineer than any other inspector in the office. For over ten years I held a flight engineer rating, with experience in numerous types of aircraft. The FAA requalified me as an engineer in jet and piston equipment several times while I flew for the airlines prior to joining the FAA. No other FAA inspector had that level of experience.

While the FAA argued that I was not qualified to evaluate United's flight engineers, the FAA counsel argued, without any evidence, that United's flight engineer training program was safe. Ironically, United eliminated their flight engineer check airmen (their standards were too high), and used check pilots to check the flight engineer's competency. Most of these check pilots did not even have a flight engineer rating.

"Dribble!" shouted the FAA attorney.

The FAA coterie repeatedly showed their contempt for the FAA's safety function. While I was associating United's many training program irregularities with the Denver crash, Boberick jumped up and bellowed: "Dribble."

During another outburst, as I was describing still other safety hazards, and submitting official documents to prove my allegations, the FAA counsel shouted: "I am not concerned with facts!"

During the hearing I testified that United Airlines management personnel denied me access to the training records, in clear violation of law. The implications were especially serious, since it was a record inspection that revealed the fraudulent training record entries and denial of legally required training to the crewmembers prior to the New York City and Denver

---

[9] He was first promoted to Regional Counsel in Alaska, and then took the position of Regional Counsel in the Southeastern District of the Federal Aviation Administration.

crashes. I stated that I suspected these records revealed United Airlines denied legally required training to their crewmembers. I testified that I reported this refusal to FAA management, and that they took no corrective actions.

Boberick jumped to his feet and said, "You're lying; if you had made any such report, federal regulations required FAA management to file a violation against United Airlines." This response, implying an inspector would deliberate falsify his findings, and then go to this much effort to support the lying, was idiotic as only an attorney could argue.

Boberick assumed that FAA management did not know of this record inspection refusal. Boberick didn't know that I could prove that FAA officials had known of the record inspection refusal. When FAA counsel discovered my ability to prove that point, like a good attorney (?) Boberick reversed his argument, and stated that United properly refused to allow an inspection of its training records.

Day after day for over four weeks I carried three large suitcases full of FAA records to the hearing room at Stapleton Airport. During the day I argued my case, and then worked long into the night preparing for the next days' presentation. And during all this I had to face the crap from these idiots!

The FAA counsel became visibly disturbed when I introduced a copy of an official government document reflecting the FAA's cover up of midair collision problems. Boberick vigorously protested my entry of the document into the hearing record. The manner in which Boberick reacted suggested that the original had been either destroyed, or removed from the official records, a common FAA tactic. The report *had* been removed from the records, but only after I made a copy of it. The unexpected appearance of my copy now irritated Boberick, though reports of far greater importance had been introduced.

I didn't put much weight on that document. But the document embarrassed FAA Administrator Halaby because it added further credibility to criticism of the FAA's handling of the midair problem. Representative Henry Gonzalez had just blasted the FAA's whitewash tactics, accusing the FAA of intimidating pilots to discourage their reporting of near midair collisions. Hiram Broiles, principle inspector for United Airlines, prepared the report shortly before his retirement. (Years later Gonzalez become famous for investigation another scandal.)

Boberick insinuated I had either written the report for Broiles, or had forced him to prepare it. Broiles was almost twenty years my senior, a titular superior, and a pilot who in the thirties was an airline captain in China. He didn't need me or anyone else to write his reports.

COVERING UP FOR A SAFETY PROBLEM THAT HAD, AND CONTINUED, TO CAUSE HUNDREDS OF DEATHS

During the hearing I described the FAA's blocking of corrective actions to prevent pilots accidentally descending into the ground due to lack of altitude awareness. Prior accident reports confirmed the existence of this problem, which I also saw during flight checks. Two crashes from this problem had recently occurred on airlines based at Denver. In one crash on Frontier Airlines, everyone was killed.

Recognizing the seriousness of this problem, and faced with pilots failing their check flights because of it, I developed a simple but effective fix. I handed the pilots a grease pencil to make two marks on the glass face of their barometric altimeter. The lower mark depicted ground elevation and the higher altitude mark depicted minimum descent altitude. Simple, but effective. It worked.

Later, I recommended permanent mechanical ring and bug assemblies attached to the face of the altimeter, to take the place of the grease-pencil marks. This pilots favorably received the recommendation. United flight instructors thought favorable of it. But the FAA Denver office ordered me to halt corrective actions, and to ignore the problem.

To show the prevalence of the serious altitude-awareness problem, I entered into the hearing record over a dozen copies of previously submitted FAA reports in which I had identified pilots inadvertently descending below the minimum altitude during approaches. One of my reports stated in part:

> The value and need for a ring and bug assembly on the altimeter to insure a more positive adherence to minimum altitude on instrument approaches was discussed with Mr. McFadden [United's Manager of Flight Operations]. Incidents were related which clearly shows the need for this installation to insure greater safety. Mr. McFadden appeared very interested, as did Mr. J. Brown [UAL Director of Flight Training] who was present and with whom this was previously discussed. Mr. McFadden stated that he would investigate this further.

I testified about conversations in which I described the altitude-awareness problem with various FAA and industry personnel. I submitted a memorandum prepared by FAA principal inspector Hiram Broiles, describing my research into the altitude awareness problem:

> Letter of Commendation—Inspector Rodney Stich. During a recent conversation with Mr. Sommermeyer, Vice President

of Line Flying for United Air Lines, he informed the undersigned that Inspector Rodney Stich's recommendations to
him regarding the placement of two bugs on UAL's altimeters for predetermining minimum altitude for a standard
instrument approach and ground elevation of the airport
have been implemented on several UAL aircraft with
favorable pilot comments.

Mr. Sommermeyer said that Inspector Stich's suggestion
would be perfected to a further degree by establishing a bug
on UAL's Radar Altimeters for lower minimums. This would
consist of a bug which, when set for a point of decision
altitude, would cause a light to burn, thus alerting the pilot
that his decision altitude has been reached.

It is also my understanding that Mr. Stich made this
recommendation to the Federal Aviation Academy at
Oklahoma City and that they, too, placed two bugs on the
altimeter of the Convair 880. Should not Mr. Stich receive
commendation for this outstanding contribution to safety?
This progressive thinking by an inspector should be encouraged, it is maintained, and credit given when credit is due.

Obviously, I was identifying a serious problem and a corrective
fix. But my official reports also showed the FAA tried to
obstruct these corrective actions. I entered into the hearing
records a copy of an FAA memorandum showing the blocking
actions:

I feel some concern that if there is any further pressure
from Mr. Stich—or any other FAA person, for Altimeter
`bugs', we may end up with a strong complaint from UAL. If
this should occur, I think we would be unable to defend such
practice to our Regional or DCA [Washington] office. Please
check with Rod, as you may think is necessary, to assure
that the `bug' project is not pushed.

The FAA person ordering me to stop this corrective action had
safety responsibility for the two air carriers that had experienced crashes due to the same problem.
    Despite these many reports, despite the accidents resulting
from the problem, the FAA legal counsel fraudulently argued
that these reports of safety problems were fabrications, that I
had never seen the problems during my official duties, and that
they did not exist! This is the type of lying that formed the
base from which hundreds of people were torn apart in crashes
from this very same cause.

Jennings went the legal counsel one better. He reprimanded me in his hearing decision for promoting this corrective action (on my own time) after FAA management improperly ordered that the serious problem be ignored (as they waited for the subsequent crashes). We didn't have long to wait; a United 727 crashed into Lake Michigan due to the altitude-awareness problem on August 16, 1965 during the hearing.

Jennings also implied that Stacy's accusations of my being hard to get along with, based in part on this altitude-awareness activity and my reports on United's training program irregularities, justified the psychiatric and other charges against me.

It is possible that the next of kin of the hundreds of persons who perished in subsequent air tragedies (it actually goes into the thousands at the time this book was sent to the printer) may have a little problem with the FAA conduct of perjury, subornation of perjury, fraud, conspiracy, coverup, establishing the official covert policy of this key government safety agency.

The FAA took the position that the serious problem did not exist. After the hearing, and after several more crashes occurred from this same problem, Washington issued a circular addressing the exact same problem:

> The increased number of accidents and incidents involving lack of altitude awareness prompted the FAA to initiate rulemaking" action for an altitude alerting device.

CROSS EXAMINATION

After presenting considerable testimony and a multitude of copies of previously submitted FAA reports, FAA legal counsel cross-examined me. The sole purpose of this cross-examination was to deceptively and fraudulently state the safety problems did not exist, and that FAA and United Airlines officials had not engaged in any wrongful acts.

These repeated deceptive tactics reflected a very serious attitude problem within the FAA that was hard-core criminal misconduct, involving the FAA Western Region, and the office of the FAA Administrator. The implications were fantastically serious. People could be expected to die as a result of this scheming. And people did die, and the specific deaths and specific air tragedies can be found throughout these pages.

The FAA didn't call any witnesses to refute my testimony and evidence. Not a single shred of evidence was contradicted by testimony or by evidence. Rules of court procedures required that my evidence be accepted as true. The official status of the documents made the evidence impliedly true.

After this cross-examination it was my turn to question witnesses. I considered Stacy my primary witness. He wasn't too bright in my opinion. But he had the power of the FAA behind him, protecting his bungling attempts to cover up the serious misconduct. His arrival in the Denver office had immediately escalated FAA efforts to stop my reporting of safety irregularities at United Airlines. Stacy was a key part of the conspiracy, and any misconduct on his part directly implicated FAA Western Region and Washington officials, up to and including the FAA Administrator.

Referring to his charges against me, I instructed Stacy to "point out the areas that indicated" the basis for his accusations. Stacy spent several days on the witness stand looking over my safety reports, seeking to justify his charges that the reports indicated I was hard to get along with. Stacy started by stating, "This is just typical," pointing to a copy of my report titled: "Hazards in Present Stall Recovery Technique and Recommended Changes."

The report was a critique citing the dangers of present stall-recovery training techniques in jet aircraft. The United Airlines technique resulted in large altitude loss during stall recovery while in landing configuration, the very time when *minimum* altitude loss is life-saving. My report recommended specific changes in the training program that would greatly reduce the altitude loss. I had practiced this technique during recurrent DC-8 training at Eastern Airlines at Miami, and we all agreed that it was a improvement over the prior method. It was simpler, and the altitude loss was almost nil.

I looked puzzled that Stacy could find justification for his accusations in that report. The hearing officer also looked puzzled. We all looked at Stacy, waiting for an explanation. No reply came. After a while I again asked Stacy what in that report indicated the serious charges he made against me. He finally conceded he could find nothing. This same poor stall-recovery technique possibly could have prevented a major air tragedy when a United jet crashed into a Chicago residential area on December 8, 1972, killing everyone on board. Mrs. Howard Hunt of Watergate fame was on board, and this crash is described in later pages.

HAZARDOUS OXYGEN MASK

Stacy turned to another report, and again testified that it justified his charges. This report described an unsatisfactory oxygen mask which United crewmembers repeatedly criticized, and found difficult to quickly put in place. To save money over the total replacement cost of a previously issued, unsatisfactory mask, United used the face piece designed for the former mask assembly, with the head piece of still another mask. It was an abortion. It was difficult to place over the face. Sharp protrusions threatened the user's eyes. It was difficult to get in place. In a high altitude depressurization, the crew could pass out before fitting the mask to the face, with possible loss of the entire aircraft due to an unconscious crew.

My report described the oxygen mask deficiencies, the complaints by United crewmembers, comments by the FAA aeronautical center research team, and my observations. They all agreed the mask was unsatisfactory and actually dangerous.

The importance of a safe oxygen mask design was illustrated by an inflight emergency occurring on a Sabreliner 40 type corporate jet flying at flight level 45,000 feet on June 24, 1967. The cabin door blew out, causing an instant depressurization. The copilot, who wore his oxygen mask hanging loose by his face (as required by regulations at that altitude), quickly donned the mask. The captain, who had his oxygen mask hanging on the storage hook, passed out before he could place the mask over his face. The loss of oxygen caused him to slump unconscious over the control wheel.

The copilot made an immediate emergency descent. One of the passengers, also a pilot, and using a portable oxygen bottle, placed the oxygen mask over the captain's face. The captain began to revive as the oxygen flowed into his lungs. But during the brief period of unconsciousness, a nitrogen bubble developed in his body, and lodged in his brain. The captain became combative, and began wildly fighting to take over control of the aircraft, endangering everyone on board. It was a wild flight, developing from a seemingly minor oxygen problem. The captain remained in critical condition for several weeks, luckily surviving, but suffering brain damage.

BRAIN DAMAGE DUE TO OXYGEN DEPRIVATION

In another instance where oxygen deprivation existed for only a short time, with the symptoms showing up later, brain damage occurred to passengers when a military Lockheed C5-A aircraft lost pressurization after a cargo door failed.[10] Before the aircraft could get to lower altitude, over 150 people suffered permanent neurological disorders from brain dysfunctions, the basis for subsequent law suits.[11] U.S. District Court Judge Louis Oberdorfer of Washington called the law suits arising from the brain damage "one of the most protracted, costly and unpleasant litigations in the history of this district."

BRAIN DAMAGE FROM HIGH ALTITUDE OXYGEN LOSS

Investigators from University of Washington School of Medicine examined 35 young mountain climbers from 1981 to

---

[10] April 4, 1975, during "Operation Babylift," airlifting 250 Vietnamese orphans, many fathered by American GI's.

[11] Law suits filed in the U.S. District Court, District of Columbia, *Friends For All Children v. Lockheed*, No. 76-0544. Also *Maupoint v. Lockheed*, No. 76-0544-68.

1984 and discovered long-lasting or permanent brain damage.

Incredibly, Stacy considered my identification of a problem that affects the crewmembers directly and the passengers in back indirectly if the pilots pass out, to be support for psychiatric charges. Obviously, *someone* had psychiatric problems!

Stacy continued to look for something in that oxygen mask report that supported his accusations. After an hour passed, Jennings asked in a sympathetic voice, "This is not, however, evidence of being hard to get along with in a work situation."

Twitching nervously, Stacy replied: "No, sir."

I would liked to have had a sympathetic voice in my behalf during this hearing.

Politely, Jennings assisted Stacy. "To remind you of what you are looking for now, Mr. Stich has asked you to point out evidence which you found in the correspondence file or memorandums which he had written, which indicated to you that he was hard to get along with in a work situation."

Stacy continued searching. After a seemingly long five minutes, with all of us growing restless, I again asked Stacy if he found any such indication. Stacy didn't answer. When it became obvious Stacy's position was becoming absurd, Jennings came to his aid and stated; "No, Exhibit 41, he has finally agreed is no evidence of an inability to get along with people in a work situation."

Stacy hadn't agreed. It was the hearing officer's benevolent action which got Stacy out of his predicament. As Stacy looked through other reports, I looked at Exhibit 41, and read into the hearing records a paragraph indicating the opposite of what Stacy had charged: "They were extremely cooperative, friendly, and helpful to this inspector in his efforts to evaluate the types of oxygen masks now in general use by industry." The friendly reference to those who helped with my attempts to focus attention on the dangerous oxygen mask hardly indicated a hard-to-get-along-with personality, or a person with a psychiatric disorder.

Stacy fumbled through more reports. Finally, after what must have been twenty minutes of searching, Stacy came up with still another report. He couldn't have picked a more classic example of serious problems at United Airlines that helped to explain its history of air disasters.

Identified as Exhibit "1" in the FAA hearing, this seven-page report listed serious United training and check program problems. It identified anything-goes competency standard that explained why almost all of United's many crashes resulted from ignorance of the systems and procedures.

Looking at the report, Stacy testified, "I find there to be disagreement between you and the Check Pilot." That there was!

The U.S. Government paid me and other inspectors to disagree and report when FAA approved company check airman had unsatisfactory standards. Obviously, there will be disagreement if the inspector does not agree with the company check pilot's standards. To insure that the FAA would not be able to later circumvent Stacy's testimony, I asked Stacy for a clarification: "Now, sir, you are referring to the fact that [the United check airman and I disagreed on the outcome of the check. Is that correct?"

"Yes."

My report described incredibly poor performance by the two captains being checked by the company check airman. It was the worse flying I had ever witnessed in my many years of airline and Navy flying. The company check pilot tried to pass as acceptable, pilots who didn't meet minimum standards, and whose flying capabilities were actually dangerous.

It would be virtually impossible to find a worse example of unacceptable standards.

I continued: "Well, not meaning to belabor exhibit number one, Mr. Stacy, where in this exhibit does it indicate I am hard to get along with?"

"As I originally stated," Stacy replied, "whether it was right or wrong, there was indications in this exhibit that there was disagreement, and there is also indications in here of questionable competency on the part of the check pilot. There are indications in here of variances in statements made by you [that Stacy could never identify] that creates an impression to me that there was disagreement, as I said originally, whether it was right or wrong, there was disagreement."

Benevolently, Jennings interjected, "You think Mr. Stich should have been able to sell his position to the check pilot?" That's a new approach, and should make great headlines:

"Poor FAA Salesmanship Responsible For New York City Air Tragedy."

My report went into detail on the need for the company check pilot to several times take over control of the aircraft to avoid a rapidly escalating out-of-control situation. It told of massive out-of-limits heading changes after a simulated engine failure. Starting with a south heading, paralleling the Rockies to our right, the heading changed 80 degrees, taking us toward the nearby mountain range. In addition to loss of heading control, large altitude losses occurred. The pilots had poor knowledge of important flight procedures. Several times the check pilot, fortunately sitting in the copilot's seat, had to take over control of the aircraft because of the dangerous attitude.

Later, during debriefing on the ground, the company check airman insisted upon grading the pilots as satisfactory, and depriving them of needed corrective training. At that point I excercised the responsibility for which I was paid and entrusted. I disagreed and did what the FAA expects inspectors to do. I stated the pilots need additional training and a recheck of their competency.

Making matters worse, the two captains being checked were senior company check airmen, setting the standards for other pilots. One pilot was from Los Angeles, and the other, from Seattle. One of the pilots was so bad that United, on their own determination, provided as much simulator training for him as the average piston pilot received during his first checkout transitioning to the jets. (And he had been flying the jets for the past four years!)

In addition, Stacy knew the same company check airman identified in that report had been identified by other inspectors as contributing to a poor safety standard at United Airlines. That same company check pilot boasted of forcing the removal of my predecessor, Frank Harrell, and had warned me, I would meet the same fate if I did not become more amenable to United's ways.

I delved further into Stacy's reasoning processes and asked him if, based upon the facts in my report, he would have suspended the company check pilot's authority. Stacy replied that he would not.

Stacy continued his search. He came up with another report, exhibit number 31. This was an FAA report describing United's noncompliance with emergency evacuation training requirements, a very serious matter. The report stated that United violated the mandatory emergency evacuation training requirements, deprived the crewmembers of this training, and falsified its records to show that the training had been given.

Additional support arose from listing the names and the statements of United instructors who admitted the noncompliance. Their office was only five minutes from the hearing room. Incredibly, if the FAA hierarchy considered its inspectors likely to lie in official reports, they could confirm the facts with the United Airlines instructors named in that report!

It was cremation of passengers in the United Denver DC-8 crash—the site visible from the hearing room windows—that caused the requirement for the training that United was now violating. Stacy thought a report of that outrageous death-causing misconduct supported his accusations against me!

Suddenly, Stacy proffered another exhibit, and he couldn't have selected a more fitting climactic report. The safety deficiencies described in that document would, during the hearing, cause a United 727 to crash into Lake Michigan, and seven months later, be the cause of death for 58 persons in an American Airlines crash at Cincinnati. My recommended corrective actions shown in that report were identical to those made in the government accident report following the Cincinnati crash of November 8, 1965; instrument changes to prevent inadvertent descent into the ground.

Referring to my report, and the recommended corrective action, Stacy testified that it showed a personality problem. He accused me of making numerous attempts to sell Gus Sommermeyer [United's Vice President of flying] on the need for altimeter instrument changes to reduce the chance of crashing into the ground from lack of altitude awareness.

I asked Stacy what in that report showed I made numerous attempts to sell Sommermeyer on this safety proposal. He looked at the report for several minutes and finally admitted he was unable to find any such indication.

Contradicting Stacy's previous statements that the report justified his charges, Sommermeyer was quoted in another FAA report Stacy already had in his possession, as accepting my recommendations. The report stated Sommermeyer was grateful for them.

I then asked Stacy: "*If* I had pressured Mr. Sommermeyer to correct this condition, do you think *that* would be wrong? Would it indicate an inability to get along with others if I had pressured Mr. Sommermeyer to correct a serious safety problem that I believe existed?" Stacy replied, "Yes."

It is important to associate the outright lying during the safety hearing, covering up for major air safety problems, with the shredding of hundreds of bodies in crashes made possible by the misconduct.

Seeking to have Stacy give his justification for the harassment actions obstructing the reporting of serious crash-causing problems was an exercise in futility. It was *obvious* that Stacy was sent from Washington to stop my exposure actions. Was Washington trying to protect primarily United Airlines, or its own dirty line? The price for these tactics went into the thousands of deaths over the next two and a half decades.

Stacy's statements during a taped telephone conversation admitted that he did *know* of the safety irregularities, that he did *believe* they existed, and that the FAA had the authority to correct them. His statements showed he did *agree* with my reports of safety problems at United, although he used these same reports in his psychiatric charges to silence an exposure of the safety problems. I testified that Stacy made these statements to me several times. But during the hearing, the FAA legal counsel and FAA Hearing Officer *denied* there were any problems, while their primary witness admitted to the accuracy of my reports during this taped conversation.

Prior to the hearing, during an evening telephone conversation, Stacy admitted the problems at United Airlines. Stacy said, "We are going to tackle this thing with United ... We have got a lot of good points to hit, some of which you recommended." Although he admitted problems with United Airlines, his actions never reflected his rhetoric. The telephone conversation continued:

> We are going to get it loud and clearly understood with United, ... We are going to hit these areas, ... and also not just United, but it is other areas, too ... we will rapidly clean up these things ... I have identified these problems to higher ups along the same lines as you have done, and this is one of the weaknesses we have had, and you identified it"

During the hearing I testified that Stacy admitted the safety problems. I submitted reports prepared by Stacy several years earlier, referring to the same problems.

The same day that Stacy admitted these safety irregularities, he used my official reports of safety violations and deficiencies as the basis for the psychiatric charges against me.

There were other exhibits in which the reasoning went along the same lines. I could have continued my questioning of Stacy, but the record was clear. He knew that serious safety violations and safety problems existed. He deliberately obstructed the air safety functions of the FAA in a conspiracy with others, and the conspiracy went right to Washington. Stacy contributed to many of the deaths that followed his clumsy tactics.

CHIEF OF THE AIR CARRIER BRANCH

Key players in the dangerous games played by the FAA Western Region was Al Butler, Chief of the Air Carrier Branch in the Western Region. He was a bit-player, doing whatever he was told. Butler held the air safety responsibilities for United's DC-8 program while the New York City and Denver crashes were occurring, and later held the air safety responsibilities for Flying Tigers when they experienced many crashes. He apparently did not require too much from the air carriers in his area of safety responsibilities.

Butler was one of the inspectors making the cross-check of United's training records at Denver and maintenance logs at San Francisco when the inspectors discovered the falsification of training records. Having made this important finding, and repeatedly witnessing other forms of misconduct during his assignment to United Airlines, and witnessing the resulting tragedies, Butler knew the consequences of the irregularities. He also knew the rewards of remaining quiet, as he progressed up the FAA management ladder.

The crux of Butler's testimony was that he had read my official reports, that I had personally reported the problems to him, that I appealed to him for help, and that he had not taken any action. Butler testified with a straight face that he did not consider any safety problems existed, despite the many crashes.

Butler knew of my report identifying United's refusal to provide the legally required emergency evacuation training. My report stated in part: "The life rafts are not being moved from the stowage location to the launching location during emergency evacuation training, as required by appropriate FAA orders, ... the training that *is* conducted is done every *three years instead of yearly.*"

This training is very important for an almost automatic response in an emergency. Three years between training is totally inadequate. The law requires *yearly training* and crew *participation* rather that simply observing. Try learning to fly a plane by watching instead of doing; it doesn't work too well.

The emergency evacuation training requirements were written in blood for Butler. He shared responsibilities for United's DC-8 safety with Frank Harrell when the Denver tragedy occurred. That crash was the catalyst for this training requirement. Butler made no complaints of any safety violations or safety problems. Grateful FAA management promoted Butler to Supervising Inspector of the Burbank air carrier district office, which included crash-plagued Flying Tigers. Flying Tigers suffered four major crashes in one year while Butler held responsibility for its safety activities. In one of these tragedies 107 persons perished. Later, the FAA promoted Butler to chief, air carrier division, at Los Angeles.

Shortly after that assignment, a Flying Tiger Constellation crashed into the residential area of the San Fernando Valley near Burbank. Butler lived close by, and should have been moved by this crash. This was the crash that happened the same night I was experiencing a near-crash on a United jet during an instrument approach to San Francisco. Everyone on board that Flying Tigers aircraft perished, along with those killed in their homes.

In another Flying Tiger crash, the flight engineer mishandled an engine problem, and ended up with *two* engines inoperative. The plane than crashed into the frigid North Atlantic. As two engines failed, the engineer turned to the captain, "I'm sorry John, I goofed." That he did; many deaths resulted.

The government accident report stated: "Details which are necessary or desirable to be performed prior to ditching were not carried out ... the Captain was asked the location in the cockpit of the release handle which actuates the life rafts stowed in the left wing compartment. He was not aware that there was such a handle. The simple actuation of a handle to release the other lift rafts may have saved many of those who perished."

Of the training programs that Butler always appeared to consider satisfactory, the accident report stated:

> Testimony indicated that scope and emphasis on training in this area was lacking. The Board strongly supports the view that crew training should encompass all features of all equipment that may be utilized to cope with emergencies in flight and thus enhance safety ... performance and testimony by surviving crew members indicated a lack of, or a low degree of proficiency having been gained from the training program designed to meet emergencies such as were encountered on this flight.

One of the FAA inspectors working on the Flying Tiger assignment approached the NTSB investigators outside the hearing room, and blasted the FAA's safety attitude associated with the Flying Tiger training program. In this way, many inspectors alert the NTSB investigators to crash-causing problems.

Again and again, death came in air crashes due to training program irregularities under the responsibility of Al Butler. He was aware of the result of inaction on training program problems.

During the Denver hearing Butler testified that he knew of United's refusal to allow an inspection of its training program records. I asked Butler: "Is it not a fact that I stated to you at this meeting, Mr. Butler, that I had been refused access to United Air Lines' training records?"

"Yes, you did tell me."

"Do you recall what your reply was?"

"No, I don't." Butler made no qualifying statement as to why he refused to act. Later, apparently pre-briefed by FAA legal counsel, Butler admitted knowing that United refused to allow the record inspection to occur, stating United didn't have to make those training records available to the FAA.

I questioned Butler as to United's dangerous safety pilot that had received many adverse reports, and which violated federal air safety laws. "We don't have a regulation that requires the safety pilot" to be at the controls.

Referring to the numerous FAA reports describing the United practice as dangerous, Butler testified, "I am not sure that you can say that a safety deficiency exists..."

I did manage to get Butler to admit that "none of the inspectors in the Denver office took to" this United procedure. That was an understatement, since it was the only time in the FAA's history that inspectors refused to get on board an airline's plane because of the dangers.

Butler even testified to being on board a United flight that experienced a near-accident. During a pilot check, the pilot mishandled the controls and placed the plane in a dangerous attitude. The safety pilot sitting in the observer's seat was almost powerless to correct the life-threatening emergency. But Butler still thought the practice safe.

Hundreds of people perished in air crashes closely related to training programs for which Butler had air safety responsibilities. Referring to United's training program problems, Butler testified, "I have found no evidence that the program is marginal."

REGIONAL TOP DOG

The top dog in the FAA Western Region was William Krieger, Chief of the Western Region Flight Standards Division. Krieger was in this sensitive air safety position when the Washington investigative team rushed into the Western Region offices to make an emergency inspection of FAA activities the year before this Denver hearing. The report of that inspection blamed the FAA Western Region for the area's high airline accident rate.

After my verbal complaints to Butler failed to obtain any satisfaction, I directed a request for an investigation to Krieger. The Federal Aviation Act and FAA directives required that Krieger conduct an investigation upon receiving my charges. The brutal consequences in thousands of air tragedy deaths also demanded an investigation. Krieger refused to conduct an investigation.

Krieger knew air tragedies are a natural sequence to uncorrected safety problems. And he had a history of them to prove the relationship. Krieger butchered air safety activities while he and his group were in control of key FAA safety functions.

Krieger's testimony followed the pattern set by Stacy and Butler. Krieger testified that he did not conduct an investigation into the reported safety irregularities because my initial complaint to him did not include the specific times, dates and places of each occurrence. Could he look into the face of the thousands of relatives who lost a family member in a crash, and state he did not make a prior investigation of alleged crash-causing problems because the allegations (referring to detailed documents) did not give the dates, times and places!

Obviously, the voluminous amount of data could not be placed in an initial complaint. Nor is it the proper place to put the detailed evidence that belongs in the investigation that follows a complaint. Krieger's legal responsibility was to conduct an investigation, which he refused to do.

Krieger knew crashes and deaths would follow if the safety problems went uncorrected. The earlier Washington report made clear that the Western Region misconduct caused or permitted many of the crashes to occur. There were no changes made. Then I made my report. And again Krieger ignored them. He knew that the consequences would be bloody. And so it was, over and over again.

Krieger thought his refusal to make an investigation ended the matter. Instead, I made imaginative use of the Civil Service Commission employee grievance system, and filed a grievance protesting air safety corruption within the FAA.

During the hearing, Krieger sought to excuse his refusal to make an investigation by testifying that I did not respond to his demands during a telephone conversation for times, dates and places. Therefore, he was justified in doing nothing about the serious safety allegations. But the FAA files, more complete than mine, contained the individual reports I submitted, and contained the recommendations making reference to the individual reports. This was a cop-out made obscene by the consequences of inaction.

Referring to United's safety pilot problem, Krieger testified that no authority existed to force United to comply with the safety requirements, or to change their practice. He was lying. The FAA had the authority to remove the unsatisfactory company check airmen; to require the airline to provide crews sufficient training to pass meaningful checks of their competency; and to require United to meet regulatory requirements, such as emergency evacuation training.

Krieger testified that he requested United to change their safety pilot practice, but that the air carrier refused. As I referred to the dangerous practice, Krieger testified, "The record doesn't prove this to be a fact." The records clearly showed this was a dangerous practice, and Krieger's previous writings referred to it as being dangerous. In one report Krieger made reference to the United Boeing jet that came close to crashing into a group of homes at the end of the runway at Cheyenne. Included in Krieger's previous writing on this safety pilot problem:

> ... several incidents [at United] has created serious safety hazards ... It is difficult to understand why UAL continues to operate their training flights in this manner. For several years there has existed a doubt concerning the safety [of this practice and] we have had several incidents in which this policy has created serious safety hazards ... The Airman

Certification Specialists who have submitted comments are unanimous in their opinion that ... a fully qualified pilot be in ... the seat during the conduct of emergency maneuvers.

After Krieger testified that the FAA had no authority to act on the problem, I asked, "Mr. Krieger, you said that we have no authority to take action. If you, today, thought we have a safety pilot situation that we consider dangerous, you feel we cannot take any action?"

"We ran into an impasse with United Air Lines on our position, and a moratorium for a period of over one month, possibly six weeks, ensued, where we didn't participate in the flight checks because of the fact that United would not put a safety pilot in the right seat."

Krieger had just testified he didn't think this was an unsafe procedure. He then testified to FAA inspectors refusing to board any United Airlines training flights for six weeks, something that had never before happened in the history of the FAA.

Krieger continued, "United Air Lines told us they are going to beat us, in the March 24, 1965 meeting they said they are going to beat us on this very point..."

Beat us? The FAA determines whether there is a safety pilot at the controls or not!

This was the meeting which Stacy referred to in his February 5th telephone conversation, where big things were going to happen. It turned out to be a dud.

"We had no authority ...."

Krieger added, "We had no authority to take any action against United, other than threatening and possibly telling them their insurance might be in jeopardy, or something of that nature."

The complex field of aviation insurance obviously wasn't included in Krieger's expertise. Nor were safety matters.

Krieger continued, "But United had many arguments in their favor, which they presented, such as the fact that they were so convinced that they were correct in their supposition, pointing out that their accident record in training wasn't as bad as other carriers who had safety pilots at the controls."

That line of reasoning can be shot full of holes. Part of that argument could be due to United's noncompliance with industry accepted training maneuvers, and a hell of a lot of luck. A paradox of aviation is that a dangerous practice may continue, escaping tragic consequences for years, before fate finally intervenes. This does not make the practice any safer than the arrival home of a drunk, without crashing, is proof that drunk driving is safe.

Hearing officer Jennings engaged in similar deceit. During the hearing, Jennings stated, after having examined the FAA directives requiring a safety pilot to be seated at one of the flight controls, that Federal laws did not require a safety pilot in the control seat.

I had submitted copies of federal directives requiring a safety pilot to be in the safety pilot seat. Also, federal safety laws are also sufficiently broad so that the FAA has the authority and the responsibility to intervene when any unsafe practice or condition is believed to exist, as reported by its inspectors. A typical example would be if a jet, let us say a DC-10, is reported by an inspector to have a faulty cargo door locking mechanism. A specific FAA regulation is not needed, directed to that particular door, for the FAA to take corrective action. Krieger and his gang in the Western Region were simultaneously approving aircraft designs that violated prior safeguards, and thousands would die over the years. That DC-10 cargo door would be one of the causes of mass-deaths.

Jennings referred to United's change in safety pilot position after the inspectors refused to be on board a training/check flight without a safety pilot at the controls. Jennings approved the presence of a safety pilot at the controls when FAA inspectors were on board, but the absence of a safety pilot when an inspector is not present. "I find nothing inconsistent in these two positions." I responded, "What about the people on the ground [or the crewmembers]!"

THE WAITING GAME

Jennings responded, "How many accidents have we had in United Airlines's DC-8 training program which can be traced to the absence of a check pilot in one of the control seats?" We have had many near-tragedies, simply waiting for luck to run out.

Jennings conveniently overlooked the many near-crashes caused by the safety pilot problem. United had been very lucky that one of its aircraft had not crashed into a housing area surrounding the airports.

Using Jennings' philosophy, numerous near-crashes requiring corrective actions could be ignored until an actual crash occurred. Then corrective actions could be considered.

WESTERN REGION COMPLICITY

While my adversaries (and yours) engaged in these dangerous games, the same group violated numerous regulatory safety requirements. This included elimination of hard backups for the flight controls and horizontal stabilizer on the DC-10 and other aircraft; reducing the strength requirements for jet engine fan blades; permitting outward opening cargo doors and eliminating design safeguards associated with these doors; eliminating fire-fighting equipment in cargo compartments; and many other safeguards.

Early in the hearing, the FAA hearing officer stated that anything testified to by me, not refuted by evidence, would be considered as the truth. The FAA legal counsel presented no witnesses or evidence to refute my official testimony and reports, and as a matter of law, they must be accepted as true. The FAA legal staff used legal trickery to deny the existence of officially established air safety problems of crash-causing magnitude. We had the paradox of qualified air safety inspectors, authorized to make these determinations, blocked by aviation-ignorant FAA attorneys, using legal trickery and intimidation to deny serious safety problems which they knew had existed for years.

TAPED TELEPHONE CONVERSATIONS

Stacy and Krieger did not know when they testified that I had taped their telephone conversations. At the end of the evidentiary portion of the FAA hearing, I made known that tape recordings of certain telephone conversations existed; that these tapes would show the existence of perjury and fraud by FAA management personnel who had already testified; and additionally, that these tapes would show them admitting to the existence of the safety irregularities that they denied in their sworn testimony.

FAA legal counsel Boberick already knew perjury existed, and probably promoted it by subornation of perjury. Boberick warned that if the tapes were submitted, showing his witnesses to be lying, actions would be taken against me for making the tapes.

An examination of the transcripts made from the tapes showed the perjury. Stacy admitted the existence of the safety irregularities that I had reported. He admitted falsely accusing me of AWOL and Unexcused Absence. He acknowledged other things that would be violations of federal laws, and would require his removal from the Federal Aviation Administration.

I complained to Jennings of the massive conflicts in sworn testimony by FAA officials, and stressed the consequences in continuing crashes. I requested that all witnesses, including myself, undergo lie detector tests. This request was not as unusual as it may sound. Government agencies have used these tests in the past. But the FAA hierarchy was now involved, and the perjured testimony was already obvious.

Jennings refused my request, glibly adding: "False testimony under oath is a crime, and if you believe that a crime has been committed, you may discuss it with the proper prosecuting officials."

The FAA's security and compliance department, for instance, was involved in the misconduct. The office of the FAA Administrator was implicated. The Executive Director of the FAA was part of the coverup. The Department of Justice knew of the criminal activities. Jennings knew that no government security department would act on the perjury.

The hearing finally recessed after several weeks of testimony. I proceeded to prepare my initial and then my closing briefs, totaling about 500 pages. I had little optimism in the outcome, even though I had proved my case. This was a Kangaroo Court!

The first section of my closing brief dealt in generalities. The subsequent sections dealt in specifics, such as the specific perjury, serious safety deficiencies, irregularities, and outright noncompliance with mandatory federal safety requirements. It stated in part:

This initial closing brief could almost be called, `The Federal Aviation Agency, a Story of Blood and Guts.' The hearing has illustrated that the Federal Aviation Agency, as it pertains to Flight Standards, and particularly the Western Region, has allowed thousands of safety violations of the regulations to exist in serious safety areas with a major air carrier. These violations of safety regulations including noncompliance with agency safety directives were accomplished with the obvious knowledge, condoning and coverup by certain FAA management personnel.

It has shown that massive and continuous violations of the important emergency training regulatory requirements have occurred since approximately 1962 in clear noncompliance with the intent and the specifics of the Agency regulations and Agency directives.

The net result is that several thousand crewmembers are now in noncompliance with this regulatory requirement with an obvious safety deficiency existing that will take several years to correct.

It has been shown that passengers are paying for the refusal of incompetent FAA management personnel who stubbornly refuse to follow their job authority and responsibilities, and who ignore Washington directives, Agency regulatory requirements, and the requirements of aviation safety.

It has been shown that certain FAA management personnel have been closely associated with numerous tragic air disasters of operational safety deficiencies, that such FAA personnel were responsible for the safety activities and standards of the air carrier, and that such personnel before and after the major air tragedies tolerated or ignored the conditions that were involved in the accidents.

United's crashes continued, as we all knew they would. Even during the hearing itself, crashes occurred in the very same area of safety problems that I identified, and that the FAA Western Region stated did not exist.

The NTSB blamed the cause of the American Airlines Cincinnati crash upon a lack of altitude awareness. This is the problem I sought to correct; the problem the FAA ordered me to ignore; the problem the FAA legal counsel stated did not exist; and the problem the office of the FAA Administrator, via his staff member Jennings, stated did not exist!

Before Jennings issued his hearing decision report on August 24, 1965, which was approved by the FAA Administrator, several more crashes occurred from the altitude-awareness problem that the FAA falsely stated did not exist.

During the hearing, FAA management alternated between stating that no safety irregularities or deficiencies existed, to stating no authority existed to correct the problems.

SETTING THE STAGE FOR MORE TRAGEDIES

The evidentiary part of the hearing was over, and we adjourned to prepare and submit our briefs. My brief was hundreds of pages long. It made reference to hard evidence of unsafe and illegal practices, corruption by FAA and United officials, the criminal coverup during the hearing, and the relationship to prior air tragedies.

In their closing brief, the FAA legal staff falsely stated that there were no safety problems; that they hadn't been reported; that they were corrected; and that suddenly the air safety picture had brightened. The FAA legal staff stated that the unsafe and illegal conditions did not exist because I had *never reported them*, even though the hearing record contained dozens of previously submitted reports.

THE MAGNITUDE OF THE TRAGEDIES

The FAA legal counsel stated during the hearing that the frequent reporting of safety irregularities "when the need was long gone" was justification for Stacy's charges against me. No one testified the problems were eliminated. FAA management testified to doing nothing about the reported safety problems. Obviously, they couldn't be gone.

Within the hearing records were three years of reports of serious safety problems, leaving no doubt they existed, and were reported. For the sake of argument only, *IF* I had not made any written reports of the safety problems prior to the hearing, and the hearing was my first report of the serious conditions, the magnitude of the consequences in air tragedies made the FAA duty-bound to make an immediate and thorough investigation.

Referring to my report of noncompliance with the emergency evacuation training requirements, the FAA brief falsely stated, in part: "It was also clearly evident in this hearing that when this condition was reported by the grievant, nearly two years ago, the necessary steps to correct this condition were taken by the personnel then responsible. Further, it was also evident that at all times subsequent to the time that the corrective action was taken, United Air Lines had been found to be meeting all the requirements of the regulations."

There were no reports or testimony showing any corrective actions were taken. FAA management alternated before stating they knew of my reports, and did nothing, to the FAA's attorney arguing that I never made the reports. Hearing Officer Jennings even read into the hearing records a paragraph showing the emergency training problem existed during the grievance hearing: "Also, it appears that the [emergency evacuation] training is only done every three years instead of yearly."

I was stunned by these outright lies by the FAA legal and management staff, knowing that crashes would continue, and that unsuspecting people would die. And die they did, for the next 15 years, not only at United Airlines, but in other crashes in which the Western Region had safety responsibilities for the known, uncorrected, safety problems!

Referring to the long-standing problems with United Airlines check airmen, the FAA counsel stated; "Grievant's testimony has proved little more than his problems encountered in connection with these [check airmen] was the result of a personality conflict between individuals." Nothing was ever stated during the hearing showing any such personality conflicts. The technical deficiencies described in the official reports showed the basis for my recommendations and supporting the unsatisfactory nature of the check airmen.

The FAA legal counsel knew the problem inspectors had with the United Airlines check airmen, who falsified training records, and had anything-goes safety standards. The problems had been repeatedly reported for years, in such reports as the sequestered report that the legal counsel had in his possession at the start of the hearing.

Of the dangerous safety pilot problem, the FAA legal counsel wrote: "Stich could not point to a single instance in which he had reported such an incident to have occurred."

I could have sat mute during the hearing, relying on submitted government reports, including my own, to prove the danger of this illegal, unsafe, practice, whose only redeeming feature was in saving United Airlines a bundle of money. One of many reports that I *did* enter into the records, contrary to the FAA's brief, stated in part: "This inspector has observed on several flights the check pilot jump to his feet and grab the throttles and the yoke to prevent an accident. The condition whereby United Airlines check pilot jumps to his feet [from the observer's seat] to take corrective action is not unusual."

TRAINING PROGRAM COVERUP

Covering up for the training program that would kill over 1000 persons before there was a temporary halt in 1978, the legal counsel's closing brief stated that "the allegations [of] serious safety deficiencies [at United Airlines did not exist and were] solely the product of Grievant's fertile imagination."

I was castigated in the FAA's closing brief for daring to make such reports. The FAA implied I was making untrue reports of safety irregularities, and that I did not understand aviation safety. But the FAA attorneys supposedly fully understood this highly technical subject!

My accusations could be summed up by the statement of the FAA legal counsel in his closing brief, that I charged FAA management "with criminal misconduct in connection with their application of Agency directives, policies and regulations."

FAA ADMINISTRATOR COVERUP

Hearing officer Jennings, Executive Director of the FAA, and a member of the Administrator's staff, reflected the level of corruption within the FAA.

Fourteen lines in that decision were devoted to a whitewash of the emergency evacuation training noncompliance, implying that the statements of the FAA counsel that it did not exist were correct.

The coverup of the safety pilot problem stated that I "did not report this [problem on my] proficiency check reports nor in any other writing." The problem was repeatedly reported in FAA writings and these writings were the subject of considerable testimony and questions during the hearing by the management trio.

Jennings covered up for the serious ground collision problem by simply implying the hazard did not exist, apparently insinuating I didn't know what I was talking about; the numerous company and FAA personnel described in my reports didn't know what they were talking about; the government accident reports didn't know what they were writing about, but that the FAA legal fraternity knew. The public paid for these legal ploys in thousands of human lives destroyed.

Jennings *praised* Stacy, whose testimony was impeached again and again during the hearing, and whose misuse of the power of the FAA was employed to fraudulently protect the United Airlines misconduct, and the corruption within the government safety agency. Jennings wrote: "I was impressed by the sincerity of Stacy."

Addressing himself to the perennial United check airmen problems, Jennings stated: "Stich never did mark a check pilot unsatisfactory." Jennings added, contradicting his previous statement, that my marking of check pilots as unsatisfactory was due to "a personality clash between Stich and the Check Pilot." Numerous reports were in evidence showing I did mark the company check pilots as unsatisfactory.

After the hearing, the crashes continued. Simultaneous with the deaths, those who cooperated in the fraud received promotions. Boberick became regional chief counsel in Alaska, and then later in the Southern Region. Stacy received merit increases.

For thousands of others, there would be life-long sorrow, as thousands of unsuspecting persons were injured, maimed, and killed in airline crashes that could not have happened without the obstruction of justice by people in positions of trust.

SEEKING HELP BEFORE AND DURING THE HEARING

Immediately prior to and during the FAA grievance hearing, I sent dozens of letters to members of the U.S. Senate and House, seeking to get them to exercise their FAA oversight responsibilities. It was an exercise in futility. I described, as a government air safety investigator, the specific acts of corruption, and associated the acts with specific air tragedies. Not a single one conducted an investigation, or made any public utterance that would focus public attention on the serious scandal, or request an investigation by the GAO, the inspector general, or the Department of Justice. They did nothing, despite the horror that would continue if my allegations were true. This government-funded coverup showed contempt for those whose death would be made possible by their acts.

Senator Mike Monroney was head of the powerful Senate Aviation subcommittee, and held the primary responsibility for oversight of the Federal Aviation Administration, when I first contacted the Senate and House members. I contacted Monroney before the start of the Denver grievance hearing, describing the FAA misconduct and the related crashes. Monroney replied:

If there are shortcomings in the FAA which are jeopardizing safety, I will, of course, want to see them corrected. Therefore, if you could give me some details and more specifics as to the exact practices or procedures which you believe are dangerous and should be changed ... I would not hesitate to investigate the FAA. I would be anxious to have such information if you feel you can divulge it to me.

"I do not doubt your honesty or your sincerity."

The FAA attack increased in intensity and frequency. I again asked Monroney for help. Monroney replied: "I would be happy to assist in any way I can to remedy the situation. I do not doubt your honesty or your sincerity." Monroney added: "I would make it clear to Mr. Halaby that you should not be the subject of recriminations merely because you had the courage to speak out on matters affecting the safety of airline passengers. Best wishes."

The attacks, and safety violations, continued.

In another letter, Monroney wrote: "I have raised your case with Mr. Halaby and assure you that the charges you have raised are being considered seriously by the Agency. I am sure the hearing officer will be objective and impartial in his consideration of them."

The FAA considered the charges, but not in the manner Monroney implied. The FAA legal and management staff, under the Administrator's control, subjected me to the indignities described earlier.

I shouldn't have raised my hopes too much. Former FAA Administrator Elwood "Pete" Quesada described in Senate hearings other forms of air safety problems caused by pressure groups, who regularly contributed funds to the same politicians. Quesada presented a 60-page list of safety problems. Monroney sided with the groups that Quesada blamed for interfering with safety.

The House and the Senate groups directly responsible for air safety ignored the warnings Quesada identified. The same group ignored my evidence of misconduct, even though criminal acts were implicated in several major air disasters. Even a moron could see the relationship.

Representative Henry Gonzales frequently spoke out against the FAA, and I made him aware of the government corruption. Gonzales replied: "For more than two years I have been speaking out on the matter of aviation safety generally."

That was the end of that. The public, who really suffered, got no relief.

In reply to my next letter, Gonzales stated: "You may be sure that I will continue to do everything within my power to bring the deficiencies in our aviation safety program to the attention of the public."

Still trying, Gonzalez responded to another letter: "If I can help in any way, I will be happy to do so."

I asked, and got the usual. Nothing.

In answer to letters putting him on notice, Representative Oren Harris, Chairperson of the House Committee on Aviation Matters, wrote: "The Interstate and Foreign Commerce Committee, as you know, has an active and continuing interest in the work of the Federal Aviation Agency. Air safety, of course, is of prime concern to the Agency and also of prime concern to the committee."

I sent evidence of the FAA and NTSB corruption, and Harris responded: "I cannot conclude that a committee investigation of your claims is warranted."

I put many members of the Senate[12] and the House[13] on notice, expecting them to respond to their responsibilities in this major air safety and government corruption. Many if not all recognized the truth of my allegations. Some, like William Proxmire, Robert Kennedy, Mike Monroney, George Miller, admitted the gravity of the allegations, and then did nothing. Some wouldn't even answer, permitting the criminal acts to continue to the repeated, final consequences.

The gravity of the allegations coming from an insider required conducting an immediate investigation. Members of Congress are constantly conducting investigations. At the very least, they could have requested the Government Accounting Office (GAO) to conduct an initial investigation, which members of the House and Senate repeated request. They all kept the lid on the scandal, either to protect some of their corporate and union political contributors, or because they had some vested interest they were protecting. Responsibility to the public came last, and by that time, other interests required ignoring the public's interests.

THE FAA CORRUPTION WAS ON A ROLL, PROTECTED BY POWERFUL CO-CONSPIRATORS IN GOVERNMENT!

Having survived this hard-core corruption directly linked to numerous deaths, the FAA coterie was on a roll. They could not now be identified by Congress, the Department of Justice, the news media, without implicating these same groups who protected the FAA prior to the earlier fraud-related crashes. A string of crashes directly linked to this misconduct was an element linking all forms of corruption, and made them all parties to the same conspiracy that lasted for years, and continues to this day.

---

[12] Mike Monroney of Oklahoma; Robert Kennedy of New York; John McClellan of Arkansas; George Murphy of California; Thomas Dodd of Connecticut; Daniel Inouye of Hawaii; Vance Hartke of Indiana; Edward Kennedy of Massachusetts; Eugene McCarthy of Minnesota; James Eastland of Mississippi; Howard Cannon of Nevada; Clinton Anderson of New Mexico; Strom Thurmond of South Carolina; George McGovern of South Dakota; Robert Byrd of West Virginia; and William Proxmire of Wisconsin.

[13] George Miller and Edward Roybal of California; John Conyers, William Ford, John Dingell, all of Michigan; and others.

SERIOUS NTSB INVOLVEMENT

Before and during the Denver hearing I notified the NTSB of the hard-core misconduct, the corrupting coverup at the Denver hearing. I stressed the need for their immediate intervention and their obligations under the Federal Aviation Act. Any person may demand of the NTSB that they conduct an investigation into alleged safety problems, and my position certainly qualified me to request such investigation.

The NTSB responded by fraudulently stating the matters I brought to their attention did not indicate any safety problems. They lied, and by their lying hundreds and eventually thousands perished in crashes caused or made possible by misconduct of officials in the FAA Western Region.

Because of their lying the safety problems continued, and the NTSB because contributing causes to the crashes because of their corrupt coverup. Every time that a crash occurred in which the NTSB's earlier coverup played a role, another nail was put in the coffin that required the NTSB to continue the coverup. To this day the NTSB is barred from ever identifying air safety misconduct without implicating itself, and implicating everyone who joined the conspiracy of silence that covered up for the serious air safety misconduct.

CASSANDRA WARNINGS

The Cassandra's warning were deliberately ignored, knowing that the criminal coverup, the conspiracy to coverup, the perjury, had a price: the deaths of thousands of persons.

Let's see who these persons were, and how this group of FAA Western Region thugs affected the lives of thousands of persons, not only in the United States, but citizens of foreign countries. Buckle up, hang onto your seats, and watch the tragedies go by.

Aircraft and occupants jammed into the front of the United
Airline DC-6 near Hayward, California.

CHAPTER FIVE

Immediate Consequences
as to UAL....

At the Denver air safety grievance hearing the FAA hierarchy fraudulently covered up for many federal safety violations and air safety problems. The FAA legal and management staffs, and the FAA Administrator, knew that crashes and deaths would follow the coverup, especially of United Airlines aircraft. But they did not expect the crashes to occur as soon as they did. Let's look at the horror and the deaths that unsuspecting victims suffered from the FAA misconduct and those whose complicity of silence made the crashes and deaths possible.

CRASH INTO LAKE MICHIGAN

Lack of altitude awareness caused one of the first crashes to occur on August 16, 1965. United Flight 389, a Boeing 727, approached Chicago on a flight from New York. Among those on board was a former president of the Air Line Pilots Association, Clarence Sayen, who obviously knew of the many problems and of my attempts to correct them. The pilots' union knew the rampant safety problems and not only did nothing about them, but they blocked corrective actions. Several times I felt their sting after I tried to correct dangerous safety problems that threatened their own members. Now their own president would shortly pay with his life for a safety problem I sought to correct, and the FAA corruption forcibly continued.

It was a dark night, and the lights of Chicago were clearly visible fifty miles away. Approaching Chicago, approach control cleared Flight 389 to descend from 35,000 feet cruising altitude to 6,000 feet. The crew acknowledged the clearance, and reported leaving its assigned altitude. The captain made the radio communications while the copilot flew the plane.

Although the clearance limit was 6,000 feet, the crew continued their descent upon reaching that altitude, apparently misreading the barometric altimeter as 16,000 feet. Within minutes of reporting leaving 16,000 feet—when they actually were leaving 6,000—the aircraft slammed into Lake Michigan, erupting in a ball of fire which was seen from Chicago and O'Hare Airport.

The bodies and wreckage were eventually recovered within a few days 250 feet below the surface of Lake Michigan. The impact with the water cut many of the passengers in half where the seat belt wrapped around their waist.

UNITED WAS AT IT AGAIN—no CVR recorder.

The cockpit voice recorder (CVR) which records sounds in the cockpit would be valuable to determine the cause of the crash. But when the searchers found the unit in the aircraft, only the *shell* of the CVR was in the wreckage; the intact shell did not have the interior recording mechanism. United had illegally dispatched the aircraft without the unit functioning.

The CVR is protected by a rugged case designed to withstand severe impact. The case was there, unopened, but the insides were missing! United apparently did not have a spare unit and simply put the shell of the unit in the aircraft to give an appearance of meeting the legal requirements. (The aircraft could not be legally dispatched without the CVR unit installed and operating.)

The NTSB report described the cause of the crash as due to lack of altitude awareness, the common problem that I sought to correct. The NTSB purposely withheld from the accident report the fact that I had repeatedly reported the same problem, and that the FAA blocked corrective actions, and fraudulently held during the Denver hearing that the problem did not exist.

The NTSB also omitted any reference to the serious problem of United dispatching the aircraft without the CVR, fraudulently inserting the shell of the unit into the receptacle to indicate the unit was installed. If the NTSB had reported the underlying causes of the crash it would have implicated itself for not taking corrective actions when I reported to the NTSB during the Denver hearing this same altitude awareness problem and the FAA corruption. The NTSB now *had* to cover up to protect itself. By doing this, it continued and pyramided the coverup that it would have to do for every subsequent crash. To this day the NTSB is unable to report air safety misconduct without implicating itself. It is no longer a properly functioning government air safety agency.

MORE OF THE SAME

Another close one. A United Airlines flight from Hawaii to San Francisco was descending from 33,000 feet to 6,000 feet. The copilot was flying and he mistook passing through 6,000 feet as 16,000, and continued the descent. As the aircraft approached what the crew thought was 10,000 feet altitude (when it was actually sea level), the captain reminded the copilot to slow down to 250 knots. (FAR requirement below 10,000 feet.) The copilot leveled off to bleed off airspeed, and unknowingly skimmed along the ocean surface while thinking they were 10,000 feet higher.

Fortunately, and saving everyone's life, the flight engineer, who wasn't paying attention to the pilots' altimeters, noticed an absence of cabin pressure differential at his flight engineer panel. He didn't realize the aircraft was at sea level and therefore the aircraft cabin couldn't be pressurized. Suddenly the engineer recognized the problem, and shouted to the crew that they were about to crash into the water.

ANOTHER CLASSIC AIR DISASTER—Salt Lake City

The beginning—or was it the end—for many passengers on United Flight 227 occurred at Denver's Stapleton Airport on November 11, 1965, an appropriate location for what was about to happen. The United Boeing 727 was being readied for its short flight to Salt Lake City, and then on to San Francisco. Among the passengers were the entire Blaisdell family of Florrisant, Oklahoma, the home state of Senator Mike Monroney, who played a key role in covering up for the safety problems that affected this flight.

A PREMONITION

Marvin Bennett, his wife Janet, and their two children, six year-old Rosa and two-year-old Marie Christiania, were returning from an assignment to Bogota, Columbia. They were making a surprise birthday visit to Marvin's mother in Silverton, Oregon. Janet felt a premonition, or perhaps she was simply afraid of flying. Whatever the reason, she left the plane and made a phone call to her grandmother in Idaho Falls, Idaho, to relieve her own anxiety. Several days before this flight, Janet felt uneasy about the trip, asking Marvin, "What would you do if by some freak accident all three of us would die?"

Unknown to the Bennetts, the coverup of the safety irregularities that would soon affect them occurred in the same building where Janet initiated the call to her grandmother. One of the warnings I entered into my closing brief stated:

Many safety shortcomings exist. There is probably no other office in the United States with the massive and serious conditions existing, affecting safety, as in Denver. Any one of these safety shortcomings can bring newspaper headlines into being. Safety is endangered by existing safety short-comings at this time, any one of which can cause a fatal or catastrophic accident tomorrow. The repercussions in the safety activities of the FAA due to perjury and the actions associated with the conditions may be paid for in blood and guts. The Agency tolerates a worsening of the existing conditions to depths never before reached, of misconduct and dereliction of duties. A sinister attempt to undermine the United States aviation security could not be any more effective than the conditions shown here.

Not only had I warned about the serious problems at United Airlines and within the FAA, but I had warned about the problems that the captain of *this* flight had with his approach technique, which would be soon be fatal for many of those boarding the flight.

United made the boarding announcement, and ninety-one persons boarded the aircraft. They had the implied assurance from the United States government, represented by the FAA and the NTSB, that United's safety standards met federal criteria and complied with federal air safety laws.

United flight 227 was soon airborne, and headed for Salt Lake City, less than an hour away. In many respects, this flight would have much in common with United Flight 857 that crashed at Denver's Stapleton Airport. That flight was also affected by similar training program problems and corruption.

Captain Gale Kehmeier, his copilot, and the flight engineer, plus the flight attendants in the cabin, were products of the airline's training and check program. Their performance reflected the adequacy of United's training and the FAA oversight responsibilities. I had reported that United Airlines denied corrective training to weak pilots, endangering the crew and the passengers. I had reported the flight engineer training and anything-goes standards as the worst ever seen. I had reported United was violating the emergency training require-ments and falsifying its records. The FAA and the NTSB covered up for these major safety violations. Now, let us look at the end results.

THE CAPTAIN WAS NO STRANGER TO ME

Earlier in the year, I reported the captain needed correc-tive training for a dangerous high sink-rate approach problem. I observed this flying technique during a route check from Chicago to Denver on that same flight number. United Airlines denied Kehmeier the corrective training, and FAA refused to require it be given. This "in-bed" relationship between FAA and United officials saved United considerable money.

I made brief reference to the enroute check in my flight log book: "Enroute Check—G. Kehmeier. High Descent rate, hard landing." The reference was to a high sink-rate approach and landing technique which United check pilots failed to correct. Since some of the check pilots had that same problem, there wasn't the proper environment to correct the dangerous technique.

Marvin Bennett sat in the left row of seats opposite his wife and two daughters. They anticipated a smooth and quick 57-minute flight to Salt Lake City. Janet was especially anxious to get there, as her mother would be waiting.

The weather was excellent, and the flight should have been uneventful. Salt Lake City's temperature was 44 degrees, the sky overcast, and the wind calm. A pleasant, crisp, autumn evening.

The passenger terminal was just to the west of the north-south runways, and now bustling with families and friends waiting for United's arrival. The clock in the terminal building showed 5:50 p.m. as United announced the approach of Flight 227. Many of those waiting for Flight 227 moved closer to the large plate glass windows, watching United's approach and landing. What they saw would eventually be a nightmare.

"It looks like he'll have to go around."

Cleared to land on runway 34 left, landing to the north, and passing immediately in front of the terminal building, Flight 227 was much too high on the approach path. FAA control tower operator Preston Hunt watched Flight 227 descending at an abnormally steep angle. Kehmeier's technique hadn't changed since I reported a similar dangerous high sink-rate approach going into Omaha. Hunt stated to a fellow controller, "It looks like he'll have to go around."

Hunt was partially right. United *should* have gone around. Kehmeier got away with this unsafe technique before, and as some of United's check airmen would say, "You can't argue with success."

With all power levers retarded to idle thrust, the gear extended, and full flaps, the aircraft sank rapidly toward the ground, in excess of 2300 feet per minute. A safe maximum sink rate at that point would be less than 500 feet per minute. Sensing the impending consequences, the copilot attempted to add power, saying, "Skipper, we are going down fast and getting slow, and I'm for putting in some power." Kehmeier waved his hand from the power levers and stated, "Wait a little, I'll do it."

The urgent need for adding engine power was suddenly evident, but it was too late. Kehmeier shoved the power levers forward, and the jet engines slowly started to accelerate. (At idle thrust most jet engines require a relatively long spool-up time to develop significant thrust.)

Too late with power application, all they could now do as the plane plunged toward the ground was wait for the crash. The jet hit the ground hard, short of the runway. Fortunately, there was no vertical sea wall, building, or immovable object, where they hit, which would have caused an explosive disintegration of the aircraft. With a loud thump, the jet hit the ground, ripping off both main landing gears, and sliding on its fuselage for three thousand feet, fish-tailing wildly from side to side, and obviously out of control.

THE ENGINEER HAD TO ACT QUICKLY

A well-trained flight engineer would immediately execute certain emergency items immediately after the initial crash. But United's crew-concept required all crewmembers to debate the subject, and there wasn't time.

The emergency required the engineer to immediately shut off the fuel valves and fuel booster pumps. Fuel lines could easily be broken by the crash, and failure to shut off the fuel valves and pumps would result in large quantities of fuel flowing in and around the aircraft.

The engineer did not turn off the fuel valves. He did not shut off the fuel pumps. He did nothing. Fuel lines had broken and fuel poured out under pressure beneath the aircraft. The sparks ignited the fuel and the stage was set for tragedy, if it hadn't already been set months and years earlier.

A SURVIVABLE CRASH

The 727 slid to a stop. In the cabin all the passengers were alive. It was a survivable crash, and could have remained that way if there hadn't been even more problems. The crew had to quickly evacuate the passengers, and their response depended upon the quality of the emergency evacuation training. But I had testified in the Denver grievance hearing and submitted FAA reports showing United withheld the legally required emergency evacuation training, and falsified its training records. The FAA legal and management staffs said these reports were fabricated, without providing any support for that statement. The NTSB wrote to me in letters that this and the other problems I raised did not constitute safety problems.

THE LEADERS—WHERE WERE THEY?

As soon as the aircraft stopped sliding, the cockpit crew, and three Denver-based FAA inspectors dead-heading in the aircraft, jumped from the aircraft. The more alert passengers did the same. But many passengers, especially women and children, sat petrified in their seats, waiting for the guidance that never came.

One confused passenger wandered aimlessly back and forth inside the darkened and smoke-filled cabin. Kenneth Geiler of Lake View Terrace, California, *crawled* through the length of the passenger cabin and into the abandoned cockpit. Unable to exit from there, he crawled back "through and under people" to the rear of the cabin, unknowingly passing the cabin door right behind the cockpit. He finally managed to find an exit over the wing and leave the burning aircraft.

Ample time existed to evacuate all the passengers to safety during this time interval. There was even time to spare. But where were the leaders? The flight crew members and three FAA inspectors, all *victims* of the emergency evacuation training program problems, were safely out of the aircraft. Inside the aircraft, 43 persons were slowly cremated alive.

FEELING THE HEAT

"It was horrible. The heat was terrible," exclaimed Ralph Nesbitt of Santa Monica, California. He stated, "A virtual free-for-all existed in the cabin." Marvin Bennett, knocked unconscious, was unable to help his wife and children. Fortunately for him, another passenger, believed to be Ned Brown, pulled Marvin's unconscious form through an emergency exit to safety. The intense heat and flames advanced on the confused passengers groping through the cabin or sitting in their seats. They screamed with pain as the scorching heat advanced.

ALL HOPE WAS LOST—or was it?

All hope had been given up for those inside the aircraft. Suddenly, a fireman pouring water on the burning plane saw a woman's arm waving through a small crack along the partly-opened rear stairway door. Stewardess Victoria Cole and two male passengers had attempted to exit the aircraft through the rear stairwell, but the position of the aircraft prevented the door from opening more than a crack. They were trapped, and felt the advancing heat.

As the flames and heat invaded their sanctuary, Vickie reached through the small crack in the rear entrance door and shouted: "Hurry, give me something to put out the fire!" One of the fire-fighters thrust a fire hose into the small opening, and the trapped passengers poured water onto the approaching flames. Thirty minutes after the crash, they left the aircraft through the burned-out cabin, passing the charred remains of people with whom they had been in conversation within the hour.

A grisly scene confronted rescuers. The effects of the high heat caused limbs to separate from bodies as they were lifted for insertion into the removal bags. The bodies were laid in neat rows at a nearby mortuary, awaiting identification by loved ones.

Outside the burning aircraft, the crisp air revived Marvin Bennett, and he realized his wife and two daughters were in the burning plane. Marvin had much in common with Dr. Guyer, who lost his entire family in the earlier Denver DC-8 crash.

The entire Blaisdell family of Florrisant, Oklahoma, perished. Also from Oklahoma, four Air Force crewmembers who had recently survived a midair collision in which three persons died, were on this United flight. Only one of them survived.

"Where's Janet and the children!"

Janet's mother and father arrived at the airport to meet the daughter they hadn't seen in several years. Instead, they found the fiercely burning jetliner. Rushing from hospital to hospital, they finally found Marvin being treated for burns.

"Where's Janet and the children?" they pleaded.

"In that plane," Marvin replied.

Ironically, as the United jet crashed at Salt Lake City, I was driving from San Francisco to Denver, and was only a short distance west of the Salt Lake City Airport when the crash occurred. I heard the news report as I drove toward Salt Lake City. I had no idea that so many of the safety problems I exposed had caused the crash and deaths.

THE USUAL COVERUP BEGAN

Everyone who concealed the facts when I appealed to them for help, asking them to exercise their responsibilities, now had to cover up. The FAA feigned ignorance. The NTSB omitted their role in this crash. They identified the immediate causes of the crash; the pilot's dangerous high sink rate technique; the engineer's failure to perform life-saving duties; and the crew's poor evacuation of the passengers. But the NTSB report deliberately withheld behind-the-scene information needed to prevent reoccurrences.

United Salt Lake City crash, one of many consequences of
government corruption.

INVESTIGATING WHAT THEY MADE POSSIBLE

By coincidence (or was it to insure a coverup), the NTSB sent Don Madole, Chief of the Accident Investigation Section, to Salt Lake City to conduct the accident investigation. (The term "accident" is used throughout these pages, even though their occurrence from the many safety problems prohibited calling them accidents.) Madole *again* saw the results of his coverup. He had covered up after Harrell came to him for help, permitting the New York City and Denver crashes to occur, among others. Madole covered up when I came to him for help, making possible this and many other crashes from the air safety outrages that the NTSB stated were no safety problems. Madole, and the NTSB, now had to cover up, and this was a crime. By the repeated warnings to Madole of serious safety violations, his refusal to act, and his observation of the resulting crashes, Madole surely must be one of the top experts in the country in the cause and effect relationship between air safety corruption and the air tragedies.

World aviation headlines would be made if the two government air safety agencies were identified in this type of criminal fraud. The corrupt nature of the FAA, the NTSB, the Department of Justice, and other government agencies, would have been exposed to the American public, and to citizens of other countries. The coverup, however, caused these people to be affected by the government corruption. Citizens of the United States, and even of foreign countries, would die from the effects of the FAA Western Region misconduct, and the complicity of silence by many others.

The NTSB coverup had a domino effect. The safety problems continued, as the FAA was now on a roll, immune from being exposed because of others that were now implicated by their complicity of silence. Congress, the new media, the networks, none could blow the whistle because of their involvement.

NON-ADVERSARY SAFETY HEARING

After the crash the NTSB conducted hearings to obtain testimony and to determine the probable cause of the crash. NTSB Board member Adams stated it would be the usual non-adversary hearing so as to identify as many causative factors as possible. The non-adversary hearing is standard practice at hearings intended to get to the cause of the crashes, and should have existed at the Denver grievance hearing. However, the hearing commenced with a pre-planned coverup intent.

The accident investigators determined from the testimony, the aircraft flight recorder, and other evidence, that the *direct* cause of the crash was Captain Kehmeier's high sink rate technique, the failure of the flight engineer to shut off the fuel valves and fuel booster pumps, and the poor evacuation of the passengers by the crew. Every one of these identified causes were directly implicated in the FAA and United Airlines misconduct.

QUESTIONABLE TRAINING RECORD ACCURACY

Referring to the questionable accuracy of United's grading system, the accident report referred to the report of a United flight instructor:

> The entire jet training record of the captain reflects a spread of grading which ranges from unsatisfactory to above average. This variation is typified in his inability to complete the DC-8 training program due to ... unsatisfactory performance in the areas of command, judgment, standard operating procedures, landing technique, smoothness, and coordination.

The accident report felt the contradictions in grading reflected a failure by some instructors to give honest evaluation of the crew member. I discovered this problem at United, as did other inspectors. For years FAA officials refused to remove the company check airmen whose standards were so low that anyone could receive favorable passing grades.

The accident report criticized the captain's failure to adhere to standard operating procedures:

> The *training records* of this captain indicated a pattern of below average judgment as well as a tendency to deviate from standard operating procedures and practices. Indeed, it is indifference toward adhering to acceptable procedures and tolerances in general, but specifically during the landing or ILS approach phases of flight.

But Kehmeier was steered into these problems by the dirty politics of air safety. Like most crew members, he never realized that the denial of legally required training and anything-goes safety standards deprived him of the valuable training that would have made him a safe pilot.

THE BOARD IS CONCERNED. Really?

The accident report identified the unsatisfactory method of pilot testing by company check airmen when it stated:

> The Board is concerned that the procedures for pilot testing prevailing at the time of the accident were such that an individual with the pilot behavioral characteristics of the pilot in this case could qualify and be retained as pilot in command.

It would be my guess that the *behavior* of Captain Kehmeier was above that of the individuals who made that crash possible, and above the members of the NTSB who knew of the problems before the crash. To absolve itself, the Board was making a character assassination upon the captain, himself a victim of the NTSB's earlier criminal coverup.

THE IMPORTANCE OF THE TRAINING RECORDS THAT UNITED UNLAWFULLY SEQUESTERED

The NTSB showed the importance of record inspections by citing these records in many accident reports, and it did this extensively in the Salt Lake City crash. These were the *same* training records that United Airlines officials illegally withheld during my record inspection. The NTSB used these same records to blame the crash on Kehmeier. My report of the record inspection refusal stated my suspicions of what the NTSB later found when United couldn't withhold the records any longer.

Regarding such record inspections, the accident report stated:

Although the FAA, as part of its inspection system, periodically spot checks the carrier's pilot training and airman records, it does not require an examination of these records as part of the certification and type rating process for each airman. The company records of this pilot were not examined as part of his B-727 flight check.

The NTSB knew that United unlawfully withheld these records in an earlier inspection attempt when similar training irregularities were suspected. The NTSB knew that FAA officials had condoned the refusal to allow its records to be inspected. The NTSB knew that United had serious problems in training falsification as evidenced in that October 16, 1960 memorandum and related reports.

MATTER OF GRAVE CONCERN

The accident report identified the obvious unsatisfactory evacuation of the passengers by the United crewmembers:

An FAA committee similar to the FAA industry task force on crash worthiness, which evolved from the UAL DC-8 accident at Denver ... has been activated to study what remedial actions will preclude loss of life in survivable accidents in the future. This is a matter of grave concern to the Board.

Matter of grave concern? The primary concern was coverup. The Board knew, from my reports before and after the Denver grievance hearing, that United was withholding emergency evacuation training with the aid and comfort of FAA officials, and that the problem would undoubtedly continue.

FLIGHT ENGINEER'S LACK OF KNOWLEDGE

The accident report identified the engineer's failure to perform:

> The entire roof and cabin area was consumed by fire which was initially supplied fuel under pressure by the operating boost pumps ... [the flight engineer] did not activate any switches or controls prior to leaving the aircraft.

The accident report omitted the FAA reports of major problems with the flight engineer training, and the FAA blocking of all corrective actions. The NTSB covered up for the FAA's tactics of charging me with psychiatric problems when I reported these same problems.

Knowing that the recommendation had been ignored in other air disasters, the Board repeated its canned recommendation urging the FAA and the air carriers to "reexamine existing procedures to the end that all feasible steps may be taken to make sure that airmen who serve as pilots in command of commercial aircraft, and in particular high speed jet aircraft ... possess not only the requisite technical skills but the necessary qualities of prudence, judgment and care as well."

The FAA announced similar reexaminations in earlier crashes, without any changes.

SNAIL PACE

The government accident report recommended improving the emergency lighting inside the aircraft. These recommendations were made for years prior to the Salt Lake City crash, and made again years after this report. Ten years after this Salt Lake City crash, in 1977, the NTSB recommended the same improvement in the emergency lighting.

Several years before the Salt Lake City crash, after investigating an American Airlines 707 incident at Los Angeles Airport, I made the same recommendation, without any corrective actions taken:

> Emergency lighting inside the aircraft cabin is too weak under smoke conditions. Investigation of a recent aircraft accident and a study of the systems used on air carrier aircraft indicates to this inspector the need for improvements in Emergency Cabin lighting and Emergency Exit lighting requirements. The changes deemed highly desirable by this inspector and the reasons therefore are as follows:
>
> Installation of floodlights, one at each end of the passenger cabin, of sufficient intensity to brightly illuminate

the entire cabin area ... the present use of low candlepower lighting ... is not considered adequate for our high density seating configuration and the need to evacuate large numbers of passengers in the shortest possible time ... the average passenger is in unfamiliar surroundings aboard an aircraft. Add to this a high density seating configuration, an unexpected crash, a darkened cabin, and confusion reigns. Add also to this, delay in setting up the evacuation chute due to improper lighting, and all the ingredients of low survival rate exist ... another important change necessary is the placement of conspicuous, brightly illuminated red exit lights located over every emergency exit ... The changes are considered of utmost importance...

UNITED ADMITS THE HIGH-SINK-RATE PROBLEM THAT THE FAA ARGUED DID NOT EXIST
United Vice-President Gus Sommermeyer was quoted in the *Denver Post* describing the frequent landing-short incidents which are often associated with high-sink-rate approaches:

I.E. Sommermeyer, V.P. for Flying United—United said Undershoots—landing short of the runway—were the most prominent among runway incidents recorded by United in 1965.

Referring to United's training program and the need for corrective action, an FAA order stated: "The FAA issued an order for all Principal Operations Inspectors to review their assigned air carrier's jet operating procedures and approved training programs." These recommendations are standard canned announcement and serve as public relations rhetoric and protect-your-rear responses.

ALMOST EVERYONE PROFITED
By not providing Captain Kehmeier and other crewmembers the proper training, and violating federal air safety laws, United Airlines saved a bundle. Shortly after the crash United reported record earnings. The insurance company paid more money for the destroyed aircraft than it was worth on the corporate books, making a profit on is loss. The FAA officials and inspectors who played the game received outstanding awards following the Denver hearing, and many received promotions. Who says air disasters are not profitable!

"You are through with flying!"
Captain Kehmeier had two meetings with United Airline officials in March 1966, at which one of them stated: "You will never fly again for United. You are through with flying." Kehmeier was given two choices. Sign a resignation effective

the end of the month, and receive $45,000 plus lifetime pension—or be fired. If United exercised the second choice and fired Kehmeier, United attorney George Foy advised Kehmeier that FAA attorney Ned Zartman, Regional Counsel in Los Angeles, was prepared to invoke an emergency suspension of Kehmeier's Airline Transport Pilot certificate. After Kehmeier resigned, the FAA revoked the ATR certificate and replaced it with a Commercial certificate.

What irony! FAA and United officials engaged in outrageous criminal acts depriving the crews and passengers of the training safeguards, and now they conspired to blame Kehmeier, a victim, for the deaths they caused. If the facts were known, and the Department of Justice had not been implicated, all could be prosecuted for crimes preceding the crash.

Much of the aviation industry, including his fellow pilots, and the public, perceived Kehmeier as causing the crash and blaming him for the deaths of those who died under such terrible conditions. Very sad.

COMPOUNDING THE AIR DISASTER CORRUPTION, AND SETTING THE STAGE FOR MORE OF THE SAME

Ironically, shortly after the Salt Lake City crash occurred, the FAA Administrator released the whitewashed decision of the Denver grievance hearing. The FAA Administrator saw the horror he could have prevented if he had not approved the fraud, corruption, coverup, occurring at the Denver hearing. He had first hand knowledge of more to come if he continued the coverup. The decision, of course, was a coverup, and set the stage for many more tragedies.

"No changes in crew training."

While the FAA issues its normal public relations releases to improve training, United stated they would not make any changes. The *Denver Post* quoted one of my frequent adversaries:

> Carl Christenson, chief of United's flight operations, said the carrier is making no changes in crew training.

Actually, there *were* changes made in United's training program after the Salt Lake City crash. Ground training, which had been 120 hours to prepare for initial check out on the plane, was *lowered* to 80 hours within two years after the crash, and then eventually to 60 hours. The FAA approved reduction in frequency of emergency evacuation training. The flight engineer shortcomings were addressed by eliminating the flight engineer on most of the two-engine aircraft. Everyone it appeared, was on a roll, encouraged by the successful coverup.

"United's approach will continue in a similar manner."

United Airlines President William Patterson said before a meeting of the Aviation Space Writers Association, shortly after the Salt Lake City tragedy,

> I don't see how the crash could have been made more survivable. United's approach will continue in a similar manner. [How well I know!]

"The carrier was remiss."

In a statement to the Society of Air Safety Investors, United Executive Vice President and General Manager Charles McErlean referred to the accident report identification of United's poor safety standards: "Implicit in that statement is speculation that the carrier was remiss in its monitoring of its day-to-day operations" Amen!

Shortly after the crash an FAA spokesman stated: "The airline passenger has to take a more active role in his own survival."

STILL TRYING TO IDENTIFY THE PROBLEM

And speaking for the FAA, the *Denver Post*, referring to the Salt Lake City crash, stated:

> Charles F. Stacy, Chief of the FAA Flight Standards Branch, Denver—Stacy said his office was attempting to identify the problem.

Quoted at a later date in the *Denver Post*:

> Charles F. Stacy, the Federal Aviation Agency's Chief of Flight Standards [promoted since the post-Denver safety hearing] for the Denver region—where United's flight training is located ... said that a program was under way to identify training or flight check problems ... but that no problems have so far been isolated.

The FAA's Director of Flight Standards, speaking before a Congressional committee, indirectly referred to the United training program problem:

> There are a series of very unfortunate circumstances in that particular accident ... very unfortunately, the fuel shutoff valves in the cockpit that would cut off the supply of fuel to those lines were not activated to shut off the fuel. Very unfortunate.

THE PILOT'S UNION (ALPA)

The Air Line Pilots Association knew the behind-the-scene causes of the Salt Lake City crash, as it did of the New York City and Denver tragedies. ALPA kept quiet about the true causes, and shifted the blame elsewhere, insuring the continuation of the problems. They let Kehmeier take the blame. They knew the problems before the crash. And now they let one of their own members take the blame for United, FAA, and NTSB officials. Kehmeier, no longer a pilot nor member of ALPA, was useless to them. They had to keep their communications open with United, the FAA, the NTSB, and others implicated in the expanding scandal.

The union fabricated a defense, but its absurd nature accomplished nothing. They said the engines failed to accelerate, knowing that those particular jet engines were known to have that characteristic, and that the pilots had to fly the aircraft accordingly.

"Dirtier with the blood of countless victims"

Never missing an opportunity for some good press, Representative Henry Gonzalez of Texas stated that the FAA Administrator's hands would "get dirtier with the blood of countless" victims of air tragedies. In response to my letter reminding him, again, of the FAA corruption and resulting tragedies, Gonzalez replied: "Your statement about air disasters, and your warning to expect worse seems to have been borne out..." Again he refused to exercise his Congressional responsibilities, engaging in nonfeasance, malfeasance, misfeasance, obstruction of justice. But who would prosecute?

One of United's officials that was responsible for the low safety standards at Denver, and one with whom I regularly sparred, was Carl Christenson. In the politics of the aviation environment, the parties give each other awards for air safety activities. Christenson was a trustee of the Flight Safety Foundation, and described by former FAA Administrator Halaby[14] as "one of the nation's top experts in air safety." If this is the quality of experts, it helps to explain the sorry state of air safety.

AN ACT OF GOD?

Several years after the Salt Lake City crash, as I prepared my first manuscript, I was in telephone contact with Marvin Bennett at his Idaho Falls home. I didn't tell him of my interest in the crash other than that I was writing a book, and wanted as much human interest input as I could get. Marvin thought back, and said:

---

[14] *Crosswinds*, Najeebe Halaby, Doubleday.

Before the flight, myself, I was a little concerned, and I
wondered what I would do if I did lose my whole family. And
I   know   before   we   left,   I   was   standing   there
commenting—"What would you do if by some freak accident
all three of us would die?"

Thinking that this accident was an act of the God that he wor-
shipped, Marvin's agony was lessened. I thought otherwise.

PREMONITION OF DEATH

Several months before boarding Flight 227 Marvin had
premonitions of events that were to occur. Marvin stated to
me: "I know, one night, I had a nightmare, and I dreamed Janet
was killed in an accident; and it seemed very realistic to me. I
remember waking up and turning over and reaching for her, and
saw she was still there. I was really grateful."

Marvin continued: "I dreamed it was something very disas-
trous. I used to, I do remember, for the last year, I used to look
in on Marie Christiania, in the crib, and she would be sleeping
there; and always I had the feeling that she wasn't going to live
very long—I don't know why—I just had that feeling."

During the time Marvin had these premonitions, I was
fighting to expose and correct the corruption that would later
kill his family. Neither Marvin, his wife, or their two daughters,
were any match for the conspiracy of government thugs who
operated under color of federal law, in corrupt acts funded by
the United States government.

"What happened to the captain," Marvin stated, "happened
two thousand years ago to Christ!" Marvin described the abuse
Captain Kehmeier received after the crash.

> The bitterness I've seen and heard would turn one's
> stomach. Some of the things I heard happen to the captain
> are not even Christian; what happened to the captain
> happened two thousand years ago to Christ.

"Beautiful [financial] horizon"

United President William Patterson later predicted "a
beautiful horizon for the airline industry," adding that he
"thinks this will be the first year in 37 years that it will realize
10% return on invested capital..." United does well financially.
More than once United earned nearly one billion dollars on
which no Federal income tax was paid. Reducing training costs
contributed significantly to these record profits.

PRAISING THE CONGRESSMAN WHO MADE THE CRASH POSSIBLE

Meanwhile, Monroney was honored for his alleged outstanding aviation contributions. A news article stated:

> Arches of Achievement Award of marble, walnut and sterling silver as Mr. Aviation from the citizens of Oklahoma City. (*Daily Oklahoman* December 3, 1966.) Robert Murphy, vice chairman of the Civil Aeronautics Board, described Monroney as "The archangel of aviation," and said Monroney was responsible more than any other individual for the nation's air safety. Present during the ceremonies were William McKee, FAA Administrator; Robert Murphy, vice chairman of the CAB.

TIME FOR HANDING OUT REWARDS

After the burial services for the victims of the Salt Lake City crash the FAA gave outstanding awards and financial bonuses to those who played a part in the Denver hearing corruption. The FAA promoted Stacy. The FAA promoted legal counsel Boberick to Chief Counsel in the Alaska region, who in 1988 had a high FAA position in the southeast region.

FAA Western Region Director, Joseph Tippets, who made many of the crashes possible, and who either engineered or approved the Denver hearing misconduct, received an honorary doctorate. Would you believe, it was awarded by Brigham Young University, in Salt Lake City (!) where many of the victims of the misconduct perished.

Graves for Janet Bennett and her two daughters.

The grim search for bodies in the United Salt Lake City crash.

CHAPTER SIX

Checks and Balances

After the Salt Lake City crash the FAA transferred me against my wishes from Denver, out of the United Airlines assignment, and into a position at the FAA Aeronautical Center at Oklahoma City. My absence aided the coverup needed to insure that I would not get to the news media and the NTSB. Subsequent events showed they need not fear, as the widespread corruption became such a major national scandal that everyone kept the lid on it.

I decided to continue my exposure activities and attempts to halt the tragedy-related corruption from Oklahoma City.

While working at the aeronautical center I met a former FAA attorney with whom I worked in the Los Angeles area; John Graziano. He was now legal counsel in charge of Security and Compliance for the FAA training center. He knew of the internal FAA problems and my attempts to expose them. During our first conversation Graziano stated, "Rod, please, don't do anything here until I can get away; I don't want to get involved."

CONTINUED COVERUP BY CONGRESS

I again renewed my contacts with members of the U.S. Senate and House. I had even more evidence now of the FAA and NTSB[15] corruption then before, and had the evidence

---

[15] Reference to the predecessor agency of the NTSB, the CAB Bureau of Aviation Safety, and to the existing NTSB, is by using NTSB throughout the book.

linking the misconduct to even more air tragedies.

Unfortunately, the additional hard-evidence of corruption and deaths also implicated the same members of Congress who had earlier covered up. Any exposure now would implicate those whose complicity of silence made the crashes possible.

Senator Robert Kennedy was one of those previously contacted, and who I again contacted, seeking to get him to exercise his moral and legal responsibilities. His involvement in the litigation and settlement of the United Airlines New York City crash (as United States Attorney General) certainly made him aware of the brutal consequences of the misconduct. The consequences of plane crashes was also brought home by an earlier crash that hospitalized his brother, Edward Kennedy.

As Attorney General, he knew of the sequestered FAA reports when he approved the settlement protecting United. I didn't realize it then, but Kennedy was Attorney General when I first made the Department of Justice aware of the criminal activities; he must have known all along of the scandal.

Following one of my earlier letters Kennedy responded: "If you have complaints against the enforcement of FAA regulations, I would be glad to make arrangements to have you talk with officials of the Federal Aviation Agency or the Civil Aeronautics Board." Obviously, since I worked for the FAA, and just completed two months of adversary hearings with key FAA management, I didn't need Kennedy to introduce me to the FAA. His attacks upon Teamster President Hoffa certainly showed more intelligence that his coverup letter to me suggested. I answered:

Your offer to help me talk with the FAA or NTSB officials is most generous. However, the charade involves the lives, and the deaths, of human beings and this includes your constituencies and those for whom you have a responsibility. As you know, I work for the Federal Aviation Agency and I certainly don't need a Senator to arrange a talk. Glib talk didn't help the 43 cremated souls at Salt Lake City, only one example, and it won't help those that have yet to pay the price with their lives.

You knew the consequences in 1965 of this side-stepping; you know the consequences NOW. The expected happened after the 1965 sidestepping which is only too tragically, a carryover from the world's worst air disaster. Your constituents didn't fare too well in that one either.

Kennedy replied:

Thank you for your March 20th letter commenting on my

offer to arrange a meeting with officials of either the FAA or the CAB. As you know, these are the agencies responsible for aviation safety, and they are the individuals most qualified to review problems in this area. Please let me know if I can be of any further assistance.

The preposterous dialogue continued; I replied:

I described to you at that time, and provided ample official evidence, of a major government scandal involving criminal misconduct in high government positions. I knew, and you knew, that this was a corollary to inevitable deaths of American air travelers. I clarified the long-standing status of this fraud, and associated it with the deaths of specific air travelers. I also provided you with previously hidden government documents that left no doubt that air travelers did meet death in fraud-tinged air disasters.

Your peculiar offer to provide further assistance takes the guise of a cruel charade. Senator Kennedy, don't you recall, and of course you do, that during mid-1965 I appealed to you for help, warning of the consequences if it did not come. I expected something other than apathy because of your astuteness and public responsibility position.

In your position as Attorney General, this tragedy was the subject of a peculiar benevolent action. (Assumption by the public of much of United's financial liability.) Matter of fact, some of your New York City constituents perished in that great tragedy. You should have shown an interest, don't you think, Senator Kennedy?

There was no doubt in my mind, nor could there have been in yours, that the criminal misconduct within the highly sensitive area of aviation safety HAD to result in deaths. I appealed to you because of your previous background as Attorney General, surely qualified to recognize the gravity of the situation. Your position as Senator with its implied responsibilities, and the fact that some of your constituents perished in air disasters tinged with fraud, made me optimistic that you would help. But your inactions were the same as others who didn't give a damn.

The consequences? Contemptuously and without compassion, responsible Congressmen actively or passively allowed the crime to rage and escalate, and in a dramatic sequence of events a mother and her two daughters were cremated in an officially forewarned, and fraud-tinged air disaster, Salt Lake City. They simply weren't any match for the collusion and conspiracy, the willful misconduct, that tinged their deaths. But then, this is routine, isn't it. The death of the little boy and 142 others in the great New York City midair collision, the Cincinnati disaster, and others, show that this is a long term, well organized conspiracy. The conspiracy is so well organized that despite the extent and gravity, the public is still denied access to the truth.

Today there is massive collusion, conspiracy and willful misconduct as the escalating crime is being hidden from the public. The question you can ask yourself, Senator Kennedy, is whether that mother and her two daughters would be alive today ... if informed Congressman responded to their public trust. The terrible part of it is that still more Congressmen are trying to shield the guilty, and the crime escalates ... By doing so, the government corruption escalates and sets a terrible precedent, and the highly sensitive aviation safety area is subjected to still more of the previous fraud.

Even FBI Director Hoover has become ensnared in this mess, as he writes to Congressmen that no crime, as alleged by me, exists; the basis for his "determination" being his alleged examination of my material. No such examination has ever been made.

If the crime that I allege does actually exist, and there can be no doubt about this, we have the additional crimes of those harboring it, obstructing justice by high Government officials and Congressmen.

Kennedy replied:

Thank you for your July 9 letter. I am sorry to have delayed in replying, and I do appreciate your taking the time to write to me again. The Federal Bureau of Investigation has told me that the information which you supplied to them and to me has been considered and indicates no violation of Federal law within the investigative jurisdiction of the FBI. I am, therefore, referring your letter to the Deputy Attorney General of the Department of Justice. You will be hearing from me again in the near future.

Senator Kennedy later advised me that he received a letter from the Department of Justice, stating in part:

Previous correspondence from Mr. Stich reveals he has made unsubstantiated charges that certain air crashes were due to deficiencies in the training program of aircraft personnel and that perjury and other offenses were committed by witnesses at the hearing at Denver on his employee's grievance complaint. Members of a Federal grand jury at Denver permitted Stich to testify before that body on

February 23, 1967, and thereafter the grand jury returned a no bill. We found nothing in his correspondence warranting action by the Department. A careful consideration of the letter Mr. Stich addressed to you presents no new facts justifying action by the Department, and the letter is returned to you herewith.

The Department of Justice had never contacted me for evidence to substantiate my allegations, and obviously had no intention of doing so. The Justice Department blocked every attempt to provide evidence. Kennedy also knew that the U.S. Attorney obstructed my presentation of evidence to the lay jury consisting of lay people, most of whom had no understanding of the law, and responded as the U.S. Attorney told them to do.

Members of Congress have the oversight responsibility for agencies they create. They have the duty to investigate my allegations which, if true, would cause the deaths of hundreds and eventually thousands of people. Under the Standing Rules of the Senate and Senate Resolution 381, the duty to investigate is stated:

the efficiency and economy of operations of all branches of the government including the possible existence of fraud, misfeasance, malfeasance, collusion, mismanagement, incompetence, corruption, or unethical practices, waste, extravagance, conflicts of interest, and the improper expenditure of government funds in transactions, contracts, and activities of the government or of government officials and employees and any and all such improper practices between government personnel and corporations, individuals, companies, or persons affiliated therewith, doing business with the government.

During his 1968 campaign for President Kennedy stated: "What this country needs is a return to individual responsibility ... Civil rights get strangled because no one will take responsibility."

Unfortunately, the public buys this rhetoric hook, line, and sinker.

AIRLINE CRASHES—SOME SEARCHING QUESTIONS

An *American Aviation* article entitled, "Safety Hearings," described forthcoming Senate hearings scheduled by Senator Clinton Anderson:

The [committee] intends to air a controversial issue of safety in air travel with testimony from FAA ... it will ask some searching questions about ... aircraft safety research to reduce fatalities in airline crashes ... the committee feels the government ought to step up its efforts to make air travel safer.

I had contacted Senator Anderson almost two years earlier and received the usual non-responsive reply:

I have your letter concerning certain conditions in the Federal Aviation Agency. I don't know what I can do to help the situation but I will be glad to submit this information and your comments to the Senate Commerce Committee for its consideration.

That was the end of that. The nature of the hearing was an excellent opportunity to give Anderson another chance at investigating government corruption within the FAA and NTSB, especially with the recent Salt Lake City crash furnishing still more support to my allegations.

"I don't know of anything I can do..."

My letter to Senator Anderson contained copies of FAA writings supporting my allegations of FAA misconduct. Senator Anderson replied: "This is to acknowledge your letter concerning conditions within the Federal Aviation Agency ... the hearings are strictly in connection with the aeronautical research and development and its relationship to the space program ... I don't know of anything I can do to be of assistance."

I then wrote to the author of the *American Aviation* article, questioning him about its authenticity. He replied: "The last word I heard, [the intention was] airing the issue of air travel safety came from a top-level committee staffer." Possibly, my intervention changed their plans.

Another article in *Aviation Week* stated:

Rep. Harley O. Staggers (D-W.Va.), chairman of the House Commerce Committee, scheduled *closed* hearings this week on several recent aircraft accidents. At the hearing, the committee will consider holding a full investigation of air safety problems.

My subsequent letter to Staggers described the FAA irregularities, showing the relationship to the Salt Lake City crash. I closed by saying, "This letter is not an appeal to your group; I've given up on that approach long ago. It is just to show you have been informed."

That same committee received air safety irregularity data before United's New York City crash and before the Salt Lake

City tragedy, but did nothing. Action now was unlikely, and they were implicated in the subsequent deaths by their coverup.

Staggers wrote: "This committee has had, does have, and will continue to have, a direct interest in the numerous subjects under its legislative jurisdiction. These include, as you are aware, an interest in the Federal Aviation Agency and the Civil Aeronautics Board, and the achievement of the highest degree of air safety attainable." He said the right words, and committed the crime of further coverup. Again, many would pay for his malfeasance.

Congressman Richard Bolling wrote, in *House Out of Order*:

> In the many years that I have been a Member of Congress, the House has revealed itself to me as ineffective in its role as a coordinate branch of the federal government, negative in its approach to national tasks, generally unresponsive to any but parochial economic interests. Its legislation is often a travesty of what the national welfare requires. It does not even fill one of its possible functions, that of being the 'grand inquest of the nation,' in William Pitt's phrase.

In his book, *Government of the People*, Senator Kenneth B. Keating stated:

> Congress is being discredited not by those working for reform, but by daily evidence of its incompetence for creative and responsible decision making, by repeated exposure of conflicts of interest and other abuses, by its inability to deal efficiently with the most routine housekeeping responsibilities. The manner in which the government carries out its responsibilities has a tremendous bearing on the whole future of our nation.

Keating detailed the corruptive influences and apathy within government. He provided sobering thoughts on our national leadership. Thinking it possible that Keating, now a judge of the New York Court of Appeals, might offer some help, I described the problem to him. He now knew of serious crimes affecting the national welfare, that would result in further deaths if he failed to act. A federal judge, more so than the average citizen, has a responsibility to act when he knows a crime has or is being committed, and if civil and constitutional rights are violated, that he could prevent or aid in the prevention.

Keating had a responsibility to bring the matter to a responsive investigative authority. Keating replied: "In my position as a Judge of the Court of Appeals, I feel I should not in any way become involved in the *problem which you have so seriously raised* and can only suggest that you communicate with either Senator Monroney or Senator Harris ... If my memory serves me right, Senator Monroney is Chairman of the Aviation Subcommittee of the Committee on Commerce so that he would have an active concern with the matter which you outline." That contact was a dead end for me. The stonewalling continued.

"I certainly recognize the immense seriousness of the problem."

The list of Congressmen aware of the scandal, and ignoring their responsibilities, who made possible the continued air tragedies and government corruption, reads like the "who's who" of Washington. Senator John Williams of Delaware wrote:

This will acknowledge receipt of your letter of May 30, ... in which you provided me with certain information concerning recent airline disasters. I have read the letter with a great deal of interest, and while I certainly recognize the immense seriousness of the problems which you outlined, I do not feel, lacking background in this field, that I could appropriately involve myself in an investigation such as you have suggested. Although I realize that other Members of Congress may show lack of interest in this particular area, I can only suggest that you take this matter up with Members of the Senate and House Commerce Committees which are most directly affected with matters concerning air safety. I regret that I cannot be of greater assistance to you, but do appreciate very much your calling this matter to my attention.

SUPPRESSING SCANDALS AND CORRUPTION

The unresponsiveness of Congress to serious wrongdoing was illustrated by their indifference to letters written by the ex-FBI investigator who exposed the My Lai massacre. He sent letters to 23 Congressmen about this outrage, and not a single one responded. Even warnings to Congressmen about threatened mass suicides and murder in the Jim Jones cult community in Guyana failed to get any reaction until much later.

Senator Thurmond stated in a television address that the government

has breached the trust reposed in it by the people. It has repudiated the Constitution of the United States ... it has violated its trust by using the power of Government to suppress information on scandals and corruption of its leaders in Government and party offices ... has used the Government as a propaganda machine to distort the truth and deceive the public to the extent that a sub-cabinet official can publicly defend the Administration's 'right to lie' and remain in office, unrebuked.

Thurmond wouldn't lift a finger when advised of the corruption within the two government safety agencies that continued to cause infliction of horror and deaths.

The purported right of government to lie is no secret. Writing in *Life Line*, Melvin Munn said of government's outright lying to the people;

> More and more it is being frankly acknowledged in behind-the-scenes Washington that one of the major troubles with our ailing international relations is the plain and simple fact that the leaders of other countries, friends and foes alike, just don't believe us anymore.

The *Life Line* article continued:

> This assistant Secretary of Defense for Public Affairs acknowledged under pressure that our government had been reckless with the truth in telling the American people what happened. It's basic, he said, that the government had a right to lie. Only 15 percent of Americans (on a public opinion sampling firm hired by a major television network) gave their government a full vote of confidence in the truth and integrity department. As one network news commentator put it: "The political lie has become a way of bureaucratic life. It has been called by the more genteel name of news management." I say here and now, let's call it what it is —LYING.

"The main victims are our own citizens."
Senator Gaylord Nelson stated in a Congressional speech that there is "an alarming trend in this country toward the use of police-state tactics ... assurances [from Government agencies] it now appears, were lies ... The worst thing about all of these tactics is that the main victims are our own citizens."

Nelson couldn't be bothered when I advised him of government-funded corruption in the air safety field.

"Crisis of Confidence Rocks Capital; Nobody Knows who's Telling the Truth," captioned a James Reston column. Describing the housecleaning needed in Congress, the *National Observer* stated: "In Paris, *Le Monde* editorialized that not a day passes any more but that the most moderate American press catches the President or his collaborators in the flagrant act of lying."

As if this criminal and morally-bankrupt misconduct were not enough, even groups outside of government play the game. The Airline Passengers Association stated in its publication; "APA is the one official spokesman for the air traveler, working directly with the airlines to achieve the safety, comfort, and convenience every passenger deserves." I was a member of that consumer group, and thought they might help. I sent them information in the 1960s, and again in the lat 1980s, explaining the government corruption that endangered and killed their members.

Attorney William Jennings, Director of Aviation Safety for the APA, replied in the early contacts, "You can rest assured that your communications will remain confidential." He then asked me to send further information, which I did, requesting that Jennings lets me know what he thought about the matter.

His assurance of confidentiality certainly existed; he kept the lid on the scandal. Six months went by without a reply. I wrote: "You must have your reasons for not responding and I'm sure they are good ones." Back came the bland rhetoric: "You can be sure that my interest is for the safety of the traveling public, which my experience has shown to be frequently contrary to the positions taken by powerful interests in the aviation industry." My subsequent letters to him went unanswered. In 1989 their coverup continued. They refused to even respond to my communications, and even refused to send me a membership application which I requested in a phone call and by letter.

The news media reacted the same way. Drew Pearson was typical and in response to my letter wrote:

> Thank you very much for your letter. I'm unforgivably slow in answering, but Senator Dodd has been keeping me busy night and day. I assure you that any information you pass on to me will be kept strictly confidential, and your name will not be used unless you give me permission to do so. The controversy over auto safety has now reached its climax, and while the public is still safety-minded, I would be happy to take up the question in relation to air carriers. I have reported on this subject in the past, but if you have documentary evidence to back up your charges, I would be grateful if you would make it available to me.

I furnished Pearson with revealing documents of government corruption and related air tragedies, sufficient to show the credibility of what I alleged. He never answered my subsequent letters. His associate, Jack Anderson, kept the lid on the scandal, up to and including 1989.

Even David Lawrence, editor of *U.S. News and World Reports*, who wrote idealist editorials, turned his back on my appeal for help. Ignoring his responsibilities, he wrote:

I have your letter of April 10 and can appreciate your feelings in this matter. Our answer still has to be the same. Our job is to report and analyze news developments, and our staff is not set up to conduct investigations such as would be essential before publishing matter of this kind. We believe this should be left to the investigative committees of Congress or other governmental agencies established for this purpose.

Yet, in one of his editorials entitled "What Can I Do?", Lawrence stated: "Public opinion is the product of what thoughtful people say and do to express their viewpoint. It is as mistaken to fail to inform oneself and express oneself on issues and candidates as it is to fail to vote ... Public opinion is, after all, the accumulation of many individual opinions."

Lawrence recognized the responsibility of citizenship and of the need to know what is going on. He could simply have reported the actions I had taken to expose the scandal, which were newsworthy; the news media does it all the time. But to have done so would have opened a Pandora's box which Lawrence for some reason apparently didn't want opened. David Susskind, William Buckley Jr., and NBC news, among others, were even less responsive.

ARROGANCE OF THOSE MISUSING GOVERNMENT

Conducting hearings into government misconduct, Senator Sam Ervin stated, "In all of our investigations, I have never seen anything to equal the outrage and indignation from government employees, their families and their friends." Senator Ervin, a former Supreme Court judge in his home state, was an astute investigator, especially of criminal misconduct. He understood the evidence I presented to him, but he refused to act on it.

Writing of government's brutality toward its own employees, reflecting its attitude toward the public, Joseph Yount wrote in a *Washington Star* article: "One of the most insidious factors [within government] of involuntary retirements is that many of them are based on mental disability charges ... Employees charge that they have been involuntarily removed through this procedure ... because they dared criticize the way things were being run in their office. Others are threatened with such actions if they' don't stay in line.'"

In one instance, Senator John Williams rushed to the rescue of a government employee who refused to remain quiet when

the Billie Sol Estes scandal in the mid-1960s threatened to
implicate President Johnson and other government officials.
Senator Williams said "She was railroaded to a mental institution because she knew too much" about the Estes scandal; she
was "guilty of nothing other than refusing to cooperate in
covering up the corruption." Robert Kennedy held the post of
Attorney General while his Department of Justice legal goons
dragged this woman to a mental institution.

Senator McClellan's committee managed to squelch Congressional investigation into the Billie Sol Estes scandal and
keep it from the public. McClellan and Kennedy both kept the
lid on this air safety scandal. As Attorney General, Robert
Kennedy transferred millions of dollars of liability from United
Airlines to the taxpayer, for the New York City disaster. With
claims totaling close to a third of a billion dollars, this relieved
United of considerable financial outlay. FAA Administrator
Halaby vigorously objected. Halaby didn't stay as Administrator
much longer.

"vast powers of the government..."

In *The Pentagon*, author Clark Mollenhoff speaks of the
political maneuvering and coercion by government, of how their
threat to close key military bases, awarding or denying multi-
million dollar contracts, can impose the will of Government on
industry and others. He explained, "the vast powers of the
government to keep powerful congressmen in line and to keep
others from complaining."

Senator John McClellan, Chairman of the Senate Permanent
Committee on Government Operations, conducted many highly
sophisticated investigations into all segments of crime. He, as
well as Kennedy, knew the gravity of the scandal, and weren't
as dumb as they made themselves sound when I made them
aware of the rampant government corruption.

Donald O'Donnell, Chief Counsel for the committee, replied
to the letter I sent to McClellan, "Senator John L. McClellan
has asked me to answer your recent communication." Implying
their interest and responsibility over the areas I had outlined,
O'Donnell stated, "The Subcommittee can assure you that the
information will remain confidential until such time as it is
mutually decided otherwise."

Three months later the Chief Counsel for this committee
wrote again: "I very carefully reviewed the material that you
forwarded to this office, and I have contacted the office of
Senator Mike Monroney who is Chairman of the Senate Aviation
Subcommittees who have jurisdiction over various matters and
to whom the subject matter has been referred." He knew that
Monroney had covered up, and that Monroney now could not
blow the whistle after his coverup made possible some of the

deaths that followed.

O'Donnell's first letter to me, knowing this was an aviation scandal, implied the matter was within the committee's area of responsibility and that he was willing to investigate with an eye toward corrective actions. The fact that he asked for detailed data supported the fact his committee had responsibilities in the area. But suddenly, his committee did not have the responsibility in the matter that he implied earlier. It was apparently too hot to handle. Or something.

Later, I wrote that I had learned of a significant FAA report that would show a continuation of internal FAA misconduct, and asked Senator McClellan and his chief counsel to assist me in obtaining a copy of it. They wouldn't even respond to my letter, or any of my others.

Speaking to the press, McClellan stated: "Mounting crime, murder, rape, robbery, theft, rioting, and civil disobedience, has reached a level and momentum that borders on open rebellion and insurrection and is the most critical internal danger confronting the nation."

In correspondence with Senator William Proxmire, I explained the matter as I had to other Congressmen, and asked for help, and for him to exercise his Congressional oversight responsibilities. He asked for more details, which I sent. His June 21st letter acknowledged receipt of my material, adding; "I can assure you that if there is any wrong-doing involved here, I shall bring it to the surface."

QUICK "INVESTIGATION"

Four working days after having sent that letter, Proxmire wrote: "I am sorry to say that after extensive research I have failed to find evidence which would warrant my pursuing further your grievance with the Federal Aviation Administration. Since you seem to have exhausted your avenues of appeal with the FAA, the Civil Aeronautic Board, the Federal Bureau of Investigation, and the Federal Grand Jury in Denver, I would suggest that if you decide to pursue this matter, that you consult an attorney." Proxmire, an astute attorney, knew that pursuing this matter via a private attorney was highly impractical, run into hundreds of thousands of dollars, and lack the subpoena power necessary to get to the full depth of the misconduct.

Proxmire replied to my next letter describing the tragic results of the coverup: "Indeed, you have every right to be angry if what you say is true; but I need the evidence." He never requested any evidence from me, even when I offered it. The gravity of the matter, the brutal shredding and cremation of hundreds and eventually thousands of people required aggressive actions on Proxmire's part. Also, I obviously couldn't ship thousands of pages of hearing transcripts, evidence, and supporting documents, and my presence to explain their significance and tie the many documents together.

The following year I asked Proxmire's help in obtaining a copy of the FAA inspection and evaluation report that I learned was a shocker, and which would show the continuation of the internal FAA misconduct. I told Proxmire that the FAA refused to send me a copy of that report, even though the Freedom of Information Act required the report be released. I described its importance and explained that it would give additional credibility to what I had previously told him, showing that the safety problems within the FAA were as bad or worse than before.

GOVERNMENT CORRUPTION IS SECRET DATA(!)

Proxmire refused to get the document for me, writing: "I have noted from the FAA's reply, this information is considered of a 'secret' nature in the public's interest and a matter relating solely to the internal management of this Agency. I do not feel it proper or wise for me to intervene in this instance. I hope you can understand my position in this matter."

Public interest! I expose criminal misconduct by the FAA, and Proxmire held that supporting documents in the FAA's possession was in the public's interest to further cover up. Proxmire was not illiterate to the extent that he failed to recognize that if the FAA corruption did in fact exist, the FAA would not cooperate in releasing any incriminating data about itself. How could withholding an internal FAA report showing FAA shortcomings related to air tragedies be in the public interest!

I replied, stating: "It is obviously ... a grave crime against the American public [it is receiving] Congressional and government assistance in its perpetration and protection ... Congressmen [are] engaging in deceitful charades and feigning excuses to prevent the exposure of this crime [and] are guilty of a crime worse than those perpetrated by the original culprits, because of their position of public trust."

"The attention it seems to deserve."

I didn't expect a reply, but Proxmire answered:

It was good of you to go into such great detail regarding your accusation of criminal malfeasance in the Federal Aviation Administration. Frankly, I think you would be well advised to submit whatever evidence you have regarding this matter to the Aviation Subcommittee of the Senate Commerce Committee. This Subcommittee is Chaired by Senator Monroney and has a great deal more experience in the field of aviation law than I have. I simply don't have the staff or the expertise to give this matter the attention it seems to deserve.

Proxmire knew that Monroney was part of the coverup, and certainly wouldn't expose himself in this worsening national scandal. Further, if a group of relatively unsophisticated citizens can conduct grand jury investigations, Proxmire certainly could understand the matter. He had Congressional investigation responsibilities as he had repeatedly exercised in other issues. I thanked the kind Senator, writing:

> Your suggestion is noted but I hardly think referring the matter to Senator Monroney would be the answer; would you submit data ... in which he was involved, with a request that he investigate them, and himself? As to not being informed on aviation matters for an excuse to look the other way, you and other members of Congress have investigated everything from tuna fish to the dance racket, and I'm sure you weren't experts in these fields. I understand, Senator, and the letters and sequence of events tell quite a story. I wish I knew ALL of the story. Care to clue me in?

The press, who knew of the scandal from my many letters, didn't help. In the Sunday syndicated paper, *Parade*, a full-page article eulogized Senator Proxmire: "HE'S TRYING TO IMPROVE THE QUALITY OF AMERICAN LIFE." Among the tributes stated of Proxmire were that he "had a strong sense of priorities, both personal and national. Proxmire's prime concern is with the priorities of the nation. Proxmire was one of the best qualified men in the U.S. Senate to conduct an inquiry into the basic economic orientation of this country. Also, one of the most shrewd, studious, industrious, and intelligent members in that sometimes illustrious body ... After more than 11 years in the Senate, nine of which he spent as a sort of institutional maverick fighting valiantly for seemingly hopeless causes. Bill Proxmire knows how to handle himself in clinch and crunch."

"How in all good conscience..."

The article certainly didn't depict Proxmire as being as ignorant as the Senator tried to appear in his letters to me. It quoted Proxmire chastising several executives who did not appear for a Senate hearing: "How in all good conscience can these men who are so intimately involved in the decisions which affect our national security ... be so sanctimonious and uncooperative."

Senator Warren Magnuson, a close associate of Monroney, who must have been aware of the FAA and NTSB corruption, was quoted in *Aviation Daily* as he eulogized the NTSB, "The Board is now functioning effective in accident investigation."

Magnuson knew that the NTSB engaged in criminal coverup prior to and after several of the air tragedies that had occurred.

"FAA can do the job..."

The next day's *Aviation Daily* quoted Senator Monroney as stating, "I know that the FAA, as now organized, can do the job in the years ahead." This assurance contradicted the picture portrayed by the evidence I had sent to Monroney.

The Congressmen knowing the most about FAA and NTSB corruption were trying hardest to cover up for those whose despicable misconduct overwhelmed those who perished.

Congressman H.R. Gross acknowledged receipt of data on the misconduct, "I will certainly look over the information you have provided at the earliest opportunity." His membership on the Civil Service committee gave him additional responsibilities in the matter. But seven months later I still couldn't get a response from the Gross.

Senator Everett Dirksen wrote, after learning of the problem, "If you feel your activities have been circumscribed, you should bring it to the attention of the United States Senate Subcommittee on Constitutional Rights, which has expressed an interest in aviation activities. I referred your previous letter to this Subcommittee."

Not hearing from this committee, I wrote to them, referring to Senator Dirksen's letter, sending a copy of O'Donnell's evaluation, and inquiring as to their intentions. No reply came back.

"Hot stuff on air safety."

Aviation Daily described an important aviation safety hearing scheduled by Senator Edward Kennedy on "how the FAA responds to safety problems. Aides to the Senator had alerted the press that the hearings would contain hot stuff on air safety." The hearing chambers were bustling with television lights and cameras as the hearing was about to begin, when suddenly, before this so-called hot-stuff could be divulged, the hearing was cancelled.

I had made it known earlier to Senator Kennedy that I wanted to testify before the hearing. He wasn't any more concerned about potential victims from coverup than he was at a later date when he drove his car into the water at Chappaquiddick and left a young woman to die.

The article stated that the hearings were suddenly cancelled because "an objection has been raised by a minority member." Under Senate rules any member can hold up a hearing by objecting. Senator Hugh Scott of Pennsylvania reportedly raised the objection on the Senate floor "at the request of other Senators."

I had earlier suggested to Kennedy in a certified letter that he investigate certain areas of FAA irregularities, but he never replied. Neither Robert Kennedy or his brother Edward Kennedy were responsive when advised of the government scandal.

Congressman Jack Brooks held the chairmanship of the important House Government Activities Subcommittee under the Committee on Government Operations, and frequently delved into FAA activities. With scant hope for developing interest, but still trying, I contacted Brooks.

Brooks replied: "As indicated in the attached news release and statement, this Subcommittee shares your deep concern over the maintenance of air safety, and we are doing everything possible, as evidenced by our recent hearings on this vital subject, to maintain air safety at the highest possible level."

The opening letter sounded great, until I read the minutes of the so-called aviation safety hearing. Except for briefly lamenting the deaths in United's Salt Lake City crash, the hearing delved into the subject of ducks and geese in the vicinity of the airport. The for-public-consumption opening statement read in part:

> The difference between safety and disaster in many ways remains obscure. Any tragedy often hinges on some apparently minor consideration which only hindsight reveals in true proportion. In matters of safety, we must constantly seek to anticipate problems rather than to react to them ... We are also concerned over the tragedy of what are classified as otherwise 'survivable' accidents ... the need for such improvements was pointed out with tragic emphasis in a plane crash in Salt Lake City last fall ... It is also of continuing interest to the committee to determine the means by which the Federal Aviation Agency, one of the largest independent agencies in Government, with an annual budget of about one billion [now 3 billion], can carry out these responsibilities with greater efficiency and economy.

Plenty of style; no substance. The hearing was a coverup. I advised Brooks earlier of FAA corruption associated with the Salt Lake City crash. Brooks then praised the FAA for its safety activities!

Friendly comments relating to the Salt Lake City crash, not likely to embarrass anyone, consumed approximately one hour of that committee hearing. FAA Administrator "Bozo" McKee, under whom the misconduct was rampant, stated, "It is crystal clear to us that we need the best thinking of industry, airmen and Government to meet the challenges to safe flight which are in the immediate future."

Bozo continued, "Safety has our highest priority, and we are moving aggressively in many ways to meet this challenge." Bozo described the order he received from former President Johnson when asked to take over the top FAA post: "Safety, Bozo, is your number one priority. Do you understand that?" And if Bozo had a tail, he would surely have wagged it as he docilely stated: "Yes, sir, and I have never forgotten it."

The criminal conduct at the Denver hearing, with the subsequent closely related deaths, occurred after this conversation occurred between Bozo and President Johnson.

Brooks stated during this hearing, "Now, General, I would like to turn to survivable accidents, an area of vital concern to all of us." Congressman Brooks briefly inquired about the United airlines Denver and Salt Lake City crashes, carefully avoiding any mention of the scandalous information that I brought to his attention earlier.

"We were considering," Brooks stated, "the evacuation studies being conducted by the FAA as a part of their continued research and efforts to improve the get-out rate in survivable accidents."

NO IMPROVEMENTS

Director of the FAA's Flight Standards Service, George Moore, was asked by Brooks, "Have you all found any noticeable improvement in the number of persons who do survive airline crashes?"

Moore replied, "Over a period of the last five or six years, as you well know, there have been survivable accidents. I cannot say that there has actually been a higher percentage of people that actually have survived in these survivable accidents."

Internal FAA reports showed continued violations of emergency evacuation requirements at various air carriers and explained why there have been no improvements in the survival rate.

Referring to the safety deficiencies and the FAA's failure to detect them, Mr. King of the Congressional group asked, "Is it not possible to ferret them out before we have such a colossal loss of life?"

They all pretended they didn't know about the scandalous corruption preceding the Denver and Salt Lake City crashes. Moore skirted the outer fringes of the scandal as he stated: "But there are a series of very unfortunate circumstances in that particular accident ... very unfortunately, the fuel shutoff valves in the cockpit that would cut off the supply of fuel to those lines were not activated to shut off the fuel. Very unfortunate." No one questioned why the FAA did not detect the reason for this poor crew performance.

With aviation safety problems now euphemistically solved, Brooks stated: "In closing, I want to say the people are entitled to the safest, most convenient, and most economical air travel the ingenuity of this nation can provide. We recognize the very heavy burden of responsibility imposed upon the FAA." It comes out like diarrhea of the mouth.

I wrote again to Senator Monroney about the air safety irregularities:

> Let's be candid, Senator Monroney; you were either deceived by all the glib talk [hardly likely] or else you willingly participated in this. Your immediate actions now will show just which it was, and where your responsibilities lie ... An airline captain is a broken man, as a result of a crime and blame that belongs elsewhere. Passengers are being set up for still further deaths by the condoning of that which just occurred. Lives entrusted to you will depend upon your integrity in this matter."

How do you explain, Senator Monroney, to the nation that looked to us as we held the public trust that these actions were undertaken with the full knowledge that death would follow? How do you explain the facts behind the world's worst air disaster, and the coverup for the damning fraud that preceded it?

Monroney never answered that letter.

Representative McVicker was from Colorado, and my home at that time was in his district. I wrote to him for help, explaining the NTSB involvement in this government scandal. I had previously sent hundreds of pages of evidence to the NTSB seeking to have it take a stand and conduct the investigation that was now long overdue.

The NTSB replied to McVicker's request, stating "our Bureau of Investigation [has] been unable to substantiate his allegations relating to safety hazards." The NTSB advised that the Congressman "will be ... advised ... if subsequent review produces any information relevant to a hazard in aviation safety."

The NTSB had access to thousands of pages of evidence, Denver grievance hearing documents, that were hard-core evidence of corruption within the FAA that far exceeded evidence used by the NTSB to reach the probable cause of many prior air tragedies. They continued their lying that they knew required the sacrifice of further lives.

Nine months later I wrote to McVicker, asking him to inquire again of the NTSB the status of their findings, which he did. The NTSB replied: "The investigator who has been reviewing this case is out of town and will not be available until the week of June 6. Upon his return a more detailed reply to your request will be prepared."

The NTSB investigator returned to Washington on June 6th and on June 12th, the NTSB wrote to Congressman McVicker stating: "There is no evidence ... that Mr. Stich's allegations as to safety hazards ... [exists]."

The NTSB is a small organization. Ironically, on May 26, at the FAA center in Oklahoma City, an old friend, Ed Jensen, invited me to have breakfast with him. At the *same* table with Jensen was none other than an investigator from the NTSB Bureau of Investigation in Washington, who was away from his investigative assignment—would you believe—*until June 6th.*

During this fortuitous encounter with the NTSB investigator, Bill Ayton, Bill raised the subject of my 3500 page hearing report, stating he had the *responsibility* for reading my material at NTSB headquarters. He said: "The report reflects poorly upon the Agency," adding, "I've worked on the material with Don Madole." This conversation showed that Ayton considered the material serious, and that he was the one the NTSB referred to as looking over the material.

Don Madole knew the relationship between air safety problems and tragedies. He knew the relationship between air safety corruption and death. He knew that the FAA was riddled with both. Madole served as the FAA attorney at the United DC-8 accident hearing in Denver in the fall of 1961. Frank Harrell had contacted him in Washington prior to that crash, and prior to the United DC-8 crash into New York City, describing the rampant corruption within the FAA and at United Airlines. By now, Madole knew as well as anyone the price the public and the crews pay for the misconduct I brought to his attention.

"The NTSB has their tit in the wringer..."

I asked, "Why didn't the NTSB act on that report before the accidents that followed, as I warned they would?"

"You sent it to the wrong section," Ayton replied. "It should have been sent to the safety division. Why don't you send it now to the Board's Bureau of Safety?"

Ayton was acting terribly naive. The matter had been referred to him by the head of the NTSB hierarchy. But for argument, the air safety misconduct was of such gravity that *any* NTSB department would of necessity recognize its importance and the need for the NTSB to investigate. Further, the fact that NTSB management gave my material to Ayton implied it was sent to the right section. Madole was head of the Hearing Section that investigates airline crashes and safety problems.

I said, "The NTSB has their tit in the wringer now, especially since the subsequent Salt Lake City accident, and it certainly doesn't want to admit *now* that it did nothing when advised, before the accident, of the problems that were later identified as the causes of the crash. It is going to take an outside investigation to bring this matter out."

Ayton stated he had possession of my material, that it was the only copy the NTSB had, that it was very serious, and that he was in the process of looking it over, adding that he would look at it again when he returned to Washington. Ayton was apparently *the* person who the NTSB told Representative McVicker was examining my material. In this conversation Ayton made clear that my material revealed very serious air safety problems.

Later that day Ed Jensen received a telephone call from an old Navy pilot friend, a United Airlines instructor I knew at Denver. Referring to the Salt Lake City crash, the United instructor stated, "It looks like Stich's warnings were correct."

The NTSB eventually responded: "There was nothing in the material offered by Mr. Stich that could be considered evidence that would warrant an investigation by the Civil Aeronautics Board ... that could be related to the investigation of the United Airlines B-727 accident in Salt Lake City."

The NTSB stated that I, a government safety expert, had reported *nothing* in 3500 pages of hearing transcript indicating a safety hazard. The entire record dealt with gross safety problems. The NTSB fraudulently continued the coverup, the effects of which continued for years, and continues to this date. The NTSB stated, in effect, that the non-compliance with the emergency evacuation training requirement was not a safety problem; the denial of corrective training to Kehmeier was not a safety problem; or the many other outrageous safety violations. This was a criminal coverup that would be paid for in the deaths of several thousand persons between the time I originally made the statement and the date this book was published.

An FAA inspector is *the* government air safety expert, and is the person whom the government relies upon to make a determination of air safety problems. If I, with my thousands of pages of hearing transcript and official government documents, did not present evidence of safety problems, both government agencies might as well shut down.

The NTSB was lying, of course, and protecting the FAA, United Airline officials, and itself. And as the NTSB knew from its many accident investigations, deaths would follow their coverup. And so it was.

As an FAA employee, I demanded in a letter to the Board that they reopen the investigation into the Salt Lake City crash. The basis was to introduce substantial data which the DAB and FAA had failed to introduce during the official investigations. The Federal Aviation Act provides that accident investigations are never closed, and new information can be entered at any time. The Board refused to do this, ignoring the legal requirement, and protecting their position.

Speaking for Chairman Charles Murphy, the Director of the CAB's Bureau of Safety, B.R. Allen, wrote to me while I was still with the FAA, and made reference to my "serious allegations of deficiencies against the Board in its investigation and accident report of the United Air Lines crash at Salt Lake City." But he refused to reopen the investigation to permit introduction of the documentary materials I had that would require changing the primary cause of the crash.

Angrily, I demanded that "we stop playing game with the lives of the public entrusted to us." In my six-page letter to the Director of the Bureau of Safety, I summarized the excuses given for refusing to act before the Salt Lake City crash, and to the sham statements that no safety irregularities were indicated. I enclosed copies of specific, irrefutable safety irregularities that no one could deny were a hazard to air safety—revealing documents from the Denver hearings.

I had the smoking gun, and the NTSB couldn't find any evidence. Those lying SOB's continued the sacrifice of human life.

Five days earlier, on June 7th, the NTSB released the accident report of the Salt Lake City crash, and omitted the volumes of hard evidence showing why the tragedy occurred. The NTSB doctored the report and omitted these criminal acts, making them accessory after the fact, adding to the accessory before the fact, crimes related to the Salt Lake City crash and many others.

"Members of Congress have no authority..."

Offering me sympathy upon receiving the NTSB's no-safety-hazard letter, Representative McVicker stated, "I am sorry that the report is not more favorable, but as you know, members of Congress have no authority over agencies of the Executive Branch, and our only prerogative is to make suggestions or recommendations."

No authority! Members of Congress have oversight authority and responsibilities over the agencies they create. They constantly conduct investigations and ask other government agencies to make investigations for them. All government departments and their officers are accountable to Congress through the statutes which created the agencies, and to the

Congress that provide for their operations and appropriations.

The Supreme Court recognized the authority and responsibility of Congress to investigate wrongdoings in government departments and agencies, especially violations of Congressional laws. In *Watkins v. United States*[16], the Supreme Court stated Congress had the power to investigate "departments of the Federal government to expose corruption, inefficiency or waste ... [and make] inquiries concerning the administration of existing laws as well as proposed or possibly needed statutes."

Representative Pete Stark and Jerome Waldie, and Senator Cranston, from my resident state of California, ignored my appeals for help and for them to act. I sent detailed letters of the FAA misconduct to many other Congressmen.[17] Some acknowledged the seriousness of the problem. Some ignored my letters. None helped and none exercised their moral and legal responsibilities. Their excuses for not acting were all basically the same, that it wasn't in their area of responsibility; none disputed the authenticity of my allegations.

ADMINISTRATIVE WATCH-DOG AGENCIES

In addition to their own responsibilities, individual members of the House and Senate frequently ask the General Accounting Office (GAO) to investigate a particular government agency, or to the inspector generals of the individual agencies. The GAO frequently makes investigations and reports of FAA activities, either on its own initiative, or upon Congressional requests. In January 1990, for instance, the GAO recommended that the FAA conduct more hands-on maintenance inspections. But the GAO refused to investigate my serious charges, as with every other check and balance of whom I made such a request.

RESPONSIBILITIES OF THE NTSB

The primary government authority over aviation safety is the Federal Aviation Act. The Act provides that the Civil Aeronautic Board Bureau of Air Safety (since renamed the National Transportation Safety Board), investigate aviation accidents, publish accident reports, and make safety recommendations to the FAA. This responsibility is stated in Section 102 which reads in part:

> The Board shall consider the following, among other things, as being in the public interest ... assure the highest degree of safety [by] air carriers ... The promotion of safety in air commerce ... The Board is empowered to perform such acts, to conduct such investigations, to issue and amend such orders, and to make and amend such general or special rules,

---

[16] 354 U.S.178.

[17] Senators McCarthy, Daniel Brewster, Stennis, Long, Gaylord Nelson, Strom Thurmond, and others.

Regulations and Procedures, as it shall deem necessary to carry out the provisions of, and to exercise and perform its powers and duties under the Act.

Essentially, the Board is required to do anything to investigate and correct air safety deficiencies or irregularities, Section 701 of the Act further states:

It shall be the duty of the Board to ascertain what will best tend to reduce or eliminate the possibility of, or recurrence of, accidents by conducting special studies and investigations on matters pertaining to safety in air navigation and the prevention of accidents.

And if the FAA requires investigating, the Board is empowered to do that. The NTSB's investigators are astute in uncovering the causes of air disasters, often having nothing more to go on other than some seemingly insignificant detail to develop the cause of an accident.

The NTSB's responsibility to conduct an investigation based upon written requests is spelled out in section 1002 of Public Law 85-726, otherwise known as the Federal Aviation Act, which states in part:

Any person may file with the Administrator [of the FAA] or the Board ... a complaint in writing with respect to anything done or omitted to be done by any person in contravention of any provisions of this Act, or of any requirement established pursuant thereto ... *it shall be the duty* of the Administrator or the Board to investigate the matters complained of."

POLITICAL PRESSURES UPON THE NTSB

Political pressures to alter accident reports is well known within the FAA and NTSB. Charles O. Miller, training seminar director of the Flight Safety Foundation, and former director of the Bureau of Aviation Safety for the National Transportation Safety Board from 1968 to 1974, stated he left the Board because of a degradation of safety and technical competence brought about by political pressures on NTSB members.

The effects of political contributions and political interests affecting the NTSB was shown in a later event. NTSB official William Gingery left a suicide note implicating Richard J. O'Melia, acting chairman of the Board at that time. In the suicide note, Gingery alleged obstruction of an investigation into illegal political contributions by airlines. The Congressional subcommittee looking into these payoffs asked O'Melia about the charges made in the suicide note, and the allegations were, of course, denied.

O'Melia then turned around and accused Board member Timm of ordering him to stop these investigations, which Timm denied. We don't know who is lying, but it suggests that the airlines can bribe the government agencies responsible for overseeing their activities, and possibly shows why favoritism affects the FAA's safety activities.

In my official investigative functions with the FAA, NTSB accident investigators frequently complained that they were pressured to omit or change the cause of a crash by political members of the Board. The subcommittee turned over to the Justice Department evidence revealing "a strong likelihood of highly improper and possibly criminal behavior on the part of the Board members themselves." The Senate subcommittee wrote that the material was being submitted "to see whether criminal prosecution is warranted."

The report continued, stating that "when the interests of the industry and those of the consumer have diverged, the board has chosen to protect the industry at the expense of the consumer."

This dovetails with my findings that the Board has covered up for accident causes. The United Salt Lake City crash is only one example of how the public safety and lives are sacrificed to protect vested interests. The relationship is often so subtle that neither passengers or crewmembers recognize it.

INDIFFERENCE TO TRAGEDY

With the change of administration when Nixon became president, I again requested the NTSB to investigate my allegations of corruption within the FAA. The Board chairman replied, "I assume that I could obtain access to the various letters to which you refer, but I see no occasion to do so."

The Board was also aware of the previous coverup and the FAA's misconduct. Appearing before the House Commerce Committee, Safety Board Chairman Joseph O'Connell stated that the safety Board's relationship with the FAA was good. He stated that he thought highly of the "quality of the response by the Administrator of the FAA" to safety needs. The relationship had better be good; they were protecting each other's necks in this scandal. Everyone I contacted protected the initial FAA misconduct as well as that of the Board, United Airlines, members of Congress, and the news media. No one knew how the public would react if it learned of this scandal.

RALPH NADER COVERUP

I tried to develop the interest of the Ralph Nader group in Washington. They sent me a telegram requesting a meeting the next day with attorney Reuben Robertson, from the Center for

Responsive Law. He flew to San Francisco and discussed my
allegations. He didn't look at my evidence, but accepted my
allegations at face value. Robertson appeared very knowledgeable in air safety. He volunteered the information that the
Civil Aeronautic Board and the NTSB recognized the FAA for
its virtually criminal behavior. After that meeting, the NTSB
created a consumer advisory council, and named Reuben
Robertson as its head. That halted Robertson's interest in
exposing the misconduct by the NTSB Bureau of Aviation
Safety.

In a later letter, I chided Robertson about this NTSB assignment, since the NTSB was deeply enmeshed in this scandal. He
replied: "Your charges and complaints appear to be most
interesting and significant. I am still interested in pursuing
them." He never did.

OBSTRUCTION OF JUSTICE BY THE DEPARTMENT OF JUSTICE

By law, the Department of Justice must enforce Federal
laws, and also protect the government and its employees in
Federal law suits. Obviously, priority must be upholding the
laws and Constitution of the United States over protecting
criminal acts of government employees or officials.

The Department of Justice is under the control of the
United States Attorney General, whose responsibility is stated
in Public Law 89-554:

> The Attorney General and the Federal Bureau of Investi-
> gation may investigate any violation of title 18 [Federal
> criminal codes] involving Government officers and employ-
> ees ... any information, allegation, or complaint received in
> a department or agency of the executive branch of the
> Government, relating to violations of title 18, involving
> Government officers and employees, shall be expeditiously
> reported to the Attorney General by the head of the depart-
> ment or agency ...

If the FAA, the CAB, the NTSB, or the Civil Service Commission, reported my allegations of FAA misconduct to the Department of Justice when I first made them, as these departments
must do by law, it is probable that the Attorney General and the
Department of Justice *knew* of my allegations before the
Denver hearing commenced. If this assumption is correct, the
conspiracy to cover up and the acts taken against me were done
with the knowledge, or at the direction, of the Justice Department.

And if that is true, then the subsequent air tragedies and
deaths arising from the criminal coverup and other wrongful

acts were funded by those in control of the government of the United States. That means in hard terms, that Mrs. Bennett and her two children in the Salt Lake City crash, died in the fiery cremation from the corrupt acts funded by those in control of the United States government, and especially the Justice Department. This is obviously even more of a scandal than what had already occurred. The following pages will irrefutably support that this is what occurred, and continued to occur.

AMONG THOSE HOLDING RESPONSIBILITIES TO ACT

The criminal perjury, subornation of perjury, withholding of information, obstructing justice, tampering with air safety, conspiracy to defraud, occurring during the Denver hearing, were all criminal acts for which the Justice Department had responsibilities to prosecute. This responsibility fell directly upon the U.S. Attorney in Denver.

I filed a complaint with the U.S. Attorney in Oklahoma City describing these criminal acts after I had changed my residence to Oklahoma. I identified myself as a government employee, briefly described the alleged criminal acts, associated them with the Salt Lake City and other crashes, and requested that they contact me for further information and evidence.

The stonewalling continued. The U.S. Attorney responded: "The matter you complained of occurred in Denver, it seems unlikely that any action by this office would be appropriate. However, we are double checking our own judgment on this with our superiors."

A private citizen does not have to run to the far corners of the country to report federal crimes. The local U.S. Attorney is responsible for making the *initial* investigation and then coordinating it with the U.S. Attorney at Denver. Apparently the Justice Department sought to stonewall me and gave me phony excuses for not investigating what would be the free-world's worst ongoing air disaster scandal.

When I received no reply I wrote again: "It is now almost five weeks since I submitted to your office allegations of a crime gravely involved in air carrier safety. Is it possible that your office has no interest in this serious matter involving the public's welfare. I think we both realize the government scandal that would be uncovered if the material that you have is actually true". Again, no answer.

A month later I wrote again, explaining the urgency of the matter and stating that irregularities "would have a very important effect upon aviation safety, and delay can have a very adverse effect." No answer.

I then wrote to the office of the U.S. Attorney in Washington, addressing it to Alfred Hantman, Chief of the Criminal Division. He wrote back:

Please be advised that your letter of September 14, 1966, directed to the United States Attorney in this jurisdiction, and relative to certain allegations of perjury committed by unidentified persons in connection with a Government safety hearing, has been referred to the Department of Justice for its consideration.

At that time I had not provided the Justice Department with any evidence. An inquiry, if they did not already know of the corruption, required that I be contacted and a thorough examination made of the evidence in my possession, along with a detailed explanation of its significance.

I wrote again on October 9th, and then on October 30th, explaining to the Department of Justice the gravity of the matter, and offering to produce my supporting data. Here I was, a government safety investigator with evidence of a national crime, and the agency responsible for investigation refused to look at my evidence. Getting no answers from the Department of Justice, I sent a certified letter to FBI Director J. Edgar Hoover, stating in part:

Possibly I should have made this request sooner [for an FBI investigation of my allegations] but I had expected other government agencies to act, who are now involved in the crime themselves. I also was not completely aware of the responsibilities specifically delegated to your bureau until analyzing the Government Organization Manual, Executive Order 10450 and other material. I am requesting an investigation into the crimes of perjury, criminal misconduct, by government personnel, especially as it preceded the tragic and expected cremation of 43 passengers at Salt Lake City from ... forcibly continued unsafe and unlawful conditions. Unfortunately, we are beyond the point of euphemistic platitudes, and immediate corrective actions, not whitewash, is required. The affront upon the public's welfare cannot continue ... I really think that at least one government agency should finally respond to this serious condition and its responsibilities before the public is made aware of the crime. Naturally, I am the one person with the information of the crime. May I have an acknowledgement from your bureau of this letter and of its intentions, Mr. Hoover?

In the meantime, Hantman replied: "I feel certain that the Department of Justice will take whatever action may be necessary in connection with the information you have heretofore furnished." Five months later, the Justice Department still had not contacted me for the details of my allegations.

WHY WERE THE CRIMES COMMITTED?

FBI agent Don Sloatt made a brief visit to me at my Oklahoma City home. He explained that the purpose of his call was to make an initial contact to determine the general nature of my allegations. He stated that it wasn't an investigative or fact-finding visit. He didn't look at my evidence, or go into any specifics.

I had the feeling his visit was to discourage me from pursuing the exposure activities. Sloatt stated that the FBI could not take action on government corruption unless they knew the reason for the crimes. "This is asinine," I retorted. "Giving the reason for the crime, much less proving it, would be virtually impossible. This requires looking into a person's inner thought processes." I added: "Your position is synonymous to a policeman standing indifferent as a crime is committed because he doesn't know the *reason* for the attack!"

Not one of the Federal criminal laws state that criminal acts go unpunished because the *reason* for the crime is unknown. Sloatt then tried to justify FBI inactivity on the basis that the accident rate wasn't very high. I hardly think Sloatt was an expert or authority on air safety. I replied, "The facts speak otherwise. Besides, that has *nothing* to do with the prosecution of the criminal acts." If the number of holdups, or rapes, is not high in a particular community, that doesn't excuse the acts that are reported.

REQUEST FOR A JUSTICE DEPARTMENT INVESTIGATION

Sloatt tried to discourage my exposure activities. But recognizing that I wasn't buying his position, he stated: "This appears to be a matter for our fraud division to investigate. I'll recommend that the Justice Department conduct further investigations."

Before leaving, Sloatt asked me to submit a letter outlining the general allegations in more detail, which I did. The usual silent treatment followed. I wrote directly to FBI Director J. Edgar Hoover, stating in part:

[My previous letter of October 31st] made reference to what I considered to be a serious crime within government that is ... creating aviation chaos with one example being the intimate association with the Salt Lake City crash of November 11, 1965. To this date I have not been contacted for the details and evidence that I possess except for a brief discussion with a local FBI agent who of course wasn't equipped for conducting the intensive investigation ... the public is getting the short end of this failure to investigate.

Hoover never responded. In a later speech, Hoover said: "The best way to solve the crime problem is by swift detection, prompt prosecution and sure punishment."

Again, while still employed by the Federal Aviation Agency, I tried to obtain a response from Hoover, stating in my certified letter: "To this date the Federal Bureau of Investigation has never once contacted me for the specifics of the alleged crime that I brought to its attention, or looked over any of my myriad evidence, facts, and other material pertaining to my allegations."

FBI OBSTRUCTION OF JUSTICE

Referring to the FBI coverup, I stated: "If the crime actually exists, and it certainly does, then we have the added problem of the felony of harboring the crime which would be attached to anyone knowing of it and acting to bring it to immediate justice." I was referring to Hoover's coverup.

I had been naive, thinking that all I really had to do was present evidence of the FAA corruption, and the Justice Department would swing into action. What especially bothered me was that they knew the serious FAA corruption would continue if a full-blown exposure did not occur and that the slaughter in preventable air tragedies would also continue.

I seemingly ran out of Federal administrative agencies to whom I could appeal. I also hadn't done well with the legislative branch, but I kept trying. I contacted Representative Jerome Waldie and explained the problem to him. (I was formerly a resident of California before I moved to Colorado and then to Oklahoma, and on that basis sought Waldie's help.) I described the FBI coverup and requested that Waldie obtain an explanation from Hoover, and this was done.

HOOVER'S CONFIDENTIAL REPLY

Hoover's reply to Waldie's letter asked that Waldie keep it confidential. Hoover implied that the FBI had contacted me and conducted an interview with me. Hoover wrote: "I have received your letter of February 10th, and copies of official communications written by Mr. Rodney F. Stich. However, I did not receive the letter sent to you by this individual. In response to your inquiry and for your confidential information, Mr. Stich has been interviewed by a representative of this Bureau. Mr. Stich has also corresponded with this Bureau, and based upon the data he has set forth there has been no violation of Federal law coming within the investigative jurisdiction of the FBI."

HOOVER COVERUP

The FBI never asked for my evidence, and they never received any. The FBI received my serious allegations, and never pursued the matter any further. They stonewalled me. Hoover lied when he stated that the FBI contacted me, and looked at my evidence. Under these conditions, it is understandable that Hoover requested his letter to Waldie remain confidential. But by error or otherwise, Waldie sent me a copy.

WHO'S LYING—HOOVER OR ME?

I replied to Waldie's letter, describing the discrepancies in Hoover's letter, and asked that Waldie pursue the serious contradiction. Waldie replied: "Although I have read and re-read your letters of March 12th and March 14th, I still cannot overcome the hurdle of J. Edgar Hoover's letter to me of February 27th. The only way that I will feel free to proceed on this matter is to assume that Mr. Hoover is misinforming me as to the fact that his agency has examined your material and has concluded that no violation of Federal law occurred. I am not willing to make that assumption. I am returning for your file, the information you have heretofore forwarded me and regret that I am not able to be of further service."

National issues were involved. Life and death issues were involved. If the FBI was lying, and sacrificing the lives that would be lost, the scandal was that much worse. Rather than let the matter drop, I replied and asked Waldie to obtain from Hoover the specific data to support his investigative claims. I asked:

1. The date that the FBI alleges to have contacted me and examined my material, from which a determination was made that no violations of Federal laws were involved. The mere coverage of the multitude of Federal criminal, safety and Civil Service laws, for which the FBI has responsibility, would take at least several hours if not longer. There are at least eight criminal laws, a multitude of Federal safety laws, and Civil Service Commission regulations included in this area of responsibility.

2. What material was examined. There are 3500 pages of hearing records, hundreds of pages of correspondence, some of which would imply fraud in statements to Congressmen. These specific areas would require considerable explanation to provide any investigator with an understanding of the allegations. To examine these, it would take at the very minimum, one day, and probably longer. I hardly feel that my memory is so bad that I recall none of these actions taking place.

Waldie surely recognized the seriousness of the implications. In an apologetic manner he asked Hoover for this information. Hoover refused to provide the requested data, stating:

As indicated in my letter to you of February 27th, information which Mr. Stich has supplied the Bureau, both through correspondence and personal interview, has been considered and indicates no violation of Federal law within the investigative jurisdiction of the FBI.

Waldie then wrote to me: "I would now suggest that you proceed through a civil court action." A civil action is not an investigation of hard-core government corruption; the matter was so sensitive no attorney would handle it; the cost to conduct such litigation would be in the hundreds of thousands of dollars; the civil litigation would not have the benefit of subpoena power; and it isn't my function to do the responsibilities for which members of the U.S. Senate and House are paid and entrusted to perform.

In a newsletter to his constituencies Waldie wrote: "It is readily apparent that there is an overwhelming lack of confidence in the integrity of the Legislative Branch. My concern with this ... stems from a conviction that each of the three Branches of Government are experiencing a similar decline in the confidence of the general public, and if this is so, the Nation is deeply threatened because self-government simply cannot function unless respect for and confidence in its basic institutions exist among the governed."

"The part played by the FBI"

In order to place into the records the discrepancy between what Hoover had stated to Waldie as the basis for denying my allegations, and what I recognized as the true facts, I wrote again to Hoover, stating: "The purpose of this letter is to place into a single communication certain important facts known to both of us. The purpose being to clarify the conflicting facts between what you reported to Congressman Waldie, and what we both know to be the truth ... [government fraud] intimately associated with the deaths of airline passengers by willful misconduct. If these allegations and facts are true, the part played by the FBI is tragically manifest."

In reply to this strong letter from a government employee, Hoover never replied. Simultaneously, Hoover repeatedly appealed to the public to show concern about crime, and to report any crimes to the proper security departments. I did both, and encountered the crime of obstruction of justice by the FBI and Department of Justice.

Learning that Representative Waldie was to be one of seven Congressmen named to a newly created House Committee to conduct an investigation of crime in the United States, I wrote:

I understand you are one of seven named to newly created House committee to conduct an investigation of crime in the

United States. The resolution as I understand it authorizes this committee, including you of course, to conduct a full and complete investigation and study of all aspects of crime in the nation ... I suppose you and FBI Director Hoover would be working together, as you did when I requested your help in exposing the serious aviation and government fraud associated with the Salt Lake City air disaster. It pains me that so many aid and abet the conspirators in this crime that has left such horrendous human suffering in its wake. It further pains me that those who give comfort and aid to the guilty, those in public positions of trust, continue their pious-appearing roles.

Waldie never answered this letter.

The criminal acts during the FAA Administrative hearing in Denver were the legal responsibility of the U.S. Attorney in Denver to investigate and prosecute. Since my residence at that time was in Oklahoma City I filed a complaint with the U.S. Attorney in Oklahoma in 1965, in which I identified myself as a government employee, briefly described the alleged criminal acts, associated them with the Salt Lake City crash, and requested that I be contacted so that I could submit my evidence and provide more detailed information. The U.S. Attorney responded: "The matter you complained of occurred in Denver, it seems unlikely that any action by this office would be appropriate. However, we are double checking our own judgment on this with our superiors." That was the end of that.

I then made a written complaint to the U.S. Attorney at Denver. I identified myself as a government investigator, described the administrative hearing that occurred in his area of jurisdiction, and described the specific criminal acts.

U.S. Attorney Lawrence Henry replied: "We cannot see that this office has any jurisdiction whatsoever in the matter, and accordingly, are taking no action."

The U.S. Attorney in Oklahoma City held that it was Denver's responsibility. Denver says they have no responsibility. The Department and the FBI stonewalled me. I started out with an air disaster scandal, and now I have other scandals to deal with.

Angered, I wrote back: "Your letter almost takes on the guise of a ploy to sidetrack your important responsibilities to the public in this matter that is taking the lives of airline passengers ... I suggest you correlate your letters with Oklahoma City as the United States Attorney [at Oklahoma City] stated it was in your area [of responsibility].

DUTY TO INVESTIGATE AND PROSECUTE

Responsibility to act is shown in part by Public Law 89-554

which states: "Each United States attorney, within his district, shall [investigate and] prosecute for all offenses against the United States." Additional responsibilities are stated—and here we have a conflict: "Defend for the Government, all civil actions, suits or proceeding in which the United States is concerned."

The U.S. Attorney, like the Attorney General, is a political appointee, and although responsible for enforcing federal law, he is part of a vast political machine that often misuses the powers of the federal government to persecute and cover up.

GRAND JURY INVESTIGATION

Unable to proceed through the nation's police agencies, I circumvented the Justice Department's stonewalling, and filed a complaint directly with the foreman of the Federal grand jury at Denver. The jury foreman then notified U.S. Attorney Henry to have me appear, and this he did. When the FAA refused to give me time off to appear before the grand jury, I wired the jury foreman, explaining the problem, and requesting that the grand jury subpoena me to appear. The grand jury issued the subpoena.

Before leaving for the Federal grand jury appearance at Denver, I contacted attorney Clyde Watts in Oklahoma City for legal guidance. He and attorney Percy Foreman had defended General Walker, whom the federal government had incarcerated in a mental institution at the time of the early civil rights movement. Watts listened attentively, but offered no encouragement. Recognizing the odds and the stacked deck I faced, he described the political facts of life.

Watts felt it was virtually impossible for me to win with the might of government against me. It surprised him that the government hadn't made trumped-up psychiatric charges against me and had me locked up, or in some manner got rid of me. The psychiatric charges *had* been made by Stacy, but had stopped there. Watts described the false arrest of General Walker by the government, the General's placement in a mental home, and the difficulty in getting him released.

According to Watts, the office of Attorney General is a vast easily influenced political machine. He explained that it was an easy matter for United Airlines to influence government officials to take action against me, by making political contributions, or outright bribes. I thought of Robert Kennedy's benevolent actions for United while he was Attorney General, involving the financial settlement in the New York City crash.

Watts gave me some tips for my grand jury presentation, assuming that the U.S. Attorney would thwart my presentation. This I interpreted as tampering with the jury. Watts apologized for not being able to help me, advising that he had to appear before the United States Supreme Court on Walker's behalf the following week.

TAMPERING WITH A FEDERAL GRAND JURY

I received a cold reception from the grand jury. These lay persons are often unsophisticated and unaware of the political role of the U.S. Attorney. They function as a jury only with the direction and guidance of the U.S. Attorney. In the complex matters I brought to their attention, they would not act unless advised to do so by the same U.S. Attorney who covered up for the multi-faceted corruption. A *Wall Street Journal* article dated August 11, 1989 described this control by the U.S. attorney over the average unsophisticated jury member: "Prosecutors can get grand juries to indict a ham sandwich, the old adage runs."

Although my presentation was ready, the U.S. Attorney stonewalled me, demanding to know the specific Federal statutes that pertained to the various criminal acts that were violated. He wanted the title and section of the criminal code pertaining to fraud, perjury, conspiracy and subordination of perjury, among others. Surely the U.S. Attorney knew these numbers from constantly working with the particular statutes. It was a delaying tactic, obstructing my testimony before this federal grand jury. I just happened to have the numbers, but when I presented them to the Attorney, he showed no interest and didn't even write them down.

It was similar to a citizen calling the police that a robbery was taking place and the police refusing to investigate unless I told them what criminal statute was violated in the robbery.

I learned that the U.S. Attorney had arranged for the FAA's Executive Director, William Jennings, to appear before the grand jury the day before I arrived. Jennings was a key part of the criminal coverup, and the Justice Department must have used him to counteract my subsequent testimony.

It became obvious that certain vocal grand jury members didn't want to hear my allegations, or even to look at any of my supporting evidence. It was as if they were shills. They were obviously under the control of the U.S. Attorney. The hostility of both the U.S. Attorney and these key jury members consti-tuted obvious and blatant jury tampering and obstruction of justice. My testimony and evidence were obviously not wanted, and the proceedings took on the bizarre air of a free-for-all proceeding.

Aggravated and disgusted at this spectacle, irritated that the U.S. Attorney would tamper with a grand jury hearing, I rose, closed my briefcase, and said:

I have evidence here of a major aviation and government

crime that is being openly harbored and protected, a crime undertaken by government personnel in positions of trust, realizing that death would occur. Death did occur, at Salt Lake City, in a United Airlines crash. Today, a former airline captain living here in Denver, is the scapegoat to protect the guilty in government.

As I started to gather my mound of documents into my two briefcases, the jury disbanded, but a few came over to me as I was packing. "There must be something behind all this," one elderly woman said to me.

"I wouldn't be here if there wasn't," I replied.

Another jury member stated, "I admire you for trying; we need more like you."

Their statements did not reflect the jury's actions, but the jury acted primarily as advised or guided by the U.S. Attorney, who in turn acted upon the advice of the Department of Justice in Washington. There was no way I could succeed in this approach. I had to find still some other way to achieve an exposure.

In *The FBI Nobody Knows*, Fred J. Cook said of this feared government bureau: "An autocracy that was superior to and above the law it was supposed to serve; an autocracy so powerful, so unchallengeable, that it intimidated, if at times it did not actually terrify, even senators and congressmen." Possibly this was one of the reasons many Congressmen shied away from this scandal.

CREW MEMBERS KNEW OF THE UNITED'S TRAINING PROGRAM FRAUD

The night before my appearance in front of the Denver federal grand, I called a United captain and personal friend from my Denver motel. He and I had started up the Rocky Mountain Chapter of the American Theatre Organ Society, composed of members who either owned one of the old theatre pipe organs, or who had a fondness for them. I explained my grand jury appearance the following morning, and discussed the problems I found at United, making reference to the falsification of training records and other problems. Possibly without thinking, he responded: "Oh, you mean the shortened training flights." His remarks added still more substance supporting the FAA report I uncovered during the FAA hearing at Denver.

HOFFA CONTACT

Attorney General Robert Kennedy was trying to send Jimmy Hoffa to prison for jury tampering at this time, and he asked the public for information that might help him. My battles with the Justice Department came to Hoffa's attention, and he sent an associate to my Oklahoma City home. It was ironic that the

Justice Department sought to put Hoffa in prison for the crime of jury tampering that was less harmful to the public than the jury tampering by the U.S. Attorney in conspiracy with the Justice Department. The public fared far worse in the government corruption and jury tampering then it suffered under Hoffa's tampering.

Hoffa's fate could have changed greatly if his associate had stayed to discover what I was trying to do. But when he learned I was a government employee, he quickly left without hearing what I could have told him. At that time I welcomed help from any source to expose the tragedy-related corruption.

SEEKING LEGAL HELP

I needed legal help to become thoroughly familiar with all aspects of this matter, an attorney with a good knowledge of aviation, and who would spend months taking a matter of this complexity through the federal courts. This was difficult to find. Also, such an extensive legal proceeding by a member of the middle class would be impossibly expensive, and costs go into the hundreds of thousands of dollars in cases far less complex than this.

Some attorneys warned me that I would be seriously hurt if I continued with these exposure activities, and that if an exposure did occur, I would have powerful interests viciously attacking me. I also encountered attorneys who admitted the seriousness of the matter, indicating they would look into it and possibly assist, and who shortly thereafter became unavailable for any conversation whatsoever. I felt the legal fraternity was under the influence of the Justice Department, a suspicion that was supported by later developments, which have yet to be described.

I contacted aviation attorney Lee Kriendler, who was highly experienced in the aviation accident field. He had written technical books on aviation accident litigation, and was a recognized authority in the field.

Kriendler wrote: "Thank you for giving me the opportunity of reviewing these materials and, since I realize their importance to you, I am returning them herewith ... Since we do share ... a common interest in aviation safety and in view of your qualifications in this area, I would like to extend an invitation to you to visit our offices and talk further with us in this area should you ever have occasion to be in New York." He declined assistance.

Kriendler appeared on the TV show, The *Aviation Revolution*, and discussed safety problems, stating airlines occasionally "sacrifice safety for economic considerations." I wrote to Kriendler, making reference to the show: "I sometimes wonder what effect upon aviation safety would have resulted if you had given attention to my case, that I presented to you last winter, more attention."

One of the attorneys I contacted had previously worked for the Department of Justice. When he first saw some of my data he acknowledged its seriousness, adding "I've never heard of anything like this!" As he was then working on the Bobby Baker case and was going to Washington in a few days, he stated he would check with his friends at the Department of Justice and get back to me when he returned.

He never called, and my attempts to reach him were unsuccessful. However, when I called and told his secretary that I would pick up the data that I had left, he was immediately available to authorize its release. When I picked up the material, his associate came to me, looked at me as if I were involved in a very serious but lost cause, and wished me "lots of luck."

Many wished me luck, but none would help.

"I wish to warn you once again..."

A Denver attorney with whom I had previous business dealings initially appeared very concerned and indicated he might be able to help. This too changed, and he wrote: "I wish to warn you once again that you are biting off an awful big piece when you take on United Air Lines and the people entrenched in the FAA. As you point out, this thing is getting bigger and bigger all the time ... There are many ramifications that might arise..."

Another of the nation's leading aviation attorneys, Stuart M. Speiser, stated he might be able to help me. He wrote, "I certainly appreciate the gravity of the situation described in your letter. In a subsequent letter he did not offer any help but stated he would "advise ... if there is anything further" he could do to assist me. On this letterhead I noted a change in the partnership; a name was added—Donald W. Madole, former Chief of the NTSB Hearing Section to whom I had appealed for help.

I concluded that was the end of that relationship, and I was right.

"The matter is so serious..."

I pressed Speiser for a reason why he could not represent me. Speiser replied:

We found from looking over the material that you sent to us that the matter is so serious and complicated it would be physically impossible for us to do justice to your positions...

These words from one of the most knowledgeable aviation attorneys in our nation added further weight to the gravity of the air safety corruption.

Using another approach, I sent a letter to the Utah State Bar Association, offering help to the plaintiffs in the Salt Lake City crash, and asked for the names of the plaintiff's attorneys. The letter was directed to President Ray Christenson and properly belonged in the files of that association when he received it. I did not receive a reply and a follow up was sent, but still no reply. Shortly thereafter, the FAA legal counsel at Oklahoma City, whom I knew from earlier days, contacted me and asked if I had been in contact with the Utah State Bar Association.

Since my exposure activities were never kept quiet from the FAA, I did not hesitate to answer yes, but his request raised questions. I wrote to the Bar Association demanding to know what had been done with my letters. At first they attempted to avoid the matter, but I finally forced an answer from them. The ethics committee wrote that "Mr. Christenson was at the time and is now retained as legal counsel by United Air Lines, and advised that he had received my letters and then sent one copy to United and one copy to the FAA.

UAL and the FAA were not only my adversaries but the adversaries of the survivors and the decedents of those killed in the Salt Lake City crash. For the president of the State Bar Association to have done this was gross misconduct, but the Bar Association refused to take any disciplinary action.

I then entered into a correspondence with the American Bar Association and its presidential assistant, James Spiro, stating: "Let me clarify the situation so that the urgency of the matter is clear to you. I had then, and I have now, factual and evidentiary material pertaining to criminal misconduct and fraud preceding the Salt Lake City disaster, obtained through my official position as government safety inspector assigned to United Air Lines prior to that expected and forewarned air disaster."

In subsequent correspondence he made a suggestion: "It is assumed that you have been in touch with the attorneys for the plaintiffs in each of the cases which have been filed as a result of the ... United Airlines crash in Salt Lake City. May I suggest you also consider contacting our Standing Committee on Aeronautical Law so it may have the benefit of the special information you have about improper airline operations. The chairman of the committee is Mr. Sidney Goldstein ... Our wish is to be of as much help as our authority permits and we do hope you are convinced of our intentions in this regard."

Spiro again reminded me in another letter to write to Goldstein, so I did. Goldstein never answered. I advised Spiro of this and he replied: "As a believer in persistent pursuit of solutions to problems, I am confident that you will be successful if you persevere." Lack of perseverance is something of which I could not be accused.

The attorneys for the Salt Lake city victims eventually learned of my existence and that I could help their clients get more financial compensation due to the misconduct causing the crash. They refused to contact me. This seemed strange. I had the virtual smoking-gun that would help their clients. The legal brotherhood continued to block every attempt to expose the widespread corruption.

The FAA's Chief of Security and Compliance at Oklahoma City, John Graziano, contacted me to find out about the contents of the letter that I had sent to the Utah State Bar Association. I told him in a friendly manner to find out for himself. But I described to Graziano the nature of the FAA corruption I encountered in Denver. He became quite concerned, apparently unaware of the serious nature of the internal FAA misconduct. He was astute in security-type activities, but naive about the misconduct within the FAA. Graziano assumed the FAA Administrator didn't know about the misconduct, and he asked me to prepare a letter for the FAA Administrator describing what I had stated to him. I felt the last thing the FAA Administrator wanted was to be confronted with more evidence of the worsening scandal. I agreed.

"This is serious!"

"That's a great idea, John!" I immediately went to work preparing a sixty page document for transmittal to FAA Administrator Bozo McKee. After Graziano read the document he exclaimed, "This is serious!" adding, "You surely keep your evidence under double lock and key, and behind locked doors."

Graziano was a competent attorney, and clearly recognized the significance of what I had reported. Several days later, as we were having lunch in the FAA cafeteria, Graziano said, "It's a lonely fight taking on the role of a crusader."

"Yes, John, I know, lonely and rough."

Graziano was later to head the nation's sky marshall program dealing with skyjackers.

I waited for the FAA Administrator's reply to my report, and after a few months, when no reply had come, I submitted a request that I be advised "of the actions, or inactions, taken on my August I report."

The FAA replied: "We ... know of no entitlement you might have to a reply..."

"You're going to get shot!"

Typical of the concern felt by some of my FAA friends was the statement by one FAA employee, "You're going to get shot! They're going to dynamite your house, or your car!"

Another thought that the gravity of the problem was such

that a hired killer would not be beyond the acts of present-day government. (Government involvement in the planned assassination of foreign leaders doesn't leave much doubt that this was a definite possibility.)

I received phone calls and letters from friends, concerned over my safety, asking for instructions as to who to contact if something suddenly happened to me. But who could I refer them to? Certainly not the FBI or the Department of Justice.

I wasn't oblivious to the possibility of physical danger. I took numerous precautions to protect myself, including keeping my not-too-docile Doberman Pinscher, "Savage," close at hand. I remembered the unsolved murder of another government employee, Henry Marshall, who uncovered the key to the Billy Sol Estes scandal in Texas. This government investigator was murdered on a remote section of farm land near Franklin, Texas. The Billie Sol Estes scandal had not yet broken and Marshall had the incriminating evidence and determination to expose it, threatening many in politics, including President Lyndon Johnson.

It wasn't until 1989 that the part which former President Johnson played in Marshall's death was revealed. This is described in later pages.

CONSTANT THREAT OF HARM

Every time I started the engine of my car I thought of how easy it would be for a stick of dynamite to eliminate the threat I represented to those involved in this scandal. Even today I wonder who may be lurking in the shadows, but I shrugged off these feelings—foolishly; the danger was real. They would eventually get me, but before then I had a lot of kick remaining.

The important aspect of the warnings by other government employees and FAA inspectors was their *belief* that such things could happen in our government today. This would of course greatly affect their willingness or ability to function effectively in air safety.

ATTITUDE OF FEAR BY FAA INSPECTORS

An example of how government inspectors are prevented from correcting air safety violations and safety problems was revealed during a telephone conversation between a senior FAA safety inspector from Los Angeles and myself. The inspector, Carl Whitman, discussed his knowledge of United's safety problems stating: "We had the problems in the [United Airlines] Boeing program, though not what it was in the DC-8" (The senior United pilots were on the DC-8 program and they possessed more clout than the junior pilots on other aircraft programs, such as the Boeing 720.) Referring to the inability to correct the safety problems at powerful air carriers, Whitman continued: "We don't have any backing. They'd crucify us"!

Referring to the experiences of my predecessor on the United DC-8 program, Frank Harrell, who tried to correct the same problems I later encountered, Whitman stated: "Harrell got into the same deal you did ... he went to Washington [to report the problems] and when the chips were down, he was by himself."

Whitman added that he and another FAA inspector, George Sheridian, attempted to dissuade Harrell from going to Washington, realizing the futility of attempting to buck well-entrenched pressure groups within the FAA. Whitman described the conversation that occurred in a Denver restaurant and bar, the Blue Onion, preceding Harrell's departure for Washington.

"Don't do it!"

"Let it die! we told him. Whatever you do, *don't do it,*" Whitman said to me. "It will take an out-of-Agency investigation ... you don't have any backing."

I well knew this, having been through the mill myself. I encountered the problems Harrell encountered, and tried to correct them. I carried the fight longer, and lost more.

Referring again to Harrell, Whitman stated, "They made it very uncomfortable for Harrell and he had to leave."

"Like a pack of wolves..."

Referring to Hi Broiles, the former Principal Inspector responsible for the United Airlines certificate, Whitman stated, "Hi is sick of all these things." He continued: "We can't be professionals right now. You know, any time any of us questions industry, automatically, they all come upon us like a pack of wolves, you know, when a wolf gets a wound. It's like a big game. It is a weird damn life. Just like the FAA Western Region, what backing do we get? None!" Referring again to the reaction when inspectors attempt to function: "That's right, coercion, they'd crucify us!"

Whitman's primary responsibilities were the training and check programs at American Airlines (who generally had a good safety attitude). Whitman was a good pilot and had an interest in promoting safety. Referring to the inability of FAA inspectors to obtain compliance with the FAA safety requirements, and the difficulty of obtaining enforcement, Whitman said: "As soon as you enforce them, it hits them in the pocket. They go to the top in Washington and put pressure upon us."

"It would implicate a lot of people if this gets out."

"Fellows admire you, they really do; we thank you for your fortitude. There are a lot of us that have bowed back, have avoided collisions with industry." He went on to state that "it would implicate a lot of people if this gets out."

Carl Whitman and George Sheridian were two men I admired from the time I first joined the FAA. They were sincere, dedicated to air safety, and had a good analysis of the problems. The FAA doesn't have many like them. Whitman showed more courage than most inspectors.

George Sheridian had also been on the jets since they first entered commercial service. In a telephone conversation following the NTSB on the Salt Lake City crash, and a year after the Denver grievance hearing, he stated his reactions to testimony given by United officials responsible for air safety: "If these are the people we have to work with at United, assign me to Edde Airlines!" This was a reference to a small charter operator whose air safety sophistication would expectedly be much less than with a large airline. Sheridian had taken the FAA assignment with United after I left the FAA, and discovered the same safety problems and FAA obstructions. Nothing had changed. It was too much for him, and he transferred back to Los Angeles.

I made the news media aware of the serious rampant corruption, from the mid-1960s to the present date. They knew of all aspects of this scandal. Never once did they print a single word about the government corruption. By their silence, they made possible many of the tragedies yet to unfold.

THOSE WHO PERISHED IN AIR TRAGEDIES ROOTED IN CORRUPTION WERE NO MATCH FOR THESE THUGS

Those who subsequently perished were no match for these holders of public trust. To this day, the public pays the price. Before Watergate, it would have been difficult to convince the average person in the street of the government corruption behind many of the nation's air disasters. Even I had trouble believing what was unfolding before my eyes. Watergate was preceded by numerous scandals, and followed by many more, including the savings and loan, HUD, Defense Department, Abscam, and other scandals. There should be no excuse for the public's failure to recognize the endemic corruption that exists in government.

AMONG THE CRIMINAL ACTS THAT WERE COMMITTED

Many crimes were committed throughout this ongoing scandal. If a fraction of these many crimes, or any one of the criminal violations that were repeatedly committed, were committed by a citizen, the Justice Department would promptly prosecute and seek imprisonment of the person. The crimes committed that are shown within these pages knowingly caused people to die. Let's look at a few of the crimes so you recognize the criminal nature of what is repeatedly shown within these pages.

ACCESSORY BEFORE AND AFTER THE FACT

An accessory is a person who in some manner is connected with a crime, either before or after its perpetration, but who is not present when the crime is committed. (21 Am J2d Crim L § 115.)

An accessory *before* the fact is a person who contributes to a felony committed by another, and is too far away to aid in the felonious act. In some jurisdictions the accessory before the fact is also charged with the crime of those committing the actual act. An accessory *after* the fact is a person who knows a felony has been committed and who comforts or assists the felon in any manner to avoid prosecution. (21 Am J2d Crim L § 126.)

ACCOMPLICE

An accomplice is a person who knowingly, voluntarily, and with a common interest with others, participates in the commission of a crime as a principal, as an accessory, or aider and abettor. Aiding and abetting is a person advising, counseling, procuring, or encouraging another to commit a crime.

AIDING AND ABETTING

Any person who "commits an offense against the United States or aids, abets, counsels, commands, induces or procures its commission, is punishable as a principal." Any person who joins any conspiracy, even if they are unaware of the actual act committed by others, or why, become equally liable for the with the others.

CORRUPTION

Corruption applies to many within these pages. It applies particularly to a government employee who acts under authority of his or her office, and who impedes or obstructs the administration of justice. (*United States v Polakoff*, 121 F2d 333.)

CONSPIRACY

Conspiracy is an agreement between two or more persons to accomplish a criminal or unlawful act or to achieve by criminal or unlawful means an act not in itself criminal or unlawful.

FRAUD

Fraud is deceit, deception, or trickery operating prejudicially to the rights of another, and so intended, by inducing him to surrender some legal right. It is anything calculated to deceive another to that person's prejudice. It is an act, a word, silence, the suppression of the truth, or any other device contrary to the plain rules of common honesty. (23 Am J2d Fraud § 2.)

MISPRISION OF A FELONY

Misprision of a felony is an offense for failure to inform the authorities as to a felony that has been witnessed or that has come to the person's knowledge. It is also the failure to prevent a felony from being committed. (21 Am J2d Crim L § 7.) The federal offense of misprision of felony is the failure to disclose a felony coupled with some positive act of concealment, such as suppression of evidence, harboring of criminal, intimidation of witnesses, or other positive act designed to conceal from the authorities the fact that a crime has been committed. It is a felony not to promptly disclose and make known to a Judge of the United States, or to the Governor or some judge of a particular state, knowledge of the commission of any felony against the United States or the particular state. (Title 18 U.S.C. § 31) It is having knowledge of the commission of a felony and concealing it, or failure to report it to a proper civil authority.

OBSTRUCTION OF JUSTICE

Obstruction of justice is the criminal offense of knowing of a crime and interfering with the administration and due course of justice. This applies to any government agency having knowledge of wrongdoing or anyone who engages in deceit, fraud, or any other act that prevents exposure of a crime.

PERJURY

Perjury is making false statements under oath. Anyone who subscribes or signs any material matter which he does not believe to be true, is guilty of perjury.

MISFEASANCE

Misfeasance is the improper doing of an act which a person can lawfully do, but done in an unlawful and injurious exercise of lawful authority. It is the doing of a lawful act in an unlawful manner.

MALFEASANCE

Malfeasance is the doing of an act which is positively unlawful or wrong, and which causes injury to another's person or property. It is the performance by a public official of an act in an official capacity that is wholly illegal and wrongful.

NONFEASANCE

Nonfeasance is the failure to act where duty requires. When a public officer neglects or refuses, without sufficient excuse, to do that which it is the officer's legal duty to do, whether wilfully or through malice or ignorance.

FALSE STATEMENTS WITHIN GOVERNMENT AGENCY

Making false statements to or within a government agency. (Title 18 U.S.C. § 1001.) It is a crime under section 1001 to make a false statement in a "matter within the jurisdiction of a department or agency of the United States. Under the Federal Aviation Act it is also a crime to make a false statement, or cover up for safety violations.

MAIL AND WIRE FRAUD

Under Title 11 U.S.C. § 1341 and 1343, mail and wire fraud

is any scheme to deprive another of money, property, their lives, by false or fraudulent pretenses, dishonest methods, tricks, deceit, chicane, overreaching, or other wrongful acts.

Among those who committed crimes, funded by the government of the United States, were FAA officials, and especially those at the FAA Denver grievance hearing; the Executive Director of the FAA, speaking for the FAA Administrator; the NTSB; attorneys with the Justice Department; members of the U.S. Senate and House; the news media, who covered up, and others. This group would be joined by others as the saga of corruption continues.

Except for the FAA who was directly implicated in the air safety crimes, the others had two basic decisions to make when I brought evidence of the government-funded corruption to them. One, they could expose and take corrective actions that would greatly reduce the number of airline crashes and deaths, but cause powerful people and powerful government and non-government institutions to be rocked with scandal. Or two, they could cover up, protect the guilty, and sacrifice the many lives, going into the thousands, who would be lost by the coverup. To this date of book publication, every known check and balance took the second option. And by doing so, they are all implicated in lesser or greater degree with causing or permitting many air tragedies to occur, along with the brutal deaths. Not a single one of the victims were any match for this group, acting in unison, their actions often funded and protected by the cloak of federal office.

THE PRICE FOR THE CORRUPTION

The price is shown throughout these pages, and continues to this day. You and many others are threatened by the misconduct described within these pages. Before reaching the last page, what has been revealed to this point will become far worse, if that could be possible. And it *is* possible; it is a fact of life in our government that has been corrupted beyond comprehension.

CHAPTER SEVEN

The Imposters—
who were they?

The forces working to prevent my exposure activities were multi-faceted. A friend of mine in San Francisco, Edith Armstrong, developed a strong interest in my crusade. She was a sales person in San Francisco, and I bought supplies from her for my apartments and rental houses. (I had numerous real estate investments acquired while I was a pilot for the airlines.) Her interest eventually involved her in one of the many strange aspects of the scandal. She devoted years of her life to support my air safety crusade. Her eventual death in 1989 may have been precipitated by actions taken against her by my adversaries.

It was several days before the Salt Lake City crash when I first described to Edith the mess I was trying to expose. While I was in the FAA at Oklahoma City seeking to force an investigation into the widening government scandal, Edith sought to obtain publicity in San Francisco by calling newspapers, radio stations, and members of Congress. Her exposure activities came to the attention of people who wanted her to stop.

THE MAGAZINE IMPERSONATORS

A person identifying himself as Ed Keating, editor of *Ramparts* magazine, telephoned Edith at her home, requesting a meeting to discuss my exposure activities. He was supposedly writing a magazine article on the corruption I uncovered and on my exposure activities. At that time *Ramparts* was not as radical a magazine as it later became. Neither of us cared about its editorial leanings, but felt that if their publicity could expose the corruption a public service would be performed.

The next day a woman representing herself as Mr. Keating's secretary phoned Edith to advise that Keating was entering the hospital for an ulcer checkup. She asked if Edith would meet with Keating's assistant, Dave Russo. That evening Edith received a call from the person identifying himself as Dave Russo, who told her that he was Keating's assistant at *Ramparts*. He indicated that he would like to meet with her as soon as possible to discuss the possibility of a story. They set up a meeting for the following Saturday at Appy Knight's restaurant in San Mateo.

Edith's daughter, Minda, drove her to the restaurant. Sensing possible danger, Edith said, "If I'm not back in two hours, call the police and then call Rodney.

THE WRONG QUESTIONS

Two men, Dave Russo, and Ted Crawford, both well dressed and in their forties, met Edith at the restaurant, representing themselves as *Ramparts* employees. They spent the first fifteen minutes of conversation on inconsequential matters, and then for the next two hours the conversation centered on my activities. But the questions were slanted not to obtain the type of data needed for an article, but instead, to determine Edith's reasons for assisting me.

The men didn't want to know the specifics of the government corruption; it appeared they already knew, and their questions reflected this fact. Edith asked them to provide identification during this meeting. Russo said they did not carry identification because of their association with the magazine and because they were trying to avoid receiving frequent phone calls at home. This excuse was absurd, but Edith decided to play along.

FALSE IDENTIFICATION

Edith and I were in almost daily telephone contact discussing the events taking place. We both suspected the men were not from *Ramparts*, and I asked her to call the magazine and verify my suspicions, which she did. Ramparts advised they didn't have any persons by that name working for them.

We decided to continue the contacts, however, in the hope that we could determine who they actually were, and what their motives were for the meetings. In hindsight we later realized that our approach should have been more sophisticated in order to be productive. We should have had another person in the background obtaining license plate numbers and other identification. But at that time I had my hands full with the FAA at Oklahoma City, making numerous appeals to people that had a responsibility to act, and I was not devoting enough time to

Edith's encounters.

WARNING—TOO HOT TO HANDLE

Two days later Russo called Edith at home, explaining that he had assimilated the information, checked into it, and found the material too hot to handle. Just before ending the phone conversation, Russo said: "I don't have a clear understanding of how close the ties are between you and Mr. Stich, but if you are wise, you will take up sewing or golf."

"I never could sew," Edith answered, "and I've given up golf long ago."

"Do you think the CIA is involved?"

Next morning Russo called again, asking for an immediate meeting. They met in the Southern Pacific passenger depot near downtown San Francisco. Russo and Rob Randall met Edith, and the questions were along the same lines as in the previous meeting. They didn't ask any details of the misconduct that would be the subject of the story they were allegedly writing. The questions centered around Edith's relationship with me; why she was being so loyal to me; do you think the CIA is involved; do you know any government agencies involved in this; will Mr. Stich carry on; are you aware of the risks Mr. Stich is taking?

Three phone calls in as many weeks followed this meeting. During the last call Russo said that Randall was also on the line, and they had a few more questions. Edith told them that I was now in town, and that they could ask me directly. Russo said they would contact me later. They never did. Russo said, "We can determine the public's reaction to the events by learning how you react," Russo said. Again, this sounded fishy, but Edith played the game.

AGAIN ASKING ABOUT CIA AND FBI INVOLVEMENT

"Do you have any knowledge of, or any material in your possession that would implicate the CIA in this matter?" Russo asked. And then, "Do you think the FBI is involved?"

"How do these questions concern public reaction," Edith asked.

"As long as you have access to information that Mr. Stich had given to you," Russo replied, "we can gain an insight into how the public will react." The excuses weren't getting any better.

"Mr. Stich is facing a stacked deck."

Randall telephoned Edith at home two weeks later, and asked for my phone number, explaining that he had been out of town, and that Russo was back east. She asked Randall for the correct spelling of Russo's name, and Randall managed to avoid answering the question. He then asked basically the same questions as in previous conversations, including whether we thought the FBI or CIA were involved. They apparently were concerned about whether we suspected these two agencies were involved.

About a week later, Russo called, and asked Edith if she had heard from Randall. He added, in almost a sympathetic voice, "Mr. Stich is facing a stacked deck; it's a rough go." Russo said that this was his last call and that he was leaving town, and again suggested that Edith and I discontinue our efforts.

This telephone call was the last contact Edith had with the three mysterious strangers. To this date we don't know their identity, or from where they came. I felt they were with one of the government's security departments, although it is possible that United might hire private investigators for a case like this. The nature of their questions concerning the CIA and FBI strongly suggests one or both of these two agencies *were* involved. Books on the CIA operation leaves little that what had occurred up to that time, and what would occur in the future, was the type of intrigue that the clandestine departments within the CIA could be expected to do.[18] The information I eventually obtained convinced me that the FBI *was* deeply involved in this matter, and not in lawful activities.

If we had been more sophisticated in the ways of private investigators, we probably would have learned much about the three men's identity. We would probably have added still another dimension to this bizarre scandal. Who could we turn to? Certainly not the FBI or Department of Justice. The imposters could have come from either of these two agencies. Or the CIA.

The intrigue continued over the years as various methods were used to silence me. What a fool I was, to continue this hopeless task in an environment of endemic government corruption.

My attempts to expose and correct the corruption within the FAA and NTSB weren't proving effective. All that I managed to do was implicate others in the scandal as they protected the guilty, and themselves committed crimes. I exhausted my appeals within the executive branch, the legislative branch, and key agencies including the FBI, Department of Justice, General Accounting Office, and others. The high government block was everywhere, it seemed.

Even my attempts to circumvent the obstruction of justice by the Justice Department, by going directly to a federal grand jury at Denver, failed. The news media kept a tight secrecy lid on this sordid scandal. I couldn't understand how the govern-

---

18 *The CIA and the Cult Of Intelligence*, Victor Marchetti and John Marks, Knopf.

ment block could silence the press. Discouraged, I didn't know where to go next.

I thought of another possibility. The government can't force a government employee to work under corrupt conditions, especially in a government agency responsible for air safety. The internal FAA corruption required that I ignore my legal job responsibilities, which caused me to violate the law by covering up for safety problems and corruption. I stopped going to work, and notified the FAA in writing of the reasons for refusing to work, and waited for the FAA to take action to separate me from government employment. Following this separation action, I would exhaust my administrative remedies by appealing to the Civil Service commission and then seek judicial relief.

This plan was unorthodox, but the law was not designed to deal with corruption of this nature. If I had not taken unorthodox actions from the very beginning, the FAA corruption would remain untold.

My plans changed. First, the FAA simply ignored my absence, although the problem had to be addressed eventually. The second was an early-morning phone call from California notifying me that the manager of my apartment complex in the San Francisco Bay Area had died. With this sudden death and the realization that I could carry on just as well in California, I decided to move back to where I originally started. I quickly sold my house and most of my furniture, and prepared for the trip west.

CALIFORNIA HERE WE COME

I rented a truck, loaded my three-manual theatre organ and certain other personal items, and towed the car in the back, accompanied by my companion, Savage, the doberman. Just before pulling away, a neighbor who worked for the NTSB accident investigative school at the FAA academy in Oklahoma City came over. She said that the NTSB investigators admired me for my activities. She told of the problems NTSB investigators have, as the political Board members try to hide sensitive accident-causing misconduct. She described the problems of one of the NTSB senior safety investigators, and the pressure from NTSB officials blocking the reports of safety irregularities during accident investigations. She described the pressures that often caused distortion of NTSB accident reports, with important safety irregularities omitted to prevent government embarrassment.

Savage and I then headed west. Years earlier I had left California with my family, having accepted the United assignment with the FAA. I was now returning without them. Eighteen months earlier (May 1964), when the FAA pressures at Denver became too great, my wife moved out of the Denver residence, and returned to her former home in Texas. We obtained an amicable divorce in 1966.

After arriving in California, I tried to learn the true identity of the three men who had contacted Edith. In a telephone conversation with *Ramparts'* associate editor, Adam Hochschild, I again confirmed that the mysterious men who had met with Edith were unknown at the magazine.

My inquiry raised Hochschild's interest. We met for dinner in Berkeley, at which time he looked at some of my material. He was especially interested in the part played by Edith and the three men representing themselves as Rampart writers. Hochschild and Edith met several times after that, discussing various aspects of the scandal and the part the three men played in it.

A couple of weeks later Edith received an excited call from Hochschild, asking her to come immediately to *Ramparts'* San Francisco office. When she arrived, internationally known detective Harold Lipset greeted her.

Hochschild briefed Lipset ahead of time on the Edith's activities. He asked Edith to prepare a more detailed list of pertinent facts, with special interest in where FBI Director Hoover might fit into the picture.

Referring to the almost incredible nature of the matter, Edith stated to Lipset: "No one would make up a story like this."

"Many would, but we've bought it," Lipset replied.

Edith described the meeting with the unknown men; the sympathetic and gentle attitude of one, and the needling by the second man. Lipset explained, "This was classic investigative procedure. Both were against you; neither was on your side." Lipset added, "This is the game they play. One tries to get the information in a sympathetic manner; the other uses an approach to get you angry, trying to get you to snap back with answers."

Lipset decided to stake out the FAA offices at the San Francisco Airport on the possibility that Edith might recognize one of the FAA people. William Buchanan, who was associated with Lipset for many years, checked the FAA offices the night before, learning the departure and arrival habits of the employees. The next morning Buchanan and Edith arrived early in a radio-equipped station wagon, and parked in a location where they could observe FAA employees coming and going. It was like looking for the proverbial needle in a haystack. As I expected, it was non-productive.

Lipset decided to do the same stakeout at the FAA Los Angeles Regional Office. The next afternoon Edith and Lipset boarded a PSA plane at San Francisco Airport for Los Angeles. When they got on the plane Edith saw a close friend, Norris Seastrom, who was also on the flight. Edith, with her overnight bag in hand, and in the presence of Lipset, stated to Norris: "This isn't what you think. I'll tell you later!"

During the week I lived in Los Angeles, working with Flying Tigers setting up their flight manual for the stretched DC-8s that they had on order. I met Edith and Lipset that evening and we speculated as to whom the three men represented. I felt that it could be the FBI, the CIA, or any segment of the Department of Justice, rather than the FAA. I thought their FAA surveillance would be fruitless.

Lipset thought the CIA's Department of Clandestine Services might be involved. Several books written on and by members of the CIA show the many forms of tactics used by the organization, their use of other government agencies and even private enterprise, in overseas and domestic operations. Investigations associated with Watergate revealed the CIA's covert activities within the United States, and its use by the President of the United States in coverup domestic operations, including the White House's burglary and coverup in Watergate.

The control of the press by the CIA has been described in such documented books at *The Invisible Government* and *The CIA and the Cult of Intelligence*. As the scheme eventually widened, the involvement of the CIA was a good probability, suggested by the questions of the mysterious imposters who repeatedly asked if we thought the CIA was involved.

Lipset's Los Angeles assistant, Harry Grimm, was to drive Lipset and Edith to the FAA regional office the next morning. But because of heavy traffic, Grimm was late. Lipset and Edith proceeded by cab to the FAA offices on Manchester Avenue. The No Admittance signs caused the cab driver to stop short of entering the FAA area. Bags in hand, Edith and Lipset walked into the restricted area, and then watched the arriving personnel. Lipset said jokingly, "If anyone asks what we are doing here, we are looking for a hit and run car."

They weren't stopped. When Grimm arrived they all sat inside his car parked in the restricted area and waited. Again, no one questioned them. After deciding they had seen enough from the outside, and that all the employees had probably arrived, Lipset said, "Come on, we're going through the building."

Inside the FAA regional office building they went from office to office on the chance that Edith might recognize one of the men they were looking for. Again, they received quizzical stares, but no one questioned them as they wandered deep within the FAA inner sanctum.

Edith didn't recognize any of them. Lipset and Edith went back to the airport and caught a flight to San Francisco. But not with United. Lipset said that he hadn't flown on United since reading of United's problems, and that he wasn't about to. (United Airlines has many excellent pilots; the problem is with those who are inadequately trained, without corrective actions taken.)

"... could be a major public scandal."

Ramparts continued their interest in the case. Hochschild continued his interest, and in one letter to me stated of the material that I sent to him: "It looks good, I read the material with considerable interest. There obviously is quite a bit of inside information here on a subject that could be a major public scandal." In another letter he wrote that he hoped the magazine would "treat your story with the attention it deserves."

After the unproductive FAA stakeout, Hochschild flew to Washington to interview FAA officials for their reaction to my charges. He talked with FAA Flight Standard officials who were part of the FAA misconduct. After talking with Joe Ferrarese, assistant to James Rudolph, Director of Flight Standards, and others, Hochschild returned to San Francisco.

Hochschild stated to me, "They said *terrible* things about you." Obviously, those exposed with corruption that played a key role in over a thousand deaths would not be talking affectionately about the person exposing their sordid misconduct. It is also possible that the politics of air safety is so ingrained that they can't accept being accused of wrongdoings.

I was becoming heavily involved with the Flying Tigers flight operating manual I was preparing. I became weary of the lonely fight. I told Hochschild, I would like to forget the matter for the time being. If the scandal was exposed, I would be fighting it all alone. It had been a losing battle. Not a single check and balance assisted me. These same checks and balances now had a vested interest in coverup, and in the event the scandal blew, then they would seek to discredit me. I had enough. Hochschild agreed to stop any further action on the story.

THE FRIENDLY SKIES OF UNITED

The crashes continued, with clear signs of the same internal FAA corruption. I slowly rekindled my exposure efforts on a small scale, preparing to write a book on the matter.

I flew my Navion Rangemaster airplane to Idaho Falls, where I visited the grave site where Mrs. Bennett and her two daughters were buried. Standing at their graves, I thought of their sad experience in the Salt Lake City crash. It stirred me to fight again. Ironically, a short distance before reaching the cemetery entrance appeared a full-size billboard advertising "The Friendly Skies of United."

The congressional contacts continued, with the same stonewalling as before. The news media continued their coverup. Nothing had changed. Occasionally, my activities would interest some low-level member of the press or the broadcast media, and they contacted me, only to drop out of sight shortly thereafter. I would give them information, and after apparently contacting some of the parties at the Justice Department, silence always followed.

A powerful source, somewhere, stopped every investigation in its track. I wondered how they did it. Were they being threatened? Were they convinced that public interest required that the scandals be kept secret? Were they warned that the scandal was so serious and involved so many key government and private enterprises that the nation couldn't tolerate the turmoil? Did the Justice Department threaten members of the House and Senate to keep them quiet? Were so many people involved that no one could blow the whistle without implicating other members of their same group? Is the nation so corrupt that coverup is the natural reaction? Were they trying to protect United, and prevent possible financial losses if the public react against the airline? These pages give the hard facts. Why the scandal was covered up by so many can only be speculated at this time.

WITHOUT FRIENDS

A San Mateo attorney advised me to forget the exposure attempts, warning that I would be virtually without friends and that I could be viciously smeared by powerful forces with unlimited funds and resources to discredit me and my exposures. He also said the Justice Department could come up with trumped up charges against me, discrediting me to the point where the news media misrepresented the facts, making me look bad in the public's eye. He said the public isn't going to believe these outrages can happen. In the end, I would be seriously harmed if I continued. The truth of his warnings came to pass several years later.

It was frightening. Some of the attorneys I contacted reminded me of the high cost of legal actions, which could easily exceed several hundred thousand dollars. As I would also find out, the high government block controlled the legal profession, and could cause my own attorney to sabotage my defenses.

I stayed busy preparing the training manual and flight operating procedures for Flying Tigers, until 1969. Flying Tigers gave me a free hand to incorporate several of my safety recommendations into the flight manual, which were well received by the pilots. Ironically, after Flying Tigers printed the flight manual for the stretched DC-8, Douglas copied some of these safety innovations, word for word, into their own flight manual. I was flattered to have the manufacturer of the aircraft copy my procedures for flying it. Douglas and Flying Tigers especially liked my high-altitude jet-upset avoidance program which dealt in specifics rather than generalities. The program reduced the chance of a high altitude loss of control.

The devices to lessen the danger of low-altitude lack-of-altitude-awareness was used in the Flying Tiger simulator, where it proved effective. Upper management delayed placement of the device on the aircraft until a Flying Tigers DC-8 crashed during an instrument approach at Guam. Unlike United, Flying Tigers immediately added the device to their aircraft.

LETTERS OF COMMENDATION ADD FURTHER SUPPORT

For personal reasons, and because the pilots' union was putting pressure on FTL management to get rid of non-union instructors (and I was one of them), I decided to resign. I received many letters of recommendations from those at Flying Tigers, and the contents of some are repeated here solely to add credibility to what is stated within these pages. An FAA inspector, Jack Druoin, assigned to FTL wrote: "I have found Rod to be well qualified in the [DC-8] aircraft and highly motivated toward the establishment of sound training standards."

A Douglas flight instructor and the key man on the DC-8 program wrote:

> The enthusiasm and dedication of Mr. Stich in the preparation of the [DC-8] training guide resulted in a document that was complete in every required detail, yet simple, straight forward and easy to use. In addition, he was not content to stop with maneuver descriptions and techniques, but researched extensively areas of performance generally overlooked or treated lightly. Mr. Stich is a self-starter, loyal, highly motivated and does not require constant supervision to assure a thorough job. He is by nature careful, conscientious and exacting.

A key FTL official wrote:

> He is a DC-8 specialist with exceptional ability in instructing crew members and preparing training material. [he] assisted greatly in preparing Normal, Abnormal and Emergency Procedures Check List, a flight training manual, and FAA approved maneuvers package. His professional workmanship in many instances have established an industry standard. A large part of the success of our DC-8 training program must be attributed to Mr. Stich, who devoted his

loyalty and untiring efforts toward the attainment of safe, efficient training. The Flying Tiger Line management, and myself in particular, are deeply grateful for the excellent service he has rendered, and we sincerely regret his voluntary decision to resign for personal reasons.

Another FTL management official wrote:

Rod was the guiding influence during our acceptance of the Flying Tiger DC-8-63 Flight Simulator. It was through Rod's constant attention to details, and his demands to have all systems work perfectly, that ours was without a doubt the best simulator ever produced by a simulator manufacturer ... The attention to detail displayed during simulator acceptance is prevalent in all work performed by Rodney Stich ... Rod has been extremely helpful in "ironing out" problems that occur in the course of normal training ... Rod Stich's relationship with others seems guided by an ethical responsibility, consequently, he is well liked by all who come in contact with him. His increased concern for competence sets an example for others that is difficult to duplicate.

A highly qualified FTL jet pilot and instructor wrote:

It would be my opinion as qualified jet pilot and instructor that Mr. Stich has exhibited a high degree of personal knowledge and skill. He certainly has exhibited the fact that he is dedicated to the furthering of aviation knowledge and safety.

A flight instructor, who later became a captain and flight instructor for Japan Air Lines, wrote:

[Rodney] accomplished this monumental task [preparation of the DC-8/63 flight operating procedures, training manuals, etc.] practically unassisted in a timely and outstanding manner. As a result of his efforts, he was soon recognized within the flying Tiger Line as the expert he is; not only concerning the DC-8, but encompassing the entire field of aviation. His judgment was frequently the basis on which company policy and procedures was decided ... His seldom equalled knowledge, patience and instructional techniques won him the respect and admiration of all with whom he dealt. If a person were searching for one word with which to describe Mr. Stich, that one word would have to be professional. Throughout my many years of experience in both military and civil aviation, I can think of no one more deserving of that title. This professionalism coupled with his enthusiasm, initiative and unquestionable integrity, combine to make him an invaluable asset to any company engaged in the field of aviation.

BECOMING A PRIVATE AIR SAFETY ACTIVIST

I left Flying Tigers and my activities branched out. I started writing a book on the multi-faceted corruption that I encountered, while simultaneously investing in real estate. I purchased motels, hotels, and apartments. I developed a truck stop and a golf course. It was these investments that supported my air safety activist activities.

In 1978 I published the first printing of the *Unfriendly Skies*. The second printing and updated version came out in 1980. These books became the basis for appearing on hundreds of radio and television talk shows throughout the United States and Canada. Simultaneously my air safety research continued, possibly more intensely than before. Having an insider's knowledge that very few people had, of the aviation corruption, my contacts with government and industry insiders, and the large source of aviation material, provided me with an unusual insight into the air safety politics.

The attempts to get checks and balances to meet their moral and legal responsibilities continued to expand the list of those covering up and committing coverup crimes.

What follows is more shocking than what you have already seen.

CHAPTER EIGHT

Selected UAL Crashes

Before we go on to crashes by other airlines, this chapter looks at other crashes experienced by United, to show the thirty-year relationship between the perennial training program programs, poor attitudes, and resulting air tragedies. These crashes are further evidence showing how crewmembers and passengers paid for these problems.

CRASH INTO MOUNTAINS DURING INSTRUMENT APPROACH TO OAKLAND

I well remember this crash, as I had just moved to California and lived several miles from the crash scene. Misreading the instrument approach chart, United Flight 615 descended too low during an ILS instrument approach to Oakland. The plane crashed into hills east of Oakland, California on August 21, 1951. Everyone perished.

At 4:25 a.m. approach control cleared the flight to make a straight-in range approach from Newark radio beacon to the Oakland airport. Two minutes later the flight reported leaving Newark radio beacon supposedly heading straight in on the southeast leg of the radio range (the terrain was basically sea-level height on this approach). But one minute later, Flight 615 hit a 1000-foot hill that was approximately 15 miles to the right of the radio range approach course for which it had been cleared. Flight 615 appeared to be making an ILS approach from another direction over hilly terrain where the 1000 foot altitude would not clear the hills. None of the radio receivers were tuned to the navigation facility required for the approach that the aircraft was cleared to make. The crew made an ILS approach over hills far to the east of the range approach over sea-level terrain for which they were cleared. The errors were major, and everyone perished.

OTHER CRASHES

United Flight 610, from Salt Lake City to Denver, crashed into a mountain near Fort Collins, Colorado, on June 30, 1951. The crew took a short-cut at night, and crashed into Crystal Mountain, thirty-five miles west of course.

United also lost a Boeing Strato-Cruiser during training near San Francisco shortly before these two crashes occurred.

"There won't be a United Airlines if these crashes continue!

During this series of back-to-back crashes I had started flying for Transocean Airlines out of the San Francisco area. The pilot grapevine disclosed that United Airlines officials held a pilot meeting in 1951 at San Francisco, warning the pilots that "There won't be a United Airlines if these crashes continue!"

But the crashes continued, and for good reason. The training program was a shambles; United deprived the flight crews of training safeguards that would have prevented the gross errors associated with these crashes and those that continued for the next thirty years.

FLAP MISMANAGEMENT

During the height of the Denver grievance hearing another crash occurred that showed the training program shortcomings. United Flight 9963, a Boeing 727, crashed during a late-night takeoff from Chicago's O'Hare Airport on August 16, 1965. The crew incorrectly set the wing flaps, increasing the stalling speed. As the captain advanced the power levers for takeoff, the takeoff warning horn sounded, indicating an improper setting of either the flaps, the speed brakes, the horizontal stabilizer trim, or auxiliary-power-unit exhaust door. The crew had missed the wing flap setting during the pre-takeoff check list.

Despite the continued sounding of the take-off warning horn, the crew continued the takeoff, while they tried to determine the source of the warning. The crew relied on the assumption that the wing flaps were in the proper takeoff position, based upon the green leading-edge flap lights being illuminated. The crew did not know that the lights only indicate that the leading-edge wing-slats are in agreement with whatever flap setting existed. An incorrect two-degree flap setting, for instance, would cause the leading-edge-slat light to illuminate, even though the flaps were not correctly set for takeoff. The correct position for takeoff was 5 to 25 degrees. None of the crewmembers looked at the flap handle or the flap position indicator.

The captain continued the takeoff, and the warning horn continued to warn the crew of a serious problem. The horn went silent after the extension of the nose-gear deactivated the warning system (the warning system is a ground-warning, and is deactivated in flight). But the malfunction still existed. The crew didn't know the mechanics of the system.

Immediately after the aircraft became airborne, another warning horn sounded. The stall warning system activated when the nose gear lifted off the ground, putting the aircraft in a flight mode. In response to the stall-warning sound, the captain lowered the nose and added thrust. But the aircraft failed to climb or accelerate. It was in a stall condition. The aircraft stalling speed increased by approximately 25 miles per hour with the lower flap setting, or approximately the margin between stalling speed and the initial liftoff speed. The aircraft crashed to the ground, narrowly missing buildings, and striking a drainage ditch, exploding into a ball of flames, killing everyone on board. This crash was the second United crash to occur during the Denver grievance hearing.

STANDARD NTSB RESPONSE

The off-the-shelf standard recommendation in the NTSB accident report was for the FAA to review the crew training curriculum and the operating procedures relative to (1) aircraft takeoff handling characteristics with various flap settings, and (2) a better understanding of the intermittent warning horn in the takeoff regime and action expected of the crew when the horn sounds during the takeoff roll.

ANOTHER MAJOR AND CLASSIC CRASH WITH TRAINING, MAINTENANCE, AND DESIGN VIOLATIONS

A crash caused by the training program problems compounded by design and maintenance problems occurred on January 18, 1969, while I watched the takeoff of United Flight 266 from Los Angeles. Flying Tigers hired me for their Los Angeles training center, which was located at the west end of the Los Angeles International Airport. During an evening coffee break outside the simulator building I watched Flight 266 pass overhead and quickly disappear into the overcast. There was nothing outwardly unusual about this flight except that within minutes everyone on board was dead.

United dispatched the Boeing 727 with one of its three generators inoperative, which reduces the margin of safety. The

727, as in most jets, has important systems and instruments that are electrically driven, including the flight instruments. Without certain attitude indicating instruments the pilots have no means of properly controlling the aircraft during instrument conditions. On United Airlines aircraft the danger of losing all flight instruments was greater than with any other known airline in the world, greater than any known military aircraft, and greater than in most general aviation aircraft.

Despite the obvious dangers, United Airlines management ordered the planes from the manufacturer without backup-powered flight instruments. This saved United Airlines considerable money, although small by comparison.

Making this decision more outrageous was the fact that United Airlines experienced numerous *complete* electrical failures on its aircraft, and lost all flight instruments. If the aircraft had been in instrument conditions, it could be expected that the plane and its occupants would be destroyed. Fortunately, every time the power failed the aircraft were in visual flight conditions. Luck only occurs so often, and then the price must be paid. It was now time to pay the price.

I first learned about this dangerous problem when I was an FAA inspector assigned to the United program at Denver, and one of the United flight instructors admitted it when I asked him about the danger. He also advised me of a total electrical failure that occurred on a training flight. The generators unparalleled due to an electrical overload, and sheared the first generator. The load for that system was taken up by the next generator, and that generator shaft sheared. This continued until all four generator shafts sheared, and the aircraft was without electrical power.

I responded by complaining to the FAA that United should be forced to immediately install backup-powered flight instruments. United and FAA officials were on a roll, and had gotten away with safety problems and the brutal consequences for many years. They weren't about to have me change their success rate.

Normally the crew should have strenuously objected and demanded changes be made. Most crew-members were not sufficiently proficient in the aircraft systems to recognize the possibility of the problem occurring. The pilots' union, ALPA, was indifferent to the problem.

At other airlines several aircraft crashed due to partial loss of electrical power, partial loss of flight instruments, and failure of the crew to determine which instruments were reliable.[19] The basic needle-ball instruments were the most reliable, but the average airline pilot's proficiency in flying by this instrument is not adequate.

ILLEGAL DISPATCH WITH DANGEROUS FLIGHT INSTRUMENT DESIGN, AND TRAINING DANGERS

United dispatched the aircraft illegally with a generator inoperative. It was legal to dispatch the aircraft with an inoperative generator from an outlying station to the first airport where there are maintenance facilities, under the minimum equipment list (MEL). But not thereafter. United, however, had repeatedly dispatched that aircraft with that inoperative generator for a total of forty-one flight hours, repeatedly passing through bases that had facilities to repair the generator. The dispatch of the aircraft was illegal.

As the United 727 entered the clouds an engine fire warning sounded in the cockpit, indicating a possible engine fire or engine pneumatic system leak on number one engine. The standard procedure is to shut down the engine and complete the engine-out check list. One of the two operating generators was on that number one engine. Shutting the engine down reduced the number of generators to only one. The lives of everyone on board would then rely upon that one generator continuing to operate. It was absolutely essential to shut off all possible electrical loads, and especially the galley power, before shutting down the engine. Otherwise, a generator overload could occur, causing the sole generator to trip off the line, or cause the generator shaft to shear at the shear-point.

The crew shut down the number one engine, but the engineer had not unpowered the galley power. The remaining generator now assumed the total electrical loads intended for three generators. Over-loading of the remaining generator occurred, causing the generator to go off the line, leaving the aircraft with no electrical power except for battery power. The flight instruments did not operate on battery power, and immediately tumbled, leaving the crew with no means to control the aircraft. The battery-powered CVR recorded the events:

"We're gonna get screwed up," the flight engineer shouted. "I don't know what's going on!"

"Keep it going up, Arnie," the copilot pleaded. "You're at a thousand feet ... pull it up!" The initial impact with the ocean was recorded on the CVR. Everyone perished, including many deadheading flight crew members.

If the crews had been better trained, they would have

---

[19] Two Lockheed Electras flown by Airlift International. Actually, power was lost to only part of the flight instruments, and the pilots refused to believe the remaining instruments.

recognized this glaring design deficiency and possibly would have demanded that United management install battery-powered backup flight instruments.

MECHANIC GROUNDED THE AIRCRAFT EARLIER

There may have been still other problems. A former United Airlines mechanic, Robert Poor, living in Sacramento, California, gave me interesting information concerning this particular flight. Robert stated he was at the airport before and during the aircraft's departure. Robert stated that the generator control panel installed on the aircraft had been repeatedly written up by the flight crew as being faulty. The mechanics at Los Angeles tried to repair it, without success, and reinstalled the unreliable unit. According to Robert, the mechanic grounded the aircraft because of the dual generator-out and electrical-panel problems. A United official reportedly overrode the mechanic's grounding of the aircraft.

After learning that the plane had crashed, Robert and the other mechanic got copies of the aircraft log showing the mechanic grounding the aircraft. They were making copies of the log sheets when United management came into the room, and took the incriminating records from them. Robert reported these facts to the FAA and the NTSB, but they showed no interest.

As the investigation process continued in the weeks after the crash, Robert reported what happened to United Airlines management, who tried to discount the significance of what he was stating. Eventually when Robert did not cooperate, Robert stated that United charged him with having mental problems. Eventually United discharged him and the mechanic who grounded the aircraft.

Both mechanics obtained legal counsel in the Los Angeles area, who then filed law suits against United Airlines. Robert stated that the court dismissed his action, claiming the attorney filed it in the wrong court.

THE NTSB REPORT

The NTSB report correctly identified the *direct* cause of the crash. The report identified the false fire warning signal, and the failure of the crew to unpower the heavy electrical loads before shutting down number one engine. They made brief reference to the inoperative generator. They omitted all details about the history of United's training program problems, and avoiding incriminating themselves in the earlier coverups.

"We don't intend to make any change!"

During a press conference reported in the *Los Angeles Times,* a United official stated, "We don't intend to make any changes in the dispatching of aircraft with one generator inoperative." United apparently was stating that they intended to continue illegally dispatching with inoperative generators, and they had no intention of installing battery-powered backup flight instruments.

United Airline had four electrical failures on the Boeing 727 jet in June and July following the crash. Fortunately, they occurred under visual flight conditions, eliminating the loss of life that would otherwise probably occur. If those aircraft had been on instruments, four more crashes would probably have occurred. Luck was with them.

An investigation of United's maintenance records showed that the inoperative generator on that ill-fated jet had been defective for numerous flights before that crash, for a total of 41 flight hours. United's senior Vice-President Marvin Whitlock stated, "I'm not proud of that forty-one hours of flight time with the improperly operating generator, but I don't feel [it affected] safety." They never learn.

"Possible crew mismanagement."

Aviation Week and Space Technology described the government's report that United's training played a decisive role in that crash, and stated: "The Board [NTSB] is looking at a number of aspects including possible crew mismanagement."

Solely because of United's refusal to correct a serious safety problem, the FAA again had to issue a mandatory directive that all airliners have a backup flight-attitude indicator powered by a separate electrical source, such as a battery. The order applied solely to United Airlines, and *forced* United to finally install what should have been specified when the aircraft was ordered. The need was obvious for years.

EMPLOYEES PAID WITH THEIR LIVES

Numerous United Airlines employees who were on deadheading on this flight perished. One of United's check airmen that I frequently encountered at our San Francisco area meetings of the Society of Air Safety Investigators lost a daughter on that flight. Again, crewmembers paid with their lives, along with the passengers. They rarely realize how they themselves are victimized by the training program shortcomings or irregularities. If the crews were aware of these dangers, they might very well have forced United to eliminate the many cost-saving practices that frequently result in disasters.

This was another crash that probably would not have happened if normal FAA oversight activities had existed. The training would have been improved; the missing flight instrument would have been ordered as mandatory equipment; the repeated dispatching of aircraft with an inoperative generator would not have occurred. The politics of air safety is an interesting science, and brutal.

ANOTHER TAKEOFF CRASH

United Flight 611, a Boeing 737-222, crashed during takeoff from Philadelphia International Airport on July 19, 1971. Flight 611 lifted off the runway, and while climbing out at normal climb speed, heard an explosion caused by the left engine disintegrating. The aircraft was already faster than the normal engine-out climb speed, and safe operation practice dictated containing the climbout. The normal practice is that if an engine fails before V1 speed, which occurs on the ground, the crew should reject the takeoff. If the engine failure occurs after V1 speed, the crew is normally expected to continue the takeoff, unless an obvious excess amount of runway remains. But in this incident, the aircraft had not only exceeded the V1 speed, but was airborne. The captain should have continued with the flight and executed the normal engine-failure procedure.

But the captain pulled the power off the remaining good engine, and tried to land on the remaining runway. The plane touched down with only 1000 feet of runway remaining. Flight 611 sped past the end of the runway, and continued for an additional 1600 feet. Fortunately there were no buildings or vertical obstructions in the aircraft path to cause instantaneous disintegration.

ANOTHER CLASSIC CRASH—PORTLAND

Shortly after Christmas, United Airlines experienced another fatal crash on December 28, 1978, that should have had a much higher death toll. Lady luck intervened for many, but not all. The captain of this flight was one of the union representatives that investigated the Denver DC-8 crash described earlier. His operation of the plane reflected the same lack of knowledge and judgment that led to the earlier crashes.

United Flight 173 approached Portland, Oregon on a flight from Denver. The crew extended the landing gear and noticed that the down-and-lock light for the right main gear was not illuminated. They also heard a loud sound as the gear went down. A visual check of the mechanical down-and-locked indicators could have quickly confirmed that the three landing gears were down and locked.

None of the crew members realized the reliability of that check, and United's crew-concept didn't work because of the total lack of knowledge by all three crewmembers. None of the crew knew the procedure for visually checking the gear as down and locked, or the significance of flying until all fuel tanks ran dry.

The crew didn't understand the peculiarities of the fuel system. They didn't realize that the plane should be on the ground before the remaining fuel got below 15,000 pounds. When the remaining fuel got below 8000 pounds there is danger of engine flameout when the aircraft has an upward pitch angle. When the fuel lowered to 4000 pounds, there was danger of engine flameout when the aircraft had a downward pitch. In an aircraft where the fuel flow at low altitude could easily reach 16,000 pounds an hour, minimum fuel doesn't last long.

It was now dark in the Portland area. Flight 173 continued to circle far south of the airport, as its remaining fuel reached a dangerous level. The only crew member voicing concern was the flight engineer, and he would shortly pay with his life. Even when the remaining fuel wasn't enough to reach the airport, the captain continued circling.

The crew was engrossed in United's *crew-concept*, holding a committee meeting as they tried to ascertain if the gear was locked in the down position, a matter that should have been resolved in five minutes. Trying to figure out what to do, the captain instructed the engineer: "Okay, on the touch down if the gear folds or something really jumps the track, get those boost pumps off so that ... you might even get the fuel valves open." There was no sense in opening the fuel valves; they should have been turned off.

The instruction to turn off the fuel booster pumps was standard procedure and good advice. But "get the valves open" was wrong. The engineer should shut off the supply of fuel from the fuel tanks by placing the fuel valves in the closed position if the gear collapsed. The valves are already open during the approach, and the goal is to shut off the fuel supply to the fuel lines, and thus prevent fuel spillage if a fuel line breaks.

ANOTHER WARNING NOT UNDERSTOOD

At eleven minutes before 6 p.m, the engineer stated, "The lights in the fuel pumps are illuminating." The captain replied, "That's about right, the feed pumps are starting to blink." But that was not right. The feed pump lights were blinking because the fuel tanks were empty and the only remaining fuel was that remaining in the small tank reservoir, which was designed to hold enough fuel for five minutes of maximum thrust engine operation. Once that light illuminated, the crew should have known that there was no fuel in the main fuel tank and that there were in perilous shape. Not taught this basic fact, the crew did not understand their serious life and death situation. None expressed concern about the flashing feed pump lights. They didn't know the significance. So much for United's crew concept.

The crew's attempt to reach a decision using United's crew-concept halted abruptly when the first of the four engines flamed out due to fuel starvation six minutes after 6 p.m. That first engine flamed out, right on schedule as it exhausted the remaining fuel in the reservoir once the wing tanks ran dry and the small tank reservoir ran out of fuel.

The engineer stated, "I think you just lost number four buddy." The copilot responded, "Better get some cross feeds open there, or something." The "or something" wasn't very informative.

Another engine ran out of fuel thirty seconds later: "We're going to lose an engine buddy," said the copilot. The captain responded, "Why?" The copilot replied, "Fuel." The captain shouted, "Open the crossfeed, *or something*." This was United's crew-concept in action. No one knew exactly what to do, and now everyone had to interject their uninformed opinions. No one had an educated knowledge of the systems.

A half minute later, the engineer stated, "We're going to lose number three in a minute too," and shortly thereafter the engineer reported the engine flamed out.

The captain pleaded with the engineer, "You gotta keep them running, Frostie." The engineer responded, "Yes sir."

A minute later the engineer shouted, "Number two is empty," followed by the sound of another engine spooling down. Three minutes later the engineer stated: "We've just lost two engines, one and two," which were the last of the engines.

At night, over Portland, all engines flamed out, and the DC-8 plunged rapidly toward the ground, with 186 terrified people in its cabin. For miles around, United's arrival in the Portland area was heralded by huge blue flashes in the darkened sky as the DC-8 snapped high-voltage lines. Flight 173 narrowly missed apartment buildings occupied by hundreds of people, as it slammed into a house on the south side of Portland. When it was all over, eleven people perished, including the flight engineer. Miraculously, 179 survived. Among the survivors were 23 who were seriously injured. Some were maimed for life.

KEEPING THE PUBLIC IN THE DARK

The Federal Aviation Act required the NTSB to conduct a public hearing, taking testimony from witnesses and gathering evidence. The intent of the hearing is to get to the direct and indirect causes of the crash, and issue safety recommendations. Much valuable information is elicited during a hearing, by questioning those who experienced the crash, or observed it, and taking testimony from FAA and company personnel. There would be testimony on United Airlines' training program, and the FAA monitoring of it. There would be the question raised of how three separate crewmembers were as ignorant as they were of basic safety requirements.

INEXPLICABLE REFUSAL TO CONDUCT A PUBLIC HEARING—COVERUP OF ITS OWN COMPLICITY IN THE CRASH

The NTSB, in an unprecedented act, refused to hold a hearing into this serious crash. A public hearing threatened to expose the corruption described within these pages. The first printing of *The Unfriendly Skies—an aviation Watergate* had been published several months earlier. I had been on hundreds of talk shows, including some in the Portland and Seattle area. A public investigation into this crash risked exposing safety problems and corruption that the NTSB had tried to sequester in earlier crashes. Conducting a public hearing on this bizarre crash could expose the scandal that now included parties in numerous government and non-government entities.

In crashes of far less significance, the NTSB conducts intensive public hearings. The NTSB devoted five days of hearings to a Pan Am 747 July 30, 1971 incident at San Francisco which entailed no loss of live.

It is probable that the NTSB refused to conduct a hearing, unprecedented in its history, out of fear that my charges would be publicized and the widespread air disaster and government scandal would be exposed.

United Airlines DC-8 crash into Portland, reflecting continuation of two decades of training program irregularities.

Without a public hearing, the NTSB eventually issued a report[20] on this Portland crash, criticizing United's training. It then issued an off-the-shelf recommendation for the FAA to monitor the training at United Airlines.

The NTSB report of United's Portland crash said in vague terms that the captain failed to use the full resources of his crew. Between the lines: the captain didn't know the procedures; the copilot didn't know the procedures; and the engineer didn't know them. By law and common sense, they *all* should have known the aircraft systems and procedures thoroughly.

NTSB support for United's crew concept!

Psychologists at the NTSB fell into the United crew-concept trap, implying that the crew should have huddled together, each contributing some speck of information (often wrong) about the system problems, and what should be done. Possibly to sound original, the NTSB psychologist called this Cockpit Resource Management (CRM). It was nothing more than another name for United's bankrupt crew-concept label to mask the problems of inadequate training. Instead of all crewmembers being fully trained, the crewmembers pooled their half-baked training to come up with the right answers—hopefully.

The NTSB recommended that the FAA "urge their assigned inspectors to ensure that flight crews are indoctrinated in principles of flight deck management, with particular emphasis on the merits of participative management for captains and assertive training for other cockpit crewmembers."

The "assertive training" was a fancy label for a natural human reaction. If all three crewmembers were property trained, assertive training would not be necessary. Instead of psychologists, the NTSB needs experts with extensive piloting and flight-instructor backgrounds to understand the causes of airline crashes and how to prevent them.

The assertive training recommendation fell right into the hands of United officials who had been promoting this concept for years. Even people in the aviation industry repeated the Cockpit Resource Management argument, unaware that the NTSB didn't know what they were talking about.

This poor competency levels of the NTSB was articulated during a news interview[21] by former FAA Administrator Donald Engen who served on the NTSB Board before becoming the head of the FAA. Engen stated:

---

[20] NTSB-AAR-79-7, adopted June 7, 1979.
[21] *Aviation International News*, September 1, 1987.

[The] NTSB is a collegial body. ... What I had to do was try to persuade my fellow Board members, who had absolutely no aviation background, to see an issue as I saw it. That was very difficult. Sometimes I had to come up with a dissenting vote because I couldn't make them understand how an accident logically happened.

CRASH WITH WATERGATE INTRIGUE

United Airlines Flight 553, a Boeing 737, experienced a crash into a Chicago residential area on December 8, 1972 that had Watergate intrigue. Numerous writings have described the events associated with that Chicago crash. I make reference to these writings, but reserve my analysis to the operational evaluation.

A Chicago group called the Citizen Committee[22] is a public-interest group that played a key role in exposing judicial corruption in the Chicago Cook County courts, which was the subject of the book, *Greylord Justice, Chicago Style*.[23] This same group believes people in positions within the federal government played a role in the crash of United Flight 553, and wanted key individuals on Flight 553 dead.

Twelve persons connected in one way or another with Watergate boarded United Air Line Flight 553 in Washington, all of whom had something in common relating to Justice Department and Watergate activities.

There had been a gas pipeline lobbyist meeting as part of the American Bar Association meeting in Washington, D.C., conducted by Roger Morea. Among those attending were attorneys for the Northern Natural Gas Company of Omaha; attorneys for Kansas-Nebraska Natural Gas Company; and president of the Federal Land Bank in Omaha. The Citizen Committee described these people as a group determined to blow the lid off the Watergate case.

For many years Chicago resident Lawrence O'Connor boarded flight 553 like clockwork. He had no Watergate connections, but he had friends in the White House. On this particular Friday, O'Connor received a call from someone he knew in the White House strongly advising him not to take Flight 553. The caller advised him to go to a special meeting instead of taking that flight.[24] Whether this was coincidental or to save his life is of unknown to me, although the Citizens Group considers it significant.

---

[22] Citizen Committee to Clean Up the Courts, 9800 So. Oglesby, Chicago, Illinois 60617.

[23] Putnam Publishers; authors James Tuohy and Rob Warden; 1989.

[24] Report by Citizens Committee Group.

U.S. Attorney General John Mitchell (who was later indicted and sent to federal prison) and the Justice Department were putting pressure on Northern Natural Gas, a firm with subsidiaries that the federal government indicted on federal criminal charges in Omaha, Chicago, and Hammond, Indiana. (September 7, 1972.) The charges included bribery of local officials in Northwest Indiana and Illinois, to get clearance for installing the pipeline through their state.[25]

Allegedly to blackmail the Justice Department out of these charges, the Omaha firm uncovered documents showing that Mitchell, while Attorney General in 1969, dropped anti-trust charges against a competitor of Northern Natural Gas—El Paso Natural Gas Co. The committee alleged that dropping these charges saved the utility 300 million dollars. Simultaneously, Mitchell allegedly obtained through a law partner a stock interest in El Paso Natural Gas Company. Gas and oil interests, including El Paso, Gulf Resources, and others, gave heavily to Nixon's spy fund, supervised by Mitchell.

Kruger, an official with Northern Natural Gas, allegedly carried these revealing documents on United Flight 553. Kruger had reportedly told his wife that he had in his possession irreplaceable papers of a sensitive nature. For months after the crash, Kruger's widow demanded that United turn over to her his briefcase. It later came out that just before the crash, Kruger had been browbeating federal officials to drop the criminal charges.[26]

The Citizen Committee reported that Krueger had been previously warned that he would never live to reach Chicago.

Among the dead were Dorothy Hunt (whose husband was on Nixon's staff and ensnared in the Watergate mess) and several others with Watergate connections. Mrs. Hunt was allegedly carrying payoff money for the Watergate participants and private papers that would implicate President Nixon in the Watergate scandal.

Traveling with Mrs. Hunt was CBS news reporter Michelle Clark, who was doing an exclusive story on Watergate, including covert details about Attorney General Mitchell and President Nixon. Ms. Clark had already gained considerable insight into the bugging and cover-up through her boyfriend, a CIA operative. Others knew of this exclusive interview, including the Justice Department.

According to some reports, Dorothy Hunt conveyed offers of executive clemency with the financial payoffs to some of the

---

[25] *Chicago Daily News* September 8, 1972.
[26] *Chicago Tribune*, May 18, 1973.

Watergate defendants. Mrs. Hunt also reportedly sought to leave the United States with over 2 million dollars in cash and negotiables that she obtained from CREEP (Committee to Re-Elect the President.)

Early in December 1972, Dorothy Hunt and her husband threatened to blow the lid off the White House if Hunt wasn't freed of the criminal charges, and if they didn't both get several million dollars.[27] Hunt claimed, according to McCord, to have evidence necessary to impeach Nixon. McCord said matters were coming to a head early in December 1972. Dorothy Hunt was unhappy with having to bribe defendants and witnesses in the bugging case, and wanted out of the mess.

The Citizen Committee reported that over a hundred FBI agents were inexplicably in the area when the plane crashed, and that the FBI kept a medical team out of the crash zone. One member of the medical team said he heard someone in the crashed plane screaming for help.[28] Witnesses near the airport reported that the FBI agents were there before the fire department arrived. Something highly irregular appeared to be going on, involving the Department of Justice.

In *Secret Agenda* by Jim Hougan (Random House) reference is made to this intrigue, and the request to the FBI by Michael Stevens (who supplied bugging devices to James McCord (allegedly under authority of the CIA) for protection. Stevens claimed he was to receive part of the money Mrs. Hunt was carrying; that his life had been threatened; and that he believed that Mrs. Hunt's death had been a homicide.

MORE POLITICAL INTRIGUE?

The day after the crash of Flight 553, the White House appointed White House aide Egil (Bud) Krogh, Jr., to the post of Under-Secretary of Transportation. His qualifications? Krogh was involved in the Ellsberg burglary caper and was part of the White House Plumbers group. In his new position, Krogh had an important safety role supervising (or muzzling) the NTSB and the FAA. He could exert political influence over the NTSB investigation into the United Chicago crash through the politically appointed NTSB Board members who establish the official probable cause of crashes.

Further control over the air safety process was demonstrated ten days later, on December 19, 1972, when the White House appointed Nixon's deputy assistant and secretary to the Cabinet, Alexander Butterfield, to head the FAA. The FAA, the NTSB, and the Department of Transportation, had political loyalties to the White House. At the initial NTSB crash investigation hearings (February 1973), Chapin reportedly

[27] See Memo of Watergate spy, James McCord, before the Ervin Committee. (*New York Times* 5/9/73).

[28] Testimony offered at the NTSB hearing on June 13 and 14, 1973.

threatened media people with reprisals if they mentioned sabotage.

Political influence could again be exerted in factors affecting the nation's air safety. Butterfield was a former CIA aviation liaison officer.[29] Five weeks after the crash, Nixon's appointment secretary, Dwight Chapin, became a top executive with United Air Lines in the Chicago home office, even though Chapin had no previous business experience. Before the crash, Herbert Kalmbach, Nixon's personal attorney, had been an attorney for United Air Lines.

Those capable of carrying out the reprisals against the news media included Clay Whitehead, Nixon's communications czar. Breakup of the networks on anti-trust charges was always lurking in the wings. In this and other ways, the government controlled the news media.

NEVER IN LIVING MEMORY

Supporting the fact that these highly irregular actions did in fact occur, NTSB chairman John Reed testified before the House Government Activities Subcommittee on January 13, 1973, testifying to Justice Department interference with the NTSB's investigative duties. Reed testified that he sent a letter to the FBI, claiming that never in living memory had the FBI acted as they acted in the United 553 crash. Reed said fifty FBI agents came into the crash zone shortly after the crash, and took over the duties assigned by law to the NTSB.

The FBI confiscated the Midway Control Tower tape relating to Flight 553, interfering with the NTSB investigation. Before the NTSB investigators could conduct their own investigations, the FBI conducted twenty-six interviews, including the surviving flight attendants. The FBI obstructed the NTSB's examination of the aircraft wreckage.

At the original NTSB accident hearings, the NTSB board members refused to consider the documentation and testimony provided by the Citizen's Committee group relating to mysterious FBI activities. The NTSB reopened the hearings after the group sued the NTSB. (June 13, 14, 1973.) The group produced over 1300 pages of documentation, and presented many witnesses, describing the FBI obstruction of the accident investigation. The final NTSB report ignored the group's testimony and evidence.

The Citizen Committee alleged that a gang known as the Sarelli group came into possession of the highly sensitive documents carried by Mrs. Hunt. This discovery was made after the arrest of gang members on January 12, 1973 for an unrelat-

---

[29] Jack Anderson's column, Chicago Daily News, 5/8/73.

ed in-flight plane robbery.[30] The Nixon Strike Force in Chicago prosecuted the case against the Sarelli mob. What they didn't know was that their star witness against the gang was a staff investigator on the Citizen's Committee, Alex Bottos, Jr.

When Bottos surfaced in the NTSB hearing during the week of February 27, 1973, federal marshals seized him, without the formality of a hearing, trial, or conviction. They reportedly sequestered him in the federal Prison Hospital at Springfield, Missouri, a maximum security prison, to quiet him.[31] Apparently the Nixon Strike Force was fearful their case against the Sarelli gang would expose parts of the Watergate scandal and its relationship to the crash of United Flight 553. The government then tried to sabotage its own case against the Sarelli aircraft robbery gang when the Sarelli mob threatened to expose the documents that Mrs. Hunt was carrying.

After considerable public clamor in Chicago, including picketing in front of the United Airlines downtown offices, the Justice Department released Bottos 40 days after his imprisonment.

The government wanted Bottos and Zale silenced, so they could not testify at the reopened NTSB crash investigation into the crash of UAL Flight 553. The hearings were held on June 13, 14, 1973. The government indicted Zale the day before the NTSB hearing, possibly to keep him from the hearing, or to seize him if he showed up. The federal government also tried to frame Bottos, and in that manner discredit his testimony at the NTSB hearing. At a later date, July 27, 1973, a federal jury at South Bend, Indiana, deliberated less than a half-hour before handing down an innocent verdict following a week of government prosecution. Buttos and Zale showed up at the NTSB hearing. Buttos wore a bullet-proof vest. They both expected to be arrested at any moment.

I know nothing about the truth of these matters claimed by the Citizens Committee and some other groups. They are intriguing, and must be considered possible in light of the intrigue revealed within these pages.

---

[30] U.S. Magistrate Balog's records, 72-41, U.S. Courthouse, Chicago.
[31] Jack Anderson's column in *Chicago Daily News*, April 9, 1973.

United Flight 553 crash into Chicago residential area, with
Watergate, FBI, and CIA intrigue.

AERODYNAMIC ASPECTS OF THE CRASH

The direct causes of the Chicago crash were revealed by the cockpit voice recorder (CVR), the flight data recorder (FDR), and the history of training program problems. During the approach to Chicago Midway Airport (an approach I've flown many times in poor weather conditions), Flight 553 reached its minimum descent altitude (MDA), and then continued to descend to the ground where it crashed.

Upon reaching the minimum descent altitude (MDA) the pilot raised the nose of the aircraft to stop the descent. But he was slow in adding sufficient power. The stall warning horn sounded, and continued sounding as the plane crashed seventeen seconds later.

Some believe that the captain used speed brakes during the descent, contrary to procedures (used only at higher altitudes for emergency descents), and then retracted them too late, possibly accounting for the failure to recover from the stall condition.

Compounding the problem, if the pilot used the stall-recovery technique taught by United, it would explain why the plane crashed. United's technique resulted in a 500 foot altitude loss. The technique I recommended resulted in virtually no altitude loss.

INTO THE MOUNTAINS AT SALT LAKE CITY

During a night approach to Salt Lake City Airport on December 18, 1977 a United DC-8 crashed into the side of a mountain, killing everyone on board. As the flight prepared for an instrument approach, the landing gear down-and-locked lights did not function, believed due to an electrical failure. The crew abandoned the approach, and notified approach control that they were trying to correct an aircraft problem.

Salt Lake City approach control cleared the aircraft to hold northwest of the Salt Lake City VOR station until they were ready to land. The crew asked if they were to hold north, which was an inaccurate request, since the question was whether the holding along the north-south course was to be on the northwest or northeast side. The controller responded, instructing the crew to hold "northwest of the VOR." United held on the opposite side, the northeast.

If the crew had looked at the terrain charts they would have seen that mountains higher than their holding altitude were on the northeast side.

Very few crewmembers check the surrounding terrain when taking off or landing, and are often unaware of high terrain. They rely upon the radio navigation charts, which often do not show hazardous terrain with the details needed for a safe flight.

Before reaching the holding pattern, the crew notified approach control that they were leaving the frequency so as to make radio contact with the United Airlines maintenance base at San Francisco. (One of their communication radios was inoperative, requiring the crew to leave the controller's frequency while they communicated with the company.) The crew sought help in figuring out a system problem.

Upon reaching the holding pattern, the DC-8 held on the wrong side of the north-south ILS approach—the northeast side—at 7000 feet, below the height of the mountains. They compounded this error by flying at 230 knots airspeed, instead of 200 knots, which extended their path over the ground, closer to the mountains. In addition, the crew flew 2 1/2 minute legs instead of 1 1/2 minutes. (The length of the flight path from the holding fix before turning inbound.)

On top of these problems, there was yet one more. The NTSB report omitted the NTSB investigators's report that the flight engineer had a blood alcohol level of .04, which decreased the engineer's performance, and undoubtedly affected his ability to handle the system abnormality.

As the controller saw on his radar screen that United was holding on the wrong side of the approach course, he tried to reach the crew by broadcasting on the last frequency used, and also on the navigation radio channel, without success. When the United crew finally returned to the Salt Lake City frequency the controller directed the crew to turn left. Twenty seconds later the controller advised the crew to climb. But it was too late. The DC-8 crashed into the 7200-foot-level of the 7665-foot mountain, and disintegrated in a ball of flames.

A post-crash investigation showed that the cockpit recorder was not working at the time of the crash, and had been inoperative for several days. It is illegal to dispatch a flight with this unit inoperative (or to dispatch the unit with the insides missing, as United had done in the 727 that crashed into Lake Michigan). The NTSB post-accident investigation revealed that there were over 89 reports of defective CVR units, many of which went uncorrected. The test procedure by the airline required pressing a test button and noting that the needle deflected to the center of the scale on the monitor. But the manufacturer requires plugging a headset plug into the unit to monitor the flight station microphone for audio test tones and United did not do this. The report did not address the inoperative radio.

DC-8 CRASH DURING TAKEOFF AT DETROIT

A United DC-8 crashed during takeoff from Detroit on January 11, 1983 killing every one on board. The captain allowed the flight engineer to make the takeoff, even though the engineer was unqualified to fly the aircraft. The flight engineer had flunked earlier pilot training. During the takeoff the flight engineer incorrectly set the horizontal stabilizer trim to a high nose-up position. Immediately after becoming airborne, the plane pitched up sharply, stalled out, and crashed to the ground.

Many other near-crashes and non-fatal crashes also occurred during the time span shown in these pages.

There were many near-crashes that avoided becoming crashes by luck. Aircraft have landed with only a few minutes of fuel remaining; they could easily have become major disasters if the flights had been a few minutes longer.

ANOTHER SUSPICIOUS AND POSSIBLE SABOTAGE INVOLVEMENT CRASH IN A CORPORATE JET

Although it did not rank in the big-league of air disasters, it had an element of intrigue along the lines of the United Chicago crash. A brief reference is made to it for its interest value. A corporate jet owned by Gulf Power Company crashed at Pensacola under mysterious circumstances. For several years the IRS and FBI had been investigating a kick-back scheme at Gulf Power Company, an electrical utility based in Pensacola, Florida. During these investigations several mysterious deaths and disappearances of key officials involved occurred in the highly sensitive investigation.

Gulf Power Vice-President Jacob Horton was the only passenger on the Pensacola plane that crashed after takeoff, killing everyone on board. The crash didn't have any clear cause.

Shortly after the crash, an unidentified caller to the sheriff's office stated: "You can stop investigating Gulf Power now, we took care of them this afternoon."

There had been several unsolved mysteries associated with the Gulf Power scandal. A former Gulf Power director, Robert McRae, and his wife, were shot to death at their home in Graceville, Florida. A former Gulf employee, Ray Howell, traveled to Atlanta for a scheduled appearance before the grand jury, and disappeared before appearing. Within several weeks of the Pensacola crash three dead yellow birds were placed outside the office and home of Horton's attorney. The attorney felt that it was a Mafia-style warning, warning him not to divulge the substance of conversations with his now deceased client.

CHAPTER NINE

Selected Crashes—
other airlines

This section addresses a selected number of crashes experienced by other airlines in the United States prior to deregulation.

AMERICAN'S PLUNGE INTO JAMAICA BAY

American Airline suffered far fewer crashes than experienced by United Airlines, and very few of them, if any, were due to the glaring ignorance of basic aircraft systems or flight procedures. The crashes that did occur arose from safety problems that went unaddressed throughout much of the aviation industry, and unaddressed, even where the training is relatively good by comparison.

Other inspectors, and myself, respected American Airlines for its training, attitude, and standards. However, an airline's safety standards and attitude can change with a change of management, especially following deregulation where greater emphasis is placed on increasing profits than on safety.

DEATH PLUNGE IN SIGHT OF THOUSANDS

American Airlines Flight One, a Boeing 707, departed New York's Idlewild International Airport on March 1, 1962, headed for Chicago. (Since then renamed John F. Kennedy International Airport.) The weather was excellent and it should have been an uneventful flight. Flight One made a noise-abatement climbout, and at 1,000 feet above the ground the captain put the 707 into a steep bank. The aircraft suddenly rolled inverted and plunged straight down into Jamaica Bay. Everyone perished.

The scenario was similar to the captain's prior flight check at Los Angeles. The captain at that time also put the aircraft into a steep 45 degree bank during the initial climb out, at approximately 1000 feet above the ground, during a relatively low-airspeed noise-abatement climb procedure. That was a dangerous maneuver, and if the check pilot had recognized the dangerous proximity to a stall, a major reaction should have followed, such as immediate cancellation of the flight check. In this way the pilot would have realized the danger of what he had done.

At a later date I flew approximately twenty flights in a Boeing 707 simulator at the FAA Oklahoma City training center, duplicating that aircraft's fatal flight, using the known airspeed, altitude, and "G" force data from the aircraft flight recorder. I added into the flight parameters turbulence which is believed to have existed when Flight One took off from Idlewild Airport. Seventeen of the simulator flights ended in an uncontrollable roll and subsequent crash immediately after entering a forty-five degree bank.

Years ago, at some airlines, if the pilot made a serious unsafe maneuver, the strict adherence to safe operating procedures resulted in the flight check stopped right then and there. The competency check was considered failed, and the aircraft returned to base. The pilot who failed the check was given additional training, and then rechecked. In this way the pilots were mentally impressed with the danger of the unsafe maneuver, and were far more cognizant of safe operating procedures.

But this strict adherence to safety is rarely followed. Returning to the base, giving additional training and a recheck, is costly. Today, the most that may be done at many airlines is either not mention it at all, or brief reference made to it, and the pilot passed as satisfactory. The pilot with the dangerous habit then has a false sense of security, and doesn't realize the danger of what he or she has done. The company takes a calculated risk, and the extra cost of retraining is eliminated.

NTSB BASED THEIR PROBABLE CAUSE ON FAR-OUT THEORIES

During the investigation into the crash of Flight One, NTSB investigators reached a conclusion on the probable cause of the crash by visiting the factory where the autopilot was manufactured. An NTSB investigator saw an assembler pulling wires into place with tweezers, and jumped to the conclusion that the use of tweezers cut into the wire's insulation, causing an electrical ground, and causing the autopilot yaw damper to give a sudden rudder deflection. The plane then became, under that theory, uncontrollable.

This was wild speculation, and wasn't supported by flight tests. Using flight-test data, the test pilots found that applying maximum yaw damper deflection in flight under similar conditions as Flight One experienced did not result in loss of control. Frequently the NTSB's official probable cause of the crash is unsupported by people far more knowledgeable in aircraft operations than the often low-experience NTSB personnel.

The NTSB investigators knew of the report in the FAA files showing the captain's dangerous steep bank, but the NTSB apparently didn't recognize its dangers. An FAA friend of mine, Carl Whitman, had observed the captain's prior flight check conducted by a company check airman, and reported that the captain put the aircraft into the same 45 degree bank during the noise-abatement takeoff at Los Angeles.

The inspector received considerable criticism from FAA officials for having put that comment into the report. They weren't concerned that the inspector had not done anything about the unsafe maneuver; they were concerned that he made an entry in the records.

AMERICAN AIRLINES CINCINNATI

American Airlines Flight 383, a Boeing 727, on a flight from New York to Greater Cincinnati Airport, made a visual night approach in light-rain conditions on November 8, 1965. In the cockpit was the usual three-member crew and an American Airlines check captain conducting an enroute check. The airport sits on a hill and pilots are susceptible to altitude-awareness problems as they judge their height above the ground by the lower ground in the adjacent valley.

During the base leg and turn to final the pilots were unaware that they had flown the plane *below* the elevation of the airport. People on the ground heard the aircraft's jet engines passing over their roofs, in some cases less than 100 feet. Flight 383 rammed into the hillside, exploding on impact, at an elevation below the airport altitude. The impact jammed most of the passengers and crew into a tight ball at the front of the plane, where most of the broken bodies were found. Only four people survived.

Three months earlier a United 727 had experienced a similar altitude-awareness problem. The 727 descended at high speed into Lake Michigan, unaware of its altitude. This is the problem I recognized, and sought to correct. The FAA Western Region hierarchy blocked my corrective actions, and during the Denver hearing held that I fabricated the existing problem.

The NTSB accident report for Flight 383 stated the probable cause of the crash was the lack of altitude-awareness:

> [T]he failure of the crew to properly monitor the altimeters during a visual approach into deteriorating visibility conditions. All events leading up to impact, including the final radio transmission from the flight, indicate that the crew was not concerned with, and were totally unaware of a dangerously low altitude situation. ... It does believe that improper monitoring of the instrument [altimeter] could possibly result in a misinterpretation and this in turn could help to explain the inappropriate descent involved in this accident.

USUAL NTSB COVER UP

The NTSB accident report covered up for the serious FAA misconduct preceding the crash that prevented earlier corrective actions. The NTSB covered up for the fact that I had repeatedly reported the altitude-awareness problem and that the FAA ordered me to ignore it and halt my corrective actions. The NTSB covered up for the fraud and conspiracy during the earlier Denver hearing. The NTSB covered up for their own complicity as their letters to me stated that the FAA conduct did not constitute safety problems. This complicity attaches to every crash described so far, and to many that have yet to occur. Even after the NTSB report was issued on this crash, the NTSB responded to my letters stating the FAA's actions in covering up for this problem, and barring corrective actions (and the many other wrongful acts) did not constitute a safety problem. They were of course lying, and had no other answer if they were to avoid blame for this and other crashes.

An *Aviation Week* article described the recommendations of the National Transportation Safety Board concerning pilots accidentally descending below minimum safe altitude: "Altimetry Improvements Urged by NTSB." The same year an FAA Advisory Circular warned pilots: "The increased number of accidents and incidents involving lack of altitude awareness prompted the FAA to initiate rulemaking action which resulted in a requirement for an approved altitude alerting device/system ..."

The Air Line Pilots Association magazine, *Air Line Pilot*, used wording almost identical to that in my recommendations: "All barometric altimeters, if not already updated, should have two indices [bugs] on the bezel of the instruments; one to be preset to the decision height [minimum safe altitude] and the other to be preset to the elevation of the touchdown point."

American Airlines 727 crash at Cincinnati, caused by problem of
lack of altitude awareness which FAA claimed did not exist.

I first became aware of the problem while I was an eighteen year-old Navy pilot in World War II during night landings on unlighted waterways, and particularly Escambia Bay at Pensacola, Florida. As a PBY flight instructor at Jacksonville, Florida frequent night landings on the St Johns River further brought this altitude-awareness home to me. Since the surface of the water cannot be seen, we must rely heavily upon our barometric altimeter to determine our height above the landing surface.

One of my earlier recommendations addressing the altitude-awareness problem included a FAA report which stated: "This inspector highly recommends altimeter bugs—a yellow bug to denote minimum altitude and a red bug to denote the ground." Another of my FAA reports identifying the problem recommended "the use of a reddish or orange bug that shows under red lights to indicate the field elevation and a white bug to indicate minimum altitude."

Under this presentation the white bug would be a positive indication to the pilot of approaching minimums, greatly eliminating the possibility of descending into the ground. The pilots are more aware of their altitude. Preoccupation with other parts of the approach procedure, and lack of any ground or minimum-altitude marks on the barometric altimeter, makes it easy to pass through the minimum descent altitude. The red bug would impress the pilot with the need to positively rotate the aircraft during a missed-approach maneuver to avoid hitting the ground that wasn't much more than a wind-span away.

I promoted this arrangement with a Western Airlines check pilot who subsequently wrote:

> This experience [as a check pilot] has confirmed to me a point which you made during our conversation. This is that a surprising number of good pilots will over or undershoot a ... minimum altitude. I am writing to you to see what information you have on an altimeter bug.

Japan Airlines also adopted my recommendation after one of their DC-8s crashed into San Francisco bay during an instrument approach. The *National Observer* reported the problem:

> Reasons for mysterious crashes: Pilots may be misreading their altimeters, Federal Agency says.
> In response to the mounting worry that pilots may occasionally—and fatally—read their altimeters. The Federal Aviation agency two weeks ago proposed a new regulation that would require airlines to install a system ... to warn a pilot when he is approaching his assigned altitude.
> ... The latest report, released last week, involves the crash

of a Boeing 727 jet into Lake Michigan killing the 30 persons aboard." Referring to the barometric altimeters, the article state what I reported in the early sixties, that they were "fairly easy to misread.

An FAA Washington Advisory Circular addressed the problem:

The increased number of accidents and incidents involving lack of altitude awareness promoted the FAA to initiate rulemaking action which resulted in a requirement for an approved altitude alerting device system on all turbojet aircraft ...

Business and Commercial Aviation reported in its February 1971 issue a similar problem:

The 707, with three captains in the cockpit, was cleared out of FL 290 to 9000 ft. After descent and level-off the captain in the right seat noticed trees just below them and shouted "pull up." A recheck of the altimeter showed they were actually at 900 ft pressure altitude.

But the story doesn't end there. The flight landed routinely at Chicago. However, the captains decided it would be better not to report the embarrassing [and near-fatal] incident. One passenger, a private pilot, also noticed how close the plane had come to the ground and noting the sudden pull up that followed surmised that something had gone awry. He later mentioned the incident to FAA, which impounded the flight recording tape of the jet—and found that only 40 ft separated an incident from a very fatal accident. The captain said that when he went through 9000 ft he thought it was FL 190 ft. [19,000.]

Everyone, it appeared, knew a problem existed, except the FAA. (What else is new!) FAA Washington headquarters finally had no choice but to admit a problem existed. They issued a proposed rule requiring installation on large aircraft and small jets of a device to "warn pilots when they approach a preselected altitude." Comments from industry on this proposal were directed to FAA's General Counsel for action. Ironically, this was the same office that obstructed the correction of this same problem, and accused me of falsifying its existence!

AMERICAN AIRLINES CHICAGO DC-10 CRASH
One of America's great air tragedies occurred at Chicago's O'Hare Airport on May 25, 1979. American Airlines Flight 191, a DC-10, carrying 271 persons, started its takeoff, heading for

Los Angeles. It didn't get far.

The copilot made the takeoff, which the passengers monitored in the cabin via the TV monitors. As the DC-10 reached rotation speed (VR), the copilot applied back pressure to the control column, causing the aircraft to pitch sharply up and lift off the runway. Simultaneously the number one engine on the left side of the aircraft ripped loose from the wing. It flew up, over, and behind the aircraft, crashing to the runway.

The crew knew they had an engine failure, but were unaware the engine ripped off the aircraft. Using standard procedures Flight 191 climbed at a very respectable 900 feet per minute. The copilot reduced the airspeed from the V2 plus 15 knots to V2, as required by the FAA and the company operating procedures. This immediately reduced the speed margin over the stall and would prove fatal.

As the DC-10 reached 400 feet something suddenly went wrong. The DC-10 went into a steep left bank, rolled inverted, and at 250 miles per hour slammed into the ground within a mile of the runway. It instantly disintegrated into a ball of flames and black smoke, killing all 271 people on board.

Fortunately the plane missed the airport terminal building and numerous hotels and other buildings containing thousands of people, and crashed in an area of auto rental businesses.

BRUTALITY BECOMES PROGRESSIVELY WORSE

Hundreds of onlookers on the ground, and those on Flight 191, watched horrified, as the DC-10 plunged to the ground and erupt in a ball of flames like a napalm explosion. As planes become larger and carry more people the death toll in airline crashes naturally becomes higher with subsequent crashes. With the higher speeds and greater amount of fuel the horror worsens. It was difficult to recognize the wreckage as an aircraft. There wasn't a single body intact; just bits and pieces, without any body-part recognizable as a face. It wasn't possible to tell if the remains were male or female, an adult or a child. Stuck to the shredded wreckage were bits of human flesh and bones. Rescuers couldn't help walking on parts of bodies. Matching body parts became guesswork. Less than a dozen bodies had heads attached to the torsos.

American Airlines DC-10 about to crash at Chicago, showing the missing engine on the left wing.

I describe this scene not for its shock value, but to emphasize that the sheer brutality of air disasters should eliminate any form of corruption or misconduct that could lead to such great tragedy. The horror of air disasters prohibits anyone from refusing to investigate the charges I made, and the evidence I offered. Aware of this horror, it makes obscene the obstructionist actions of the Justice Department, the NTSB, members of Congress, the news media, and everyone else who failed to act when they were made aware of the charges.

WHY DID THE CRASH OCCUR?

The pilots of Flight 91 went by the book, and did everything they were suppose to do, including the recommended procedures that had built-in safety hazards. But one simple mistake triggered the disaster.

Despite the missing engine, Flight 191 rapidly climbed at approximately 800 feet per minute. This performance tripled what some of our four-engine propeller aircraft accomplished with all four engines running. I remember many a takeoff from Pacific Islands on a hot day or night, in which our climb rate was less than 300 feet per minute, with all engines operating.

For 22 seconds the DC-10 climbed at an excellent rate, and it looked like everything was under control. The copilot's right foot continued to deflect the rudder to keep the aircraft going straight. He had not yet applied trim tab which would have eliminated having to manually apply right rudder.

The captain then took over the aircraft that was flying straight, not realizing the copilot still had right rudder applied. Without checking that the captain had also applied right rudder, and without slowing easing the pressure on the right rudder pedal to insure that directional control existed, the copilot released his pressure on the right rudder pedal. The rudder then slammed to zero deflection, causing the aircraft to yaw to the left from the unsymmetrical engine power.

When the plane yawed, the right wing developed greater lift than the left wing,[32] causing the right wing to rise, and the left wing to lower. This downward movement of the left wing increased the angle of attack in relation to the relative wind, causing a higher angle-of-attack on a wing that was already stalled or near-stalled. The captain instinctively applied right aileron to lift the left wing, which is a normal reaction, but dangerous when the wing is near the stall. At near-stall speeds, trying to life a low wing with the aileron causes the low-wing aileron to lower, increasing the angle of attack.

---

[32] The increased lift on the right wing resulted from it moving faster as it advanced due to the yaw, and greater frontal area. The left wing initially moved slower, and the yaw caused less of the wing to be exposed to the resulting wind.

The stall worsened, and the plane continued rolling until it was upside down, and the nose plunged toward the ground.

I know of no airline that teaches this basic knowledge. It is one of those subjects that is not covered even on the airlines with relatively good training programs. The pressure to keep training costs down generated by airlines with low-training costs (such as United) precludes another airline from raising the training costs to cover the many other possible emergencies that may arise. A calculated risk is taken and considerable money saved.

WHAT SHOULD HAVE BEEN DONE?

This is not to criticize the crew, as this scenario is one that is rarely, if ever, covered during training flights. The basics of flight control application during stalls are taught in primary training, but long forgotten by many airline pilots.

Once the mistake was made, and the rudder slammed to zero, it was necessary to take special corrective actions. Right rudder should have been applied immediately, simultaneous with lowering the nose to reduce the angle of attack from the steep 14 degree pitch-up. Another precaution, taught in primary training, is to avoid using the ailerons to raise the low wing until the angle of attack is reduced.

FAA DIRECTED UNSAFE ENGINE-OUT PROCEDURE

On training and check flights the FAA required the pilots to go to V2 speed during the climb-out. This is fine if there is an obstruction in front of the aircraft, which there rarely is. I too looked for the pilots to climb out at that speed, *if* the pilot had not already exceeded that speed before recognizing and reacting to the simulated engine failure. When time permitted I advised the pilots that their rate of climb, or maximum altitude in a given distance, was greater and safer with the higher speeds, such as V2 plus ten or fifteen knots (on most aircraft). I suggested that they climb out at this higher speed because of the greater safety. But my comments were a voice in the wilderness, as the FAA refused to qualify the engine-out climb speed. Also, there were so many other problem areas that this more sophisticated area simply couldn't be properly addressed. Besides, very few in the FAA know this simple fact of flight. In this tragedy that seemingly minor flight technique became fatal for 291 people.

The pilots should have maintained the V2 plus 15 knots that had already been reached, and should not have reduced the airspeed. The higher airspeed gave the plane greater protection from the stall. American Airlines, and all the other airlines I encountered, followed the practice, and had their flight director command bars programmed to guide the pilot for a V2 climbout after engine failure.

Compounding the pilot's controllability problems (which could have been compensated by climbing out at the higher airspeed) was the retraction of the left wing leading-edge slats due to loss of hydraulic pressure. (Instead of using screw-jack design that firmly holds the slats in place, Douglas relied upon hydraulic pressure, without providing any protection against inadvertent retraction.

CONTRIBUTING CAUSES

In addressing why the engine ripped loose from the aircraft the NTSB investigators discovered what the FAA already knew; American Airlines used an unacceptable engine-removal and reinstallation procedure, which violated recommendations by the Douglas Aircraft company. To save time and money, American removed the engine and pylon as a single unit, rather than removing them separately. Also, they used a fork-lift, instead of a cable hoist, increasing the risk of damaging the aircraft structure. Douglas disapproved of this procedure, which they held could damage the engine mounting assembly.

Subsequent investigation revealed that the ill-fated DC-10 engine mounting assembly had cracks, arising from the improper engine removal and re-installation. Investigation of other DC-10 aircraft found additional cracks and manufacturing defects. United Airlines found a DC-10 with an upper spar web in a wing pylon cracked in half, with 25 bolts completely missing. Several months earlier Continental suffered aircraft damage from using this same unauthorized procedure which the FAA allowed to continue.

The NTSB also found that Douglas's quality control was poor, indicating sloppy workmanship. Engine pylons were not produced according to blueprints; vital parts failed to meet metal stress and strength standards; Douglas inspectors used defective measuring and drilling tools; Douglas workers failed to follow proper procedures; parts were missing or misaligned; and other forms of unacceptable workmanship.

During a five hour talk show on radio station KABC in Los Angeles with Ray Briem, a listener called in who worked as an aircraft riveter at Douglas's Long Beach assembly plant where the DC-10 was built. He described a practice of putting chewing gum in oversized rivet holes to hide the defect, allowing the metal parts to loosen. Obviously, this practice can lead to fuselage failure; or, engines ripping loose.

SUICIDE

The lead mechanic who performed the engine removal and installation on the DC-10 using the unapproved method committed suicide just hours before he was to appear at a deposition relating to the crash. It is believed that he knew of the damage to the aircraft when the engine was reinstalled, and that suicide was his way of dealing with the problem.

NO CHANGES, AND A NEAR-DISASTER

It was obvious after the DC-10 Chicago holocaust that certain changes must be made on the DC-10s. Contributing to the Chicago crash was the retraction of the leading-edge wing slats on the left wing when hydraulic lines ruptured. To prevent this retraction that increases the stalling speed, several remedies were available. The easiest was to install a hydraulic fuse plug that locks in the hydraulic fluid and pressure if excessive flow is sensed.

The FAA did not require any changes. Two years later, on September 22, 1981, an Air Florida DC-10 commenced a takeoff from Miami International Airport, and at 90 knots, before liftoff, an engine disintegrated, causing failure of two of the three hydraulic systems. The leading edge wing slats then retracted due to loss of the hydraulic fluid necessary to keep them in position.

Fortunately, the pilot recognized the engine failure and rejected the takeoff. The number three engine cable controls and fire protection systems failed due to the damage. The Air Florida crew tried to extinguish the engine fire, without success. The line carrying the fire extinguishing agent to the engine was severed by the disintegrating engine, as was the fuel shutoff valve cables. The fuel was shut off by shutting off the fuel tank valve that fed the engine.

The FAA certified the DC-10-30 on November 21, 1972, and on that date Douglas submitted a letter[33] stating that the redundancy and separation of critical systems minimized the possibility of damage to critical systems from engine disintegration. But repeated engine failures and repeated rupturing of fuel and hydraulic lines showed that this assurance was not valid, and that design changes were urgently needed.

Government regulations require[34] that "The motion of the flaps on opposite sides of the plane of symmetry must be synchronized unless the aircraft has safe characteristics with the flaps retracted on one side and extended on the other." The Chicago crash showed that the DC-10 design did not meet this requirement. Nothing was done. The 1981 Air Florida mishap again showed the design requirement did not exist.

CAUSE OF THE ENGINE FAILURE

The investigation into the Air Florida mishap showed the engine experienced a catastrophic disintegration. The cause? The mechanics overhauling that engine left a metal wrench

---

[33] McDonnell-Douglas Letter No. MDC C1-25-7362.
[34] 14 CFR 25.701(a).

inside the engine during overhaul. United Airlines maintenance base at San Francisco did the overhaul.

TWA CRASH INTO MOUNTAINS

TWA and American were two airlines with relatively few crashes in their history, and even fewer resulting from ignorance of aircraft systems. However, the TWA crash about to be described was an aberration, and not typical of the few crashes TWA experienced.

A few weeks before Christmas, on December 1, 1974, TWA Flight 514, a Boeing 727, approach the Washington, D.C. area for landing at Dulles Airport. About a half hour before reaching their destination air traffic control gave TWA the following clearance: "TWA 514, you're cleared for a VOR DME approach to runway 12."

For years pilots understood the mechanics of an approach clearance like that. The clearance gave the pilot the discretion of when they would start their descent, requiring the pilots to comply with the various minimum crossing altitudes from their present position, right on down to the minimum altitude over the airport. Its a basic common-sense rule that the various enroute and approach altitude restrictions had to be met.

An example would be receiving a clearance over Sacramento to proceed to Reno, and to make an ILS approach. In event of light traffic this clearance would not be improbable. This clearance gave me the option of descending at my convenience, respecting, naturally, the minimum enroute altitudes enroute.

It was expected that I would follow the standard procedures, arrive over Reno at whatever altitude I wanted, from the last assigned altitude to the lowest permitted enroute altitude, and then comply with all subsequent altitude restrictions. I couldn't simply descend at San Francisco to the lowest approach altitude at Reno; there was the problem of the Sierra Mountains between my present position and the Reno Airport. But the TWA crew didn't understand that basic aviation term. The captain thought he was cleared to the final approach altitude of 1800 feet. But that was not what the clearance stated, and that was not what was permitted by the enroute and approach charts. The enroute chart depicted a 1930-foot mountain directly in front of Flight 514. Disregarding these factors, the inexperienced captain instructed the copilot to descend to 1800 feet. (Flight engineers and pilots were on the same seniority list. The captain had been a flight engineer during much of his employment with TWA, and had been upgraded to captain without the normal copilot on-the-job training. He did not know many basic flight procedures.)

Crash scene of American Airlines DC-10 at Chicago.

"... this dumb chart ..."

During the descent the captain looked at the enroute chart and said, "You know, according to this dumb sheet, it says thirty-four hundred to Round Hill ... is our minimum altitude." He continued, "When he [air traffic control] clears you, hell, that means you can go to your ..."

"Initial approach," volunteered the copilot.

"Yeah."

This exchange showed that both pilots were ignorant of one of the most basic rules of instrument clearances. It also didn't reflect a great amount of judgment when the crew ignored the 1930-foot mountain shown directly ahead of them, and continued descent to 1800 feet.

"We're out of twenty-eight [hundred] for eighteen," the copilot said aloud. The mountain was straight ahead.

The altitude-warning horn sounded, indicating descending through 2500 feet above the ground. The crew continued the descent. The altitude warning horn again sounded, as the radar altimeter indicated passing through 500 feet above the ground, when they should have been thousands of feet higher. Could it be that the mountain on the chart actually existed? It wouldn't be long!

At nearly 270 miles per hour, TWA Flight 514 slammed into the mountain depicted on their enroute charts, and instantly disintegrated.

ROUTINE COVERUP BEGINS

Vested interests appear at every accident investigation, protecting themselves. The NTSB said nothing about the obvious failure of the FAA to insure higher level of crew competency. The Air Line Pilot Association denied the ignorance of the pilots, which arose from the inadequate training. And so it goes, right down the line. They all try to divert attention from the real cause of the tragedy, and in the coverup process the denial of costly adequate training remains unaddressed. Crews and passengers continue to pay the price.

The pilot's union blamed the air traffic controller for this crash, even though the clearance was no different than that given for years. Other pilots, including a United Airlines pilot, testified at the NTSB hearing that they had done the same thing as the crew of Flight 514, but missed the mountain by a few hundred feet. This testimony didn't say much for their piloting knowledge. It also showed the nearness to death experienced by other people, in flights that were statistically safe. In its accident report the NTSB stated:

The Board has been advised by the Federal Aviation Administration that the agency has taken action to require its air carrier inspectors to assure that all air carrier pilots understand that an Air Traffic Control clearance is not authority to descend below any established minimum altitude.

This canned response was window dressing. The NTSB knows their recommendations will accomplish nothing. First, the individual inspector cannot reach the hundreds of pilots employed by the airline. Second, as I found, FAA management blocks any corrective actions inspectors may take, unless the airline willingly makes the changes of their own accord.

Air traffic controllers were then instructed to take extra precautions to protect the pilots against the mistakes made by those who are less-informed.

TWA NEAR-FATAL DIVE

TWA Flight 841, a Boeing 727, was cruising at 39,000 feet on a night flight from New York to Minneapolis-St.Paul Airport on April 4, 1979. The speed was Mach .80 and an indicated speed of 250 knots. Over Saginaw, Michigan, the pilots felt a slight buffeting, and noticed that the autopilot was turning the control wheel to the left, while the instruments indicated the aircraft was in a bank to the right. The aircraft was in a stall condition, with the right wing going down, and the autopilot tried to recover by applying left aileron. Rolling opposite aileron in a stall condition with the wing falling to the right worsened the stalled condition. The pilot encountered a high-altitude stall and was on the verge of a high altitude jet upset. The flight was too high for the existing weight and airspeed. Either a lower weight or possibly a higher airspeed would have prevented what was about to happen.

As the aircraft entered the stall the right wing dropped. Not recognizing the stalled condition, the captain tried to lift the wing with left aileron, which simply aggravated the stalled condition. He then did the next worst thing; he pulled the power levers back to flight idle, which slowed the aircraft and put it firmly into a stall, after which a jet upset could be expected.

The correct reaction would have included advancing the power levers to increase the speed, lowering the nose and reducing the altitude while simultaneously making an emergency request to ATC for a lower altitude.

Similar to United's O'Neill jet upset, the 727 first pitched up and then rolled over on its back. It then started to roll a second time, and then plunged out of control toward the ground below. The airspeed rapidly increased, and exceeded its design speed, losing 34,000 feet in about 65 seconds, exceeding any known commercial aircraft rate-of-descent.

Trying to regain control, the captain extended the speed brakes. Nothing happened; he retracted them. As the aircraft rocketed through 15,000 feet the captain called for the landing gear extension. Parts of the aircraft ripped loose during this frightening descent in the pitch-black night-time environment.

In the cabin people were screaming. The high "G" forces kept them from moving their arms and legs. One of the flight attendants, Carlos Machado, was able to get his hands together and start praying. He said, "God, don't let me die, please." Passengers were asking the flight attendants, "Are we going to die; what happened?"

Seconds before plowing into the ground, the captain recovered the aircraft. He then diverted to Detroit's Metro Wayne County Airport. During the approach, as the wing flaps were lowered, the aircraft rolled sharply to one side. They were immediately retracted, and a no-flap landing made.

After landing, and before reaching the terminal, the captain reportedly stopped the aircraft, applied the parking brake, and pressed the cockpit voice recorder erase button. This erased all conversation recorded during the last 30 minutes of flight.

PILOT GRAPEVINE RUMORS

Rumor had it that the initial problem started when the captain tried to increase the stability of the aircraft at the high 39,000-feet cruising altitude. The captain reportedly extended the leading edge wing slats without extending the wing flaps. This is a non-approved procedure occasionally used by pilots to increase stability at high altitude.

Normally, the wing flaps extend with the wing leading-edge slats extension. But to circumvent this design arrangement, the flight engineer reportedly pulled the circuit breaker for the wing flaps, allowing the leading-edge slats to extend without the trailing edge flaps extending. The pilot grapevine reported that everything was proceeding normally, until the flight engineer noticed the pulled circuit breaker and without thinking, pushed it back in, causing the wing flaps to extend. This is believed to increased the drag and caused the plane to stall.

If this is what happened, it was admirable that the captain tried to fly the plane at its most economical altitude. However, safe airline operations require that crewmembers follow standard procedures for flying the aircraft. Despite demonstrating poor judgment in using the unauthorized procedure, the captain must be credited with saving the aircraft from the resulting near-fatal consequences.

EASTERN'S FAMOUS EVERGLADES CRASH

One of the first jumbo-jet crashes occurred during a night visual approach to Miami International Airport. Movies and books were written about the tragedy that befell Eastern Airlines Flight 401, a Lockheed 1011, and the senseless deaths arising out of the crash.

It was late evening as Flight 401 approached Miami from New York on this eventful December 29, 1972. The crew extended the landing gear, and one of the green down-and-locked lights did not illuminate. The problem was easily handled. Either replace the probable burned-out light bulb, or visually check the nose-gear mechanical down-locks. The crew tried to replace the light bulb, and advised approach control that they would circle west of the field at 2000 feet.

The captain instructed the copilot to engage the autopilot and maintain 2000 feet altitude, which the copilot did. As the copilot leaned forward to replace the light bulb he put pressure on the control column, which disengaged the altitude-hold function of the autopilot. All three crewmembers concentrated on replacing the light bulb, and none noticed that the aircraft was slowly descending toward the ground.

When the light bulb could not be removed, the captain instructed the flight engineer to go into the electronics bay just below the cockpit and make a visual check of the nose landing gear down-and-locked indicator.

During these activities a brief warning sounded which indicated the aircraft had deviated over 250 feet from its set altitude. But none of the crew members paid any attention to the warning signal. The aircraft continued descending. The Miami approach controller noticed the aircraft's departing from the 2000 foot altitude, and descending through 900 feet. He said nothing, even though the crew had advised they would hold at 2000, and even though it was very strange for a large jet to be that low over the Everglades. The controller radioed, "How are things coming along out there?"

The crew responded by requesting clearance to land, unaware they were close to hitting the ground. While turning to a heading of 180 the copilot suddenly recognized all was not well. "We did something to the altitude," he warned.

"What?" the captain replied. The copilot, supposedly flying the aircraft, said, "We're still at two thousand, right?" The captain exclaimed, "Hey, what's happening here?" Five seconds later, the altimeter warning indicated close proximity to the ground. Suddenly the captain and copilot recognized the problem, and shoved the power levers forward, trying to stop the descent. But it was too late.

While in a left bank, Flight 401 plowed into the Florida Everglades, instantly disintegrating, and scattering wreckage over an area 1,500 feet long and several hundred feet wide.

Miami Control Tower personnel saw the fire and sounded the alarm. Coast Guard crews arriving on the scene in helicopters with powerful flood lights saw bodies scattered throughout the area, with survivors huddled in the darkness.

The first Coast Guard pilot reaching the scene later said, "The first person I saw was still sitting in his seat strapped in his safety belt with nothing around him but knee-deep water." The pilot continued, "He was talking to a girl sitting in the water next to his seat. They didn't pay any attention to us. It was like they were in such deep shock that they were oblivious to us and the bodies lying in the mud around them."

Miccosukee Indians living in the swamp area helped with the rescue, but refused to allow the bodies to be placed in their school house. They said that their customs required them to tear down the schoolhouse building afterwards.

Of the 176 people on board, 101 suffered fatal injuries. Some suffered permanent crippling injuries.

SAS INTO PACIFIC OCEAN
A similar crash occurred to a Scandinavian Airlines DC-8 that crashed into the Pacific Ocean several years earlier. Making a night approach from over the water to Los Angeles International Airport on January 13, 1969. The crew had the same landing-gear-light problem, and all three crewmembers abandoned flying the aircraft to concentrate on the light bulb. The aircraft descended without anyone knowing it, and crashed into the Pacific Ocean, with heavy loss of life.

EAL CHARLOTTE
On September 11, 1974 Eastern Airlines Flight 212, a DC-9, crashed during an approach to Douglas Municipal Airport at Charlotte, North Carolina. The crewmembers were preoccupied with conversations having nothing to do with operating the aircraft while conducting an instrument approach. They talked about used cars, politics, and other matters not related to the approach procedure they were conducting.

The aircraft was 50 knots too fast on the approach, where the normal tolerance is 10 knots. The altitude over the final approach fix was a dangerous 500 feet too low. Instead of being 1080 feet above the ground at that point, the aircraft was only 500 feet above the ground. The non-flying pilot failed to make the required altitude reports. Even when the altitude warning horn sounded, alerting the crew they were too low, the crew continued to descend and continued to chatter.

The weather conditions were sky partially obscured with one and a half mile visibility in ground fog, making a non-precision VOR approach that demanded full attention from the crew to the complexities of the task. Preoccupation with personal conversation, contrary to good judgment, company directives, and FAR regulations, distracted the crew during the instrument approach. The aircraft hit the ground over three miles from the runway and 100 feet below the runway elevation. Of the eighty-two persons on board, seventy-two perished in the usual brutal fashion.

MOUNTAIN RAMMING
During an approach to La Paz, Bolivia on January 1, 1985, an Eastern Airlines Boeing 727, Flight 980, crashed head-on into the side of a 21,000-foot mountain in the Andes, at the 20,000-foot level. The crew was cleared to descend from 25,000 feet to 18,000, on the airways that would take them to the side of the mountain. The crew obviously did not follow the airways, became careless, and are to this day embedded in the side of the mountain, along with everyone on board who were obviously killed. The official cause remains in doubt; the Bolivian government announced it lacked the funds to recover the aircraft and bodies from the difficult crash site.

WESTERN AIRLINES MEXICO CITY
Shortly after midnight, Western Airlines Flight 2605, a DC-10, took off from Los Angeles International Airport on October 31, 1979, headed for Mexico City's Benito Juarez Airport. Both pilots had made many approaches into Mexico City. Before departure, Western's flight dispatch office told the pilots that one of the two main runways at Mexico City, number 23 left, was shut down due to construction. This required landing on 23 right, which was 600 feet to the right. The Notices to Airmen also notified the pilots of this runway closure. Attached to the crew's flight plan was a notice of the runway closure.

Approaching Mexico City, approach control notified Flight 2605 that runway 23 left was closed. The tower operator also notified the crew, and instructed the pilots to land on the right runway, "Western 2605, land on 23 Right." The tower then told the pilots to "advise [when] runway in sight" for clearance to land. Scattered ground fog obstructed visibility.

The tower operator saw the landing lights of Western 2605 to the left of the extended centerline for runway 23 Right. He radioed, "Western 2605, you are to the left of the track." Western replied, "Just a little bit." The controller said, "Advise [when] runway in sight, there is a layer of fog over the field."

Again the tower advised Western, "Approach lights are on 23 left, but that runway is closed to traffic." Western acknowledged. That was the third warning by the tower.

VIOLATING NUMEROUS SAFEGUARDS

Western's instrument approach procedures, as well as FAA rules, require executing a missed approach procedure if the runway is not visible when the aircraft descends to 600 feet above the ground. But when the pilots descended to the 600 foot-height, they didn't see the runway. They descended in instrument conditions below the minimum altitude, without having visual contact with the runway. Company procedures required that the pilot not handling the controls call out the descending altitudes, and the Decision Height (DH). The non-flying pilot did not make the call-outs.

Western also failed to call the tower for landing clearance, and didn't have clearance to land. Without clearance to land, without the runway in sight, and after having ten notices that runway 23 left was closed, the airplane struck the ground to the left of runway 23 left. After hitting the ground, the DC-10 veered to the right and crossed onto the closed runway, ramming into a truck loaded with 10 tons of dirt. The crew tried to miss the truck by shoving the power levers forward to climb above the obstruction. They didn't succeed.

The right main landing gear crashed into the side of the truck, demolishing the vehicle, and ripping the landing gear off the aircraft, along with part of the wing flap and part of the right lower section of the tail. The DC-10 veered to the right, crashing into another ground vehicle. Out of control, the Western headed for the terminal building where three aircraft were in the process of loading passengers. The right wing tip ripped into the side of a maintenance hangar, splitting open the fuel tanks, and stopping the aircraft in a ball of flames. Those in the terminal were spared by this impact with the building.

The crash killed everyone on the DC-10 except a few people seated in the rear section. One of the flight attendants, and an amateur weight lifter, had to pry metal apart to escape. The flames burned away part of the weight-lifter's mustache.

The many errors made by the crew were inexplicable. Western Airlines' training had been good in the past and the abominable performance on this flight didn't jive with what I had seen at Western (although there certainly can be exceptions.) My thoughts turned to a Los Angeles call-in television show a year earlier in which I appeared on *Midmorning Los Angeles.* Meredith McRae and Robert Hilton hosted the hour-long show, during which a Western Airlines employee tried to call in to describe her observations of crews flying under the influence of alcohol.

She did not succeed in getting on the show because of busy lines, but she left her phone number for me to call. Following the show, I called her, and she described the many times that crewmembers showed up at flight dispatch with alcohol on their breath. At first she didn't give me the name of the airline, but as we talked, I recognized it as Western Airlines. When I suggested that it sounded like Western Airlines, she acknowledged it was.

LOOKING FOR ANSWERS

I wrote to the Mexican aviation authorities to get the results of the blood alcohol test of the crew. But the Mexican authorities refused to release the information. That was suspicious, as data on accident reports is not confidential information, but available to the public.

There is also the possibility that fatigue due to the late night flight played a key role in this crash. I encountered the problem on middle-of-the-night training flights. Even early morning flights also have that problem. During a Western Airlines training flight in a Lockheed Electra some years earlier, that took off from Los Angeles International Airport at 5 am in the morning, I noticed that none of the crew was especially alert. During a recovery from a full flap stall, the aircraft did not accelerate properly and none of the pilots responded. I sat behind the pilots, and although I may not have been much more awake than the crew, I was in a better position to see the flight instruments. I could see that the crew had forgotten to raise the wing flaps from the full-down to the take-off position. I pointed at the flap-position indicator and everyone became slightly more alert.

MIDNIGHT TRAINING FLIGHTS

A midnight training flight spelled disaster for the crew and people on the ground in New Orleans when a Delta Airlines DC-8 training flight crashed into a motel on March 30, 1967, killing 12 people on the ground, including nine high school girls from Juda, Wisconsin. Just prior to the crash the crew was conducting simulated two-engine-inoperative approaches with five pilots and an FAA inspector on board. This type of approach requires strict adherence to speeds to avoid loss of directional control. The lack of alertness at two a.m. caused the pilot being checked to let the airspeed fall below the minimum, and the check and safety pilot did not respond in time. Directional control was lost, and the DC-8 flipped and dived into the motel.

I opposed middle-of-the-night flight training because of the dangers, and wrote a report shortly before this crash, after completing DC-8 recurrent training with Pan Am at the same New Orleans Airport, and experienced the problem.

TWA crash approaching Washington's Dulles Airport.

LONG-STANDING PAN AM SAFETY PROBLEMS

Pan Am had its share of senseless crashes, and was probably a close second, or equal, to United Airlines, for senseless crashes. Their crashes did not get media attention because many of them occurred overseas. My experiences with Pan Am included receiving recurrent DC-8 training from them; as a pilot for Transocean Airline who flew many overseas flights on the same routes; and via the pilot's grapevine.

A typical example of a near-disaster, reflecting the inadequate knowledge of aircraft operations, occurred during a Boeing 747 takeoff at San Francisco on July 30, 1971 that almost caused the loss of the entire aircraft.

The crew incorrectly figured the takeoff and rotation speeds for the flap-setting they selected. They set on their airspeed indicators and their takeoff data card airspeeds for a lesser flap setting that they actually selected. This caused the aircraft acceleration to be slower, and caused the crew to pass the speed at which the aircraft could have been rotated. By the time the pilots lifted the aircraft off the runway it was too late to miss the steel piers holding the runway approach lights. The crew also did not realize that the aircraft could, if needed, be rotated at a speed less than the normal rotation speed.

The 747 then ripped into the steel beams, several of which penetrated the 747, destroying three of the four hydraulic systems that furnished power for the flight controls. The fourth hydraulic system was almost destroyed. If that fourth system had been lost, the plane would probably have become uncontrollable. Two passengers were impaled by the steel beams as the beams passed through the aircraft and exited out the top and rear.

Several years later, after four fatal crashes within a years time, the publicity forced the FAA to conduct an investigation of Pan Am's training program problems, which it knew had existed for years. The publicity caused the pilots' union to conduct an unheard of investigation into Pan Am's safety problems, and caused Pan Am management to hire a private group (The Thomas Group) to conduct the investigation. Never before had anything like this occurred.

FAA inspectors had already identified the problems. Anything-goes competency standards deprived pilots of the training intended by federal law. But FAA inspectors responsible for Pan Am had the same problems I had at United.

All three investigative teams reported what had been known for years. The training program was notoriously weak; the competency standards were low. After the investigative groups made their reports the Pan Am pilots were rechecked. The competency level was so bad that over a third of the captains given flight checks observed by members of the investigative groups failed the check rides. Many captains took early retirement rather than take training to raise their skills.

The reports also focused attention on the deterioration of the flight engineers following the changeover from professional engineers to pilot-engineers. The report criticized the upgrading of Pan Am flight engineers to pilots, when they had very little piloting experience. (This had been the probable cause of the TWA crash near Washington.)

The private reports described Pan Am's practice of assigning strong copilots to weak captains. The reports addressed the fears of other crewmembers who addressed the dangerous captain competency levels by "specifically avoiding having a flight schedule assignment ... with substandard captains." This opportunity to avoid unsafe captains was an employee benefit not available to the public.

Indicating the obvious, that the FAA had knowledge of these safety problems, the private reports stated:

> FAA inspectors at San Francisco Air Carrier District Office had knowledge and some records to verify that the captains in the Pago Pago and Tahiti crashes were also substandard. It was common knowledge that the captain killed in the B-707 cargo accident at Manila was also considered substandard.
>
> The failure rate of captains is five times higher when an FAA inspector is on board the aircraft/simulator observing or conducting the proficiency check," then when the government inspector is not present. In this manner, "numerous substandard airmen have been approved to continue in line operations.
>
> There is definitely a need for initial and recurrent emergency evacuation training improvement for all crewmembers. ... it has been years since any of the crewmembers have had the opportunity to physically handle the emergency equipment. [The law requires hands-on training.]
>
> In summary, it is the team's opinion that Pan American Airlines, in comparison with the air carriers to which the team members are assigned, is below the 'state of the art,' in air carrier management, training, cockpit procedures, standards, coordination and adherence to established procedures by airmen.

The reports reflected badly upon Pan Am and the FAA. Pan Am requested a federal judge to seal the reports, keeping them from the public. The judge accommodated Pan Am and the FAA, and sealed the records. As often happens, the federal judge protected this influential corporation—and the FAA—and kept the sensitive information from the public.

The law relating to sealing of court records is intended to protect an innocent party from embarrassment, and not protect wrongdoers. Federal judges have turned the law[35] into something it was not intended, protecting powerful corporations that spend large sums with the legal profession. In this manner other people threatened with harm, or who experienced harm, are deprived of information with which to protect themselves.

Pan Am's safety problems were addressed in a *CBS Evening News* broadcast with Walter Cronkite on April 4, 1980. Guests charged high-level Pan Am management with hiding the unsafe pilot training and aircraft maintenance problems that had been identified in the court-sealed investigations.

I had heard of Pan Am's safety problems since 1951 when I was a pilot for Transocean Airlines flying many of the same overseas routes as Pan Am.

The guests on the Walter Cronkite program described instances of fuel mismanagement (which happens on most airlines), where engines ran out of fuel even though there was ample fuel on board the aircraft. In one instance the aircraft was forced to land when an engine flamed out from a dry tank, while thirty tons of fuel still remained in the aircraft. The guests explained management indifference to safety matters.

Pan Am's maintenance also became very shoddy after deregulation. When United Airlines purchased many of Pan Am's aircraft in the last 1980s they found that the aircraft were in far worse condition than they realized, and had to spend considerable money to bring the aircraft up to standard.

Washington politics were such that Pan Am was denied the routes necessary to stay profitable. I felt sorry for Pan Am, that they pioneered many of the routes that helped make the United States the aviation leader that it was, and then because of these politics it lost money and was unable to maintain its former role in the nation's aviation scene.

NORTHWEST AIRLINES CRASHES AND NEAR-CRASHES

Northwest started its post-World War II air safety history with numerous crashes. Northwest experienced three Martin 202 crashes in a row when it started flying the hot two-engine airliner. The crews were dissatisfied with the safety of the aircraft, and the planes were subsequently purchased in 1951 by Transocean Airlines. I was a pilot for Transocean, and

---

[35] Federal Rule of Civil Procedure 26 (c) provides that a federal judge "may make any order which justice requires to protect a party or person from annoyance, embarrassment, oppression, undue burden or expense, ..."

started flying the aircraft. It was a high performance aircraft compared to the DC-3 and DC-4 aircraft in operation until that time.

Transocean lost two of them in crashes, but these were due to pilot error. In one instance during a low circling approach during bad weather at Tucumcari, the pilot let the aircraft get too low on the base leg during a snow storm and the left wing hit the ground. The plane cart-wheeled along the ground and miraculously only one passenger died.

In the other crash, Transocean pilots flying the aircraft for newly started Japan Airlines crashed into an island south of Tokyo. They were flying a thousand feet too low during instrument flight conditions and rammed into the side of a volcano. It was Japan's first postwar air tragedy.

Northwest experienced a needless crash when the captain ditched a Boeing 377 Stratocruiser into Puget Sound. Buffeting commenced after takeoff when the wing flaps were raised, and the captain thought the plane was uncontrollable. Actually, the only problem was that the flight engineer failed to close the engine cowl flaps to the takeoff position when the check list was accomplished. None of the crew members recognized the obvious cause of the buffeting. They didn't recognize that the buffeting was associated with retracting the wing flaps, and didn't try extending the flaps to see if the buffeting stopped. Either closing the cowl flaps or extending the flaps to the position that they were at before the buffeting commenced would have halted the buffet. The plane was ditched and broke apart upon water contact.

TRAINING—INDUCED IGNORANCE AND CARELESSNESS

An air tragedy, with all its accompanying horror, is especially tragic when the cause is so easily preventable. A Northwest Boeing 727 crashed into the hills near Yonkers, New York, shortly after taking off from New York's Idlewild Airport. The crew overlooked the pitot tube[36] heater switch on the pre-takeoff check list, and the pitot tube iced up during climb. The ice blocked the pitot tube opening, locking the existing impact air pressure into the pitot tube. As the aircraft climbed the pressure locked in the lines increased in proportion to the static air pressure, causing the airspeed indicator to read a much higher speed than normal, and accompanied by an equally erroneous rate of climb indication. The erroneous readings were unrealistically high, beyond the capability of the aircraft in its

---

[36] Pitot tube directs impact air pressure to various aircraft flight instruments, such as the airspeed indicator.

current configuration. The cause of the problem, why it was occurring, and what to do about it, should have been obvious to the crew.

The pilots had the use of the attitude indicator, showing that the aircraft was maintaining a normal attitude for that part of the flight. With that normal pitch attitude and power setting the airspeed indicator advanced from its normal 300 knots to the top of the scale, exceeding 450 knots, and climbing at a rate of climb that would be almost impossible to achieve.

The crew reacted by pulling off the power, and raising the nose of the aircraft to as high as 30 degrees, trying to get the airspeed to return to a normal reading. The stall warning indicator sounded when the stall warning system sensed the aircraft was in a stall from the high pitch-up attitude and reduced power setting. Simultaneously, the overspeed clacker sounded from the erroneous airspeed indication.

If the crew had been properly trained in the aircraft systems, they would have immediately known the false readings were probably due to a blocked pitot tube. They would have independently known that the three attitude indicators were reading correctly, and maintained a normal flight attitude, with the power set where it normally would be. The aircraft stalled, and fell 18,000 feet to the ground near Yonkers. Everyone on board was killed.

NORTHWEST BOEING 720

In another incident, a Northwest Boeing 720 became one of the first jets to crash due to inflight turbulence. In this February 13, 1963 crash the crew is believed to have concentrated on maintaining a given airspeed in an extreme turbulence condition instead of flying attitude. In doing so, excessive stress was applied to the wings.

One of the nation's most brutal air tragedies occurred in 1987 when a Northwest crew took off without extending the wing flaps. This is described in later pages.

CHARTER AIRLINE CRASHES

For balance, let's address several charter airline crashes. Having flown for charter and supplemental airlines during my flying career, I personally know some of the problems they faced. Canada's worst aviation crash was the crash of a charter airline from the United States. An Arrow Air DC-8, carrying United States service men from the Middle East crashed during takeoff from Gander. The plane had stopped at Gander, Newfoundland, for fuel on December 12, 1985.

The DC-8 was barely airborne from Gander when it crashed

to the ground within half a mile of the end of the runway, leaving a trail of debris. All 256 persons on board perished, including 248 soldiers from the U.S. Army's 101st Airborne Division.

The Canadian Aviation Safety Board investigated the crash. The Board sharply divided as to its cause. Five members blamed the crash on ice adhering to the wings. Four other members thought the crash was due to a bomb. Another Board member, Roger L. Lacroix, quit under protest, claiming that evidence was withheld from the crash investigation. At least five of them had the courage to disagree, rather than the NTSB coverup as is routine, and which makes the American NTSB a contributing cause to subsequent crashes.

Those blaming the crash on the bomb cited evidence of a bomb blast, and several parallels between the Gander crash and the bombing of Pan American flight 103 at Lockerbie, Scotland (which we have yet to describe). Herb Gray, the Liberal Party leader in the House of Commons at Ottowa, Ontario, claimed there was a coverup.

Included in the evidence supporting the coverup theory was a February 24, 1986 memo written by Michael Mendez, Director of Maintenance for Arrow Air, to Betty Batchelor, wife of the airline's owner. In the memo Mendez described his arrival at Gander the day after the crash, and being denied admission to the crash site. The secrecy was allegedly requested by U.S. Army Major General John S. Crosby, who had arrived from Washington, D.C. with his staff. Later that day, Crosby, members of the Canadian Aviation Safety Board, the FBI, and the U.S. National Transportation Safety Board toured the accident site, and again refused Mendez access to the accident site.

BLOCKING A CRASH INVESTIGATION

Contrary to crash investigations, Major General Crosby wanted to immediately bulldoze over the crash site, even though an investigation had not been made, and evidence would be destroyed. Mendez described some strange events concerning the accident investigation, including pressure from the U.S. Army to immediately plow the wreckage under the ground.

Transport Canada's critique of both the majority and minority report on the accident stated that many factors were overlooked in both reports by the Canadian Aviation Safety Board. Canada's Transport Minister, Benoit Bouchard, requested former Canadian Supreme Court Justice, William Estey, to make an informal review of the accident investigation. (*Aviation Week & Space Technology*, July 31, 1989.)

Estey looked over the record and concluded, without calling any witnesses, that nothing was overlooked in the investigation. This contradicted the split opinion of the Canadian Aviation Safety Board (CASB) and Transport Canada's report.

Estey's report stated: "The testimony and material gathered by the Board [Canadian Aviation Safety Board] does not show that ice contamination of the leading edge or upper surface of the wing was the cause of the accident. Furthermore, nothing in the material placed before the Board reveals the cause of the accident." Without ordering further investigation, Estey then concluded that the crash-cause could not be determined.

The incomplete status of the record showed the need for taking testimony, which the judge refused to do. He simply refused to allow the investigation to proceed, despite the unusual issues raised that demanded an investigation. Parliament member, Don Boudria, responded to Estey's report, stating his party would ask for Senate hearings on the Gander crash when Parliament reconvened in the fall.

In the United States, two congressmen, Representative Robin Tallon of South Carolina, and Representative C.W. Young of Florida, requested an investigation to determine what the U.S. government knew about the Gander crash. Young asked the investigative staff of the House Appropriations subcommittee on defense to check government archives for any information about the Gander crash, including classified reports. Earlier, Young requested Secretary of State James Baker to request Canada to reopen the investigation into the crash. Baker refused to do so, claiming that U.S. government aviation authorities had no reason to doubt the Canadian investigation reports. Three and a half years after the Gander crash, in July 1989, Tallon requested Attorney General Richard Thornburgh to release the *censored* portion of the FBI report.

The subject is certainly intriguing. If there was no bomb-sabotage, the most likely cause of the crash was either frost or a thin layer of ice on the wing. The absence of any deicing during the freezing-drizzle weather conditions makes this a strong probability. However, without the testimony of any reliable witness as to whether there was or was not ice on the wings, the cause will never be officially known.

CRASHING ON MAJOR STREET IN RENO

On January 21, 1985 a fully loaded Lockheed Electra crashed on a main city street in Reno around midnight, after taking off from Reno's Cannon Airport. The plane carried a charter group of gamblers from Minneapolis to Reno, and was beginning the return flight. Reno Flying Service refueled the plane, and provided the ground power to start the engines. After the ground personnel removed the air hose from the fuselage, they did not latch, or improperly latched, the small access panel. If left open, this small panel causes buffeting of the aircraft at certain speeds. It doesn't threaten the aircraft's controllability, but is annoying. The crew did not understand the possibility of buffeting from this small door, and mishandled the abnormality.

Shortly after becoming airborne the aircraft started buffeting. The pilot radioed Reno Tower advising that they would be returning. Thinking the vibrations might be an engine problem, the captain retarded all four power levers, reducing the engine power below that needed to maintain flight. The aircraft settled toward the ground, and crashed into buildings, narrowly missing a large apartment complex. It slid through a recreational vehicle sales lot, and then onto South Virginia street. The disintegrating fuselage ejected bodies along the path of destruction.

The impact threw seventeen-year old George Lamson from the aircraft as the fuselage broke apart. He unstrapped his seat belt and ran, just as the airplane's fuel tanks blew up. His father suffered severe burns, but survived. The other survivor was Robert Miggins, a high school teacher in Plymouth, Minnesota. He also ran from the wreckage, with his clothes on fire, suffering burns over 90 percent of his body. Three of the 71 initially survived. Only George Lamson survived the injuries.

Within nine months of the Reno Electra crash, two other Electras crashed; one on May 30, 1984 near Baltimore and another one near Ogden, Utah, with the loss of all on board. One Electra broke up over Pennsylvania, and the other crashed during an approach to Kansas City Airport. Earlier, two Electras crashed near Salt Lake City after the electrical system shorted out, causing partial loss of the flight instruments. The crew failed to determine which instruments were giving correct readings, causing the planes to crash during instrument conditions.

FOREWARNED TAHOE CRASH

A tragedy that I forewarned occurred on March 1, 1964 to a fully loaded Lockheed Constellation of Paradise Airlines that crashed into the mountains surrounding Lake Tahoe. The captain attempted a visual approach to Tahoe Airport during marginal visual conditions, flying in and out of clouds, one of which contained a mountain peak. Almost a hundred people perished in that tragedy.

Several months before the crash I conducted an enroute check of Paradise Airlines from the San Francisco Bay area to Tahoe, with a return the next morning. My FAA report stated that the captain was inattentive during flight, actually drowsy, rarely looked out, and flew in marginal visual flight conditions. The report had greater significance than normal, since the captain was the chief pilot for the airline, and set the pattern of acceptable conduct for other pilots.

The FAA report received the usual FAA hostility. The FAA principle operations inspector contacted me at Denver after I submitted the report, and chastised me for making the unfavorable comments. I had been aware of earlier problems with that airline; shortly after I joined the FAA, I accompanied the FAA principal operations inspector for Paradise Airlines on several inspections. That inspector had an insurance business on the side, and was soliciting business from airlines over which he had air safety responsibilities.

During the accident investigation, the FAA and NTSB sequestered my reports which made the FAA look bad for not acting on it. Since my report had more relationship to the crash than any other report or testimony, the NTSB was engaging in a coverup of important behind-the-scene, crash-causing problems.

Before the crash, numerous complaints were made of Paradise Airlines' operations. The company doing the maintenance warned the airline in a letter two months before the crash that "if you continue the maintenance as you have in the past, you are going to lose a plane full of people." The airport personnel at Lake Tahoe Airport, including FAA tower personnel, frequently saw the aircraft taking off or landing at below minimum weather conditions. The aircraft lacked deicing boots; the leading edge of the wings were simply painted black to look like boots.

WORLD AIRWAYS

World Airways DC-8 crashed into the side of Mount Dutton, eighteen miles east of Cold Bay, Alaska on September 8, 1973. The plane was cleared for the approach, and then descended too soon, without clear radio navigational guidance, crashing into the mountains.

In an earlier crash World lost a plane load of passengers when it made a night takeoff at Guam, and then made a right turn instead of a left turn; it rammed into the side of a hill. This is not an infrequent occurrence. It arises because pilot often don't look at the terrain charts around airports to get a mental picture of where high terrain is located.

On January 23, 1982 another World crash occurred at Boston when the crew landed faster than it should have, and landed further down on the icy runway. It slid off the end of the runway into the water, causing the loss of one passenger, whose body was never found.

Eastern Airlines Flight 401 crash into Florida Everglades.

CHAPTER TEN

Foreign Victims

Citizens of other countries have paid with their lives for continuing corruption within the United States. Unlike U.S. citizens, who could have prevented these air tragedies by forcing their Congressional representatives and agencies to take corrective actions, and punish those committing the air safety corruption, the foreign citizens didn't have that opportunity to defend themselves. This chapter focuses on several tragedies in which foreign citizens paid with their lives for the rampant corruption within the United States, described in part within these pages.

THE INFAMOUS DC-10

Lives were knowingly sacrificed by violating regulatory and common-sense design safeguards in the DC-10, in an environment of corruption by the FAA Western Region hierarchy. These are the same officials and mentality described within these pages, and especially in the Denver grievance hearing. Shortly after that Denver hearing the same FAA management officials covering up for major safety violations extended the same mentality to eliminate formerly required federal design safeguards. The DC-10 was one of their pets, and is riddled with effects of the FAA corruption. These violations extended into the design of other aircraft, and into other areas of design, maintenance, operations.

Design safeguards formerly considered mandatory were ignored and violated. These acts saved money for the aircraft manufacturer and the airlines, although the amounts saved were relatively small in comparison to the overall cost. These savings were offset by imposing unacceptable safety hazards upon air travelers; a situation that resulted in an occasional air disaster.

There were several major design safeguards that were violated. These affected the flight controls and the horizontal stabilizer; the outward-opening cargo doors; the locking mechanism for the cargo doors; engine strength; and fire protection in the cargo compartments.

Hydraulically powered flight controls were standard for many years, and always had hard backups to control the pitch of the aircraft permitting a safe landing if the hydraulic system failed, as they occasionally do, and always will. The pilots' control inputs go from the control column and rudder pedals via cables to hydraulic valves that meter hydraulic fluid under pressure to actuating cylinders which move the flight controls and the horizontal stabilizer. Prior to the certification of the DC-10 by the FAA Western Region, there were hard backups for the flight controls and for the horizontal stabilizer.

The former backups consisted of cable connections directly to the flight control trim tabs, which then aerodynamically positioned the control surfaces. The large hydraulically-actuated horizontal stabilizer had either an electric motor (in the DC-8), or hand-crank control in the cockpit (for the Boeing 707).

On the smaller jets Boeing backs up the hydraulic controls with manual reversion, in which the cable control to the trim tabs provides pitch-control via aerodynamically actuated flight controls.[37] In this manner all hope would not be lost for the occupants in the event of a total hydraulic failure.

The Lockheed 1011, which was the competitor to the DC-10, had four safeguards over and above the DC-10: (1) an additional hydraulic system, making a total of four; (2) an electric motor to position the horizontal stabilizer; (3) a hand crank to position the horizontal stabilizer; and (4) direct cable connections to the trim tabs which use aerodynamic forces to position the elevators.

Federal regulatory design safeguards requires that there be virtually no chance of a total control failure. Repeated hydraulic failures clearly showed that relying on hydraulic systems did not provide the fail-safe design needed to permit approval of flight controls without a hard-backup.

Douglas, with the approval of the FAA Western Region hierarchy, eliminated the four additional protections that Lockheed considered necessary for a safe flight. The elimination of these backups violated federal regulatory design safeguards that had been industry accepted for years. Solely to save a

---

[37] Flettner tabs, which are servo tabs on the trailing edges of control surfaces that can be flown by the pilot, and which in turn move the main control surface.

relatively small amount of money required to provide the backup safeguards, Douglas eliminated these protections and subjected tens of thousands of people to the risk of horrible consequences when the hydraulic systems fail. And they will fail.

SAFETY DOESN'T PAY

In eliminating these flight control and cargo door safe-guards, Douglas offered the airlines a lower-priced aircraft, but with built-in hazards that almost anyone in aviation recognized as endangering lives. Lockheed refused to endanger lives in that manner. Not only did Lockheed have four hydraulic systems for pitch control, but they installed an electric motor to position the horizontal stabilizer in the event of hydraulic failure; they installed a hand-crank in the cockpit to position the stabilizer in the even electrical power is also lost; and they installed tabs on the flight controls for aerodynamic boost. The airlines rewarded Lockheed for these safeguards (that raised slightly the cost) by ordering the cheaper DC-10s. Due to lack of sales, Lockheed discontinued production of the excellent 1011 flying machine in the early 1980s. That was surely a lesson to other manufacturers.

CERTAINTY OF EXPLOSIVE CARGO DOOR OPENING

Another serious design problem existed in the outward-opening cargo doors that presented a constant threat to the safety of the crew and passengers. Rather than install a safe inward-opening plug-type door Douglas incorporated an outward-opening hinged door. It cost less to manufacture, and provided a sales advantage by allowing cargo to be stored behind the door that was not possible with the safer inward-opening door.

EXPLOSIVE PRESSURE CHECK

The first hard-evidence showing the dangers, and the consequences, of outward opening cargo doors occurred during a fuselage ground-pressure check at the Douglas plant in Long Beach, California on May 29, 1970. As the pressure increased inside the aircraft, simulating pressure differential existing at approximately 12,000 feet altitude, a cargo door suddenly exploded open, causing considerable damage that if the aircraft had been in flight, it would probably have been lost.

This is what happened: the cargo door handle had been placed in the closed and locked position, but the locking pins only partly engaged in the door frame. As the pressure inside the fuselage increased, and pressed outward on the cargo door, with possible stretching of the fuselage also, the door locking pins disengaged and the cargo door with tons of air pressure pushing outward, slammed open.

This caused a rapid depressurization in the lower part of the fuselage, causing tons of air pressure on the upper half of the fuselage to press down on the cabin floor, ripping it open. When this happened, flight control cables jammed or sheared, hydraulic lines ruptured, and other damage occurred.

This incident proved that the cabin floor was dangerously weak, which they already knew from engineering calculations. It proved that the equalizing vents between the upper and lower compartments were too small, preventing rapid equalizing between upper and lower fuselage pressures in the event of a fuselage opening. This was also known. It proved that the placement of the control cables in the cabin floor was unsafe. That was known. It proved that the absence of hard backup for the flight controls and the horizontal stabilizer would cause loss of control. That was known. It proved that the outward-opening cargo door was unsafe. This was known, and obvious. The aircraft was not safe to certify without major changes.

Obviously, planes and their occupants would be lost if the aircraft did not have major design changes. The FAA Western Region officials knew of these serious design dangers. Douglas presented the aircraft for FAA certification, and the FAA certified it as safe. Douglas and the FAA knew otherwise.

OTHER PREDICTIONS OF TRAGEDY

Other people knew the DC-10 design was unsafe. Consolidated Aircraft Company, a division of General Dynamics, contracted with Douglas to build part of the fuselage section, which included cargo doors, following specifications set by Douglas. Early in the construction process Consolidated conveyed their concerns to Douglas over the dangerous cargo door locking mechanism, the weak floor, the equalizing venting problem, and the position of the flight control cables.

After the plane went in service there were many reports of cargo door closing problems. The reason for the doors not locking were that the pins were not lining up and going into the door frame. In some cases the cargo handlers forced the door handles. This either forced the locking pins into the door frame, or the long linkages connecting the door handle to the locking pins bent sufficiently to where the handle could be moved into the locking position without the locking pins fully locked.

FOREIGN GOVERNMENTS AND FOREIGN AIRLINES KNEW OF THE SERIOUS PROBLEMS

Foreign airlines and foreign governments knew of these serious design problems and said nothing. Their revenues depended on received the DC-10s that were on order. Exceptions were several employees in the Netherlands Department of Civil Aviation (RLD), who became concerned about the dangers of the inadequate floor venting and inadequate floor strength.

"You are waiting for an accident to happen."

In one letter to the FAA they wrote: "You are waiting for an accident to happen." The FAA responded that so far that hadn't happened. The FAA wanted a plane load of people to die before they would do something about it.

In response to these same complaints Douglas responded that the wires for the autopilot ran along the ceiling of the aircraft, and that if the control cables were lost, the autopilot could control the aircraft. But if the hydraulic lines in the floor were severed, the autopilot signals to the hydraulic valves porting hydraulic fluid to position the actuating cylinders (that in turn move the flight controls and horizontal stabilizer) would accomplish nothing.

The complaints by the RLD employees were stonewalled by KLM Airlines, who had DC-10s on order. The airline would lose a competitive position if the planes were not delivered on time. (KLM was part of a consortium of Dutch, Swiss, and Scandinavian interests.) The Swiss and the Scandinavians said they were not in a position to take a strong stand, and were contractually required to recognize the FAA certification of the aircraft (no matter how unsafe it may be). This isn't so; in 1989 several European countries refused to recognize the FAA's certification of the Boeing 747-400 until the nose-section was strengthened.

ONE LAST WARNING

Everyone who knew of the serious design problems waited for the first DC-10 disaster to occur. The first victim was American Airlines. Loading bags into the cargo compartment, the baggage handler had trouble closing the cargo door on American Airlines Flight 96, as the plane prepared to leave Detroit for Buffalo, New York on June 12, 1972. The cargo door handle refused to close, as happened the day before on that same aircraft. The pins wouldn't fully enter the door frame.

Three American Airlines employees, including a mechanic, worked on the door. Finally, the baggage handler put his knee to the handle, and forced the door handle into the locked position. Unfortunately, the door locking cams and pins did not fully enter the locked position. Unknown to the crew or the baggage handler, the door locking handle went into the locked position by bending the actuating tubes inside the door between the handle and the pins, making it seem like the door was locked. With the cargo door problem seemingly solved, Flight 96 took off from detroit, heading for Buffalo.

What had threatened tens of thousands of people for the past two years finally happened. Climbing through 12,500 feet, approaching Windsor, Ontario, the cargo door suddenly exploded outward, and ripped off the aircraft. The cabin floor collapsed. The flight control cables were jammed.

In the cockpit the crew heard the explosion, and saw the rudder pedals slam violently to the full left position, causing the plane to quickly yaw to the left. Engine fire warning lights illuminated for the number two engine, along with numerous other warning lights and horns. The captain notified air traffic control that an emergency existed, requested clearance to Cleveland, and requested that emergency equipment stand by.

CABIN FLOOR COLLAPSE

As Douglas, the FAA, the Dutch RLD, and Consolidated knew would happen, the cargo door exploded outward, the cabin floor collapsed, and control cables jammed. Ejected out the bottom of the aircraft from the cargo compartment were a coffin and passenger baggage. Two flight attendants were almost ejected out the bottom of the aircraft and fell into the hole caused by the collapsed floor. Looking down, they could see the clouds going by.

The damaged floor did not collapse as much as it otherwise would, as the absence of passengers reduced the weight on the collapsed floor.

The captain, Bryce McCormick found the flight controls only partly effective. Some control cables were jammed, and some severed. There were no procedure given by the manufacturer, the airline, or the FAA, for this emergency. Passengers and crew were lucky that Captain McCormick was the pilot. He had been concerned about possible loss of control on the DC-10, and scheduled time in the DC-10 simulator practicing what he would do if flight controls were lost. McCormick had discovered that by manipulating the engine power levers that he had partial control of the aircraft pitch attitude and could make shallow turns by varying engine power.

McCormick found that advancing the power on the two wing-mounted engines resulted in the nose pitching upward, and the reverse occurring when power was reduced. Also, by retarding the engine power on one side, turns could be made. McCormick became adept at the technique. He was able to fly the simulator from shortly after takeoff and return for a landing, without using the flight controls that were simulated jammed in a neutral position.

Approaching the airport, McCormick made a long shallow approach to Cleveland Airport, touching down at approximately 190 miles per hour. Shortly after touchdown the aircraft veered off the runway and headed toward the terminal building. Fortunately, the soft ground slowed the aircraft before any buildings were hit. Everyone luckily survived.

The near-disaster exposed the serious design problems, and the FAA's elimination of previously required safeguards. The airlines and Congress did nothing. Douglas did virtually nothing.

The NTSB did very little. The big one was yet to come.

COVERUP AND INDIFFERENCE

The head of the FAA Aircraft Engineering Division in Los Angeles, Richard Sliff, suspected that Douglas withheld information about the cargo door problems prior to this incident. Sliff asked Douglas on June 14, 1972 how many cargo door malfunctions had been reported by the airlines. Douglas responded that they had only a few reports. Sliff didn't believe this, and asked for the files on the problem. Sliff then discovered that the airlines sent over 100 reports of cargo door closing problems to Douglas. Each problem had been a potential disaster.

Neither the FAA Western Region officials nor FAA Washington headquarters required any meaningful corrective actions to prevent a repetition of this near-tragedy. James Rudolph, director of Flight Standards Service in Washington, composed a relatively innocuous telegram to the DC-10 operators, advising them of the problem, but not requiring any meaningful corrective actions. The telegram instructed the airlines to conduct a one-time inspection of the cargo doors; check the operation of the doors; check the door warning systems; and check for structural failure or deformation of the door and door frame. None of these checks addressed the design problems.

Douglas did issue a series of Service Bulletins, but they were more of the nature of band-aids. None of them addressed the primary problem of the unsafe outward-opening cargo doors; the Rube Goldberg door-locking mechanism; the absence of backups for the flight controls and horizontal stabilizer; the inadequacy of the venting between the upper and lower fuselage; the weak cabin floor design; the dangerous placement of critical hydraulic lines and control cables under the cabin floor that could be expected to be destroyed when the cabin floor collapsed.

One Service Bulletin that FAA Administrator Shaffer and Douglas President McGowen decided during an evening telephone conversation was heavier electrical wiring to the door-closing motor.[38] Another was to place a couple of one-inch view holes in the cargo doors for the baggage handlers to make a subjective evaluation of whether the complex locking mechanism was safely closed.[39]

---

[38] The theory being that more electrical current could get to the motor, and therefore the motor would have greater strength to hopefully fully lock the doors.

[39] This check would be conducted by baggage handlers who may not know what they were looking for, an unlighted small opening, looking through dirty glass, while standing on a high platform at night, during cold, often raining conditions, while people on the ground are shouting to hurry.

Another one required installation of an inexpensive metal guide that prevented the long cargo door locking rods from flexing when the baggage handler applied pressure to the cargo door handle. In this manner the locking handle could not go into the locked position if the locking pins and cams did not move into the locked position.

Consolidated's head engineer on the project, F. Applegate, who had earlier expressed concern about several of the design problems, wrote a memorandum to his superior:

> It seems to me inevitable, that in the twenty years ahead of us, DC-10 cargo doors will come open and cargo compartments will experience decompression for other reasons, and I would expect this to usually *result in the loss of the airplane* ... It is recommended that overtures be made at the highest management level to persuade Douglas to immediately make a decision to incorporate changes in the DC-10 that will correct the fundamental cabin floor catastrophic failure mode.
>
> Correction will take a good bit of time. Hopefully there is time before the National Transportation Safety Board (NTSB) or the FAA ground the airplane which would have disastrous effects upon sales and production both near and long term. This corrective action becomes more expensive every day as production continues. However, it may well be less expensive than the cost of one plane load of people.

BUT WHOSE GOING TO PAY FOR IT!

In response to Applegate's warning, Consolidated's DC-10 Support Program Manager, J. Hurt, wrote:

> We have an interesting legal and moral problem, and I feel that any direct conversation on the subject with Douglas should be based on the assumption that as a result, Convair may subsequently find itself in a position where it must assume all or a significant portion of the costs that are involved.

NTSB RECOMMENDATIONS

The NTSB, who knew of the DC-10 problems since their inception, did very little to prevent the major holocaust that would happen, even though its responsibilities included making recommendations to prevent air safety mishaps. After the NTSB made an initial investigation into the American Airlines Windsor accident, it sent a safety recommendation[40] to FAA Administra-

---

[40] A-72-97 & 98, June 23, 1972.

tor Shaffer, recommending that the DC-10 cargo door be modified to make it impossible to position the locking handle in the locked position without the cams and locking pins being in position. It further recommended the installation of relief vents between the cabin and aft cargo compartment to minimize the pressure loading on the cabin floor in the event of sudden depressurization of the cargo compartment. FAA Administrator Shaffer did not require any corrective actions, and the NTSB didn't give it enough priority to follow up until a year and a half later.

After eighteen months, the NTSB against questioned the FAA, on September 13, 1973, as to what was done to correct the DC-10 problems. Not hearing from the FAA, the NTSB again requested a reply two months later. Again, the FAA refused to respond. It was now almost two years after the American Airlines near-tragedy.

Airline management didn't worry about the consequences; nineteen months after Douglas issued a voluntary Service Order on the cargo door that prevented forcing the cargo door handle into the locked position, the modification had not been made to most of the 130 DC-10s in service. Neither were any changes made to many of the DC-10s on the production line at Long Beach. Some of the newly constructed DC-10s left the factory without the service bulletins completed on the cargo doors.

CAMPAIGN CONTRIBUTIONS

Douglas made numerous campaign contributions before and after the Windsor mishap. Donations were made two days after the American Airlines near-disaster, and on the same day that the FAA discovered that Douglas was withholding information on the cargo door problems. Contributions were also made the day after the head of Douglas entered into an agreement with FAA Administrator John Shaffer, which relieved Douglas of any meaningful corrective action.

Aircraft and human parts in the Paris DC-10 crash.

The airlines continued reporting cargo door locking problems; the FAA continued to ignore the problem, as did the NTSB. Everyone waited for the inevitable.

Luck finally ran out. Instead of U.S. citizens paying the price for the corruption, it was citizens of foreign countries.

On March 3, 1974, bags were loaded at Paris onto Turkish Airlines Flight 981 for a short flight to London. The baggage handler closing the rear cargo door had trouble placing the locking handle in the closed and locked position. Finally, to get the door locked, he applied pressure with his knees to the cargo door locking handle, causing the handle to go into the seemingly locked position. Unknown to him, the pins were not fully engaged.

There was a placard alongside the locking handle instructing the baggage handlers to look at the complex locking mechanism inside nearby unlighted viewing holes. The untrained baggage handler had to look in the holes and to make a subjective analysis that the locking pins upon which the lives of everyone on board depends, are in the locked position. The instructions were in English. The baggage handler closing the doors on this flight spoke two languages; neither were English.

Shortly thereafter Flight 981 took off for London. While climbing through 12,000 feet, it again happened, just as forewarned many times, and worse than experienced by American Airlines. Instead of an empty passenger cabin over the rear cargo-door area, as in American's Windsor incident, there was an additional 25,000 pounds of passenger weight. The increasing pressure inside the pressurized aircraft and the expansion of the fuselage forced the *partially* latched cargo door to burst open with an explosion-like sound.

The huge cargo door ripped off the aircraft; the cabin floor collapsed and ripped apart; six passenger seats—with their human occupants—ejected out the bottom of the aircraft; the cables for controlling the position of the flight controls and the horizontal stabilizer were moved to a nose-down position; the three hydraulic systems were ripped apart and failed. The sequence followed the prior patterns at Long Beach and over Windsor, just as many knew it would.

Before losing the hydraulic systems, the horizontal stabilizer and elevator controls were moved to a pitch-down position. Flight 981 went into a steep 22-degree nose-down attitude.

PANIC IN THE CABIN

The cabin floor collapsed and broke apart, creating a huge hole in the cabin floor. People screamed. Some cried. Some preyed. Some clutched the hands of loved ones in their own. The fear was indescribable. Most knew they would never again see loved ones left behind.

"We've lost it."

The flight deck crew heard the sound of the explosive decompression and searched for clues as to what happened. From their previous nose-up climbing attitude, the DC-10 pitched downward, going into a steep dive toward the ground, with a rapidly increasing airspeed. The cockpit voice recorder showed the sequence:

Klaxon sounded as the plane exceeded the never exceed speed.

Capt. Berkoz: "What happened?"

Capt. Ulusman: "The cabin blew out."

"Are you sure?"

Captain Berkoz shouts: "Bring it up, pull her nose up."

Captain Ulusman: "I can't bring it up—she doesn't respond."

During the next sixteen seconds, Berkoz sings the catch-line from a famous Turkish TV commercial: "Aca-ba, nedir" (Wonder what it is, what is it?)

"Nothing is left."

Berkoz asks: "Hydraulics?"

"We have lost it ... Ooops, oops."

Berkoz: "It looks like we are going to hit the ground."

Berkoz: "Speed." (Tape suggests he tried to raise nose by juggling throttles, then pulled all power back.)

Berkoz: "We've lost it."

Sound of impact signifying the brutal end to 346 lives.

This disaster, with its roots in the FAA Western Region, remained the world's worst air disaster for over a decade. (Until it was replaced by a worse one, caused by the same basic problem, and also with roots in the FAA Western Region.)

HORROR BEYOND DESCRIPTION

Within an hour after Flight 981 plunged to its moment of destiny rescuers found the crash scene in a wooded area. The forest was strangely silent as the rescuers arrived. Over 100 tons of fuel had vaporized upon impact after a brief massive fireball. After the immediate terrible sound of impact, it became death-like quiet. There were no cries for help; no screaming; no moaning. Just deadly silence in the forest.

The aircraft's death plunge had been followed on radar, and air traffic control personnel alerted the local police force who then went looking for the crash scene.

Two Hands Clasped In Death

Arriving rescuers had no one to rescue. No known aircraft containing so many people had plunged into the ground at such a high rate of speed, in the history of the world. Pieces of bodies were everywhere; in the trees; on the ground; impaled on parts of shredded metal fragments. Among the thousands of bits of bodies were two hands clasping each other, withstanding the destructive forces that tore apart the remainder of their bodies. The tightly joined hands of a man and a woman were all that remained of these two lovers. Another set of clutching hands were found nearby; those of a woman and a small child.

A gory mixture of human remains covered the area. Legs, arms, heads, trunks, pieces of viscera, hanging from aircraft fragments and trees. Torn segments of human beings were entangled in the underbrush. Rescuers slipped on moist human remains. A photographer, taking pictures, inadvertently stepped on a human brain laying on a bed of moss, stamping the soft mass into pulp. Another rescuer stepped on a two-foot long backbone, cut from the remainder of the body as if by a butcher. Mixed with this carnage were pictures, letters, and other personal belongings, of people that had no further use for worldly goods.

Many of the bodies were cut in half by the seat belts. Very few heads were still attached to the trunks. Most of the bodies were without limbs. Stomachs and intestines were ripped open, and the contents drained and mixed with the blood. One fireman climbed into a tree to dislodge a headless bust from an overhead branch. As he pulled on the body, the innards poured out on top of him. He climbed down the tree and threw up. Some of the rescuers fainted on the spot. Others became irrational and disoriented. A spectator reached down, picked up a hand, and put it in his pocket. It was ironical that hours earlier they were all living human beings, enjoying life, with plans and dreams, and loved ones waiting for them.

COLLECTING BODY PARTS

Heads were collected and put on stretchers. Sometimes a dozen heads at a time were transported in this manner to a temporary morgue. At the morgue, the body parts were placed together that appeared to match, relying on hair color, skin pigment, sex, and other signs to match them together. Huge piles of shredded and bloodied clothing accumulated in heaps.

Individual burials were impractical. There weren't enough parts of bodies to join together. A mass funeral service was held in which most of the human remains were buried together at a single site near Orly Airport, marked by a monument placed in their memory. Many Japanese newly-weds were on this flight, and the marker in remembrance of the victims is regularly visited by loved ones from Japan.

The above description is not placed here to be gory. The description is to shock the American public out of its complacency, realize the harm that endemic government corruption within the United States is causing; and that further indifference, complacency, by the American public will make possible more of the same!

Very few suspected that the terrible sufferings had their

roots in the dirty, filthy, politics of air safety. Very few knew that these, and many other deaths, had their origin in an environment of corruption within the FAA Western Region. Very few suspected that these and many other deaths were made possible by endemic corruption within the government of the United States of America, and that hundreds of people in and out of government made these deaths possible by their complicity of coverup. Those who knew, had a reason to keep the lid on the scandal. They wanted to protect their own involvement, or for some particular self-benefit arising out of coverup.

The results of misconduct already described within these pages made these deaths possible. The FAA Denver hearing; the internal FAA corruption; the coverup by the NTSB; Department of Justice; members of the U.S. Senate and House; the press. Not a single one of the poor souls whose body parts were scattered in this forest near Paris were any match for the group-conspiracy that helped make their deaths possible.

FALSIFIED RECORDS

The French discovered during the investigation that the inexpensive metal guide to prevent closing of the cargo door handle without the locking pins and cams in position had not been installed on this plane. Falsified records at the Douglas plane in Long Beach, California showed the fix had been installed before delivery while the plane was at the Long Beach factory.

French investigators made a quick check of the sister ship to determine if the fix on that door had been installed, as Douglas records indicated had been done. Incredibly, the inspection of the other plane showed that the Service Bulletin had *not* been accomplished!

CONGRESSIONAL KANGAROO INVESTIGATION

The House of Representatives conducted a Kangaroo-type hearing of the FAA's conduct relative to this great tragedy. The same committee conducting the investigation had covered up for the FAA corruption when I repeatedly requested them to intervene. The FAA misconduct, and their coverup, played a role in the Paris DC-10 holocaust which surely could not have happened except in an environment of total coverup.

The Special Subcommittee on Investigations issued a January 1975 report signed by none other than Congressman Harley Staggers, head of this committee who repeatedly ignored my warnings and the evidence I submitted of hard-core FAA misconduct related to other air tragedies. The report described the FAA conduct in part:

Abdication of responsibility ... A threat to public confidence. ... There have been instances when appropriate FAA actions in furtherance of air safety have been unreasonably delayed, or omitted entirely, because of an oversolicitous attitude on the part of some within the agency concerning the economic well-being of the aircraft industry or the air carriers" The report made reference to the so-called "Gentlemen's agreement," [in which FAA Administrator and the head of Douglas ignored the requirement for a hard-fix and ignored the requirement of a mandatory AD]

The findings of the Subcommittee is that the agency's performance was completely unsatisfactory and involved non-regulatory expedients which must not be resorted to again in any future situation of similar import.

As a result of this departure from the clear and proper regulatory response which the agency should have made, the lives of thousands of air passengers were needlessly and unjustifiably put at risk for almost two years.

After these harsh words, the report was then toned down, and a mild label put on hard-core criminal misconduct:

The Subcommittee found throughout its inquiry—from the DC-10 crash to its most recent investigation ... a tendency for the agency to avoid the role of leadership in advancing air safety which the Congress intended it to assume ... In some instances, this abdication of responsibility has been coupled with an administrative lethargy—a sluggishness which at times approaches an attitude of indifference to public safety. This must stop.

Defusing the highly sensitive issues that had criminal underpinnings, the report then—would you believe(!)—then praised those who outrageous misconduct made possible the deaths of 346 people:

The United States can be justly proud and appreciative of the contributions made by the aircraft industry to the safety of air travel ... The pre-eminent position which the United States has achieved has also been largely due to the high standards of Federal regulations pertaining to air safety which has been maintained over the years by the Federal Aviation Administration.

The indications, which have appeared relatively recently, of erosion in the agency's traditional insistence on excellence and attention to detail constitute a threat to public confidence and to the continued worldwide acceptance which has heretofore been accorded to American aircraft. It is time for the FAA to reassess all of its policies and procedures relating to air safety and to reaffirm the predominant and primary importance of this aspect to its regulatory mission.

In the future there must be no resort to non-regulatory procedures, self-regulation, or "Gentlemen's agreements" in matters affecting air safety.

The Senate, who also covered up for the FAA misconduct, and whose coverup made the tragedy possible, also conducted a hearing. The Senate panel published a bland report on June 27, 1974, charging that circumvention of government regulatory processes was involved in the DC-10 tragedy, putting it in a poor judgment category rather than in a criminal class where it belonged. In its report the Senate criticized the FAA, the National Transportation Safety Board and McDonnell Douglas for failing to meet their responsibilities.

The Senate and House had to protect the FAA. Otherwise, they themselves would be implicated in the many criminal acts committed by the FAA during the Denver grievance hearing and elsewhere. If they had identified the repeated criminal acts by the FAA, and the NTSB's criminal coverup, they would then implicate themselves in the deaths. Accessory before the fact and after the fact, misprision of felonies, and other crimes, were the criminal laws violated by these members of the House and Senate. They had to cover up.

The FAA personnel whose misconduct made these deaths possible, and primarily the FAA Western Region coterie already identified within these pages, remained in their safety-sensitive positions, and were actually promoted into even more sensitive positions.

The FAA Administrators that assisted in bringing about the great tragedy took advantage of the revolving door syndrome. The industry interests that they protected then hired Shaffer and Butterfield. The attorneys for the next-of-kin made a bundle out of the settlements, including Donald Madole, an attorney with a large law firm. If Madole had met his responsibilities when he was head of the Bureau of Aviation Safety, when I brought the FAA corruption to his attention, he would have had far fewer clients when he later entered private law practice as a plaintiff's attorney in air tragedies.

To this date, the deaths of these 346 persons have not been avenged.

NO MEANINGFUL CHANGES

Following the Paris DC-10 crash, the FAA issued orders addressing a few of the many design problems that caused this tragedy, and gave the airlines until December 31, 1976—almost three years after the crash—to make the very limited corrections. Nothing was done about the absence of a hard backup for pitch control. An electric stabilizer motor, or a hand-crank in the cockpit, or both, would have eliminated the awesome dangers of loss of pitch control. Almost two decades later, the problem still exists.

Some changes were made. The Rube Goldberg door locking mechanism was changed, but the outward-opening cargo door remained. The equalizing vents were installed, and the cabin floor strengthened. Despite the life or death nature of these design changes, FAA Flight Standards Service Deputy, Joe Ferrarese, issued an extension on October 4, 1976, giving the airlines an additional year to comply with the important modifications. It was then, almost four years after the Paris crash, before partial corrective actions had to be taken.

Industry observers quickly questioned whether the amount of money saved for the air carriers from lost revenue by this extension warranted continuing the danger to tens of thousands of air travelers. The NTSB, upset with this further delay, asked in a written request to the FAA on October 20, 1976 for "information ... to assist the Board in our understanding the rationale underlying the issuance of the year extension."

FRIEND-OF-THE-COURT BRIEF

The numerous law suits filed in federal courts as a result of the Paris DC-10 crash were consolidated into Multi-District Ligation heard in the District Court at Los Angeles, before Judge Peirson Hall. Because I had an insider's knowledge of the FAA misconduct and could show the hard-core deeply ingrained pattern of FAA misconduct that made the crash possible, I filed a friend of the court brief.[41] An amicus curiae brief is provided by Federal Rule of Civil Procedure 37.1 if the brief brings "relevant matter to the attention of the court ..." Since I was the only party in the litigation that had the insider knowledge of the FAA misconduct and corrupt environment that caused and made the DC-10 crash possible, and in the interest of justice, my intervention should have been accepted.

Lee Kreindler of the law firm of Kreindler and Kreindler, wrote: "Thank you for your letter of July 3, 1974 and enclosing the *amicus curiae* brief. I am pleased to see it."

LONG-STANDING OBSTRUCTION OF JUSTICE BY THE JUSTICE DEPARTMENT

Continuing its practice of coverup, the most misnamed department in the federal government—the Department of

---

[41] July 3, 1975, number 74-808-PH and entitled, Motion to Intervene as Amicus Curiae.

Justice—filed a brief objecting to my motion to intervene as *Amicus Curiae*. The only purpose of my intervention was to promote justice, bringing out facts that would show criminal misconduct that made this crash possible. No one else had this information who was willing to come forth. Any impediment to bringing out the misconduct would cause the misconduct to continue, and result in many other similar tragedies.

The only possible reason the Justice Department could have to oppose my attempts to cover up for the criminal misconduct by the FAA, the wrongful acts of powerful United Airlines, the coverup by the NTSB, members of Congress, the press—and itself.

The Department of Justice blocked my exposure activities since the mid-1960s, and are implicated in many crashes and deaths occurring from that date to the present date.

"A conspiracy that is shocking."

An attorney for some of the families involved in the DC-10 crash stated to the court:

> We have come over ... some of the most incredible evidence of almost a conspiracy that is shocking. I thought I was shocked when we first got into this case, but what has come to light in the last month is just beyond belief ... [it is] literally a conspiracy to conceal the fact that they {Douglas] were fraudulently certifying this aircraft.

"Some of the testimony would have been sensational."

Judge Peirson Hall, who heard many of the law suits arising out of the Paris DC-10 crash, and was privy to much of the behind the scene shenanigans, kept the lid on the scandal. In answer to reporter's questions after the cases were settled, Judge Hall stated, "Some of the testimony would have been sensational." But the 85 year-old judge refused to open the files to the public. When asked whether he would fly on a DC-10, Hall responded, "Sure I would ... I just don't give a damn." Ironically, a close member of Judge Hall's family was killed in an airplane crash.

Judge Hall issued an order denying my motion to intervene as a friend of the court, stating I did not have a "justiciable" interest in the matter. Judge Hall knew that I was the only one with the hard evidence, willing to come forward. Hall knew that a coverup would cause or permit to occur more of the same horror as occurred in the brutal Paris crash. Hall became one more person involved in the complicity that would play a role in many airline crashes and thousands of deaths, that could be linked to the widespread air disaster corruption.

Reflecting what many in industry felt about the FAA and the

DC-10 tragedy, reporter Bob Kahn of the San Francisco Bay Area newspaper, *Contra Costa Times*, taking a refreshingly moral stand, wrote:

MCDONNELL-DOUGLAS AND THE COVERUP ON THE DC-10. With the collusion of courts and the newspapers in the United States, much of the news was suppressed. After all, not only is McDonnell-Douglas a big advertiser in publications like Business Week, Forbes, Wall Street Journal, and the like but the airlines, using that wonderful DC-10 in which McDonnell-Douglas permitted many Americans to unnecessarily risk their life, are BIG advertisers in daily newspapers.

Ironically, the same *Contra Costa Times* kept the lid on the scandal for years thereafter. When a reporter for the same newspaper chain prepared a story on me in August 1988, including hours of picture taking, the story was suddenly killed before the publication date. The lid stayed on the scandal. United Airlines was the San Francisco area's seventh largest employer. The publisher, Dean Lesher, was himself an attorney, and the legal fraternity was deeply implicated in this worsening scandal.

CONGRESSIONAL INVESTIGATIONS INTO OTHER DC-10 PROBLEMS

There were hearings by Congressional committees into other aspects of the DC-10 design problems, including the frequently disintegrating engines and their questionable certification. In one report forty-five pages were devoted to the serious engine design problems, and the FAA's disregard for design strength requirements.

The committee findings included numerous warnings by FAA technical personnel of probable catastrophic damage to the aircraft from disintegrating engines. The report described the questionable certification of the General Electric CF-6 engines used on the DC-10, Boeing 747, and other aircraft. The engines failed to pass the bird-ingestion test because the fan blades were not strong enough. This serious problem was circumvented by simply using smaller birds until the engine passed the tests!

During the first engine certification test for resistance to ice damage, one engine suffered moderate damage and another suffered severe damage. This failure was circumvented by replacing the engines and then making a second icing certification test in stratus cloud conditions, causing softer rime ice to accumulate (and which tends to crumble) rather than the more damaging clear ice. The soft rime ice did not meet operational or legal requirements, but the FAA considered the tests satisfactory.

When the GE engines were flight tested in Europe on the A-300 Airbus, one of the two engines suffered moderate damage and the other suffered severe damage. Two engine failures on a twin-engine aircraft is a frightening experience. The FAA European office issued an order refusing to accept the test as satisfactory. FAA Washington headquarters countermanded this decision and ordered the FAA European office to approve the failed engine tests as satisfactory, even though the engine failed the test and was considered dangerous.

Other FAA reports also identified the dangerous engine problem. One report stated that a "survey of the service record of this blade indicates that a significant hazard exists when these fan blades are used."

An FAA engineering chief, reflecting the concern of the FAA technical personnel responsible for certifying the DC-10, issued a proposed Airworthiness Directive (AD). The proposed AD cited a long test and experience history showing that serious engine problems existed with the GE engine containing drilled fan blades. The proposed AD warned of catastrophic damage to the aircraft from the engine problems, and recommended prompt replacement of the weak engine fan blades with heavier units:

> The resulting damage to the engine and the aircraft is considered excessive and presents a serious threat to the safety of the aircraft.

Industry protested the corrective fix as being too costly, claiming that it would cost 47 million dollars to replace the drilled blades with solid ones. It proposed instead that the drilled blades be replaced at the normal scheduled replacement, which the Congressional report estimated to be as late as 1988, fourteen years later.

MORE OF THE SAME COVERUP

The FAA rescinded the proposed AD, claiming "the agency has determined that an unsafe condition does not exist." Previous reports said the very opposite. By law the FAA engineering personnel have the technical and legal responsibility for making determination of safety problems. The FAA technical personnel had *already* made such determination as stated in the proposed AD.

When Congress investigated the cancellation of this engine AD by high FAA management officials, the FAA attempted to justify the cancellation by claiming insufficient machines existed to manufacture the solid fan blades in the time limit provided by the proposed Airworthiness Directive. When the committee checked with the blade manufacturers it found this excuse was a fabrication. Lying by FAA management is not unknown.

The concern by the congressional committee over the GE engine problems and the FAA's obvious coverup caused them to take the unusual step of requesting the NTSB to investigate the problem and the FAA's mishandling of it. The same congressional committee refused to investigate my far more serious charges by requesting an NTSB, GAO, Congressional, or any other investigation. The consequences were sufficiently important to them.

The congressional request stressed the importance of the engine problem, but then warned of the possible harm to the engine manufacturer if the public became aware of the problem. The Congressional request to the NTSB to get to the facts was thereby tempered with a warning not to cause corporate interests any adverse publicity.

A year after this congressional report was released on the DC-10 engine problems, an Overseas National Airlines DC-10-30F taking off from New York's JFK airport on November 12, 1975 came close to becoming a major disaster. The General Electric engine experienced a catastrophic disintegration when birds were ingested during the takeoff roll and the weak engine blades disintegrated, severing fuel and hydraulic lines. The crew fortunately recognized the engine failure just prior to liftoff and rejected the takeoff. The aircraft burst into flames and everyone barely got out before the entire plane was engulfed in flames. This catastrophic event could just as soon have happened after the aircraft became airborne.

Several years *after* the sterile Congressional investigation into the engine problems, the NTSB issued a safety recommendation (A-76-59 through 64, April 1, 1976) stating:

> Until ... a remedy is developed, the Safety Board is concerned that the CF6 engine is being operated worldwide, not only on DC-10 aircraft, but also on the A-300 and some 747 aircraft, in an environment that may at any time initiate conditions leading to another catastrophic engine failure.

Referring to an earlier safety recommendation, the Board stated: "On March 25, 1975, in its Safety Recommendation A-75-24, the Safety Board expressed concern regarding the adequacy of the bird ingestion certification criteria for large turbofan engines." This weakness would also be associated with the inability to tolerate ice damage, and susceptibility to disintegration from other causes. Earlier Congressional hearings identified the same problems. The Board added:

The Safety Board now concludes that the bird ingestion test procedures of Advisory Circular 33-1A, as they were used for the certification of the CF6, were inadequate. ... the approach used in the tests to demonstrate compliance ... meets neither the spirit nor the intent of the Advisory Circular. ... the current provisions of 14 CFR 33.77 do not provide adequate safeguards against the ingestion potentials of future large turbofan engines.

The Board then recommended "immediate retest of the General Electric CF6 engine to demonstrate its compliance with the complete bird ingestion criteria of AC 33-1A. (Class I—Urgent Follow-up.)"

Not much was done to correct the problem. Engine disintegrations continued, and in 1989, for instance, a major mishap occurred at Sioux City, Iowa from an engine disintegration and associated DC-10 design problems.

JAL 747 CRASH
the world's worst single-plane air disaster

A run I frequently flew as a Japan Airline captain was the relatively short flight from Tokyo to Osaka. It is normally a very uneventful flight. But for Japan Airlines Flight 123, a Boeing 747-100SR, it turned into the world's worst single-plane air tragedy in number of deaths, and also one of the heart-rending of all air tragedies. As with the Paris DC-10 crash, citizens of foreign countries paid with their lives for the same elimination of design safeguards committed by the Federal Aviation Administration.

JAL Flight 123 departed Tokyo on August 12, 1985 with 524 people on board. (Most international carriers configured the 747 to carry 420 passengers, while United States' carriers normally configure theirs to a maximum of 380 seats.) Shortly after Flight 123 reached its cruising altitude of 24,000 feet over Oshima Island (the site of JAL's first air tragedy), the crew and passengers heard a loud explosive decompression at the rear of the aircraft.

The pressure bulkhead had blown out at the rear of the aircraft. In the process the explosive blowout destroyed all four hydraulic systems, causing the plane to lose its flight controls and horizontal stabilizer, similar to the Paris DC-10 crash. The FAA had permitted Boeing to build the Boeing 747 without any hard backups for the flight controls and the horizontal stabilizer. The price would again be paid for this money-saving design compromise.

Immediately after the explosive blowout the flight deck

crew quickly donned oxygen masks, and started a descent. They quickly discovered that the aircraft did not respond to control movements. The flight engineer's panel was aglow in lights, each one indicating an abnormality or emergency in some particular system. The engineer hollered that the aircraft lost all hydraulic pressure. The pilots didn't believe him; "All lost?"

In the Paris DC-10 crash the horizontal stabilizer had been moved to the nose-down position before all hydraulic pressure was lost. In this mishap the horizontal stabilizer was frozen in the cruise position. The aircraft started a series of continuous up and down oscillations, and the wings rocked from side to side. Partial pitch and directional control could be obtained by advancing and retarding engine power, but this gave crude and unreliable control over the gyrations.

Pitch control was similar to standing on a basketball and trying to maintain balance. Fortunately the captain was a former Boeing 747 flight instructor, and had capabilities beyond that which a non-instructor could be expected to have. (The captain was checking out a copilot upgrading to the captain's position.)

The instructor repeatedly advanced and retarded the power levers to provide limited pitch control. The aircraft repeatedly porpoised to extreme nose-up and nose-down attitudes. At one point the nose pitched up 39 degrees, seemingly straight up. The 747 went into extreme bank angles, oscillating from side to side, while simultaneously pitching up and down.

For thirty minutes the crew kept the plane in the air, as the 747 made wild rambling oscillations. The uncontrolled gyrations conveyed ominous warnings to the passengers that there was very little chance of survival.

Approaching mountains northwest of Tokyo, the captain shouted for maximum power, trying to get the plane to pitch up. But it was no use. The 747 hit glancing blows on the ridges of two mountains, and then the huge plane impacted on the third one, slamming into the side of 5,400-foot Mount Osutaka, 70 miles northwest of Tokyo. The plane loaded with 524 people exploded into many huge parts and millions of little pieces, in the usual disaster scene.

"Don't go to sleep mother! Stay awake, or you'll die."

It wasn't until fourteen hours later, the next morning, that rescuers reached the crash-site. Arriving rescuers found 200 to 300 bodies tightly wedged into the front of the unrecognizable wreckage. Unable to tell the living from the dead, the rescuers hollered for anyone who was alive to speak out, raise their hands, or move their legs. Almost all were dead. Among the four survivors were a flight attendant, a twelve-year old girl, Keiko Kawakami, found in the branches of a tree, and eight-year old

Mikiko Yoshizaki, strapped in her seat, next to her dead mother, Hiroko.

During the night Mikiko kept shouting at her mother to stay awake until rescuers arrived. "Don't go to sleep mother! Stay awake, or you'll die!" Mikiko later described that as the plane began to fall, passengers cried out in pain from the pressure of the seat belts on their abdomen.

WATCHING HER FAMILY DIE

Keiko Kawakami, the 12 year old girl, recalled that before the crash her father shouted, "Keiko, cut your belt with a knife." Keiko replied, "What! a knife?" Keiko recalled hearing the sound of people unbuckling their belts, and her father, who "yelled at me with a voice so loud I've never heard before." Her father was screaming at her to unfasten her seat belt, and to cut it open if she couldn't do so. It was probably fortunate she couldn't get the belt unbuckled. Keiko's father, Eiji, and her sister, Sakiko, survived the initial crash, but died during the night before rescue crews arrived.

"I can't help you now," she remembered her father saying, when she called out for him. "I'm stuck." Keiko recalled. She recalled smelling spilled fuel, and many people and children crying from pain. She said later, "I heard murmurs from many people and children crying. I felt parts of my body with my hands, and they were all there. I thought, 'I am alive.'"

Keiko stated, "My father, who was lying next to me, told me to move my legs. He said, "I'm trapped. I really can't help you because I can't move.'" Keiko added, "After a while, I asked Sakiko (her younger sister) if mother was dead. She replied, 'Mother is cold. She's dead. Father is also dead.' I touched my father, and knew that he had died."

"It hurts; it hurts!"

"Sakiko then told me she was in pain, and I tried to cheer her up by telling how we can live together back home with grandmother, even though mother and father were dead." Keiko stated her younger sister cried:

It hurts, it hurts. Suddenly, I heard Sakiko make a vomit-like sound and she stopped talking. I then knew I was alone. I kept losing consciousness until morning. I awoke with sounds of helicopters. I saw the sun and trees through the pieces of metal. I thought 'I am alive.' I tried to get out. I tried and tried. I remembered what father had told me. 'Keiko lost patience since she entered junior high.' So I kept trying. I heard people calling: 'If you are alive, please move your hands or feet!' Somebody came over, and called out 'It's a boy!' maybe because I had short hair and was wearing shorts.

The family of a businessman who died in the crash released his last message, scrawled across the creased pages of a notebook found in the wreckage. His final words to his 2-year-old son: "Live strongly, Tetsuya, grow up to be a fine man." Several other passengers wrote notes to their families, knowing that death was coming.

"I don't want to fly anymore. God, please save me."

Another passenger, Hirotsugu Kawaguchi, scribbled in a notebook as the 747 plummeted through the sky: "I don't want to fly anymore. God, please save me."

The family of another victim, Kazuo Yoshimura, received a blood-stained note, in which he asked his wife to look after their three children:

> Dad probably will not survive. I don't know the cause. It's been five minutes now. I don't ever want to get on an airplane again. Please, God help us. Who would have thought that our meal together yesterday would be our last. Tsuyoshi, I'm depending on you [referring to his only son]. Mariko Tsuyoshi, Chiyoko, please help each other, and help mother. I'm truly grateful that I've had a happy life until now.

Another passenger, Taniguchji Masakatsu, wrote on a disposal bag during the last moments: "Machiko, please take care of our children. Osako Minoo. Taniguchji Masakatsu. 6:30." The blood-stained disposal bag was turned over to his family.

JAPANESE REACTION TO TRAGEDY

The Japanese show great consideration for those who suffer from a plane crash in marked-contrast to the disregard and lack of care shown to next of kin in the United States. After the crash, Japan Airlines flew relatives to the vicinity of the crash scene. JAL President Yasumoto Takagi stood at the bottom of the airplane ramp, bowing and apologizing to relatives.

The rigid customs of Japan's highly group-oriented society take many forms. People who fail to live up to their responsibilities face shame or condemnation. In times of disaster, Japanese custom dictates unique and often dramatic response from those responsible or otherwise involved. Mr. Takagi stated that when the investigation was settled and his presence was no longer necessary, he would resign.

JAL officials transported the relatives to a town near the crash site, where they were housed until the remains were recovered and identified. The motivation for this gathering near the crash scene reportedly stems partly from Buddhist belief that the spirit does not immediately separate from the body, and remains an integral link to the deceased's family.

Buddhism also teaches that a person must have a proper burial, so the spirit may rest in peace. This belief accounts for Japanese continuing to make pilgrimages to remote South Pacific islands in search of soldiers' bones, decades after the end of World War Two.

Japanese custom also obligates companies to offer consolation payments to victims, an act that in some countries would be interpreted as an admission of liability. In Japan, it is simply an act of good faith. After the DC-8 crash into Tokyo Bay, the company offered more than $400,000 to relatives of each of the persons killed in the crash.

STARTLING FINDINGS ADVERSE TO THE INTEGRITY OF THE GOVERNMENT OF THE UNITED STATES

The subsequent investigation into the cause of the crash discovered that the rear pressure bulkhead failed due to a defective repair made in 1978 by Boeing Aircraft Company personnel. Boeing contracted with JAL to repair a damaged rear pressure bulkhead resulting from a prior hard landing that had injured 30 persons. The repair required replacement of the lower half of the rear pressure bulkhead. Three rows of rivets had to be installed, according to the engineering drawings, to fasten the replacement pressure bulkhead to the upper existing bulkhead.

The crash investigation discovered that the third row of rivets did not pass through the overlapping repair section, making for a weak connection, subjecting the entire rear of the plane to an explosive decompression. Compounding Boeing's gross errors, JAL's inspectors did not detect cracking of the rear pressure bulkhead that commenced after Boeing made the faulty repairs.

THE PRIMARY BLAME FOR THESE DEATHS

There is no excuse for eliminating the relatively inexpensive hard-backup for the flight controls and the horizontal stabilizer. The installation of an electric motor to control the horizontal stabilizer would have eliminated the danger of an uncontrollable aircraft and the deaths that happened here.

CHAPTER ELEVEN

Foreign Crashes

The safety standards for foreign airlines vary much as they do in the United States. Some have excellent safety practices and records, and some have a long way to go to reach acceptable standards. Changing management and changing policies alter safety practices. Corporate officials at Swissair and Lufthansa, for instance, provide their flight crews with vigorous training and achieve high safety levels.

An *Aviation Week & Space Technology* article dated July 4, 1988 described Australia's "keen attention to safety and its enviable record—no fatal accidents involving large commercial aircraft in more than 20 years." Swissair, KLM, Lufthansa, for instance, rarely have crashes. They have high safety standards and don't tolerate the air safety corruption that is rampant in the United States. In this manner the crews and the passengers are protected, rather than victims of the politics of air safety. Even the Russians, for instance, reportedly have strict safety standards, and there is some evidence to indicate that the repeated crashes the United States experiences from lack of knowledge—caused by withholding training—rarely exists.

Compare this record to the shenanigans described within these pages, and the outrageous nature of the tragedy-breeding misconduct starts to sink home. There is no reason American crewmembers and passengers should be threatened and sacrificed as has become the practice within the United States.

Air France had a bad reputation for safety many years ago, until rigid training and competency standards were reportedly imposed.

JAPAN AIRLINES

Japan Airlines is one of the foreign airlines with changing safety practices and changing safety standards. I was one of the first pilots with Japan Airlines, and hold one of the first pilot licenses issued by Japan, Airline Transport Pilot number 170. I had first-hand knowledge of the safety attitudes, conditions, and comparisons with other airlines in other parts of the world. In 1951 I was a pilot for Transocean Airlines, which had contracted with the Japanese government to start up a national airline.

It was ironical to fly a Japanese aircraft with a rising sun emblem on the tail, sharing the cockpit with Japanese copilots with whom I engaged in aerial combat six years earlier. During World War II I flew Navy patrols out of Midway Island in a search pattern toward Wake Island, while the Japanese did the reverse from Wake. Occasionally we met in the middle, and exchanged gunfire. There were only a few pilots on each island, and it was paradoxical that we now flew together as a crew.

The chief pilot for Transocean Airlines (Claude Turner) set high training and check standards, which kept the accident rate very low. This was even more remarkable in light of the adverse conditions in which we flew, throughout the world, into strange airports, usually without ground-support personnel. These safety standards carried over to Japan Airlines.

The only crash at Japan Airlines, while American pilots flew as captains, occurred more from fatigue that resulted from late night partying activities. A Martin 202, flown by two of our pilots, rammed into the side of an inactive volcano on Oshima Island (1951) near Tokyo. During the early morning flight from Tokyo to Osaka the two American pilots flew at too low an altitude and crashed into the side of the mountain.

Except for that crash there weren't any fatal crashes for the first ten years of Japan Airlines's existence. This is all the more remarkable because of the harsh weather conditions existing in Japan in the winter months. The safety standards changed after Japanese management acted to check out more of the low-time Japanese pilots to meet the expanding airline requirements. The pilots lacked background experience, and suffered unnecessary crashes. Alcohol was reportedly implicated in several of the crashes.

JAL SAN FRANCISCO CRASH

During a DC-8 instrument approach to San Francisco Airport, JAL pilots misunderstood the operation of the flight director, and did not cross-check the raw-data navigational indicators. The plane crashed into San Francisco Bay as the pilots followed flight director commands that were not giving them the ILS guidance that they thought was given.

The JAL crew had the aircraft on autopilot, set for a glide path capture. The flight director had been set to maintain a given *pitch* attitude, and would indicate to the pilot that he was properly flying the command bars as long as he maintained that pitch-setting, even though the aircraft may be descending like a rock.

As the raw-data ILS glide slope needle on another instrument (ILS indicator) started to move toward the center (on-glide-slope position) the pilot prematurely lowered the gear and flaps, reduced the engine power, and took it off autopilot, flying the flight director command bars. But the flight director had not yet captured the glide slope, and was still giving pitch-commands rather than commands to maintain the glide slope. The pilot did not cross-check the raw-data glide-slope signals, and didn't realize the ILS on-course position was far above where he was. He then compounded these errors by ignoring the minimum descent altitude and continued to descend into the bay when the runway was not in sight.

Several weeks before that crash I observed the same mistake made by pilots I was checking in the Flying Tigers DC-8 simulator. I promptly changed the flight manual to emphasize the danger.

DC-8 CRASH INTO TOKYO BAY

Japan Airlines had a bizarre DC-8 crash into Tokyo Bay during an approach to Tokyo's Haneda Airport on February 9, 1982. The Japanese captain, who had a history of psychiatric problems, placed the inboard engines into reverse during the approach, which could be expected to cause the plane to crash. (On the DC-8 the inboard engines could be placed in reverse during flight, and is intended only to expedite the loss of altitude during emergency descents from high altitudes.) The plane did crash, killing 23 people. During rescue operations the captain hid among the passengers, and then disappeared.

OTHER FOREIGN CRASHES

Other foreign airlines were experiencing crashes. In England, British Airtours (owned by British Airways), experienced a fatal crash on August 22, 1985. This crash occurred when a Pratt & Whitney JT8D engine on the Boeing 737 exploded during takeoff at Manchester Airport in northwest England. The pilot fortunately recognized the engine failure while still on the ground and rejected the takeoff. Unfortunately, the exploding engine severed fuel lines, and the rear of the aircraft caught fire. Fifty-four people perished.

The engine problem was in the combustor cans where air and fuel are mixed and ignited. After the crash, the world fleet of more than 1,000 Boeing 737s were ordered grounded for reinspection of the Pratt & Whitney JT8D-1 to JT8D-15 engines for combustor can integrity.

Several years later on January 12, 1989 a Boeing 737-400 experienced an engine disintegration and subsequently crashed during approach to East Midlands Airport near Kegworth, England. The left engine (CFM-56) disintegrated in flight, but the signal sent to the cockpit was that the right engine (the good engine) had failed. The crew shut down the good engine. Without power, the plane crashed into an embankment during approach to the airport, killing 44 persons. (The wrong signal was believed due to poor quality control at Boeing, which is described in later pages.)

SETTING NEW RECORDS

The record for the number of people killed in a single air disaster occurred ironically on the ground, when two Boeing 747 aircraft collided on March 27, 1977. Due to a bomb explosion in the passenger terminal at Las Palmas Airport in the Canary Islands, tourist flights to the airport were diverted to nearby Tenerife. When the situation at Las Palmas was under control, aircraft started leaving Tenerife during dense fog conditions. Among the aircraft taxiing to the takeoff position via the active runway were a KLM and a Pan Am Boeing 747. KLM was taxing down the active runway to the takeoff position, with Pan Am behind him. The visibility was only 1/8 of a mile; the planes had to rely heavily upon radio communications with the tower.

When KLM reached the takeoff position at the end of the runway, and had completed the pre-takeoff check list, the KLM captain advanced the power levers for takeoff into the fog bank that had hidden the Pan Am 747. The KLM 747 started to roll forward into the fog. The copilot shouted, "Wait a minute. We don't have ATC clearance!" Neither did they have the tower clearance for takeoff.

The copilot received the instrument clearance, but not the takeoff clearance. While the copilot read back the clearance for confirmation, the KLM captain *again* advanced the power levers for takeoff. *Again* the copilot and engineer told the captain they had not received the takeoff clearance from the tower. In the midst of this irresponsible conduct the copilot hurriedly tried to determine if they were cleared for takeoff. The need for *extra* caution was dictated by the nearly zero-zero visibility, and the knowledge that Pan Am was right behind KLM taxing down the active runway.

The copilot radioed to the tower, "We are now at takeoff." The tower replied, "Okay. Stand by for takeoff. I will call you." The Pan Am copilot, hearing this radio call, and still on the active runway in the fog, radioed, "We are still taxiing down the runway."

Like a pit-bull just released from his cage, the KLM captain advanced the power levers and started the takeoff into the fog. The KLM flight engineer worriedly asked, "Is he not clear, that Pan American?"

The Pan Am crew sensed KLM's anxiety to take off. The copilot stated, "Yeah, he's anxious, isn't he?" Suddenly, the Pan Am crew saw KLM looming out of the fog and closing in fast.

"There he is!" shouted the Pan Am captain. "Look at him! God damn! That son-of-a-bitch is coming!!" The Pan Am copilot shouted to get the plane off the runway, "Get off! Get Off! Get off!" The Pan Am pilots shoved the power levers full forward in a futile attempt to avoid a collision.

It was too late. KLM managed to get barely airborne, but its landing gear slammed into the fuselage of the luckless Pan Am 747. The Pan Am 747 exploded into a huge fireball. KLM crashed 500 feet down the runway, slid a thousand feet, and erupted into a second fireball. All 248 persons on KLM perished. Of the 394 people on Pan Am, 326 perished. If both planes were full, almost a thousand people could have died.

KOREAN AIRLINES

Korean Airlines doesn't even get to the starting gate with safety because of their numerous air disasters. Two of them resulted from gross navigational errors. In one instance on April 20, 1978, KAL Flight 902, a Boeing 707, experienced a gross navigational error ending in tragedy. The 707 departed Paris on a transpolar flight to Anchorage; it never arrived. Shortly after taking off from Paris at night, Flight 902 crossed the European coastline heading in a northwesterly direction. The crew put the plane on autopilot and then made several mistakes. Unobserved by the crew (were they all sleeping?), the plane made a 180 degree turn during the night. As the sun rose next morning, one of the passengers stated to another that the sun was rising on the wrong side of the aircraft; the left side instead of the right. The planned route of flight was in a northwesterly direction and the sun rising in the east should have been on the right side of the aircraft.

Flight 902 crossed into Russia in the vicinity of the major navy base at Murmansk on the Kola Peninsula. The plane was flying at 35,000 feet, and should have been detected by Russian radar while it was 500 miles out. Somehow Flight 902 crossed into Russian territory before it was discovered. Fighter aircraft took off and fired missiles at Flight 902.

One missile hit the aircraft, ripping holes in the side of the fuselage, depressurizing the plane, killing two passengers, and forcing Flight 902 to make an emergency descent due to the depressurization. The steep descent apparently caused the Russian fighter pilot to think he shot the aircraft down, and reported this to his base. However, Flight 902 continued flying, looking for a flat area to make a forced landing. Eventually Flight 902 crash-landed on a frozen lake in Russia.

THE FAMOUS FLIGHT OF KAL 007

KAL's navigation did not improve. On a North Pacific flight from Anchorage to Seoul on September 1, 1983, KAL Flight 007, a Boeing 747, strayed several hundred miles to the right of course, and entered Russian territory. Again, as before, a Russian fighter shot missiles at the Korean jet, and this time blew it apart. The debris and occupants fell into the Sea of Japan, killing all 269 persons on board.

The Russians at first denied shooting down Flight 007. One of their later radio broadcasts claimed the United States government put a bomb on board to make it look as though the Russians shot it down.

There were all types of theories as to why KAL was off course. Politics aside, the most probable cause was that the pilots had inserted the wrong coordinates into the INS navigational computers; or they failed to place the autopilot on the proper function, keeping it on a heading mode rather than the INS navigational mode. The crew obviously did not check the INS to cross-check their actual position as the flight proceeded. Nor did they turn on the radar which would have indicated the Russian coastline. It is also possible that the entire crew was asleep while the errors occurred.

OTHER KOREAN AIRLINES MISHAPS

A Korean Airlines 747 carrying 226 persons departed Los Angeles for Kimpo International Airport near Seoul on November 18, 1980. It crashed into a military vehicle upon landing, killing 12 persons and injuring 15. A Korean Airlines DC-10 crashed into an Alaska commuter plane upon taking off from the wrong runway at Anchorage on December 23, 1983. Both planes were destroyed. Miraculously, every one survived.

In another crash, which can *not* be blamed on the crew, a Korean Airlines 707, Flight 858, was blown up in flight by a bomb left behind by passengers. The explosion, on November 29, 1987, killed all 115 persons on board. An older man and a young woman, posing as his daughter, boarded the flight at Baghdad airport, without checking any baggage, certainly a suspicious sign. During a fuel stop at Abu Dhabi, the couple left the plane, leaving a bomb on board. Flight 858 left without the two passengers, and near the Thai-Burmese border the bomb exploded.

NOT THE ONLY PLANE WITH NAVIGATIONAL PROBLEMS

Korean Airlines wasn't the only airline with navigational errors. They simply had more of them, and they occurred while in hostile airspace. Several weeks after the Korean Airlines 707 crash into Russia, a United States overseas airline departed a major European city for a North Atlantic flight to Gander, Newfoundland. (1978.) The crew failed to make the three Loran fixes to validate the doppler navigation system, and eventually found themselves over—would you believe—North Africa! The crew then recrossed several busy Atlantic routes and landed in another country for fuel. Compounding the crew negligence was a significant compass error.

On a night Transocean Airlines flight from Milan, Italy, to Shannon, Ireland, with a full load of passengers (1958), flying at 10,000 feet, the crew made a heading change over Paris that nearly had fatal consequences. Instead of continuing in a northerly direction along the airways, the crew turned to a southeasterly heading, toward the Swiss Alps. Fortunately, someone woke up to the fact that they were going in the wrong direction before they rammed into the mountains.

A Thai Airways 747, carrying 391 people, kept the navigational fiascos going. On a flight from Seattle to Tokyo (December 21, 1989), and when 400 miles west of Seattle, unknown to the crew, the plane *reversed* course over the hostile northern Pacific Ocean, and ended up 600 miles from its intended flight path. Instead of heading west, the 747 was heading east. Air traffic controllers advised the crew it was heading in the wrong direction and was far off course. The flight returned to Seattle to refuel, as it no longer had enough fuel to reach its destination. The question has not been answered as to whether the three INS navigational systems failed, or the crew simply made operational errors. It is difficult to fault the equipment when the crew did not detect that they were flying in the wrong direction. Shades of wrong-way Corrigan of the 1930s.

WHITEOUT AND BAD JUDGMENT IN ANTARCTICA

Another major crash occurred from extremely poor judgment. A New Zealand Airlines DC-10 sightseeing trip to the Antarctica on November 25, 1979 crashed into the side of 12,400-foot Mount Erebus at the 1,500-foot level. The death toll was 257 people. The pilot had instructions not to descend below 16,000 feet, and should not have been at the 1,500 foot elevation.

The moment I heard of the crash, I suspected the pilot flew into a whiteout condition, where he could not see the surface. Whiteout is a phenomenon in snow-covered areas that occurs when the ground and the sky blend together, and resembles what seems like the inside of a milk bottle. The official accident report identified white-out as the cause of the crash.

The New Zealand Royal Commission, headed by Judge P. Mahon of the Auckland high court, blamed this crash primarily on airline management for not telling the crew the computerized routing fed into the aircraft's inertial navigation system had been changed hours before the aircraft departed New Zealand. (*Aviation Week & Space Technology*, May 18, 1981.) But this change was relatively minor, and did not justify the pilot descending from his 16,000 feet minimum altitude to 1,500 feet, or into a whiteout environment.

The judge listed several contributing causes. Among them were failure of the crew to see Mt Erebus; descent of the aircraft below the published minimum en route altitude (14,500 feet too low); uncertainty of the crew about the true position of the aircraft.

Chairman M.R.Davis of Air New Zealand allegedly discovered the night of the crash that the computer printout given to the pilots were off from the coordinates put into the aircraft navigational system. Davis allegedly passed the word that information of this error must not surface, and ordered all documents relating to the flight collected and impounded. He purportedly ordered all other documents not pertinent to the flight destroyed. The deviations in the computer readouts were actually of no consequence because of the other restrictions that protected the flight. But when the company changed the coordinates (only a few miles) without notifying the crew, it became an arguing point.

THE MISSING BODY

One of the pilots with whom I flew on a commercial military operation in the 1950s, Airlift, had been in a Curtis C-46 that crashed during a whiteout condition in Canada on the early warning radar system (DEW). The plane had been cruising in a whiteout condition, and descended into the ground at cruising speed. Rescuers found the wreckage and removed the bodies and then returned to base, where it was discovered that they were short one corpse. They returned to the wreckage, and in the mangled plane found the other pilot, with many broken bones. Ironically he survived, and returned to flight status.

SAS DC-8 CRASH NEAR LOS ANGELES

A Scandinavian DC-8 approached Los Angeles International Airport for a landing to the east, approaching from over the Pacific Ocean during a night visual approach on January 13, 1969. When the crew extended the landing gear, one of the three down-and-locked green lights did not illuminate.

All three crewmembers concentrated their attention on this relatively minor problem. The aircraft descended, unnoticed, and fifteen people died.

CHAPTER TWELVE

Windshear

Windshear has caused many deaths in airline crashes throughout the world.[42] It is a rapid change in the horizontal or vertical wind speed or direction within a short distance. This phenomenon is further defined as downbursts, or microbursts. The subcategory of microburst pertains to a violent downward rush of air that flattens out when it hits or approaches the ground, and spreads in all directions. They are often of short duration, believed to be as little as 5 to 10 minutes.

Although windshear has always existed, crashes due to the problem did not occur to any great extent, or receive any publicity, until jets were introduced in 1958. In propeller aircraft the result of windshear was less severe. Application of engine power on propeller aircraft produced an almost immediate increase of lift as airflow over the wings increased by advancing the power levers. With the jets, the engines must first spool up, and then the aircraft must be propelled through the air with greater speed or the pitch-attitude increased to counteract the effects of the windshear.

One of the earliest reported windshear crashes was that of an Iberia Airlines DC-10 during approach to runway 33 left at Boston's Logan International Airport on December 17, 1973.

---

[42] e.g. Continental Airlines 727 at Denver, August 7, 1975; Allegheny Airlines DC-9, Philadelphia, Pennsylvania, June 23, 1976; Continental 727 at Tucson, Arizona, June 3, 1977; Iberian Airlines DC-10, Boston, December 17, 1973.

The DC-10 first struck approach lights 500 feet short of the runway, then struck an embankment at the airport perimeter. It then landed on the runway and skidded to a stop 3,000 feet beyond the runway threshold. Luckily, most passengers survived.

EASTERN WINDSHEAR CRASH AT JFK

The windshear problem received major recognition with the June 24, 1975 crash of Eastern Airlines Flight 66, a Boeing 727. The flight approached New York City's JFK Airport during thunderstorm activity and encountered severe downdrafts that caused it to crash and disintegrate.

The severe turbulence associated with the storm caused an earlier flight, a Flying Tiger DC-8, to abandon the ILS approach. The FTL captain radioed to the control tower, "I'm just telling you that there's such a severe wind shear on the final to that runway that you should change it to the northwest. You have a tremendous wind shear down near the ground." The wind at the control tower was only 15 knots when Flying Tigers reported the severe turbulence, as the effect of the thunderstorm had not yet reached the airport.

Right behind Flying Tigers was Eastern Airlines Flight 902, who also experienced severe turbulence, and who also executed a missed approach. Behind both of these flights was Eastern Flight 66, landing to the southwest. The approach controller asked the crew of Flight 66 if they heard the report by Flight 902, and if they wished to continue the approach. The captain of Flight 66 chose to continue the approach.

The tower and approach controllers should have changed the approach from another direction, which would have avoided the thunderstorm that was northeast of the airport. This was not done.

The primary reason for not changing the runway was that the airport received many noise complaints when using the runway 31 approach. The airport noise abatement program called for switching runways after so many hours of use, and runway 31 had been used earlier in the day for six hours.

Flight 66 continued its approach. When it was several hundred feet above the approach lights the aircraft encountered the same severe turbulence and downdrafts experienced by the two earlier flights. The violence of the turbulence caused the captain to struggle with both hands on the controls, trying to keep the aircraft under control. The captain suddenly shouted, "Take-off Thrust!"

That command can mean either take *off* the thrust, or, apply maximum rated or available power. Taking off power when the captain wanted maximum power could be deadly. It's unknown whether the copilot responded by taking the power off, or added maximum power. What is known is that the plane crashed.

Flight 66 fell into the steel beams supporting the approach lights, and split apart, ejecting passengers out of the disintegrating aircraft. The death toll was 113 people.

CONTINENTAL WINDSHEAR CRASHES

Less than two months later, on August 7, 1975, a Continental Boeing 727, Flight 426, encountered windshear, and crashed during takeoff at Denver's Stapleton Airport.[43] The Continental crew knew that earlier aircraft reported windshear during the climbout as they passed through 200 feet above the ground. Despite these reports, the captain made the takeoff with a low airspeed noise-abatement climb and using reduced engine power. These procedures should have been abandoned for safety reasons in the presence of windshear.

Shortly after passing the end of the runway, Flight 426 encountered the windshear, and promptly lost 40 knots of airspeed, and crashed to the ground about a quarter mile north of runway 35. It hit the ground at a speed exceeding 150 miles per hour. Fortunately, there were no buildings where the aircraft crashed, and fortunately there was no fire. Miraculously there were no fatalities, but numerous injuries. On statistically records that flight was listed as a safe flight because of the absence of deaths.

The NTSB investigated the crash and in its accident report criticized the airline for its windshear training; for its poor passenger evacuation; and the FAA's failure to implement windshear training recommendations arising from earlier crashes. The report criticized the flight and cabin crew, stating that "the evidence indicates that the flight crew abandoned the cockpit through the sliding windows as rapidly as possible. The safety board concludes that the flight crew's performance in this respect did not conform to the standards of professional crewmembers." The report stated that only two of the seven flight attendants stayed on board the aircraft to evacuate the passengers.

After this crash the NTSB issue its off-the-shelf recommendation that the FAA issue an air carrier operations bulletin requiring that principal operations inspectors review the emergency evacuation training programs of their assigned air carriers. In that way the NTSB protected itself.

---

[43] During training flights in this same area I frequently encountered windshear conditions, but never threatening the flight. I used these encounters during debriefing to make the pilots more aware of windshear problems (which had received very little publicity at that time).

Continental's safety activities were under the control of the FAA Western Region.

In another safety recommendation issued on June 9, 1976, the Board stated:

> The safety Board's accident experience has shown that a crewmember's response to an emergency depends almost entirely on his training. Flightcrews must understand that they must lead the evacuation and that they must act swiftly and aggressively to assist passengers. In order to do so, each crewmember must have a firm understanding of his duties and responsibilities and of the duties of other crewmembers so that his effects will complement theirs.

Similar recommendations were made throughout the 1960s.

Continental experienced another windshear incident during takeoff from Tucson, Arizona on June 3, 1977. The crew started the takeoff 500 feet down the runway, rather than at the start of the runway. The aircraft required the entire runway to safely miss the obstacles at the airport perimeter. The aircraft remained on the ground longer than the pilots anticipated. The bottom of the aircraft struck power lines and utility poles at the far end of the airport, and barely missed crashing to the ground. Miraculously, a major disaster did not happen, and another safe flight was chalked up on the accident statistics.

PAN AM AT NEW ORLEANS

A major windshear tragedy occurred to Pan Am Flight 759, a Boeing 727, taking off from New Orleans for Las Vegas on July 9, 1982. There were rain showers in the area when the copilot made the takeoff into the expected windshear conditions. The captain advised the flight engineer to turn off the air-conditioning packs during the takeoff to eliminate the loss of engine thrust caused by operating these units.

The captain advised the copilot to "let your airspeed build up on takeoff" as a precaution against windshear. Shortly after becoming airborne the copilot leveled off the aircraft at roof-top level to increase the speed, rather than increase the height above the ground obstacles. Subsequently, Flight 759 encountered severe down drafts and never climbed above 150 feet.

During this critical phase of flight the captain continued coaxing the copilot, "Come on back [with the control column], you're sinking, Don ... come on back!" The power levers should have been slammed to their stops, beyond the arbitrary maximum-rated power setting.

The Ground Proximity Warning System (GPWS) sounded, "Whoop ... whoop ... pull up ... whoop ... whoop." Half a mile beyond the end of the runway Flight 759 stuck trees and houses in Kenner, Louisiana, erupting in a huge fireball. The death toll was 145 people on the plane and eight on the ground.

Several *hours* after the crash, a rescue worker searching through the rubble in one of the houses noticed a mattress move. He lifted it, and there was a 16-month-old-girl, wide awake and crying. She was the only survivor in that house, having lost her four-year-old sister and 26-year-old mother. The father was at work at the time of the tragedy.

DELTA AT DALLAS

Another tragedy that served as the basis for movies and books was Delta Flight 191, a Lockheed 1011, which crashed during approach to Dallas/Forth Worth Airport on August 12, 1985. It was a typical muggy summer afternoon with scattered thundershowers when Flight 191 made its approach from the north, landing on runway 17 left. Northeast of the airport, and moving west into the flight path of the landing aircraft, was a rapidly developing thunderstorm.

The Delta crew saw the lightning in the clouds ahead of them. Previous pilots had not reported any turbulence because the thunderstorm developed to the east of the approach path, but had not yet moved into the path of the landing aircraft. The one exception was a Delta crew that had just landed, but had not yet reported the turbulence to the controller. That crew experienced extreme turbulence and had trouble controlling the aircraft.

Watching the developing thunderstorm was the approach control radar operator who suddenly noticed the rapid worsening of the storm. He did not notify the controllers.

Despite the threatening nature of the rapidly developing thunderstorm, the crew of Flight 191 did not turn on their radar, which would have shown the developing intensity of the storm. Possibly the conversation the with female flight attendant in the cockpit, relating to non-flying matters, diverted attention from the problems at hand.

The relative calm of the winds at the airport gave no indication of the ferocity of the winds on the approach path north of the airport. The airport's Low Level Windshear Alert System (LLWAS) provided wind direction and speed measurements on the ground at different airport locations, and indicated relatively calm wind conditions. This system has serious limitations for detecting windshear.

DOPPLER RADAR

Doppler radar had the capabilities of detecting dangerous micro-burst and windshear activities, and could prevent some of the crashes from occurring. But the aviation trust fund money that had been collected from passengers and aviation users to purchase the equipment was not released. The reason? Make the federal deficit look less horrendous. The adverse affect upon air safety, and this crash, was intangible, and not recognized by the public.

Making an approach ahead of Flight 191 was another Delta aircraft, Flight 963. The pilots encountered the ferocious nature of the thunderstorm, but managed to land safely. The pilots said, after landing, "Looks like a tornado or something. I've never seen anything like it." Unfortunately, they had not yet relayed this information to the control tower or the flight right behind them.

Flight 191 entered the thunderstorm several miles north of the airport. The copilot was making the approach, coaxed by the captain, who told the copilot to add more power. Shortly, the captain again reminded him to add still more power.

The difference between a safe flight and a crash is often the subtle application of power at the right time and applying subtle pressures to the control column to maintain a delicate balance of airspeed and altitude control. Any delay in application of control pressures, sometimes not discernible to the pilot watching, can have fatal consequences. Sometimes it requires relaxing nose-up or nose-down pressures; or making minute speed adjustments; or flying the aircraft at the nibble of a stall-warning stick-shaker. At critical times the captain should be in control of the aircraft, wherein the pilot actually flying does not have to second-guess what another pilot may want done. The captain is the crewmember who can best make this decision, and he should have made the approach.

"Pull up! Pull up!"

Flight 191 experienced abnormally high altitude-loss as it approached the airport, causing the aircraft altitude-alert warning system to sound off: "Pull Up, Pull Up." Despite corrective actions Flight 191 hit the ground hard, over a mile from the runway, and the tires sank into the soft ground. The aircraft bounced, and hit again, three hundred feet away. The CVR recorded the sounds of the fuselage ripping apart.

During the series of ground-contacts Flight 191 hit a car on State Highway 114 that runs along the north edge of the airport. The driver was decapitated.

The plane then crashed into a tall water tank on the airport itself, causing the fuselage to break into several major pieces. The fuel tanks burst open, exploding into a huge fireball like exploding napalm. The aft fuselage section broke loose from the forward sections that were now engulfed in flames.

KNEE-JERK REACTION

The control tower operator panicked upon seeing the

aircraft hit the ground, and shouted, "Flight 191, go around!" This instruction was probably a knee-jerk reaction to the tragedy unfolding before his eyes. At that point the tower operator had no say in the actions taken by the crew. The controller sounded the crash alarm, sending emergency equipment rushing to the crash.

One of the first to reach the crash scene was Bob Sonnamaker, who was driving near the airport when the car radio announced that a plane had just crashed. A few second later he saw the flames, and rushed to the crash scene.

Later, he said, "It was very, very frustrating not to have anybody to help. It was probably 15 minutes before I found somebody alive." In a section of three upside-down seats, he found Kathy Ford, badly burned, but still breathing. "There was just an arm sticking out," he said. "Then the arm moved." He began cutting her loose from the wreckage. Her jacket was twisted over her head, covering her face.

Also arriving at the scene was Zantop International Airways employee Jerry Fenske. He later recalled how a little baby lay hidden in the debris for hours before rescuers discovered the badly injured girl and rushed her to a hospital. By then it was too late.

Triage stations were quickly established to provide emergency treatment to the survivors who might be in shock, who may have traumatic injuries, burns, or profuse bleeding. There were very few to treat. Most were dead.

Emergency Medical Technicians (EMTs) estimated that without this quick triage treatment, at least 50 percent of the surviving passengers would have died from their injuries.

When it was over, 135 persons perished. The few persons who survived were in the rear section. Many of the twenty-nine survivors were critically injured. Four days after the crash a Florida teacher died from the effect of her burns and fractures, and the complications of an amputated leg. In 1988, several years after the crash, Kathy Ford still lay in a Dallas Hospital, brain-dead, with no chance of recovery.

The tower controller later stated, "It's just a feeling of helplessness." He added, "You're standing there looking at an airplane explode and you know that people are dying. You don't have any idea how many. There's not a damn thing you can do for them. Zero. It's just total helplessness."

Airport tower controllers later reported that they had no idea of the wind's severity in the flight path. When the thunderstorm moved over the airport, the controllers reported that the 200 foot tall tower was shaking. They stated that if the plane had not crashed they were ready to close the airport to all takeoffs and landings, and evacuate the control tower.

Removing body parts from DC-10 crash at Paris.

Depositions and court testimony brought out ironies. Three tower controllers changed shifts during the rapidly developing thunderstorm four minutes before Flight 191 crashed, without overlapping coordination. Richard Douglas, a National Weather Service meteorologist, testified that he left his radar unmonitored for 45 minutes while he ate dinner. He returned shortly after the crash. Another FAA controller testified that he didn't realize his radar scope was set to filter out indications of minor rain storms, which was how the storm looked until several minutes before the crash.

"We just want our share [of the bodies]!"

Dallas funeral directors squabbled over division of the corpses. A group of about 20 business owners charged racism and favoritism in the distribution of bodies to area funeral homes. "We're not demanding anything. We just want our share," said Nat Clark, a Dallas funeral home owner. "It's greed on the part of a few owners, flat greed."

The group said the president of a mostly white funeral home association deliberately left them off a list of funeral homes authorized to prepare and transport the bodies of crash victims. Delta paid funeral homes $390 for each body they handled.

THE LEGAL FRATERNITY SHOWED UP

By Sunday morning after the crash the San Francisco law firm of Melvin Belli dispatched two lawyers, one of them Mr. Belli's son, to set up a temporary office in the hotel where most of the victims' families were staying. They filed their first claim for damages against Delta the following Tuesday in federal district court in Florida.[44] Florida juries are noted for their high damage awards, causing plaintiff's attorneys to file in Florida whenever possible.

The State Bar of Texas disclosed it opened a preliminary investigation into the Belli firm's activities in Dallas. Another man used the crash to wangle a free ride from Florida to Dallas, claiming to be the fiancé of a victim. When Delta escorted him to the hospital where the woman's family was awaiting news, the family said they had never seen him before.

NTSB REPORT

The NTSB reported the probable cause of the crash as the:

flight crew's decision to initiate and continue the approach into a cumulonimbus cloud that they observed to contain visible lighting; the lack of specific guidelines, procedures and training for avoiding and escaping from low-altitude

---

[44] Based upon Florida being where the passenger boarded, and where Delta had corporate offices.

wind shear, and the lack of definitive, real-time wind shear hazard information. This resulted in the aircraft's encounter at low altitude with a microburst-induced, severe wind-shear from a rapidly developing thunderstorm located on the final approach court.

The NTSB again used the off-the-shelf recommendation that the FAA insure that airlines provide better windshear training to the crews. Also, that the FAA install more Doppler radar units at airports experiencing frequent thunderstorms.

The blame belonged in many places, and the extensive distribution of blame shows what happens when a government safety agency is riddled with problems as exists in the FAA. The FAA knew training was inadequate. It had the responsibility to take immediate corrective action. It had the capability of detecting the sudden blossoming of the thunderstorm, and said nothing. The Weather Bureau radar should not have been abandoned at that critical time. Doppler radar should have been installed at Dallas/Forth Worth Airport on the basis of the frequent thunderstorms and heavy traffic at that location.

The training should have emphasized the importance to the crew of turning on their radar. Good cockpit discipline should be emphasized, including elimination of distracting people and conversations in the cockpit. But inspectors cannot function to achieve these goals under the continuing FAA mentality that punishes inspectors for reporting these shortcomings.

IMPROVEMENTS IN PREVENTING WINDSHEAR CRASHES

Pressure caused by the public and the news media prompted Congress to order the FAA to install more Doppler radar units so as to minimize windshear-type crashes.

The goal of avoiding windshear (and downdraft or micro-burst) includes (a) avoidance; (b) training; and (c) cockpit equipment. Avoidance will be helped by ground Doppler radar (and flight Doppler radar).

Boeing obtained FAA certification of wind-shear cockpit aids in 1986, commencing in the 737-300 and then in the 767-300, with subsequent modifications in other aircraft.[45] The system can be retrofitted to many other jets. The equipment gives the pilots warning of a wind shear when it may not yet be recognized by the crew. These improvements will help, but the coordination needed to address the overall windshear and other problems require massive changes in the FAA itself.

LAW SUITS

A federal judge in Forth Worth, Texas[46] rendered a decision in a lawsuit filed against the U.S. Government as a result of

[45] *Aviation Week & Space Technology*, October 7, 1985.
[46] September 1989. *Connors v. U.S.*, No. 4-87-060-K.

this crash. The 113-day trial developed over 20,000 pages of testimony after months of deliberations. The federal judge protected the U.S. Government and held that the government was not at fault. He said nothing about the FAA's responsibility to force correction of the training program inadequacies that was known to the FAA. He said nothing about the FAA's failure to notify the crew of the mushrooming thunderstorm seen on the weather radar. He protected the government who had the capability of promoting him into higher judicial positions.

If the federal judge had not ruled as he did, a precedence would have been set that made the federal government liable for the settlement costs. Many federal judges are former attorneys with the Department of Justice, whose function it is to protect government against law suits. Many federal judges are noted for rarely ruling against the government that decides which judges are promoted to higher appellate court positions. The judge blamed the pilots for the crash, and disregarded the other parties who contributed heavily to the tragedy.

DAMAGE CONTROL

A *Wall Street Journal* article described how the injured and the survivors were treated by various attorneys and by Delta Airlines. In the beginning, Delta showed compassion to the victims. Then the attorneys took over, and commenced practicing their standard tools of the trade. After the funerals, the attorneys examined the victims' lives, looking for character flaws to decrease the value of any financial settlement. They scrutinized the marriages, looking for infidelities, homosexual tendencies, relationships with children, and any other gossip. Then they misused the information against the victim or the victim's family.

During court depositions the attorneys examined the victims' lives, and put the most unfavorable slant and fabrications on anything possible. The husband of a Delta flight attendant killed in the crash found that attorneys and their investigators had combed the neighborhood shortly after the funeral, asking neighbors whether the couple fought or had drinking problems. Senior vice president of United States Aviation Underwriters Inc., claims these tactics are a "search for the truth." The truth is that this court-sanctioned conduct was totally immoral.

Asked about these tactics, Delta stated that it had input into the conduct of the attorneys, but doesn't necessarily get involved in each case. Like a Kafka novel, it is impossible to place individual responsibility.

Delta treated the family of Harold Ageloff with respect, until the family filed a law suit to protect their legal interests. Delta's attorneys then investigated the deceased, and threatened the family with making public the homosexuality of their son if they did not settle for what the airline offered.

Ageloff's attorney filed a motion in the U.S. District Court for the Southern District of Florida requesting an order barring Delta from mentioning the victim's sexual preference in the pending jury trial. Delta's attorneys responded in its opposition that it was important to bring out his homosexual life style. They argued that if Ageloff had AIDS (and Delta offered no evidence that he did), that "in the present environment of 100-percent-fatal-AIDS, it becomes a critical, relevant subject." Delta's attorneys argued that Ageloff's "sexual preference may be relevant from the standpoint of his employability."

Ageloff's attorney accused Delta of raising the issue "only to harass, oppress, intimidate and blackmail the plaintiffs into dropping their lawsuit in order to avoid embarrassment and humiliation." Attorney Alpert replied, "Not so. We wouldn't raise an issue if we didn't intend to use it in court."

Alpert's statement shows how low an airline will stoop to protect its profit margin. It is therefore not surprising that they trade lives for the almighty dollar with no regrets.

"What Delta did to her and her two children ..."

The attorney representing Kathy Ann Reynolds, who gave birth to her second child three days after her husband and his brother died in the Delta crash, said, "What Delta did to her and her two children makes Karen Silkwood look like a fairy tale." He demonstrated that the airline and the insurance company tried to find unfavorable information not only about crash victims, but also about the survivors.

During a jury trial to determine the damages to be paid to the wife of a deceased passenger, Delta's lawyers stated to the jury that Mrs. Reynolds was "sleeping with another man within 10 weeks of her husband's death."

A San Francisco attorney who had several cases against Delta complained that the families don't realize when they pour out their souls to an adjuster or airline employee that these same people, pretending to be friends, may use the information against them to reduce the compensation to the survivors for the death of their loved one.

AFTER DEATH OF A LOVED ONE, HARASSMENT.

These immoral ghouls are even proud of their conduct. For example, some attorneys referred to the practices as the "Delta Plan." They called it a state-of-the-art blueprint for insurance companies to follow in subsequent crashes. Record all the negative information they can obtain while acting as a friend. Then, if the families refuse to settle on the airline's terms, show them just how painful a lawsuit can be.

CHAPTER THIRTEEN

Midair Collisions

One of the first significant midair collisions occurred when a P-38 flown by an employee of the Bolivian Embassy in Washington collided with an airliner that was approaching Washington National Airport. Later, an Air Force fighter collided with a United DC-7 near Las Vegas, Nevada on April 21, 1958. A month after that a Maryland Air National Guard fighter crashed into a Capitol Viscount over Brunswick, Maryland. A Marine Corp fighter jet rammed an Air West plane (June 6, 1971) with the loss of everyone on board the airliner. The list goes on and on. We'll now look at a few of the high-fatality midair collisions.

MIDAIR COLLISION POLITICS

Even one of the United States' Presidents wrote a letter expressing concern over the midair collision problem to a commission empowered to investigate the threat. The letter stated in part:

For some time now I have been seriously concerned about aircraft accidents, both commercial and military, that have occurred in the takeoff and landing of aircraft, especially in heavily-populated areas. I have been concerned about the loss of life, and I have been concerned about the anxiety in some of our cities. I have decided to set up a temporary President's Airport Commission to look into the problem of airport location and use.

A report on the midair collision problem was later submitted to the President of the United States by the commission, and it made forty-seven recommendations that covered the entire field of air safety. Included in the recommendation was that aircraft "should have some form of light and reliable airborne radar to guard against midair collisions." The date of that report? May 16, 1952. The report was submitted to concerned President Harry Truman.

Eight years later the December 26, 1960 issue of *Air Transport* magazine carried a multi-page report headed: "Collision Avoidance Progress Reported," in which the FAA briefed the news media on the progress in developing a collision avoidance system. After the FAA failed in getting collision-avoidance equipment on airlines, and almost *forty years* after Truman's actions, Congress passed legislation forcing the airlines to install collision avoidance equipment by the early 1990s.

MIDAIR COLLISION THAT BROUGHT ABOUT THE FAA

The grand-daddy of midair collisions occurred over one of the most scenic spots in the world—the Grand Canyon, on June 30, 1956. This tragedy focused public attention on air safety, and forced Congress to address the lingering air safety problems. In response to public pressure, Congress enacted the Federal Aviation Act, and created the Federal Aviation Agency, which has since been renamed the Federal Aviation Administration. The Act transferred safety functions from the former Civil Aeronautic Administration (CAA), and used the same government personnel to carry out the safety duties. Unfortunately, its legislative authority and responsibility over the government safety agency was either ignored, or misused, just as Congress misused HUD and other government agencies.

The Grand Canyon tragedy occurred when United Airlines Flight 718, a DC-7, overtook and rammed TWA Flight 2, a Lockheed Constellation. The DC-7 had taken off from Los Angeles International Airport slightly after the Constellation, and both headed for New York City, using the same airways. Both aircraft were cruising at 21,000 feet when they reached the Grand Canyon area. In the 1950s air traffic control system, the instant communication between the aircraft and the air traffic control centers was not what it is today. There was no long-range radar coverage. The only enroute radar was located at Newark Airport in New Jersey, and this was a World War Two surplus item. Air safety had low financial priority.

As the United DC-7 approached and caught up to the TWA plane, none of the crewmembers were looking outside the aircraft. The propellers of the DC-7 cut into the Constellation, ripping off its triple tail, causing TWA to plunge almost straight down into the Grand Canyon. United soon followed, allowing the pilots sufficient time to send its last radio message: "Salt Lake, United 718, ... we're going in!"

By today's standards the 128 deaths are low, when others go into three hundred, five hundred, seven hundred, and who knows what will come next. However, in those days the public reacted to these many deaths, forcing changes in the government's air safety actions. We were not yet a people satiated by the instant coverage of tragedies on television. We were still a nation of concern and, as individuals, we assumed responsibility for each other and for our institutions.

ANOTHER RAMMING INTO TWA BY UNITED

The next major midair occurred over the New York City area, as described in the first chapter, when a United DC-8 rammed into a TWA Constellation.

Other major midair collisions followed. A TWA 707 rammed into an Eastern Constellation over Carmel, New york on December 4, 1965. Following the collision, the Eastern Captain found the flight controls jammed, and executed a crash-landing. The captain partially controlled the descent of the aircraft and the pitch-attitude by power manipulation. The captain stayed in the plane after it crashed and came to a stop, trying to save a trapped passenger. Captain White and the passenger were the only deaths, that the captain's skill and courage prevented from escalating.

LACK OF ALERTNESS

Numerous articles have been written identifying the problem of pilot inattention to outside traffic. The problem was admitted years ago by the Air Line Pilots Association as they attempted to justify another pilot in the cockpit. They stated in an *Airline Pilot* article:

> [the study showed] that on takeoff the Captain was looking out only 12% of the time while he was flying and the non-flying co-pilot was able to look out only 26% of the time. On landings, the figures were 15% and 32%. Assuming that the looking-out times were not concurrent, it would seem to indicate that no less than 62% of the time, no one would be looking out on takeoff, and on landing, no less than 53% of the time...

Corrective action includes evaluating the crew's alertness when conducting enroute checks of their performance. FAA reports of poor cockpit discipline were received no more favorably than reports of safety violations and irregularities. As an FAA inspector, during an enroute flight check of a Western Airline flight crew from Denver to San Francisco, I noted very poor outside vigilance by both pilots. I made the required written report of my observations, stating that

> the Captain and crew were so thoroughly relaxed that they placed their aircraft seats into the most rearward position which is intended for ground use to facilitate entering the seat. From this rearward position the relaxed crew could not properly actuate the flight controls, especially the rudders, creating a hazard should a near midair incident suddenly occur, or a high altitude upset occur, or any one of a myriad of other inflight emergencies.

I further reported that both pilots spent considerable time reading personal material and union newsletters. The report stated that for as long as twenty minutes at a time neither pilot looked out for other traffic. Several times I watched as other traffic passed close by, at closure speeds of over one thousand miles per hour, with the crew unaware of the nearby aircraft. Included in my report was the copilot's habit of reporting to air traffic control that the aircraft was passing through and leaving an altitude, when in fact it hadn't even reach the altitude, let alone passed it. This created a potential midair collision problem. It was terrible cockpit discipline.

These and still other careless cockpit habits were discussed with the captain when the flight terminated at San Francisco. It was done tactfully and in a friendly spirit. But the captain responded in a cocky and antagonistic manner, an attitude fostered by the known lack of inspector support by FAA officials. FAA management was more interested in placating the industry to whom they looked for a high paying job after their departure from government. In response to that enroute report of lax cockpit discipline, I found myself on the carpet during a subsequent staff meeting in the Denver FAA office for alleged misconduct during this flight. The misconduct? The crew reported my comments to another FAA inspector, who relayed the comments to FAA officials. I should not have said anything, nor reported the problems. This same FAA person inserted this harassment in an FAA bulletin:

> INSPECTORS CONDUCT IN THE COCKPIT: Because of critical complaints regarding the conduct of some FAA field inspectors by ATA—discussed previously at the August 14th staff meeting—and because we have received a complaint from a flight crew regarding the conduct of an enroute inspection by one of our inspectors, I decided to again discuss the need for courteous professional, businesslike conduct of all our business in the cockpit.

The lack of crew alertness to outside traffic never ceased to amaze me. I noticed this years ago when I first started flying with the airlines as a crewmember, as crews caught up on their personal reading during flight. This casualness is reflected, in part, by crewmembers sleeping at their duty stations, or engaging in frivolous conversations that are not related to the operation of the aircraft. The seriousness of their profession simply is not impressed upon them. They have very little comprehension of the crashes occurring, and the need for professional actions. It is shown by aircraft overflying their destinations, such as the United DC-8 overflying Los Angeles and proceeding out to sea, the entire flight deck crew asleep. That was only one of several incidents that came to my attention as an airline pilot.

FRIVOLITY WITH DANGEROUS CONSEQUENCES

An example of how lack of cockpit discipline can result in near-tragedy occurred one night in 1948 on an American Airlines DC-4 east of El Paso. A company check pilot, Chuck Sisto, seated between and slightly behind the two pilots being checked, engaged in some cockpit merriment. He engaged the aircraft gust lock without the pilot's knowledge, locking the flight controls. This lock is *never* applied in flight. It is used on the ground only, to keep the wind from whipping the controls back and forth. Many aircraft have crashed during takeoff when the gust lock was inadvertently left on during takeoff.

After applying the gust lock in flight, the aircraft pitched upward. As it did, the captain—unaware of what the check airman had done—started applying nose-down trim, trying to bring the airplane's nose down to normal attitude. But now that the flight controls were locked, the nose-down trim worked in reverse, causing the plane to pitch up even more, to a scary nose-high attitude.

Recognizing that things had gotten out of control, the check pilot quickly took the gust lock off. And when he did, the plane reacted as he should have known it would. The maximum nose-down trim setting now worked as it was intended to do, and the aircraft went from a steep nose-up to a steep nose-down attitude, making part of an outside loop.

Neither the captain or the check pilot had their seat belts fastened, and they fell against the propeller feathering knobs on the overhead panel as the plane reached an inverted position. This caused two of the four engines to literally shut down. Fortunately, the copilot had his seat belt fastened and managed to get the plane upright, but not a second too soon. The descent was halted just as the plane was about to crash into the ground. The pull out was so close to the ground that the glow of the engine exhaust illuminated the surface.

Trying to cover up for what had actually happened, the company check pilot reported that the autopilot malfunctioned, and that the crew miraculously saved the aircraft; they were heroes. The public was unsophisticated in aviation matters, and accepted the concocted story. However, others in the aviation field didn't buy it, and the true facts came out. Captain Sisto, a senior company check pilot, was fired, and the FAA revoked his pilot certificate. Some years later, upon getting his license back, Sisto was hired by Transocean Airlines, and was my copilot flying Moslem pilgrims to Mecca in 1952.

In another incident, one of my friends, an NTSB accident investigator, described a form of cockpit merriment he encountered while employed as a captain for the airlines. On a flight from Miami, a dead-heading captain on his flight crawled into the cargo compartment through the cabin emergency hatch (Curtis C-46) and in a playful episode started moving the trim control back and forth. Many pilots are unaware of the tragic consequences of unprofessional conduct.

EXCESSIVE SPEED

Another major midair disaster occurred when a TWA DC-9 rammed into a corporate aircraft near Urbana, Ohio on March 9, 1967. The DC-9 was traveling almost 300 miles an hour at low altitude in airspace occupied by numerous small planes. The DC-9 rammed into a twin-engine Beechcraft Baron, killing everyone on both planes. After that accident, the NTSB proposed a maximum speed of 250 knots (288 miles per hour) below 10,000 mean sea level, and the FAA responded. The news media blamed the small plane for crashing into the airliner.

Among the other midair collisions were the Allegheny Airlines DC-9 that rammed into a small Piper Cherokee just southeast of Indianapolis. All 83 persons on both planes perished. An American Airline jet rammed into a Cessna 150 at 3000 feet near Newark, N.J. on January 9, 1971. A Continental 707 rammed into Cessna 150 on August 4, 1971 over Compton, California. An Eastern DC-9 crashed into a Cessna 206 on December 4, 1971 near Raleigh, North Carolina. Then we had two catastrophic air disasters in southern California which are described shortly in more detail.

SAN DIEGO—ANOTHER GREAT AIR DISASTER

The greatest number of people killed in a previous United States air tragedy was the United Airlines crash into New York City. This record remained until a Pacific Southwest Airlines (PSA) Boeing 727 jet crashed into a San Diego residential area on September 25, 1978. PSA Flight 182 departed Sacramento at 7 a.m. on a flight to Los Angeles, and then on to San Diego.

Among those boarding the flight at Sacramento was Helen Rhea and a mortgage banker friend, Lee Johnson, of San Diego. During the flight to Los Angeles a flight attendant, Debbie McCarthy, who had gone out with Lee several times, chatted with Lee and Helen.

Debbie complained to them of being very tired. She stated she had been at a party in one of the crew motel rooms at the Sacramento Airport from eleven p.m. until 5 a.m., shortly before the flight left Sacramento. Debbie stated that the entire crew had been there. She stated that large quantities of Johnny Walker Red Label was consumed. She stated that the party had been given on behalf of a captain and a flight attendant who had been dating. Debbie stated that the crew was very tired, and that they had less than two hours sleep. Before leaving, Debbie stated, "All I care about is getting home; I'm tired. All of the crew is really hung over."

"... our lives in their hands, and they're hung over!"

After Debbie left, Lee said, half joking and half angry, "I can't believe this! These pilots have our lives in their hands, and they've been out partying, and have been up until five a.m. this morning!" Lee added, "They have our lives in their hands, and they're hung over!"

Helen went to the rest room after Debbie left, and while waiting for it to become available, she overheard another PSA flight attendant talking about the same party described earlier by Debbie McCarthy. Helen overheard the flight attendant, whom she described as "looking bad from lack of sleep," describe the party, further confirming that it did in fact occur.

Flight 182 landed at Los Angeles, and Helen left the plane. She was half tempted to continue on to San Diego with Lee, but changed her mind and got off. Lee continued on to San Diego.

In the cockpit of Flight 182, before leaving the terminal at Los Angeles, the cockpit voice recorder recorded the following conversation between a female flight attendant and the captain, as the flight attendant referred to the captain's tired appearance: "Tired, are you?" The captain responded, "I'm dragging. It was a short night."[47]

APPROACHING SAN DIEGO

San Diego's weather was excellent as PSA approached Lindberg Field at 9 a.m. Approach control cleared Flight 182 to the downwind leg, heading east, for a visual approach to land on runway 27, to the west.

Other airlines were radar vectored to the final-approach course east of the field, for a straight-in approach. This avoided the hazard of descending into other aircraft in the Lindberg traffic pattern. But PSA reached an understanding

[47] Published in *Forum*, magazine of Society of Air Safety Investigators, Volume 17, 1984.

with the FAA to make a close-in downwind approach. This saved a few minutes flight time, but increased the hazard of descending onto other traffic and causing a midair collision as the airliner descended in its blind spot where other traffic was heavy. It was a dangerous procedure.

When the jets first came out and other airlines were flying under instrument flight rules from airport to airport, PSA continued flying under visual flight rules, creating a midair collision problem. The FAA Western Region approved this dangerous practice, but the Washington FAA offices finally put a stop to it.

Approaching Lindberg Airport, several dead-heading crewmembers were in the cockpit engaging in constant non-flying conversations, diverting the flight crew from the important business of flying the aircraft. The captain did not stop the diversionary chatter.

As PSA Flight 182 descended into the Lindberg traffic pattern, the air traffic controller twice advised PSA that they were overtaking and descending onto a small plane going in the same general direction. The controller gave PSA the bearing, the distance, and the altitude of the traffic. Twice PSA reported they saw the small plane. The controller then cleared PSA to maintain visual separation with the aircraft, and instructed PSA to change over to Lindberg tower frequency for landing clearance.

Upon contacting Lindberg tower, the tower controller also advised PSA of the other traffic. But the PSA crew had lost sight of the plane. The PSA captain radioed, "I think he's passed off to our right." But they really didn't know. The small plane was in PSA's blind spot under the nose of the aircraft. PSA should have halted the descent until the small plane was sighted again. They did not do this.

Suddenly, the copilot, who was flying the aircraft, exclaimed, "There's one underneath!" But he didn't try to maneuver the aircraft, possibly because of fatigue which dulls the senses and dulls the reaction. Shortly thereafter the captain exclaimed, "Whoop," which may have been the reaction from seeing the impending collision. The copilot moaned, "Ahhh," coinciding with the sound of impact as PSA rammed the small plane from the rear.

"What have we got here?" the captain asked. The copilot, looking at the damaged right wing which was now engulfed in flames, answered, "It's bad. We're hit, man, we *are* hit!"

PSA rammed the small plane from the rear just as the Lindberg Tower controller assured the small plane pilots that PSA had them in sight, and was maintaining visual separation. Simultaneous with this assurance, the Cessna disintegrated, falling 2700 feet to the ground.

PSA going down into San Diego residential area.

"Ma, I love you."

The impact damaged the leading edge of PSA's right wing, and the jet immediately plunged seemingly straight down into the city of San Diego. The captain sighed, "This is it, baby."

"Ma, I love you," cried one of the crewmembers, realizing he was about to die. With a terrible thunderous thump Flight 182 crashed into the heavily populated residential area, splitting apart into millions of pieces. Its human cargo instantly disintegrated, flinging headless corpses and dismembered bodies through car windows, into houses, onto rooftops, on lawns, and into the street. Walls were splattered with human remains. One body smashed through a car's windshield, killing a mother and her daughter inside the car. It was a typical air disaster crash scene, with horror that has probably never been fully conveyed in any writings!

Ironically, the first printing of *Unfriendly Skies* had just occurred, and numerous promotional copies had been sent to talk show hosts and reviewers several days before this crash. The night of the crash I was a guest on KGO radio in San Francisco. A truck driver who had just driven from the San Diego area called in, and described watching the death plunge of PSA. He was crying.

Rescuers familiar with tragedy would be receiving psychiatric treatment for months and years thereafter. Indifferent to it all were the plunderers stealing from the dead.

DIVERSIONARY TACTICS

The usual diversionary tactics of shifting responsibilities followed this great tragedy, insuring that the direct and indirect causes continue to play a role in crashes yet to come. The pilot's union (ALPA), who surely knew of the partying, which would be the primary underlying cause of the crash, obstructed disclosure of the evidence. ALPA first placed the blame on the FAA's failure to require collision avoidance systems (CAS) in aircraft. ALPA knew that the PSA pilots had been given almost as much help and information by the air traffic controllers as the CAS could have done. ALPA argued that the PSA pilots' attention had been diverted by another aircraft which they mistakenly thought was the aircraft they were to follow. But the crew fatigue—and the reason for it—was withheld, insuring that the practice that killed other crewmembers and the passengers would continue.

NEWS MEDIA PROTECTING THE AIRLINES

The press distorted the facts. And in doing so, gave the small plane capabilities that it did not possess. The press accused the small-plane pilots of ramming into PSA. But the small plane was rammed from the rear by PSA, the very opposite of what the press reported. The press protected their valuable airline advertisers. In 1978 the airlines spent over 300 million dollars for advertising, much of it in newspapers.

The small plane pilots were portrayed as incompetent and guilty of wrongdoings. The press called them student pilots, even though each pilot in the small plane had more flight time than many airline copilots. A *Newsweek* article showed the small plane *overtaking* the jet from the rear, even though the small plane was physically incapable of going that fast, and the evidence was clear that PSA rammed the small plane from the rear, and not the way the article fraudulently stated.

"Somebody committed murder..."

Columnist Jim Bishop shifted the blame for this tragedy from those who caused it onto the two victims in the small plane. Bishop wrote: "Somebody committed murder when that little Cessna slammed into the 727 at San Diego." The article, full of falsehoods, inflamed readers against general aviation pilots, and diverted attention away from those actually responsible. In this manner, Bishop and others contributed to subsequent tragedies.

In a follow-up article, Bishop continued discrediting the small plane pilots as he wrote of "the many dead private pilots showing a high alcoholic blood content." This was especially ironical since the evidence showed PSA pilots partied much of the night before.

Donald Bain, a former public relations writer for American Airlines, authored the book, *The Case Against Private Aviation*, blaming midair collisions on the small plane-pilots. The book was published by *Cowles Book Company, Inc.*, whose chairman, Gardner Cowles, also sits on the board of directors for United Airlines. (*AOPA Pilot* January 1970.) Although Bain identified himself as an air safety expert, *AOPA Pilot* magazine stated he had forty-one hours of small-plane flight time, which made him about as much of an amateur as one can get.

Columnist Jack Anderson published a similar article in the October 26, 1969 Sunday supplement, *Parade*. Anderson and his boss Jack Anderson had covered up for the FAA corruption since 1965, making possible many of the crashes that followed.

THE MOST PROBABLE CAUSE OF THE CRASH

The first inkling of what may have been the primary cause of this crash was suggested by a press release issued shortly after the tragedy. Most newspapers refused to print the report, but I happened to see it in a small-town newspaper at Yuba City, California (*Morning Herald*) on November 28, 1978 when I visited a motel I owned. The article made reference to comments made to an NTSB investigator by passenger Helen Rhea, who left Flight 182 after it landed at Los Angeles. The article stated:

Also presented at the hearing was a report from the NTSB's human factors group which included an interview with an unidentified woman passenger who got off the plane in Los Angeles before it continued to San Diego. She was asked by investigators whether she noticed anything unusual about the crew. "She heard a flight attendant say they had been up late at a party ... and that they were very tired and had only a couple of hours sleep.

That article also referred to Helen Rhea's statement about overhearing crewmembers describing the partying. The statements were dynamite, but the press put the lid on it, and public interest then ceased. Most of the news media refused to publicize the revealing and explosive comments. Unless the press emphasizes a story, and more or less tells the public to get angry, that's the end of it, unfortunately. In that manner the press kept the lid on not only the PSA scandal, but the entire air safety corruption I had sought to expose.

A subsequent *Los Angeles Times* article dated November 28, 1978, written by George Frank and Cilla Brown stated:

NTSB chief investigator Rudy Kapustin disclosed that toxicological reports showed varying amounts of ethanol alcohol in tissue samples from the remains of the crew members of both the 727 and the Cessna.

Laboratory toxicological examinations revealed significant ETOH levels in some of the cabin and cockpit crewmembers. The copilot's muscle tissue ETOH level was a significant 46 mg%, and one of the flight attendants had a 83 mg% lung tissue level. The captain's body was too shredded to be identified.

REFUSING TO ACCEPT EVIDENCE

Helen Rhea, who had gotten off PSA 182 after it landed in Los Angeles, was outraged when she heard the flight had crashed. She still remembered Lee's statement, "Our lives are in their hands, and they're hung over!" Helen immediately contacted the FAA Western Region to give a report on the conversations related to all-night crew partying. The FAA put her off and wouldn't talk to her. Helen then contacted the NTSB Los Angeles office. They wouldn't talk to her. Helen then contacted an attorney, and paid him money to arranged for the NTSB to take her statement.

Reluctantly, the NTSB took that statement, and conducted virtually no questioning of her. On her own, Helen prepared the following statement, which I later acquired from the NTSB:

On the flight returning from Sacramento, I got off in Los

Angeles. On the flight, Lee [a mortgage banker friend], who knew Debbie McCarthy, who was a flight attendant for PSA. Debbie was telling Lee, who I was sitting next to, that they had been up late at a party drinking Johnny Walker Red Label. My understanding was the whole crew was involved, and that they were very tired, and had only a couple of hours sleep. I went back to the restroom and heard the other flight attendant speaking of how tired they were, speaking of being at a party. Lee went on to San Diego.

START OF THE NTSB COVERUP
The NTSB released selected *parts* of the cockpit voice recorder transcript in response to public demand. This crash was the nation's worst air disaster at that time, and the public wanted to know what happened. The NTSB released part of the CVR recording, carefully omitting the sections reflecting absence of sleep. Not until many months later when attorneys obtained copies of the cockpit voice recording were the revealing comments discovered. A critical segment of the CVR recorded a flight attendant talking to the captain: "Tired, right?" The captain responded, ""Uh, huh. Dragging, I'm tired. Short night."

THE AIRLINE AND THE FAA KNEW OF THE WIDESPREAD PARTYING AT PSA LAYOVER STATIONS
As I later discovered, it was well known to people in the aviation industry close to PSA that partying was a standard practice among some crewmembers at overnight layovers. The company couldn't help but know this. FAA inspectors would be privy to it. It was accepted. A woman whose acquaintance I met in California told me her daughter was a PSA flight attendant and that partying did occur that night at Sacramento, and that it was a common practice.

At this point it was obvious to the NTSB that they had a very serious and a very sensitive problem on their hands. Release of the information that the crew had partied much of the night before the tragedy would outrage the public, and risk public clamor for an investigation of the entire air safety process. This would threaten many people involved in the air safety corruption and the coverup that I had tried to expose.

UNPRECEDENTED COORDINATION WITH THE JUSTICE DEPARTMENT TO BLOCK CRASH INVESTIGATION
I didn't know of an unprecedented act taken by the NTSB until a later date, and this will be described shortly. On September 30, 1978—five days after the crash—the head of the NTSB contacted the United States Attorney General for advice concerning the evidence of all-night crew partying. This was an unprecedented request, as the NTSB is an autonomous agency,

and does not seek the advice of any other government agency as to how to pursue an investigation into an airline disaster, especially when the NTSB is by law the topmost expert on the matter.

The facts indicate that the NTSB *knew* that partying existed; knew that this was a scandal; knew that the repercussions threatened to expose every government agency engaged in the ongoing air disaster scandal which I sought to expose with the first printing of the *Unfriendly Skies*. Apparently the Attorney General of the United States advised the NTSB to cover up, which of course is a criminal act. In the air safety field, the consequences of coverup are more air disasters and more deaths.

PSEUDO INVESTIGATION OF CREW PARTYING

Testimony from the maids cleaning the motel room where the party allegedly occurred would make the probable occurrence more obvious. Making an appearance that the NTSB made an investigation, the NTSB sent three people to the Host International Hotel at Sacramento where the crew partying reportedly occurred. Would you believe, one of the three so-called investigators was a PSA pilot and union member, who would be strongly motivated to cover up for extreme pilot irresponsibility associated with the nation's worst air tragedy.

Accompanying the PSA pilot were two physicians, who had no investigative experience, and could easily be stonewalled. There was no need to send two people with medical background who had no hard-investigative experience, to investigate a matter of this gravity that required highly experienced and motivate independent investigators.

Possibly to further insure coverup, the NTSB notified PSA the reason the three people were going to San Diego, and PSA was asked to further them transportation. PSA officials reached the hotel before they arrived, and convinced (or pressured) the hotel manager to block the investigation by denying access to the motel maids who cleaned the room where the partying reportedly occurred.

When the three pseudo-investigators arrived at the Host International Hotel, the manager *refused* to allow them to contact the maids who cleaned the rooms occupied by the PSA crew. This refusal was unheard of in an NTSB investigation, and even more so in light of the reason for that investigation. The hotel manager could be charged with obstructing justice, besides obstructing an air safety investigation and covering up.

The importance of the NTSB investigation into the cause of the tragedy made it mandatory that the NTSB issue subpoenas forcing the maid, and the hotel manager, to appear for questioning. This was not done. The NTSB made no effort to obtain the maid's testimony, and to determine whether PSA blocked the accident investigation. It was however, apparent that this was done.

There was already sufficient evidence of crew partying, and the testimony of the maids would simply be additional support for what already existed.

The NTSB later released a report on the crash that could not offend anyone, as it simply reported what was obvious. The covert facts were withheld. In this manner the NTSB committed several criminal acts, including coverup, falsifying the accident report by omitting key facts, obstructing an investigation.

By their wrongful acts the NTSB encouraged the continuation of the drinking problem that could have been greatly diminished if crewmembers recognized this relationship. Flight attendants and others would be less tolerant of crew partying and drinking if they realized they may end up as those people on Flight 182 ended up.

"The NTSB just shut me up."

Thereafter, I investigated the crew partying on my own. Helen Rhea had moved, and I couldn't locate her. A friend of mine, Ginger Cowan, contacted a psychic who led me to Helen's mother in Long Beach, California. I eventually reached Helen who by that time lived in Calgary, Canada. Helen gave me additional information on the conversation of the PSA Flight 182 crew from Sacramento to Los Angeles.

Helen stated to me, "I had so much anger in me," remembering the things she had been told about the crew partying, "and I wanted to let the public know." She described her problem trying to get the NTSB to take her statement. "They just shut me up. I contacted an attorney and asked him who could I go to." The attorney arranged for Helen's statement to be taken by a reluctant NTSB. Helen had to pay an attorney to get the NTSB to take a deposition showing the primary cause of the crash that was the nation's worst at that time.

REFUSAL TO DENY THE TRUTH OF DRINKING

I sent letters to the Host International Hotel and PSA, giving them an opportunity to deny my findings. The letters stated that I had evidence that crew partying existed; that PSA and the Host International Hotel blocked the NTSB investigation; and that they both covered up for this important information. I described my appearances on radio and television shows—which PSA already knew—because they had refused to appear with me on some of them. I wrote that I would be discussing these findings and suspicions on subsequent shows, and in subsequent printings of the book. I wrote that if my information was incorrect, I would make known their denials. Both refused to answer, which I equate with an admission that these allegations were true.

PARTYING WAS, AND IS, A STANDARD PRACTICE

At certain airlines drinking is more of a problem than at others, and PSA was one of the airlines that had the problem. Another indication of the prevalence of partying at PSA was reflected by a law suit filed in Superior Court at San Diego, in which a female flight attendant was awarded damages against a PSA captain in a slander action. The PSA captain entered a Long Beach hotel room occupied by several PSA flight attendants, and demanded that they go for a drink with him to the hotel bar. When the flight attendants refused, the captain spread rumors that the flight attendants were lesbians, and they were "getting it on" when he entered the room.

The point is, drinking is done openly at layover points, and has been going on for years. The NTSB's coverup of the relationship between drinking and crashes deprived the crews of realizing the dangers, and contributed to the ongoing problem and resulting crashes.

CIRCUMVENTING THE HIGH GOVERNMENT BLOCK

After the NTSB released its deceptive report on the probable cause of the PSA San Diego crash, I filed a seven-page petition with the NTSB, demanding that they reopen the investigation and enter my evidence of the crew partying. Under the Federal Aviation Act, aircraft accident investigations and reports are never closed, and must be reopened any time any party wishes to introduce evidence pertaining to the cause of the crash. Reopening the PSA investigation risked exposing not only the NTSB coverup, which was serious by itself, but also the entire on-going air disaster scandal, and those who became a part of the coverup.

INADVERTENTLY GIVING AN IMPORTANT CLUE

NTSB Chairman James B. King refused to reopen the investigation, and refused to receive my evidence. But his response inadvertently gave a clue that showed the scandal to be even bigger than I thought. His November 26, 1980 letter stated:

We have reviewed your letter of September 14, 1980, and the enclosed petition to reopen the investigation of the mid-air collision between a Pacific Southwest Boeing 727 and a Gibbs Flite Center Cessna 172 at San Diego, California, on September 25, 1978.

The allegations to which you refer were known to the Board 5 days following the accident and were thoroughly investigated by the Board.

Additionally, the matter was discussed with the Deputy U.S. Attorney General, and on behalf of the Department of

Justice, he declined to take any further action. The Board remains convinced, based on its own original investigation and the decision by the Department of Justice not to pursue this matter, that the allegations are not supported by substantial evidence. Therefore, your petition to reopen the investigation and hearing is hereby denied.

Thoroughly investigated? He was lying. Boy scouts could have made a more meaningful investigation of the alleged partying. But even more revealing was the statement that the NTSB contacted the Attorney General of the United States concerning the matter. This is never done. The NTSB investigation of airline crashes do not require advice from the political Attorney General of the United States.

The NTSB must have recognized the danger of revealing the crew partying in the nation's worst air tragedy, and coming on the heels of the ongoing air disaster scandal that I sought to expose with the recently published *Unfriendly Skies*. There is no other reason for contacting the highest security office in the United States when the NTSB has the responsibility and competency to make investigations relating to airline crashes. The Attorney General has no expertise, no legal responsibility, and no right to interfere or influence investigations of airline crashes.

EVIDENCE FAR IN EXCESS OF WHAT THE NTSB NORMALLY RELIES UPON TO REACH THE PROBABLE CAUSE OF AN AIRLINE CRASH

The NTSB often states as the probable cause of a crash causes for which there are no hard-evidence, and rely upon speculation (and political considerations). In this crash the evidence of crew partying far exceeded probable causes stated in other crashes. The NTSB had the CVR recording showing extreme fatigue that should not exist. They had Helen Rhea's statement of specifics concerning the crew partying. They had the toxicological reports showing alcohol in the bodies of several crew members. They had the blockage of an investigation by the hotel manager where the crew partying reportedly took place.

COVERUP CONSPIRACY BETWEEN NTSB AND JUSTICE DEPARTMENT

The first printing of the *Unfriendly Skies* had just come out shortly before the PSA crash. I was appearing on the first of many radio and television appearances. The book and my appearances exposed the government corruption related to a series of major air tragedies that implicated the Department of Justice and the NTSB. The horror of the PSA crash was front-page news for many months. Exposing the PSA partying and the coverup activities had the potential of causing public outrage, and expanding into the other areas of air safety misconduct.

The biggest block to exposing the air disaster corruption was the U.S. Department of Justice, under the highly political office of the United States Attorney General.[48] The Justice Department refused to conduct an investigation when I made formal complaints as a government air safety investigator in the mid-1960s. The Justice Department blocked my 1965 attempts to get a federal grand jury at Denver to conduct a grand jury investigation. The Justice Department blocked my attempted exposure and corrective actions in the 1974 law suit against the FAA. Now, the Justice Department blocked my attempts to expose the NTSB coverup. This coverup continued and expanded for years thereafter, including today. In the 1990s the Justice Department obstruction of justice, and actions taken to silence the scandal, plays a key role in some of the nation's most brutal air tragedies.

Under federal statutory and case law, a party can file a federal law suit to force a government agency to comply with the law. I exercised that right, and filed a law suit against the NTSB.[49] The law suit sought to compel the NTSB to perform its duty, and in this case, reopen the accident investigation into the PSA crash and several other crashes, and admit evidence of misconduct as the causative element in the crashes that occurred.

ASSISTANT U.S.ATTORNEY SUPPORTED THE LAW SUIT

After I filed the 1980 action, assistant U.S. Attorney George Stoll in the San Francisco office contacted me by phone, and agreed with me that the NTSB should be required to reopen the investigation. During this conversation, Stoll stated:

> It's ridiculous that the NTSB did not investigate further into the reported partying. ... The investigation should be reopened. ... I am going to bring pressure on them [NTSB] through the Department of Justice to see if they won't reopen the investigation. ... the government has responsibility to see to it that its agencies do their jobs. ... I can go ahead and file a motion to dismiss in the next few days, but I'm not satisfied with that because I don't think in this case the government's skirts are totally clean, and I don't think it's my job to cover up. ... I agree with you that what she

---

[48] This office has been occupied by such persons as Mitchell, who was later indicted and sent to federal prison; Edwin Meese, linked to Webtech and other scandals; and others accused of serious wrongdoings.

[49] *Stich v. National Transportation Safety Board*, 685 F.2d 446 (9th Cir.)(table), cert. denied, 459 U.S. 861 (1982).

said [PSA passenger Helen Rhea] was far more than an investigator in many cases is reasonably likely to hear. It certainly is pregnant with some very serious implications. ... it is ridiculous [referring to the NTSB coverup].

Stoll stated that he was recommending to his superiors in Washington that the government support my action, and that the NTSB be ordered to reopen the investigation and admit evidence of the crew partying. He also stated that he was recommending that the NTSB be investigated, as was obviously necessary.

Morally correct but naive, Assistant U.S. Attorney Stoll was unaware of the long history of air safety misconduct, and the part played in it by the Department of Justice. I knew that Stoll's recommendations would be denied. If Stoll was not blocked, the free-world's worst ongoing air safety scandal would be exposed, implicating high government offices with corruption and sacrificing lives by their coverup.

The Department of Justice instructed the U.S. Attorney at San Francisco to file a motion to dismiss the action against the NTSB. Although Stoll earlier admitted the NTSB misconduct, he was overridden by Justice Department politics. Reversing its earlier position and statements made to me, the office of the U.S. Attorney at San Francisco argued in the motion to dismiss: "There is no question in this case that the Board has performed its duty and conducted a substantial investigation." A coverup like this would put the average citizen in prison.

The complaint against the NTSB had been assigned to federal Judge Stanley Weigel in the Northern District of California at San Francisco. During the various motions by the U.S. Attorney to dismiss the law suit, Wiegel admitted the gravity and probable consequences of the allegations in my complaint. Under federal case law, the allegations in the complaint must be accepted as true in opposing motions to dismiss.

The law suit could be dismissed only if my allegations did not state facts constituting a federal cause of action. Judge Wiegel dismissed the action, falsely stating that I was appealing an order of the NTSB, and that it came under federal statute, Title 49 U.S.C. Section 1903(d). I did not file my cause of action under that statute. I did not appeal an order. I filed it under Title 28 United States Code Section 1361, giving federal courts the authority to force an administrative agency to comply with the law, and halt unlawful acts.

Judge Wiegel stated in part, "This is a matter that is properly before the Court of Appeals, and in a way I am sorry, because it is a fascinating subject and I would like very much to have it before me. But under the law, I don't think I properly can."

Judge Wiegel stated that it should have been filed in the U.S. Court of Appeals. That was incorrect. But, if the complaint was filed in the wrong federal court, under law he was required, in the interest of justice, to transfer the case to the Court of Appeals, rather than dismiss the action.

REPEATING EARLIER CONSEQUENCES

Judge Wiegel knew of the many deaths in the Paris DC-10 tragedy arising from the FAA and NTSB misconduct, and the many other fatal crashes that would not have occurred without the judicial coverup. The deaths to which he would become a party didn't appear to bother him in the least.

I then filed an appeal which was heard by Judges James Browning, Joseph Sneed, and Mary Schroeder, who also admitted the gravity of my allegations. In their May 27, 1982 decision, the judges dismissed my appeal, stating:

Although appellant's concern for the safety of future airline passengers is commendable, in view of the recent decision of the United States Supreme Court in *Valley Forge Christian College v. Americans United for Separation of Church and State, Inc.*, 102 S.Ct. 752 (1982), the judgment [of dismissal] must be affirmed.

Article III of the United States Constitution limits federal court jurisdiction to "cases or controversies." Consistent with this limitation, litigants may not make claims for relief in federal court without showing an actual or threatened personal injury. "[A]t an irreducible minimum, Art. III requires the party who invokes the court's authority to 'show that he personally has suffered some actual or threatened injury as a result of the putatively illegal conduct of the defendant ....'" *Valley Forge, supra*, 102 S.Ct. at 758, *quoting Gladstone, Realtors v. Village of Bellwood*, 441 U.S. 91, 99, 99 S.Ct. 1601, 1608 (1979). Even absent an article III bar, this court should refrain from adjudicating disputes based on generalized grievances shared by all citizens. *Warth v. Seldin*, 422 U.S. 490, 499-500, 95 S.Ct. 2197, 2205-06 (1975).

Stich's concern, the risk of future airline crashes, is real enough. That concern does not, however, rise to the level of an actual or threatened injury. The risk is shared by Americans generally. Absent an injury which threatens Stich in a way which distinguishes him from the populace as a whole, federal court action is barred.

[Dismissal is] Affirmed.

The judges knew I was the only person with the hard evidence and willingness to produce it, relating to matters that if not addressed, would continue to result in the deaths of thousands of persons. I then filed a petition for writ of certiorari with the United States Supreme Court,[50] seeking to vacate the dismissal by the district court. The Justices of the U.S. Supreme Court covered up—misprision of a felony being one of the crimes—and denied to hear my petition. In this manner the deaths of many people whose lives could have been saved would be on their hands.

Another federal statute that requires federal courts to exercise jurisdiction when the Federal Aviation Act is violated is Title 49 United States Code Section 1487.

> Any party in interest may apply to the district court of the United States ... for the enforcement of ... this Act, or such rule, regulation, requirement, ... such court shall have jurisdiction to enforce obedience thereto by a writ of injunction or other process, mandatory or otherwise, restraining such person, his officers, ... from further violations of such provision of this Act or of such rule, regulation, requirement ... and requiring their obedience thereto.

My present law suit fell under that statute, among others, as did law suits that I would file in the future which addressed violations of federal law relating to air safety.

In an earlier action against the Federal Aviation administration,[51] the same judicial coverup occurred. (And helped make this and other crashes possible.) In that earlier action against the FAA, the Ninth Circuit Court of Appeal judges were Herbert Choy, Warren Ferguson, and Anthony Kennedy (who was later appointed to the U.S. Supreme Court). These Court of Appeal judges covered up for the FAA corruption and dismissed my appeal, stating in part:

> Stich appeals the dismissal of his petition for a writ of mandamus by the district court. He argues that the district court had jurisdiction and that he had standing to sue. Although appellant's concern for the safety of future airline passengers is commendable, in view of the recent decision of the United States Supreme Court in *Valley Forge Christian College v. Americans United for Separation of Church*

---

[50] No 82-93.

[51] *Stich v. United States, et al.*, 554 F.2d 1070 (9th Cir.) (table), cert. denied, 434 U.S. 920 (1977).

and State, Inc., 102 S.Ct. 752 (1982), the judgment must be affirmed.

Article III of the United States Constitution limits federal court jurisdiction to "cases or controversies." Consistent with this limitation, litigants may not make claims for relief in federal court without showing an actual or threatened personal injury. "[A]t an irreducible minimum, Art. III requires the party who invokes the court's authority to 'show that he personally has suffered some actual or threatened injury as a result of the putatively illegal conduct of the defendant ....'" *Valley Forge, supra*, 102 S.Ct. at 758, *quoting Gladstone, Realtors v. Village of Bellwood*, 441 U.S. 91, 99, 99 S.Ct. 1601, 1608 (1979). Even absent an article III bar, this court should refrain from adjudicating disputes based on generalized grievances shared by all citizens. *Warth v. Seldin*, 422 U.S. 490, 499-500, 95 S.Ct. 2197, 2205-06 (1975).

Stich's concern, the risk of future airline crashes, is real enough. That concern does not, however, rise to the level of an actual or threatened injury. The risk is shared by Americans generally. Absent an injury which threatens Stich in a way which distinguishes him from the populace as a whole, federal action is barred. [district court's dismissal is] Affirmed.

Every level of the federal courts blocked my attempts to prevent the litany of major air disasters arising from the internal FAA and NTSB corruption.[52] They all violated criminal statutes that apply to judges as much as to anyone else, if not more so. They all willingly sacrificed the lives that would be lost by the coverup.

The district and appellate judges held they had no right to interfere in government functions, although statutory and case law specifically required them to do so when citizens brought complaints under the law. The same federal judiciary ordered the Transportation Department to reopen its investigation of

---

[52] *Stich v. United States, et al.*, 554 F.2d 1070 (9th Cir.) (table), *cert. denied*, 434 U.S. 920 (1977)(addressed hard-core air safety corruption); *Stich v. National Transportation Safety Board*, 685 F.2d 446 (9th Cir.)(table), *cert. denied*, 459 U.S. 861 (1982))(addressed repeated falsification of official airline accident reports, omitting highly sensitive air safety misconduct); Amicus curiae brief filed on July 17, 1975, in the Paris DC-10 multi-district litigation, *Flanagan v. McDonnell Douglas Corporation and United States of America*, Civil Action 74-808-PH, MDL 172, Central District California.)(addressing the long standing FAA misconduct, of which the coverup of the DC-10 cargo door problem was one of repeated instances of tragedy related misconduct); U.S. v. Department of Justice, District of Columbia, Nos. 86-2523, 87-2214, and other actions.

alleged safety defects in Ford Motor Company cars made before 1979 (*Associated Press* September 9, 1987), and in numerous similar cases. The U.S. District Court of Appeals in the District of Columbia ruled that a lower federal court judge improperly dismissed a lawsuit by the Center for Auto Safety to force the National Highway Transportation Safety Administration to reopen the investigation of transmissions in 23 million Ford cars.

In this action against a federal agency relating to auto safety oversight responsibilities, the appellate judges said

> denials of petitions to investigate alleged safety defects ... are subject to judicial review under the Administrative Procedure Act" to assure that the agency properly enforces its auto safety standards.

This holding made my allegations associated with specific corruption and specific air tragedies especially timely. The case stemmed from the Center for Auto Safety's efforts in 1985 to force a new investigation of Ford transmissions that critics contend slide from park to reverse when the engine is running.

The federal courts stonewalled every attempt I made to expose the corruption in the two government air safety agencies, and the coverup by the Department of Justice.

CONGRESS WAS AWARE OF THE CRIMES

Throughout the last two decades I repeatedly brought evidence of the worsening air safety corruption to the attention of Congress. Each subsequent coverup permitted more tragedies to occur, and further solidified the need for Congressional stonewalling to protect their own involvement. I sent a letter to Mayor Pete Wilson of San Diego on April 17, 1980, along with a copy of *Unfriendly Skies* so that he knew the details of the corruption. Pete Wilson never answered; he covered up. He continued to cover up after he became a Senator from California, and refused to respond to subsequent letters and petitions.

A *San Francisco Chronicle* article dated January 12, 1990 stated of Senator Wilson:

> He took his first special-interest payment barely two weeks after he became a United States senator. And during his first year in Washington ... he collected nearly $70,000. Or to put it another way, in 1983 the special interests paid him more for being a United States senator than the people did. ... Wilson has accepted more than $200,000 [in honorariums] money that went straight into his pocket."

Another article in the same paper on February 6, 1990 charged
Wilson with accepting $105,000 in contributions from the
scandal-plagued savings and loan industry, and charging him
with the same guilt as charged to the Keating-Five Senators.

NTSB INTRIGUE ... OR CORRUPTION

NTSB coverup has been well established within these pages.
These acts were crimes. These acts continued air safety
problems, violations, and corruption. These acts made possible,
caused, contributed to, subsequent air tragedies and deaths.
The nature of the misconduct is a crime with international
implications. Citizens of foreign countries have died, and will
continue to die, as a result of these crimes.

The politically appointed members of the National Transportation Safety Board are part of a political cesspool, tampering
with airline accident reports, omitting crash-causing air safety
misconduct, covering up for FAA and its own corruption bribes.

BRIBING OF NTSB BY AIRLINES

Exposing one tentacle of the political machine and bribery
in the NTSB, William Gingery, a member of the NTSB Board,
left a suicide note referring to the NTSB's politics adversely
affecting air safety. The note implicated Richard J. O'Melia,
acting chairman of the Board at that time, alleging obstruction
of an investigation into illegal political contributions by various
airlines. The Congressional subcommittee looking into these
payoffs asked O'Melia about the charges made in the suicide
note. As expected, O'Melia denied the allegations. O'Melia
then turned around and accused Board member Timm of ordering
him to stop these investigations, which Timm denied.

In 1971 President Nixon appointed Richard Spears as chief
administrator of the NTSB. His qualifications: none in air
safety, but he was a Republican political aide. Weiss proceeded
to interfere with the NTSB's safety functions. The White House
also tried to change the classification of the NTSB head from
civil service to political appointee to gain further control of
this government agency.

Shortly after the White House moved Speers into the head
of the NTSB, Speers wrote a letter on NTSB letterhead to
Robert Six, President of Continental Airlines, seeking a job for
a White House aide, Harry Fleming. The letter reminded Six
that Fleming had good connections with the White House and
could be very productive.

EMASCULATION OF NTSB INVESTIGATIVE FUNCTIONS

The number of accident investigators were reduced, but the
administrative staff that had nothing to do with accident
investigations was increased. Spears set a policy ignoring the
Accident Prevention Branch within the NTSB that was often
critical of the FAA in its reports. The staff was systematically

destroyed. They were denied training courses and ignored for promotions. On March 1, 1974, the valuable branch was abolished.

In an earlier 1972 report, James Reed, the head of the NTSB, recommended to Congress that the NTSB be made completely independent of the Department of Transportation. Before the report was sent to Congress, Egil Krogh, Jr., a White House aide, warned NTSB Chairman Reed that his proposed recommendation was looked at in disfavor by President Nixon. Krogh warned that if the recommendation was not withdrawn, the Republican members of the NTSB Board would be disciplined. When the Senate learned of the threat, it investigated, and stated at the hearing:

> This is no matter of bureaucratic nicety. The NTSB was established to insure the optimum safety of the travelling public. To the extent that the Board's voice has been muted, to the extent that the Board has failed to monitor those operating agencies charged with the safety of the traveling public, and to the extent that the board has failed to press for compliance with its recommendations for safety-related reforms, the safety of the public was well as the integrity of the governmental process have been gravely compromises.[53]

What were Krogh's abilities in the air safety field? He was an attorney with John Ehrlichman's Seattle law firm; headed the Plumbers unit in Nixon White House; worked with Gordon Liddy and other Watergate participants; involved in the Ellsberg break-in.

On March 14, 1973, President Nixon appointed Alexander Butterfield to be FAA Administrator. Butterfield had been a little-known aide to Bob Haldeman, who was later involved in the Watergate fiasco. Ironically, it was Butterfield, who several months later[54] revealed the existence of the White House tapes, that eventually led to Nixon's resignation.

During Butterfield's first year as FAA Administrator, the same hit and miss safety measures favoring specific manufacturers and airlines continued. The DC-10 problems remained uncorrected. Voluntary service bulletins were issued, when airworthiness directives were required by the urgency and nature of the dangers. The end result were the deaths of 346 people in only one of many related air tragedies.

---

[53] Oversight Hearings before the Aviation Sub-Committee of the Senate on the duties of the National Transportation Safety Board, May 21, 1972.
[54] July 16, 1973.

The NTSB was under political attack from Nixon's White House gang to back off on its pressure on the airlines and manufacturers. In 1972, fund-raiser Buckley Byers for the Committee to Re-Elect the President (CREEP), asked FAA head Shaffer for a list of aerospace people who might contribute to Nixon's campaign. Shaffer didn't endear himself to the White House when he advised Byers that a list of aerospace executives would be found in the World Aviation Directory.

President Nixon had shortly before sent Shaffer a glowing tribute for "bringing credit not only on yourself but on my administration." After Nixon's reelection, Nixon accepted Shaffer's resignation (which are routinely submitted after every presidential election). Shaffer than cashed in his chips in the revolving door syndrome, and became a director of Beech Aircraft Corporation on March 13, 1973—while he was still Administrator of the Federal Aviation Administration.

Before joining Beech, Shaffer had been protective of Beech by refusing to force correction of serious design problems that led to numerous deaths, including the infamous V-tail Bonanza aircraft tail assembly. (Over 200 inflight disintegrations have occurred due to that design problem.)

In April 1974 a Senate committee received testimony that the Accident Prevention Branch was rendered ineffective "because they were one of the principal 'over-view' activities ... critical of the FAA." The White house was shown as covering up for FAA misconduct.

In 1975 both Houses of Congress passed legislation removing the NTSB from the Department of Transportation. It was however, still run by political appointees, and Mr. Spears remained as general manager

These politics may explain why the NTSB covered up with deadly consequences the hard-core misconduct, much of it criminal, that caused and permitted to occur some of the air tragedies described within these pages.

The public has seen years of government corruption; it has seen the nation's greatest financial debacle in the savings and loan corruption. Should it be so hard to understand that corruption after affects the two government air safety agencies?

This chapter looks at government corruption, and industry coverup that makes it possible. Possibly then the reader will not find the sordid air tragedy related corruption so hard to understand.

Among the many check-and-balance coverups that kept this scandal going for the past 25 years and longer were members of the United States Senate and House. I advised many of them of the FAA corruption in 1965. As in the HUD, the savings and loan, and other government scandals, they all covered up. And many people paid with their lives for this duplicity.

Most of those I contacted admitted the gravity of my allegations, as they should; I was an insider, and had the government position to make such determinations. I had the hard evidence. I had nothing to gain, and everything to lose, by coming forth. Repeated air tragedies supported my allegations.

The brutality of the consequences was so serious that refusal to act would be obscene, with death consequences for thousands of people. The life and death consequences, if my allegations were true, made the refusal to investigate inexcusable. Every check and balance showed contempt for the terrible consequences by refusing to conduct an investigation.

THE NEXT BIG ONE—CERRITOS

California had another big midair collision not more than 100 miles from the PSA San Diego tragedy. August 31, 1986 started out as a beautiful Sunday morning in the Los Angeles area. A small plane (Piper PA 28-181) took off from Torrance Airport heading east for Big Bear Lake. On board was the pilot, William Kramer, who had several thousand hours of flight time. With him were his wife and daughter. The small plane was passing an area near the Los Angeles suburb of Cerritos, where a thin sliver of restricted airspace (1000 feet) protruded out from the Terminal Control Area (TCA) where aircraft must have permission to enter. The fragmented nature of the TCA at Cerritos made it difficult to know precisely where the boundaries were. Many planes entered the airspace unknowingly every day, making it obvious to the FAA changes had to be made, and that the airspace could not be considered inviolate.

Entering the Los Angeles area from the south was an Aeromexico DC-9, Flight 498, for landing at Los Angeles International Airport. The DC-9 pilots, without a flight engineer, were busy reading to each other the approach and before-landing checklists, checking their radios, and setting up frequencies and radials. They weren't looking out for other traffic, a common problem due to the absence of the engineer.

Both the small plane and the DC-9 were on the air traffic controller's radar screen. But for some reason the controller did not advise the DC-9 of the other aircraft's presence. The small plane had a transponder, but it did not transmit altitude information. Despite the urgency for an altitude reporting transponder, the FAA never required it.

The DC-9 pilots, on a northwesterly hearing, headed straight at the small plane that was flying on an easterly heading, approaching the small plane from slightly aft of the right wing. The small plane appeared in the windshield of the DC-9 for at least a minute, but neither DC-9 pilots saw the plane; probably due to their high cockpit workload caused by the FAA's removal of the flight engineer requirement.

The fast-moving DC-9 coming in from the right side of the small plane was not obvious to the small plane pilot. A pilot simply does not look out the extreme left and right sides of their aircraft as much as they look forward.

Accidentally, the small plane penetrated the thin sliver of restricted airspace between 6,000 and 7,000 feet as dozens of others have done. This time the space was occupied.

BRUTAL IMPACT!

The DC-9 rammed into the side of the small plane with its horizontal tail surfaces shearing off the top of the small plane and decapitating the pilot, his wife, and daughter, coating the top of the small plane's wing with their blood. The horizontal stabilizer ripped off the DC-9, destabilizing the jet, and causing it to plunge almost straight down.

The DC-9 impacted directly onto a house in which a party had gathered. The house instantly disintegrated, killing 15 people on the ground. The brutality was similar to that in the PSA San Diego crash.

The NTSB investigated the crash and issued its report. The blame was placed on the difficulty of visual separation; the small plane pilot's entry into the restricted airspace; and the controller's failure to notify the DC-9 pilot of the small plane's presence.

OMITTING A PRIMARY CAUSE OF THE CRASH

Nothing was stated in the NTSB report about the increased workload placed on the DC-9 pilots by the FAA's elimination of the previously required flight engineer, which increased the workload of the airline pilots, contributing to their failure to see the small plane. Identifying the flight engineer problem would cause major financial costs to be inflicted upon the airlines and have major political repercussions. Changes to the cockpit arrangement would be required (although the problem could be partly addressed by having the flight engineer sit between the pilots, as in the DC-6 and DC-7 aircraft). Too much money was at stake to address the dangers arising from elimination of the flight engineer. The problem continues, and is getting worse. Disregarding the dangers arising from eliminating the flight engineer, the FAA approved the huge Boeing 747-400, carrying as many as 500 persons, to be certificated without a flight engineer.

MANY NEAR-COLLISIONS

It is difficult to understand why there have not been more midair collisions in light of the many near-collisions that missed becoming major holocausts by as little as fifty feet. The potential for such tragedies is huge. A few examples. An American and TWA aircraft avoid a collision by the quick reaction of one of the pilots. The planes missed each other by a matter of less than 100 feet. The fortuitous spotting of the other aircraft, and instantaneous reaction of the American Airlines crew, avoided what would have otherwise been an aviation disaster. Unfortunately, the violent evasive maneuver seriously injured three people on the American Airlines flight.

Two Pan American wide-body jets approached each other head on, with a closure speed approaching 1000 miles an hour, due to controller mistake, and missed each other by a hundred feet. A United and TWA flight passed within 100 feet of each other when a radar controller failed to notice that one airplane was overtaking the other at the same altitude. On that same day two other planes, a North Central Airlines Convair 580 and a twin engine Cessna nearly collided when two radar controllers failed to coordinate their control activities. Seven days later an Eastern Airlines jet and a military fighter nearly crashed into each other when controllers allowed the two planes to occupy the same altitudes at the same location.

On New Year's day, January 1, 1984, two Pan Am planes carrying 496 people avoid a midair holocaust in the last few seconds when one of the pilots sees the other, and dives to avoid the collision. It was estimated by some that the planes missed each other by as little as fifty feet. ATC controllers assigned both aircraft to the same altitude on the same route, by error. A Pan Am flight narrowly missed experiencing a midair collision with American Airlines, approaching each other head-on at 29,000 feet, at combined speeds exceeding 1,000 miles per hour. This was another error of both planes assigned the same altitude on the same route.

An American Airlines DC-10 and a Transworld L-1011 almost collided at 35,000 feet near Carleton, Michigan on November 26, 1975, at night in instrument conditions. The American crew saw the impending collision through the clouds and made an emergency evasive maneuver, narrowing missing a midair collision, and resulting in serious injuries to several occupants.

These aren't isolated examples; they happen all the time. Luck has simply been on our side.

DEREGULATION'S EFFECT ON MIDAIR COLLISIONS

After deregulation the midair collision danger increased due to the change in route structure, in which the airlines adopted a hub and spoke system to replace the former direct routing. Added to this problem is the inadequate number of airports and runways to handle the ever increasing traffic. In 1988, for instance, there were virtually no new airports planned, despite the urgent need for them. The FAA, who should emphasize and focus attention on this serious problem, remained quiet.

EFFECT OF FATIGUE ON AIR SAFETY

Fatigue plays a part in crashes, and is rarely identified by the NTSB. A crewmember may be on duty for 16 hours, or twice the working day of the average person. And that long duty time may not *start* until the end of the day, when the pilot had already been awake for many hours. The consequences are either fatal, or near-fatal. The PSA San Diego crash is of course a good example of fatigued-induced disaster.

A little-publicized fatigue incident occurred when a United DC-8 flight from New York to Los Angeles overflew their Los Angeles destination. The entire cockpit crew was asleep. The pilots lowered the volume on their radios to the point where they couldn't hear the radio transmissions from the air traffic controllers, who tried to give United clearance to descend. An alert (and possibly understanding) controller notified United Airlines that the overflying crew could not be reached by radio. United then called the crew by company radio, which alerts the crew by chimes in the cockpit. The crew woke up, and then contacted Los Angeles Approach Control. The newspapers kept the incident quiet.

COLLISION AVOIDANCE EQUIPMENT

The collision avoidance system that was promised in the early 1950s finally became a reality and required installation commencing in the early 1990s. In 1960 the *New York Times* had headlines proclaiming the imminent installation of collision avoidance equipment. Thirty years later, with the prodding of Congress, the collision avoidance equipment became a reality.

For the collision avoidance equipment (TCAS) to be fully effective, all planes, large and small, should have altitude-encoding transponders. At the present time this is required only in selected locations. Therefore, if a small plane inadvertently strays into airspace requiring an altitude-encoder transponder, the air traffic controller is unaware of the plane's altitude, and the airliner's collision avoidance equipment is ineffective.

For many years there were usable collision-avoidance systems on the market, one of which was extensively used by the Army, and which were relatively inexpensive. The FAA procrastinated and refused to approve any of them.

"Dirtier with the blood of countless victims"

Speaking of the FAA's mishandling of the midair collision problem, Congressman Henry Gonzalez stated on the floor of the House of Representatives: "[The FAA Administrator's] hands are not as clean as he would like them to be, and they will, in my judgment, get dirtier with the blood of countless victims of air tragedies if his policies are allowed to continue."

Gonzales claimed the FAA was playing "Russian roulette with the lives of people in the skies over Texas" by closing an unneeded ATC facility in Gonzales's district.[55] This was public posturing.

THE TARGET OF GONZALEZ'S WRATH

Gonzalez's rhetoric wasn't to improve safety; it was to get Halaby. The charges Gonzalez made against Halaby failed to focus on the hard-core internal FAA and NTSB problems. Halaby had ordered the removal of an FAA office from Gonzalez's district in a consolidation move, and Gonzalez objected.

Halaby[56] wrote about this aspect of the political fallouts from air safety decisions in his book, *Cross-Winds, an Airmen's Memoir*. He also described other aspects of the political pressures from ALPA, the airlines, members of the Senate and House. He eulogized some of those within the FAA and even at United that were most responsible for the air tragedies that made repeated headlines. He describes the attitude of airlines and others refusing to discuss air safety problems on the assumption "if we don't talk about it, the problem may go away attitude."

Halaby described his error in blaming the captain of a Continental Airlines 707 that crashed due to a bomb explosion, and his examination of the wreckage:[57]

I remember lifting up a metal piece of the top of the cockpit in the hole the cabin had bored into the ground, and there was the open skull of the captain with the red-warm, almost live brains draining out. I almost threw up; I was terribly shaken. [Halaby then described his error of blaming the crash on the pilot] "That's what happens when you fly through thunderstorms." There was no thunderstorms involved in the crash. A bomb blew off the tail.

INTERNAL FAA COMPLAINTS OF MIDAIR PROBLEMS

Just before reaching retirement, an FAA employee friend wrote:

The undersigned is in receipt of information that indicates refusal on the part of United Air Lines flight crew members to report near midair incidents. Violations filed against UAL

---

[55] Gonzales won his Congressional seat in a district that was heavily dependent on federal largesse, including FAA facilities.

[56] Administrator of the FAA after Quesada was ousted until July 1, 1965 (during my exposure of hard-core FAA corruption). Halaby then became chairman and chief executive officer of Pan American World Airways, until March 22, 1972.

[57] Centerville, Iowa, May 22, 1962.

flight crewmembers for reporting near midair incidents is the reason given by United flight crews. The number of subject reports previously reported to this office by United also indicate that near midair incidents are occurring but not being reported. The near-miss incidents will not be corrected by merely sweeping them under the rug. It is therefore suggested that higher authority in the Western Region assist in attempting to alleviate this condition.

By coincidence this report was dated the same day Congressman Gonzalez blasted the FAA's position on the floor of the House of Representatives. I obtained a copy of that report before it too, disappeared from the FAA files.

Referring to the midair collision problem and the FAA's handling of it, *Federal Times* said of warnings by the air traffic controller group, "The arguments they presented were convincing—and frightening. The controllers charged that near misses are a regular occurrence ... as many as five to nine each week take place in the Washington-Boston air corridor."

WORLD'S WORST AIR DISASTER—ALMOST

A Delta Airlines Lockheed 1011 narrowly—extremely narrowly—missed ramming a Continental 747 by an estimated *fifty feet* in July of 1987. Delta was sixty miles off course, and slowly overtaking the Continental jet which was going in the same direction. The Continental 747 was visible in Delta's windshield for at least ten minutes, without any of the three Delta crewmembers aware of the other plane's presence. The near-collision was so close that passengers in each aircraft could see the rivets and the faces in the other aircraft.

Although the Continental pilots were blameless, passengers rushed up to the flight station door and pounded on it, demanding to know what was going on.

The Delta crew was off-course because the pilots programed the navigation system incorrectly, and then compounded that by failing to check their position as they passed each checkpoint. On top of these errors they failed to look outside the aircraft for other traffic.

These errors were then compounded. After the near-collision, the Delta captain radioed to the Continental crew and asked them to keep the near-collision a secret. Over 600 persons witnessed their near-deaths, and the Delta captain thought the matter could be kept secret! In addition, the radio communication was heard by crewmembers in other aircraft over thousands of square miles, making it ridiculously improbable that the near calamity could be kept secret.

COLLIDING WITH GROUND OBJECTS

A few other collisions: A B-25 twin-engine Air Force bomber

rammed into New York City's Empire State Building in July 1945, with parts of the aircraft exiting out the other side. The crash killed thirteen persons, instead of the hundreds who would have perished if the crash happened during the week when the offices were heavily occupied.

A similar ramming of a sky scrapper nearly occurred when an Argentina Boeing 707 misunderstood the air traffic controller's clearance, and descended to 1500 instead of 2700 feet. Flying in instrument conditions with low ceilings, the 707 headed straight for the World Trade Center which was 250 feet higher than the 707 was flying. The automation of many ATC facilities included an altitude warning horn, which sounded, drawing the controller's attention to the impending crash. The controller immediately radioed the 707 to confirm its altitude, and when advised that it was 1500 feet, instructed the 707 in a frantic voice to immediately turn right to a heading of one eight zero degrees and climb to 3,000 thousand feet.

COLLISION THREATS ON GROUND

Collisions between aircraft are not confined to the air. Ironically, the world's worst collision between two aircraft occurred on the ground at Tenerife in the Canary Islands. A KLM 747 jet took off on a fog shrouded runway without a takeoff clearance, knowing that a Pan Am 747 had been on the runway. The KLM captain, over the objections of the other two crewmembers, stubbornly ignored them. The death toll was 583 people. Numerous ground collisions, and near-collisions, have since occurred.

Many actual and near-ground collisions between aircraft occur in the United States. In one of numerous Tenerife-like incidents, the *flight engineer* on a Northwest DC-10 taking off at Minneapolis International Airport, on June 1985, hollered, "Don, there's a whale going right across the runway!" Right before their eyes there was another DC-10 crossing the runway. The pilot had just received training describing the ability of a plane to lift-off before the normal rotation speed, and he tried it out to avoid ramming the other plane. "Jesus Christ!" exclaimed the captain of the DC-10 who was almost rammed. The planes missed either other by less than fifty feet. It was that close to being another Tenerife. NTSB Chairman Jim Burnett called it *almost* the worst United States air tragedy in history.[58]

A Pan Am shuttle 727 at Boston also pulled up abruptly during takeoff to avoid hitting another plane, missing it by less than fifty feet, in 1988. A Japan Airlines 747 rammed into a

---

[58] *Aviation Week & Space Technology* July 1, 1985.

commuter plane at Anchorage in December 1983, injuring eight people. In the same month, a Boeing 727 and DC-9 collided in Madrid, killing 115 persons. An Emery DC-8 rammed into an Airborne Express DC-9 at Stewart International Airport at Newburgh, New York on August 20, 1987, severing the tail of the DC-9. At LaGuardia two planes nearly collided when a DC-9 taxiing down the runway was almost rammed by a corporate jet taking off on the same runway going in the opposite direction on August 29, 1978. A landing Flying Tiger 747 suffered considerable damage as it swerved off the runway to avoid hitting a Delta Airlines 727 at Chicago's O'Hare Airport on February 15, 1979. A Korean Airlines DC-10 and a commuter plane were destroyed following a ground collision at Anchorage on December 23, 1983. The Korean crew tried to take off on the wrong runway.

A fatal crash occurred at Chicago's O'Hare Airport on December 20, 1972, when the tower controller failed to insure that the runway was clear before issuing a takeoff clearance. During poor visibility conditions (half mile visibility and 200 foot-ceiling), the tower controller cleared a North Central DC-9 for takeoff. But a Delta 880 jet was not clear of the runway. Just prior to liftoff, at over 150 miles per hour, the DC-9 rammed into the Delta 880 with fatal consequences.

The tower controller cleared a TWA 707 for takeoff at Greater Cincinnati Airport without checking that a previously landed Delta DC-9 was clear of the active runway. The DC-9 had taxied off the runway and missed the taxiway, becoming bogged down in the mud, with its tail in the path of planes taking off. The TWA 707 hit the tail of the other aircraft during the takeoff with serious damage to the aircraft.

A fatal crash occurred at Atlanta's Hartsfield Airport at night on January 18, 1990, when a landing Eastern 727 crashed onto a twin-engine Beechcraft Kingair that had just landed. The entire top half of the Kingair was sheared off, killing one of the pilots and seriously injuring another. Minutes earlier the controller's attention had been diverted by a reported hydraulic problem on an approaching Eastern flight.

A Tenerife-type crash in the United States is only a matter of time.

CHAPTER FOURTEEN

Air Traffic Control

The airspace and runways are obviously becoming more cluttered. Numerous factors led to conditions which cause traffic congestions and delays. Airlines' scheduling changes from direct flights to hub-and-spoke operations increased congestion at hub airports.

The greater competition on heavily traveled routes forced airlines to schedule more frequent flights to remain competitive. Since these frequent flights carried fewer passengers than under previous scheduling practices, the airlines used smaller aircraft. Results: greater air traffic control problems. Compounding the problems was the FAA refusal to address the inadequate number of airports and runway.

GREAT STRIDES IN AIR TRAFFIC CONTROL

The air traffic control system has made great strides from its early days. The system dates back to 1934 when Glen Gilbert, generally regarded as the father of air-traffic control, instituted a flight-following system for American Airlines. Several years later the government purchased the system. The air traffic control system remained primitive for many years, as the ATC system was hampered by inadequate equipment, official indifference, and congressional refusal to provide money. The system was far behind the needs. The primary event changing the government's attitude toward the air traffic control system was the 1956 crash over the Grand Canyon between United and TWA Airlines.

The air traffic control system was primitive by today's standards. Air traffic controllers determined the position of aircraft by moving "shrimp-boats" and paper strips. Enroute position reports were made either to Airinc[59] or to the local FAA radio facility.

INTEGRITY PROBLEMS

As in other segments of aviation, there are hostile influences affecting the air traffic control system. One of the worst was the militant air traffic controllers' union, PATCO. This union endangered air safety by hostile acts. Unfortunately, the attitude fostered by the militant union heads harmed many air traffic controllers.

In the 1960s and 1970s controllers felt the effect of the internal FAA problems which the inspectors felt in a different form. The traffic controllers turned to unionization to obtain relief from the autocratic and often-times corrupt FAA hierarchy. The Air Traffic Control Association (ATCA) was the first air traffic controllers' union. With President Kennedy's signing of Executive Order 10998 authorizing the creation of federal employee unions, ATCA became more militant. But ATCA wasn't militant enough for some of the younger controllers. They formed a splinter group known as the Professional Air Traffic Controllers Organization (PATCO).

ATCA eventually faded, and PATCO engaged in air traffic slowdowns and work stoppages that almost brought air transportation to a halt in the summer of 1968. Highly publicized attorney F. Lee Bailey counseled the militant PATCO, and under his influence, PATCO became increasingly militant to the extent that air safety was compromised. Seeking to obtain higher pay scales than that provided by law, the controllers engaged in slowdowns, computer sabotage, and other unsafe acts.

The slowdowns caused airlines to make unscheduled landings as fuel reached the danger point due to deliberate traffic slowdowns. In one instance, a TWA flight from Kansas City to O'Hare was twice forced to land at Rockford, Illinois to refuel. Even after planes made it to the ground at Chicago O'Hare's airport, the controllers continued to harass the pilots and passengers by holding the planes on the taxiways, and withholding clearance to taxi to the terminals.

The danger of delaying flights and causing a fuel depletion was made brutally evidence in the 73 deaths arising from the Avianca 707 crash onto Long Island on January 25, 1990.

The sabotaging of the ATC computers endangered flight

---

[59] Private company under contract with most scheduled airlines for forwarding messages between the aircraft and the company.

crews and passengers. A Braniff jetliner was deliberately vectored toward a thunderstorm; controllers sabotaged the ATC computers, including the incident on January 18, 1980 that caused a Russian jetliner, Aeroflot Flight 315, to stray into an unprotected area. The flight flew for six miles at the wrong altitude in the New York area, and ATC supervisors were forced to take over. FAA officials announced that the sabotage included removing the numbers and letters identifying the flight, its altitude, and airspeed. The FAA announced plans to fire one air traffic controller and suspend another in connection with this sabotage.[60]

Striking controllers threatened working controllers who did not sympathize with PATCO's militancy, or who refused to engage in slowdowns or strikes. They damaged the homes, the cars and properties of the less-militant controllers. False radio signals sent to planes by striking controllers endangered air safety. ATC equipment was damaged, such as shots fired into the radar building at the Oakland airport, damaging the normal and backup power supplies.

THREATENING TO CAUSE A MIDAIR COLLISION

Air traffic controller Taso Anthan sued the air traffic controllers union for damages following union harassment that threatened to cause a midair collision. Anthan alleged in his law suit that the union and some of its officers in St. Louis harassed him because he disagreed with their hostile attitudes. Anthan charged that another controller (who was a union official) deliberately directed a Frontier Airlines plane into the airspace above Lambert Field occupied by a TWA plane that Anthan was directing. The June 25, 1975 incident occurred during a thunderstorm. Anthan testified, "My heart was in my mouth. I began to get nervous. I stood up and screamed at the supervisor."

After hearing the evidence, senior U.S. District Judge Roy Harper stated the air traffic controllers union was guilty of "outrageous conduct (and) intentionally or recklessly causing severe emotional distress" to Anthan. Judge Harper added, Anthan was run out of St. Louis "by ostracism and hostility" from PATCO members. "The incident on June 25, 1975 is so extreme in degree that it is beyond all possible bounds of decency."[61] Harassment of Chicago area controllers by fellow controllers was described during a congressional panel.[62]

The militant controllers threatened air safety. The FAA

---

[60] *Associated Press* article appearing in September 23, 1980 *San Francisco Chronicle*.

[61] *United Press* article appearing in *San Francisco Chronicle*, August 12, 1981.

[62] *Chicago Tribune*, June 21, 1988.

couldn't control them. Congress wouldn't act; they didn't wish to alienate the powerful labor unions who furnished money and election help. The nation was falling hostage to the militancy of certain controllers. Something had to be done, as I pointed out in my first and second printings of the *Unfriendly Skies.*

The militant traffic controller union, PATCO, was accused by the FAA of "traffic in threats" and defiance of statutory and regulatory laws. Seeking to defend their financial demands by placing a safety label on the issues, air traffic controller spokesman Stanley Lyman charged that flight was reaching "a point of public peril. We are fortunate that we don't have the collisions now. Ninety percent of this is pure luck. Its a luck system."

When the FAA replied that the charges were "exaggerated completely out of context," the controller group called on Congress to make a "full-scale Congressional investigation of the FAA," charging "mismanagement to a point of public peril." Then the controllers showed their "concern for public safety" by their slowdowns, computer sabotage, and other union tactics.

After inflicting these dangers upon the public, the union heads, including Robert Poli, chief of the Professional Air Traffic Controllers Organization (PATCO), sought to bring the nation's air traffic to its knees by going on strike on August 3, 1981. Over 11,000 of the nation's air traffic controllers walked off their jobs to enforce their financial demands. President Ronald Reagan responded to this illegal act by giving the controllers 48 hours to return to work. When they failed to return, Reagan fired them, and started rebuilding the ATC system.

The rebuilding started with a cadre of 7,000 controllers and supervisors who had stayed on the job. Air traffic was slowed down, and greater separation between aircraft permitted the less-qualified controllers to gradually increase their proficiency.

Most of the professional pilots noticed an immediate improvement in the attitude of the remaining controllers, which they equated with a greater safety level. Controller insolence, hostility, slowdowns, computer sabotage, were gone. The skies became safer.

Even the airlines and business community, which stood to lose millions of dollars because of the strike, supported the firing. Public opinion polls showed widespread support for Reagan's reaction to the strike. An Associated Press-NBC News poll in mid-August showed 64 percent of the public approving

Reagan's actions.[63]

REPORT DOCTORING

The FAA was not blameless in the controller dissatisfaction. When the controllers went on strike, the FAA found this a convenient time to get rid of other controllers that were not on strike, and who had offered to return to work. Under the urging of numerous union officials, a Congressional panel charged[64] that FAA officials lied under oath about payroll records prepared during the 1981 controllers' strike. The panel charged that the FAA doctored time sheets to deny employment to controllers who were falsely charged with joining the 1981 controllers' strike.[65] The House Public Works and Transportation subcommittee on investigations and oversight charged in a 66-page report that FAA officials used fake evidence against the fired controllers during their appeals before the Merit System Protection Board. The report alleged that FAA officials sought to cover up the falsification during the subcommittee's investigations.[66]

The internal FAA misconduct deprived the government air safety agency the requirements for safety cooperation, contributing to the controller dissatisfaction.

CREDIT TO THOSE AIR TRAFFIC CONTROLLERS CONTRIBUTING TO SAFETY

Credit is given to those air traffic controllers whose attitudes reflected well on the controller profession. Many controllers have saved small-plane pilots from possible crashes by their assistance. But the internal FAA problems permitted breakdowns in normal discipline and conduct.

CRASHES CAUSED BY CONTROLLER CARELESSNESS

Controller indifference, or controller problems such as drugs, union hostility, indifference, caused and permitted to occur fatal crashes. A corporate Kingair making an instrument approach into Washington National Airport was observed by the controller to be far below the safe altitude. The controller said nothing, and the plane subsequently crashed. A Miami controller saw an Eastern Airlines Lockheed 1011, Flight 401, descend from the previous 2000 feet holding altitude through 900 feet toward the ground on December 29, 1972. Inexplicably, he remained silent. In the PSA San Diego midair collision, neither of

---

[63] *Associated Press* September 4, 1981.

[64] Committee chairman Representative Glenn Anderson (Calif.), and aviation subcommittee chairman Representative James Oberstar (Minn.) and other House members urged the Justice Department to "investigate and prosecute those that have violated" the law. 1989.

[65] *Associated Press*, September 16, 1989; *Washington Post* article appearing in *San Jose Mercury News*, September 16, 1989.

[66] *Aviation Week & Space Technology*, September 18, 1989.

the two tower controllers whose medical certificate required them to wear glasses were wearing them. Possibly the impending collision between the two planes within their field of vision could have been prevented if they worn their glasses.

NEW HOPE, GEORGIA

Many fatalities occurred in the small town of New Hope, Georgia, on April 4, 1977, when a controller's indifference made possible the crash of a Southern Airways DC-9. Prior to the crash, Flight 242 encountered severe weather and had its outer windshield cracked by hail. This problem was followed by failure of both engines on the two-engine jet.

The crew desperately sought help from the air traffic controller: "Atlanta Approach, [this is] Southern 242, we've lost both engines. How about giving us a vector to the nearest place. We're at 7,000 feet."

"Stand by"

Although there was an airport almost directly under the plane, and a military field within gliding distance, the controller did not give this information to the pilots. Instead, he advised the DC-9 plunging to the ground without any engine power to stand by. Despite the gravity of the emergency, and the need for the controller's undivided attention, the controller continued to handle other traffic as if no emergency existed, and delayed giving information to the falling aircraft.

The controller should have advised other controllers to take over the handling of all other traffic, and transmit a general announcement to all other aircraft to change frequency. He should then have devoted his entire attention to the DC-9 that was in a life-or-death emergency. The desperate pilots radioed, "I can't tell you the implications of this. We've only got two engines. How far out are we now?"

The controller advised Southern they were nineteen miles from an airport, and then continued issuing traffic to other planes. The Southern pilots continued to request urgently needed information that the controller should have anticipated. "Stand by," said the controller! When the controller finally gave the Southern pilots information on available airports, the plane was already too low to reach them in their unpowered flight. The Southern pilots advised the controller: "I don't know if we can make [the airport] or not." The controller responded nonchalantly: "Roger," and then proceeded to handle other traffic while Southern descended toward impact with the ground in the small community of New Hope, Georgia.

Approaching tree-top level, the Southern pilots saw a winding country road. The crew made the last radio transmission they would ever make, "We're putting it down on a highway. We're down to nothing." The controller responded as

if it was a routine event: "Putting it down on a highway, roger."
He then proceeded to handle other traffic!

At approximately 150 miles per hour the DC-9 crashed onto
the winding road, ripping a path of destruction through the
center of town. The left wing ripped through a service station,
shearing off the gas pumps, ripping open the aircraft's wing
fuel tanks, and starting a spectacular conflagration. Flames
shot high into the air over. Before it was over, seventy-two
persons in the aircraft and nine on the ground perished.

Also sharing a small part of the blame were the pilots in
other planes who heard this unfolding tragedy and did not step
in and tell the controller to devote his attention to the extreme
emergency that existed.

FRANK SINATRA'S MOTHER

Pilot and controller error caused the death of Frank
Sinatra's mother near Palm Springs, California on January 1977.
Sinatra's Learjet crashed at high-speed into the side of San
Gorgonio mountain. The controller issued an instrument departure clearance requiring the Learjet crew to make a right turn
shortly after takeoff from the northwest 30 runway, and
proceed northeastward on the 051 radial. The crew failed to
make the right turn after takeoff, and headed straight for the
towering mountain, reporting to the controller that they were
crossing the radial, and not established on it.

The controller failed to respond to this position report
suggesting the crew was heading toward the mountain. Then, as
the crew leveled off at 9000 feet, heading straight for the
mountain, they twice asked the controller if they were cleared
to proceed out the 051 radial, which they had long passed. The
controller should have realized the crew's error, and alerted
them to immediately turn. The plane disintegrated against the
mountain. As so often happened, the pilots failed to check the
surrounding terrain before takeoff and therefore lacked the
knowledge that the plane could not continue on the northwest
heading.

Similar errors: A charter plane crashed during takeoff from
Bishop, California. The plane took off to the north at night, and
then made a wide right turn to head south for Los Angeles. They
rammed into the side of high terrain shown on the maps. A
World Airways passenger flight made a wrong turn during a
night takeoff at Guam, crashing into the side of a hill. A plane
made a right turn from a south takeoff at Lajes Airport in the
Azores, crashing into the high mountain west of the field.
Numerous military planes crashed into the side of the mountain
west of El Paso. All were senseless crashes that could have
been prevented if the crews had been better trained to make

them aware of the need to check ground obstacles.

CONTROLLER CLEARANCES SENDING AIRCRAFT INTO THE SIDE OF MOUNTAINS

Controller carelessness caused numerous crashes. In one instance a controller gave headings to a twin-Cessna, causing it to crash into the side of a mountain near Nogales, Arizona, in May 1977. The plane was on a flight from Nogales to Fresno, California. A military C-130 jet was given radar vectors into the side of a mountain near Seattle in 1981.

"You're going to kill us all!"

A single-engine plane was radar vectored into the side of a hill near Salinas, California. Two single-engine planes were radar vectored into the side of a mountain east of Los Angeles. "You're going to kill us all," the pilot stated to the controller as the pilot was flying in the narrow east-west corridor just east of the Los Angeles basin. The pilot was right; within minutes they were all dead, crushed against the side of the mountain. A twin-engine private plane was vectored into a hillside near Monterey, California, when the controller failed to properly identify the aircraft.

In another similar crash in the Burbank area, the controller vectored a light plane into the side of a mountain ten miles northeast of Burbank. The plane was on a flight from Van Nuys to Santa Monica Airport. The controller put the plane on an eastbound course, at 3,000 feet, toward mountains that were 5,000 to 6,000 feet high.

After the crash the controller refused to cooperate with the accident investigators from the NTSB. The nation's two air safety agencies exchanged charges. (*Los Angeles Times* October 1986.) The NTSB stated that controllers in the Burbank facility refused to be questioned by the NTSB because the NTSB wanted to record the interview for the sake of accuracy (as is normal investigative practice).

FAA spokeswoman Barbara Abels stated in a formal statement that the refusal to be interviewed was in the interests of fairness to the controllers. (*Los Angeles Times* October 18, 1986.) Fairness? What about the people killed by controller error! People employed in air safety don't have the luxury of refusing to submit to questioning concerning accidents. The FAA release showed the contempt for peoples' lives as they protected the controllers:

> The FAA believes that the controllers should have sufficient time to prepare final statements for the record and have the right to have the assistance of legal counsel in any proceeding in which their involvement may be substantial.

That is not the procedure in air safety and crash investigations. The intent under law of such immediate hearings, without the manipulation by legal counsel is to get to the cause of a crash, and to prevent further crashes from similar problems. This has been standard procedure for years. The FAA was protecting its personnel while subjecting the public to more deaths. The FAA also stated they were asking the controllers to voluntarily submit to alcohol and drug tests, but did not know when this would be done. Obviously, any evidence of alcohol and/or drugs would disappear with the passage of time. The same FAA expects crewmembers to immediately submit to alcohol and drug tests.

The NTSB responded that immediate drug tests are routine in aircraft accidents, and indicated that the NTSB was upset by the controllers' refusal to submit to informal taped interviews. NTSB spokesman Ira Furman stated:

> It is their [the investigators'] option to ask that [such] an interview be recorded. Investigators are issued tape recorders ... it [the recorder] isn't a cattle prod.

The NTSB stated that formal depositions are not an adequate substitute for informal interviews "because they delay the investigation."

A combination of controller and pilot errors came in a group at Los Angeles Airport during the last week in December 1987. There was a near-collision between two planes on approach that missed each other by an estimated *ten* feet! A Mexicana airline and a Westair commuter, making approaches to parallel runways nearly collided at 2000 feet when the Mexican plane failed to make a turn ordered by controllers. There was the incident where a Delta aircraft that was supposed to be on a taxiway ended up on a runway as a United jet took off and at over 200 miles per hour passed 200 feet above the Delta plane. Three hours earlier a Westair flight which had just landed crossed the runway on which a Delta flight was taking off.

FAILURE TO RESPOND

Air traffic controllers failed to respond to the pleas of an Avianca 707 crew on a flight from Medellin, Columbia to Kennedy Airport at New York City on January 25, 1990. Several times during the last 90 minutes of flight the crew advised enroute controllers that they were short on fuel. ATC had the aircraft hold enroute for approximately 90 minutes, due to weather and traffic delays at Kennedy. Fifty minutes before the aircraft ran out of fuel the crew made the first of several calls notifying the controllers of their fuel shortage. Apparently enroute controllers did not relay the urgency to the approach controllers at Kennedy. Adding its role to the problems was under-staffing at the New York City air traffic control facilities.

MANY DEATHS FOLLOWED

At night, in rain, the 707 ran out of fuel and crashed into a residential area on Long Island. The rescuers who quickly arrived found bodies on top of bodies, and had to pull the dead away to reach the living. Seventy-three people died, and many were badly injured. Heavy television coverage did its part in making the public more aware of the consequences of the many problems described within these pages, although they did not associate the deaths with the problems. There was no one to tell them, certainly not the networks that had done such an efficient and deadly job of coverup for many years.

The FAA responded to NTSB criticism for failure to come to respond to the numerous requests for clearance to land due to running out of fuel, stating the crew didn't use the magical words. Different FAA people had different responses to what the magic words should be. President of the National Air Traffic Controllers Association, Steve Bell, defended the controllers refusal to respond to Avianca's pleas concerning low fuel. He stated that the magical words, "fuel emergency, or "minimum fuel," would have triggered a response. This is the type of mentality that exists in the present FAA mentality. The words running out of fuel has one connotation; emergency!

Possibly the FAA excuses the failure to give life-saving heading information to the Southern DC-9 that crashed in New Hope, Georgia, on the fact that the pilots didn't use magic words in describing what they wanted. They only stated that all engines were out and they were going down, without using the word "priority" or some other magic word!

MANY NEAR FUEL-EXHAUSTION TRAGEDIES

There have been many near-fuel exhaustion incidents in which the Avianca death toll could have been multiplied several times over. For instance, a United 747-100 landed at Tokyo following a non-stop flight from Los Angeles, with three of its four engines shut down because of lack of available fuel. The fuel system was mismanaged. (24,000 pounds of fuel in number 2 main tank; the others were dry.) United suffered a similar reported near-tragedy when a 747 lost all four engines on July 5, 1981. A United 747 landed at Seattle, with barely enough fuel to make it to the terminal. NTSB records show seven incidents involving fuel starvation of United States aircraft since 1981. Pan Am made an emergency landing in Tampa when the flight engineer and ground personnel did not properly refuel the plane at the last fuel stop. Any one of these, and many other near-crashes, could have been fatal flights.

CHAPTER FIFTEEN

Alcohol and Drugs

Alcohol and drugs play their part in air safety problems. Alcohol misuse has always been a part of the aviation scene, as it has been throughout society. Many crew members spend frequent days and nights away from home, staying in hotels, often with little to do. Partying and alcohol is one way to pass the time. The percentage of crewmembers that fly under the influence of alcohol is small, but the numbers are far greater than they should be. In the military, alcohol misuse is especially high, even though the Air Force has a 24-hour bottle to throttle rule.

THE LAW RELATING TO CREW DRINKING

Formerly, the Federal Aviation Regulations (FAR 91.11) barred a person from acting as a crewmember within eight hours of consuming alcoholic beverages, or while under the influence of alcohol. "Under the influence" is a subjective term, and not capable of meaningful enforcement. The FAA came under pressure to do something about the alcohol problem as the news media publicized the large numbers of licensed pilots arrested for drunken driving. The FAA stalled for several years, and then finally changed the rules in April 1986. It relaxed the rules!

The new regulation retained the eight-hour rule, which prohibited a pilot from flying within eight hours of alcohol consumption. But it relaxed the former rule by permitting a pilot to fly with a blood-alcohol level not over .04 percent by weight of alcohol in the blood. But dozens of studies showed that pilots are adversely affected by *any* blood-alcohol level.

METHODS OF EXPRESSING ALCOHOL LEVEL

The most common method of expressing the alcohol content of blood is grams percent or just percent, often shown as 0.15% (grams of alcohol per 100 milliliters of blood).

A single average highball, or a 12-ounce can of beer, will cause an approximate blood-alcohol level of 0.015, or 15 mg%, in a 160 pound person. It is oxidized at approximately .01 to .015 per hour. The blood-alcohol level depends on body weight, quantity of ethyl alcohol consumed, and time since ingestion. Food in the stomach affects the speed with which alcohol is absorbed into the blood. Other factors determine an individual's tolerance to intoxication at a specific blood-alcohol level. Women appear to be affected more by ingested alcohol because their stomach lining contain smaller amounts of an enzyme called alcohol dehydrogenase. As a result, more alcohol from each drink passes into women's bloodstreams than into men's.

The body oxidizes alcohol in the blood faster than it can diffuse from the urine, cerebrospinal fluid and brain. Therefore, the effects of alcohol may still be evident when no alcohol is present in the blood. This partly explains hangovers. Another factor is that the liver, kidneys, and certain other tissues contain alcohol dehydrogenase, the enzyme which converts alcohol to harmless carbon dioxide and water. The brain does not share in this activity, and is affected longer than the remainder of the body. Additionally, the brain has an enzyme that slowly converts the alcohol to acetaldehyde, which is more toxic than alcohol.

It is possible that many people who test legally intoxicated do not realize they drank that much. Drunkenness would probably decrease if everyone knew the number of drinks required to reach the legal intoxication level.

CRASHES RELATED TO DRINKING

We've already discussed some crashes associated with alcohol, and the PSA San Diego crash appears to be the classic. The after-crash test of the blood-alcohol level of the deceased American captain following the crash of a Japan Airlines DC-8 during takeoff from Anchorage on January 13, 1977 was .028 percent (or nearly three times the legal intoxication level in most states and almost four times the intoxication level in California, Oregon, Utah, Maine, and Vermont. Effects of the alcohol was shown throughout the short flight. During taxi from the terminal the captain taxied to the wrong runway; he had difficulty understanding the radio transmissions; he mishandled the plane during takeoff; and the plane crashed, with the death of everyone on board.

Before the flight, others saw the captain in an obviously inebriated condition, but none intervened. The captain reportedly staggered from the hotel in Anchorage as he went to the taxicab. He smelled of alcohol. He was obviously drunk. The copilot made a feeble comment on the captain's state of inebriation, but was gruffly rebuffed. The entire crew then proceeded dutifully to the airport.

After leaving the crew at the terminal, the cab driver reported the captain's condition to the company dispatcher, who in turn called JAL's flight dispatchers. They already knew of the captain's inebriated condition and did nothing to stop the flight. After the crash, the flight dispatch personnel stated to the NTSB that they did not see any signs of alcohol. What else could they state after their acts of omission played a key role in the subsequent deaths.

DRINKING BY FAA PILOTS

Those responsible for enforcing government safety regulations are sometimes the worst violators. FAA inspectors frequently receive flight training from the airlines or the military, and occasionally appear for flight while under the influence of alcohol. During flight training at Mather Airforce base the FAA inspector who joined me for flight training often showed up with liquor on his breath. The flight training was vigorous, with repeated simulated engine-out emergencies, creating a hostile environment in which no pilot should be impaired by alcohol. That particular plane, a Convair 340, also flew very poorly on a single engine, and needed a pilot's full facilities to safely handle the simulated emergency.

"What do I do when the captain shows up under the influence of alcohol?"

During my hundreds of radio and television appearances many listeners called in to report having seen crewmembers drinking shortly before leaving for a flight. During an appearance with Ray Briem on KABC in Los Angeles, a flight attendant identifying herself as Pat called and addressed the drinking problem she encountered. She asked for advice as to what she could do when the captain showed up for flight smelling of alcohol, or obviously under the influence. The flight attendant described an occasion when another flight attendant complained of a captain's drinking, and was then fired. Unfortunately this is not uncommon.

During a television call-in show on *Mid-Morning Los Angeles,*[67] a woman who formerly worked in the flight dispatch office of a major airline in the Los Angeles area called to describe the many times that crewmembers showed up for a flight smelling of alcohol.

An *Aviation News Digest*[68] article stated:

ALCOHOL INVOLVEMENT IN TRANSPORT ACCIDENTS
Alcohol is a growing safety and efficiency problem in many industries and more prevalent in air transport than most airlines and pilots care to admit, states an editorial in London-based *Flight International.*

The statement was prompted by a finding of the U.S. National Transportation Safety Board (NTSB) that the captain of a cargo DC-8 that crashed when taking off from Anchorage, Alaska, in January 1977, was under the influence of alcohol. *Flight* said the DC-8 crew had been worried about the captain's condition, noting that "loyalty, compassion and respect for authority are decent instincts but in the case of this killer disease they can be taken to tragic extremes."

An inebriated Northwest Airline captain flew a flight from Las Vegas to San Francisco on August 1, 1982, carrying 73 passengers.[69] The captain was tested later that morning, and had a blood alcohol level of 0.13 percent. Calculating the burn-off rate per hour, the blood alcohol level must have been close to 0.20 percent while piloting the flight.

During a scheduled layover in Bangor, Maine on January 9, 1985, a Delta captain and other cockpit crew members began consuming alcohol the evening before the flight. The drinking continued until shortly after midnight, when the captain became unconscious. The next morning, the captain did not wake up in time to leave for the airport with the remainder of the crew for a scheduled seven a.m. departure. The crew, minus the captain, left for the airport to get the plane ready. The captain arrived later, and boarded the aircraft, still under the influence of alcohol. The copilot and flight engineer covered up for him, even though they knew he was in no condition to fly.

---

[67] July 16, 1979.

[68] June 8, 1979.

[69] *Dallas Morning News* article reprinted in January 29, 1989 *San Francisco Sunday Examiner.*

The flight left Bangor with the impaired captain in command. During the flight one of the flight attendants discovered the captain's condition and became concerned. The copilot and flight engineer unlawfully disconnected the cockpit voice recorder to eliminate any trace of the conversation dealing with the captain's intoxication. When the flight landed in Boston, a passenger and several flight attendants reported the problem to Delta's Chief Pilot. The airline then ordered a blood-alcohol test for the captain, which showed a level of .13 grams at the time he flew the aircraft.

Delta fired the captain the next day for violating company and FAA regulations concerning drinking. The company suspended the copilot and engineer from duty for covering up, and for unlawfully turning off the cockpit flight recorder (CVR).

The captain then filed a grievance, and the Airline Pilots Association (ALPA) defended the captain. The pilots' union argued that the captain's operation of the flight while under the influence of alcohol was insufficient cause for his discharge. The next of kin in the PSA crash might question that.

The pilots' union took the dispute to the System Board, which held that Delta discharged the captain without just cause. The Board ordered the captain reinstated. The pilots' union supported the inebriated captain and, in effect argued that Delta should condone intoxicated pilots, thereby becoming an accessory to the wrongdoing. Delta appealed the decision to the U.S. District Court,[70] which upheld Delta's dismissal of the captain, but required Delta to pay for the captain's alcohol rehabilitation program. The Court of Appeals affirmed the district court's ruling. No one, it appears, condemned the outrageous acts of the captain.

DRINKING IS ESPECIALLY BAD IN THE MILITARY

When I was a young Navy pilot I came face to face with heavy drinking among the military crews. A Navy pilot crashed into a crowded hotel in 1972 during an early morning flyby demonstration in the South Pacific, killing many hotel occupants. He was reportedly drinking heavily the night before. A congressional study released by Representative Joseph Addabbo (New York) revealed that as many as 20 percent of the Navy's aircraft crashes were due in part to alcohol abuse. Articles make reference to the problem[71] and feedback from military pilots tell me of its continued existence. In the same article, Representative Robert Dornan (California) warned that drug use among GI's in Europe is nightmarish. Possibly the alcohol use

---

[70] *Delta Airlines v. Airline Pilots Association International*, No. 87-8839 (11th Cir., December 8, 1988).

[71] *U.S. News & World Report*, September 28, 1981.

had a major bearing on the unprecedented suspension of all Navy activities in December 1989 when the Navy was plagued with crashes and mishaps.

AIRLINE ALCOHOL PROGRAM

The Air Line Pilots Association developed an alcohol-treatment program with the cooperation of several airlines that rehabilitated about 1,000 pilots. The 15-year-old program is suppose to use peer pressure to identify pilots with alcohol problems. But many alcoholic pilots revert either frequently or occasionally to their old habits, endangering the lives of everyone on board. The failure rate for recovering alcoholics who are airline pilots exceeds twenty percent.

Northwest Airlines challenged the alcoholism program as a violation of FAA regulations. "We are attempting to demonstrate that alcoholism is a disqualifying medical condition in light of studies that show an extremely high rate of recidivism," said Philip Lacovara. The former counsel to the Watergate special prosecutor represented Northwest Airlines. "In our view, the FAA's program, as it has been administered, does not provide a long enough period of rehabilitation before granting medical exemptions," he said. "The air surgeon is treating pilots as his clients instead of the traveling air public."

Under California law, a person with a blood-alcohol level between .05% and .08 is presumed under the influence of alcohol, and legally intoxicated at .08. However, the FAA says a blood-alcohol level just short of .04 is satisfactory for a pilot, even though any amount of alcohol adversely affects flight performance. Many pilots don't realize the effects of liquor last longer than beyond the legal requirements of FAR Part 91.11.

Aware of the pilot drinking problem, the General Accounting Office (GAO) recommended for years that Congress pass legislation to *force* the FAA to compare National Drivers' Register (NDR) records on drunken drivers with the pilot list. This legislation would require the FAA to access these records, and compare them with the FAA's list of active pilots. The FAA had the authority to do this on their own, and never did. Since they refused to do so, GAO sought legislation to force the FAA to act.

The *National Enquirer*[72] estimated that 12,500 pilots had lost their *driver's* licenses because of drunkenness, but continued to fly. The NTSB embarrassed the FAA[73] by comparing the FAA's pilot roster against the National Driver's Register, and

---

[72] January 30, 1979.
[73] 1987.

found that 10,000 active pilots had driver-license suspensions or revocations due to driving while intoxicated. The cross-check found that more then three-quarters of the pilots did not report their drunk-driving convictions on their medical certificates, thereby falsifying the medical applications.

The Department of Transportation forced the FAA in 1989 to compare NDR records with the statements made by pilots on their physical renewal applications. This comparison showed many pilots falsely denying prior drunk-driving convictions. Many of those pilots were then charged with perjury by U.S. Attorneys in different parts of the United States. Despite these pressures, the FAA relaxed the regulations that addressed pilots who drink and fly.

In 1988 the FAA prepared a sanction schedule addressing those crewmembers who falsely state on their medical application that they had not been arrested for drunken driving. The punishment provided for revocation of current medical certificates and suspension of any airman or ground instructor certificates for 60 days for a single Driving-Under-the-Influence (DUI) conviction. In the case of a single drug conviction for simple possession, the schedule provided for revocation of the medical certificate and suspension of the airman certificates for 180 days. For drug convictions that do not involve falsification of the medical certificate application, the schedule provided 120 days of suspension for a single conviction. For two or more convictions, the schedule provided for revocation of any airman or other certificates.

WIDESPREAD TOLERANCE OF DRINKING

The widespread toleration of drinking was shown in the Exxon Valdez tanker mishap near Anchorage in 1989. Exxon knew Captain Joseph Hazelwood had an alcohol problem, and did nothing about it. Other crew members knew of it, and most said nothing. Those who did report it to Exxon officials were ignored. Several hours after the tanker ran aground, the captain's blood-alcohol level reportedly tested .022.

The public paid hundreds of millions of dollars in various costs for the Exxon spill, due entirely to the captain's drinking. The public paid heavily in the PSA San Diego crash that reportedly had its roots in the all-night crew partying. Many train crashes occur from drinking. The auto-death toll from drinking is over 25,000 a year, with many others permanently crippled. Excessive drinking is tolerated by many people.

Chuck Yaeger's drinking exploits sound exciting in a book or movie, but deadly in real life.

OTHER COUNTRIES HAVE SIMILAR PROBLEMS

Japan Airlines, for instance, had several crashes associated with crew partying. Drinking is prevalent in the Japanese society and is prevalent among the Japanese crewmembers (as well as other foreign airlines). Unfortunately, many of the American pilots who started up Japan Airlines had a history of drinking and partying.

It is believed that Japan Airlines' first crash resulted from late night partying by the two American pilots. On an early morning flight from Tokyo to Osaka, under instrument conditions, the crew flew the route segment from Tokyo to Oshima Island one thousand feet below the minimum instrument altitude. At Oshima Island, the Martin 202 rammed into the side of an inactive volcano, killing everyone on board.

Other Japan Airline crashes followed, in which alcohol or late-night partying was suspected. A Japan Airlines DC-8 crashed during takeoff at Moscow, following reported late-night partying by the crew. The cockpit voice recorder readout showed the crew joking during the critical takeoff phase of the flight. The copilot responded to the captain's Gear-Up command by reaching forward and pulling back on the ground spoiler handle, rather than lifting the gear handle which was immediately ahead of the spoiler control. The death toll was heavy.

A Canadian Snowbird pilot was killed in 1988 in a one a.m. car crash after leaving a party at the home of Seward Mellon, an heir to the Mellon banking fortune. The pilot had a blood alcohol level of .191 percent, nearly twice the legal intoxication level. Fourteen hours later he was to have performed in a precision aerobatics performance above the heads of thousands of people, at which time he would still have been impaired by alcohol.

What could have happened to the spectators later that day, if the car crash didn't kill him, was reflected in the high death toll in the 1988 Ramstein airshow tragedy in Germany. A miscalculation by Italian pilots, combined with an unheard-of flight path toward the thousands of spectators, resulted in severe injuries to several hundred people and over fifty deaths. One of the planes crashed directly into the crowd.

An Air India Boeing 747-200B crashed into the sea moments after takeoff from Bombay, India on January 1, 1978, killing all 213 persons on board. The Indian Court of Inquiry faulted the pilot for responding solely to what it called a malfunctioning attitude director indicator (ADI), and the copilot for failing to provide assistance. Federal Judge James Fitzgerald in Seattle contradicted the findings, and ruled that a Bombay police official's attempt to discover if the captain had been drinking the night before the flight had been "conducted in a superficial manner." The judge cited testimony by a Bombay bartender who claimed his life had been threatened if he admitted serving drinks to Kukar.[74] Who is telling the truth?

ALCOHOL TERROR ROUTES

Even the passengers abuse alcohol. "We have to see what can be done to keep this problem in control," stated Captain Viktor Jauernig, chief of Lufthansa's airline pilots association. He described increasing cases of drunkenness and rowdy behavior by passengers emboldened by cut-rate drinks sold aboard international airliners, or tippling from bottles bought at tax-free airport shops. He stated, "What's typical for excursion boats has become normal in air travel; boozing on board. Lufthansa pilots recognize veritable terror routes."

A Lufthansa stewardess stated, "Especially on the long routes, passengers drink as if it was their last drink." She stated that one drunk had to be tied to his seat on the Hong Kong-to-Frankfurt run when he got out of hand. "We all have the same problems. Why deny it?" Lufthansa spokeswoman Sigrid Votteler told the Associated Press.

THE DRUG PROBLEM

Drug abuse is increasing in the aviation environment, and it should be no surprise. The industry doesn't work in a vacuum, and has its share of substance abusers. Among mechanics, the adverse affects of substance abuse is reflected in the poor quality of maintenance and inspection work. One can only wonder what part drug abuse played in some of the past airline crashes that started with aircraft malfunctions.

Substance abuse also injures the quality of aircraft construction. Rivets may be installed improperly. Wires and piping may be incorrectly fastened. Inspectors may write off an item as being completed when it is not. Paper checks may be made when the work is not actually performed. I know of no studies on this, and I doubt that any factual statistics exist.

An *Aviation Safety Institute* article (Number 77-11) reported a typical problem:

> We are reminded of the major air carrier [believed to be United] which suffered a series of fatal accidents in years past and where one of its major maintenance facilities was found to be the haven for a drug-peddling ring.

The San Francisco Chronicle and San Francisco Examiner had reported drug raids at United's San Francisco maintenance base in the late 1970s.

---

[74] *Aviation Week & Space Technology*, November 11, 1985.

The NTSB issued a February 1, 1989 report citing cocaine use as contributing to a commercial aviation crash. During a night approach to Durango, Colorado a Metro 3 aircraft belonging to Continental Express, a commuter airline, crashed at night on January 19, 1988. At a point where the aircraft should have maintained 8,400 feet altitude, it hit the ground at 7,220 feet, five miles short of the runway, and over a thousand feet too low. The NTSB report stated that the captain was a heavy user of cocaine and that traces were found in his blood and urine. It is a proven fact that cocaine-use induces insomnia, poor judgment, lack of attentiveness, and forgetfulness. NTSB chairman James Burnley called the incident "a tragic reminder that not even commercial aviation is exempt from the drug abuse problem which plagues our society."

Blood tests found marijuana in the bodies of two pilots flying a Central Airlines commuter Learjet that crashed at Newark, New Jersey Airport on March 30, 1983. The investigation found that the captain was under the influence of marijuana and the copilot had been exposed to marijuana in the past 24 hours.

Pilots have been caught smuggling drugs into the United States. I remember my first experience with this. I had been furloughed from Transocean airlines in 1951, and I was to be the next pilot recalled. The police arrested a working pilot selling drugs in Oakland, and it resulted in my recall.

Police arrested a veteran TWA Airlines captain at Kennedy International Airport in New York on July 1, 1987, and charged him with smuggling heroin into the United States from India. The captain brought in seven pounds of heroin on each of two other occasions in 1986. The captain was about to retire.

DRUG AND ALCOHOL USE ON THE TRAINS

Other methods of transportation have alcohol and drug problems, with no regard for the lives at risk. The railroads experienced many drug-related accidents over the years, especially in 1987 and 1988. A Conrail locomotive crashed into an Amtrak passenger train near Baltimore on January 4, 1987, killing 16 persons and injuring 175. The Conrail locomotive ran through several warning signals and a stop signal, before speeding into the path of an Amtrak train traveling at 105 miles per hour. The speed of the Conrail locomotive was substantially higher than the allowable speed near the track interchange.

Tests showed the Conrail crew had marijuana in their system at the time of the accident. Federal Railroad Administration officials stated that marijuana can remain in the body for 30 days or longer. A former head of the National Institute for Drug Abuse said the levels of marijuana in both men were two to three times higher than transportation industry standards for the amount that impairs behavior. The engineer had been cited the month before for drunken driving in Maryland. Blood and urine samples from the engineers on both trains were sent to the FAA's Civil Aeromedical Institute in Oklahoma City. Because of internal FAA problems (which are explained shortly) the tests were inconclusive.

The men riding in the caboose of a Seaboard System freight train in southern Indiana were killed when their train was rammed from behind by another Seaboard freight on September 14, 1983. The engineer on the second train had a blood-alcohol level of 0.27 four hours after the crash, and the brakeman had a level of 0.04. The coroner stated that at the time of the crash their blood-alcohol levels were 0.33 and 0.10 respectively. Crash after crash occurred on the railroads under substance abuse conditions.

The Department of Transportation issued regulations requiring drug testing of certain transportation related personnel. Beginning in 1990 the Transportation Department required all airlines to conduct random and periodic drug testing of pilots, flight engineers, navigators, flight attendants who perform cabin crew duties, flight and ground instructors, flight test personnel, aircraft and ground dispatchers, and maintenance personnel.

The plan requires pre-employment testing of all new hires in covered positions. It requires testing all covered employees holding FAA medical certificates as part of the regular physical. Testing of all covered employees is required within 32 hours of an accident. They must submit to testing for reasonable cause if at least two supervisors reasonably suspect them of using drugs. Unannounced testing of 50 % of all covered employees after first year of the program is included. Unannounced testing of those returning to duty after failing a drug test is mandatory.

Federal judge Marilyn Petal in the Ninth Circuit federal courts held in May of 1988 that mandatory drug testing was unconstitutional. The judge invalidated Federal Railroad Administration rules mandating drug tests after accidents. The Ninth Circuit Court of Appeals decision held: "Accidents, incidents or rule violations by themselves do not create reasonable grounds for suspecting that tests will demonstrate alcohol or drug impairment." The federal judges in the Ninth Circuit and I constantly disagreed on safety matters. Obviously, passengers and other crew members in any mode of transportation, and certainly in aviation, have a right to a drug-free operation of the aircraft.

FRAUD IN THE FAA DRUG TESTING LABORATORY

The Transportation Department sent many of the blood, urine, and body-tissue samples from transportation crashes to the FAA Oklahoma City medical unit for testing. Accuracy is obviously important in this testing area. It was in this area that another FAA scandal surfaced. The FAA medical laboratory routinely falsified alcohol and drug test results.

A detailed article in the *Wall Street Journal* dated July 31, 1987 described the falsification of alcohol and drug tests conducted by the FAA medical unit at Oklahoma City. Officials in the FAA and other government agencies knew serious problems existed, but they all covered up. The problems came to a head after a Conrail locomotive ran into an Amtrak passenger train near Baltimore on January 4, 1987. The crash caused 16 deaths and over 170 injuries, invoking considerable media attention and public interest.

The public was clamoring to know if the Conrail engineer had any drugs in his system. Because of the importance of the tests in accident investigations, the Transportation Department used a government laboratory that it thought would be reliable. They selected the FAA laboratory at Oklahoma City, thinking that the test results would be more reliable than those from a private testing laboratory. Because of the importance of the test in this most-disastrous of train accidents, swarms of federal officials were at the facilities waiting for the results.

Biochemist Delbert Lacefield and his assistant worked throughout the night to come up with the report—that should have taken a relatively short time to complete. There was a problem: Neither biochemist Lacefield, nor anyone else in the lab, knew how to use the sophisticated equipment needed to perform the test.

Lacefield submitted a fuzzy and contradictory report that raised questions about the integrity of the testing. An investigative team from the Federal Railroad Administration investigated the Civil Aeromedical Institute (CAMI), and made startling discoveries. The investigators discovered that the laboratory fabricated the results of seventeen blood tests during a nine-month period.

Federal Railroad Administrator John Riley down-played the gravity of the fraud. But the problems at the lab were actually much worse than publicly admitted, as high FAA officials covered up for the fraud. It turned out that FAA supervisory personnel knew of the problems nearly a year earlier. They refused to take corrective actions, and protected those falsifying the test results. It wasn't until the Philadelphia Amtrak tragedy that public attention focused on the fraudulent lab reports.

Accident investigators said the work by CAMI was so shoddy that accident investigators will never be sure whether drug-use by the engineer played a role in the Amtrak tragedy, or in any of the hundreds of post-accident lab tests that CAMI performed on airplane crews over the past 20 years. Blood, urine, and tissue tests for years are now suspect, and no one knows how many airplane and train crashes may have been due to alcohol or drugs, and not reported by the FAA laboratory.

In the Philadelphia Amtrak crash, CAMI's workers reached conclusions using improperly calibrated equipment, which they did not know how to operate. They lost—or destroyed—the computer data that backed up their findings. Therefore their work could not be verified. The FAA laboratory squandered the entire blood sample taken from the engineer soon after the train accident, preventing further testing by a competent lab.

The engineer's urine sample was split, and a sample sent to a private lab. This tested positive for marijuana. But lab experts say that without the more precise blood test, there is no way of knowing whether the engineer was drug-impaired at the time he pulled his Conrail engine in front of a fast moving Amtrak train carrying 600 people.

A year earlier, in June 1986, the Armed Forces Institute of Pathology reported to FAA officials that the FAA laboratory lacked safeguards, that the personnel were unqualified, that their tests were inaccurate, and that proficiency training and tests by an outside group were necessary. The FAA ignored these warnings, and protected those fabricating the test results.

Even CAMI's own employees tried to alert higher FAA authorities to the lab's incompetence and falsifications. FAA supervisors rebuffed medical technologist Claudia Ryan when she reported the lack of quality control to Mr. Lacefield's supervisors. The supervisors rebuffed her; therefore she did not mention the falsification of reports. She chose not to become a "whistle-blower."

During the subsequent investigation, three of the lab's four laboratory technologists testified that they complained to FAA officials about numerous problems without result.

In a 1984 airplane crash near Laredo, Texas, CAMI reported that the pilot had a blood alcohol level of .406, a condition that is close to death, and far beyond a pilot's ability to even try to fly. A nearby hospital found only about a quarter of the amount of alcohol reported by the FAA laboratory, which is still serious.

When the railroad administration picked CAMI to run its post-accident testing program, they knew that the FAA lacked a device called a gas chromatograph/mass spectrometer that is necessary for sophisticated blood testing. The FAA promised to subcontract blood tests to a nearby nongovernment laboratory, but it never did. None of the FAA employees knew how to extract a test sample from blood plasma, which was a necessary first step before an outside lab could analyze the fluid. The FAA simply falsified and fabricated the test results. The head of the lab had worked at CAMI for 21 years, continually operating in this manner, fraudulently fabricating test results.

Despite the fraud involved in these years of tests, and the knowledge of the fraud by FAA officials, no one was punished. The Transportation Department shut down the FAA lab, and transferred all post-accident railroad and airline testing to a non-government laboratory. The guilty went unpunished.

AIR TRAFFIC CONTROLLER DRUG PROBLEMS

A significant drug problem exists within the FAA air traffic control facilities. This problem first surfaced following a midair collision between a Hughes Air West and military aircraft under control of the Palmdale ATC facilities. After the crash, the FAA removed several controllers to desk jobs, based on suspicion of drug use. Except for the local Lancaster newspaper, the press did not report this story.

Several years later, the FAA again removed thirty-four air traffic controllers at the Palmdale facility near Lancaster, California for the same reason. Don Early, the manager of the Palmdale facility, 65 miles northwest of Los Angeles, stated the controllers would be required to take urine analysis tests to determine if they used cocaine or hashish.

The allegations against the traffic controllers stemmed from information gathered from internal and external sources during a two-week investigation. The investigation stemmed from a narcotics arrest on July 8, 1986 when police and FAA investigators served a search warrant at the home of Steven and Karen McIntosh in Palmdale.[75]

The extent and gravity of the drug problem among controllers was described in an investigative reporting article in the *Wall Street Journal* article. (1988.) The article described the large numbers of drug users among controllers; how some controllers sit by their radar screen in a literal stupor, requiring others to cover for them.

LAX ALCOHOL SAFEGUARDS

Federal Aviation Regulations (FAR) 91.11 required the pilots to *submit* to a test to indicate the percentage by weight of alcohol in the blood, when requested by a state or local law enforcement officer. That regulation required the crewmember

---

[75] UPI article, August 23, 1986, appearing in Las Vegas Sun.

to *release* to the FAA the results of each test taken within four hours after acting or attempting to act as a crewmember.[76] The regulation was poorly written. The wording indicates that only a state or local law-enforcement officer may require a pilot to undergo a blood-alcohol test; it does not allow the FAA to demand a test.

Section 91.11(c)(2) requires that the airman authorize the release of the blood tests, taken within four hours of acting or attempting to act as a crewmember, the results requested by a state or local law enforcement officer of tests relating to blood-alcohol content. Section 91.11(d) authorizes the medical facility to furnish or release to the FAA the results of each test taken within four hours after acting or attempting to act as a crewmember.

FAR 61.15 provides penalties for the violation of any Federal or state statute relating to the growing, processing, manufacture, sale, disposition, possession, transportation or importation of narcotic drugs, marijuana, or depressant, or stimulant drugs or substances. It provides that any of these violations is ground for denial of any application of any certificate or rating for one year after the date of final conviction and suspension of any rating or certificate. It also provides that the violation of FAR 91.11(a) (alcohol use) or 91.12(a) (drugs in aircraft) is grounds for denial of an application for a certificate or rating for up to one year after the date of that act, or suspension or revocation of any certificate or rating.

FAR 61.16 relates to refusal to submit to an alcohol test or to furnish test results when requested by a State or local law enforcement agency in accordance with section 91.11(c), or refusal to furnish or authorize the release of the test results requested by the FAA in accordance with section 91.11(c)or (d), is grounds for denial of an application for any certificate or rating for a period of up to one year after the date of that refusal, or suspension or revocation of any certificate or rating.

TRUCK DRIVER DRUG AND ALCOHOL USAGE

Test of the bodies of drivers in one of every three fatal truck crashes indicated detectable usage of cocaine, marijuana, alcohol, or stimulants, according to a *New York Times* article of February 6, 1990. The study covered the period from October 1987 through September 1988, covered one-fourth of the truck crashes occurring in that period, and covered 182 accidents in which 310 people were killed.

---

[76] Test that indicates percentage by weight of alcohol in the blood.

President James Johnston of the Owner/Operator Independent Trucking Association opposed testing of truck drivers for alcohol and drugs, stating, "As far as we're concerned, we still have not seen any evidence that it is a substantial problem."

JUSTICE DEPARTMENT PROTECTS ITS OWN DRUG DEALERS AND USERS

The Department of Justice, who is in the forefront of the war on drugs, covers up and protects its own employees who are caught using or selling drugs. Prison officials at the federal penitentiary at Long Beach's Terminal Island prison, which houses many drug dealers, sold and used drugs (as in many other federal prisons). When the Justice Department discovered their criminal acts, the Justice Department protected them from exposure. The punishment? The Justice Department withheld promotions from several of the federal employees, but did not prosecute any of them. The CIA uses drug dealers and actually protects them in some of their covert operations.

DRINKS (TWO-HOUR PERIOD)

Weight — 1½ ozs. 86° Liquor or 12 ozs. Beer

Weight											
100	1	2	3	4	5	6	7	8	9	10	11	12
120	1	2	3	4	5	6	7	8	9	10	11	12
140	1	2	3	4	5	6	7	8	9	10	11	12
160	1	2	3	4	5	6	7	8	9	10	11	12
180	1	2	3	4	5	6	7	8	9	10	11	12
200	1	2	3	4	5	6	7	8	9	10	11	12
220	1	2	3	4	5	6	7	8	9	10	11	12
240	1	2	3	4	5	6	7	8	9	10	11	12

BAC TO .05%   .05-.09%   .10% & UP

Source: NHTSA

CHAPTER SIXTEEN

Sabotage

Threats to air safety come from all directions, including hijackings and bombings. There was a period in time when hijacking in the United States was rampant, but then came to an almost virtual halt as the FAA required airlines to take stricter security measures. Aircraft bombings in the United States deceased more of its own volition than from any actions taken by the FAA. The bombings were the work of individuals, and not terrorist groups as is common in the Middle East. This respite from aircraft bombing can change at any time because of the political climate, and can approach the magnitude of the threat experienced in the Middle East and elsewhere.

Hijackings and bombings against U.S. airlines operating overseas find much of their basis in the conflict between Israel and the Arab countries, and in our government's heavy support of Israel. Sooner or later these two dangers will expand to the United States. With the general breakdown in global law and order, many terrorist authorities believe the bomb threats within the United States will escalate. The dangers comes from many sources, including the drug cartels in South America, the Middle East terrorists dissatisfied with our support for Israel, and other terrorist or dissatisfied groups.

THE BOMB THREAT

One of the first known bombings of an American aircraft occurred on October 10, 1933, over McCool, Indiana, on an early Boeing 247-D. The explosion killed ten people. A bomb was placed on a Canadian Pacific Airways DC-3 in Canada in 1949, by a jeweler who wanted to kill his wife in order to marry another woman. He succeeded in causing his wife's death and that of 22 others.

The next year, a laboratory technician, John Grant, put his wife, two children, and a bomb, on a United Airlines plane in Los Angeles. He wanted to marry a flight attendant. Fortunately for his family and others, he lost his nerve. Rushing to the plane, Grant screamed a warning to baggage handlers, causing the bomb to be removed from the plane.

A bomb exploded on a United Airlines DC-6B, Flight 629, after it left Denver's Stapleton Airport for Portland on November 1, 1965. Jack Graham had given his mother a heavy bag before she boarded the flight; he had stated it was a gift to be opened upon her arrival at Portland. Instead of a gift, the bag contained 25 dynamite sticks, a timing device, and two blasting caps. Flight 629 took off into the night and proceeded northwest. But before it was out of sight it blew up, causing a bright flash in the sky that was visible from Denver's Stapleton Airport.

The subsequent investigation found traces of the bomb that exploded in the rear cargo compartment that held mail and baggage loaded at Denver, reducing the scope of the investigation. Investigators found parts of the explosive device, including a tiny gear from a travel alarm clock used as a timing device for the bomb. The investigation found insurance policies purchased at the airport, showing that John Graham had purchased three policies on the life of his mother, Daisie King, just prior to the flight's departure. He had killed his own mother and a plane full of people to profit himself. A jury later convicted Graham, and he was executed.

In 1957, retired jeweler Saul Beinstock, went into the lavatory of a Western Airlines Convair flying from Las Vegas to Los Angeles. He carried with him a bomb which he detonated. The explosion ripped a large hole in the side of the fuselage, and ejected Beinstock out of the aircraft. Fortunately the aircraft continued flying and made it to a safe landing.

National Airlines (which later merged with Pan American), lost two aircraft by bomb explosions within two months of each other. The first bomb exploded on a Douglas DC-6B, Flight 967, on November 16, 1959, between Tampa and New Orleans, while the aircraft flew over the Gulf of Mexico. Investigations into aircraft bombings have routinely centered on airport insurance machines to determine if anyone stood to profit from the crash. Among those purchasing insurance policies before boarding the flight was a salesman, William Taylor. But he was not listed on the passenger manifest for the flight. His divorced wife received the insurance policy in the mail, naming her son as the beneficiary. Another passenger appearing on the passenger manifest who presumably perished on the flight was Dr. Robert Spears, a Naturopath from Dallas, Texas. The insurance dispensing machine at the airport showed Dr. Spears taking out a large policy.

Taylor and Spears were friends, and had done time together in prison. They were both in Tampa prior to the flight's departure. Spears suggested that Taylor use Spears' plane ticket, and Spears would drive Taylor's car to Dallas. Taylor had to get to Dallas for medical treatment, and accepted the offer. Taylor agreed to check Dr. Spears' suitcase on the flight, and have it waiting in Dallas when Spears arrived. After the loss of Flight 967, Spears dropped out of sight, and was presumed killed in the crash.

Two months after the downing of Flight 967, National Airlines experienced another bomb explosion on January 6, 1960 on Flight 2511 from New York City to Miami. On board was attorney Julian Frank, a former Assistant U.S. Attorney. Ironically, he also was a friend of Dr. Spears. Frank kissed his wife goodbye, and boarded the flight. Shortly after 2 a.m, as Flight 2511 cruised at 18,000 feet altitude, a violent blast lit up the night sky, scattering aircraft parts and bodies over Bolivia, North Carolina. Despite the severity of the blast, the aircraft continued flying, suggesting that it might land safely. But that was not to be. The weakened fuselage came apart and crashed in a ball of flames.

Investigation of the bodies showed that the blast severed both of Frank's legs below the knee. Bits of wire and fabric were embedded in Frank's flesh, and his face was reddened, indicating a nearby explosion, possibly from a handbag under the seat. Leg fragments belonging to Frank were found in the plane, further suggesting that the bomb exploded near his body. Frank was probably an unwitting bomb carrier, possibly for Dr. Spears. During the investigation into these two crashes, an unknown informant notified National Airlines that numerous life insurance policies had been purchased on the life of Julian Frank by Robert Spears.

Dr. Spears performed abortions before they became legal, and he tied in with Dr. Donald Loomis of Los Angeles, who was also in the illegal practice. Eventually they were indicted for their abortion activities. Dr. Loomis and Dr. Spears were co-defendants in a pending criminal trial. Before trial, Loomis suggested to the FBI that there was a tie between Dr. Spears, who was thought to have been lost on the National flight that plunged into the Gulf of Mexico, and the dead lawyer, Julian Frank. Further investigation showed Spears had a long criminal record before he eventually moved into abortions as a business.

Spears later turned up in Phoenix, Arizona, making an unexpected visit to an old friend, Dr. William Turska, at Turska's desert home. When asked about the Gulf of Mexico crash, Spears told Turska that Taylor has planned to drive his car to Dallas for treatment of pains in his head. Supposedly, Taylor asked to use Dr. Spears' plane ticket, and Spears agreed to drive Taylor's car to Dallas. But Dr. Turska didn't buy the story, and notified the FBI, who then arrested Dr. Spears. Unfortunately, the FBI never did convict Spears of any part in the bombings, and could only convict Spears for car theft.

Ironically, from 1949 through 1951, I supplemented my pilot salary by working as a pharmaceutical detail-man and sales-man, calling on medical doctors, osteopaths, and naturopaths, in the Dallas area. Spears was one of the doctors on whom I occasionally called.

A Transocean Airlines DC-6B is believed to have blown up on July 12, 1953, about 300 miles east of Wake Island on a flight to Honolulu. I had started out with that same crew when the plane left Burbank and had gotten off at Oakland, prior to the crew continuing on to Guam. Among the debris recovered by the Coast Guard in the shark-infested waters was a plywood panel from the navigator's table upon which was written the words, "Falling in."

The writing reminds us that those on board doomed aircraft fully realize their impending death and have plenty of time to think of their fate. Other crashes have records of last-minute farewells written as they waited for death to occur. Few were as sad as the messages written by some of the 520 people who perished in a Japan Airlines 747 crash near Tokyo.

BOMBINGS IN THE JET AGE

A Continental Air Lines 707 was one of the first jets downed by a bomb on May 22, 1962. It occurred on a flight from Chicago to Los Angeles. Over the small town of Centerville, Iowa, the bomb exploded, and the jet vanished from the air traffic controller's radar screen.

Another jet, an American Airlines 727, experienced a bomb explosion in 1967 after an executive with a soft drink company planted a bomb in his wife's luggage before she boarded the Chicago bound flight at San Diego. The bomb detonated but the aircraft remained intact, and landed safely.

In 1967 a bomb exploded on a British European Airways Comet over the Mediterranean, blowing a large hole in the fuselage. For a while it looked like the plane might hold together, but the strain of the emergency descent caused the fuselage to come apart in the air. Everyone was lost.

The danger of further aircraft damage is one of the reasons why a pilot is faced with the decision of making an emergency descent at a slower airspeed to avoid further structural damage. The correct decision is made more difficult as brain damage can occur to those not using oxygen. It is not generally understood that even short periods of oxygen deprivation can cause permanent brain damage with symptoms appearing at a later date, and the cause usually not recognized.

START OF THE MAJOR LOSSES

The really big disasters from bombings started in the 1980s. An Air India Boeing 747, Flight 182, blew up on June 23, 1985 at 31,000 feet on a flight from Toronto to London, 150 miles southwest of Ireland. The explosion and crash killed 329 people. After great effort and expense, the CVR and digital flight data recorder were recovered by a robot submarine at the bottom of the Atlantic Ocean at 6,500 feet. Unfortunately, the tapes ended when the explosion caused electrical failure, and didn't provide any significant information. However, the search uncovered sufficient evidence to indicate a bomb explosion had downed the aircraft.

Terrorists—possibly the same ones—placed a bomb that same day on a Canadian Pacific airplane at Vancouver, for transfer to an Air India plane in Tokyo. But the bomb exploded on the ground in Tokyo while baggage handlers transferred the bags to the Air India plane. The explosion killed two workers and injured four others. It was suspected that the bombs had been placed on both planes by Sikh fugitives wanted by the FBI in connection with an alleged plot to assassinate Indian Prime Minister Rajiv Gandhi.[77] Another group, the Kashmir Liberation Army, claimed responsibility for the Air-India crash. The liberation army is a terrorist group seeking independence for Kashmir, India's northernmost state.

A Korean Airlines Boeing 707, enroute from Baghdad, Iraq to Thailand, on November 29, 1987, blew up about 200 miles southeast of Rangoon, near the coast of Burma. The death toll was 115 people. Investigators found evidence of a bomb explosion in the wreckage, which was carried on board at Baghdad by an older man and a young woman posing as his daughter. They left the bomb under a seat when they got off at Abu Dahabi. They came under suspicion following the explosion. During questioning at Bahrain the man swallowed poison and immediately died. The other, Kam Hee, daughter of a North Korean diplomat, also swallowed poison, but lived. She later admitted placing the bomb under one of the seats.

TWA Flight 840, a Boeing 727, enroute from Rome to Athens with 122 people on board, experienced an explosion as the jet

---

[77] *Washington Times* June 25, 1985.

descended from 29,000 feet through 15,000. Terrorists, who had been aboard a previous flight had left a bomb under the seat. The explosion tore a huge hole about nine feet by four feet in size in the right side of the aircraft, just forward of the wing leading edge. The explosion expelled four American passengers from the aircraft, near the town of Argoes in Greece.

Many other bombings occurred,[78] but few people in the United States know of their occurrence.

SECURITY MEASURES

There are many steps that can be taken for minimizing the terrorist dangers. Non-passengers should be kept out of domestic and international concourses. Intensive training exercises must be conducted to train and check security personnel. Airports should have security people constantly checking the airport environment for security breaches. These security personnel should not be under the control of those responsible for getting the plane out on time. The entire airport security should be under the control of one entity, to avoid different entities acting independently, and with some areas not properly protected.

Baggage carried on board or placed in the cargo compartment should be carefully examined. X-ray equipment and the high-technology units, such as the Thermal Neutron Analysis (TNA) and computed tomography X-ray (CT) scanning system devices should be used to detect plastic-type explosives. Dog-sniffers for bomb detection are a great help. Curb-side baggage check-in should be eliminated. Bags should not be allowed to sit unattended in the terminal. It is too easy for terrorists to insert a bomb in someone else's bag, or to substitute bags. The passenger boarding the flight should personally identify every bag going on board the aircraft. Some airlines question each passenger to determine if people other than the traveler packed

---

[78] Air France 747, January 18, 1984. Explosion in cargo hold with major damage, but landed safely; UTA DC-8, March 10, 1984. Explosion in baggage compartment while on the ground, with twenty-four injuries; Lloyd Aereo Boliviano B-727. January 23, 1985. Explosion in lavatory. One killed. Landed safely; Royal Jordanian L-1011. March 9, 1985. Explosion in baggage compartment while plane was still on the ground; Air India B-747. June 23, 1985. Explosion in cargo hold. Destroyed in flight over North Atlantic with 329 deaths; American Airlines B-727. Explosion in baggage compartment while on ground in Dallas; Trans World B-727. April 2, 1986. Explosion in cabin area. Four killed, nine injured; Air Lanka L-1011. May 3, 1986. Explosion in cargo hold on ground in Colombo. Sixteen killed and forty-one injured; Thai Airways Airbus A300. October 26, 1986. Explosion in rear lavatory. Sixty-two injured. Plane landed in Osaka; Korean Airlines B-707. November 29, 1987. Explosion in cabin area. Aircraft destroyed in flight with 115 deaths; BOP Air Bandeirante. March 1, 1988. Explosion in cabin area with aircraft destroyed in flight. Seventeen killed; Pan Am 747. December 21, 1988. Explosion in baggage compartment. Aircraft destroyed in flight with 259 deaths in the plane and eleven on ground; UAT DC-10 September 19, 1989. Explosion in baggage compartment. Aircraft destroyed in flight with 171 deaths.

the bags or had access to them.

The destination of the bags should always be the same as the destination of the passenger. Otherwise, the passenger can get off at an interim stop, with the bomb set to detonate during the subsequent flight. If a passenger, ticketed for a further destination, does not reboard the aircraft at an enroute stop, the departure must be halted, that person's bags removed from the aircraft, and the aircraft searched for possible bombs. Once the airline checks the baggage, passengers must be denied access to the bags. Well-trained personnel at each ticket counter must be alert for any suspicious activities—a subjective analysis that is fraught with pitfalls.

Flight attendants should check the aircraft under the seats and in the overhead racks for baggage left behind. But this creates a major problem. How does one determine what belongs to a passenger who left the aircraft? The small size of plastic explosives makes detection difficult.

Admittedly, some of these recommended practices are not fool-proof. The sheer number of passengers makes strict adherence difficult. It is not unusual for a passenger to book a flight to a distant city, and then get off at an enroute stop, especially when the fare structure makes this practice profitable.

The United States has put the cost and responsibility for security upon the airlines themselves, even though much of the terrorist activity is due to government policies. In most other countries the government provides security, and has one agency responsible for the security at all levels of airport operations.

Human error is almost unavoidable when employees must check hundreds of bags on each flight. Complacency and fatigue become important factors. It is easy to conceal plastic explosives in the lining of bags, or in electronic gear, with the timing device embedded where it is not detectable.

CARGO SHIPPED BY COMPANIES

Bombs placed in cargo or mail shipments are a more difficult security problem. The use of X-ray is difficult or not practical. Dog-sniffers are only partly effective, and cannot detect the plastic type explosives used by most of today's terrorists. The danger is lessened, but certainly not eliminated, by accepting shipments only from recognized shippers. One of the answers may be to exclude cargo from passenger-carrying aircraft. Even after all practical security measures are in place, a resourceful terrorist can still place a bomb on the aircraft.

PAN AM 103—LOCKERBIE

At first the American public paid little attention to the bombings of aircraft overseas. That serenity has changed. Shortly before Christmas of 1988 Pan Am Flight 103 suffered the same type of inflight bombing that had affected other airlines. The flight started at Frankfurt, Germany as a Boeing 727 and changed at London to a Boeing 747, bound for New York. The flight was booked almost solid, until a series of last-minute cancellations by U.S. State Department personnel. They had inside knowledge of a possible bombing on Pan Am, and a state department memorandum suggested they use other airlines, which many did. This warning was not made available to other passengers.

Several weeks earlier, on December 5, 1988, the U.S. embassy in Helsinki had received a phone tip that a bomb would be placed on board a Pan Am plane at Frankfurt shortly before Christmas, connecting with a Pan Am 747 leaving London for New York. Four days later the U.S. Information Service notified the FAA, other U.S. Embassies, and Pan Am, of the threat.

On December 21st Pan Am people loaded baggage on a Pan Am 727 at Frankfurt that would change to a Boeing 747 at London, continuing on to New York. It is believed that on board that plane was a Lebanese passenger carrying a Toshiba radio casette player. And concealed in that player was a bomb made of plastic explosives, believed weighing less than one pound, along with a well-concealed detonating device.[79]

BARBECUE PARTY BY SECURITY PERSONNEL WHILE THE BOMB WAS PLACED ON THE PLANE

Despite the bomb threat, Pam Am's Frankfurt security department had a barbecue on that same December 21st,[80] and only twenty-four pieces of luggage were checked for the 124 passengers who boarded the flight. The barbecue was a retirement party given by Pan Am's security personnel for Pan Am's Frankfurt security director, Hanz Leuinger. It was on that afternoon that the bomb-carrier checked his bags at Frankfurt Airport, destined for New York. (Other theories have also been advanced as to who placed the bomb on the aircraft at Frankfurt.)

At London, baggage handlers transferred the bags from the 727 without making another security check, assuming that Pan

---

[79] Another theory is that the bag containing the bomb originated on a flight in Malta, and the *unaccompanied* bag was transferred to the Pan Am 727 in Frankfurt. Allowing the bag on the plane, without being personally checked in by a passenger on the flight, violated international air regulations.

[80] *Spotlight*, June 26, 1989.

Am's Frankfurt people had properly inspected the bags. Flight 103 departed London's Heathrow Airport, heading for New York City. As it approached Lockerbie, Scotland, cruising at 31,000 feet, the plastic bomb located on the left side of the forward cargo compartment exploded. The explosion ripped open a section of the 747 fuselage, which then peeled back from the force of the airflow outside the aircraft. The 747 then broke into several major parts, with the cockpit separating and plunging almost straight down.

The main portion of the 747, with the wings and fuel tanks attached, crashed into the center of the little town of Lockerbie, Scotland. It dug an enormous crater into the ground, killing 11 people in Lockerbie. The cockpit containing the crew crumpled onto the ground ten miles away from where the main fuselage fell. The tail section fell fifteen miles away.

During the crash-investigation the cockpit voice recorder was recovered, but revealed only the initial sound of the bomb explosion before electrical power halted the recording.

After months of intensive investigation, the investigators identified the suitcase containing the explosives, and the passenger who checked the bag. The bomb-container was identified as a Toshiba radio-tape recorder as having contained the plastic explosives.

FINDINGS DURING LITIGATION

During subsequent litigation, depositions uncovered facts that would otherwise not have been discovered or exposed. Lee Kreindler's law firm[81] obtained the deposition of Oliver Koch, who worked for Alert Management Systems, Pan Am's security affiliate at the Frankfurt Airport. Koch worked in Pan Am's baggage security, and he was responsible for training and supervising security personnel who checked baggage for explosives. Koch testified that he had not seen the "Helsinki warning," the name given to the reported bomb plot alert, until the morning *after* the Lockerbie tragedy. Withholding this knowledge from Koch prevented extra security measures being implemented that might have discovered the bomb in the casette player.

The federal judge ordered Koch's testimony sealed, acquiescing to Pan Am's motion, protecting Pan Am from public criticism. Lee Kreindler, an attorney for many of the relatives of Flight 103 victims, summarized the deposition before U.S. District Judge Thomas Platt, stating:

The night of Lockerbie he [Koch] got an emergency call

---

[81] *Jack Anderson Column*, July 28, 1989, appearing in *San Francisco Chronicle*.

from his boss, [Ulrich] Weber. And Weber said come in early the next morning. And he comes in early the next morning, and there is, obviously, confusion and concern. And he is asked to work on Weber's desk with his computer. And he looks down and he sees the Helsinki warning on Weber's desk. And he goes crazy. And he says, "What is this?" And Weber says: "Oh, my God, don't worry, don't worry, it's nothing, forget it." So Koch says, "How can I forget it? This is a warning of a potential bomb. It is my job." "Just forget it. Be quiet or you will get in trouble."

It was standard procedure at Frankfurt to date-stamp all correspondence on the date received. Koch testified there was no date stamp on the Helsinki warning when he found it the morning after the Lockerbie disaster. Kreindler continued:

A few days later the FAA was supposed to arrive, and in Koch's presence Weber takes out a date stamp, backdates it to December 9, which is when he received it, and stamps it. And that apparently was the one given to the FAA. Koch has the original one without the date stamp.

After the crash, meaning well, but using questionable judgment, Pan Am promoted a barbecue party at Lockerbie for those who missed their Christmas because of the crash. The barbecue site was 200 yards from where many of the bodies were cremated in the crash of Flight 103. Many thought the idea ghoulish, and public outrage caused Pan Am to cancel the event.

SHOULD TERRORIST THREATS BE PUBLICIZED?

When the public heard that many State Department personnel had warning of the bomb threat, and changed their reservations to other airlines, the question arose about whether or not Pan Am, or the government, had the moral responsibility to make the bomb threat public. This is a difficult question. Obviously, if one group of passengers is notified of the bomb threat, then all the passengers should be notified. But notifying the public every time the carrier received a bomb or terrorist threat could escalate the number of threats, and could very easily lead to chaos. Hundreds of bomb threats are already received by the airlines every year; this could escalate into thousands if publicity is given to each one. Tight security is the best measure.

FAA'S RESPONSIBILITIES TO INSPECT

The FAA's responsibility under law is to monitor an airline's safety practices, and to inform the airline if any shortcomings exist. This includes checking security measures at various airlines, and making recommendations. The FAA is itself responsible when safety problems or violations that the FAA should have detected (and probably did), were not brought to the airline's attention with a requirement that they be corrected.

The FAA's success rate in this area was as bad as it is in every other area. If the FAA met its responsibilities, and used its resources to supervise and advise as to proper security measures at the airlines, it is very possible the Pan Am 103 tragedy would never have happened.

The FAA has a legislated duty to inspect safety practices and make recommendations to correct the deficiencies they find. One of the FAA's duties is to find safety problems overlooked by the airlines (or crewmembers) and bring these to the attention of the proper people to prevent a repetition. But the FAA abdicates this responsibility, and instead, punishes the airlines (or the crewmembers), rather than helps. After the FAA failed in doing its own duty to check Pan Am's security before the Lockerbie crash, the FAA then proposed a heavy fine of $630,000 against financially ailing Pan Am World Airways.[82]

The FAA said that Pan Am did not follow proper security screening procedures in Britain and West Germany for passengers on Flight 103. The FAA also stated that its post-crash security was inadequate. The FAA said that Pan Am failed to properly determine whether thirty-one passengers who boarded the airline's Flight 103 in London needed further security screening. In addition, the FAA claimed Pan Am did not perform follow-up screening on five passengers who boarded at Frankfurt and four other passengers who joined the flight from other airlines. These charges are very subjective, and probably could be charged of most other airlines.

The FAA claims that as a result of these oversights, the airline did not assure that the passengers, their checked baggage and carry-on items, received additional scrutiny as called for in Pan Am's security program. The FAA stated that the airline's security personnel at Heathrow used a hand-held metal detector rather than perform required search procedures for carry-on baggage identified for follow-up screening. In the tens of thousands of passenger boardings the FAA could make this charge against many airlines.

Senator James Exxon, of Nebraska, who I repeatedly informed of internal FAA corruption—that would naturally affect its willingness or ability to meet its air safety responsibilities—praised the FAA for assessing the fines.[83] Exxon said

---

[82] September 20, 1989.
[83] *Associated Press*, David Briscoe, September 21, 1989.

the fines would "serve notice not only on Pan Am but all other airlines that we are going to be insistent, on not only proper maintenance of the aircraft, but proper screening of passengers and baggage that goes on airplanes today." Too bad Exxon couldn't use the same moralizing on himself and have acted on my pleas for him to exercise his Congressional responsibilities on the other crash-causing problems within the FAA.

Claims and counterclaims! Whose telling the truth? Ohio congressman James Traficant reported to the press on November 7, 1989 that West German intelligence alerted the CIA that they saw suspicious activities around the baggage loading area when the bomb was reportedly put on board the Pan American 727. Accompanying Representative Traficant at the news conference was a former CIA officer, Victor Marchetti, who obtained the report.[84]

Excerpts from the report released by Traficant described a West German intelligent agent watching baggage handlers an hour before the flight left Frankfurt, who singled out a suspicious suitcase and decided "something was very wrong." West German intelligence immediately passed the information and concern to a CIA unit in Frankfurt, which relayed it to an unidentified "control," stated the excerpt from the insurance investigator's report. The "control" replied, "Don't worry about it, don't stop it, let it go."

Representative Traficant stated several days earlier that the report concluded that the CIA was "covering up a drug run." The CIA was reportedly protecting the terrorists' Frankfurt-to-New York heroin route in exchange for contacts that might lead to freedom for American hostages. In this environment of intrigue, the public never knows whether government statements or denials are truth or lies.

Pan Am sought to defend itself against more than $300 million in law suits by filing documents with the court that the United States received warnings from West German and Israeli intelligence about the bomb, and failed to relay the information to Pan Am. The Justice Department blocked discovery by attorneys representing the family of the victims, who tried to determine if the government actually received information concerning the warnings, and failed to act.

Pressure generated by the relatives caused President Bush to appoint a Presidential Commission on Aviation Security and Terrorism, which conducted its first hearing in November 1989. Relatives of victims testified that their inquiries into the

---

[84] Marchetti left the CIA in 1969 and later wrote a critical book, "The CIA and the Cult of Intelligence."

bombing had been met with "lies, half-truths, denials, allegations, revelations, and enormous amounts of buck-passing and finger-pointing" by numerous government agencies and the Bush Administration.[85]

United States international policies make United States airlines target for terrorists. U.S. airlines and U.S. citizens pay the consequences. Pan Am suffered heavy financial losses in numerous sabotage actions because of the government's mid-East policies.

Many American companies advise their employees to travel on foreign airlines to avoid the bomb and terrorist threats. Foreign carriers enjoy the financial rewards of higher passenger loads and profits as Americans shun their own airlines.

BOMB DETECTORS

As the bomb threat increased, the FAA gave more attention to detecting bombs. Prior to Lockerbie, the bomb detectors were conventional X-ray machines and dog-sniffers. But the increasing use of plastic-type explosives by terrorists resulted in the development of high-technology detection equipment.

The plastic explosives make detection very difficult. They can be easily molded into literally any shape, even as flat as a sheet of paper. It is a mud-like material that can be easily molded by hand. Unsuspecting carriers often bring these bombs on the aircraft, in baggage, radios, or other objects. The plastic explosives are almost odorless and dogs can't sniff them out. A pound of plastic explosives, easily concealed, can bring down the largest of aircraft. It is approximately twice as powerful as dynamite.

High-technology has developed equipment to detect plastic explosives. However the machines that were installed in airport terminals in the early 1990s could not reliably detect small amounts of plastic explosives. One machine, called a thermal neutron analysis detector (TNA)[86] was programed to sound an alarm for two and a half pounds of plastic explosives. Less than one pound can destroy a Boeing 747. Further, many items commonly found in luggage also sound the alarm, including boots, cheese, wool, nylon stockings, and other material.

THE BOMBINGS CONTINUED

The next major bombing occurred when the French airline, UTA, had an aircraft blow apart. This DC-10 was the third jumbo jet destroyed by a bomb in four years, with a total loss

---

[85] *Aviation Week & Space Technology*, November 27, 1989.

[86] These machines sense, rather than see, the explosive material. One type of machine bombards the explosives with low energy neutrons to make them give off identifying radiation. The elements become temporarily radioactive after bombardment by the nuclear radiation, and this radioactivity is then detected by electronic sniffers.

of 770 lives.[87] UTA's DC-10 departed the Congo for London, with a stop in Chad. It exploded shortly after departure.

Immediately after the crash, two anonymous telephone calls claimed responsibility. One caller identified himself as representing the Islamic Jihad, an organization of Shiite Moslem extremists headquartered in Lebanon, who claimed responsibility. A caller to a Western news agency in London read what was reported to be an Islamic Jihad statement. The speaker said his group bombed the UTA aircraft in retaliation for Israel's abduction the month before of a Shiite cleric in southern Lebanon, and to enforce demands for his release.

"We are proud of this action, which was very successful," the caller said in English. "We would like to say the French are warned not to exchange information regarding Sheik Obeid with the Israelis no [sic] more. We demand the freedom of Sheik Obeid and otherwise we will refresh the memories of the bombings in Paris of '85 and '86. Long live the Islamic Republic of Iran."[88]

This reference was to the terrorist bombings that shook the French capital in 1985 and 1986, and which killed a dozen people and wounded more than 150.

A Columbian Boeing 727 belonging to Avianca Airlines blew up shortly after takeoff from Bogota on November 28, 1989. It was reportedly caused by a bomb left in the cabin by a passenger who boarded the aircraft. But then he dashed off the aircraft before it taxied out, a tell-tale sign to remove the passenger's baggage and search the plane before proceeding.

MANY NEAR-BOMBINGS

There were numerous bomb attempts that could have made headlines bigger than the Pan Am 103 tragedy. Terrorists placed a time bomb on a Saudi Arabian 747 on November 24, 1989. But it failed to go off when an internal wire in the bomb detonating device jarred loose. Without the luck of that loose wire, 248 people would probably have died.

HIJACKINGS

Between 1930 and 1958, there averaged less than one hijacking a year. During the early 1970s the average jumped to 100 per year. The hijacking incidents escalated in 1969 and 1970, when there were 150 in a two-year period. The modern history of hijacking commenced in 1959 when Fidel Castro seized power in Cuba. Anti-Castro Cubans began seizing airliners, escaping from Cuba. The press lauded them at first as

---

[87] June 1985 Air India Boeing 747 blew up en route from Toronto to London, killing all 329 aboard; Pan Am's 747 over Lockerbie on December 21, 1988.

[88] *Washington Post*, September 21, 1989.

heroes. But in May 1961, as the hijackings started in the other direction, the media coverage became critical of hijackers.

In one incident a pro-Castro hijacker armed with a long knife seized a National Airlines convair 440, and diverted the flight to Cuba. Many others followed. Three months later, on July 24, 1961, a hijacker diverted an Eastern Airlines Electra to Havana. Castro initially seized the aircraft and released the crew and passengers. Several weeks later he relented, releasing the aircraft.

A hijacker boarded a Pacific Air Lines DC-3 at Chico, California on July 31, 1961, shooting a loading agent. He then forced his way into the cockpit, where he shot the captain, permanently blinding him. Following this incident, the pilot-union pressured Congress to pass an air piracy act, providing for stiff penalties. The FAA issued a requirement that the door to the cockpit be locked, a common-sense action that should have been taken much earlier.

Opposing this and other measures, including the screening of passengers, was the Air Transport Association (ATA). The Air Line Pilot Association tried to get Congress to add an amendment to the Federal Aviation Act of 1958, requiring detection procedures to detect concealed weapons on boarding passengers. ATA opposed any kind of passenger screening or search. The public soon forgot the prior tragedies, and nothing meaningful was done.

Pacific Airlines experienced another inflight sabotage with fatal results for all on board. Pacific Airlines Flight 773, a Fairchild F-27, was returning to San Francisco from Reno. Shortly before seven a.m. on May 7, 1964, as the aircraft approached the San Francisco Bay area, passenger Francisco Gonzales forced his way into the cockpit. He shot both pilots, causing the plane to go into a near-vertical dive, plunging into the outskirts of the little town of Danville, California, within a mile of where I lived. The plane crashed into the hillside at an estimated 400 miles per hour. The gunman, who had purchased life insurance before boarding the plane at Reno, had bragged for the past several days that he was going to kill himself.

Most of us remember the famous D.B. Cooper who hijacked a Northwest Airlines Boeing 727, and made a bizarre exit. Upon receiving $200,000 in cash, Cooper forced the plane to depart Seattle and, at night over wooded and mountainous terrain, opened the rear airstair door and parachuted out. He was never found. Years later hikers found some of the money along a mountain stream.

Between 1968 and 1972 over 160 hijackings of U.S. airlines occurred. Congress finally passed the Anti-hijacking Act of

1974. While waiting for Congress—or the FAA—to act, hijackers murdered an airline pilot and wounded eight others. Again
Congress refused to act until the threat of a work stoppage by
all U.S. airline pilots forced them to address the issues.

Other incidents occurred, including the hijacking of a
Southern Airlines plane on March 18, 1970. A passenger forced
his way onto the flight station of a DC-9 at gunpoint and forced
the crew to fly eastward over the Atlantic Ocean, with the
intent of forcing the aircraft to ditch into the ocean. Unable to
reason with the gunman, the pilots attacked him, and during the
process the gunman killed the copilot and shot the captain, who
barely remained conscious until landing the DC-9 at Boston.

Practical gun detection equipment had been available since
1960, but the FAA refused to require its use. FAA had appointed
a special group to study the electronic screening of passengers
prior to boarding the aircraft; then the FAA buried the study.
In spite of this delaying action the copilot's death focused
public attention on the hijacking problem. Electronic screening
became a reality and hijacking dramatically decreased. Senator
Vance Hartke, a powerful force in Congress during the 1960s,
repeatedly attacked the screening of passengers, citing civil
liberty violations. Could that be why Hartke covered up for the
FAA and NTSB corruption when I brought it to his attention?

News media publicity and resulting public pressure forced
the FAA to act. The large number of hijackings also caused
initiation of the sky marshal program under the control of the
FAA. Marshalls were placed on random flights.

Three hijackers diverted a Southern Airlines DC-9 on
November 1972 after it took off from Birmingham, Alabama.
The hijackers forced the crew to land at Detroit, where they
demanded $10 million from city officials. While waiting for the
money, the hijackers got drunk, and forced all male passengers
to disrobe. They terrorized everyone on board. After obtaining
the money, the hijackers then forced the crew to takeoff, flying
to places in Canada and finally Cuba.

The hijackers didn't like the appearance of the Cuban
troops, and again forced the aircraft to takeoff and land at
Orlando, Florida. FBI agents shot out the tires. In retaliation
the hijackers shot the copilot, and forced the captain to make
a takeoff with flat tires. Somehow, despite the drag of the flat
tires, the plane made it off the ground, trailing smoke from the
burning tires. The DC-9 then landed for the second time back
at Havana.

The regulations initiated in 1973 requiring screening for
guns lowered the number of hijackings. In the five years
preceding 1973, there were 133 hijacking attempts. In the
following ten years, there were only 73. The numbers continual-

ly decreased, lowering to 50 by 1985.

In one of the few subsequent hijackings, a hijacker took over a Northwest Airlines 727 on January 20, 1983, but was shot and killed by an FBI agent.

A former mental patient boarded an American Airlines 727 at Los Angeles International Airport, on May 27, 1989, enroute to Miami, with a stop at Dallas-Fort Worth Airport. Although the security at Los Angeles International Airport is supposed to be among the nation's best, this former mental patient slipped through security carrying a bulky starter pistol, two knives, and a pair of scissors. He was dressed in military combat fatigues. Surely this attire should have raised suspicions. Approaching Miami, the hijacker forced the plane to head for Havana. When the pilots pleaded with him that the plane was running out of fuel, he allowed them to land at Miami. After 90 minutes of negotiation with the FBI, the hijacker surrendered. Fortunately, this drama ended peacefully for all 157 people on board. Not all such hijackings end without loss of life.

American Airlines did not detect weapons in 24 security tests in 1988, the worst performance among the 26 carriers tested. An American Airlines spokesman stated afterwards, "We really have no reason to question the effectiveness of our security in Los Angeles."

THE OVERSEAS PICTURE WAS DIFFERENT

Overseas, the Arab-Israeli problem caused bombings and hijackings to increase. Hijackers took over an El Al airliner in August 1968, and forced the pilots to fly to Algeria. Pressure from many sources resulted in the release of the aircraft, its crew and passengers. Radical Palestinians then used violence. In December 1968, two gunmen opened fire on an El Al airliner in Athens, Greece, killing one passenger and seriously wounding a cabin attendant. The two gunmen were captured and convicted, but released by the Greeks when terrorists threatened violence to Greece's airlines. A continuing series of terrorist incidents followed.

Israeli security grabbed two suspected Algerian terrorists off a British airliner making an enroute stop in Israel in August 1970. This precipitated Arab retaliation, and Arab terrorists hijacked four international flights simultaneously on September 6, 1970, including El Al, TWA, Pan Am, and Swissair. The El Al jet had an Israeli security guard on board, who shot it out with the hijackers, killing one, and seriously wounding a woman hijacker who had smuggled two grenades on board the aircraft in her brassiere. The plane and passengers were saved from destruction by defective fuses in the grenades.

Terrorists seized an Alitalia jetliner on September 25, 1982 during a flight from Algiers to Rome. Terrorists seized a Cyprus

Airways jetliner on January 8, 1985 and held 12 hostages at Beirut Airport. In 1984, according to U.S. State Department records, there were over 700 terrorist incidents throughout the world, an increase of forty percent over 1983.

Pro-Iranian militants hijacked TWA Flight 847 on June 14, 1985, with 153 people on board. Three of the hijackers had arrived in Athens from Beirut the night before. They spent the night in the airport lounge, and prepared to board the TWA plane. Police detained one, but two others slipped through security. They carried two grenades and a pistol onto the plane wrapped in fiberglass insulation material and a nylon traveling bag, which were not detected by security people. The terrorists took over the jet after it picked up passengers in Beirut. They ordered the captain to fly to different destinations in Europe and the Middle East, including Beirut, where the control tower operator twice denied the plane permission to land. Authorities eventually relented, and agreed to refuel the aircraft in exchange for the release of 17 women and two children. The aircraft took off, and then returned, with only about one minute of fuel remaining. The ordeal lasted four days.

During this hijacking, the terrorists badly beat some of the passengers. They killed U.S. Navy diver Robert Stethem, and dumped his body out of the aircraft onto the ramp. Eventually one of the militants, Mohammed Ali Hamadei, was brought to trial in a West German court, and on May 16, 1989, he was sentenced to prison. The day before the sentence, terrorists kidnapped three West Germans in Lebanon, seeking to put pressure on the Frankfurt court. The terrorists demanded freedom for 17 Shiites imprisoned in Kuwait for bomb attacks, and the release of hundreds of Shiite guerrillas transferred south to Israeli prisons before Israel's withdrawal from southern Lebanon.

Terrorists seized a Kuwait Airways jet on April 5, 1988 as it was flying from Bangkok to Kuwait, and forced it to land at Cyprus. A week later the terrorists were still holding the plane and passengers hostage. Terrorists killed two of the passengers, and dumped them out of the aircraft at Cyprus. As the terrorists threw the bloody bodies from the airplane, the airport was operating in a business-as-usual atmosphere. The tragedy unfolded within sight of crowds of vacationers. Tour groups went by the plane as the bodies lay on the ramp. A Scandinavia Airlines jet landed and discharged passengers, without noticing the hijacked jet, or the bodies laying on the pavement.

Hijackers took over an Indian Airlines 737 enroute to Lahore, Pakistan on July 5, 1985, which had earmarks of an earlier aircraft diversion from India to Pakistan on January 30, 1971. In the earlier hijacking the Pakistani government granted the hijackers asylum and treated them as heroes. This time the hijackers were jailed. Hijackers took over an Egypt Air jet in 1985, which resulted in sixty deaths when Egyptian troops stormed the plane in Malta.

Horror and death were the fate of many in the hijacking of Pan Am Flight 73, a Boeing 747. This tragedy occurred while the plane was on the ground at Karachi, boarding passengers bound for Frankfurt. As the passengers were boarding, a van pulled up and four men leaped out. They boarded the plane, spraying gunfire. They immediately shot one passenger and threw him out of the plane to the ground. The flight deck crew, hearing the commotion, locked the cockpit door and climbed out the pilot's windows to safety. The hijackers were stranded, and unable to go to their planned destination at Cyprus.

Angry, they set a deadline for a new flight crew to arrive. As it grew dark, the on-board fuel-driven electrical power unit ran out of oil, causing it to fail. This in turn caused the emergency lights to shift to battery power. The air conditioning unit stopped operating, resulting in stifling heat build-up in the cabin. Eventually, the batteries went dead, causing the lights to go out. When this happened, the hijackers panicked, and shot their high powered guns point-blank at the passengers, blowing some of them to pieces. The hijackers threw hand-grenades among the passengers, killing sixteen people and seriously wounding fifty others. It was a gruesome blood bath.

In the panic, hundreds of passengers leaped from the plane through the emergency exits. Outside, encountering Pakistani security forces, the passengers screamed for them to stop the killing going on inside. Instead, the Pakistani forces waited for ten to fifteen minutes, as the killings continued, before entering the plane.

In another Pan Am 747 hijacking, the terrorists forced the crew and passengers to fly to Cairo, where passengers evacuated by emergency chutes, and the terrorists blew up the plane in a spectacular explosion and fire. Hijackers forced two aircraft to an abandoned World War II airstrip in Jordan, forcing the occupants to stay in the aircraft for nearly two weeks, without air conditioning or sanitation necessities. The hijackers wanted the British to release a wounded woman hijacker, which the British refused to do.

Another team of hijackers then seized a British airliner, and flew it to the Jordanian airfield. Through international pressures, and the subsequent release of the wounded female hijacker, the terrorists finally released their captives. The hijackers then blew up the planes. The hijacking was later fictionalized in the movie and novel *Black Sunday*. This bizarre series of hijackings was given the name "Black September."

Hijackers seized a Kuwaiti airliner on a flight from Kuwait to Pakistan, killing three passengers while on the ground at Teheran Airport. The terrorists dumped the victims from the plane as if they were sacks of potatoes.

WHAT WILL THE FUTURE BRING?

It is hard to predict what the future will bring in the way terrorists attack. United States support of Israel has made the Arabs desperate. On top of that we have the war on drugs and the powerful drug cartels. FBI spokesman Oliver Revell stated in an interview[89] that U.S. security officials expect the Colombian drug cartels to launch terrorist attacks against Americans and American interests, because of the drug wars. "I expect bombs," he said, adding that "They certainly have the capabilities to do these things."

Revell stated in testimony before the Senate Government Affairs Committee that attempted attacks within the U.S. can't be ruled out, and would be extremely difficult to head off. He testified that U.S. borders are porous and the cartels have shown in the past that they can carry out killings within the U.S. The easiest and most dramatic targets are aircraft, and this is probably the most likely arena for retribution upon American interests.

LONG PERIOD OF AIRCRAFT TERRORISM AHEAD

Senator David Boren of Oklahoma, chairman of the Senate Intelligence Committee, said in an interview that "I think we're in for a long period of problems with the cartels, and potentially some terrorist retaliation."

---

[89] *Wall Street Journal* September 21, 1989.

CHAPTER SEVENTEEN

Deregulation

The Deregulation Act was signed into law by President Carter on October 24, 1978. The Act started to take effect in 1982, by eliminating the Civil Aeronautic Board's (CAB) control of routes that the airlines could fly. The next year the CAB's control over pricing stopped. And on January 1, 1985, the CAB ceased to exist, after decades of regulating the growth of airlines. Price stability ceased. The price charged for a particular flight was something like a flea-market, where the prices changed by the hour, depending upon the demand for seats.

Regulation had a stabilizing effect upon an industry highly sensitive to safety problems. Deregulation destabilized an industry where safety of flight is highly sensitive to economics and intangibles affected by economics. If the two government air safety agencies had been strong, with a high degree of integrity, and maintained impeccable safety standards, deregulation probably would not have brought about the vast increase in safety problems that has occurred.

Deregulation compounded the safety problems that previously existed, and which often had gone unaddressed. In addition to the former safety problems, additional safety problems started making their presence known.

ECONOMIC BENEFITS—A MYTH?

The greater economic efficiency that was expected from deregulation was a figment of Congress's fertile imagination. In many areas airline costs increased. Airline routing changed from direct flights from point "A" to Point "B," to a hub-and-spoke operation. This increased the flight time, the fuel consumed, and the number of employees required over the former routing. To prevent loss of passengers to the competition, airlines went to more frequent scheduling. In addition to higher costs, the scheduling changes increased airport and airway congestions, and increased safety hazards.

These costs, of course, are passed on to the passengers. Confusing and discriminatory pricing became rampant, with some passengers paying two or three times more than the person seated next to them on the plane. Widely advertised discount fares were limited to a few seats on the heavily traveled routes, and only for those who could make reservations a week or more in advance. Routes served by only one or two airlines experienced rapid fare increases far out of proportion to inflation.

Passenger service deteriorated. Passengers occasionally arrived at terminals to discover the flight was cancelled because not enough seats were sold.

Small towns across America that were formerly linked by long-established airlines lost the first-class service, and either ended up with no air service, or second-rate service by small airlines. Many of the old airline names that pioneered and built up the nation's airline industry disappeared.[90] In their place we have small commuter airlines, often operating smaller aircraft that do not meet the former standards of the larger planes. They are often piloted by young, inexperienced, captains, who should have had years of on-the-job training before they upgraded to their present position.

Those promoting deregulation argued that the new start-up airlines would keep the large carriers on their toes, and keep fares low. This was true, initially, on heavily traveled routes on a small number of advertised seats. But the established airlines, with their greater financial base, met the low fares of the new airlines, and forced many of them out of business, or forced them to merge in order to survive.

To break into established markets, new airlines were confronted with all types of start-up problems. They were under-capitalized. They didn't have a strong marketing program. They couldn't compete with the larger airlines' greater frequency of flights or their "frequent-flier" program that rewarded those who travel with one airline. The large established airlines control computer systems used by travel agents, and controlled

---

[90] Among them were Allegheny, Lake Central, PSA, Mohawk, Piedmont, North Central, Frontier, Trans Texas, Southern, Ozark.

much of the business.

Since 1978 over 200 new airlines started up. Very few are left. Large airlines could survive the fare-wars, while the upstarts could not. So much for the advantages to the consumer tooted as the justification for de-regulation.

It would be safe to wonder what was actually behind the airline deregulation; what airline or group expected to profit by it; and who paid what to which member of the Senate and House to bring about deregulation.

As the smaller airlines were forced out of business, fewer airlines dominate a greater percentage of the flights. Eight giant airlines now control about 90 percent of the market. At a fortress hub, where a single carrier dominates the market, the fares often go up as the service gets worse.

The established airlines kept out competition. How? The major airlines locked up twenty to forty year leases on passenger-loading gates at many big airports. Any airline wanting to sublease gate space must pay huge sums. In Detroit, for instance, Southwest Airlines pays Northwest Airlines $150 per flight to use two gates, and the total monthly charges reportedly total about 20 times what Northwest pays the airport authority to lease the space.

Sky-gouging is common in today's deregulated environment, with some passengers paying as much to fly a 500-mile trip as others pay for 3000 miles.

DECEPTION

Deception arises when passengers book a flight on a major airline and then find themselves transferred to one of the smaller, less-safe, commuter operations, before they get to their final destination. After deregulation many of the major carriers discontinued their short haul operations. But then they discovered that they lost the benefit of the feeder traffic. The large airlines addressed this problem by entering into marketing agreements with small regional airlines to feed passengers from the smaller cities to the hub airports.

Many professional pilots won't fly as passengers on these smaller airlines. The type of aircraft they fly, the low-experience level of the pilots, the sometimes poor safety discipline, training, and adherence to federal regulatory safeguards, results in a deterioration of safety. The pilots only remain with the smaller airlines long enough to build up enough flight time to be hired by the larger airlines. Some small airlines experience a complete turnover of pilots every twelve months.

Airlines frequently cancel flights at the very last moment if insufficient tickets are sold, and if the flight is not needed at the destination to meet some other schedule. The passengers are an expendable commodity, and are often treated as such, subjecting them to unnecessary dangers. Gambles are taken with the lives of the crew and passengers.

AIR SAFETY WAS AFFECTED

During hearings on airline economic deregulation, Congress asked FAA officials if they could maintain an adequate level of safety if airlines deregulated. The same FAA personnel described within these pages testified the way the White House wanted them to testify. FAA officials testified that they could maintain the same level of safety as before. Any astute FAA inspector knew otherwise.

Congress knew the FAA couldn't handle the greatly increased safety problems accompanying deregulation. Congress already knew that the deeply ingrained FAA problems would only worsen with deregulation. But a bundle of money and powerful interests lobbied for deregulation. It is a safe bet that money probably exchanged hands, just as it did in the savings and loan, HUD, Abscam, and other government scandals.

Worse yet, after deregulation, the FAA greatly *decreased* the inspector force, when it should have been doubled or tripled it. In 1978 the inspector force was approximately 2,000; it dropped within the next five years over thirty percent. The number of FAA air traffic controllers was also reduced, from 13,000 in 1977 when ATC centers handled over 25 million flights, to a lesser number in 1989 when controllers handled over 30 million flights.

In addition to reducing the number of inspectors, the quality of the inspectors deteriorated. Instead of hiring experienced pilots, affirmative action quotas were set for minority and women, regardless of their experience. Many of the experienced inspectors retired. Add to this the air safety politics, and the ingredients for out-of-control safety exist.

Compounding the problem, the government air safety responsibilities for feeder or regional airlines were turned over to the General Aviation District Offices (GADO). Their responsibilities before deregulation consisted of primarily conducting basic pilot checks in general aviation, including small single engine personal aircraft. The GADO inspectors had no experience, or very little, with airline standards, and didn't have the knowledge or experience to set airline standards.

PILOTS FEEL THE EFFECTS OF DEREGULATION

Today's aviation environment is hostile. The pilots are the first to sense it, and its intangible effect upon air safety. Modern corporate management is often not attuned to the intangible needs for a safe aviation environment, and the long-term effects of good training and competency standards. Their concern is primarily lowering costs. They neither know, nor care, about the long range effects imposed upon air safety by the implementation of such cost-saving methods. Lowering safety by reducing training, reducing competency standards, reducing spare-parts inventory, and reducing maintenance costs, are all a part of the new deregulation environment. Passengers are a commodity. If there is a crash, insurance pays for it, and there is usually a profit from the tragedy.

Airline officials pressure pilots to fly under unsafe conditions. Pilots are pressured to fly with less fuel, since it takes more fuel to carry the additional weight of reserve fuel. For this reason 747s and other planes frequently land with only minutes of fuel remaining, averting a crash by the narrowest of margins and lady luck. Five additional minutes of air time and they could have crashed into the heart of a major city. Pilots are pressured to fly with important equipment inoperative or malfunctioning.

Disasters and deaths arising from these calculated risks are a part of doing business. Management can always point the finger at the crew, blaming them, when, in reality, the problems are elsewhere. The United Salt Lake City tragedy was a classic example of those most responsible for the crash blaming the captain.

FATIGUE

Fatigue is not a new problem with deregulation, but deregulation has worsened the problem. The new management mentality looks on the crewmembers as factory production workers, seeking to maximize the duty time and output. But it doesn't work that way in the hostile aviation environment.

With deregulation, many crews are making more takeoffs and landings, working longer hours, under more difficult conditions. And this especially applies to the small regional airlines. Many crewmembers are on duty for sixteen hours, sometimes starting duty late in the day.

I remember many times when I started work late in the afternoon, and being on duty for the next sixteen hours. This is like working through two shifts of the average employee, and not even starting to work until after having been awake many hours. Not many crewmembers can sleep throughout the day and then wake up in time to start a sixteen-hour duty period in early evening, under difficult flying and working conditions. Compounding this schedule may be frequent instrument approaches under difficult conditions, no meals, working at cabin altitudes of 5000 feet or more, in noisy cockpits. Deprived of a flight engineer, the crew is often overworked, fatigued, and on a poor diet. It is a wonder that more crashes do not occur.

On overseas flights it is often even worse. Some FAA regulations permit flying until a suitable rest stop is reached. This has been interpreted on some routes as when the crew returns to base. I remember flights from California to India or the Middle East, for instance, with a three-pilot crew, where the only time on the ground during a five or seven-day flight occurred for refueling or off-loading cargo. Needless to say, the crew was very fatigued. This type of fatigue is FAA and company-induced, and the crew can't be blamed for the consequences of what was forced upon them.

Night flights have their own problems. The fatigue that seems to accompany night flights is one of the reasons for the entire cockpit crew simultaneously sleeping. A United freighter from New York to Los Angeles overflew Los Angeles—its entire crew asleep, and proceeded west over the Pacific due to this problem. I have heard of other instances through the pilot grapevine. The most difficult time to stay awake appears to be when the sun is rising after flying all night.

CHAPTER EIGHTEEN

Post-Deregulation Crashes

AIR FLORIDA—bringing air tragedy to Congress's doorstep
The Washington, D.C. afternoon rush hour had started early
due to poor driving conditions, and many commuters stuck in
traffic would shortly be part of a major air tragedy. Snow was
falling as Air Florida Flight 90, a Boeing 737, started takeoff
from close-in Washington National Airport on January 13, 1982.
Despite the threatening weather, and despite the short slippery
runway, the captain instructed the copilot to make the takeoff.

The copilot advanced the power levers until the engine EPR
gauges read the engine pressure ratio[91] calculated by the crew
to develop maximum rated thrust. This is an arbitrary engine
thrust setting below that which the military uses for the same
engines. It is intended to prolong engine life. In the event of an
emergency needing more power, the crew could shove the power
levers full forward to get additional thrust, although this is
often not done.

As the copilot advanced the power levers to the calculated
EPR setting, he noticed that it was reached before he advanced
the power levers to their normal position for that power
setting.

---

[91] EPR or engine pressure ratio is the difference in air pressure at the inlet to the
engine, called the Pt2 probe, and the pressure sensed by the probe at the rear of the engine.
Any errors in determining this setting, or errors in reading the pressure ratios, affects the
engine output.

As the 737 slowly accelerated, the copilot, referring to unusual engine instrument readings (resulting from the engines only producing approximately 2/3 of their normal power) said, "God, look at that thing. That don't seem right, does it?" The captain replied, "Yes, it is." The copilot replied, "Naw, I don't think that's right. Ah, maybe it is. I don't know." Sounded like Air Florida's version of United's crew-concept.

If those two pilots had the level of engine knowledge concerning their profession that many teen-agers have about their cars, the crew would have—and should have already done so—checked the engine N1 and N2 percentage of maximum engine revolutions (which read low), checked the engine fuel flows (which read low), and the checked the turbine inlet temperatures (TIT) (which also read low). Any one of these abnormal readings, and certainly all three of them together, indicated that the engine thrust they thought they had did not exist. This conclusion was further suggested by the unusually short forward movement of the power levers.

Air Florida used much more runway than normal before it became airborne, and at Washington National there just doesn't seem to be any excess runway. Once in the air, the aircraft pitched up sharply; the wings started rocking violently; the stall-warning stick-shaker actuated. They were in a stall and about to crash, and didn't know what to do.

Skimming along the ground in the congested Washington, D.C. area, the Lincoln Memorial and other Washington buildings immediately ahead of them, the aircraft refused to climb, and never reached a hundred feet altitude; less than their wing-span. Ground effect kept them in the air, but it wouldn't last much longer. Unless something was done, they would shortly crash.

The first and most obvious thing to do was to shove the power levers forward. Even a little-old-lady driving up a steep hill knows to increase power. This crew displayed incredibly dangerous lack of knowledge of the complex equipment they were flying before lifting off, and now didn't do any better. The poor training, the absence of experience, and the low check-standards—all known to the FAA, would shortly result in brutal deaths for almost a hundred persons, and make television history.

Flying in a dangerous nose-high attitude, the captain tried "talking" the nose down: "Forward, forward. Come on, forward, Forward!" The plane continued skimming over the ground and getting further behind the power curve.

"We're going down."

Still not thinking of advancing the power levers from the far-back position to the full forward position, the copilot said:

"Larry, we're going down, Larry!" They didn't have the benefit of an open field. Instead, the plane hit the 14th Street bridge that crosses the Potomac River. Near down-town District of Columbia, the bridge was crawling with traffic.

Stuck in the bridge traffic jam was McKinley Maggette, a passenger in a friend's car. Air Florida slammed into the guard rail with its main wheels. It flattened and sheared the roofs from several cars, before it slammed into the Potomac River. The sound was like a giant plate glass dropping flat and breaking apart.

On the bridge four people perished immediately. One driver was decapitated, others were badly injured. One person got out of his car, saw the bloody carnage, and passed out. A woman nearby fainted from shock.

Rescuers quickly arrived. Some pried pieces of metal from the cars that Flight 172 had flattened, to free those trapped inside. People on the river banks screamed for blankets, rope, two-way radios, and other emergency supplies and equipment. The rescue operation continued for hours under the glare of lights and the scrutiny of national television. When it was over, the death toll was seventy-two on Flight 172, and four on the ground. Many were injured; some permanently crippled.

One person later said, "I saw one guy ... he was laying on his back with his eyes open. His arms were spread, his head was in the water, the water was red. He was bleeding from the head."

THE CAUSE

Going back and examining the errors made by the Air Florida crew, the first mistake was using reverse engine thrust to back the aircraft from the terminal. The ground was covered with loose snow, which whirled onto all parts of the aircraft, including the wings and the engine Pt2 probes. Basic knowledge that comes with experience and good training, which was very bad at Air Florida, would have advised against this procedure, which was also prohibited by the airline's flight manual.

The next mistake was in radio procedures. Before getting taxi clearance to leave the terminal, it was standard procedure at Washington National Airport (and most other airports) to contact clearance delivery to start the process of getting instrument clearance. The crew had taxied the aircraft from the terminal to the deicing pad without notifying Washington Airport clearance delivery. It wasn't until the aircraft had been deiced that the call was made. Air traffic control then factored in sufficient time to permit Air Florida to get deiced, which was no longer needed. By the time the clearance would arrive, the effect of the deicing was lost and the aircraft started accumulating ice all over again.

The aircraft was incorrectly deiced, and none of the crew checked the deicing procedure. American Airlines deiced Air Florida under contract, applying a weak mixture of water and ethylene glycol. This spray was not followed by an anti-ice mixture that would have prevented ice formation for a short period of time. Further, one wing is believed to have not been deiced at all, and none of the crew members checked the deicing.

Canadian and European operators apply a heavy anti-icing mixture, known as Type II fluid, after first deicing the aircraft with Type I fluid. This method prevents ice formation for up to thirty minutes, giving the crew time to get in the air and get the wing heaters working.

If the FAA had met its responsibilities it would have required an anti-icing spray be applied when there is probability of falling snow, sleet, or rain adhering to the aircraft after deicing; it would have encouraged or required deicing to be done near the takeoff position; and required that a competent person check the deicing procedures.

The manufacturer of the deicing equipment, the company that furnishes the deicing fluid, the Boeing Aircraft Company, and earlier NTSB reports, recommended a second application of primarily glycol, for its anti-ice effect. Neither one of the pilots went back to the cabin to check for ice or snow buildup on the aircraft, a job that is normally done by the flight engineer.

FRIGHTENING IGNORANCE OF THE MOST BASIC KNOWLEDGE!

Recognizing whether the engines are putting out rated power is obviously one of the most basic of all piloting knowledge requirements. Without adequate power the aircraft doesn't take off and climb as shown by the charts and for the weight and runway conditions. The crew had no knowledge of how to check that they had the required engine power. Power is set in accordance with the pressure ratio between the engine probe at the engine inlet (PT2) and the probe in the turbine area. If the inlet probe is iced over, the pressure ratio reading will be considerably higher than normal, falsely indicating maximum rated power before the power levers are advance far enough to produce that amount of thrust. In this case the crew had less then seventy-percent rated power.

I discovered that this lack of knowledge was common among the crewmembers in the mid-1960s, and tried to train the crews in its importance during simulator checks. Almost every takeoff was a simulated crash, as none of the crew members were trained to recognize the problem. My recommendation to include the simulated problem in the crew training and check requirements was ignored.

Another problem: The check list, the company operating manual, and good judgment, required that the crew turn on the engine anti-ice during taxi and for takeoff. If this had been done, icing of the EPR probe icing would not have occurred and the false reading would not have occurred. The check list called for the engine anti-ice to be turned on. The captain responded to the check list call-out by answering, "off," when "on" was the correct response and action.

AIRCRAFT DESIGN PROBLEM

The crew experienced a little-publicized design problem inherent in the early Boeing 737 wing design that made the plane more susceptible to wing contamination (ice or snow) than most other aircraft. Little-publicized operational incidents showed a sharp pitch-up during takeoff if the wings have even a small amount of ice or snow adhering. The pitch-up was due to the wing being nearly stalled due to leading edge contamination, and is a common reaction on most jet aircraft to a stall or near-stall condition.

The frightening pitch-up and wing-rocking that occurred shortly after liftoff caused European aviation authorities to require the airlines to increase takeoff airspeeds when there was danger of wing contamination. The FAA ignored this safety requirement. To have required the airline to do this would occasionally cause the aircraft to be dispatched at a lighter weight, and this could reduce the payload, resulting in reduced profits.

Boeing knew about the problem, but only gave it enough notice to be able to claim in the event of a crash that they notified the airlines. The FAA knew of the problem, as did the NTSB, and the airlines. They all kept quiet.

AGAIN IDENTIFYING THE WING PROBLEM

After the crash, the NTSB issued a report identifying the pitch-up tendency of the 737, and recommended increasing the takeoff speed. Although European operators had encountered the problem for years and had required corrective actions, FAA Administrator Lynn Helms replied that the FAA hadn't yet determined whether the 737 is "more sensitive than other airplanes" to pitch up. The NTSB identified the icing of the PT2 probe, and the inadequate icing procedure by American Airlines.

WANTING PRAISE FOR CONTRIBUTING TO THE CRASH

American Airlines' president, Robert Crandall stated in a June 1989 speech[92] that the Department of Transportation

---

[92] *Wall Street Journal* June 9, 1989.

should issue a monthly award to the airline with the best maintenance. American suggested a "Golden Wrench" award, implying it would be eligible to receive it. This could boomerang. Maybe Crandall forgot that it was American's unsafe maintenance procedures that led to the Chicago DC-10 crash; it was American's deicing of the Air Florida Boeing 737 that contributed to that tragedy. In 1985 American Airlines paid a $2.5 million fine, the largest in aviation history at that time, for a series of maintenance-related violations.

NORTHWEST CRASHES

Northwest Airlines had a fairly good safety record, with occasional lapses. Immediately after World War II, Northwest experienced several crashes, but then the airline corrected the problem. Northwest experienced three Martin 202 crashes in a row when it started flying the two-engine airliner. Northwest's crews disliked the aircraft, and California-based Transocean Airlines purchased them in the same year that I started flying for the airline, 1951. Compared to the DC-3 and DC-4 used by the airlines at that time, the Martin 202 was a high performance aircraft. Transocean lost two of them, but this was due to pilot error. One plane crashed at Tuccumcari, New Mexico, during a low-altitude circling approach during a snowstorm. The pilot lost his altitude awareness and descended into the ground. The second plane was lost while Transocean pilots, flying at the wrong altitude, flew the aircraft into the side of an inactive volcano on Oshima Island south of Tokyo. (The plane and crew had been furnished to Japan Airlines when it started up in 1951.)

Northwest had a DC-4 crash during an engine-out landing at Sandspit, British Columbia. Northwest experienced a needless crash when the captain ditched a Boeing 377 double-deck Stratocruiser into the water shortly after takeoff from Seattle. As soon as the wing flaps were raised, the plane experienced buffeting. The flight engineer had failed to position the engine cowl flaps to the takeoff position just prior to takeoff, causing buffeting to occur after the pilots raised the wing-flaps. None of the crew members recognized the obvious cause of the buffeting, nor recognized that raising the wing flaps brought on the buffeting. Common sense suggested checking the cowl flap position, or extending the wing flaps to the takeoff position where buffeting did not occur. Instead, the captain ditched the plane into Puget Sound where is ripped apart.

YONKERS

Another senseless air tragedy occurred when a Northwest Boeing 727 crashed near Yonkers, New York. The crew failed to turn on the pitot heat switch during the pre-takeoff check list at La Guardia Airport. This simple failure, compounded by lack of understanding of the important pitot-static system and flight characteristics, led to tragedy.

The pitot tube feeding impact air to the various flight instruments, including the airspeed indicator, iced up, trapping air in the lines. This trapped air *expanded* as the aircraft climbed, causing the airspeed indicator to increase from the normal approximately 280 knots to 450 knots. The rate of climb indication was also much higher. The captain reacted to this high airspeed by increasing the pitch angle to thirty degrees from a more normal ten to fifteen degrees, and reducing all engine power to idle-thrust.

A basic understanding of the pitot-static system would have promptly alerted the crew to the *cause* of the symptoms, and the simple corrective action to be taken.

The captain should have kept the normal pitch-attitude and power setting for that segment of flight, and then trouble-shoot the system. The most-obvious cause for the incorrect readings was an iced-up pitot-tube. A quick check of the pitot-heat switch would have shown it to be off. Turning it on would have removed the blockage within seconds. A backup check if the pitot-switch had been on would be to check the circuit breakers.

The stall warning indicator sounded when the stall warning system sensed the stall. This gave a correct reading and was separate from the pitot-static system. Simultaneous with the stall-warning indication, the overspeed clacker sounded from the erroneous high airspeed reading. The crew had the worst of two worlds, which would have been instantly recognized if any one of the three crewmembers knew the aircraft systems.

The 727 stalled from the extreme high-nose-attitude and the power off, and then plunged 18,000 feet to destruction near Yonkers, New York. Obviously, everyone perished.

DETROIT

It was early evening on August 16, 1987 when Northwest Airlines Flight 255, a DC-9-82, took off from Detroit's Metro Wayne County International Airport. This flight, which started poorly, would make next-morning's headlines. During taxi to the takeoff runway, the crew failed to make a radio frequency change, a relatively minor error. The crew turned onto the wrong taxi way. Another not-unknown error. The main errors were failure to extend the wing-flaps during taxi, which should be as intuitively obvious as extending the landing gear before landing; failure to make visual checks of the important takeoff items shown on the pre-takeoff check list; failure to complete the before-takeoff check list.

The crew violated the sterile-cockpit rule that prohibits conversations unrelated to flying when below 10,000 feet above the ground. The crew entertained an attractive flight attendant who sat in the cockpit, contrary to company regulations. The crew discussed personal matters, diverting their attention from important matters such as the before-takeoff check list and the many other considerations that go through a pilot's mind at a key phase of flight such as takeoff.

As the aircraft started the takeoff roll, it took almost twice the normal runway length to become airborne, the first indication something was not right. The pilot had to raise the nose of the aircraft to an unusually high pitch-up position to get airborne, the second indication that something was wrong. The wings started rocking violently as soon as they were airborne, as if the plane was in a stall attitude, being the third indication. The stall-warning sounded, being the fourth indication. The plane was obviously in a stalled condition. Unless the right actions were immediately taken, the plane would probably crash.

The crew also found that the auto-throttles refused to operate after liftoff. (The crew also forgot to turn the system on during the pre-takeoff check list.) The crew did nothing to recover from their precarious predicament. They didn't check the wing-flap handle and flap-position indicator to insure that the wing flaps were set for the eleven-degree takeoff setting required for this takeoff. They didn't advance the power levers to the full forward position to get additional engine thrust. They just sat there.

Fourteen seconds after liftoff, the 737 was only about 45 feet in the air. Flying like a projectile at tree-top height, the 737 hit a light pole in a National Car Rental lot, ripping open the wing fuel tanks and bursting into flames. It then hit a light pole in an Avis car rental agency, rolled 45-degrees to the left, scraped the roof of the Avis building, and cart-wheeled into a concrete embankment. It burst into a giant fireball seen for miles around.

The airplane disintegrated into many large sections and millions of little pieces. The cockpit section broke off and skidded down a two-lane road, sliding under a railroad trestle and under two spans of the I-94 freeway.

Local hospitals were alerted for the arrival of victims. But rescuers found only bodies and parts of bodies. There was one exception. Fire fighter Dan Kish thought he heard moaning from among the bodies. Firemen turned off the hoses and pumps, and listened. The sound appeared to be coming from a man who was dead. The moaning continued. "We spotted a woman lying on some debris," said Roy Brindamous. "We lifted a seat off of her and I put my face to hers to check for breathing; but she was not alive."

Suddenly an arm moved under one of the seats. It was a four-year old girl, badly injured, and covered with blood. The fire fighters unbuckled her seat belt and removed the little girl. A doctor cut away her charred white dress and checked for signs of life. She was alive.

The rescuers rushed the girl to the hospital, where her identify was unknown for 24 hours. The nation's news media identified her unusual purple nail polish, which was the clue needed to identify her as Cecelia Cichan. Her grandmother had applied the unusual purple color at Philadelphia the weekend before the family's return to Phoenix via Detroit. The only survivor, Cecelia lost her mother, her father and her brother.

After the tragedy, witnesses recalled the horror at the crash scene. "There was fire all along the highway," said Delilah Schultz, who lives near the airport. "The whole house shook. The plane exploded twice after it hit. The whole road was nothing but flames. I heard a lady scream, 'Somebody help us. Somebody help us.' She was on the highway overpass. Then she stopped screaming."

Pam Hughes was helping a customer at the Avis Rental Car agency at the Detroit Airport when a man shouted, "Get out of here!" She looked up and saw the burning jetliner careening toward the building. In the Avis parking lot employees were cleaning cars and filling gas tanks when suddenly "everything went orange." Jeff Williams stated, "It lit up the sky."

"Oh God! It was awful!"

"We could hear the passengers screaming from the outside," Pamela Galvin, a waitress at a nearby motel stated, wiping tears from her eyes. "It was horrible. Oh God! It was awful!"

Adding to the miseries, and drumming up business for attorneys, a man impersonating a priest appeared at this crash scene, as he had appeared at numerous others, soliciting legal business for a Florida attorney. Bodies were being pulled from the crash when the priest, identifying himself as Father John Irish, appeared on the scene, seeking legal clients. He was right from central casting—soft-spoken and comforting—wearing a sandy beard and soulful gaze. His line was well rehearsed. The supposed priest hugged crying loved ones, and talked of God's rewards in the hereafter. He even sobbed with family members during the aftermath of the Detroit crash. He then handed out the business card of a Florida attorney.

The press reported that Father Irish held a mail-order divinity degree from a church that recruits clergy through advertisements placed in supermarket tabloids. The pseudo priest is thought to have first shown up at a funeral following a September 1985 plane crash in which the pilot and 16 skydivers perished. Father Irish was identified in the Detroit crash when Fred McLaughlin flew to Detroit to identify the remains of his son. Father Irish introduced himself to McLaughlin as they walked through the airport. "I showed him a picture of my son, and he put his arm around me and started crying," said Mr. McLaughlin. "I was impressed. He was a very sensitive person." McLaughlin stated Father Irish "deepened and perverted our personal tragedy."

POST-CRASH ACTIVITIES

This Detroit crash became the second worst air disaster in the United States, in the number of fatalities, behind American Airlines DC-10 Chicago crash that killed 273 people. The severity of the disaster caused over 100 investigators to converge on the scene, many with a vested interest to protect. They charted and photographed the 3500-foot long wreckage path. It didn't take long to discover that the wing flaps were in the retracted position instead of the 11 degree setting.

Interfering with determining the cause of the crash was the statement by a Northwest copilot, in another plane, who later insisted he saw the flaps extended as Flight 255 commenced the takeoff. The Cockpit Voice Recorder (CVR), the Digital Flight Data Recorder (DFDR), the examination of the physical wing flap mechanism, the performance of the aircraft, showed otherwise. However, the contradictory statement by the copilot shifted public attention from the actual cause of the crash while the crash was still foremost in the public's mind.

PETITIONING THE COURT TO REOPEN THE ACCIDENT HEARING

The highly sensitive aspects of an airline crash, if they are revealed at all, often come out in subsequent law suits. McDonnell Douglas filed a petition on April 1989 with the National Transportation Safety Board to reopen the crash investigation, based upon new evidence uncovered. The petition stated that the two pilots on Flight 255 had deliberately pulled the circuit breaker that silenced the takeoff warning horn (which would have sounded an alarm during the takeoff, warning the crew that one or more of several aircraft systems were not property set for takeoff).

The petition stated that it was standard practice for the

two pilots on Flight 255 to pull the warning circuit breaker. The petition stated that another Northwest pilot found the circuit breaker pulled on a MD-80 jet piloted by the same two pilots, John Maus and David Dodds, just two days before the Detroit crash. The petition also cited the statement given by an off-duty dead-heading pilot who heard the warning system sound as the plane taxied at Saginaw, just two hours before the accident.

Investigators told reporters for WJBK-TV that the take-off warning sounded earlier after the plane arrived in Detroit from Saginaw when the crew shut down one engine to conserve fuel while taxiing. The investigator reported, to silence the warning horn, that the "crew disabled the alarm system, which also monitors the wing flaps, by disconnecting a circuit breaker." The investigator stated to WJBK "We know that for a fact." If this is so (and it isn't uncommon), the crew apparently forgot to reset the circuit breaker during the departure from Detroit a short time later.

The petition cited an FAA study that showed pilots were routinely pulling circuit breakers to shut off the "nuisance warnings." The pilots' union knew of the hazardous practice, and knew that the pilots on Flight 255 had done this on earlier flights. Yet, the union sought to place the blame on a mechanical problem, obstructing corrective actions.

The FAA had interviewed dozens of MD-80 pilots and determined that pilots routinely pulled the circuit breaker to stop the nuisance warnings. FAA inspectors conducting the tests found that flight crews demonstrated unusual familiarity with the location of that particular circuit breaker, something that would ordinarily not exist unless the pilot had frequently pulled the breaker in the past.

"We've got to rededicate ourselves to professionalism in this industry," FAA Administrator McArtor stated at a related news conference. He added, there had been a sharp increase in the number of incidents or near-accidents. In that same year there were 31 scheduled airline crashes in the United States, the highest number since 1974.

LABOR DISPUTES AND SAFETY

During the investigation into the Northwest Detroit crash it was revealed that labor unrest caused numerous acts of sabotage to planes and equipment. Sabotage of aircraft from labor unrest was also occurring at the McDonnell Douglas plant in Long Beach, California; four MD-80 jets were sabotaged in an eight-day period.[93] Douglas Aircraft Company spokesman

---

[93] Eight-day period ending July 26, 1989.

reported about fifteen separate incidents of vandalism on planes, including such critical components as damaged hydraulic cables. During the Eastern Airlines strike, while the machinists were out on strike, bomb threats were telephoned to the news media and to Eastern Airlines. One labor-dispute related bomb threat was for Flight 90 from Portland to Atlanta.[94]

DELTA AIRLINES

Before deregulation, Delta had a fairly good safety record, with very few crashes. But after deregulation, top management applied pressure to reduce costs, and training was reduced. This was followed by numerous near crashes and actual crashes. During the late 1980s, Delta experienced the results of the reduction in training costs and lower standards. During a two-week period, Delta experienced numerous embarrassing near-accidents, two of which could have been major air disasters. In one incident occurring on June 30, 1987 that was a near tragedy, just after liftoff at Los Angeles, while the aircraft was over the ocean, the pilot accidentally shut off both engines on the two-engine aircraft. The aircraft, with 205 people on board, plunged from 1,750 feet above the Pacific Ocean to 500 feet; shortly before ditching would have occurred, the pilots fortuitously restarted the engines. That was close. The accidental engine shutdown resulted from a combination of poor training, and poor placement of the engine controls, a problem that FAA inspectors surely should have detected ahead of time.

In another incident, Delta landed at the wrong airport in Kentucky on July 7, 1987, landing at Frankfort, Kentucky, instead of Lexington, 19 miles away. The passengers eventually reached their destination—by bus. In another incident, Delta landed on the wrong runway at Boston's Logan Airport on July 12, 1987. In another incident occurring at Boston, a Delta 727 took off without a takeoff clearance, endangering other aircraft. In still another, Delta nearly crashed into another plane on the ground at Nashville.

A Delta spokesman, Jim Ewing, stated to the press, "There's no connecting thread between" the incidents. But there was a connecting thread. That was the breakdown in the training and competency standards, a condition apparent to the FAA inspectors. They were either inexperienced and would not recognize the problem, or were afraid to report the training deficiencies. Another problem that gets very little attention, is the absence of a flight engineer on board many of the aircraft, thereby placing a greater work load on the remaining two crewmembers.

---

[94] November 25, 1989.

The numerous near-accidents forced the FAA to send a Washington inspection team to Delta. The team spent several weeks on a paper inspection of the carrier. The real test was the day-in and day-out examination of their flight checks and enroute flights that were the responsibility of the assigned FAA inspectors at Atlanta. After the inspection, the FAA reported that Delta's "lack of clear cut" management guidance to pilots was largely responsible for shortcomings found during a five-week review of the carrier's flight operations." The FAA expressed concern over the performance of Delta's pilots, a concern that should have been shared by the public.

Delta responded that it was increasing their training and strengthening the internal monitoring of training and standards. However such changes take years, and Delta had run out of time and luck. The near-tragedies would shortly turn to actual tragedies.

DELTA 727 CRASH AT DALLAS

We've already described Delta's 1011 crash at Dallas. Delta had another crash at the same airport. Delta Flight 1141, a Boeing 727-200, taxied from the passenger terminal to the takeoff runway, for a flight to Salt Lake City on August 31, 1988. During taxi, instead of concentrating on the before-takeoff check list, the crew talked upon personal matters for twenty minutes out of the thirty minutes elapsed time. They talked about a co-worker's dating habits, about the earlier Delta crash at the same airport, about politics. They talked about the CVR recordings of crew frivolity in the Continental Denver crash. They joked that they should be careful since their comments could become public if the plane crashed. A female flight attendant was in the cockpit during the taxi and takeoff, violating company procedures.

These personal conversations distracted the crew's attention from the operation of the aircraft. It violated company procedures; it violated federal aviation regulations that came about from the same distracting conversations and the deaths of many hundreds of people.[96] As in these other crashes precipitated by the same type of cockpit carelessness, they too would shortly suffer the consequences of their inattention to duty, taking with them many other people.

---

[96] Eastern Airlines crash at Charlotte, North Carolina, the Continental DC-9 crash at Denver, and the Northwest Airlines Boeing 737 crash at Detroit.

HEADED FOR DISASTER

Upon receiving the takeoff clearance from the tower, the crew commenced the takeoff. The normal takeoff point, 4500 feet down the runway, went by, and the plane was still on the ground. Something was wrong. At 8500 to 9000 feet down the runway, the plane finally became airborne, requiring an unusual nose-high attitude to lift off. That unusual attitude was the second clue something was wrong. As the main wheels left the ground the captain heard two explosions; another clue. Then, the aircraft started to roll violently, the fourth clue. None were recognized.

The explosions heard by the crew were engine compressor stalls caused by disturbed airflow to the engines, resulting from the unusually high nose attitude.

The aircraft did not climb with the normal initial 12-degree pitch-up angle, and required an unusually high pitch-up before the plane showed any inclination to climb. Another sign something was wrong. The stall-warning sounded. It was now obvious that the most probable cause was absence of wing flaps or an incorrect setting.

A well-trained crew would have promptly recognized the problem, promptly looked at the wing-flap handle position and the flap indicator position, and then promptly moved the flap handle to the proper takeoff position. The crew did nothing but hang on.

The airplane skimmed along the ground at approximately 180 miles per hour, almost 50 knots above the stalling speed (providing the wing flaps had been properly extended). For 21 seconds the flight continued skimming the ground, in nose-high attitude, with the wings wobbling, and the stall-warning sounding.

Instead of concentrating on the life-or-death predicament to figure out what was wrong, the copilot radioed to the tower that they had a problem. The tower was of no help at that critical time, and would only distract the crew even more with questions.[96] The crew couldn't answer the questions they now faced, let alone having to answer questions posed by the tower.

21 SECONDS TO CORRECT THEIR MISTAKE

The crew had twenty-one seconds to recognize and correct their mistake after liftoff. At almost 200 miles per hour, the right wing dipped and scrapped the ground; the female flight attendant screamed; and the airplane hit the ground, bouncing once, and then exploded in a fireball.

------

[96] A friend of mine, Roger Magleby, died in a single-engine plane crash during takeoff from Palm Springs in 1984 when he experienced an engine failure at 100 feet altitude, and instead of concentrating on flying, he concentrated on talking to the control tower.

People on nearby aircraft had a clear view of the horror unfolding on Runway 18L. "We were just landing, and Boom!" said Shaesby Scott, who watched from another plane as Delta Flight 1141 crashed and burned on a parallel runway. "It went up in flames," Scott said. "It looked like a bomb."

Gene Metzig was aboard a commuter flight that had just landed at Dallas-Fort Worth Airport. "His right wing was coming straight at us. It was probably no more than a foot or 18 inches off the ground," Metzig said. As other passengers watched, Flight 1141 struggled to get off the ground. They began to cheer, thinking the plane would make it. "It was like a football game," Metzig said. "We were cheering this guy to get that plane off the ground. It was very emotional. Plus, we were in danger of our own lives. We were rooting for that pilot to get that plane up. But there was just no way," he said. "I don't know how the hell he missed us, but he missed us." The crash killed fourteen people, and injured many more.

ROUTINE COVERUP

Following this crash, the pilots' union (ALPA) blocked the NTSB investigation by falsely stating to the NTSB investigators that the flight engineer was too badly injured to receive visitors at the hospital. The naive NTSB investigators took the union's word for this. But the union knew the crewmembers *were* receiving numerous visitors, including airline management, ALPA attorneys, and others. The NTSB later learned the truth, and responded to this blocking of a safety investigation by doing nothing.

Although it was obvious the pilots failed to extend the wing flaps, ALPA leaked information to the press that there were double engine failures on the aircraft, and thus the crew raised the flaps to try to stay in the air. That was dangerous nonsense. The so-called engine failures were compressor stalls caused by disturbed airflow into the engines from the high-pitch-up attitude. Raising the flaps immediately after takeoff at the low airspeed that existed would be the worst thing the pilots could have done. The aircraft was already on the verge of a stall. Raising the flaps would increase the stalling speed by at least fifty miles per hour, and surely cause the plane to crash to the ground.[98] Either the ALPA representatives were aviation

---

[98]   The initial climbout speed with an engine failure is V2, which is approximately 20 percent over the stall speed with the extended flaps, or roughly speaking, approximately 30 knots. If the flaps are raised at that slow airspeed, the stalling speed is approximately 50 knots above the flap extended stalling speed. This means that as the flaps were retracting, the aircraft would stall and crash. Obviously, retracting the flaps and crashing is not the correct pilot response. No aircraft manual provides for such a procedure. The aircraft manuals, based upon certification data, requires the pilot to maintain the V2 speed until reaching a safe altitude, maintaining the flaps at the takeoff setting.

illiterate to have stated that, or they were lying.

CVR—PRIVATE PROPERTY OF PILOTS?

In response to the public's right to know whether the crew is operating in a professional and legal manner, the NTSB released selected segments of the CVR recorder transcript. In response to this release, ALPA President Henry Duffy threatened on August 2, 1989 to issue an order for pilots to turn off the CVR recorders. This would violate federal air safety laws, and eliminate the intent of the recorder (which was to get to the true cause of the crash, and take measures to prevent reoccurrences). ALPA made this same threat years ago when release of the crew conversation showed the crew's frivolity that contributed to a fatal crash involving Eastern Airlines at Charlotte.

Duffy argued that the tape's release was an invasion of the crew's privacy. But the lives of other crew members and the passengers superseded the right of certain crew members to have their unprofessional and improper conduct protected. The crew gave up that privacy when they choose to become airline pilots.

Duffy tried to justify his stance by stating the release of the CVR tapes violated an agreement with the FAA that only transcripts of material related to the accident investigation would be made public. That is not what the law provides. Federal law (FAR 121.359) states that the "Administrator does not use the record in any civil penalty or certificate action."

Federal Air Regulation 121.359 requires continuous operation of the CVR recorder from engine start to engine shutdown, and provides that pilots cannot be punished for what is found on the recording. Nothing is stated in the regulations that the cockpit voice recorder contents be kept secret or kept from the public.

Duffy later stated that he had rescinded his earlier comment for the crews to disable the CVR because the FAA and NTSB assured him that they would seek legislation prohibiting the release of the tapes.

If withholding the contents of the CVR becomes law, the FAA and NTSB will be able to withhold highly sensitive air safety violations and safety problems from the public. The public has every right to know when aircraft are flown in an unsafe manner. The past history of FAA and NTSB coverup demonstrates that the public must fight to insure its right to know what causes air disasters.

WITHHOLDING CRITICAL INFORMATION

The NTSB had released only parts of the cockpit voice recordings, claiming the remaining portions were not relevant. They were lying. The NTSB deliberately withheld from the public critical, nonprofessional, and dangerous deviation from acceptable flight deck duties.

Following a request by the *Dallas Morning News*, the federal district court ordered the release of the entire tape recording. It was then discovered that the NTSB had deliberately and deceptively covered up for nonprofessional flight handling, as the NTSB had done in other crashes.

The pilots' union, the FAA, and the NTSB, argued in unison that these distracting, dangerous, unlawful, cockpit conversations were not relevant to the crash investigation!

ALPA head Duffy said the public's right to know was not at issue since federal investigators release all relevant information from crash tapes. ALPA made this statement right after the exposure that the NTSB deliberately concealed from the public relevant portions of the CVR to show why the pilots made so many mistakes.

The truth is that the NTSB routinely hides key segments of the cockpit recorder tapes. The NTSB did it in the PSA San Diego crash, and they did it in this tragedy. The NTSB released this recording only after the federal courts ordered the release of the tapes.

DANGEROUS FUEL LINE ROUTING

During the crash, pressurized fuel lines routed along the ceiling of the aircraft—separated from the passengers by a thin layer of insulation and highly-flammable decorative paneling—split open, spraying fuel under pressure directly upon the trapped passengers. The fuel lines were formerly routed in the belly of the aircraft. But the FAA ordered the fuel lines rerouted *through the passenger cabin* after the United Boeing 727 crash at Salt Lake City. In that crash, the fuel lines ruptured after the hard landing, pumping fuel to the outside of the aircraft. In response to that problem, the FAA ordered Boeing to reroute the fuel lines through—would you believe—the cabin where the harm to passengers would be much worse.

LEGAL TACTICS

Delta used an unusual legal tactic after this Dallas crash. Delta admitted in a July 19, 1989 news release that the crew was at fault (ignoring their part in withholding adequate training).

We at Delta deeply regret this tragic accident. After an exhaustive investigation, during which every other possible explanation was carefully analyzed, Delta has reached the conclusion that the flight crew failed to set the aircraft's flaps and slats in the proper takeoff configuration as required by established Delta practices and procedures. ... [Delta] "accepts responsibility for the accident on that basis."

Attorneys speculated that Delta apparently decided it would save money by admitting its liability and settling the law suits, rather than paying several years' legal fees to fight the cases in court.

The legal fraternity took various positions in response to the airline's unprecedented action in admitting fault. Aviation attorney Lee Kreindler of New York suspected less noble motives, stating: "They know they're dead in the water, and I suspect this is an attempt by Delta and the insurance carrier, U.S. Aviation Insurance Group, to engage in some good public relations."

Several days later the real reason for Delta's unusual admission became evident. A court order forced the NTSB to release the entire CVR recording, showing the breakdown in cockpit discipline by the flight crew.

IMPEDING SAFETY

Air Line Pilots Association spokesman Captain Jim Gray, stated he was shocked at the manner in which Delta fired the crewmembers: "It is unprecedented that they would take this step. I've never heard of a major airline admitting responsibility in advance of an official probable cause. Delta officials summoned the pilots to the Delta chief pilot's office in Dallas on July 18, 1989. When the pilots and their wives arrived, a Delta vice president handed the pilots notice of their termination. The next day the airline issued a statement admitting liability for the crash.

The pilot's union took the position that the crew set the flaps, but that by some unknown reason the flaps and the flap handle had retracted. The union stated the airline's actions were an attempt to garner "some good PR, ... you know, a courageous airline taking responsibility for the crash while it leaves its flight crew twisting in the wind."

NEARLY THE WORLD'S WORST AIR CALAMITY

A near-calamity occurred over the North Atlantic just east of Gander, Newfoundland, at 31,000 feet altitude as Delta was westbound on a flight from London to Cincinnati. Delta strayed off-course by sixty miles, venturing into protected airspace occupied by a Continental 747. Delta was slowly overtaking

Continental that was right ahead of it and in full view of the crew. But none of the three Delta cockpit crewmembers were looking outside the aircraft. The Continental passengers saw the approaching tragedy as their windows filled with the frightening sight of the Delta about to crash into their aircraft- —but missing by a hair-thin 50 feet! Even the slightest air turbulence could have caused the two aircraft to crash together.

After the Delta aircraft slid under the Continental flight, the Delta crew suddenly realized the near-collision had occurred. Compounding their errors, the Delta captain broadcast over the radio requesting Continental to keep secret what had almost been the world's worst air disaster, and not report it. Almost 600 persons had just witnessed the near-ending of their lives, and this pilot thought he could keep the incident a secret! Besides those witnesses, pilots in other aircraft heard the radio transmissions that covered a thousand or more square miles of airspace. Upon hearing the transmission to keep the incident a secret, an Air Force pilot radioed ahead to report the near-tragedy. When the Delta pilot requested that the Continental pilots keep the near-tragedy secret, Continental's captain replied that he had outraged passengers banging on the flight station door, wanting to know what was going on.

It was later determined that the pilots caused Delta's navigational error by punching the wrong coordinates into the plane's computerized navigational system.

"High Anxiety and Rage" stated the article in *Time* magazine on July 20, 1987. The article described the panic of passengers on the Continental 747 as they watched the Delta 1011 approaching and nearly ramming into them. Almost 700 persons had just witnessed near-death. The *Time* article stated that "a crew member moved discreetly around the Continental cabin, seeking to soothe passengers who had noticed the near disaster. 'He told me they were aware of it in the cockpit,' said passenger Candi Meacham, 'but asked that I keep it their little secret' to avoid upsetting other passengers."

OTHER DELTA CRASHES

Some of Delta's earlier crashes included the DC-8 that crashed into a New Orleans area motel at Kenner, on March 30, 1967, with heavy loss of life. Another fatal accident occurred during approach to Greater Southwest Airport at Fort Worth, Texas. The DC-9 encountered the wingtip vortex of another aircraft, and lost control, killing everyone on board. Another Delta plane crashed during approach to Chattanooga, Tennessee on November 27, 1973. Shortly thereafter, a Delta DC-9 crashed during approach at Boston on July 31, 1973, with the loss of 88 lives. For some reason the news media never gave these crashes much publicity.

Delta's willingness and ability to improve its safety activities was questioned in January 1990, when the FAA charged Delta with illegally and unsafely dispatching a Boeing 727 from Fresno, California to Los Angeles. The main hydraulic system (A) was inoperative, prohibiting dispatch of the aircraft. The Delta flight took off from Fresno, purportedly to continue to its Reno destination as shown by its flight release. But instead of flying to Reno, it flew to Los Angeles, without a dispatch release for that destination.[99]

COMMUTER SAFETY

The lowest level of safety is found in the commuter or regional airlines. Many of the pilots are building up flight time to move on to a larger airline, and are glad to get the job. They can be easily influenced to ignore safety regulations. Management pressure upon the pilots to violate minimum altitudes on instrument approaches, take off over-weight, and ignore duty time limitations is an every day occurrence. Pilot training is at a minimum, and often a farce. The drinking problem is worse with the smaller airlines. The training is not as good. Discipline is less, and standardization cannot be established with the rapid change in personnel. Some of the aircraft flown by the smaller airlines have lower design standards, and are more suited for general aviation activities.

The pilot turnover rate among these airlines is very high. At some of the regional or commuter airlines the yearly turnover rate of low-time pilots and captains is fifty to one-hundred percent a year.

ANOTHER UNTRAINED PILOT

Typical of many low-time pilot crashes was the crash of a Midwest Express DC-9 on September 7, 1985. The copilot had just taken off from Milwaukee when an engine failed. It is believed that the copilot applied the wrong rudder, causing the plane to roll inverted and plunge to the ground. The FAA inspector charged with surveillance of the airline's flight operations was inexperienced in turbojet air carrier operations, and not rated in the DC-9. He lacked the experience to evaluate the airline's training and competency checks.

In another crash showing terribly poor judgment and knowledge, an Air Illinois British Aerospace HS 748-2A crashed during an IFR flight on October 11, 1983 from Springfield to Carbondale, Illinois. Shortly after takeoff and during instrument conditions, the plane lost all electrical power, and had

---

[99] *Aviation Week & Space Technology*, January 15, 1990.

only enough battery power to power the flight instruments for a short period of time. The survival of everyone on board depended upon the electrically-driven flight instruments continuing to operate. But the battery power would be dissipated within twenty minutes or less. Rather than immediately return for a landing the captain continued on, in instrument conditions. Eventually the battery power was exhausted; the flight instruments failed; the plane crashed; just as they all should have known would happen. Everyone on board perished.

NEAR-CRASHES THAT ARE STATISTICALLY "SAFE FLIGHTS"

Statistics do not reveal the many near-tragedies that occur. Statistics do not show the near-crashes from airplanes landing with only a few minutes fuel remaining, with death for hundreds narrowly averted by the flight landing five minutes before the fuel was exhausted. A United 747 landing at Tokyo in May 1988 came within five minutes of a major air disaster, as it touched down with only minutes of fuel remaining. A similar United near-mishap occurred as a 747 landed at Seattle several years earlier. Two Republic DC-9s lost power on both engines and made emergency landings due to fuel exhaustion in early 1983. A Pan American DC-10 made an emergency landing at Tampa due to fuel exhaustion. A Trans-Southern commuter plane crashed in a field while approaching Atlanta's Hartsfield Airport due to fuel exhaustion. There were many more. An Avianca Boeing 707 crashed on Long Island on January 25, 1990 when it ran out of fuel as the crew desperately sought priority for landing at Kennedy International Airport at New York City.

Fuel exhaustion near-accidents, for instance, arise from several problems. Some are unavoidable, such as unexpected adverse enroute winds, weather delays, ATC delays. Other causes include corporate pressure to fly with minimum fuel, without allowing for expected traffic and other delays. The heavier the aircraft, the greater the fuel burn-off. By decreasing the reserve fuel corporate officials increase the profits. United Airlines, for instance, like many airlines, put considerable pressure on the crews to fly with minimum fuel, lower than good judgment dictates. Some lack-of-fuel emergencies arise from planning or fueling errors, partly compounded by the absence of a flight engineer who normally takes part of this responsibility. A flight engineer has more time to monitor the fuel usage and fuel remaining in flight. With the elimination of the engineer, this safeguard is reduced.

Other examples of near-disasters includes a Continental Boeing 747 taking off from London's Gatwick airport on February 1, 1988, with 455 people on board. The 747 barely missed hitting obstructions after takeoff. The stall-warning sounded, the wings oscillated up and down rapidly, fire came out of the end of number one and number four engines. A crash seemed certain. The pilots shoved the power levers full forward, as the flight engineer (fortunately this 747 had one) immediately starting dumping fuel without going through the check list.

In another example, an Eastern 727-225 lifted off at New Orleans and failed to climb as expected. The jet came over the residential area so low that the engine thrust knocked down a woman on the ground and snapped tree limbs. It came close to duplicating the Pan Am 727 New Orleans tragedy.

CHAPTER NINETEEN

Design and Aging

Many of the safety problems causing some of the world's worst air tragedies resulted from violations of federal regulatory safeguards found in Federal Air Regulation (FAR) 25 and others. These officials approved aircraft designs that were inherently unsafe. Included in these violated safeguards were outward-opening cargo doors; cargo compartments without fire protection; flight controls and horizontal stabilizers without hard backups in the event of total hydraulic failures; jet engines that do not meet design requirements;[99] unprotected fuel and hydraulic lines near exploding jet engines; flammable aircraft interiors; seats that rip loose in crashes; eliminating the flight engineers on complex aircraft; and more.

The reason for eliminating previously recognized design safeguards was to increase profits. The offset was increased dangers to those who fly, and occasional massive deaths. And that has been the history of this cost-cutting activity. The money saved is a small part of the overall cost of the aircraft. Ironically, much of the money saved was subsequently lost by the increased inspections and maintenance, and the adverse publicity arising from the air disasters caused by eliminating recognized design safeguards. The public and most crews never got wise to the scheme.

---

[99] 14 CFR 25. 903(d)(1), 14 CFR 33.

The greatly increased dangers associated with these design compromises didn't register with the public, even when they resulted in spectacular air tragedies. The FAA and NTSB shifted attention away from the design flaws that caused or permitted the crashes to occur. In some cases an aging-aircraft label was placed upon problems that were more attributable to design than to age. For example, unsafe outward-opening cargo doors are aggravated by aging of the aircraft, but are more a design than an aging problem. Loss of hydraulics and loss of aircraft control can happen on a new aircraft, and would not be an age problem, although age will worsen the problem. Fires in cargo compartments that lack fire extinguishing equipment can occur on the first flight of an aircraft.

Placing an age-label on design compromises takes attention away from the air safety chicanery and avoids public outrage. The aircraft manufacturer and the airlines who save a relatively small amount of money by eliminating the electric motor and/or hand crank for backups on the horizontal stabilizer, are not held accountable for the great loss of life and horror resulting from the compromised design decisions. They cite statistics showing total hydraulic failures occur infrequently. But they do occur, threatening everyone who flies under those conditions. And air travelers continue to die because of the cost-saving safety irregularities that otherwise would not exist.

Never in the history of aviation have so many design problems killed as many people as have been killed, and will continue to be killed. Many, if not most, of the current safety problems got their start in the FAA Western Region that figures so prominently in the exposures within these pages.

EARLY DESIGN PROBLEMS

As the post-World-War-II aviation environment commenced, deliberate design safeguard compromises and coverups were relatively few. The shenanigans that we have today had their beginning on a minor scale in the CAA, the FAA predecessor.

The first in a series of mishaps occurred on October 24, 1947 when a United Airlines DC-6 crashed near Bryce Canyon, Utah. This crash was shortly followed three weeks later, on November 11, 1947, by a near-crash of an American Airlines DC-6 which landed at Gallup, New Mexico, with flames streaming from the aircraft. All DC-6s were subsequently grounded until the cause could be found. It was discovered that when transferring fuel from one wing fuel tank to another, and the receiving tank filled up, the extra fuel went out the overflow and entered the air intake for the gasoline-fired cabin heater. The fuel then ignited when the cabin heater cycled on. It is difficult to comprehend that this flaw was not recognized by the engineers and the approving CAA.

At that time the Civil Aeronautic Board (CAB) Bureau of Aviation Safety had responsibility to determine the cause of airplane accidents. The Board blamed Douglas and the FAA for carelessness in building and certifying the aircraft, and made the obvious recommendation that the fire problem be corrected, which it was. But while investigating the problem, the Board also recommended that the fire-fighting capability for cargo compartment fires be improved. Douglas made this change by installing carbon dioxide CO_2 bottles to discharge into the cargo compartments. CO_2 fights fires by replacing oxygen, and causes the fire to go out for lack of oxygen. Obviously, it was necessary to seal off the cargo compartments to insure that no CO_2 leaks into the cockpit or cabin. But Douglas did not do this, taking the position that the gas was not toxic to human beings. Douglas's position was medically unsound and contrary to known facts. The CAB condescended to Douglas and failed to issue a recommendation to correct the problem. The public paid for this with threats to their lives and experiencing indescribable mass horrors and deaths. The results soon followed.

Douglas installed the fire-fighting system in the DC-6, and then ran a series of tests using the system in January and February 1948. During one test flight a Douglas test pilot discharged CO_2 to one of the baggage compartments to fight a simulated fire. The gas seeped into the cockpit area, causing the pilots to suffer serious physical discomfort, and almost lost control of the aircraft. The pilots then conducted another test, using the normal rebreathing oxygen masks that added oxygen to the air in the cockpit environment. The same crew incapacitation occurred.

Now alerted to the problem, Douglas hired the Lovelace Clinic in Albuquerque, New Mexico, to conduct tests on the toxicity of CO_2. The tests were conducted by Dr. Clayton White, who subsequently sent the test results to Douglas. The report held that CO_2 was highly toxic to human beings and lethal if the concentration was high enough. Such a condition could be expected in the confines of an aircraft. The report stated that it was very important that the aircraft be designed so that none of the gas could get into the crew compartment.

The report stated that the tests run by Douglas were inadequate, and urged that the testing methods be refined and additional tests conducted. The report stated the importance of prompt system changes and testing, to "avoid embarrassment at a future date." (i.e., a fatal crash.) The report continued:

Maximum allowable CO_2 concentrations for habited compartments in aircraft should be established in commercial aviation. ... that the report be made available to the CAA, the aircraft industry, the Airline Medical Directors' Association and the Air transport Association, as an aid to establishing and accepting industry-wide regulations in this regard.

Shockingly, Douglas did the opposite. They wrote across the face of the White report: "Do not discuss with the CAA." Douglas did indeed withhold the critical information from the FAA, the airlines, and the flight crews. Douglas installed the CO_2 system without the safeguards, and then compounded this with another design flaw. The CO_2 bottles were fitted with pressure-relief valves in the lines so as to relieve excessive pressure when the system was not in use. But the relief valve was designed so that the crew had to manually close a second valve before discharging fire-extinguishing agent in the event of a fire. If the crew failed to take this step to compensate for the design flaw, the fire extinguishing agent would be discharged into the cockpit rather than into the cargo compartment.

Douglas sought to compensate for this poor design by installing a warning sign requiring the crew to shut off the valve before discharging the fire extinguishing agent. When the crew is busy with a fire there is no justification for adding to their work load a task that, if omitted, could result in the loss of the aircraft.

In addition to that problem, Douglas knew that lethal quantities of CO_2 would seep into the crew compartment when the fire-extinguishing agent was discharged into the cargo compartment. Disregarding this life-threatening problem, Douglas presented the DC-6 to the FAA for recertification in March 1948, implying the design was safe, when they had proof that it was not safe. The pilots were kept in the dark of this danger.

Two months later, a TWA crew discharged CO_2 into the cargo compartment of a Constellation, and almost crashed when they became incapacitated. Since this was the same type of fire extinguishing agent used in the DC-6, the lethal nature of the agent was again recognized.

TWA conducted an investigation, and sent its findings in a warning letter to the Air Transport Association, which acted as a clearinghouse for the airlines. In turn, the ATA sent a warning notice to all airlines, advising the crews of the CO_2 problems on the Constellations, and advised that the danger also existed on the DC-6.

Douglas reacted to the ATA recommendation by pressuring the ATA to change the warning notice, falsely stating that the problem did not exist on the DC-6. Douglas knew that the problem existed on their aircraft, but they sought to represent their product as safe, thereby obstructing corrective actions. In response to Douglas's assurances, ATA advised the airlines on June 15, 1948 that the CO_2 danger had been tested by Douglas, and on the basis of "extensive testing under varied conditions" the danger did not exist on the DC-6.

Death followed this deception. United Flight 624, a DC-6 on a flight from Chicago to New York, experienced a cargo compartment fire warning. Over Pennsylvania, while in radio contact with La Guardia Approach Control, the crew discharged CO_2, which incapacitated the flight crew, as Douglas knew it would. The crew transmitted to La Guardia approach control a frantic message heard by a nearby United flight:

> New York, New York, Flight 624, this is an emergency descent. Fire in forward cargo compartment. ... Coming down. I ... ah ... ah ...

Near Mount Carmel, Pennsylvania, Flight 624 crashed into high-voltage power lines and exploded on a nearby hillside, bursting into flames, and killing everyone on board. In response to La Guardia's repeated calls, the other United flight radioed: "Flight 624 stands in no further need of clearance. They crashed at Mount Carmel."

Among those killed were showman Earl Carroll and his girl friend, Beryl Wallace.

As often happens, the problem and its coverup came out in federal litigation during depositions filed by the family of a passenger who was killed.[101] During the litigation, Donald Douglas Jr, a senior Douglas executive, testified that he had told United's Mr. Christenson, about the White report. Christenson denied this. (Christenson and I fought frequent battles at United's Denver training center.)

The jury ordered United and Douglas to pay damages to the passenger's family. Federal Judge Clarence Galston protected the corporate defendants, and changed the jury's award. He set aside the judgment against United Airlines, and reduced the award against Douglas. But he did articulate the problem:

> It is difficult to dismiss the thought that it was human failure, negligence, that caused the death of forty-three people; and that had Douglas distributed the White report to

---

[101] *DeVito v. United et al.,* Civ. No. 9555, U.S. District Court, Eastern District of New York. (1955)

those in the aviation industry, and particularly to the CAA and United, and followed its recommendations, the catastrophe might never have happened.

CORRECTIVE ACTION:ELIMINATE THE MEANS TO FIGHT THE FIRE

Fires in flight are a serious threat to survival. Despite this danger, Douglas addressed the cargo compartment fire problem by obtaining FAA approval to eliminate the fire detection and fire-fighting systems in the large class D compartments. In this way the problem was eliminated. If a fire occurs, the deaths are attributed to the fire rather than the fire-extinguishing agent. Money was saved.

The aircraft manufacturers and the FAA argued that any fire that started in the supposedly air-tight compartment would extinguish on its own from lack of oxygen. A simple fire test would have shown this theory to be non-existent. Animals live in that compartment and are not short of oxygen. Further, any fire would quickly eliminate the integrity of the plastic liner, allowing air to enter the cargo compartment through the many holes in the aircraft metal structure.

One of the tragedies arising from this design compromise was a Lockheed 1011 that landed in Riyadh, Saudi Arabia (1985) with an uncontrollable fire in the cargo compartment. The crew was unable to put out the fire since there was no fire extinguishing agent in that compartment. Even though the aircraft was not over a half hour from a suitable landing field, all 301 people perished in that aircraft. In another major tragedy a South African (SAA) Boeing 747 crashed after it experienced a cargo compartment fire on November 28, 1987.

All types of inflammable material is unlawfully shipped in cargo or baggage compartments, posing a serious threat of fire (which cannot be extinguished because of the elimination of fire fighting equipment). Matches and liquid-reservoir cigarette lighters are carried in abundance and occasionally cause a fire. In one instance at San Diego (Delta Airlines, August 1988), baggage handlers discovered smoke coming from a passenger bag being loaded into the baggage compartment. Kitchen matches ignited due to friction, and started a fire. Fortunately, the fire was caught on the ground. Shippers sometimes deliberately mislabel shipments in order to avoid having the prohibited inflammable or toxic material rejected by the airline.

Mislabeled chemicals loaded aboard an American Airlines aircraft in 1988 caused a fire in the baggage compartment that injured eighteen people. A Pan American 707 crashed on November 3, 1973, during approach to Boston Airport when an on-board fire was no longer survivable.

The primary solution to the problem is to install fire-fighting equipment in the baggage and cargo compartments. In addition, all hazardous material should be banned from passenger flights. Passengers are not carried on oil tankers, and passengers should not share the confined space of aircraft with hazardous materials.

THE LOCKHEED ELECTRA DESIGN COMPROMISE

The Lockheed Electra was an excellent flying machine when it was introduced in the late 1950s. Four jet engines drove propellers and the technology spanned the gap between piston aircraft and the jets. During the design of the Electra, Lockheed officials put pressure on the engineers to reduce the weight in the engine mounting assembly, over vigorous opposition from the engineers. This resulted in a less-rigid mounting assembly between the jet engine gear-box and the propeller at the end of a long shaft. A condition developed under certain conditions wherein a vibration or whirl developed between the gear-box and the propeller. This led to an off-center whirling motion that rapidly worsened and ended with the engine and propeller causing an out-of-balance condition that caused the wing to rip off the aircraft within a matter of seconds.

The first crash resulting from the design compromise was a Braniff Electra enroute from Houston to Dallas. Flying at 15,000 feet, the weak support assembly permitted the engine and propeller assembly to start whirling, followed by huge unbalanced forces causing the wing to rip from the fuselage. While Lockheed and the Bureau of Aviation Safety conducted an investigation, another Electra came apart on March 17, 1960 over Tell City, Indiana.

Grounding the Electras was demanded by the press. This would have been financially costly to Lockheed and to the airlines. FAA Administrator Pete Quesada, a former Lockheed official, refused to ground the aircraft. Instead, he issued an order limiting the maximum speed to 275 knots—which was the normal cruise airspeed. Public criticism forced Quesada to reduce the maximum speed to 250 knots. He took a gamble with people's lives and fortunately, Lockheed found and corrected the problem before more Electras crashed.

THE PIONEERING BRITISH HAD THEIR STRUCTURAL PROBLEMS

In the fifties the British put the first commercial jet aircraft, called the Comet, into service. A fuselage structural design defect led to several Comets exploding in the air when the inside pressurized air found a weak spot and blew the fuselage apart. By the time the manufacturer found the cause of the problem the public had lost confidence in the Comet and

Britain lost the lead in commercial jet sales.

THE START OF MAJOR DESIGN COMPROMISES

In the 1960s, while I was with the FAA in the Western Region, many design safeguards that had previously existed were eliminated. This action saved Douglas Aircraft Company and the airlines considerable money, and greatly increased the dangers faced by the crew and passengers. The FAA eliminated design safeguards previously required under the Federal Aviation Regulations (FAR), and this caused a domino effect. Eliminating a previously required safety requirement, such as backups for the flight controls, forced other manufacturers to do the same in order to remain competitive.

OUTWARD OPENING CARGO DOORS

The outward-opening cargo doors have already been described. There is no justification for subjecting tens of thousands of people to the constant and ever-increasing risk of explosive-opening cargo doors just to save a relatively small amount of money. Lockheed spent the additional funds to provide a safer aircraft, and installed semi-plug doors.

AGING PROBLEMS, OR FAULTY DESIGN?

In the early 1960s Boeing deviated from the previously used method of aircraft construction by actually gluing the fuselage sheets together, and reducing the number of hard fasteners (rivets and doubler plates) to hold the tons of air pressure inside the aircraft. Boeing also used thinner skin panels. This change reduced the weight of the aircraft, reduced the cost of aircraft construction, but obviously entailed serious risks.

Boeing initially used a cold-bonding adhesive applied to the overlapping fuselage sections. Boeing started getting reports on premature corrosion and deterioration in the bonding along lap joints of 737s as early as 1970. Two years later it stopped using the cold-adhesive and went to a hot-bonding method. Airlines throughout the world made numerous reports to Boeing by 1974 of the severe corrosion and skin cracking problems.

The problems were three-fold. The corrosion ate away the already-thin skin of the fuselage; the structural strength from the adhesives ceased to exist; and the fuselage panels starting cracking. A serious loss of fuselage strength occurred, in the presence of tons of air pressure upon the fuselage seeking to blow out like an inner tube. The loss of strength when the aircraft came unglued was a serious structural problem threatening a blowout of the aircraft fuselage similar to an inner tube or tire-blowout.

Boeing also discovered that the skin panels were starting to fail at the rivet line, evidenced by hair-line cracks along the line of rivet holes. The cracking skin panels, in addition to the unbonding of the fuselage panels, constituted a serious danger to flight. Boeing and the FAA knew that it had a serious structural problem on its hands and knew that explosive destruction of Boeing aircraft was a real possibility.

A GOOD REASON TO ALWAYS KEEP YOUR SEAT BELT FASTENED

One of the first jets to explode in the air due to this ungluing of the aircraft was a Far Eastern Air Transport (FEAT) Boeing 737-200, while flying at 24,000 feet, near Taiwan that blew apart on August 22, 1981. A skin panel separated in flight, and the internal fuselage pressure caused the entire aircraft to disintegrate, hurling 110 people to their deaths.

A subsequent investigation by the Republic of China correctly identified the cause of the crash, and recommended replacing the skin sections in the forward part of the fuselage with heavier skin panels. The report stated that simply increasing inspections to detect corrosion and skin cracking would not by itself be adequate. The report stated that the corrosion and associated skin cracking are often hard to detect.

The Taiwan government required its airlines to replace the skin panels at the front of the aircraft with heavier panels.

Boeing played down the danger, accusing FEAT of carrying open containers of material that caused corrosion, seeking to absolve itself of blame. The airline vigorously denied the charge. If Boeing was deliberately making false statements, or unsupported speculation, Boeing would be contributing to coverup of a serious problem that would mask the need for corrective actions, and set the stage for other preventable tragedies.

Boeing and the airlines had large financial investments in 737 aircraft, and the last they wanted to hear was anything jeopardizing the value of their investments.

Boeing apparently recognized the need for heavier skin panels, and commenced to manufacture subsequent 737s with heavier panels and also used conventional construction methods. Boeing also offered a kit to the airlines to replace the weak skin panels on existing 737 aircraft.

The FAA didn't require this repair for aircraft certificated in the United States. The FAA settled for the very thing the Republic of China stated was ineffective, and which any mechanic could have recognized. The FAA recommended that the airlines check the fuselage for corrosion and cracks, knowing that these problems are difficult to detect.

DANGEROUS STATE OF ITS AIRCRAFT

Among the airlines that ordered the thicker skin panels was Aloha Airlines. But they failed to install the kits; the FAA had not required the replacement. In November of 1987 Boeing made an inspection of Aloha Airlines' aircraft, which the airline had requested. After the inspection Boeing inspectors stressed the need for immediate replacement of skin panels on some of the aircraft. One of its Boeing 737s had been manufactured immediately after the one that blew apart over Taiwan, and the Aloha 737 had almost three times the number of pressurization cycles as the FEAT had when it blew up in the air.

In December 1987, an FAA "white glove" inspection team from Washington inspected Aloha Airlines' maintenance, and discovered many of the maintenance problems. It then issued a report requiring the Honolulu FAA office to take corrective actions, which was not done. Instead, the FAA gave Aloha an extension of time to make structural repairs, when either grounding or immediate repairs were needed.

Despite the critical condition of the fuselages, and warnings from Boeing officials of possible in-flight disintegration, Aloha cancelled its plans in March 1988 to speed up the maintenance schedule.

Boeing personnel again met in Honolulu with Aloha officials in April 1988, to describe the critical condition of the Aloha 737 aircraft. When the FAA Principal Operations Inspector heard of this meeting he showed up. Boeing and Aloha refused to allow him access to the hearing. The two corporations then withheld from the FAA the critical condition of the aircraft which could at any time blow up in flight due to the numerous structural weaknesses in the badly corroded fuselages.

LONG AWAITED SEQUELA TO THE B737 DISINTEGRATION

On April 27, 1988 two passenger boarding an Aloha Airline Boeing 737 at Honolulu saw bubbles in the fuselage skin near the rivets aft of the entry door. Another passenger who flew on that same aircraft on the same day saw a two-inch-long separation between the overlapping skin panels in the same general area. This passenger reported the crack to a flight attendant, but Aloha ignored the serious signs of impending structural blowout. Later that day, one of the flights on that particular aircraft had to return with a pressurization problem caused by the fuselage leak.

No one at Aloha showed any concern. Neither the pilots who should check the aircraft before the start of each day's flight; the maintenance personnel who should have an eagle-eye to spot such problems, especially when they are so obvious that passengers bring the defect to the airline's attention; and there was no flight engineer on board who could also have detected the problem.

The day after these glaring signs of impending disaster,

three passengers noticed bubbles and a crack in the fuselage skin while boarding the aircraft. On that same day, April 28, 1988, the expected happened. Flying at 24,000 feet at approximately 300 miles per hour, the aircraft literally exploded. A twenty-foot long section of the aircraft ripped away, from below the cabin floor on one side, up and over to below the cabin floor on the other side. The disintegration commenced where the passengers noticed the skin separation.

The rapid depressurization ejected a female flight attendant out of the aircraft through the shredded metal. Another flight attendant was hit by flying metal and suffered serious injuries, as were several passengers. Winds exceeding hurricane-like force buffeted the passengers, and serious injuries resulted from the thrashing metal stringers. Fortunately the passengers in that section had their seat belts fashioned, and were not ejected out of the aircraft as was the one flight attendant. The passengers found themselves seated in a seemingly surf-board type environment, with no sides or top to the aircraft cabin. Those seated next to where the windows were formerly located could look straight down at the ocean almost six miles below.

The pilots heard a loud "clap" or "whooshing" sound, followed by a wind noise behind them. The cockpit door ripped off, and the pilots could see clear sky in the cabin where the side and top of the aircraft should have been. The captain put on his oxygen mask, extended the speed brakes, pulled the power levers back to idle, and commenced an emergency descent, while the copilot actuated the switch opening the passenger oxygen bottles.

The exploding aircraft ripped out the line to the passenger oxygen masks, keeping them from getting oxygen. The loud wind noise in the cockpit kept the crew from communicating with each other during the emergency descent. The crew made radio transmissions in the blind to Honolulu air traffic control, and moved the transponder switch to the emergency 7700 position.

After the crew got the plane to lower altitude they contacted Maui Airport tower and told them an emergency existed and that they would shortly land.

When the flaps were extended beyond five degrees the plane became less controllable, causing the crew to retract them to the five-degree extended position. The crew had to use a higher 170 knots approach speed for controllability, causing them to come in 35 knots faster than normal. During the approach the pilot noticed a yawing motion and determined that the left engine had failed. The plane landed without further damage.

Luckily, the entire plane did not break up in flight. Equally lucky that only one person was lost. Sixty one were injured, several seriously.

The initial FAA reaction was to place an aging aircraft label on the incident. The problem was in the flawed decision to assembly the aircraft with adhesives, and the FAA's failure to take corrective actions when the danger was discovered after the series of unbonding reports and after the FEAT 737 disaster.

NTSB APATHY TO THE EXPLODING FUSELAGE PROBLEM

The NTSB thought so little about the earlier FEAT disintegration that it didn't keep it on file or follow up on it, even though the problem constituted one of the worst threats to the structural integrity of large numbers of aircraft. The *Wall Street Journal* report in its May 31, 1988 issue that "The U.S. agencies haven't much to say about that report today. In Fact, they apparently didn't even keep it on file."

The Aloha fuselage disintegration focused attention on the method used by Boeing in the second generation jets.

BREAKDOWN IN NATION'S AVIATION MAINTENANCE SYSTEM

The subsequent NTSB investigation report described the monumental breakdown in the FAA regulatory system to prevent such failures. The report described a breakdown in the nation's aviation maintenance system that contributed to the in-flight loss of the upper fuselage section of the Aloha 737. The report implicated Aloha, Boeing, and the FAA. The NTSB faulted Boeing for not instituting a final fix for the problem when it was first discovered in the 1970s. The NTSB report absolved the NTSB of its failure to follow up after the FEAT disaster.

Even after this serious breakup, the FAA limited corrective actions to further inspections, knowing that this would not detect the delamination of the skin panels or the cracking of the fuselage skin. Eventually industry recognized that it had to do something about the problem and held meetings to determine what should be done, inviting the FAA to attend. The industry group decided on actions to take, and the FAA came out with mandatory requirements to do what industry finally agreed to do.

OTHER STRUCTURAL PROBLEMS

In March 1984 an American Airline Boeing 727 flying at 37,000 feet suddenly noticed the aircraft losing pressure. Upon landing at Dallas, inspectors discovered a 9-by-11 inch hole had developed in the fuselage forward of a cargo door. Fortunately a larger section had not ripped out. However, the 727 was built stronger than the 737; its skin was heavier.

In December 1987 an Eastern DC-9 split apart after landing at Pensacola, Florida. This breaking into two parts doesn't raise great confidence against explosive disintegration at altitude when there are tons of air pressure acting upon the fuselage. Douglas blamed the fuselage splitting apart upon a hard landing. Aircraft have been making hard landings for years, and may cause a collapsed landing gear, but never the aircraft breaking apart. The question arises, if a hard landing can split the fuselage apart, it can also weaken the fuselage to the point where it doesn't quite break, but cause metal distress. This weakened condition can then result in the aircraft splitting apart in the air when a weak spot develops in the fuselage, such as ungluing of the aircraft fuselage.

In 1981 a Boeing 707 cargo plane flown in Africa by British-based Dan-Air disintegrated in the air due to structure failure. This accident was so frightening that it produced a new inspection program for older jets called Supplemental Structural Inspection Documents, or SSIDs.

WAITING FOR THE NEXT INFLIGHT DISINTEGRATION OCCUR

Following the Boeing 737 mishap over Hawaii the FAA required high-frequency electronic inspections—eddy current inspections—of all aircraft that accumulated 50,000 landings or more, and on aircraft that showed evidence of cracking or corrosion. This would not have detected the FEAT 737 that blew apart, as it had fewer hours and fewer pressurization cycles.

In October 1988, while Continental Airlines stripped one of its 737s of paint for a repainting of the fuselage, inspectors discovered a one foot long crack in the skin, and many smaller cracks, that could easily have caused an explosive decompression and the loss of all on board.

On October 27, 1988 the FAA went part of the way and issued a notice of proposed rule-making requiring replacement of rivets on a small part of the aircraft fuselage. Until the rivets were replaced, the aircraft had to fly at a maximum altitude no greater than 26,000 feet, where the pressure differential is less than at the higher altitude.

During replacement of an air conditioning duct on a Navy plane that was previously owned and operated by the FAA, a ten inch long metal stringer section that ran along the length of the plane to support the frame and skin, was found to be almost completely corroded out. If that air conditioning duct had not been removed, the fuselage could have ruptured during pressurized flight.

METHODS OF CHECKING FOR DEFECTS

Methods of checking the aircraft for cracks include electronic and ultrasonic probes, X-rays, and penetrating dyes, which have limitations. The electronic rays use a pencil-sized electronic probe to scan large sections of a jetliner, are very time-consuming, fatiguing, and susceptible to personnel oversight. When the Eddy current method of inspection is used, the mechanics shoots an electric current through the plane's skin with a pencil-sized probe, looking for small cracks. The ultrasound method sends a sound beam into the metal, and measures the time that it takes the beam to bounce back. If a crack exists, the time interval for the current to return is changed. This is a very tedious job when large area must be inspected, making for boredom, complacency, and overlooking of cracks.

The surfaces must be clean, and free from paint, for maximum reliability. The accuracy of the eddy current or ultrasound inspections depend upon the ability, the alertness, the absence of complacency, of the person performing the inspections, which often occur in adverse temperature conditions and in difficult to reach areas. Another inspection method is applying dye to the surface of the aircraft and then wiping it off. If there are cracks, the dye will remain and be visible.

OTHER CAUSES OF DISINTEGRATION

In the seventies a Boeing 707 came apart in the air near Mount Fuji, Japan, in turbulence, when the vertical tail ripped off the aircraft. Everyone perished. An Air Canada DC-9 experienced an explosive decompression in flight when the rear cabin pressure bulkhead blew out. The rear of the cabin was gone; the rear pressure bulkhead had blown out.

ENGINE DESIGN PROBLEMS

Under Federal Aviation Regulations (FAR) jet engines must meet damage-tolerance tests before the FAA can certify the engines. These tests include resistance to bird-ingestion and ice damage. FAA officials violated the specifics of the regulatory requirements, and approved engines that had failed the tests. The design compromises commenced with certification of the General Electric CF-6 engine used on the DC-10s and other aircraft. The fan blades were light and of inadequate strength to resist foreign object damage (FOD) such as birds and ice. When the blades fail the engine often suffers catastrophic damage that threatens vulnerable systems on the aircraft, such as the fuel and hydraulic lines, and the aircraft controls.

The General Electric CF-6 engines received considerable notoriety in the early 1970s, continuing for years thereafter. During a 1970 check of the CF-6 engines, the FAA evaluated the tests, and the FAA Western Region issued a type certificate on September 16, 1970, thereby approving the CF-6 engines.

Segments in the FAA Washington headquarters and in the private sector raised questions that the icing tests were not adequate because test icing conditions were too light. In response, the FAA conducted a second set of tests (March 28, 1971) *after* the engines were already certificated by the FAA Western Region. The results were startling. After a test flight slightly over an hour in duration, which would be a normal occurrence in line operation, three blades of one engine and 26 blades of another engine were severely damaged.

Another test conducted on the two-engine A300B Airbus in Europe on March 29, 1973, using the same engines, resulted in damage to both engines. The FAA European representative in France sent the following letter to FAA headquarters:

> To preclude damaging the fan blades when operating in icing conditions, we will require, as a condition of A300B certification, that its CF-6-50A engines have only the undrilled blades.

FAA Washington headquarters immediately responded, demanding a retraction. If a retraction was not forthcoming, it would have costly financial effects due to engines already certified for operation in the United States. The FAA European office was forced to rescind its requirement for the stronger engine blades on February 13, 1974.

Two days later, on February 15, 1974, during a meeting of the FAA Chief of Aircraft Certification in Europe, the FAA prepared a memorandum:

> Advise FAA Headquarters that the A300B airbus is particularly vulnerable to FOD because both engines are subjected to the same operating environment and icing conditions. [Damage to a second engine] could be disastrous.

The chief of the Propulsion Branch in the FAA Washington headquarters wrote:
> Aircraft damage from shrapnel trajectories forces can be such as to puncture cowling, damage fuselage and disable systems.

When engines disintegrate, as they occasionally do, they often destroy nearby fuel and hydraulic lines, causing serious fire and control problems. The NTSB recommended placing a protective shroud around the hydraulic and fuel lines in the area of the rear engine. But the FAA refused to require this safeguard. The FAA issued a *proposed* AD requiring all DC-10 aircraft to have a protective shield around the fuel and hydraulic lines near the center engine. Fires, loss and near-loss of DC-10 aircraft had already occurred. The urgency of protecting vital system components near the three engines was obvious. Heavy armour plate was necessary. But this was not installed. A major tragedy followed, that is described in later pages. Industry and Congressional pressures on the FAA caused the FAA to rescind the proposed AD, despite the probable loss of aircraft and lives.

Representative Harley Staggers conducted a four-day hearing on the DC-10 engine problems. After the hearing, Staggers wrote to John Reed, Chairman of the National Transportation Safety Board, stating:

> A key official in the Western Region FAA stated that "Service and test experience indicate that the drilled GE CF-6 engine fan blade is very sensitive to FOD. The resulting damage to the engine and aircraft is considered excessive and presents a serious threat to the safety of the aircraft."

The committee questioned FAA Administrator Butterfield after many FAA reports by FAA personnel were introduced into the records describing the dangers of the drilled engine blades. Responding to questions raised about why the FAA had not issued an AD on the engine, FAA Administrator Butterfield testified, "We do not consider it an emergency situation." He added that issuing the AD would ground the fleet and affect the income of the airlines and the manufacturers. This was the real reason.

Butterfield was the Administrator when the stage was set for the DC-10 cargo door design that threatened tens of thousands of air travelers. He gave the same glib response in addressing the DC-10 cargo door crisis as he supplied for engine problems. Apparently the 346 deaths at Paris didn't phase him.

Butterfield testified during this Congressional hearing that the FAA would not consider issuing an AD on the engine. But the FAA had already issued a notice (NPRM) that it was considering doing the very thing Butterfield stated he would not do. Butterfield didn't seem to know what was going on, just as he didn't seem to know what was going on with the DC-10 cargo door before the DC-10 Paris crash that took 346 lives.

Representative Pickle responded, "This is very important now for us to understand. Are you saying to us that you, the FAA, might withdraw that proposed AD?"

Butterfield testified he would not issue an AD. Then, when confronted with the proposed AD, Butterfield answered, "No, I am not saying that." But that *is* what he was saying.

"Why did you mention it, then?"

In typical FAA double-talk, "I am saying it is not a directive. We are not directing the industry to do anything at this time." But an AD is a mandatory directive.

"But it is your interest to issue such, is it not?"

"Yes, it is." But that is not what Butterfield stated, until backed into the corner.

FAA Administrator Butterfield sent Representative Staggers a letter several months later, stating that the "FAA has withdrawn the Notice of Proposed Rule Making that would require installation of solid fan blades. Solid fan blades will continue to be installed on an optional basis."

Several months earlier the DC-10 experienced the catastrophic crash near Paris that arose from violated design-safeguards. The FAA covered up the multiple problems leading to the Paris crash, and was now doing the same stonewalling with the DC-10 engine problems. The same FAA Western Region hierarchy had approved the violation of regulatory safeguards; hazardous outward-opening cargo doors; the rube-goldberg DC-10 door locking mechanism; elimination of the hard-backup to the flight controls and horizontal stabilizer; the absence of cargo compartment fire-fighting equipment; and other money-saving design hazards. This mealy-mouth double-talk made possible the brutal deaths of thousands of people.

PROTECTIVE NEWS MEDIA

Eventually the news media down-played the engine problem, and it continued unnoticed. The lack of protection around the vulnerable fuel and hydraulic lines went uncorrected.

Problems later arose in the General Electric engines (CFM-56) made by CFM International. The engine was made by a consortium of a General Electric unit and Snecma. The engine is also used on the Airbus Industrie A-320. The engine problems were primarily related to the FAA's failure to require engine fan blades strong enough to resist foreign object damage (FOD). The tests imposed on the engines did not meet the requirements to resist damage from birds or from clear ice, as required by the FARs.

A sampling of jet engine failures: A Piedmont Airlines[101] Boeing 737 physically lost its right engine while climbing through 1000 feet at Chicago's O'Hare International Airport on

---

[101] Merged with U.S. Air in 1989.

January 27, 1989. Luckily, the heavy engine didn't crash onto any buildings or people, and instead crashed onto vacant property within the airport boundary. The Piedmont Airlines 737 engine separation was the third such incident in three years and the 15th related to a failure in the bolts that hold the engine to its mount. An engine ripped off a Northwest 727 shortly after takeoff from Miami on December 4, 1989. A US Air Boeing 737 lost its right engine at an altitude of 4,000 feet after taking off from Philadelphia International Airport on December 5, 1987. An engine broke loose on a Southwest Airlines Boeing 737 taking off from Love Field in Dallas January 1986, but didn't separate completely from the aircraft. At that time Boeing reported 12 other incidents of cone-bolt failures on the 737s as a result of metal fatigue or improper bolt installation, but those incidents didn't result in engine separation.

An engine failed on a United Express commuter plane, and while the aircraft was returning to Denver another engine failed, causing an emergency landing. A DC-9 physically lost an engine in the southwest, when the engine became unbalanced due to ingesting ice that broke off from a fuselage drain ahead of the engine. This sudden engine stoppage caused a severe torque, which caused the engine to rip off the aircraft. Engine mounts are designed so that engines can rip off the fuselage or wing if a sudden out-of-control vibration threatens the structural integrity of the wing or fuselage. There is no such protection for the center engine, which must rely on non-existing shielding to prevent loss of critical aircraft systems. On January 6, 1990 an engine ripped off of a Northwest Airlines 727 over Florida, due to the same leaking fuselage drain problem that had not been corrected.

The British and U.S. aviation agencies grounded all Boeing 737-400s in July 1989 that were powered by the CFM56-series of engines. Several forced landings caused by engine failures prompted the move. A British Midlands 737-400 crashed earlier in the year due to an engine failure when the good engine was shut down instead of the bad one. This error was believed due to cross-wiring of the fire-indication system by Boeing.

FALSE ASSURANCES

Despite many engine problems—some of them serious—the airlines, the aircraft manufacturers, the engine manufacturers, and the FAA argue that jet engines rarely fail. They don't fail as often as the former piston engines, but they certainly do fail. The aircraft manufacturers and the airlines now use this argument to justify long over-water flights (ETOP or extended over-water operations) with two-engine aircraft, thereby eliminating the previous safety requirement of a minimum of three engines.

The FAA reduced the former safety requirement of not over one hour from land for twin-engine operation. Twin-engine operations with several hundred people on board are now permitted if not over *three hours of single-engine operation* is required to reach a suitable airport. Making this ripe with dangers is the fact that survivability in the North Atlantic waters is figured in minutes. Also, the weather on the North Atlantic is very changeable, and can go from ceiling and visibility unlimited to zero-zero in a matter of minutes. The one airport that is used to justify the three hours on a single engine may be zero-zero conditions when the aircraft arrives. Statistics of infrequent engine failures are used to justify this danger. Many potential problems require an immediate landing.

INCREASED STALLING SPEED AND CRASHES

The early Boeing 737 jets have a design fluke that significantly increases the stalling speed when there is only a small amount of wing contamination from ice or snow. This design problem creates danger of a stall after takeoff, unless the FAA requires the airlines to increase the takeoff speeds, as is required by European airlines.

GENERAL AVIATION DESIGN PROBLEMS

FAA indifference to airline safety problems extends into other FAA functions, including general aviation aircraft. For many years one of the worst examples of uncorrected design problems was in the Beech V-tail Bonanza. Over 220 of these popular single-engine aircraft came apart in the air due to an obvious design flaw. The FAA had not required the corrective fix that a back-yard mechanic could have done, and which went uncorrected for over three decades. A weak design permitted the rear flight control assembly to rip off the aircraft, causing the aircraft to pitch down and plunge to the ground. Each of these 200-plus aircraft disintegrations were a horror story of sadness by themselves.

In 1987, about forty years after the first Bonanza came off the Wichita assembly line, and after years of criticism by knowledgeable people in industry, and after pressures upon the FAA escalated to a level where it had to act, the FAA finally issued an airworthiness directive. At first the AD required restricting the airspeed. Then the FAA ordered a structural modification, which greatly reduced the danger.

The problem came about because Beech constructed the rear stabilizers (stabilators) on the V-tail Bonanza with a spar running parallel to the leading edge, but about eight inches back. The long section ahead of the spar was unsupported, and not attached to the airframe, permitting heavy air loads to twist and rip the entire rear flight control assembly off the aircraft.

Beech knew the serious problem existed for *forty years*, but resisted all efforts to correct the obvious design deficiency. Beech officials blamed the aircraft disintegration upon pilot error, even though other aircraft without that design problem were not failing. The identical Beech aircraft, an F33, but with conventional control surfaces, had virtually no in-flight breakups. Just like the tobacco industry, Beech denied a safety problem existed, sacrificing hundreds of people to the horror of falling to their deaths.

Even the NTSB played the game. In the several hundred related crashes they invariably blamed the crashes on pilot error, even though the NTSB knew of the structural design problem. The FAA protected Beech, and never required the manufacturer to make the structural change.

The fix was simple; an 18-year old high-school kid with mechanical ability could have made the fix in one afternoon. The fix consisted of riveting the unsupported leading edge to the side of the fuselage with a metal fitting that was easy to improvise. This reduced the tendency of the stabilator to bend under the air loads imposed by flight.

Although pilots are familiar with the basics of aviation, the average pilot was either unaware of the problem, or blamed the dead pilots for not operating the aircraft properly. They were no more an air safety expert than a truck driver is a highway safety expert. While pilot error may be true in some instances, a 24 to 1 ratio of aircraft disintegration compared to other aircraft without the unsupported leading edge overhang prevents blaming the repeated disintegrations on pilot error. Some of the pilots were highly experienced. Some were airline pilots.

It wasn't until the *Aviation Consumer* magazine commenced a long campaign starting in the early 1980s, exposing the deadly problem, that public pressure forced the FAA to address the V-tail problem. Oddly enough, few pilots were aware or concerned over the problem. Several years after *Aviation Consumer* magazine started exposing this problem, one of their own contributing editors, Bernie Lafferty, his wife, and two children, perished in a V-tail Bonanza at Charlottesville, Virginia on February 17, 1984.

In 1987 the FAA finally issued an airworthiness directive, some forty years after the fact. It required that the metal cuff securing the long stabilator overhang to the side of the fuselage be installed.

OTHER UNCORRECTED GENERAL AVIATION PROBLEMS

Numerous other general aviation problems went uncorrected. Beech built many of their fuel tanks without any internal baffles, allowing the fuel to slosh away from the tank exit going to the engine. With a partially empty tank, the fuel could shift momentarily to the far side of the tank, away from the fuel tank opening to the engine (a condition referred to as unporting). This unporting of the fuel tank outlet caused air to enter the fuel lines. When the air bubble reached the engine, the engine stopped. This often happened just as the aircraft became airborne, and flying over buildings that were unsuitable for emergency landings.

Publicity from large jury verdicts and *Aviation Consumer* magazine reached the point where the FAA could not ignore the problem. The FAA issued an order requiring installation of a placard on the instrument panel, warning the pilot not to make sharp turns shortly before taking off. This FAA order was not a good fix. In flight, during turbulent conditions, the unporting of the fuel could occur without any sharp turns. One such incident occurred near Monterey, California, causing stoppage of both engines, and ending in a fatal accident.

Among the many other crash-causing design problems that the FAA refused to address was the combination fuel selector and off valve on small aircraft. Many crashes and many deaths resulted from a pilot inadvertently moving a fuel selector (which on some aircraft must be frequently changed in flight) to an off-position. Sometimes the valves were located where it was hard to see, or so poorly designed that the pilot couldn't tell which end of the pointer indicated the valve position.

QUALITY CONTROL PROBLEMS

In addition to other safety problems, we have the problem of poor workmanship. Japan Airlines sent a strong protest letter to Boeing Aircraft Company in 1987 concerning poor workmanship on some of the new 747 aircraft delivered by Boeing. Japan Airlines reported finding electrical wiring and plumbing of important emergency systems crossed. This could result in a fire in one engine indicated on the flight station to be a fire in another engine. It could also cause discharge of fire extinguishing agent to the wrong engine in the event of a fire. These safety problems were serious.

At the same time, British Airways also sent a strong complaint to Boeing, complaining of similar quality control problems. The complaining letter asserted that production employees at one plant "seem oblivious that they are building aircraft where any mistake not properly corrected, or hidden, represents a direct compromise with safety."

Shortly after receiving the quality-control letters, a British Midlands Airways B737-400 experienced an engine fire and engine disintegration on January 8, 1989, on a flight from London to Belfast. The fire warning light indicated the right engine was on fire, when actually the fire was in the left engine. The pilots shut down the right engine, just as the disintegrating left engine totally failed. The plane then crashed due to loss of all engine power. The preventable accident resulted in heavy loss of life when the 737 rammed into an embankment and broke apart. It is believed that cross-wiring was at fault.

Following this incident the FAA issued an AD requiring the airlines to check the wiring on all Boeing 737s. That check revealed cross-wiring of engine or cargo compartment fire-warning systems existed in four other aircraft. The FAA ordered the airlines on January 8, 1989 to check all Boeing 737, 747, 757, and 767 aircraft built since December 31, 1980, for cross-wiring and cross-plumbing.[102] The FAA assessed a fine of $200,000 against Boeing in November 1989, charging them with miswiring engine fire extinguishers in 94 new airplanes and failing to adequately report the problems to the FAA.

In the early 1980s some listeners in the Los Angeles area called the talk shows on which I appeared, and complained about poor quality control at Douglas on the DC-10s. One employee called and complained about the practice of putting chewing gum in oversized rivet holes, to make them pass inspection. It seems like a comical story until one considers the tragic consequences. Shortly thereafter the Chicago DC-10 crash occurred, in which the subsequent NTSB accident report identified poor quality.

OTHER CAUSES OF DISINTEGRATION

Structural failure occurred to a Boeing 707 in turbulent air near Mount Fuji, Japan. The vertical tail ripped off the aircraft with fatal consequences for all on board. During Boeing flight checks on a Navy E-6-A jet (a derivative of the Boeing 707) a section of the tail ripped off. Repairs were made, and another test flight conducted. Again, the tail ripped off the aircraft.[103] An Air Canada DC-9 experienced an explosive decompression in flight when the rear cabin pressure bulkhead blew out, giving the occupants a frightening view of the outside world through the missing rear of the aircraft.

In March of 1984 an American Airline Boeing 727 flying at 37,000 feet experienced a loss of pressure when a nine by eleven-inch section of the fuselage exploded open. In December of 1987 an Eastern DC-9 split apart after landing at Pensacola, Florida. Douglas blamed the fuselage splitting apart upon a hard landing. But did this explain the problem? Aircraft have been making hard landings for years without breaking in

---

[102] This required checking approximately 741 aircraft, including 472 Boeing 737s, 33 Jumbo 747s, 123 757s, and 113 767s.

[103] *Wall Street Journal* October 2, 1989.

half. The question arises, if a hard landing can split the fuselage apart, what prevents it from splitting apart in flight during turbulence?

The hard landing reflected the co-pilot's poor knowledge of the aircraft systems. During the approach for the landing, the captain saw that the copilot had not placed the ground spoiler lever in the normal armed position (in which the ground spoilers automatically extend upon main-gear touchdown). The captain reminded the copilot to arm the spoilers with the short statement, "spoilers." The copilot knew so little about the systems, and the effects of doing what he was about to do, that he manually extended the ground spoilers while in flight (destroying the wing lift). The aircraft plunged to the ground, and broke in half. Fortunately, the aircraft was in its flare over the runway rather than flying over buildings.

POOR QUALITY CONTROL IN MAINTENANCE

There is the problem of sloppy maintenance practices and poor inspection of the work completed. All three engines failed on an Eastern Airlines Lockheed 1011 on an over-water flight to Bermuda. Mechanics replaced the engine magnetic metal detector plugs on the three engines without the "O" ring installed, causing the loss of lubricating fluid from all three engines. The engines self-destructed from loss of lubrication. The plane almost ditched in the shark-infested Atlantic, but managed to limp back to Miami on one engine before it also failed. The same maintenance error had occurred numerous times before, with destruction of the engines.

A TWA 747 in the middle of the North Atlantic had to shut down[104] two of its engines due to loss of oil pressure; maintenance personnel failed to replace the oil filler caps, and the lubricating oil went overboard. (All four engines could just as well have failed.) A Delta DC-9 touched down at Atlanta and its nose-gear collapsed. A mechanic installed the hydraulic lines incorrectly. A TWA 707 made an emergency landing[105] due to two fires started in one of the engines because the maintenance crew neglected to refasten parts of the engines being inspected.

United Airlines San Francisco maintenance base overhauled a General Electric CF-6 engine for Air Florida, and one of the mechanics left a metal tool inside the engine. During a subsequent takeoff of an Air Florida DC-10 at Miami, the engine overhauled by United disintegrated, destroying nearby unprotected fuel and hydraulic lines and cables. Two of the three

---

[104] July 23, 1977.
[105] October 27, 1977.

hydraulic systems failed. The hydraulic system failure caused the right wing leading-edge slats to retract, similar to what happened in the American Airlines DC-10 crash at Chicago. Fortunately, the engine failure occurred on the runway during the takeoff, and the pilot rejected the takeoff.

During engine removal to meet inspection requirements, American Airlines mechanics used a procedure prohibited by Douglas, damaging the engine mounting assembly on the aircraft. This caused the engine to later rip loose, leading to the American Airlines Chicago DC-10 crash. United Airlines mechanics used power tools to manually close the cargo doors on the Boeing 747, contrary to manufacturer recommendations. They failed to conduct the physical check of the door mechanism after every manual closing, as required by an FAA directive. An exploding cargo door ejected nine passengers to their death over the Pacific Ocean near Hawaii, as a result of noncompliance with inspection requirements. The list goes on and on, showing the poor control over the aviation industry by the corruption-riddled FAA.

The American Airlines crew that deiced Air Florida with a primarily water solution did not meet recognized standards, and played a role in the deadly crash occurring nearly on the steps of Congress.

Important DC-10 cargo door modifications on aircraft were signed off as completed at Douglas; it was later found that the work was never done. The resulting death total was 346. On a sister ship that Douglas records showed had the important door modification completed, it was found not installed.

FAA PAPER INSPECTIONS

If FAA maintenance inspectors went into the field and actually checked the work performed, they would discover many of the maintenance and design problems before a crash or near-crash occurred. However, the FAA policy is to check for record-keeping violations and is primarily a paper inspection.

Maintenance inspectors active in the field can pass along useful information, check the quality of the maintenance work, and improve the quality of the workmanship and adherence to federal regulations. This requires knowledgeable FAA inspectors. Concerned aircraft mechanics recognize the value of FAA inspectors in the field doing on-site physical inspections. Aircraft mechanics have called in on talk shows where I have appeared and lamented that they never see an FAA inspector.

After industry admitted it had a serious structural problem in 1989, the FAA announced hiring maintenance inspectors to do what they should have done for years, get into the areas where the work is done. Later, the NTSB issued a report[106] showing concern about the qualifications of the newly hired inspectors and their training. The NTSB stated that because of the limited number of qualified candidates with extensive air carrier backgrounds, the FAA hired people with general aviation or military backgrounds and/or transfer inspectors from general aviation assignments who are not familiar with air carrier maintenance programs and practices.

OBSTRUCTIONS TO REPORTING SAFETY PROBLEMS

The obstruction to meaningful corrective actions arises in all spheres. For instance, it is common knowledge that airline mechanics cannot report maintenance violations or dangerous practices to the FAA. Numerous instances have occurred where mechanics felt compelled to report serious maintenance violations to the FAA when their companies refused to comply with safe practices. The FAA forwarded the letters to the employer, who subsequently fired the mechanic. It could be stated that in this area the FAA acts as a spy agency for the airlines and helped punish whistleblowers who have valid safety concerns. This problem was detailed in an *Aviation Week & Space Technology* article dated July 17, 1989 which stated:

> Two years ago three Eastern mechanics called our Hazard Reporting System [Aviation Safety Institute] office to report serious breaches of safety on several Boeing 727s. After pleadings that we should contact the FAA and report the incidents (and warnings by us that their jobs would immediately be endangered), we called the FAA. Within two weeks, two of the mechanics were fired. The maintenance issues were never fully resolved, and the FAA did very little to correct the deficiencies.

On many talk shows during the past eleven years, aircraft mechanics had called in and reported similar problems. When the FAA imposes a huge fine upon a carrier following adverse FAA publicity, it is not as much interested in safety, as it is in whitewashing its image before the public and Congress.

During 1987 and 1988 Eastern Airlines pilots were so concerned about the maintenance problems at their airline that they paid for newspaper ads to make the public aware of the dangers. This is a ridiculous situation that never would have been necessary if the FAA had been doing its job. Part of this problem could be related to Eastern's perennial labor problems over the past decade. There is considerable evidence that the

---

106 *Aviation Week & Space Technology* November 6, 1989.

maintenance deterioration exists. Airline pilots have testified in Congressional hearings, sent letters to the FAA and NTSB, and I've talked to former Eastern Airlines' officials who admitted the problems, including orders to falsify inspection or maintenance records. This shouldn't shock anyone; it was done in the Paris DC-10 tragedy. Its part of the game at some airlines and aircraft manufacturers. What should shock the public is that a publicly supported government safety agency condones and conceals this conduct.

FAA Administrator Allan McArtor, attending a hearing chaired by Senator Ernest Hollings, chairman of the Senate Commerce, Science and Transportation committee, testified that the FAA receives "a lot" of complaints from pilots who claim they are being forced to fly planes that should be grounded. The FAA Administrator excused the FAA's failure to take corrective actions on the argument that the complaints were sparked by labor disputes. In some cases this may be true, but many times the complaints are valid.

CHEAPEST WAY TO GO

Endangering tens of thousands of crewmembers and passengers to save a few bucks is accepted practice. Rather than install the hard backups for the flight controls and horizontal stabilizer, or fire extinguishers in the cargo compartments, or the many other design compromises, these safeguards were eliminated by the FAA Western Region gang.

Some manufacturers wouldn't subject people to these terrible dangers. In their 1011, Lockheed installed four hydraulic systems to control the pitch of the aircraft; an electric motor to control the aircraft when the hydraulics failed; and in the event the of combined hydraulic and electrical failures the 1011 had an additional hand-crank to position the horizontal stabilizer. The 1011 had semi-plug type cargo doors, eliminating the constant danger of explosive opening of the doors. These previously required safeguards cost extra money. The airlines bought the cheaper DC-10, accepting the occasional loss of crewmembers and passengers. Lockheed had to discontinue their 1011 for lack of sales.

Corporate officials find it cheaper to have crashes and for insurance companies to pay the claims. The money saved by the design compromises is immediate, and identifiable with the person making the decision. The consequences in tragedies are not recognized or are soon forgotten.

The September 1989 issue of *Air Line Pilot* made reference to concern stated by FAA Administrator James Busey over the absence of backup flight control systems on all existing and future widebody aircraft. That was the first indication of concern for this obvious problem; none of the news media gave publicity to this concern.

PROFITABILITY OF AIRLINE CRASHES

Airline crashes are profitable. This isn't to say that anyone deliberately causes an airline crash to occur. But the profitability of the crash, the profitability of taking safety shortcuts, are factors that certainly do not work to promote safety. When a crash occurs, the insurance for replacing the aircraft is almost always more than the aircraft is worth on the books, or the aircraft initial cost. Most policies pay the replacement cost of the aircraft in the event of a crash with major damage or total destruction.

Insurance pays liability for passenger injuries and deaths (except for punitive damages, which are rarely awarded, but should have been awarded in many of the crashes described within these pages). Crashes that were profitable includes National Airlines, who declared a $1.2 million dividend after receiving the insurance proceeds following its 727 crash into Escambia Bay near Pensacola; American's Chicago DC-10 crash showed a $26.2 million profit, based upon the difference between the $10.8 million book value of the aircraft and the $37 million insurance check. World Airways was almost bankrupt when its DC-10 crashed at Boston.

Aloha Airlines Boeing 737 disintegration.

CHAPTER TWENTY

Radio and Television Appearances

In an attempt to circumvent the high administrative block, the high judicial block, the high legislative block, I sought to reach the public via exposé books and appearances on radio and television. The first printing of the *Unfriendly Skies* came out in 1978, and was distributed to book reviewers and talk show hosts a few days before the PSA San Diego crash occurred. The first printing was reprinted in 1979, and then in 1980 the updated printing came out, with even worst coverup by all the parties involved. The books formed the basis for appearances on hundreds of radio and television shows in the United States and Canada. The appearances described intrigue and complicity associated with air disasters unheard of by most listeners. The subject matter apparently incurred considerable interest, as over 1500 appearances occurred between 1978 and 1990.

To look at the light side for a moment, let's examine the mechanics of talk show appearances. The length of the usual radio appearance was one hour. My first talk show with Bill Miller on 50,000 watt WGY in Schenectady, New York, was three hours long. The longest radio appearance was with Ray Briem on KABC in Los Angeles (syndicated for several years from coast to coast); and lasted five hours, from midnight to five a.m. I was surprised at the number of alert and sophisticated listeners who called on these shows. The more sophisticated listeners called on shows in large cities such as Los Angeles, Seattle, Dallas, Atlanta, Chicago, Boston and New York.

The talk shows are a great vehicle for reaching millions of listeners, and they serve a valuable public service. They act like ombudsmen and are the best sources for exposing government misconduct. Ray Briem once remarked to me that in the Los Angeles area alone, there would be over a million listeners. When he went syndicated coast to coast, the number of listeners skyrocketed into many millions. It was a good way to get the message across.

Radio appearances are either in-studio, or by phone. Although the radio hosts prefer in-studio guests, this was not always possibly for me, and many appearances were by phone to all parts of the United States and Canada. On a tight schedule, and especially immediately after an airline crash, there could be eight or ten shows a day, and sometimes in the middle of the night.

PROMOTING AIR SAFETY VIA TALK SHOW CIRCUIT

Many interesting experiences happen on the talk shows. Callers described their own air safety experiences. Mechanics called in to report pressures by their companies to violate federal safety requirements; their attempts to force corrective actions by writing to the FAA, only to have their letters forwarded to their employers.

Flight attendants called in to describe crew drinking. Flight instructors called to describe company pressure to reduce training and competency requirements. Pilots called in to describe pressure by company officials to violate safety requirements, including flying without sufficient reserve fuel.

One caller on the Ray Briem show called and complained of the chewing gum placed in oversized rivet holes on new-plane construction at Douglas in Long Beach, which of course weakened the fuselage. Twelve months later NTSB investigators reported evidence of poor quality control in the American Airlines DC-10 that went down at Chicago.

A retired United Airlines official called in and reported the internal meetings shortly after the first printing of *The Unfriendly Skies* came out. The meetings were to determine how best to handle inquiries concerning the exposures relating to United that I described in the book.

During a radio appearances on Hollywood's KMEX with host David Moorhead on March 9, 1980, I debated with U.S. Representative Jim Lloyd (who represented part of Los Angeles). The Congressman stated he would investigate my allegations and get back to the show, and to me. He never did.

GREEN ROOM

Many interesting people are met in green-rooms, the name given to the guest waiting rooms in radio and television stations. Among the various people I met in that manner were producer John Ford, singers Glen Campbell and Roy Clark, Erica Jong (author of *Fear of Flying* and other books), and many others. I remember that when I first heard of her title I purchased a copy in order to keep up with other author's comments on matters relating to flying. Those who read the book know that it had nothing to do with flying, but was related to sex.

These shared appearances added interest to the otherwise gruelling talk-show circuit. Often I appeared on talk shows with hosts that had hosted earlier shows in other cities, and it was like meeting old friends. During a radio appearance at the Tropicana Hotel, the host described just missing the United Airlines flight from Chicago to New York on which showman Earl Carroll met his death. The host also described his experience watching American Airlines Flight One plunge into Jamaica Bay while sitting on the roof of his apartment building in New York.

The subject material is so diverse that there could be multiple appearances in a given city, and each show would be different. Each host had their own way of asking questions, and would get into only a small number of the many areas involved in this multifaceted scandal. Very few appearances were dull. The hosts prefer that the guest add to the questions asked, within limits, and this kept the show lively. Having been in aviation for so many years, under such varied circumstances, and in possession of such a great amount of insider information not known to the general public, or even many of the crewmembers, there was no lack of interesting material. Many times the host stated off the air that "this is going great."

HOST OFTEN DETERMINES THE DEPTH OF THE SUBJECT

The questions asked by the host, and how they respond to my answers and statements determined the depths to which I could go into the corruption. Some hosts were not comfortable with exposé type material, and with them I confined my subject material to direct safety problems. Other hosts could handle sensitive subjects and issues; and still others seem to thrive on it. With them the appearances were one of a kind that most listeners had never heard before.

TELEVISION APPEARANCES

Television appearances are quite different from radio. The normal length is only seven minutes, making it difficult to get much of a message across. Fortunately, many of my TV appearances were much longer, and many were an hour in length. Television appearances are far more of a production. Some have makeup rooms and makeup artists to prepare the guests. This can be embarrassing when one forgets to remove the makeup and then goes out into the public.

Twice I appeared on the Los Angeles television show, *Mid-morning Los Angeles,* in 1978 and again in 1980, hosted by Meredith MacRae and Bob Hilton. These were call-in. During one appearance a woman employee of a major airline called in to report the many times crewmembers showed up at flight dispatch for a flight, smelling of alcohol.

Former actor, and then producer, Jackie Cooper, heard me on the second *Mid-Morning Los Angeles* show, and we got together for an all-day meeting. Cooper wanted to do a three-part television series on the problems I encountered as an air safety activist. Numerous letters and phone calls followed. Finally, Cooper stated he still wanted to do the show, but he could not get any financing for a network television show because of reaction from airline advertisers. Cooper was a former Naval Aviator, as I was, and we had many sea-stories to exchange. We had planned to fly out to Catalina Island in my plane for breakfast, but that never came about.

GRATIFYING LISTENER RESPONSE
I sometimes stated that I wish I had the talents of the fictional television anchorman in the movie, *Network*, and could motivate the listeners to stop taking it, and do something about the government corruption that I described. Some shows with more responsive listeners had gratifying responses, and listeners showed concern and asked what they could do to help. A typical instance occurred on a Los Angeles radio show in June of 1989 when a listener called in, stated he was taping the show, and that he would make the tape available to those who may wish a copy to send to their two California Senators, Alan Cranston and Pete Wilson. The listener excitedly referred to the one million or more people then listening, and suggested that if enough listeners wrote to their two Senators and enclosed a copy of the tape, they could force an investigation.

I appreciated his call, and then had to remind him that Senators Cranston and Wilson already knew of the scandal and had been keeping the lid on it for years, as they had the savings and loan and other scandals. However, I did suggest actions they could take to force an investigation. These actions are described in later pages of this book.

Many listeners wrote to me expressing appreciation for what I was doing. If only more of them had written, and each listener had done more, the present air safety crisis and government corruption would not be in the stage that it is today. Possibly I did not encourage them enough. In the early days of my appearances, when asked what the listeners could do, I replied that because of the extent of the corruption and coverup, there wasn't anything they could do. I eventually changed my thinking on that, and advised them that there were actions they could take.

Among the positive actions listeners could take included writing complaints to their representatives in the United States Senate and House, realizing that they would be initially stonewalled. They had to persist, and make their persistence obvious. The investigations could be conducted as an internal Congressional investigation (which are often Kangaroo proceedings); conducted by the General Accounting Office (who have been covering up for this scandal for years); conducted by the Inspector Generals of the Department of Justice (relating to misconduct by people in the Department of Justice, and who also knew of the internal corruption), and the Department of Transportation (as it related to FAA and NTSB misconduct, agencies who also knew of the misconduct). The public could demand that Congress request appointment of *several* special prosecutors; this is often done with investigation of government officials. I recommended that they continue to call talk shows bringing up the subject of air safety and government corruption, making reference to my exposures, and request that the host have me appear on the show.

HOSTILE TECHNIQUE

Occasionally a hostile host is encountered, but this is rare. I can only remember two in my 1500 guest appearances; one was on the *Seattle PM* television show. Several guests had been on before me, and the host used this tactic with them. The guest immediately before me was a professor who was knowledgeable on Afghanistan; his appearance was immediately after Russia's military intervention in that country. The host harangued the guest, implying he was not an expert on the matter: "If you are such an expert on the subject, how come President Carter hasn't called upon you?" This was a stupid question and stupid logic. But typical of his confrontational style. Such host technique didn't address the serious problems that I sought to expose and correct.

When the first book came out, and during my early talk show appearances, I encountered several callers who appeared to be plants to discredit my exposures. The tactic didn't work, and it soon ceased.

I often used my plane to make the out of town appearances, and then rented a car at my destination. The plane helped meet a tight schedule. In one tight scheduling period I appeared all day long on shows in the Hollywood and Los Angeles area, the last aired at ten p.m. I then had to get up at five a.m, and take off from Burbank Airport in my Twin Bonanza airplane for San Diego, to make an eight o'clock television appearance. Burbank was fogged in, but I managed to get out on an instrument clearance. When I reached San Diego, the weather had not cleared as forecast, and I had to circle until the weather reached minimums to permit an ILS approach. Fortunately Lindberg Field opened up in time for me to land and make a quick dash to the television station; I arrived there in the nick of time. It was hard work, but I felt like I was doing a public service. In retrospect, the failure of the public to act aggressively made my years of sacrifice appear in vain.

During a San Francisco talk show with Jim Eason at KGO radio, I met a psychic coming off the earlier show, and got into a brief discussion with her. I don't believe in psychics, but I also cannot explain their uncanny powers. This psychic told me things she would have no way of knowing; I did not discuss them on the air. She told me of problems that are described in later pages, and that I would have a very rough time—which I did—but that I would eventually prevail. Well, it has been six years since she said that, and things are getting gloomier and gloomier for me. I can't say whether her prediction that I will eventually prevail will come true. It doesn't look good.

There was humor too. I remember a series of television shows I did in San Jose, California, when the very attractive hostess asked me what I thought of Flying Saucers. I chuckled, stated I didn't believe in them, and lightly said that if I *did* see what appeared to be one, I wouldn't tell anyone about it, for fear of losing credibility. She believed in Flying Saucers.

INTRIGUE

Following a multi-guest television appearance in Hollywood, all the guests decided to go to Charley Brown's restaurant for lunch. During the drive over to the restaurant, one of the guests noticed we were being followed. After lunch, we all went in different directions. The stranger trailing us then had to make a decision about whom to follow. He chose another person, and after that person went into his apartment house, the man trailing him made inquiries of his apartment manager. We never learned who he was.

THREAT TO MY ADVERSARIES

These radio and television appearances were a threat to my adversaries, and to those engaging in the duplicity of silence. Simultaneously, the exposure in my books and on the talk shows of coverup by federal judges and people within the Department of Justice gave me very strong enemies; enemies who could destroy me. These adversaries had the power to destroy people, to frame them, railroad them to prison, and destroy them financially. I didn't realize that; neither does most of the public. In my future there lay a terrible fate, engineered by these two groups, and it constitutes a scandal equal to or greater significance than the ongoing air disaster scandal.

Until late 1982, I thought I was protected by the laws and constitution of the United States. I believed in the pledge of allegiance which states, "with liberty and justice for all." I had no idea that the wording was meaningless.

I would discover what corrupt people in control of government can do to silence a citizen who threatens powerful groups. I would experience fear, suffer harm, and a taking of human rights, unlike anything I had ever read or experienced while a resident of third-world countries. I would experience the outrages that a corrupt government can inflict upon a citizen, while the press kept a lid on the outrages. Subsequent chapters show government corruption that if it was described in a novel rather than a non-fiction book, many of the readers would find difficulty believing it could happen in the United States of America.

I was to discover what it was like to be the modern day equivalent of the fictional Philip Nolan in the *Man Without a Country*. I was to learn the power and arrogance of those in control of our government today, made possible by the news media coverup. Many of the remaining pages show how this is done, juxtapositioned with bloody air disasters that these same people made possible.

Human cost of air safety problems.

CHAPTER TWENTY ONE

PART THREE

Judicial Attack

The air disaster scandal and those implicated in either its perpetration or coverup, were threatened by the 1978, 1979, and 1980 printings of the *Unfriendly Skies*; and my hundreds of radio and television appearances. Those threatened by the exposure activities included the FAA and NTSB, many members of the U.S. Senate and House, federal judges, Justice Department attorneys, the news media, and probably the CIA. A scheme was engineered by one or more of these groups to silence me. Before it was over, they would all be part of a conspiracy that willingly sacrificed the lives of thousands of people to keep the lid on the scandal. The scandal became the world's worst, ongoing, air disaster scandal, and the worst judicial and government scandal in the western world. My personal life became a shambles, and I would be financially destroyed.

Every one of dozens of relevant right and protection under the laws and Constitution of the United States were openly and repeatedly violated. When I objected and exercised procedural due process, judges called me a frivolous and vexatious litigant. In a crude form of sophistication, the legal and judicial fraternity destroyed me, seeking to silence forever my exposure of the multi-faceted scandal that heavily implicated the legal and judicial fraternity.

INADVERTENTLY GIVING THE CLUE

I inadvertently gave my adversaries the clue as to how to stop my threatening exposure activities. During several radio and television appearances the hosts asked me, "Aren't you afraid of what they might do to you?" The question inferred physical harm, but I sidestepped it, "As long as they can't get to my money, I'm OK." I felt there was *no way* that my adversaries could get the assets which funded my exposure activities. After all, we are a country in which citizens are protected by laws and Constitution. Aren't we?

At the beginning of the 1980s, the market value of my real estate properties was close to ten million dollars, and my net worth was over five million dollars. Most of my properties were located in the San Francisco area, and they were rapidly increasing in value. Foolishly, instead of just enjoying life and these assets, I continued my air safety activist activities trying to expose the government corruption that continued to play a role in air tragedies. I was the only one with the inside evidence and the willingness to fight this awesome corruption that had parallels in the HUD, savings and loan, and other scandals, but which lacked the brutality and deaths.

THIS IS HOW IT STARTED

The scheme to silence me was judicially engineered and carried out, and involved an ingenious and legally preposterous law suit. I wouldn't recognize the relationship between the sham law suit; the total suspension of all due process; and the air disaster scandal, until several years after it started. The participants were federal judges, the Justice Department, and members of the legal fraternity.

The scheme commenced with a sham law suit filed[107] by the San Francisco law firm of Friedman, Sloan, and Ross, who had close connections to my adversaries in the Justice Department and to the Ninth Circuit judges at San Francisco.[108]

The law suit stated a cause of action that the United States Supreme Court had held unconstitutional for the past half century. Numerous federal statutory and case laws, as well as fundamental constitutional rights, barred the cause of action. Several dozen California statutes, rules of court, and doctrines of law, also barred the action. Under California law, California judges lacked jurisdiction over the cause of action in the manner that it was filed. However, it served as a base from

---

[107] Filed in the Superior Court, Solano County, Fairfield, California. Action No. 83472.

[108] The major partners were employed by the Justice Department at San Francisco during the time the U.S. Attorney was blocking my attempts to expose the corruption within the FAA and NTSB, and also worked as law clerks for federal judges involved in the coverup.

which cooperating judges could render orders stripping me of the assets which funded the exposure activities.

THE ACTUAL CAUSE OF ACTION

The law suit alleged that I was married to Friedman's Texas client, my ex-wife, Emma Stich, from whom I had been divorced for twenty years. The law suit alleged that she wanted a dissolution of that marriage, and stated that all my assets were community properties. Using that law suit as a base, the Friedman law firm filed a law suit seizing control of the assets used to fund my exposure activities.

There were many legal obstacles to that law suit. The main one was that I had been legally divorced for the last two decades, since 1966, and my former wife continued to declare herself divorced from me in her resident State of Texas. Five divorce judgments showed I was divorced, and that my personal and property rights had been established two decades earlier. My former wife had resided in Texas since she left Colorado in 1964 to move back to Texas where she had many relatives; she had continually declared herself divorced from me since we had obtained an amicable divorce in 1966, and gave constructive notice of that divorced status by declaring herself divorced in numerous real estate purchases and sales. Neither of us resided in California when the 1966 judgment was rendered.

When I later changed my residence to California, I had the 1966 divorce judgment entered and confirmed as a California judgment.[109] In turn, the California judgment and the 1966 judgment were entered as local judgments in the courts of Nevada, Oklahoma, and Texas. It was safe to say that I was legally divorced. Federal law controls whether a state will recognize a prior divorce judgment when a person exercises the constitutional right to change his residence to another state. And federal law prohibited the California law suit on the basis that I was already divorced, for the past two decades. It was as if a probate action was filed to distribute my estate, ignoring the fact that I was still alive. In this case, a divorce action was filed against me, ignoring the fact that there was no marriage. But the action was filed regardless, as it served as the basis for rendering orders stripping me of the assets I used to fund the exposure activities.

The Friedman law firm argued in the law suit that these divorce judgments were void, that the termination of the marriage in 1966 was invalid, and that I was still married to their Texas client. Further, since we were still "married," the

---

[109] As provided by California Civil Code Section 1699 and Civil Code Section 5164.

ten million dollars in real property assets I acquired after the
1964 separation and 1966 divorce were actually community
properties, in which Friedman's client had a fifty percent
ownership (and Friedman had a percentage interest in the
"take").

"VOIDING" TWO DECADES OF PROPERTY RIGHTS ON SHAM BASIS

The argument the Friedman law firm used to void two
decades of property rights acquired by prior divorce judgments
and as a divorced person could be applied to most divorced
persons. The law suit argued that the tens of thousands of
divorce judgments rendered by the 1966 court were void
because the court exercised personal jurisdiction upon the basis
of my five month's residence in the divorce court's jurisdiction.
Friedman argued that California judges would not recognize
divorce judgments rendered on that basis. Since the laws of all
fifty states, and court practice, exercise personal jurisdiction
in divorce cases almost exclusively on the basis of residence
(one day, 90 days, six months, etc.), the cause of action was
obviously a sham, and should be immediately thrown out.

Friedman argued that the prior judgments were void; that
the properties I acquired during two decades of divorced status
were not my sole properties as insured by title policies; and
that I was still married to their Texas client.

Friedman raised an argument that had been held unconstitutional for the past fifty years, and which, if applied across the
board, would remarry many divorced persons to their first
spouse. Friedman argued that the laws in the 1966 divorce
court did not require persons getting a divorce to acquire
domicile status,[111] and therefore California judges would not
recognize the tens of thousands of divorce judgments rendered
by that court (or any other court in the fifty United States).
The residence basis for exercising personal jurisdictions was
used throughout the fifty United States, used in all known free-
world countries, and established by statutory and case law in
California. California judges exercised personal jurisdiction in
thousands of divorce cases on the same residence basis.

Domicile is for academic purposes (and used in probate
proceedings) the place where a person intends to live for the
remainder of their lives, or, who has no intent to ever change.
The Friedman law firm, and especially their attorneys Jeffrey
Ross and Lawrence Gibbs, argued that since I had not purchased property in the 1966 divorce court jurisdiction, I had

---

[111] Legal definition defining a place where a person intends to reside for the remainder
of their lives, or from where they have no intention of leaving.

not acquired domicile status. Therefore, I could never obtain a divorce.

Since I, like many other people, changed my residence many times during my marriage, and in some moves never acquired property, I was permanently barred from obtaining a divorce that would be recognized by California judges. This was preposterous and as phony as a four-dollar bill. But the scheme to strip me of my assets got considerable mileage from that phony law suit.

Using that argument, persons who could never obtain a divorce include renters; those who move either by choice or by economic necessity; or any of the thousands of other reasons that cause people to change their residence.

The Friedman law firm argued that California judges would only recognize personal and property rights established by prior divorce judgments rendered by courts foreign to California, over residents of such foreign court jurisdictions, if the foreign courts required domicile for exercising personal jurisdiction. The U.S. Supreme Court held that argument to be unconstitutional a half century ago, and no state requires domicile status to obtain a divorce.

The law suit was filed under the California Family Law Act, which permits the California judges to immediately take over the assets on the basis that they are protecting the assets for the other party who allegedly has a community property interest. But the admission in the law suit that there were prior divorce judgments immediately deprived the California judges of personal and subject matter jurisdiction under the Act.

VIOLATIONS OF FEDERAL AND CALIFORNIA LAW

Federal law controls when rights protected by federal law and the federal Constitution are violated. Federally protected rights barred the California law suit. Federally protected rights barred the refusal to recognize residence as a basis for exercising personal jurisdiction in a divorce action. Years ago the U.S. Supreme Court put a stop to state judges voiding divorce judgments rendered by other courts.[111] Constitutional Full Faith

---

[111] *Vanderbilt v. Vanderbilt* (1957) 354 U.S. 416 (requiring the recognition of *ex parte* divorce judgments; *Estin v. Estin* 334 U.S. 541 (1948)(requiring the recognition of prior divorce judgments); *Sherrer v. Sherrer* (1948) 334 U.S. 343; *Coe v. Coe* (1948) 334 U.S. 378 (requiring the recognition of prior divorce judgments); *Perrin v. Perrin*, 408 F.2d 107 (3rd Cir. 1969) (prohibiting denying recognition to prior judgments when exercised on residence, including one day's residence).

and Credit Clause (Article IV, Section 1) and the full faith and credit statute (Title 28 United States Code Section 1738) require all state judges to recognize the California, Nevada, Oklahoma, and Texas divorce judgments. The attack violated fundamental constitutional rights and protections.[113]

CALIFORNIA LAW ALSO PROHIBITED THE ATTACK

California statutory law prohibits collateral attacks upon *any* prior divorce judgment, and requires mandatory recognition of each of the prior divorce judgments.[114] California Supreme Court decisions prohibited attacks upon prior divorce judgments, and barred judicial refusal to recognize residence as a basis for exercising personal jurisdiction.[115] California statutory law specifically provides that residence is a proper basis for exercising jurisdiction.[116] Further, the statute of limitations prohibits an attack upon prior judgments three years after they are rendered.

---

[113] Right to unabridged interstate travel, arising in the Privileges and Immunities Clause, Article IV, Section 2, and in the Fourteenth Amendment (right to change residence without losing rights adjudicated and acquired in prior jurisdictions); Fourteenth Amendment, relating to due process and equal protection, giving all persons the right to obtain a divorce, and adjudication of personal and property rights; laws respecting property rights.

[114] Mandatory divorce judgment recognition statutes (Civil Code §§ 4554, 5004, 5164; Code of Civil Procedure §§ 1699(b), 1713.3, 1908, 1913, 1915 (effective when the 1966 judgment was rendered and for nine years thereafter); Evidence Code §§ 666, 665, 622; (statute of limitations, Civil Code §§ 880.020, 880.250; Code of Civil Procedure §§ 318, 338, 343; Statute of limitations: Code of Civil Procedure 318, 338, 343; Civil Code §§ 880.020, 880.250; mandatory requirement to recognize that the prior court acted in the lawful exercise of its jurisdiction when the judgment is under attack two decades after its exercise of jurisdiction, and the acceptance of the benefits by both parties: Evidence Code §§ 666, 665, 622.

[115] Prohibiting attacks upon prior divorce judgments on refusal to recognize residence, or for any other basis: *Rediker v. Rediker* (1950) 35 Cal.2d 796 ("it must be presumed that the foreign court had jurisdiction and that its recital thereof is true ... is not subject to collateral attack on a showing of error in the exercise of that jurisdiction ... The validity of a divorce decree cannot be contested by a party who ... aided another to procure the decree."; *Scott v. Scott* (1958) 51 C.2d 249 ("There should be no implication ... that would preclude contacts with the foreign country other than domicile as a basis of jurisdiction. ... Section 1915 of the Code of Civil Procedure provides: "A final judgment of any other tribunal of a foreign country have jurisdiction, according to the laws of such country, to pronounce the judgment, shall have the same effect as in the country where rendered, and also the same effect as final judgments rendered in this state [which are final and conclusive of the rights and obligations of the parties--C.C. § 4554]"; *Spellens v. Spellens* (1957) 498 C.2d 210 ("The principle of estoppel is applicable [when] the divorce decree was alleged to be invalid for lack of jurisdiction ... The validity of a divorce decree cannot be contested by a party ... who aided another to procure the decree ..."); *Whealton v. Whealton* (1967) 67 C.2d 656 ("When both parties to a divorce action are before the court ... it is questionable whether domicile is an indispensable prerequisite for jurisdiction. ... the prerequisite of domicile may be easily avoided at the trial by parties wishing to invoke the jurisdiction of a court, with little fear in most instances that the judgment will be less effective than if a valid domicile in fact existed.").

[116] Civil Code Sections 4530(a)(b), 4531, Code of Civil Procedure Sections 410.10, 418.10(a), 1713.5; Rule of Court 1230(a)(3), 1241, 1262.

SUSPENSION OF SUBSTANTIVE AND PROCEDURAL DUE PROCESS

Despite the unconstitutionality of the cause of action, its prohibition under California statutory law, despite the absence of jurisdiction under the Family Law Act, California judges[117] repeatedly protected and rewarded the Friedman law firm, and blocked every attempt to defend against the bizarre action. Something was radically wrong. To support the violations of blocks of substantive laws, the California judges blocked every procedural defense. They denied me the right to file appeals; refused to render mandatory statements of decision addressing my defenses; refused to allow me to obtain depositions of Friedman's Texas client, and much more.

The California Court of Appeal judges repeatedly dismissed my appeals. Sometimes without accepting my appeal briefs, or simply denying them, despite the outrageous civil and constitutional violations requiring appellate relief. All rights and protections in the California judicial proceedings were suspended, and openly violated by blocks of judges in the Solano County Superior Courts, the judges in the Division Five appellate court at San Francisco, and the California Supreme Court. Every lawful and constitutional outrage was protected by every level of the California judicial process. It was bizarre.

After being served with the bizarre law suit, I filed on February 17, 1983 the sole and specific remedy provided by California law. I filed a motion to quash,[118] addressing the judges absence of jurisdiction under the Family Law Act to attack the prior judgments; to attack my two decades of divorced status; to remarry me to Friedman's Texas client; to attack property rights I acquired under the rights and protections of the laws and Constitution of prior states of residence and of the United States.

Under California law, immediately upon filing the motion-to-quash, the California judge lost personal jurisdiction over me. I was protected by special appearance status, and the only authority the California judges possessed was to conduct a brief hearing to receive evidence of the prior divorce judgment. Immediately upon receiving evidence of that judgment, the judge's absence of jurisdiction under the Family Law Act is established, and he has to dismiss the law suit.

California law requires the judge to conduct the hearing on the motion to quash within 20 days of the date I filed the

---

[117] Judges Dwight Ely, Michael McInnis, William Jensen, John DeRonde, Richard Harris, William Peterson.

[118] California Rule of Court 1230(a)(2) and Code of Civil Procedure 418.10(a)(1).

motion, which was filed on February 17, 1983. When I appeared on the date set to hear the motion to quash, February 25, 1983, Judge Dwight Ely refused to conduct the mandatory hearing. He refused to receive a copy of the divorce judgment, and in that manner sidestepped the legal requirement to dismiss the action.

Instead of conducting the hearing to determine his challenged jurisdiction, Ely subjected me to a trial on the underlying law suit, for which a general appearance had not been made, and for which he lacked jurisdiction. The trial was on Friedman's order-to-show-cause, to determine how much money I would pay the Friedman law firm to finance the law suit against me, and how much money I would pay to support Friedman's Texas client while the law suit continued. Under California law, in marital dissolution actions, the judge can order either party to pay the legal fees of the other party. But I was not married to the party, and thus he had no authority to make such an order, or jurisdiction to hear the law suit.

Several months later, without any testimony whatsoever on any matter other than how much money the Friedman law firm wanted, and how much money I had, Judge Ely rendered a decision on May 10, 1983, denying the motion to quash. He never conducted a hearing on the matter. The same order required me to pay Friedman's legal fees and costs, and to support Friedman's Texas client.

Ely's order stated that California judges would not recognize any prior divorce judgment rendered on the basis of residence, while he simultaneously exercised jurisdiction on the same residence basis in divorce actions appearing before him. His decision voided millions of divorce judgments rendered throughout the United States and in most foreign countries.

SUSPENSION OF APPELLATE REMEDIES

The appellate court remedy for a judge's refusal to dismiss an action following a motion to quash is to file a petition for writ of mandamus with the California Court of Appeals. And then, if denied, file a petition for hearing with the California Supreme Court.[119] If the lower court lacks jurisdiction, the upper court *must* grant the petition.[120] Even though the lower court judges clearly lacked jurisdiction, the California court of appeal judges denied the petition for relief. The judges of the California Supreme Court also upheld the massive violations of state and federal laws and constitutional protections.

The remedy under California law for the order to pay money is by appeal. I appealed. The Court of Appeal judges, Donald

---

[119] California Code of Civil Procedure § 418.10(b).
[120] Code of Civil Procedure Section 1086.

King, Harry Low, and Zerne Hanning, appointed by California governor, sometimes called "moonbeam" Brown, rendered a published decision[121] protecting the violations that also permitted California judges to remarry most previously divorced persons. That decision was published, and is case law in the State of California today.

This published decision makes all prior divorce judgments subject to voiding by California judges if either party changes residence to California. This was a major constitutional setback, and upheld by the California Court of Appeal judges and California Supreme Court judges justices. This little-noticed decision affects everyone who exercises their constitutionally protected right to change residence to California, making them fair game for losing their personal and property rights; their wives adulteress; their children bastards.

FRIVOLOUS TO EXERCISE DUE PROCESS RIGHTS

The Court of Appeal judges held in their published decision that it was frivolous for me to exercise my remedies under California law (motion to quash, petition for writ, and appeal). The decision held that I should have willingly submitted to the jurisdiction of the California judges (who under law had no jurisdiction under the Family Law Act to attack prior divorce judgments); that I should have agreed to be remarried; that I should have agreed to undergo another divorce proceeding, and have the properties and assets I acquired during two decades of divorced status divided with Friedman's Texas client and the Friedman law firm (on the basis of the contingency agreement between Friedman and their client).

Based upon this published decision and the holding that it was frivolous for me to object, the three appellate judges ordered me to pay $50,000 attorney fees and financial sanctions. This order was shortly followed by another order that I pay $170,000 attorney fees to the Friedman law firm.

"They can't do that!"

Many attorneys stated to me that the California judges couldn't do what they were doing. I agreed, but they were doing it anyhow. At this stage I had not yet recognized that the California law suit was a scheme engineered to strip me of the assets I relied upon to fund my exposure activities.

"They could just as well have filed a probate action!"

One attorney stated that filing a divorce action against someone who has been divorced for the past two decades is not much different from filing a probate action on a person who is still alive. Neither action has the required pre-requisite to give

---

[121] *In re Marriage of Stich*, 164 Cal. App. 64 (1985).

the judge jurisdiction. Either would have been equally ridiculous. It was bizarre; fabricate a preposterous cause of action and then deny me every protection in law.

SIMULTANEOUS DIVORCED AND MARRIED STATUS

Eight years of intensive litigation followed (which continues at this date). I was probably the only resident in California that was legally divorced in one county; divorced in other states; whose former wife repeatedly declared herself divorced from me in her resident state; and simultaneously subjected to a marriage termination action in a state where I was already recognized as divorced. The Friedman law firm and California judges were using her as a catalyst in a cause of action to terminate an alleged marriage which she denied existed.

DOZENS OF ILLEGAL LIS PENDENS

During the next seven years the Friedman law firm filed dozens of lis pendens upon my business and other properties. These lis pendens stopped my real estate investment business in its track, inflicting heavy losses upon me and my business. Mortgage loans came due, and could not be refinanced. Notice of foreclosures were filed, and trustee sales were held. I was bleeding to death, losing everything I acquired during the past twenty years. Even on the eve of losing valuable properties due to mortgage foreclosures caused by the lis pendens, the Friedman firm refused to remove them. They preferred that over a million dollars in property equities be lost, rather than remove the unlawfully filed lis pendens. If the Friedman law firm actually represented my former wife's interests, they would have lifted the lis pendens to permit the mortgages to be refinanced. That wasn't their goal. Their goal was to destroy me financially.

The persecution was continuous. Almost daily for eight years legal papers were arriving by mail or process server. These papers, and my defending briefs, fill three drawers of a legal filing cabinet, representing heavy work loads of seven days a week, often fourteen hour days, year after year. Constant legal research and legal briefs consumed my every living moment. A full-size book could be written about the California judicial corruption, not only as it was used to silence my exposure activities, but to expose the corruption per se and its effect upon all other California judicial activities.

OPEN HEART SURGERY

The constant judicial abuses; the humiliation; the loss of valuable properties; the harm to my business; the recognition of the judicial gridlock combined with judicial anarchy; watching the efforts of years of work go down the drain; the loss of my personal life; the loss of my retirement home; the adverse effect upon personal relationships; the effect upon my children;

were stressful. Possibly it precipitated the need for surgery. In April 1985 I underwent open-heart surgery for six coronary bypasses.

Before I left for surgery I notified the California Court of Appeal judges, King, Low, and Haning, of the hospitalization, and requested that they delay their decision on the appeal of the May 10, 1983 order until after I got out of intensive care. Otherwise I would not have time to request a rehearing from the California Supreme Court judges.

I was barely out of intensive care, and had just arrived home, when the Court of Appeal judges rendered their decision. Several attorney friends described the decision as the closet thing to a poison-pen letter that they had ever seen. I rushed to prepare a petition for hearing to the California Supreme Court. But the Supreme Court judges had known of and protected the judicial abuses since 1983. There wasn't much hope, as judge protected judge and the brotherhood.

The published decision[122] fabricated facts out of whole cloth. It refused to address any of the California or federal laws that I raised in defense. The decision upheld the right of California judges to void prior divorce judgments of any party moving to California, and to seize their properties and convey it to former spouses and the California attorneys representing these former spouses. They held they had the power to destroy.

The published decision eulogized the Friedman law firm who filed the bizarre action that was prohibited by law. The decision eulogized my ex-wife who openly committed fraud and perjury by simultaneously declaring herself married to me in the California action while declaring herself divorced from me in her resident State of Texas.

THE LITIGATION WAS ENDLESS

It seemed like the litigation would never end. In 1985 California judge William Jensen ordered me to undergo a bifurcated divorce trial to relitigate the exercise of personal jurisdiction by the 1966 divorce court. But this was specifically barred under the California Family Law Act, by California statutory and Supreme Court decisions, and under the Federal Supremacy Clause of the United States Constitution, barred by federal law. To insure an unfavorable ruling for me, Judge William Jensen held that I had to prove in 1985 that my mental thought processes in 1966 constituted domicile (even though the domicile invalidating argument was specifically barred by California and federal laws.

---

[122] *In re Marriage of Stich*, 169 Cal.App.3d 164.

PRE-TRIAL SUSPENSION OF DUE PROCESS

The suspension of due process was everywhere. Judge Jensen refused to order my former wife to appear for a deposition, which was an important pre-trial requirement. This deposition was especially important as my former wife declared herself divorced from me in Texas while her attorneys argued that she sought a divorce from me in California. A deposition would reveal the perjury by Friedman's Texas client who was making contradictory declarations of her marital status. While denying the right to take her deposition, Judges Jensen and Harris ordered me to appear for three depositions relating to my properties, even after statutory law halted depositions 30 days before the trial.

Several days before the start of the trial, the Friedman firm produced an "expert" witness long after the 70 day before-trial cutoff date. The judge had the right to waive this cutoff, but must grant me an extension to get deposition of the other party. Judge Harris refused to grant the extension, and I was therefore denied a deposition of this late-listed witness. The witness was an attorney who would testify that the 1966 court violated the law. This was a new approach. The Friedman law firm paid this attorney over $3,000 to appear for one day and testify that the 1966 court acted in violation of law. The paid attorney acted as an appellate process 22 years after the fact, to determine whether the judicial acts of the 1966 court were legal! Nothing was too bizarre for the California judicial brotherhood.

CHANGING THE LABEL ON THE TRIAL

The Friedman firm had filed an at-issue memorandum setting the case for trial, identifying the trial as a bifurcated divorce trial to relitigate the exercise of personal jurisdiction by the 1966 court. The nature of the trial was also established by a written stipulation dated April 27, 1985. Further, Judge Randall identified the trial as a bifurcated divorce trial during the trial-setting hearing held on May 1, 1985. He also stated that the action would be quickly dismissed. Friedman later circumvented this by disqualifying Judge Randall at the start of the trial. No reason need be given for a one-time disqualification.

After disqualifying Judge Randall, Judge Jensen became the trial judge. Just prior to the start of the bifurcated divorce trial, the Friedman group submitted what appeared to be a prearranged letter to Judge Jensen, stating that the trial was not a bifurcated divorce trial, but on my motion to quash.

The reason for changing the label of the trial was that a motion to quash has no appeal remedies, and higher court defenses were limited to a petition for writ, which could be denied without giving any explanation. A bifurcated trial had appeal remedies, and required the appellate judges to more openly violate the laws prohibiting the law suit.

There were other irregularities with that change of label. A motion to quash hearing is limited to introducing evidence of the prior divorce judgment, and does not permit relitigating the issues litigated twenty years earlier. A motion to quash must be heard within twenty days of the filing of the motion, and it was now almost three years since I filed the motion to quash. Further, Judge Ely's May 10, 1983 decision denied the motion to quash (even though he didn't conduct a hearing on the matter). There were many other irregularities, and these are stated to give examples of the lawlessness existing in the California courts.

After a five-day trial that was riddled with procedural irregularities, Judge Jensen rendered a decision on January 13, 1986. He held that my five months residence in the 1966 divorce court jurisdiction did not constitute domicile, and that California judges would not recognize that judgment—or the tens of thousands of others in which prior courts exercised personal jurisdiction on the basis of residence (which are most of the divorce judgments rendered in the United States and most foreign countries).

By this decision Jensen held that I was married to Friedman's Texas client; that my properties were community; and that the five divorce judgments were not valid. He had no authority to make any decision violating state and federal laws.

BENCH WARRANT FOR MY ARREST

The orders *never* stopped. In addition to the earlier order that I pay $50,000 to the Friedman law firm, Jensen ordered me to pay $170,000 attorney fees. The legal cloud on my properties, and the filing of dozens of lis pendens, denied me access to my own properties to obtain funds. My income had been halted. I couldn't pay the money orders. Since I couldn't pay the money orders, Judge Jensen sentenced me to county jail for contempt of court. Similar orders were later rendered by California judge William Peterson (who was later promoted by California governor George Deukmejian to an appellate judge).

Another scheme was concocted to put me in jail. Jensen ordered me to appear in court on May 9, 1986, a date that he knew I was calendared to be in federal court at Sacramento. That action was a Civil Right action I filed against Jensen on the basis of violating my rights under state and federal laws and causing me harm. Jensen retaliated against me for exercising these rights by ordering me to appear in court to answer why I should not be held in contempt for failure to pay the judgments which he knew I couldn't pay. I was repeatedly in

Catch-22 situations.

I filed papers in the Solano County court notifying Jensen of this defense, along with the illegality of the money orders and the judges absence of jurisdiction. I also advised Jensen of what he already knew; that I could not physically appear because I was previously calendared to be in federal court on that same time and date. Jensen was a defendant in that federal civil right violation action, and it was no secret to him that I could not simultaneously appear in state court. I also advised Jensen that an attorney would appear for me at that hearing, as was permitted by California law.

At the hearing Judge Jensen held me in contempt of court for not being present. He issued a bench warrant for my arrest. Since I resided in Nevada, this bench warrant kept me from appearing in California for the next year and a half. Seeking relief from the bench warrant, I submitted petitions for relief to the California Court of Appeals and the California Supreme Court. Despite the many defenses, they denied me relief.

INVOKING FEDERAL REMOVAL PROTECTION

Federal law provides for removal of state actions to federal court if federal issues are involved, or if a party cannot get due process in the state courts. After Judge Jensen rendered the bench warrant for my arrest, I filed a petition for removal with the U.S. District Court at Sacramento, which immediately halted all state jurisdiction over the case.[123] Federal Judge Milton Schwartz immediately dismissed the removal action. I then filed an appeal to the Ninth Circuit Court of Appeals, which kept the removal action in federal court, where it remained until the end of 1989. Until that removal action was returned by the Court of Appeals, the California judges lacked jurisdiction to take any action.

Even though the California judges lacked jurisdiction during the time that the state action is removed to federal court, the California judges continued to render orders as if the removal had never occurred. I again sought relief from the California Court of Appeal and California Supreme Court (which I had done at least a dozen times earlier) on the basis of the removal to federal court, the absence of jurisdiction under the Family Law Act, and the blocks of California and federal laws barring the action. Again and again the judges in the California Court of Appeal and California Supreme Court denied me relief. They had me judicially gridlocked.

I also sought relief from the United States Supreme Court by filing petitions for writ of certiorari, arguing that the

---

[123] Title 28 United States Code Sections 1441-1446.

California judges were rendering unlawful and unconstitutional orders, and rendering them while the federal removal action stripped them of additional jurisdiction. Again and again the Justices of the U.S. Supreme Court protected Friedman and the California judges, and tacitly approved the actions which threatened thousands of divorced people with loss of personal and property rights, and those who marry them.

A NEW SCHEME

While I was recovering from open heart surgery, and residing in Nevada, the Friedman law firm obtained an order for me to appear in San Francisco for the third lengthy deposition on my property rights.[123] The filing of the appeal of the bifurcated divorce trial decision halted all trial court proceedings, making the deposition request void. But the California judges continued to render orders as if the appeal had never been filed. I also argued in my motion that my delayed recovery from open heart surgery was affecting my ability to travel to San Francisco, and thus I could not appear. California law limits deposition orders to 150 miles from the parties residence. I lived over 200 miles from San Francisco.

Simultaneously, Judge William Peterson ordered me into default, wherein the seizure of my multi-million dollar estate could be ordered without allowing me to defend.

When I did appear for the deposition, Judge William Peterson refused to let me defend against the bench warrant and order-to-show-cause. Instead, he ordered me to jail.

RENDERING A SHAM ORDER TERMINATING THE NON-EXISTING MARRIAGE

Without my knowledge, the Friedman law firm and California Judge Dennis Bunting conducted a hearing on July 28, 1988 to terminate the non-existing marriage and order the taking of my properties. During that hearing, Judge Bunting rendered a judgment that described the cause of action as a dissolution of marriage action (even though it was clearly an attack upon prior divorce judgments). Having "established" that Friedman's Texas client was married to me, Bunting then rendered an order holding that all my assets were community properties (when, as a matter of law, they were not community properties even if, for argument, I had been married to Friedman's client). The same order required me to pay $2500 monthly spousal support for life (when the five existing divorce judgments showed there were no spousal support obligations). That order was rendered while the federal courts still had the removal action which further stripped the California judges of jurisdiction.

---

123 California statutory law limits depositions to one.

There were now six divorce judgments; five showing me divorced since 1966; that showed all properties to be separate; and holding that neither party had any spousal support rights or obligations.

STATE JUDICIAL CORRUPTION IS RAMPANT

The rampant judicial corruption is rarely described in the press, who for some inexplicable reason will often sequester evidence of widespread judicial misconduct. Judicial misconduct exposing a single judge without implicating the entire system occasionally gets reported. One of these exceptions was the in-depth *Wall Street Journal* article dated November 1, 1989 describing the arrogance of a Pennsylvania judge. The article described the inability and unwillingness of anyone to do anything about it. Describing the corruption of Judge Joseph O'Kicki, the article described the vulnerability of many small communities under the thumb of domineering judges. Nine months after the judge was sworn in as President Judge of Cambria County, the Pennsylvania state Attorney General finally stepped in and indicted him on a sweeping array of charges alleging more than ten years of official oppression. Although this was justified, it is highly unusual as the system protects its own and usually nothing is done to protect the public from the resulting harm.

The 80-page grand jury report handed up to the state Attorney General charged Judge O'Kicki with extorting cash from lawyers, pressuring banks for favorable loans at below-market interest rates, refusing to repay loans, and threatening the banks with adverse decisions if they pressed for payment. The judge reportedly owned secret and illegal interests in a beer distributorship, and hidden ownership interests in real estate that caused conflicts of interest which he sought to hide by setting up dummy corporations. Lawyers who frequently appeared before the judge feared alienating him or appealing his decisions, for fear of judicial reprisals. Attorneys sabotaged the interests of their clients to protect their legal careers.

The typical judge-protect-judge pattern developed. Pennsylvania Supreme Court Justice John Flaherty called judge O'Kicki one of the finest judges "not only in Pennsylvania but in the United States." Other judges voted Judge O'Kicki president of the Pennsylvania Conference of State Trial Judges.

Johnstown attorney Richard Green loaned the judge money, which was never returned. When Green won a $240,000 verdict in a land condemnation case against the state in June 1983, Green stated Judge O'Kicki unexpectedly awarded him an additional $100,000. After the courtroom cleared, Judge O'Kicki walked up to the attorney and suggested a kickback. "Don't you think I ought to get a commission, Judge O'Kicki said, "or part of your fee in this case?"

Judicial arrogance is everywhere, and the public doesn't know their rights to defend against it. Few attorneys would be brave enough to stand up to the corrupt system in which judge protects judge, where attorneys grovel at the feet of the judges seeking a favorable ruling.

"I am God," stated one of the judges in *Greylord Justice, Cook County Style.*[124] *Greylord* was a story of judicial corruption in Chicago, which can be found in various forms in courts throughout the United States, including the federal courts. The federal judicial corruption described within these pages—with more to follow—inflicts far greater harm upon our form of government, and upon individual citizens, than the corruption described in *Greylord*, which was confined to Chicago.

THERE ARE LAWS TO PROTECT THE PUBLIC, BUT THE SYSTEM DEPRIVES THE PUBLIC OF THEIR PROTECTION

There are federal laws giving people the right to obtain federal relief from state judges who either act without jurisdiction, or violate state or federal law, causing harm. Few attorneys will exercise these remedies, fearful of retaliation by state and federal judges who want no threat to their self-proclaimed right to steal and bully. Many attorneys are unaware of these federal rights. Further, federal judges, formerly state judges, usually protect their judicial namesakes in state court.

Not even the Mafia's Godfathers are appointed for life, as are our federal judges. Federal judges can commit legal and constitutional atrocities, sit in judgment on their own acts, and hold themselves immune from the consequences. This is not what the laws and Constitutional state, but what the self-protective judges hold, in open defiance of the law. They use their power to corrupt, and the cowering public takes it.

---

[124] *Putnam Publishing Company,* by James Tuohy and Rob Warden.

Destruction of Overseas National Airline DC-10 following
engine disintegration and severing of fuel and hydraulic lines at
JFK Airport, New York City.

CHAPTER TWENTY TWO

Greylord Judicial Corruption

Federal Style

Federal statutory and case law, and the U.S. Constitution, provides relief to people in federal court when state judges act without personal or subject matter jurisdiction; or violate clear and settled state or federal law; or violate rights and protections under the U.S. Constitution; or if a person cannot obtain due process in state courts.

When state officials, including judges, and private individuals acting under color of state law, cause these violations to occur, citizens have the right to relief from federal judges. (Titles 42 United States Code Section 1983,[125] 1985,[126] and

---

[125] Title 42 U.S.C. § 1983: Every person who, under color or any statute, ordinance, regulation, custom or usage, of any State of Territory, subjects ... any citizen of the United States ... to the deprivation of any rights, privileges or immunities secured by the Constitution and laws, shall be liable to the party injured in an action at law, suit in equity, or other proper proceeding for redress.

[126] **Title 42 U.S.C. § 1985 Conspiracy to interfere with civil rights—Preventing officer from performing duties.**

(1) If two or more persons ... conspire to prevent ... any person from accepting or holding any office, trust, or place of confidence under the United States, or from discharging any duties thereof; or to injure him in his person or property on account of his lawful discharge of the duties of his office, or while engaged in the lawful discharge thereof, or to injure his property so as to molest, interrupt, hinder, or impede him in the discharge of his official duties.

(2) If two or more persons conspire ... for the purpose of depriving, either directly or indirectly, any person ... of the equal protection of the laws, or of equal privileges and immunities under the laws ...in any case of conspiracy set forth in this section, if one or

1986.[127]) Federal court jurisdiction arises under federal statute[128], under federal case law, and under the Constitution of the United States. When people act in a conspiracy committing two or more predicate acts the RICO statutes provide relief (Racketeer Influenced and Corruption Act[129]). People acting under color of federal law—federal judges, prosecutors, federal officials—can be sued under the Constitution (as articulated in a *Bivens* action), and under the Federal Tort Claims Act.

Multiple federal causes of action arose in the sham California law suit, including repeated and violations of personal and property rights protected by federal law. Any single *one* of the multiple violations committed by the Friedman law firm and federal judges was sufficient to invoke mandatory federal court jurisdiction, including violations of (a) Federal statutory and case law, and federal rights; (b) constitutional rights and

---

more persons engaged therein do, or cause to be done, any act in furtherance of the object of such conspiracy, whereby another is injured in his person or property, or deprived of having and exercising any right or privilege of a citizen of the United States, the party so injured or deprived may have an action for the recovery of damages occasioned by such injury or deprivation, against any one or more of the conspirators.

[127] **Title 42 U.S.C. § 1986. Action for neglect to prevent conspiracy**

Every person who, having knowledge that any of the wrongs conspired to be done, and mentioned in the preceding section [42 USCS § 1985], are about to be committed, and having power to prevent or aid in preventing the commission of the same, neglects or refuses to do so, if such wrongful act be committed, shall be liable to the party injured, or his legal representatives, for all damages caused by such wrongful act, which such person by reasonable diligence could have prevented; and such damages may be recovered in an action on the case; and any number of persons guilty of such wrongful neglect or refusal may be joined as defendants in the action, and if the death of any party be caused by any such wrongful act and neglect, the legal representatives of the deceased shall have such action therefor, and may recover not exceeding five thousand dollars damages therein, for the benefit of the widow of the deceased, if there be one, and if there be no widow, then for the benefit of the next of kin of the deceased. But no action under the provisions of this section shall be sustained which is not commenced within one year after the cause of action has accrued.

[128] **Title 28 U.S.C. § 1343**

(a) The district court shall have original jurisdiction of any civil action authorized by law to be commenced by any person:

(1) To recover damages for injury to his person or property, or because of the deprivation of any right or privilege of a citizen of the United States, by any act done in furtherance of any conspiracy mentioned in section 1985 of Title 42;

(2) To recover damages from any person who fails to prevent or to aid in preventing any wrongs mentioned in section 1985 of Title 42 which he had knowledge were about to occur and power to prevent;

(3) To redress the deprivation, under color of any State law, statute, ordinance, regulation, custom or usage, of any right, privilege or immunity secured by the Constitution of the United States or by any Act of Congress providing for equal rights of citizens or of all persons within the jurisdiction of the United States;

(4) To recover damages or to secure equitable or other relief under any Act of Congress providing for the protection of civil rights, including the right to vote.

[129] Title 18 United States Code Sections 1961 and 1962.

protections; (c) state laws; or (d) inability to obtain due process in the California courts. The only source of relief was in the federal courts, and the federal judges had the mandatory responsibility to provide relief and protection. Federal law provides declaratory relief, injunctive relief, and/or damages. I sought all three remedies from federal judges who were paid to provide the relief, and entrusted to do so.

MANDATORY DUTY TO PROVIDE RELIEF

I filed the first federal action[130] in the United States District Court, Eastern District of California, at Sacramento.[131] Although I had years of legal experience working with attorneys, and filed federal actions against the FAA and NTSB, and could have filed this law suit in pro se, I hired attorney James Reed to file the action. He taught civil and constitutional law at McGeorge School of Law in Sacramento, California, and was shocked at the number of civil and constitutional violations committed against me (as were most attorneys who knew of the judicial actions taken against me).

The law suit[132] sought declaratory and injunctive relief to vacate the orders rendered by the California judges and to force the California judges to recognize the personal and property rights under federal law. Injunctive relief requires a state judge to halt the violations. Damages are available under federal law against the Friedman law firm and the California judges who acted under color of state law and violated civil and constitutional rights.

The law suit wanted the California judges to recognize my personal rights as a divorced person in accordance with federal and California law. I wanted my property rights recognized under federal and California law, predicated upon the five divorce judgments, and the acquisition of properties as a divorced person, under federal and state due process rights.

The law suit sought to declare my constitutional right[133] to

---

130 January 10, 1984.

131 January 10, 1984. *Stich v. California Superior Court; Dwight Ely, Judge; Friedman, Sloan and Ross*, C-84-0048 RAR.

132 1984.

133 Under Title 28 U.S.C. §§ 2201, 2202. Among the constitutional rights violated were the rights and protections in the Fourteenth Amendment due process, equal protection, property, liberty, freedom rights; Privileges and Immunity Clause rights under Article IV, § 1, and under the 14th Amendment (depriving right to obtain divorce on universally recognized residence basis, and right to change residence); right to unabridged interstate travel, without losing rights and privileges acquired in prior jurisdictions of residence; Article IV, § 1 (Full Faith and Credit Clause, and Title 28 U.S.C. § 1738, requiring recognition of the personal and property rights in the California divorce judgment, its entry for recognition as local judgments in the courts of Nevada, Oklahoma, and Texas.

change residence without suffering a taking of my personal and property rights. This right is protected by the constitutional right to unabridged interstate travel. Without that constitutional protection, people changing residence risk losing previously adjudicated and acquired personal and property rights.

The law suit sought financial damages against the California judges and the Friedman law firm. In that same year, the U.S. Supreme Court clarified the right to sue state judges who violate state or federal law, or who act without jurisdiction.[135] The court clerk assigned the law suit to Judge Raul Ramirez, a former California municipal court judge in Sacramento until President Carter appointed him to the federal bench.

THE START OF THE FEDERAL DUE PROCESS GRIDLOCK

The Friedman law firm and California Judge Dwight Ely filed a motion to dismiss the law suit. They argued that the California action was a divorce action, and therefore the federal courts must abstain. The mere fact that I was subject to a divorce action when federal law established that I was already divorced constituted numerous violations of federally-protected rights, and invoked mandatory federal court jurisdiction. Further, numerous federal laws, and over two dozen California statutes and Rules of Court were violated, constituting federal causes of action. Further, even if I had been married, which I wasn't, Federal court jurisdiction does not cease when federally protected rights are violated.

REPETITION OF THE FRIVOLOUS ARGUMENT

The standard tactic used by the California judges when I exercised my legal remedies was to call the exercise of constitutionally protected rights a frivolous act, and then to call me a vexatious litigant for seeking relief. They then compounded these outrages by ordering me to pay heavy financial sanctions for exercising constitutionally protected rights specifically provided by state law. The federal judges did the same, and enlarged upon the tactic.

Judge Ramirez held that it was frivolous to seek relief, even though federal statutory and case law clearly provided that any single one of the multiple issues I raised invoked federal court jurisdiction. Again using the frivolous label as a base, Ramirez ordered me to pay the Friedman law firm over $10,000 financial sanctions. If the action was really a frivolous action, case

---

[135] *Pulliam v. Allen*, 104 S.Ct 1970 (1984). Followed by other federal decisions: *Harlow v. Fitzgerald*, 457 U.S. 800 (1982); *Dykes v. Hoseman*, 743 F.2d 1488 (11th Cir. 1984). In *Dykes v. Hoseman*, 743 F.2d 1488 (11th Cir. 1984), the Eleventh Circuit federal district court held that a state judge could be sued for money damages when he renders orders without either personal or subject matter jurisdiction.

law relating to Federal Rule of Court 11 limits the fines to the attorney signing the papers. This was attorney James Reed.

The United States Supreme Court and other federal decisions[135] defined the term frivolous as any complaint, appeal, or any other motion, for which there is not an arguable point. The U.S. Supreme Court held that they are not frivolous if "*any of the legal points [are] arguable on their merits ...* " *Haines v. Kerner* 404 U.S. 519, 521-522 (1972). Obviously, the federal complaint alleging state orders were repeatedly rendered without jurisdiction, violating dozens of state and federal laws, violating federally protected rights under federal statutes, case law, and under the Constitution, could not be called frivolous.

Federal law prohibits dismissing an action if the complaint states federal causes of action.[136] Under federal pleading

---

[135] *Anders v. California* (1967) 386 U.S. 738 ("An appeal [or complaint] is not frivolous if "*any of the legal points [are] arguable on their merits ...*"); *Christiansburg Garment Company v. EEOC*, 434 U.S. 412, 416-416 (1978) ("where the alleged claim under the Constitution or federal statutes clear appears to be immaterial ... where such a claim is wholly insubstantial and frivolous" *where absence of a defense is obvious from the pleadings*."); *Haines v. Kerner*, 404 U.S. 519, 521-522 (1972)("allegations ... however inartfully pleaded, are sufficient to call for the opportunity to offer supporting evidence. We ...allegations of the pro se complaint [are held] to less stringent standards than formal pleadings drafted by lawyers ... "[dismissal is barred unless] it appears beyond doubt that the plaintiff can prove no set of facts in support of his claim which would entitle him to relief."); "so clearly and palpably bad and insufficient as to require no argument or illustration to show the character as indicative of bad faith upon a bare inspection." *Strong v. Sproul*, 53 NYU 497, 499. "A *suit without purpose* to determine an actual controversy, as where the parties control by interest both sides of the litigation." 1 Am J2d Actions § 56."; California Code of Civil Procedure § 907 ("Frivolous" means (A) *totally and completely without merit* ..."); *In re Marriage of Flaherty* (1982) 31 Cal.3d 637 ("whether any reasonable person would agree that the point is totally and completely devoid of merit, and therefore, frivolous ... an appeal is not frivolous if 'any of the legal points [are] arguable on their merits' ... [if] it can be said that 'any reasonable person would agree that [it is] totally and completely devoid of merit ..."); "For the purposes of determining whether a complaint is "frivolous, the court presumes that the plaintiff's allegations are true." *Franklin*, 745 F.2d at 1228. In addition, courts must construe allegations in pro se complaints liberally. *Shapley v. Nevada Bd. of State Prison Comm'rs*, 766 F.2d 404, 408 (9th Cir. 1985)." *Hernandez v. Denton*, 88 C.D.O.S. 8132, 9th Cir, 1988.

In *Townsend v. Holman Consulting Corporation* (C.D Calif, Auagust 7, 1989, the court held:

> ... in determining whether a pleading is frivolous, the proper scope of inquiry is the *entire* pleading; the court must determine whether the pleading as a whole, not merely "a particular argument or ground for relief," is frivolous within the meaning of the Rule, *Golden Eagle*, 801 F.2d at 1540.
>
> Second, ... the mere fact that a claim does not prevail, or that a court ultimately determines that a lawyer's view of the law is "wong," is insufficient to warrant sanctions under any aspect of Rule 11.

[136] *Dennis v. Sparks* 449 U.S. 24 (1980)("a section 1983 complaint should not be dismissed unless it appears that the plaintiff can prove no set of facts which would entitle him to relief ... For the purposes of testing sufficiency of the complaint, the allegations of the complaint must be accepted as true."); *Gardener v. Toilet Goods Assn.*, 387 U.S. 167, 172 (1967). (An action, "especially under the Civil Rights Act, should not be dismissed at the pleadings stage unless it appears to a certainty that plaintiffs are entitled to no relief under any state of the facts, which could be proved in support of their claims." *Escalera v. N.Y.*

practice, federal case law require that federal judges accept the allegations stated in the complaint as true for opposing a motion to dismiss.[138] If any single federal cause of action is *alleged*, the case cannot be dismissed. This due process right was routinely violated, denying me the rights and protections under the Fifth Amendment to the U.S. Constitution.

Ramirez stated in his order of dismissal that the California action was a domestic relations action, for which federal courts should abstain. The California action did not qualify as a domestic relations action under the California Family Law Act. Besides, under federal law, any of the five prior divorce judgments, the rights established in the judgments, and the properties I acquired during two decades of divorced status, were protected by federal rights. Ramirez was paid to enforce and protect these federal rights.

The constitutional right to change residence without suffering a loss of previously acquired or adjudicated personal and property rights were violated. California judges were refusing to recognize rights I acquired years earlier in other jurisdictions. This violated my constitutionally protected right to change residence.

The California law suit violated rights protected by the Full Faith and Credit Clause of the U.S. Constitution and federal statutory law,[139] which required all state judges to recognize the judicial acts of another state. The divorce judgments confirmed in California and entered in the judicial records of the States of Nevada, Oklahoma, and Texas must be recognized under the full faith and credit protections.

The cause of action violated due process and equal protection, in that millions of other people exercise personal jurisdiction to obtain divorce judgments on the same residence basis. The cause of action violated decisions of the U.S. Supreme Court.[140]

Housing Auth., 425 F.2d 853, 857 (2nd Cir. 1970). See also *Conley v. Gibson*, 355 U.S. 41, 45-7) 1957); *Sherman v. Yakahi*, 549 F.2d 1287, 1290 (9th Cir. 1977); *Mark v. Gross*, 521 F.2d 1376, 1378 (9th Cir. 1975); *York v. Gross*, 521 F.2d 1376, 1378 (9th Cir. 1975); *York v. Story*, 324 F.2d 450, 453 (9th Cir. 1963). Obviously, plaintiff is entitled to relief.

[138] *Gardener v. Toilet Goods Assn.*, 387 U.S. 167, 172 (1967). An action, "especially under the Civil Rights Act, should not be dismissed at the pleadings stage unless it appears to a certainty that plaintiffs are entitled to no relief under any state of the facts, which could be proved in support of their claims." *Escalera v. N.Y. Housing Auth.*, 425 F.2d 853, 857 (2nd Cir. 1970).

[139] Title 28 U.S.C. Section 1738.

[140] *Vanderbilt v. Vanderbilt* (1957) 354 U.S. 416 (requiring the recognition of ex parte divorce judgments; *Estin v. Estin* 334 U.S. 541 (1948)(requiring the recognition of prior divorce judgments; *Sherrer v. Sherrer* (1948) 334 U.S. 343; *Coe v. Coe* (1948) 334 U.S. 378 (requiring the recognition of prior divorce judgments); *Perrin v. Perrin*, 408 F.2d 107 (3rd Cir. 1969) (prohibiting denying recognition to prior judgments when exercised on one day's

SUSPENSION OF APPEAL REMEDIES

In response to Ramirez's dismissal, I filed a timely appeal with the U.S. Court of Appeals at San Francisco. This was the same appellate court that had wrongfully dismissed my law suits against the FAA and NTSB in 1974 and 1980. These same judges made possible some of the nation's most brutal air tragedies as the air safety misconduct continued unabated after their dismissal of my actions. My exposure actions threatened this powerful arm of government with a major scandal.

Federal appellate law requires the Court of Appeals to vacate the order of dismissal, and the frivolous holding, if the complaint alleges at least one federal cause of action for which federal courts can grant relief. On appeal, the law requires that the Court of Appeals accept the allegations stated in the complaint as true.[141] If the complaint states federal causes of action for which federal courts are empowered to provide relief, the court of appeal judges must vacate the lower court's dismissal and frivolous label. These appellate court responsibilities are clear.[142] These were openly violated. The complaint stated *many* federal causes of action.

The Court of Appeal judges upheld the gross violations of civil and constitutional rights by the California judges, and upheld the wrongful dismissal by Ramirez, which violated federal law. They upheld the $10,000 financial sanctions that punished me for exercising protected rights. They upheld the voiding of prior divorce judgments, the remarrying of persons, the seizure of property rights, and the other related human right violations on the sham argument that residence is not a valid basis for terminating a marriage (although millions of divorce judgments and personal and property determinations are rendered on this same basis).

I repeatedly sought relief from the Justices of the United States Supreme Court. In the same coverup as they did in the action against the FAA and NTSB in 1974 and 1980, the Supreme Court justices gave tacit approval to the outrages, and refused to hear my petitions for writ of certiorari. They were

---

residence).

[141] *Gardener v. Toilet Goods Assn.*, 387 U.S. 167, 172 (1967). An action, "especially under the Civil Rights Act, should not be dismissed at the pleadings stage unless it appears to a certainty that plaintiffs are entitled to no relief under any state of the facts, which could be proved in support of their claims."

[142] "In our view, a decision to give less than full independent de novo review to the state law determinations of the district courts would be an abdication of our appellate responsibility. Every party is entitled to a full, considered, and impartial review of the decision of the trial court. *Matter of McLinn*, 739 F.2d 1395 (9th Cir 1983).

aiding and abetting a *pattern* of judicial corruption, judicial subversion of the laws and Constitution of the United States.

Just as the Supreme Court Justices made possible the continuation of the air safety corruption, which then made them accomplices to the subsequent crashes and deaths, they supported and made possible the actions taken against me by the combination California and federal judges.

ESCALATION OF CIVIL AND CONSTITUTIONAL VIOLATIONS

The dismissal of my federal actions seeking relief, and the approval by the Ninth Circuit Court of Appeals and the Supreme Court, gave the California judges and the Friedman law firm carte blanche approval to continue the violations and the harms I was suffering. As if they were on a roll, the Friedman law firm and the California judges escalated the frequency and severity of their attacks upon me. I continued to lose valuable properties. My personal life was a shambles.

SEEKING RELIEF FROM JAIL SENTENCE

Emboldened by the protection given to them by all levels of the federal judiciary, California Judge William Peterson sentenced me to jail for five days. This arose from Judge Jensen's earlier order for me to show cause why I should not be held in contempt for failure to pay the money judgements to the Friedman law firm. (That was the order upon which Judge Jensen ordered the bench warrant for my arrest when I was in federal court before Judge Schwartz rather than in state court.) My defense to the contempt was that the California judges and the Friedman law firm had all my assets tied up. But Peterson refused to allow me to even defend myself, refusing to allow me to testify. When I appeared in court he sentenced me to five days in jail for refusing to pay the $50,000 money judgment to Friedman.

REPEATED SEEKING OF RELIEF

As the civil and constitutional outrages increased, and as I suffered terminal destruction of my personal and property rights, I exercised federal remedies whenever new causes of action arose. Other federal judges duplicated Judge Ramirez's due process gridlock.[143] Federal complaints seeking relief were dismissed without a mandatory hearing, in open violation of statutory and case law and constitutional due process. My complaints were unfiled, another denial of procedural due process for which there is no provision in law. When I appealed the unlawful unfiling, the Ninth Circuit responded there was nothing to appeal!

---

[143] Federal Judges Marilyn Petal, Samuel Conti, Charles Legge.

Federal judges ordered court clerks to deny me the right to file complaints seeking relief. Injunctive orders were rendered barring me from seeking relief from the continuing series of grotesque violations, forcing me to watch my own destruction without access to law.

I repeatedly sought relief from the U.S. Supreme Court on the basis that major constitutional violations had become a pattern in the Ninth Circuit federal courts. The Supreme Court had a mandatory supervisory responsibility over the lower courts,[144] and a responsibility to intervene when civil and constitutional rights were violated. The Supreme Court engaged in cheap tactics to deny filing of my petitions for writs of certiorari. In one instance they refused to file briefs (that cost almost $500 to have printed) on the allegation that the spacing between the footnote lines was less than required. (I couldn't even measure the difference.) It was obvious federal judges had me gridlocked.

SUDDENLY RECOGNIZING THE JUDICIAL CONSPIRACY

I was too close to the trees to see the forest. I suddenly recognized that the California law suit was engineered by powerful interests somewhere in the federal branch of government, using the Friedman law firm as a front, and using California judges to carry out the scheme. When I unexpectedly sought relief in federal court, the federal judges who were obviously part of the scheme then had to protect the scheme and the schemers. To do this, every right and protection under the laws and Constitution of the United States had to be denied to me, and openly and repeatedly violated by federal judges. And this went all the way up to and including the Justices of the United States Supreme Court! The scandal grew immensely.

REQUIREMENT FOR EXTREME COVERUP ACTIONS

Once I recognized the relationship between the underlying air disaster scandal, the sham California action, and the federal due process gridlock, I made these facts known in federal briefs. The government corruption now took a worse turn. An entire branch of government—the federal judiciary—was aiding and abetting, passively and actively, corruption that took the lives of several thousand persons world-wide in air disasters linked to the FAA Western Region misconduct. The scandal of government-funded corruption grew alarmingly.

I filed another federal law suit[145] seeking declaratory and injunctive relief from California orders rendered since my prior federal complaint. The law suit described the relationship

---

[144] Supervisory responsibilities over lower federal courts under Supreme Court Rule 17; responsibilities to uphold the laws and constitution of the United States;

[145] Eastern District of California, at Sacramento, 86-210 MLS.

between the sham California action and California judicial due process gridlock, the federal judicial due process gridlock, the air disaster corruption (and Justice Department and federal judiciary coverup). Now that I identified this relationship, it became urgently necessary to bar me from seeking relief in any court, to avoid the possibility of exposure.

This action was assigned to federal Judge Milton Schwartz at Sacramento. During the first hearing on May 9, 1986 Schwartz admitted the gravity of the allegations stated in my complaint. Schwartz stated, "Mr. Stich, these allegations are very serious. If you wish, I will continue the hearing and give you time to hire legal counsel." But no legal counsel would touch the case; it was too sensitive. Besides, my funds were tied up by the California action, and I had no funds to hire legal counsel.

RAPID CHANGES IN POSITION

Within a month after Judge Schwartz admitted the gravity of the allegations stated in the complaint, the Friedman law firm and the California judges filed a motion to dismiss the complaint. Despite the multiple federal causes of action alleged in the complaint, despite their seriousness, despite the criminal acts made known to Judge Schwartz, and despite the obvious continuation of brutal air tragedies if my charges were true, Judge Schwartz ordered my law suit dismissed.

The dismissal openly violated federal law which bars dismissing law suits stating a single federal cause of action; mine stated many federal causes of action. Judge Schwartz compounded these violations by placing a frivolous label on my attempt to obtain relief (clearly violating the Supreme Court criteria for the label), and ordered me to pay the Friedman law firm over $10,000 legal sanctions. The total financial sanctions that federal judges ordered me to pay the Friedman law firm now exceeded $150,000.

Seeking to totally bar me access to the courts, and suspend even more rights under the laws and Constitution of the United States, Judge Schwartz rendered an unlawful injunctive order[146]

---

[146] The May 30, 1986 injunctive order stated in part:

IT IS HEREBY ORDERED that plaintiff, Rodney F. Stich, is *barred from filing any action or actions in any United States District Court, or in any state court,* until his current state court action, Solano County Superior Court No. 83472, becomes final and he has exhausted all his state court appellate remedies, against defendants Emma W. Stich, Friedman, Sloan & Ross, P.C., or any attorneys or employees of Friedman, Sloan & Ross, P.C., Lawrence A. Gibbs, Jeffrey S. Ross, the judges of the Superior Court of the County of Solano, State of California, Judge William Jensen, Neil Crawford, Clerk, Solano County, or the Superior Court of the County of Solano, State of California, which in any way relates to issues raised in *Stich v. Stich*, No. CIVS-84-0048 RAR, *In re the Marriage of Stich*, Superior Court of the State of California in and for the County of permanently barring me from filing any action in any state or federal court. It applied to seeking relief from past, present, and future violations committed by the Friedman group, the California judges, or federal judges.

THE LEGAL BASIS FOR AN INJUNCTIVE ORDER

The purpose and authority for rendering injunctive orders are to protect a party suffering great and irreparable harm, who has no monetary remedies against those committing the harm. In my case, the injunctive order did not protect the party *suffering* harm. It protected the parties *committing* the harms. It simultaneously deprived the injured party of lawful remedies for relief.

I filed a timely notice of appeal of the dismissal and the injunctive order. The Ninth Circuit Court of Appeals at San Francisco continued to support the outrageous judicial acts, which required protecting the serious wrongdoings described in the complaint. They upheld the judicial anarchy and corruption, just as they had done since the initial coverup of the FAA and NTSB corruption.[146]

I sought relief from the Justices of the Supreme Court via emergency requests for injunctions and via petition for writ of certiorari. The Justices of the Supreme Court approved the constitutional outrages that now were the standard policy of the entire Ninth Circuit federal courts. In these law suits I named as defendants the FAA, NTSB, Department of Justice, and Judge Milton Schwartz.

While these outrages continued, and while federal judges protected the air safety corruption, numerous air disasters and near-disasters occurred. The mishaps were clearly linked to the FAA and NTSB misconduct. The aviation community, the press, and the public, became concerned about the repeated tragedies and near-tragedies. Addressing the underlying causes of several of the air tragedies and seeking relief to prevent future tragedies, as well as seeking relief for myself, I filed addition-

---

Solano, No. 83472, and *Stich v. California Court of Appeal*, United States District Court, Northern District of California, Action No. C-85-3600-MHP, or in the instant case. ... after the judgment in that state court action has become final and all appellate processes have been exhausted, this bar to further actions shall still apply to any and all claims precluded by the doctrines of res judicata and/or collateral estoppel.

[146] *Stich v. United States, et al.*, 554 F.2d 1070 (9th Cir.) (table), *cert. denied*, 434 U.S. 920 (1977); Amicus curiae brief filed on July 17, 1975, in the Paris DC-10 multi-district litigation, *Flanagan v. McDonnell Douglas Corporation and United States of America*, Civil Action 74-808-PH, MDL 172, Central District California.) *Stich v. National Transportation Safety Board*, 685 F.2d 446 (9th Cir.)(table), *cert. denied*, 459 U.S. 861 (1982); appeal of the dismissal by federal Judge Raul Ramirez (E.D. Cal. No. 84-0048 RAR; CA No. 84-2583.)

al law suits in federal court.[147]

CHARGING ME WITH A CRIME FOR REPORTING A CRIME

The Department of Justice and federal Judge Milton Schwartz then turned the power of the Justice Department and the federal courts upon me. They charged that *I* committed three crimes by filing the federal law suits *exposing* the air disaster corruption, and for seeking relief for myself and for those who would be affected if the corruption was not addressed.

Anyone who knows of a crime and does not effectively report it, is guilty among other things of misprision of a felony or coverup. The Justice Department and federal judges would charge me with crimes for refusing to commit the crime of coverup.

JUDICIAL CARTEL OF CORRUPTION

These federal judges engaged in a cartel-like agreement between themselves to carry out the scheme commenced in the California courts, and then to bar me from the numerous federal statutory and constitutional remedies to protect myself. The judges openly engaged in acts that constituted major and repeated violations of civil and constitutional rights and protections, violated criminal statutes for which judges are as liable as any other citizen, if not more so due to their position of trust.

The question arose as to where in the federal government the coverup scheme originated. In the mid-1960s the Department of Justice was obviously involved, and remained involved. Federal judges became involved in the mid-1970s, and remained so to this date. In 1982, with the start of the sham California action, federal judges again became involved, with their involvement escalating to outright persecution, with the aid and abetting of the Justices of the Supreme Court. Obviously, powerful people were behind this air disaster corruption, and jumped across all three branches of government. This was becoming more frightening for the nation—and for myself—all the time.

The judicial cartel openly engaged in a massive conspiracy that continued to obstruct justice as it related to the air disaster corruption, and obstructed justice as it related to the RICO acts taken against me.

---

[147] U.S. District Court, District of Columbia. (*Stich v. Federal Aviation Administration, National Transportation Safety Board, Department of Justice*, No. 86-2523, and 87-2214); U.S. District Court, Northern District of California, No. 86-6046 (Against California judges, including Judge William Jensen).

CHAPTER TWENTY THREE

Prison!

The attorneys in the Department of Justice responded to the law suits that I filed in the United States District Court at Washington, D.C.,[149] which named the Justice Department, the FAA, the NTSB, and Judge Schwartz, as defendants. I filed the law suits as the crashes arising from the FAA and NTSB corruption were escalating, seeking relief for others. I sought relief from the rampant government-funded corruption that misused the federal branch of government, and the attorneys in the Justice Department, against me, to silence my exposure actions. Since I was the only insider with the hard evidence, and willingness to expose the misconduct, I exercised the rights and the responsibilities in law.

Without being melodramatic, the brutality of the air disasters that would not have occurred without the government corruption required unusual steps to circumvent the total block by all three branches of government.

The complaints alleged that the FAA committed corrupt acts related to a series of fatal air disasters; that the National Transportation Safety Board falsified government accident reports covering up for air safety misconduct, and becoming a contributing cause to subsequent crashes; that the Justice Department obstructed the exposure and correction of the air

---

[149] No. 86-2523; 86-2214.

safety misconduct; and that Judge Schwartz unlawfully obstructed justice by unlawfully dismissing an earlier action (No. 86-210) seeking to expose the worsening air disaster corruption and superimposed Justice Department and judiciary coverup.

Another federal law suit was filed in the district court at San Francisco,[149] seeking declaratory and injunctive relief, and damages, from California judges violating my civil and constitutional rights in the sham California action.

The Justice Department, working with Judge Schwartz, turned around and used the awesome powers of the government against me. Judge Schwartz issued a March 1986 Order-To-Show-Cause (OSC) for me to appear in federal court at Sacramento on April 23, 1986, to explain why I should not be held in civil contempt for filing the federal law suits. Schwartz argued that I was in contempt of court for filing the federal law suits when his May 30, 1986 injunctive order permanently barred me from seeking relief in any state or federal court (i.e., suspending the rights and protections under the Constitution and laws of the United States).

Two days before I was to appear, Judge Schwartz's senior law clerk, Jo Anne Speers, telephoned me at my Nevada residence, and spent fifteen minutes convincing me not to personally appear, but to appear by legal counsel. "But the order requires that I personally appear," I stated. "I talked to Judge Schwartz," Ms. Speers answered, "and it was decided that you do not have to personally appear."

I told Ms. Speers that I didn't have an attorney. She replied that I should get any attorney to appear, and that he didn't have to know anything about the case. "This is odd," I thought.

The reason for avoiding a personal appearance was that California Judge William Jensen had issued a bench warrant for my arrest, which was still in effect. Every time that there was an appearance calendared for me, the Friedman group alerted the Solano County sheriff's office, and sheriff deputies waited to arrest me.

"They're setting you up!"

I stated to a friend in Reno, Laura Link (who use to practice law in California) what Judge Schwartz's law clerk had stated. "They're setting you up," Laura stated. "Oh, come on," I responded, "I know they're a bunch of bastards, but they wouldn't do anything that obvious."

By making some quick phone calls, I obtained legal counsel to appear for me; Joel Pegg. But when Pegg appeared on April 23rd, as Judge Schwartz's law clerk suggested, Judge Schwartz

---

[149] *Rodney F. Stich v. Rose Bird; Allen Broussard; et al.* No. 86-6046.

already had a multi-page order prepared, charging me with *criminal* contempt for not personally appearing. Schwartz and his law clerk had set me up, just as Laura warned! Schwartz then ordered me to appear in federal court on May 7, 1987, on a charge of *criminal* contempt, and warned that if I did not appear, a federal bench warrant would be issued for my arrest.

ARRAIGNED ON CRIMINAL CHARGES

I appeared on May 7th with attorney Joel Pegg, and was promptly arraigned, based on a criminal information filed by the Justice Department. The Justice Department charged me with a three-count criminal indictment; one for each of the law suits.

Federal marshals then surrounded me and marched me to magistrate Esther Mix, where I was officially charged with the purported crimes. The Justice Department sought to have me imprisoned in the federal penitentiary for 18 months for trying to halt the air disaster slaughter, and for seeking relief from the government-funded persecution!

HIGH FLIGHT RISK?

Assistant United States attorney Peter Nowinski sought to deny me my freedom pending trial, arguing that my crimes made me a high flight risk, and that I had a record of not appearing in court. Magistrate Esther Hix asked why I was considered "a flight risk?"

"He failed to appear before Judge Schwartz ... on April 23rd, 1987," replied assistant U.S. Attorney Novinski. This was the hearing at which Judge Schwartz' law clerk stressed I should not personally appear, and at which I appeared by legal counsel.

The U. S. Attorney then argued that I failed to appear before California Judge William Jensen in Fairfield, on May 9, 1986, and that there was an outstanding warrant for my arrest stemming from that. That was the date when I appeared before Judge Schwartz, and physically could not be in two places at the same time. The United States Attorney continued: "The Government also has information that Mr. Stich kidnapped a grandchild from Texas and threatened his wife, with whom he was litigating, that she would never see the child again, if she did not terminate the litigation."

ALLEGEDLY KIDNAPPING A LITTLE FIVE YEAR OLD BOY

The alleged kidnapping was a farce. One of my three daughters, Linda, moved to California from Texas, taking her two children with her. More about this in a later chapter.

Magistrate Esther Mix read my rights to me, as if I was a criminal, and warned me of the consequences if I tried to flee. I was treated like a hard-core criminal. After arraignment, and after signing a stipulation vacating my right to a district court trial, and agreeing to a trial before a U.S. Magistrate, I was released on bail. I had to convey a house to the United States government for bail pending trial. I was then booked, my fingerprints and pictures taken. Unknown to me, there was still more trouble waiting outside.

FRIEDMAN ALERTED THE CALIFORNIA AUTHORITIES

Waiting to arrest me and take me to Solano County jail were two sheriff deputies from Solano County. They had the bench warrant for my arrest rendered by California judge William Jensen. Fortunately I had bail money handy. This was paid to the sheriff's deputies. The sheriff deputies were apparently alerted either by the Friedman law firm, California Judge William Jensen, federal Judge Milton Schwartz, or all of them together. Friedman was always pulling these tricks. At another time he called the Solano County Sheriff's office when I was appearing in the California action, and stated I would appear carrying a gun. This phone call was part of the pattern of constant harassment by the Friedman law firm.

KANGAROO TRIAL

To avoid a Kangaroo trial it was important that I receive a jury trial on the criminal contempt charge. Otherwise, I would be prosecuted by the Justice Department, and tried by federal judges. Hardly an unbiased tribunal.

It was ironic. Brutal air tragedies were continuing to occur; I sought to expose the hard-core criminal acts that played a part in them; I identified the misconduct with specifics; and now the federal branch of government and the legal cohorts in the Justice Department sought to silence the one person who could force a change in the deadly pattern. I identified criminal acts committed by the Justice Department and by federal judges (which under law the allegations must be accepted as true at that stage of the pleadings), and now those I exposed turned around and charge me with crimes for identifying them! It was hard to believe that this could happen in the United States. Only a silent and cooperative press could make this government tyranny possible, somewhat akin to the rise of Nazi Germany.

During my initial arraignment, attorney Pegg instructed me to sign a waiver to a trial before a district court judge, permitting the trial to proceed before a United States magistrate. That was a dumb thing to do, as the part-time federal magistrate was employed, and retained, only so long as he pleased my adversaries in the Justice Department and the federal judges. The saving grace was that the waiver was predicated on obtaining a jury trial.

CONSTITUTIONAL RIGHT TO A JURY TRIAL—DENIED

Under the Sixth and Seventh Amendment to the United States Constitution, a person is entitled to a jury trial, and also a trial before a fair and impartial jury. But federal judges have ignored this constitutional protection for years, and held in federal decisions that this constitutional right does not apply if incarceration does not exceed six months. They call this long incarceration to be punishment for a "petty" crime. There is nothing petty about six months in prison, while one's business, his properties, his home, his assets, and maybe his family, are lost.

The Justice Department sought to have me imprisoned for 18 months. Before the start of the trial, my attorney reminded Magistrate John Moulds that I had requested a jury trial. Assistant U.S. Attorney David Flynn responded that I wasn't entitled to a jury trial if the requested imprisonment did not exceed six months; he then reduced the requested imprisonment from 18 months to six months.

But that reduction in prison sentence had nothing to do with the written stipulation for a jury trial, which arose when I signed a waiver to proceed before a U.S. Magistrate. Like every other right to which I was entitled during the past several years, that right was also violated. Magistrate Moulds denied me a jury trial, and the trial commenced without a jury on September 16, 1987. I had notified several of the news services and numerous radio and televisions stations in the San Francisco and Sacramento area, of the government attempt to railroad me to prison for reporting the air disaster and government corruption. Not a single one showed up.

Attorney Pegg raised arguments that held I couldn't be found guilty, but omitted the hard-core constitutional violations associated with Judge Schwartz' injunctive order. Pegg omitted reference to the set up by Judge Schwartz and his law clerk, and to the other issues that would expose the misconduct of the Justice Department and federal judges.

"I find you guilty"!

Magistrate Moulds concluded the trial by declaring I was guilty of the crimes charged. Moulds set a November 4, 1987 sentencing date. Attorney Pegg then abandoned me, making no effort to submit briefs for reconsideration as provided by law.[151] I then filed my own motion to reconsider.

RAMPANT CONSTITUTIONAL VIOLATIONS

In my motion for rehearing I raised numerous defenses, none of which attorney Pegg had raised. These included:

1. It was not a criminal act to exercise constitutionally protected rights specifically provided by legislated statutes, to seek relief in federal court to report air safety corruption,

---

[151] Motion to alter or amend, Federal Rule of Criminal Procedure 60.

or to seek relief from the litany of civil and constitutional violations that were destroying my personal and property rights.

2. I could not be imprisoned for exercising moral and legal responsibilities to report crimes. On the contrary, I would have been guilty of misprision of felonies and other crimes if I had not reported them as I did via the federal law suits. The same crime attaches to anyone else who knew of the criminal acts and did not report them to the proper authorities.

3. It was not a criminal act to seek relief from terminal destruction of protected personal and property rights.

4. The underlying federal law suit seeking relief did not meet the common sense or legal criteria for being a frivolous action. (86-210) It was the frivolous label placed upon that law suit upon which Judge Schwartz sought to support the injunctive order. That complaint stated multiple federal causes of action of constitutional magnitude, all of which must be recognized as true for opposing dismissal. The law suit was unlawfully and unconstitutionally dismissed by Judge Milton Schwartz, and then compounded with the infamous injunctive order.

5. Dismissal of the underlying action (86-210) violated federal case law barring dismissal if federal causes of action are alleged (and many were alleged). It was that unlawful dismissal which Judge Schwartz used as the basis for rendering the injunctive order.

6. The legal criteria for rendering injunctive orders was reversed. The limited authority for rendering injunctive orders required that it be to protect a party against great and irreparable harm. Judge Schwartz reversed that criteria, and used it to deprive relief to the person suffering irreparable harm, and protect the parties committing the harm. (Friedman law firm, the cooperating California judges, and the air disaster and government corruption.)

7. Case law provides that a person cannot be charged with criminal contempt for exercising a right that would otherwise be lost. If the federal actions had not been filed, I would have lost the right to try to protect myself, and lost the right to report the government corruption.

8. A federal judge has no authority to suspend the rights and protections under the Constitution and laws of the United States, or to force a person to suffer terminal destruction of human rights recognized in other free countries.

9. A federal judge cannot force a person to be a silent witness to the continual slaughter occurring in the air tragedies when he had knowledge of corrupt causes.

10. A judge cannot void a written stipulation to a jury trial, as was done by John Moulds.

11. A person cannot be prosecuted and tried, without a jury, by the same government officials who are threatened with exposure by the person's actions.

12. A party cannot be punished for contempt when the injunctive order is on appeal. Judge Schwartz himself admitted he had no jurisdiction to hold me in contempt while the injunctive order was on appeal. (The Solano County legal counsel sought to have me held in civil contempt for filing the federal action.) During a November 13, 1987 hearing, Judge Scwhartz, who rendered the May 30, 1986 injunctive order, held that my appeal of the injunctive deprived the court of jurisdiction to hold me in contempt.

> This court lacks jurisdiction to entertain the motion for contempt since the underlying judgment in this case rendered by this Court is currently on appeal. The Ninth Circuit follows the general rule with some exceptions not relevant here, that the filing of a proper and timely notice of appeal divests the district court of jurisdiction over those matters that are not on appeal or subject to the appeal.

Judge Schwartz then made reference to the applicable federal law.[152] The November 13th verbal order was reduced to a written order filed on December 9, 1987, and stated in part:

> The Court denies the Motion of Defendants, Jensen and Superior Court of Solano County for an Order Adjudging Plaintiff in Contempt, ... because it is this Court's conclusion that it lacks jurisdiction to entertain the motion since the underlying judgment in this case rendered by this Court is currently on appeal.

This holding, and the law cited, made the contempt proceedings before magistrate Moulds illegal. But Moulds apparently had his orders, and on November 4, 1987, sentenced me to prison. Under law there is a statutory *right* to a stay of imprisonment pending appeal if any arguable issues of fact or law are raised on appeal.[153] I obviously had many arguable issues. But Moulds refused to grant me bail, arguing that he did not think the Court of Appeals would vacate his judgment. Federal case law makes it plain that bail cannot be denied on the belief by the judge who rendered the judgment that his decision will be upheld. Otherwise, granting bail would depend

---

[152] *Donovan v. Mazaola*, 761 F.2d 1411, 1414, 1415 (9th Cir. 1985; *Matter of Thorp*, 655 F.2d 997, 999 (9th Cir. 1981).
[153] Title 28 United States Code section 3143.

upon the judge rendering the judgment also believing that his judgment will be overturned on appeal.

INVALIDITY OF UNDERLYING WRIT, ORDER OR DECREE.

If an order is beyond the power of the court, such as suspending civil and constitutional rights and protections under federal and constitutional law, the order is void, and the court has no right in law to punish for any contempt of its unauthorized requirements. One of the first Supreme Court decisions addressing void orders was *Ex parte Rowland*.[154] A void order carries no authority and a person cannot be punished for either deliberately or accidentally violating it, according to well settled law.

A judgment which is void upon its face, and which requires only an inspection of the judgment roll to demonstrate its wants of vitality is a dead limb upon the judicial tree, which should be lopped off, if the power to do so exists. *People v. Greene*, 71 Cal. 100 [16 Pac. 197, 5 Am. St. Rep. 448].

In *Bache v. Wallace*, 102 Minn. 169 [112 N.W. 366], the court said: "Proceedings outside the authority of the court, or in violation or contravention of statutory prohibitions, whether the court has jurisdiction of the parties and subject matter of the action or proceedings, or not, are utterly void. The court continued:

It has been held that the mere fact that the court has jurisdiction of the subject matter of an action does not justify an exercise of a power not authorized by law, or a grant of relief to one of the parties the law declares shall not be granted ... Although every exercise of power not possessed by a court will not necessarily render its action a nullity, it is clear that every final act, in the form of a judgment or decree, granting relief the law declares shall not be granted, is void, even when collaterally called in question. The case of *Ritchie v. Seyers*, was cited in *Michel v. Williams* (*Id.* at 200) involved a collateral attack on a judgment, wherein the rule was brought under attack that the judgment of a court having jurisdiction of the parties and the subject matter of the action, cannot be collaterally attacked. The court stated of the rule:

That may be conceded, but the question is, did it have jurisdiction to enter the particular decree and judgment that it did enter? As we have seen, we reach the conclu-

---

[154] (1882) 104 U.S. 604, 26 L.Ed. 861.

sion that the particular judgment could be entered, and it is a well settled principle that, although a court may have jurisdiction of a case, yet, if it appears from the record that it did not have jurisdiction to enter the particular decree and judgment, it may be collaterally attacked."

The *Michael* court held that the trial court was without authority to enter a judgment that was prohibited by law, even though it had personal and subject matter jurisdiction.

EVEN THE MAGISTRATE ADMITTED THE CIVIL AND CONSTITUTIONAL VIOLATIONS

Magistrate Moulds had to find that the underlying Civil Right Act violations from which the injunctive order was rendered, did not exist. If they did exist, there was no basis for Schwartz holding that the complaint was frivolous, and no support for the injunctive order based upon the frivolous holding. Three years earlier, in 1984, I contacted Moulds in his private practice at Sacramento, seeking help in obtaining relief from the civil right violations. Moulds specialized in civil and constitutional law, and admitted after examining my material that the violations were serious. But he then stated he could not represent me in federal court because of his part time magistrate position. Since that time the civil and constitutional violations greatly worsened.

I filed a motion for bail pending appeal with Judge Ramirez, whose wrongful dismissal of the first federal action in 1984 made possible the crisis that subsequently developed. Ramirez also denied mandatory bail, holding that he didn't think his judgment would be overturned.

DO WE HAVE A CRIMINAL ON THE SUPREME COURT?

I was then ordered to turn myself in on January 14, 1988. I had to act fast. Over the Christmas holidays I prepared a petition for mandamus to Judge Anthony Kennedy in the Ninth Circuit Court of Appeals (before he became a Justice of the United States Supreme Court). I worked feverishly on Christmas day to finish the petition for submission to Kennedy the following Monday. Kennedy had testified at great lengths during his televised Senate confirmation hearing for appointment to the Supreme Court, expressing repeated concerns for due process, equal protection of the law, respect for privacy. Kennedy uttered all the right statements, implying his support of the laws and constitution of the United States, which were now outrageously violated while simultaneously sacrificing lives in the underlying air safety scandal. Surely Kennedy would provide relief. Ha!

Judge Anthony Kennedy was already involved in the corruption that made prior air tragedies possible. Kennedy was on the appellate panel that heard my appeal of the district court's dismissal of the 1974 federal action against the Federal Aviation Administration. Kennedy knew the consequences of coverup in such tragedies as the Paris DC-10 crash that wouldn't have occurred if he and other federal judges had acted upon the FAA corruption, as they were paid and entrusted to do. The respect he articulated for important constitutional rights were a sham for public consumption. Within 24 hours of submitting the request for statutory right to a stay pending appeal, it was denied. Prison stared me in the face.

I then filed a second motion for stay-pending-appeal with Judge Ramirez, which was certainly a hopeless cause. When I appeared before Ramirez on February 16, 1988 on the motion, he delayed rendering a decision, continuing the matter until March 4th, 1988, the date I was to be imprisoned. I asked Ramirez to grant a continuance of the incarceration date, to permit me to request bail pending appeal from the United States Court of Appeals if he denied my motion. Ramirez assured me that I could request a stay from him on March 4th, if he denied my bail at the hearing. He implied he would stay the sentence, and added that I was assuming he would deny the bail motion.

I was appearing without legal counsel. The Justice Department and federal judges seized all my assets (as discussed in later pages). I was without funds to hire other legal counsel. I was entitled to appointment of legal counsel, which I requested. Judge Ramirez appointed assistant federal public defender Carl Larson to represent me, whose employer was the same Department of Justice who desperately wanted me in prison, if not dead.

Larson's loyalties were to his employer and the deeply involved legal and judicial brotherhood. Larson made no effort to prepare a defense to the multitude of issues that made the guilty verdict a gross miscarriage of justice. Larson took the position that I was guilty, and advised me to prepare for prison. He refused to request bail pending appeal, which is a statutory right in federal case law. He refused to file motions to reconsider, or to file an appeal. He supported each of the multitude of state and federal violations described within these pages, and many that are not described here.

When Larson learned that I was to appear as guest on a talk show on air safety and government corruption, he became furious, and ordered me not to appear. I appeared. Larson's sole interest was protecting the government corruption. I finally had to dismiss Larson and appear in pro se status so as to get the defenses on the record.

"Bailiff, do your job!"

I appeared before Judge Ramirez at the March 4, 1988 hearing without legal counsel, expecting to receive a stay pending appeal. Unexpectedly, Ramirez denied my request for bail pending appeal, and simultaneously refused to give me time to prepare a motion to the Court of Appeals, as he had earlier assured me he would do. Ramirez knew that without legal counsel it was improbable in the harsh prison environment that I could prepare the legal briefs.

Even though it was two hours before I had to turn myself in, Judge Ramirez sarcastically bellowed, "Bailiff, do your job!" Two husky marshals than seized me, led me to a dirty prison cell in the basement of the federal building, and stripped me of all my belongings.

ENCASED IN SHACKLES

I was in a state of shock, and could hardly move. The marshalls led me to a sheriff's car, and transported me to a county jail facility at Yuba City, California, in what would be one of several prisons that was my "home" for the next two months. Driving up to Yuba City we passed a motel that I owned. Staying at the motel was my dear friend, Edith Armstrong (who appears in the earlier chapter, The Imposters). I hadn't seen Edith for a couple of years because of Judge Jensen's bench warrant for my arrest.

THINGS ALWAYS GOT WORSE

No matter how bad life became, it always seemed to get worse, at least for the first month of my imprisonment. Twenty four hours a day, you sit, sleep, eat, on a thin filthy mattress, if you are lucky to have one, and eat under filthy conditions. Life appears hopeless, and you think of ending it all.

POSSIBLY SEEKING MY DEATH?

There was also another possible reason for my incarceration. I was recovering from open heart surgery (six coronary bypasses). My two main coronary arteries were 95 percent blocked; one of the sub-arteries was totally blocked, and the other three sub-arteries were almost blocked. Any stress could constrict those almost-blocked arteries, and cause collapse of the bypasses. This could be fatal. My death would then, seemingly, end the threat of exposure. There was no one else with the evidence and the willingness to continue the fight.

THE CALIFORNIA OUTRAGES CONTINUED

While I was in prison and out of circulation, unable to defend myself, the Friedman law firm and the California judges had a field day rendering orders dividing my multi-million dollar estate.

DEBATE WITH ACLU WHILE IN PRISON

My contact with the outside world while in the Sutter County jail was by mail and through a telephone in the crowded cell-block. Each prisoner was limited to a scheduled 15 minute call. During a late evening call with a friend, the friend advised me that she arranged an appearance for me on radio station KOH in Reno, hosted by Fred Taft. I was to call the station collect the following morning, and would be on the air for an hour.

In the meantime Taft arranged that the executive director of the Nevada ACLU, Shelley Chase, would be on the show. On an earlier show, my friend described the refusal of the ACLU to provide me relief from the government attacks, and the ACLU's coverup of the constitutional outrageous that affected me and those victimized by the government corruption.

I told my friend that it was highly questionable whether I could be on the talk show. I was confined in prison, in a crowded cell, with 16 other prisoners, and limited to a single 15 minute telephone conversation. I explained the situation to the other prisoners, some of whom were bank robbers and drug dealers, and that I had the opportunity to debate with the ACLU. The prisoners were very cooperative, and encouraged me to get on the show. Everyone waived their telephone schedule so that I could make the one-hour talk show possible. Of course, the prison officials knew nothing about it. If they had, they would have put an immediate stop to it.

There were some unusual sounds during the show. Clanking of cell-block doors, screaming of prisoners, and a fight ensuring in my cell block about seven feet from the phone.

During this talk show, ACLU Executive Director Shelley Chase protected the Justice Department, protected the federal judges, protected the California judges, and in effect, made a shambles of civil and constitutional rights. The ACLU protected the corruption that had, and would continue, to result in repeated air tragedies. The head of the Nevada ACLU, who continuously seek financial donations for allegedly promoting civil rights, protected those who committed some of the most outrageous violations of these rights.

For reasons I can only speculate, the ACLU had been covering up since 1965 for the government corruption that not only ended in death for many, but concurrently violated the civil and constitutional rights of those who perished. I frequently advised the ACLU of the misconduct, and civil and constitutional violations that they claimed to protect. Never did they show any concern or offer any help. Instead, they covered up. If they had acted, or if anyone else had done so, who could have focused publicity on the scandal, major changes would have occurred in the rampant government corruption. Such action probably would have changed the nation's air disaster history, and could have played a key role in preventing the endemic government corruption that exists today in all three branches of government.

Talk show host Fred Taft expressed outrage over the government conduct on the two prior shows. He even described the government abuse of his cousin, who was sentenced to prison on a tax charge. But during this show Taft changed his colors. He upheld the ACLU's clearly untenable position. I wondered if the station had been pressured by its government licensing agency, or by the Department of Justice, who in turn might have pressured Fred Taft. Something certainly changed.

START OF DIESEL THERAPY

After spending several weeks in the Sutter County jail I was put on the Diesel route. I was transferred to the infamous old Sacramento County jail, where filth, overcrowding, inhuman conditions, takes on a new meaning. I wondered how it compared to the infamous Devil's Island prison. During the frequent changes in prison, I once found myself in a cell with 12 bunks, and occupied by over 30 people. You spend every minute of the day or night sitting or sleeping on the concrete floor, unless you are lucky and have a thin mattress to lay on. The stench of the dirty mattresses is sometimes unbearable. In the Sacramento jail the open toilet was positioned along a glass wall with constant passing of male and female guards, without any screening or privacy.

Most of the prisoners looked as if they hadn't washed or changed their clothes in weeks; they resembled something out of a horror story. Food came in unsanitary containers that resembled feeding time in a dog kennel.

SILENCING TECHNIQUES IN PRISON

The Justice Department has their bag of tricks to break a prisoner, or keep him from his legal counsel, *if* he has counsel. His communication with his family or friends are halted during this "diesel therapy" tactic. It is common practice in the federal prison system to move prisoners from prison to prison, for weeks at a time, and no one knows where he is. In this manner, prisoners can be lost for weeks at a time, without any contact with family or legal counsel, and without access to a law library and legal facilities. After Judge Ramirez ordered my incarceration, he sought to keep me in the county jails where there was no access to legal facilities. In this manner, I could not conduct legal research and prepare legal papers to obtain my own release.

BRUTALITY OF PRISON

Prison has its own peculiar sounds. The constant slamming of heavy metal doors, night screams, fights in the cells. You live, eat, and exist, like caged animals. Many respond accordingly. There obviously is no privacy. I spent 24 hours a day on this bunk, and was lucky to have a bunk to myself. I slept, ate, and survived, within five feet of a dirty, seat-less toilet, used, by over a dozen occupants. Modesty didn't exist.

Anyone who hasn't been in prison doesn't know the degradation, the humiliation, that goes with it. The first thing that happens is that you are hand-cuffed, and often, leg irons are installed with a Martin Chain fitting around your waist, connecting the leg irons to handcuffs and around your waist.

You are stripped of all belongings, including your watch, rings, identification, and then put into a holding cell. The filthy toilet conditions indoctrinates you to what is yet to come. Finger prints and mug shots are repeatedly taken at every new jail or prison, and you are stripped naked and subjected to embarrassing body-cavity examinations. Smelly and over-crowded prison cells became routine. The smell of urine and god knows what else, is overpowering. One's appetite is easily lost.

BROKEN, LONELY, DYING MEN

Under these conditions broken, lonely, and dying men are found in the medium and high-security prisons. Torn from their families, some for twenty and thirty years, or forever, their lives literally come to an end. There are no hopes, no plans, nothing. In the cases of those framed by the Justice Department attorneys, it became especially pathetic that this could happen in the so-called land of liberty and justice!

I looked at the scribblings on prison walls, made by de-ranged, dejected, and morbid prisoners. Broken men, lonely, and some dying. Despite the overcrowding, it was terribly lonely, and all meaning to life appears to have been lost. For many, all hope was gone. Under these conditions, a day or a week seems forever. It gave me an entirely different perspective of those in prison, and of those who have corrupted our government. Many of these people in prison were railroaded by the misnamed Justice Department, and prosecuted for offenses far less onerous then committed by those charging and sentencing them.

My entire life passed before me. I thought of those I loved, who helped me. I thought of those who didn't seem to care. I thought of the attorneys I hired to defend me, who then conspired with my judicial and Justice Department and judicial adversaries, all a part of the vicious air disaster scandal. I sometimes wondered what part United Airlines officials played in these events, thinking of how General Motors secretly went after Ralph Nader when Nader wrote the book, *Unsafe At Any Speed*.

"My God, this can't be!"

Many times I thought to myself, "My God, how can this be happening to me! This can't be!" I couldn't believe that what started out with correcting air safety problems at United Airlines could have such devastating consequences. I thought of people such as Stevie Baltz, and wondered if perhaps I was relatively fortunate in comparison. Stevie was no match for these thugs, and it seemed neither was I.

How could I in prison for refusing to commit the crime of coverup? Where was the press, the so-called protector of government tyranny? Where was Congress? I sent out hundreds of flyers before leaving for prison, notifying these parties that had a check and balance responsibility. I appealed to the ACLU, the Ralph Nader group, civil right groups, and other checks and balances. Every single one refused to help. They all aided and abetted the criminal subversion of our form of government.

It was all so incomprehensible. I had been financially well off. I had a good life. I had a reputation throughout the United States as an air safety activist, and suddenly I am in prison for trying to help others. I kept thinking this must be a dream, and I'll wake up, and it will all be over. But I never seemed to wake up.

Prison life is especially hard on older persons. Medical care is incredibly bad at most prisons. Heart attacks receive virtually no priority, and a dying person suffering a heart attack can linger for hours before being taken to medical facilities. Often it is too late. Older persons have various medical problems which prison life aggravates. Older prisoners also become prey to young bullying inmates.

SUICIDE

Sometimes I just wanted to die. The strain of all this was getting to me. Flung into prison, things looked bleak. Everything was accumulating. The six years of judicial persecution, the loss of my home, my business, my assets, the humiliation, the character assassination, the loss of privacy, and the hopelessness. There is only so much a person can stand. It caused me to think more than once of ending it all. I had been through World War II as a Navy pilot in the Pacific. I had flown for almost fifty years, experiencing all types of aircraft emergencies. I was in the center of an Iranian revolution. All of these stressful conditions, put together, did not equal the fear that I now experienced. God bless America, the home of the corrupt! I was angry.

I looked at the plastic bags in my cell which are used for laundry and other purposes. I thought how peaceful things could suddenly become if I simply slipped a bag over my head and ended it all. The main force stopping me was the hope that I could break open the secrecy lid and in some manner expose the endemic corruption within the government of the United States. What a dreamer I must have been. With the average apathetic American, obsessed with his ball games and other trivia, there wasn't a chance to wake up this group.

JUSTICE DEPARTMENT CORRUPTION

While in prison I learned much more about Justice Department corruption, and how it affects innocent Americans. I had already seen the misconduct of the Justice Department in its coverup of the air disaster corruption and its sacrifice of others in the air disaster scandal.

There are many people in federal prisons who were either falsely convicted by the lies of the Justice Department attorneys, or who suffer longer prison terms because of the lying by the Justice Department attorneys seeking to establish a high conviction record. I discovered that attorneys in the Justice Department are given bonuses for the cases they successfully prosecute. Small time drug users or occasional dealers complained to me how they were framed, by having marijuana dumped on their property, or planted in their cars or airplanes.

There are many persons in prison for non-violent crimes who are there because of a lying U.S. Attorney. I got a taste of it several times, as the U.S. Attorney sought to deny me bail, sought to incarcerate me for longer periods of time, by making false allegations, such as charging me with kidnapping my grandson. In prison, I heard many stories from inmates who admitted the crimes that they actually committed, but who described the fraudulent planting of evidence by Justice Department attorneys.

TRAVELING IN CHAINS

From the old Sacramento County jail I was transported in chains to several other prisons, and eventually reached the Terminal Island federal penitentiary at Long Beach, California. For as long as twelve hours at a time, I was totally chained and shackled, unable to properly feed myself, or to use the toilet, or any of life's other activities. I ate in the back of crowded prison wagons, stopping at fast-food places for hamburgers. For rest room stops we stopped at service stations, and I was paraded in chains and leg irons before people who probably wondered what type of heinous crime I had committed.

Eventually I reached Terminal Island prison at Long Beach. Approaching Long Beach's Terminal Island, I could see the tourist attractions that I formerly visited during happier times. I use to visit these same areas when I appeared on radio and television shows as an air safety activist. Now, to stop these activities, the government-funded corruption had me in the same areas, but now in chains. How times had changed.

The federal prison at Terminal Island reminded me of pictures I had seen as a child of Sing Sing and Alcatraz. Standing at the bottom of the four story building in unit "J1," all I could see were cell block after cell block, four stories high. It was an eerie feeling.

THE RIGHT TO COUNSEL MYTH

The Sixth Amendment to the United States constitution, and federal statutory and case law, entitles a party to effective legal counsel. But what exists in writing is often ignored in practice. Many inmates were denied this constitutional right. A federal public defender is often appointed, who works and is paid by the Justice Department, the same department seeking to put the party in prison. If the Justice Department attorneys really want a person put in prison, attorney loyalty to a client by the federal public defender doesn't exist.

INSIDIOUS LOSS OF FREEDOMS

The justice department and their legal brethren on the federal bench confiscate without a hearing the assets of people accused of a drug crime or RICO violation. Without assets, the party is unable to hire legal counsel. Valuable properties are seized and taken, even if minute amounts of drugs are found. Your home, for instance, can be seized, on the basis of drugs fraudulently planted by Justice Department attorneys or government agents. A favorite stunt of the Justice Department is to charge the wife or an aged parent with a crime, who are not involved, to force a person to either plead guilty who is not guilty, or plead guilty to a more severe charge than the facts justify.

The Supreme Court in June 1989 upheld the right to seize all assets of a suspected drug dealer, whose crime, if any, had not yet been proved. This includes the assets needed to hire legal counsel. The Supreme Court's fuzzy argument is that the Sixth Amendment right to appointment of legal counsel will insure proper legal representation. But the appointed legal counsel is often times hired and paid by the Justice Department, and when the Justice Department wants a person incarcerated, the appointed legal counsel prepares a totally inadequate defense, insuring the person's incarceration. That is what happened to me. Each of the three counsels appointed to represent me sabotaged my defense. As in my case, the Justice Department, with the help of the federal judiciary, doesn't think twice about fabricating a crime, seizing a person's assets, and then appointing legal counsel who carries out the Justice Department's intent to incarcerate the person.

The Justice Department has tremendous influence, and can destroy persons who don't play ball their way. Federal Judge Claiborne was impeached in 1986 on a relatively minor income tax oversight. Federal Judge Robert Aquilar of the Ninth Circuit district courts was indicted by the Justice Department in June

1989 on charges of being friends with criminals. The Justice Department was dissatisfied with earlier decisions of both judges, who ruled against the Justice Department.

The mere investigation by the FBI can cause a member of the U.S. Senate and House to lose an election. Possibly this was one of the reasons every member of the U.S. Senate in 1988 and 1989 refused to respond to my multi-page petition to investigate the air disaster and government corruption I brought to their attention.

BUYING AND SELLING HUMAN LIVES

In cases where hard-core criminals come before the courts, the judges, prosecutors and attorneys buy and sell cases and human lives, as if they were commodities. Judges are paid off to rule favorably on particular cases. A clerk can lose a key file or piece of evidence. The court reporter can change the transcript to where the reverse of what actually was stated is shown on the records.

Attorneys often sell their own clients down the river, allowing them to be convicted, to satisfy a debt to his adversary's legal counsel, or to placate the desire of a judge who may want the other party to prevail. Trading of human life, in court, or in the air safety environment, is like kids trading marbles. Prosecutors will let a defendant go free, but in exchange for the life of another man. Criminal attorneys will plead a man guilty just to pay back a prosecutor for the not-guilty holding the day before. Prosecutors will lie to imprison an innocent person, or to sentence him to prison for years longer than would otherwise occur. Cases are fixed over the phone by paying judges, prosecutors, police, and others. In some parts of the country this misconduct is worse than in others. In the east, in Chicago, in the south, it is especially wretched and corrupt.

Some Justice Department attorneys justify their lying using the argument the defendant lies, so why shouldn't they lie. But a defendant may lie to avoid prison for himself. Prosecutors lie to imprison innocent persons, or to greatly increase the length of sentence for the purpose of making his record look good, irregardless of the human tragedy it brings.

The public doesn't perceive this misconduct as a threat to their liberties. When the Justice Department prosecutes a party for an alleged crime, the average public, including the Grand Jury, assumes that the party is guilty. Otherwise the accused would not be charged, or so they think. I fell into that trap in the past, until I discovered that the Justice Department is corrupted by attorneys who lie and cheat as a standard tactic. As a Wall Street article once stated, the Grand Jury would indict a ham sandwich if the prosecutor told them to do so.

DESTROYED FAMILIES

The victims become beaten, their families destroyed, and for the remainder of their lives they suffer. A facade is made of preventing the imprisonment of a party who may be innocent, while behind the scenes innocent persons are routinely put in prison by lying prosecutors and conniving judges.

It doesn't take long for those attacked by the corrupt system to be mentally, emotionally and physically beaten. I'm sure that Judge Ramirez, Judge Schwartz, and the Justice Department, planned that I too would be destroyed.

The public is led to believe that the justice system goes to great length to prevent the imprisonment of innocent persons. Just as the lawful function of the FAA and NTSB is corrupted by people employed by these government agencies, so it is with the Justice Department, although the latter is more easily corrupted because of the nature of the legal brotherhood. The Justice Department and the United States Attorneys prosecute and imprison innocent men and women by knowingly and routinely lying in court. Rarely are these attorneys accused of perjury. The legal fraternity protects themselves and those who are part of the system, and as such have no one to prosecute them. Just as judges hold themselves immune from prosecution for their acts—even though criminal laws pertains to them as well as others—the Department of Justice attorneys hold themselves immune from their criminal acts. The Civil Rights Act, for instance, applies to everyone. However, federal judges by their own decisions, hold themselves immune, despite statutory and constitutional protections that state otherwise.

The indictment of many state judges in the Greylord Cook County judicial corruption reflects the corrupt judicial conditions throughout the United States, including California. The method of bribery may differ, but the corruption is there.

Violation of criminal offenses carry different punishment if perpetrated by those entrusted to carry out the law. In the federal prison system numerous prison officials have been caught using or selling drugs, but are never prosecuted. The Justice Department protects their own.

COMFORT FROM SEVERAL FRIENDS

Edith Armstrong, the lady from the earlier chapter, *The Imposters*, who had sought to help me in my early battles, developed heart trouble about ten years earlier. I advised Edith that she could live in one of my apartments at no charge, and that if she wanted she could oversee some of my business properties. She lived in an apartment at my Yuba City motel, and enjoyed herself. But the abuses inflicted upon me created considerable stress upon Edith, which caused her heart discomfort. Edith often said that the Friedman firm constantly harassed her with threatening telephone calls.

POSSIBLE CIA INVOLVEMENT

The sinister nature of the government corruption appeared to be more like the tactics and intrigue of the Centra Intelligence Agency (CIA), and especially the Clandestine Unit, applying against selected U.S. citizens what they practice overseas. Many books on the CIA describe the covert activities against our own citizens. In *The CIA and the Cult of Intelligence* (Knopf) the authors, Victor Marchetti (fourteen years with the CIA) and John Marks, describe the immoral, vicious, clandestine activities, overseas and domestically within the United States. They describe the covert empire running wild, accountable to no one. I am reminded of the strangers who appeared in the earlier chapter, *The Imposters*, who several times asked if Edith and I suspected the CIA was involved in the government corruption I had uncovered. Other books have similar messages.[155]

SEEKING HELP FROM CONGRESS

While I was in prison I wrote letters to Senators Alan Cranston (Majority Whip from California); John McCain (Arizona); Banking Committee Chairman Donald Riegle, Jr. (Michigan); Government Affairs Committee Chairman John Glenn (Ohio); Dennis DeConcini (Arizona). These five, later called the "Keating-Five" in the savings and loan scandal, didn't answer. Senator Sam Nunn wrote on July 6, 1988 thanking me for the information on government corruption and related air tragedies, and then did nothing. Others guilty of misprision of felonies and coverup included Senators Joseph Biden; Edward Kennedy; Pete Wilson; and many others. They all covered up, knowing very well the continued price paid by innocent people for the coverup. They left the stage set for more tragedies and more corruption.

I wrote from prison to NTSB Secretary James Burnley, and described to him (again) the corruption within the FAA and the NTSB, and the actions taken to silence my exposure of them. Same response; coverup.

A PAINFUL MARK OF DISTINCTION

The United States of America is probably the only free-world country that has ever imprisoned an air safety activist for trying to prevent deaths from air safety corruption. What surprised me was that during many talk shows, very few talk-show hosts expressed outrage at what was happening. It was easy to understand how Hitler rose to power, as those who could have prevented it said nothing. The same exists within the

---

[155] *The Invisible Government* authors David Wise and Thomas Ross. (Random House).

United States in a different form. Like the saying goes, they didn't protest when they came for the jews; nor when they came for the catholics; nor when they came for the protestants. And when they came for those who didn't protest, there weren't anyone left to protest. That may be the way the United States is going with its endemic corruption and the public's silence except when it affects something that directly affects them.

ANOTHER PRISON TRANSFER

Eventually I was transferred to Lompoc Prison Camp near Santa Maria, California, where there is a law library that I could use. Judge Ramirez had sought to have me confined to the harsh conditions of county prisons in California where there was no adequate access to the law library for preparing legal briefs. Without legal counsel, I would rot in jail while they finished me off in another manner, which has yet to be told.

Some of the nation's most distinguished prisoners ended up at Lompoc. Former United States Attorney General John Mitchell, Wall Street financier Ivan Boesky, and others, spent time at Lompoc. Boesky and I worked together on several prison details. The living conditions there were markedly different, but I was still suffering the humiliation, the loss of my liberties, and other constitutionally protected rights.

RELEASE ON BAIL FROM PRISON

Access to a legal library and equipment were lacking until I reached Lompoc. On April 13, 1988 I again filed a motion for bail pending appeal with the United States Court of Appeals at San Francisco. By coincidence, Reno talk show host Fred Taft called in on the nationally syndicated Owen Spann show out of San Francisco, and described my predicament. It is very possible that this talk show was heard by federal judges. The next day the United States Court of Appeals ordered me released pending appeal.

On Thursday, April 16, 1988, the Court of Appeals rendered an order releasing me. But the Bureau of Prisons, under the Department of Justice, refused to release me. I didn't even know of the release order until four days later, when I called Sacramento from inside prison, and learned that I should have been released almost a week earlier. I then went to the prison authorities at Lompoc, California, and discovered that the order existed. They gave me the lame excuse that they couldn't find me. Can you comprehend a prison, with bed checks four times a day, and they were unable to find me!

MORE OF THE SAME

The federal courts appointed Sacramento legal counsel Clifford Tedmon about a month before my release to represent me. But he did nothing. As with the other counsel appointed by the Justice Department, Tedmon's interest was protecting the Justice Department and the federal judges. He did nothing to seek my release or to file an appeal.

Immediately after the Court of Appeals rendered the order granting me bail, the Department of Justice submitted an unusual motion seeking to have the Court of Appeals rescind their release order. They were apparently desperate to keep me in prison; I was still a threat to the corrupt Justice Department officials and attorneys, especially on the many talk show appearances. The Justice Department continued misstating the law, and holding that the Court of Appeals lacked jurisdiction to release me.

The Justice Department argued that I had not filed a notice of appeal of the March 4, 1988 order by Judge Ramirez denying my motion for bail, and thus the court lacked jurisdiction to grant bail. But the law clearly stated that only one appeal need be filed of the sentence holding me guilty, which I did file. With that filing, the Court of Appeals had jurisdiction to render any order associated with the appeal, including an order releasing me on bail.

Waiting for me in the mail was a letter, similar to what I have received over the years, that was heart-warming. Oddly enough, it was from a former United Airlines management official: The letter stated in part: "Many times I've thought about Rodney Stich and his identification with John the Baptist crying in the Desert" but you do make a difference and without you whistle blowers our world gets completely out of synch, so don't ever give up because you do make a tremendous difference!"

CHAPTER TWENTY FOUR

The Little Pawn

Shortly before going to prison, one of my daughters became targeted in this scheme. The conspiracy needed one of her children to keep the scheme going, and they took her five-year old boy from her.

In different ways the corruption affected all three of my daughters, emotionally and financially. Linda, one of my daughters living near Dallas, suffered the loss of her five-year-old son. Linda was the only daughter that had any contact with my former wife, who in turn received considerable joy out of baby-sitting Linda's five-year-old son, Heath. For convenience, Linda often left the son in her care.

Linda grew tired of the hatred generated by my former wife's participation in the scheme fronted by the Friedman law firm. In 1986 Linda suddenly moved to California with her two sons. My former wife became distraught after Linda moved, because of the loss of Heath's companionship. After Linda left Texas, my former wife decided to call an end to the scheme. However, Friedman warned her that she owed them tens of thousands of dollars, and could not pull out. The Friedman group promised that if she continued with the California action, they would obtain for her legal custody of Linda's boy, Heath.

The Friedman law firm then engaged Texas attorney Gayle Oler, to submit affidavits to the Texas courts in a petition to obtain emergency custody of Heath. The attorneys declared under oath in the petition that Linda was guilty of contempt of court, by taking Heath from my former wife. The petition fraudulently stated that my former wife had legal custody of the boy, without providing any evidence. The affidavit stated that Heath was in great danger, and that Linda was an unfit mother to care for the boy. Actually, Heath was having the time of his life living at Lake Tahoe, where Linda took up residence and looked for a job. Truth was never one of Friedman's notable traits.

The affidavit claiming Linda was an unfit mother made no reference to Linda's two-year-old son, Dustin. My former wife only wanted Heath. Linda was apparently fit to raise the little boy that was not needed to placate Friedman's Texas client. The affidavit stated that the attorneys did not know Linda's whereabouts, and thus could not give her notice of the hearing. But the Friedman group knew where Linda resided, and knew that Reno attorney Jonathan King was representing her. At least, he was suppose to do so.

TEXAS JUSTICE!

In this environment, and without any evidence other than the utterings of an attorney, Judge Hartman of the Dallas Municipal Court rendered an order taking Heath from Linda, and granting custody of the five-year old boy to my 68 year-old former wife. California judge William Jensen then converted this Texas order to a California order during a secret hearing in Solano County, without Linda's knowledge. Reno Judge McGee converted the California order to a Nevada order. He either did not know what was going on, or willingly participated in the scheme.[156]

Friedman planned the seizure of the little boy with the precision of a drug raid on professional criminals. The Friedman law firm flew my former wife to California from Texas, coordinated with the Washoe County Sheriff's Office in Reno, and with the custody order signed by Reno Judge McGee, the group converged upon Linda and her two sons at their Lake Tahoe home.

"They're taking Heath!"

It was 10:30 a.m. when Linda frantically called me on February 18, 1987. "They're taking Heath," Linda cried. She said the house was full of people, and they were taking Heath out the front door. A sheriff's deputy turned the frightened boy over to my former wife. With the Friedman group, they rushed the boy to Reno Airport for an immediate flight to Dallas before I could obtain a court order stopping them.

I tried to get immediate help from Reno attorney Jonathan

---

[156] He refused to respond to a letter requesting an explanation, or deny that he knowingly played a role in the boy's seizure.

King, who had been earlier hired to protect Linda's interest. He was as useless as any other attorney I had obtained.

FRIGHTENED, AND OFF INTO A BLIZZARD

Linda was frightened. The legal papers served upon her advised that a hearing to determine Heath's custody was taking place within 36 hours in Dallas. Linda frantically packed her belongings, her son Dustin, her German Shepherd, and drove off into the night during a raging winter snow storm.

Over the desolate mountainous roads of Nevada, Linda drove all night in blizzard conditions, seeking to reach Texas in time for the custody hearing. She failed to realize that she could not possibly reach Dallas in time. This became a certainty when Linda became snowbound in the mountains. Fortunately, she didn't break down on a desolate road in Nevada and freeze to death.

My oldest daughter, Stephanie Stadtler, quickly caught a plane for Texas, and appeared in court on Linda's behalf. Stephanie advised the court that Linda would not be there in time for the appearance, and obtained a continuance of the hearing.

REFUSING TO ACCEPT EVIDENCE

Linda was confident the court could not take Heath from her. She, like most people, was unaware of the covert powers of the legal fraternity, and naively thought the law protected her. I didn't want to scare Linda, and have her worry unnecessarily. But I wanted her to realize she was facing a formidable group that would stop at nothing, including ruining her life and that of her five year old son, to continue a scheme that was now out of control.

I told Linda we were dealing with thugs in the legal fraternity that had the awesome power of the United States government at their disposal, and who would stop at nothing to keep the scheme going to protect the scheme that was now out of control. I stated that the scheme needed my former wife's cooperation to continue the sham California action. And if this required taking Linda's child, they would not hesitate for a moment to do so. Unless they could hand the boy over to my former wife, their scheme was in danger of going up in smoke, exposing themselves in the process.

"Linda, federal judges and the justice department are already involved in your case," I said. "They aren't going to let you have your son back. There is too much at stake!"

I told Linda to fight, but for her to realize what she was up against. I told Linda that federal judge Milton Schwartz[157] had

---

[157] Eastern District of California.

already cited the Texas custody case[158] in a federal district court action I filed in the District of Columbia in March of 1987. Judge Schwartz and the Justice Department cited the custody case in a motion seeking dismissal of the Washington law suit. The Dallas custody decision hadn't even been rendered yet, and Schwartz argued that Linda lost custody of her boy!

The purpose of citing the custody case was to imply that I had filed the action taking Linda's boy from her, and that the case was decided adversely to me, and showed a pattern of dismissed actions. The Dallas judge hadn't heard the custody case when Schwartz argued in the federal brief that Linda had already lost custody of her son.

The Washington law suit addressed the sequence of air safety corruption and the actions taken to silence me. In that law suit I attempted to obtain a writ of mandamus against the FAA and NTSB to force them to halt their air safety corruption.

REFUSING FAVORABLE TESTIMONY

Dallas Judge Hartman conducted a custody hearing[159] at which I testified, along with my three daughters. We tried to introduce evidence in the form of pictures, videos, and testimony, showing that Linda and her two boys had a loving and pleasant home life in Nevada. Judge Hartman refused to accept the testimony, the video, or the still pictures, and didn't want to hear our testimony. Judge Hartman obstructed entry of evidence into the record that reflected favorably upon Linda. In every court proceeding, California, federal, and now Texas, we were totally gridlocked. The power of the judges in the United States joined together in this awesome scandal, that showed the great dangers facing our form of government from this deadly judicial branch.

The Texas case worker, without any knowledge of Linda's Nevada housing accommodations, recommended that the 68-year-old grandmother get custody of the five year old child, emphasizing that the grandmother had a brick home. With this comparison, California residents and their stucco houses wouldn't stand a chance in a Texas custody battle!

DESTROYING LINDA'S FAMILY

Based on the self-serving arguments of Friedman's attorney, and Friedman's Texas client, Judge Hartman ruled that Linda was unfit to have custody of the five year old child. He gave no consideration to Linda being the boy's natural mother, or to the testimony of Linda's two sisters, myself, and the evidence that the boys were happy. Heath became a pawn in this intrigue. In

---

[158] No. 82-9280-V. *In the Interest of Heath Ashley Mulvey.*
[159] March 1987.

this environment of fraudulent affidavits, Judge Hartman then changed custody of the five-year-old boy to the 68-year old woman.

A LEGACY OF SUICIDE AND HATE

Linda had her share of hard times. Most of her problems arose from her failure to break the ties with her domineering mother. After Linda gave birth to her first child, Shawn, my former wife developed a fondness for the child. She wanted Shawn, and schemed to get him. Linda and her husband lived in San Antonio, where the husband was in the Air Force. Linda's mother missed the child, and pressured Linda to leave her husband. Linda foolishly did that, and moved back home with her mother. My former wife acquired the first of her play toys; Shawn.

I had met Linda's first husband before the breakup, during one of my frequent flying trips to visit the children in Dallas. He was a caring individual, deeply in love with Linda. I took him and Linda flying into little airports throughout Texas during my Texas visits.

SUICIDE

After Linda left, her husband became despondent over their separation. Every attempt at reconciliation was thwarted by my former wife. One night he wrote a suicide note. He parked his car behind the place where Linda worked, and then with the engine running lay under the exhaust pipe, breathing the fumes, and committed suicide. My former wife now had greater assurance Shawn would remain with her.

The suicide distressed Linda, and ironically, she became more dependent upon the person most responsible for her sorrows. Rather than put distance between herself and her biological mother, Linda allowed herself to become more dependent upon the mother, and be further harmed. Many times Linda's mother would accuse Linda of causing the death of Linda's husband, in front of Shawn.

SCHEMING TO GET LEGAL CUSTODY OF SHAWN

Linda's mother wanted legal custody of Shawn, and consequently the survivor's pension paid by the government to the boy. She accomplished this by having Linda sign documents that allegedly enrolled Shawn in the local school district. After obtaining Linda's signature, Linda's mother applied to the court for legal custody of Shawn, arguing that Linda was an unfit mother, was on drugs, and that Linda had voluntarily signed over custody. Without requiring Linda's presence, Texas Judge Hartman ordered custody taken from Linda and granted to the grandmother.

Linda didn't learn about this custody document and loss of legal custody, until her sister, Patty, living in Waxahachie,

Texas, later described what happened. Without money, and depressed, Linda didn't know what to do.

Linda's mother than applied to the government to have the monthly survivor's check changed from Linda's name to that of Linda's mother. When Shawn became older, and was no longer the cute little boy, his grandmother lost interest in him. He became embroiled frequently with the law, and showed contempt for his own natural mother, Linda.

It was ironical that after scheming to take Linda's first child, Linda's mother then schemed with the Friedman law firm to take Linda's second child. The Department of Justice and federal judges assisted in the scheme, which was financed by the United States government! Texas judge Hartman knew about the first fraudulent taking of Linda's boy, and of the fraudulent affidavit that took Linda's second child. In true Texas-justice style, this brave Texas judge ordered Linda's second child taken from Linda, and given to Linda's mother. Friedman won out again.

The judges involved in this scheme were all aware of these outrages. Before writing this book, I accused them of deliberately participating in the scheme, and gave them an opportunity to explain. None of them responded.

CHAPTER TWENTY FIVE

Still Other Scandals!

Between the time that federal judge Milton Schwartz charged me with a crime for exercising constitutional remedies, the Justice Department and federal judges subjected me to still other government-funded outrages. The sham California law suit and the suspension of all California and federal due process threatened were financially destroying me, like a cancer. Friedman's lie pendens prevented me from refinancing the mortgage loans that periodically came due on my properties, resulting in repeated losses of valuable assets. It was like a new-car dealer unable to refinance or sell his stock of automobiles. Stripped of due process relief by every level of the California courts, and every level of the federal courts, I exercised relief intended by Congress in Chapter 11 of the bankruptcy act.[160] This relief was intended to provide people with sizeable assets additional time to pay their bills during a temporary cash bind.

I didn't have financial problems. But I exercised the Chapter 11 relief to have a Chapter 11 federal judge provide me with the relief from the violations of federally protected rights.

---

[160] Chapter 7 is for people seeking relief from their debts. They usually have no equities in their assets, and need cancellation of their debts. They are not victimized by the bankruptcy racketeering enterprises since there are no assets to loot. Chapter 11 is for people with large assets who simply seek time to pay their debts and intend to pay them in full. These are often business people, many of whom are semi-retired. Chapter 13 is for the wage earner and people with lower net worth who seek time to pay their bills.

I may have set an historic first by seeking relief in chapter 11 from an onslaught of civil, constitutional, and RICO violations inflicted in a government-funded conspiracy to silence my exposure of massive corruption by government officials.

I had no idea at that time that government corruption was also rampant in Chapter 11, and that it was one of the worst racketeering enterprises in the United States. The press kept such a tight lid on the scandal involving large sections of the federal judiciary and the legal fraternity that they caused their own readers to be victimized by this awesome racketeering activity.

Unaware of the Chapter 11 corruption, I filed two Chapter 11 cases in May of 1987; one for my personal assets, and one for my corporate assets.

The clear language of the statutes and legislative history insured that those who seek relief in Chapter 11 remain in control of their business and assets, and are given time to pay bills that came due. But this relief was misused as a criminal enterprise by federal judges. Chapter 11 was used as a carrot to induce people, many of whom had only a minor financial problem affecting only a small part of their assets, to file Chapter 11. Then, instead of being allowed to remain in control of their business, properties, and assets, as intended by statutes, Chapter 11 judges, judge-appointed trustees, and cooperating attorneys, seized the assets, threw the people out of their properties, and proceeded to loot the life's assets of the people.

Many of the victims were elderly, who invested in small businesses to obtain retirement security. Instead, they were converted into paupers by the legal and judicial fraternities who corrupted the judicial process. Every level of the federal courts, up to and including the Justices of the U.S. Supreme Court, knew of the corrupt racketeering enterprises, and aided and abetted it by depriving the victims of relief. The newspapers played their part by keeping the lid on the nation-wide scandal.

THIS IS HOW THE SCHEME WORKS

The scheme was aided by attorneys in positions of trust sabotaging people who came to them for legal help. People with large assets, encountering a temporary cash shortage, consult attorneys who specialize in Chapter 11 proceedings. The attorneys often advise the unsuspecting and trusting clients to seek relief in Chapter 11. The attorneys assure them that they will remain in control of their business and possessions while given time to pay their bills, as the statutes and legislative history provides. But after filing Chapter 11, either their own attorney, or attorneys for creditors, will routinely accuse them of gross mismanagement or dishonesty, and on this excuse deprive them of the Chapter 11 protection. The federal Chapter 11 judge appoints a private trustee to liquidate the business, even though the statutes 11 U.S.C. § 1104, related case law, the legislative history, prevents this from happening (unless the person is guilty of dishonesty or gross mismanagement that deprive the creditors of the security).

The people whose expertise built up the business are then ordered off the premises by the judge-appointed trustee; the business is then grossly mismanaged by the trustee who knows nothing about the business, cares nothing about it, and whose income primarily derives from liquidating the assets. The appointment of the trustee then commences the destruction of the valuable estate which may have been the people's retirement income.

Assets are sold at distressed prices, often to straw men with whom the private trustee or judges have covert financial ties. Cooperating attorneys reap a harvest by submitting huge legal fees which go unquestioned by the federal judges that are part of this lucrative scheme.

Federal statutory and case laws, and constitutional protections are openly violated by the federal judges and judge appointed trustees. Constitutional due process becomes a mockery. The higher courts approve the outrages, and rarely provide relief. Those whose assets were seized, are now without funds to hire legal counsel, and are defenseless against this rampant racketeering activity that permeates the entire federal branch of government, either as perpetrators, or protectors.

The once healthy business becomes a shambles; the owners life's work and earnings destroyed. Those seeking relief suddenly find themselves paupers, often at the time of retirement. Their businesses, their homes, and their assets, are gone. People, sometimes widows, leave the court crying, having lost the money they accumulated during their life time, and upon which they expected to survive their remaining years. Their estates are looted by the conspiracy of federal judges, attorneys, and trustees, deceiving the victims through Chapter 11 trickery. Chapter 11 becomes a cruel carrot to ensnare people.

How can this prevail on a large scale without the many checks and balances intervening? Every level of the federal judiciary covers up for the profitable racketeering enterprise. They look upon Chapter 11 as a feeding trough, in which the assets generated by people are plucked, like feedlot chickens. The entire federal judiciary, up to and including the Justices of the United States Supreme Court, protect their judicial brethrens at the lowest levels. Its like a police chief protecting police officers engaging in robberies, rapes, killings, and ignoring the desperate pleas of citizens seeking relief. Calls for help via appeals and petitions are ignored.

The press withholds information on this judicial racketeering activity, in which banks and other institutions are often a part, and in that manner harm their own readers, just as members of Congress harm their own constituents by refusing to take corrective actions over those criminalizing the legislation they passed.

The federal government finances this Chapter 11 racketeering enterprise by paying the salaries of the federal judges that are entrusted to uphold the law; the salaries of the U.S. Trustees who are paid to prevent corruption; the salaries of the U.S. Department of Justice attorneys who are paid to prosecute those committing the wrongful acts; the salaries of members of the U.S. Senate and House who have oversight responsibilities; and others, including the inspector generals in various government agencies who are expected to ferret out corruption.

THOUSANDS OF VICTIMS COMPLAINED; NO ONE ACTED!

Thousands of people complained to the Department of Justice and to the members of the U.S. Senate and House, pleading for relief from the judicial corruption in the Chapter 11 proceedings. Many sought relief by appeals and petitions to higher federal courts, including the U.S. Supreme Court.

Everyone who had a responsibility to intervene acted instead to cover up. They all protected the powerful judicial and legal fraternity. In addition to denying relief, federal judges rendered self-serving decisions holding that the judges, the U.S. Trustees, and the judge-appointed trustees were officers of the court and immune from the consequences of their acts. They impliedly held that the same protection enjoyed by despot dictators carries over to the federal judicial officials and those who act on their behalf.

Public pressure forced Congress to change the law in a facade purporting to halt the judicial corruption. Congress passed the Bankruptcy Reform Act of 1978, creating the office of the U.S. Trustee, charged with the responsibility of preventing fraud and corruption. These U.S. Trustees, usually attorneys, protected the system instead of the people.

The public outrage and pleas for help continued. Except for minor investigations and refusal to take corrective actions, Congress again refused to investigate the corruption. When the public pressure again reached a crescendo, Congress went through the motions, and changed the law, passing the Bankruptcy Act of 1986.[160] The legislative history of that Act

---

[160] Public Law 99-554.

addressed the past judicial misconduct in guarded terms, and gave the impression that the new legislation addressed the corruption. The legislative history[161] reemphasized that the U.S. Trustee was to prevent corruption:

> The U.S. Trustees were given important oversight and watchdog responsibilities to ensure honesty and fairness in the administration of bankruptcy cases and to prevent and ferret out fraud. ... in carrying out critical watchdog responsibilities, such as preventing fraud and other abuses and in monitoring debtors-in-possession in Chapter 11 reorganization cases ...

Congress knew that the rampant Chapter 11 judicial corruption was known to the Department of Justice; that the Justice Department attorneys protected their legal brethrens on the federal bench, the U.S. Trustees, judge-appointed trustees, and cooperating attorneys. Congress knew that the Justice Department misused Chapter 11 proceedings through their control over the U.S. Trustees, as it would do against me. The Chapter 11 judicial racketeering activities continued as before. The news media continued to keep the lid on the scandal, insuring its continuation, and insuring that their readers pay the awesome price.

EXERCISING CHAPTER 11 RIGHTS

This judicial racketeering activity was unknown to me when attorneys suggested that I seek relief in Chapter 11 from the actions taken by the Friedman law firm and the California judges that violated my civil and constitutional rights. Because I had a residence in Las Vegas, I filed the two cases in the Las Vegas federal bankruptcy court, at which time the cases were assigned to federal Judge Robert Jones.

The intent of filing the two Chapter 11 cases was to have federal judges establish my personal and property rights under the five divorce judgments and under federal law (and as subsequently provided by California statutory law). But instead of providing relief, Judge Jones protected the Friedman law firm and the California judges, just as other federal judges had done for the past four years. Jones refused to address the violations of the federally protected rights for which federal judges had jurisdiction and responsibilities. He ordered that I seek relief from the California judges—whose repeated civil and constitutional violations forced me to seek relief in Chapter 11.

---

[161] House Report No. 99-764.

However, Jones did provide some relief. During a hearing on September 11, 1987, Jones rendered an order refusing to accept jurisdiction over the two Chapter 11 cases, and ordered that he was abstaining from the cases. He delayed executing the order dismissing the two Chapter 11 cases for sixty days, ordering the removal of the lis pendens filed by the Friedman law firm. This permitted me to refinance mortgages that had come due, and eliminated the immediate need for having sought Chapter 11 relief.

I then obtained a firm refinancing commitment to pay off the $550,000 in mortgages that had come due,[162] and felt a sigh of relief that part of my problems were now addressed. My relief was short lived.

SECOND THOUGHTS

Someone apparently got to Jones after his September 11th decision. Subsequent events indicated these parties included federal judges and the Department of Justice.

The attorneys I hired to protect my assets did not notify me that there was a court hearing on September 28, 1987 for the personal bankruptcy case. This hearing was on a motion by a mortgage holder, Robil, Inc. of Hayward, California, to obtain relief from the automatic stay so that they could foreclose on several of my properties.[163] That hearing had to be limited to that issue, and to that personal Chapter 11 case. The corporate case containing the ten million dollars of properties was not on the calendar for any hearing, and therefore no orders could be rendered addressing that case. Further, since Judge Jones refused to accept jurisdiction at the earlier September 11th hearing, he had no jurisdiction to hear any new matters on either of the two cases, including the removal of the automatic stay on the personal case that was on the court calendar.

Unknown to me, one of the attorneys that I paid to protect my assets, Las Vegas attorney Joshua Landish, had been meeting secretly with my adversaries, and planned to cause the judicial seizure of my assets and subsequent liquidation. I had hired him, and paid him, to protect the assets. He was secretly doing the opposite, apparently with the knowledge of federal judges.

Immediately upon the start of the hearing on September 28, 1987, Landish requested Judge Jones to vacate his earlier order providing me relief. Landish requested that the court order seizure of my business, my home, my assets, in both the personal and the corporate cases. This sabotage of a client was com-

---

[162] Superior Home Loans-Robil, Inc., Hayward, California.
[163] Held by Superior Home Loans and Robil, Inc. of Hayward, California.

pounded by the gross violations of federal statutory and case laws, and fundamental constitutional rights to a hearing and due process protection of property laws.

OPENLY VIOLATING CONSTITUTIONAL AND STATUTORY SAFEGUARDS

Federal statutory law[164] required certain safeguards before judges can strip a person of his assets. There must be a noticed hearing, to permit the party to defend against the taking of the property. There must be legally recognized cause; a judge cannot simply seize a person's life's assets and leave the person penniless. At least, that's what the law says.

In Chapter 11, the only provisions for seizing a person's properties through appointment of a trustee (which is usually fatal to the business) are (a) gross mismanagement; or (b) major dishonesty. Then, additional protections exist in law: (a) creditors must be at risk; (b) the request must be made by a creditor; (c) it must be made in the interest of the estate and the creditors and not harm these interests; (d) the seizure must not violate the specifics and the intent to keep the debtor in possession.[165]

Not a single creditor was at risk. They were all protected by mortgages and substantial equity in the estate which exceeded five million dollars. All bills and all mortgages had been paid, except for the payoff of the mortgages that had come due. And the only reason they weren't paid off was that Friedman's California action and lis pendens prevented their refinancing.

I couldn't be accused of mismanagement. It was my efforts that increased the assets from zero value twenty years earlier, to ten million dollars at the time of filing for Chapter 11 relief. There was no dishonesty, and none was alleged. None of the creditors requested the appointment of a trustee; my own attorney made the request, and obviously in conspiracy with my powerful Justice Department and judicial adversaries.

"Stich is going to be very unhappy when he hears about this."

Disregarding the numerous protections under the Constitution and laws which supposedly constitute the backbone of our form of government, violating these many protections which he

---

[164] Title 11 U.S.C. Section 1104.

[165] Title 11 United States Code Section 1104, for instance, states in part:

§ 1104. Appointment of trustee or examiner.

  (a) At any time after the commencement of the case but before confirmation of a plan, on request of a party in interest or the United States Trustee, and after notice and a hearing, the court shall order the appointment of a trustee—

    (1) for cause, including fraud, dishonesty, incompetence, or gross mismanagement of the affairs of the debtor by current management, ...

lacked power to do, Judge Jones rendered two orders seizing my life's assets in the personal Chapter 11 case (which was on the calendar solely for consideration of removal of the automatic stay); and seizing the assets in the corporate Chapter 11 case.

The official court audio tape and reporter's transcript shows Federal judge Robert Jones saying, "Mr. Stich is going to be very unhappy when he hears about this."

Jones lacked jurisdiction to violate clear and settled statutory law. Further, he had ordered abstention, refusing to accept jurisdiction over the two cases at the prior hearing. That order had never been changed, and no hearing conducted to make the change or oppose any change.

Immediately after rendering the order seizing my assets, Jones was confronted with another problem. The five attorneys that were my adversaries at that hearing (including Landish), presented Judge Jones with the written order of abstention that Judge Jones rendered at the previous September 11th hearing. He now had to sign an order refusing to accept jurisdiction *after* he had just verbally rendered an order seizing the assets. Not constrained by protections in law, or fearful of charges of judicial corruption, Jones openly manipulated the court records. Judge Jones signed an order seizing the ten million dollars of properties on October 8, 1987, fraudulently stating in the order that the hearing occurred on October 8th. There was no hearing on that date, and the court records clearly showed that. Judge Jones openly lied.

The racketeering activities in Chapter 11 proceedings were so firmly embedded into the judicial process, and the higher federal courts had protected it for so long, that none of the conspirators felt any fear from their corrupt acts.

Landish withheld from me the information that Judge Jones ordered the seizure of my business, my properties, my bank accounts, all my assets. When I accidentally discovered that Judge Jones had rendered the order—but not knowing that it was Landish that requested the seizure, I instructed Landish to file a petition to remove the trustee. Landish agreed to do this, and then stalled, waiting for the appeal period to pass. Finally, I filed my own motion, and discharged Landish on November 10, 1987 for sabotaging my case.

Even though Friedman had no claim to my assets, in response to a motion by the Friedman group, Judge Jones transferred the Chapter 11 cases from Las Vegas to Oakland, California.

TURNING MY LIFE'S ASSETS OVER TO A KNOWN EMBEZZLER

Judge Jones appointed private trustee Charles Duck to seize my assets. Duck ordered me off my business properties that I had founded and developed over the past twenty years. He stopped making mortgage payments on most of the ten million dollars in properties. He then canceled my refinancing, which would have corrected the problem for which I had sought Chapter 11 relief. Duck diverted the $60,000 per month income to self-serving uses, the location of which is still unknown.

United States Trustee Anthony Sousa and United States Attorney Anthony Russoniello, both with offices at San Francisco, refused to investigate Duck's corrupt activities related to my cases. To do so risked exposing the Justice Department's two decades of corrupt activities relating to the air disaster scandals and the actions taken by their employer, the Justice Department, to silence me.

After Duck refused to make the mortgage payments, dozens of requests were filed by mortgage holders to foreclose on valuable properties. Federal Judge Edward Jellen approved the foreclosures, even though statutory and case law prohibited removing the automatic stay if the creditors were secured.

CORRUPTLY SEIZING MY ASSETS, AND THE VOIDING MY LAWFUL PROTECTIONS

After seizing my assets, Judge Jellen rendered unlawful and unconstitutional orders barring me from seeking relief from the seizure, and the subsequent liquidation of my assets and business. I properly ignored the unlawful order and filed oppositions and appeals. Jellen unfiled them, another unlawful act.

REWARDING THOSE WHO HELPED SEIZE MY ASSETS

When Landish submitted a claim for many thousands of dollars of attorney fees, after secretly sabotaging my legal defenses, Judge Jellen unfiled my objections to the claim, and approved payment of thousands of dollars to the attorney. Every party who had a role in the corrupt seizure of my assets were judicially protected, and I was barred from objecting. Jellen financially rewarded everyone who participated in destroying my assets, and who cooperated in the lawless and corrupt seizure of my assets. Any claim against me was automatically approved, and my objections unfiled.

The corrupt actions of the Friedman law firm that caused me years of grief, the void judgments of the California courts, were approved and paid, even though they were obviously unlawful and unconstitutional orders, rendered by judges lacking jurisdiction, and obvious void orders.

Jellen was insuring the success of one of the worst judicial scandals in U.S. history and the superimposed air disaster scandal.

I sought to circumvent these outrages by filing petitions with the United States District Courts at San Francisco, the United States Court of Appeals, and the United States Supreme Court. Every one of them protected the conspiracy and denied me relief. They aided and abetted the outrages that not only destroyed me, but continued the Chapter 11 corruption that destroyed others, and indirectly continued the air disaster corruption. Federal judges, including Judges Marilyn Petal and Charles Legge, among others, charged me with being a vexatious litigant for *seeking* relief from these outrages.

DESTROYING MY LIFE'S ASSETS

Several months after federal judges seized my assets and started liquidating them, other federal judges sentenced me to prison for having filed the actions seeking relief for myself and the future air disaster victims. While in prison, federal judge Edward Jellen (Oakland, California) commenced fire-sale liquidation of the assets. Charles Duck of Santa Rosa, California was appointed by the judges to seize and liquidate my assets. While I was in prison, Duck unlawfully ordered my mail diverted to his office and opened. These acts violated additional constitutional protections, for which I had no remedies in the stonewalling federal courts. The postmaster at Alamo, California, Dennis Hughes, later stated to me after I got out of prison that many federal officials came to the post office checking on my mail, and that he expected to be subpoenaed because of the irregularities in opening the mail.

CHAPTER 11 TURNED INTO A CRIMINAL ENTERPRISE BY FEDERAL JUDGES

The corrupt, illegal, and unconstitutional acts inflicted upon me extended the already-existing judicial corruption in Chapter 11 proceedings that had been known for years, and which had been protected by every known check and balance. People destroyed by the Chapter 11 judicial corruption complained to United States Attorney Russoniello at San Francisco since 1980. Instead of prosecuting and preventing the corruption by legal fraternity members on the bench and those acting as trustees and attorneys, Russoniello protected the scheme, enabling thousands of people to be stripped of their life's assets as the "bankruptcy club," as it became known, got rich on the corpses of Chapter 11 filings.

Most of the news media knew of the corruption, and refused to report it. In this manner they deceived their readers, some of whom lost their life's assets by being unaware of the judicial racketeering activities. Members of the Senate and House knew of the corruption, as their constituents pleaded with them to investigate. The legal fraternity in Congress protected the legal fraternity in the Chapter 11 corruption, and made possible the financial destruction of their own constituents.

There were a few exceptions. The *Indianapolis Star* published numerous reports on the Chapter 11 racketeering enterprises, commencing in 1987. As a result of the exposures, one federal Chapter 11 judge in Indianapolis was sentenced to prison. However, the system continued and flourished, and the maverick U.S. Trustee whose effort put the judge into prison was terminated by the Justice Department. The small-town paper, *Napa Sentinel* near San Francisco published articles on the relationship of the Chapter 11 racketeering and the covert government activities. The *Santa Rosa Press Democrat* ran articles on the Chapter 11 corruption. But the major newspapers, including the *San Francisco Chronicle*, the *Wall Street Journal*, and others, kept the scheme going by not reporting it to their readers.

The articles by the *Napa Sentinel* and the *Santa Rosa Press Democrat* linked the Chapter 11 corruption with numerous drug enterprises, including federal judges, judge-appointed trustees, the Department of Justice, and the CIA. This book doesn't go into that area, but raises tantalizing issues, especially in light of the revelations of government-protected drug activities by the CIA, overseas and domestically.

The articles commencing in April 1987 by the *Indianapolis Star* described the judicial corruption that most newspapers kept quiet. In a April 19, 1987 article the system was described as follows:

The [Chapter 11] court system is burdened with cronyism, political favors and conflicts of interest while a "club" of bankruptcy attorneys reaps the largest fees. ... Critics—including other lawyers—use the harshest terms. One described the system as incestuous. ... subverts the judicial system. ... Direct and indirect financial relationships between three judges and lawyers or others to whom they award fees. ... Forged, fraudulent or misleading documents ... fraud ... At stake is the fate of thousands of economically distressed companies and people as well as the financial interests of hundreds of thousands of companies and individuals ...

The Senate Permanent Subcommittee on Investigations, chaired by Senator Sam Nunn, conducted a limited investigation into the Justice Department's misuse of Chapter 11 against a small individually-owned company named Inslaw. The committee issued a report on the Inslaw matter, dated September 29, 1989. The report concluded that the Justice Department politicized Chapter 11, misused the U.S. Trustee program as a corruption tool, rather than for preventing corruption, and persecuted individual citizens in the process.

The report concluded that the Justice Department politicized the U.S. Trustee program to force the Inslaw company, with whom it did business, into bankruptcy. It did this by refusing to pay $1.5 million owed for work already performed. Then, when the refusal to pay legitimate bills forced the small company to seek relief in Chapter 11, the Justice Department misused its powers to liquidate the company in Chapter 7. The motivation appeared to be the desire by a high Justice Department official to get the rights to Inslaw's computer program which was used by the Justice Department and other law-enforcement agencies. That government official had ties with another company that wanted the Inslaw program, and sought to buy it at distress prices in Chapter 11 liquidation.

After Inslaw sued the Justice Department, and the bankruptcy judge ruled in favor of Inslaw and against the Justice Department, the Justice Department extended its obstruction of justice. The justice department terminated the appointment of the Chapter 11 judge that ruled against the Justice Department. The Justice Department attorneys then pressured the law firm defending Inslaw to fire the attorney handling the case. This was done. Next, the Justice Department got a federal judge to reverse earlier testimony that was unfavorable to the Justice Department.

The Senate report stated the U.S. Trustee was an office for political cronies and that it was misused against political enemies and others. The report described the pressures put on federal bankruptcy judges to render decisions desired by the Justice Department, and that the Chapter 11 and 13 proceedings were misused against individual citizens. The report described the removal of U.S. Trustees and federal bankruptcy judges if they did not render decisions wanted by Justice Department officials.

Director Thomas Stanton of the U.S. Trustees, employed by the Justice Department, reportedly pressured U.S. Trustees to ignore the corruption and protect those committing the criminal acts. The report agreed with the findings of U.S. Bankruptcy Judge George Bason, Jr. who blasted the Department of Justice in his decision, which stated in part:

[The Justice Department] took, converted, stole, [the plaintiff's property] by trickery, fraud and deceit. [made] an institutional decision ... at the highest level simply to ignore serious questions of ethical impropriety, made repeatedly by persons of unquestioned probity and integrity, and this failure constitutes bad faith, vexatiousness, wantonness and oppressiveness. ... engaged in outrageous, deceitful, fraudulent game of cat and mouse, demonstrating contempt for both the law and any principle of fair dealing.

The Senate report included articles appearing in *Barron's*[167] and *The American Lawyer*[168] which went into great details describing the Justice Department and U.S. Trustee misconduct. One article in *Barron's*[169] described the Justice Department's attempts to bankrupt and destroy Inslaw, misusing the U.S. Trustees and the bankruptcy judges to carry out their scheme. The article stated in part:

Justice officials proceeded to purposefully drive the small software company into bankruptcy, and then tried to push it into liquidation, engaging in an "outrageous, deceitful, fraudulent game of cat and mouse, demonstrating contempt for both the law and any principle of fair dealing. ... Ultimately, the series of "willful, wanton, and deceitful acts" led to a cover up. Bason called statements by top Justice Department officials "ludicrous ... incredible ... and totally unbelievable."

Some of the evidence against the department came from one of its own. During the course of the litigation, Anthony Pasciuto, deputy director of the department's Executive Office for United States Trustees, told ... how the Justice Department had pressured Trustee officers to liquidate [Inslaw]. Later, a superior confirmed Pasciuto's story. But at the trial, a horrified Pasciuto listened while his superior changed his testimony. Close to tears, he, too, recanted.

Judge Bason ... ordered Justice to pay INSLAW about $6.8 million in licensing fees and roughly another $1 million in legal fees. ... In November, Judge Bason rejected a Department of Justice motion to liquidate INSLAW. ... one month later, the Harvard Law School graduate and former law professor discovered that he was not being reappointed.

---

[167] March 21, and April 4, 1988.

[168] December 1987.

[169] March 21, 1988.

Describing how government officials hang in until the press drops the subject, and then continue the misconduct, the article stated:

> It seemed as if the controversy was winding down. ... It would follow a natural course in the press, and then fade from view. Inslaw would become another shocking event that slinks off into obscurity: Someone occasionally might dimly remember and idly ask, "What ever did happen to Bill Hamilton and those Inslaw people? A real shame ... I heard the judge was back teaching law somewhere..."

The *Barron* article described the efforts of Anthony Pasciuto, a Department of Justice insider, who blew the whistle on the Justice Department's misuse of this powerful federal agency against Inslaw and his small company:

> ... in an interview with *Barron's* ... Pasciuto explained how the Justice Department blacklisted Inslaw. It was a tale that involved two U.S. trustees, a federal judge who told two versions of the same story, and a Justice Department that routinely refused to pay certain suppliers.
>
> Pattern of harassment [by the Justice Department] that helped drive Inslaw into Chapter 11. ... the Justice Department was trying to starve Inslaw. They didn't just push to bankrupt the software firm, ... they wanted to liquidate it, converting it from Chapter 11 to Chapter 7, as soon as possible. Why?
>
> Tony Pasciuto [said] that his boss, Thomas Stanton, director of the Justice Department's Executive Office for U.S. Trustees, was pressuring the federal trustee overseeing the Inslaw case, William White, to liquidate Inslaw.
>
> ... Cornelius Blackshear, the U.S. Trustee in New York at the time of Inslaw's Chapter 11 filing, knew all about Stanton's plan. Pasciuto said that Judge Blackshear had repeated this tale of pressure in the presence of United States Court of Appeals Judge Lawrence Pierce in the judge's chambers in Foley Square in New York.
>
> Blackshear met with a Justice Department representative, and signed a sworn affidavit, recanting, and said that he had confused Inslaw with another case—United Press International, which had also been involved in bankruptcy proceedings in Judge Bason's court.
>
> Cornelius Blackshear left his position as United States Trustee and became a United States bankruptcy judge the

following fall.[170]

Thomas Stanton, the Director of the U.S. Trustee program in the Department of Justice, until his dismissal in November 1989, was described as misusing his position in pressure tactics corrupting the federal trustee program.

In a following article on April 4, 1988, *Barron's* described the Rogue Justice in the Justice Department. The article described the practice of hiring political appointees as attorneys in the Justice Department, giving them career status, and have them serve as "moles" in the next administration. In this position they would then report to the former administration what the next administration was doing.

> They were instead a hostile crew, inspired apparently by old scores and private interests. Whether carefully organized or spontaneously launched, the attack was successful—for a while, anyway. When the principals and the department were suddenly in danger of exposure, ... the cover-up spread out to embrace the Justice Department bureaucrats, the IRS, ... "They circled their wagons," Judge Bason wrote. The defense became an offense, and an attorney, a Justice Department whistle-blower, and the judge himself all lost their jobs.
>
> The move to keep the U.S. Trustee program was flagrantly political. "It was a way of getting cronies into office. There would be 50 or 60 positions to be filled." Stanton, the director of the Trustee program, seemed well-protected within Justice. This former Pasciuto colleague adds: "It was always puzzling to me how [Stanton] got away with what he got away with. He'd do things that were blatantly wrong and no one would question him—its kind of scary." Another former employee confirms. "Irrespective of the law, or anything, if Stanton wanted something, he had the ear of the right people at the highest level—straight from Burns to Meese. If he could not get what he needed, he went to Burns."
>
> Justice Department bonuses [were] awarded after the trial was over. ... "The whole thing smacks of a police state. This case scares the hell out of me." ... "Scary" is the word most often used by victims of the Inslaw affair. They are angry, but they also can't quite believe it happened. That the Justice Department could engage in a vendetta that

---

[170] For those who cooperate with the Justice Department, federal judgeship positions are the carrot.

would end the career of a federal judge, bankrupt a company, force a partner out of his law firm, cause another federal judge to recant under oath, and reach down and wreck the career of a 21-year government service employee—that's the stuff of a spy novel set, one would hope, in another country.

COVERUP BY SENATORS NUNN AND HOLLINGS

After issuing the report, the Senate committee did nothing to correct the Justice Department's Chapter 11 corruption. In late 1989 I had brought to Senator Nunn's attention the Justice Department's corrupt misuse of Chapter 11 to silence my exposure of the air disaster scandal. He refused to answer. I contacted at the same time Senator Ernest Hollings, Chairman of the Committee on Commerce, Science, and Transportation. He was responsible to investigate and correct air safety problems, and certainly the criminal acts I brought to his attention. Instead of meeting his responsibilities as a United States Senator and under various criminal laws, he covered up, making possible some of the nation's worst air tragedies. In a December 1, 1989 reply to my letter describing the air disaster and Chapter 11 corruption, Hollings' canned reply stated, "Many thanks for your recent letter on aviation safety and your allegations of a cover-up. As before, my primary concern in aviation is ensuring safety for the traveling public." The non-responsive response constituted criminal coverup.

An extensive article on the Justice Department and Inslaw corruption appeared in *The Recorder*, a legal newspaper published in San Francisco, on February 5, 1990. The article criticized Michael Shaheen, Jr. head of the Justice Department's Office of Professional Responsibility, for coverup on the Inslaw and other internal irregularities. The article described criticism by the Senate, judges, and others, of the misuse by attorneys of the Justice Department in their vendetta against Inslaw.

The Senate called into question Shaheen's coverup of the Inslaw and other internal problems. Federal inspector generals in other government departments are nominated by the president and confirmed by the Senate. But the article described Shaheen's employment by the U.S. Attorney General under whom the misconduct was rampant, and that Shaheen's employment can be terminated at any time. Obviously, the position is useless if the person being investigated can terminate the person conducting the investigation.

The article described federal judge George Bason's characterization of the Justice Department in the Inslaw matter as "outrageous, deceitful, fraudulent."

Bennett Gershman, professor at New York's Pace University School of Law and author of *Prosecutorial Misconduct*, was quoted as stating "It is a joke to say Justice polices itself."

BRIEF NEWS COVERAGE AND THEN SILENCE

A shocking scandal gets brief news coverage, and then the press drops it. The Chapter 11 corruption destroys thousands of people while enriching those committing the wrongful acts, and continues uncorrected. Congressional scandals and government abuses continue, stripping the public of billions of dollars to support the government-funded corruption. Saddled with billions, if not trillions, in debt arising from open corruption, the public does nothing.

Furnishing more support for the Chapter 11 corruption, a December 1987 article in *The American Lawyer* substantiated the articles in *Barron's* and what the Senate committee discovered:

> No sooner had the Justice Department awarded INSLAW a $10 million contract than things began to go wrong. Hamilton couldn't understand why. Suddenly INSLAW's finances were in shambles. By February 7, 1985, the government had withheld payments on $1.77 million in costs and fees. INSLAW, the market leader, filed for bankruptcy. Hamilton says he was mystified. How could everything he had built fall apart so fast—and with no explanation? [Inslaw said] "I think, in a perverse way, I was ... slow to catch on. I feel silly. I wasn't paranoid enough."
>
> A story of government conniving and manipulation ... and in Elliot Richardson's words, "complemented and allowed to run its course by ill will at the higher level," meaning former deputy attorney general Jensen. [Now a federal judge at San Francisco.]

The Senate report and the investigative report by the magazine further supported my observations that the attorneys at the Justice Department were fully capable of misusing the government facilities to engineer the sham California action against me; and then manipulate the federal judges to carry out the scheme.

EXAMPLES OF OTHER VICTIMS

In one case the Department of Justice forced a publishing company—exposing government misconduct—into bankruptcy. The companies were set up for the purpose of spreading political ideas, and the Justice Department attorneys did not like the exposures. Presidential candidate Lyndon LaRouche informed the public via the publications, *Campaigner Publications, Caucus Distributors,* and *Fushion Energy Foundation.*

The Justice Department obtained an ex parte order, without a hearing, forcing the companies into bankruptcy. The companies argued that the law required three parties to force a person or company into bankruptcy, and sought to have the seizure overturned, without success. The Justice Department used its control over the U.S. and private trustees, and federal judges, and forced the company into a Chapter 7 liquidation.

Then, the Justice Department secured indictment of LaRouche and six associates for mail fraud. The basis for the criminal charge was that the companies did not pay earlier loans. LaRouche argued that the loans could not be paid back because the Justice Department forced the company into bankruptcy. The Justice Department attorneys obtained a fifteen year prison term for the 67-year-old LaRouche, which amounted to a literal death sentence.

Fortunately, LaRouche had friends outside of prison willing to fight for him. While LaRouche and his associates were in prison, federal Judge Martin Bostetter ruled in a 106-page decision on October 25, 1989 that the Justice Department's seizure of the assets and the involuntary bankruptcy action were illegal and a fraud upon the court.

ANOTHER VICTIM

In another case, the husband-and-wife publishing house of *Stein & Day* was induced by attorneys to seek relief in Chapter 11 when a major customer refused to pay a large bill owed to them. Their 26-year old business had run a small but respectable operation that brought out about 100 books a year. Sol Stein, the publisher, encountered a temporary financial setback due to the dispute with a distributor. Their business was good and they were otherwise financially strong.

Instead of providing time to pay his bills, the system, in clear violation of Chapter 11 intent and specifics, seized his assets, and set the wheels in motion to destroy the assets while the attorneys feasted. The husband-and-wife team experienced corruption on a level that if committed by a citizen would result in criminal prosecution. Stein lost everything he accumulated for the past three decades. Incensed, Sol Stein wrote about the judicial Chapter 11 corruption in the book, *A Feast for Lawyers,* subtitled *Inside Chapter 11: An Exposé.* Stein described the Chapter 11 courts as inhabited by hacks, vultures and scoundrels who feed on productive companies and people. The corruption caused the loss of his life's savings, his business, and his home.

PUBLIC PRESSURES REQUIRED APPROPRIATE RHETORIC

The Chapter 11 corruption was rampant in the Ninth Circuit at San Francisco, and possibly worse than in any other part of the United States. Thousands of victimized people sought relief from the higher federal courts; from U.S. Attorney Russoniello in San Francisco; from members of the Senate and House, with no success. United States Trustee Anthony Sousa—an employee of the same Justice Department who protected and misused the Chapter 11 racketeering activities—arrived in the San Francisco area at the end of 1988, with the responsibility to prevent corruption. After looking at only a small portion of the Chapter 11 cases, and before he even got to my case, Sousa's chief investigator, Gregg Eichler, uncovered massive corruption, reflecting what I had been reported for two years; that judge-appointed trustee Charles Duck and the judges were engaged in massive corruption that had financially destroyed thousands of people in gross violation of federal statutory law.

"Largest embezzlement ever ..."

After Eichler examined only a few of the cases handled by Duck, his boss, Sousa, made a report to the Director of the U.S. Trustee program, Thomas Stanton (who had himself misused the Chapter 11 program). Referring to Duck, Stanton stated in a press release: "We believe this is the largest embezzlement ever charged against a court-appointed bankruptcy trustee." Stanton showed shock at corruption that was partly of his own making; he jumped on the publicity bandwagon.

Duck's corruption was known for years to the federal judges, who, by collusion, protected Duck. Duck could not have operated without the aid and protection of the federal judges. No actions were taken by the U.S. Trustee, or the U.S. Attorney, against the higher ups, the judicial Godfathers, federal judges. Identifying Duck was similar to arresting drug peddlers on the street while letting powerful drug lords go scot free; then stating the crime was solved.

SLAPPING THE WRIST IN THE NATION'S WORST CHAPTER 11 CORRUPTION

The U.S. Attorney at San Francisco, Joseph Russoniello, deliberately watered down the charges against Duck. Instead of charging Duck with hundreds of charges for the many millions of dollars of assets he destroyed and embezzled, the Department of Justice only charged Duck with two counts.

Since 1975 the Department of Justice protected Duck when citizens pleaded with U.S. Attorney Russoniello to provide them relief. In 1986 the Department of Justice refused to indict Charles Duck during the Centennial Savings and Loan scandal.

After U.S. Trustee Sousa was forced to removed Duck from the Chapter 11 cases, including mine, Sousa then appointed another trustee over my cases, Jerome Robertson. This was done even though Sousa knew that Judge Jones' order seizing my assets occurred under corrupt conditions, and that as a matter of law, the orders seizing my assets were void.

REFUSING TO TURN OVER RECORDS OF EMBEZZLEMENT

Sousa instructed Duck to turn over the records on my cases to the next trustee. Duck refused to do so, and no efforts were made to make him comply. There appeared to be at least a million dollars missing from my cases, and nothing was done to charge Duck with theft. To have done so would have drawn attention to the judicial misconduct, and eventually, to the awesome air disaster scandal. Duck refused to turn over the records, claiming a Fifth Amendment right to avoid self-incrimination.[170] The Justice Department protected Duck's position, and did not seek to prosecute Duck for looting my estates.

Ironically, after Duck was exposed as engaged in the nation's worst Chapter 11 embezzlement, Duck was defended by former assistant U.S. Attorney, Peter Robinson. Robinson was an Assistant U.S. Attorney in the San Francisco office from 1984 through 1988, and surely knew of Duck's corrupt activities.

Although Duck refused to turn over the records, his attorney Peter Robinson, argued before U.S. district judge Stanley Wiegel[171] that his client cooperated extensively with the U.S. trustee.

EMBEZZLER PROTECTED BY DEPARTMENT OF JUSTICE

The Justice Department acted to limit the fallout from the newspaper exposure of Duck's corrupt activities. They sought to protect their own coverup and protect the judicial hierarchy that made Duck's activities possible. U.S. Attorney Russoniello announced to the press on September 25, 1989 Justice Department approval of a plea-bargain with Duck and his attorney. Duck's attorney, Peter Robinson, stated to the press[172] that Duck agreed to cooperate with authorities as part of a plea bargain to include his guilty pleas. In exchange, federal prosecutors would seek a short jail term for Duck.

---

[170] *The Recorder*, May 15, 1989.

[171] One of the judges covering up for the FAA and NTSB misconduct in my early federal cases.

[172] *San Ramon Times*, September 28, 1989.

Duck paid Robinson an initial legal fee of $175,000, much or all of it coming from the assets of my estates that the judges unlawfully seized with Duck's assistance. What a system! Robinson was now defending Duck, something similar to Robinson's de facto protection when Robinson was an Assistant U.S. Attorney, and did nothing when dozens of people pleaded with the Justice Department to do something about the Chapter 11 racketeering activities.

The Department of Justice protected Duck and the attorneys and judges that constituted the Chapter 11 racketeering enterprises. In this way the investigation halted before it reached the higher ups.

Immediately after the U.S. Attorney announced the plea bargain, Duck and his attorney repeatedly stated that no one else was involved, as if they were protecting higher ups. These repeated assurances were quoted in the press:

> No one else really knew what he was doing. Duck was on his own on this. He offered to take a polygraph test because the FBI had questions about others being involved. They're satisfied no one else was involved.[173]

Entering a plea bargain before completing the investigating into Duck's criminal acts, including the crimes against me, had one obvious intent. Protect Duck from further criminal charges as it relates to the misuse of the Chapter 11 system against me by the Justice Department and federal judges.

Over two million dollars embezzlement were alleged in just the few cases investigated. But this was only a fraction of the money lost by those swindled in the Duck cases. For every thousand dollars Duck looted, there was probably a hundred times that much in equities that people lost. Tens of millions of dollars of assets of private citizens were destroyed, and their owners put into a state of poverty. Now the system grouped together to protect one of their own.

The Justice Department and the United States Trustee made no effort to look for the million dollars plus missing from my estate. They made no effort to get the records of my estate from Duck. They protected Duck against the criminal acts committed in my estate, probably to cover up for the Justice Department and judicial acts taken against me through Duck.

---

[173] *San Ramon Times*, September 28, 1989.

A revealing newspaper article in the *Santa Rosa Press Democrat* on February 1, 1990 stated that on July 21, 1989, two days before the FBI started to investigate the criminal acts by Duck, initially uncovered by U.S. Trustee Sousa, that the Justice Department at San Francisco signed a plea bargain agreement with Duck providing for a light prison sentence, which then halted any further FBI investigation.

JUSTICE DEPARTMENT DEFENDED THE CRIMINAL ACTIVITIES

I filed several federal law suits[174] against Duck and the law firm of Goldberg, Stinnett, and MacDonald (whose assistance made Duck's activities possible), and against the subsequent trustee, Jerome Robertson, who continued to loot my estate. The civil action addressed the criminal acts that Duck already admitted to perpetrating on other estates. Federal judges then dismissed every action I filed. In one action,[175] Judge Eugene Lynch ordered the action unfiled.[176] There is no provision in law for unfiling an action. In another action filed in the U.S. District Court in the District of Columbia (No. C 89-2974) Judge Stanley Sporkin dismissed the action against Duck without a hearing, violating the mandatory right to a hearing before dismissing an action, violating the bar to a dismissal if federal causes of action are stated.

The Department of Justice intervened to protect Duck in other actions I filed. An action that I filed against Duck in the Superior Court of the State of California in Alameda County at Oakland, California, was wrongfully dismissed by federal judge Edward Jellen, without a hearing. The system was protecting itself from one of the worst judicial scandals in the nation's history.

Additionally, Judge Jellen ordered that my assets, that were corruptly seized and turned over to Charley Duck, be used to pay the legal fees to defend Duck and his retained San Francisco law firm of Goldberg, Stinnett, and MacDonald. By March 1990 Jellen ordered over a quarter million dollars taken from my assets to pay legal fees solely to protect the trustees and their law firm from their activities in destroying my illegally-seized assets, and these legal fees were rapidly accelerating. The intent was to totally destroy all my assets. Simultaneously, they deprived me of funds from my own assets to pay dental

---

[174] Jerome Robertson of Los Altos, California.

[175] *Stich v. Charles Duck, Trustee, Merle C. Meyers, Goldberg, Stinnett & MacDonald, Does 1 through 100, Defendants.* C-89-150-Misc EFL

[176] October 3, 1989.

and medical bills.

Simultaneously, I had no funds to hire legal counsel, and had to represent myself in a corrupt judicial system that had me stonewalled while it was misused to criminally destroy all vestiges of constitutionally protected rights. Indirectly, this corruption affection everyone in the United States.

JUDICIAL HOLDING THAT THE CRIMINAL, CHARLES DUCK, WAS AN OFFICER OF THE COURT, AND IMMUNE FROM LIABILITY TO THE PUBLIC HE DEFRAUDED

Federal judges of the Ninth Circuit at San Francisco held that the private trustees, including Duck who committed the nation's worst Chapter 11 corruption, were officers of the court, and were therefore immune from liability! In effect, the federal judges held that federal judges and those acting on their behalf could inflict any type of civil, constitutional and criminal act upon the public, and the public had no remedy!

One of the many people I encountered who was victimized by the judicial corruption was Thomas Read of Connecticut. Read had not sought relief in Chapter 11, but was affected by Charles Duck, and the federal judges seeking to protect the admitted embezzler. Read obtained a Connecticut judgment against Duck. Bankruptcy Judge Alan Jaroslovsky of Santa Rosa, who had protected Duck's criminal activities, issued an injunction forever barring Read from enforcing the judgment. Read argued that the injunctive order exceeded the judge's authority. Read filed an appeal with the Ninth Circuit Bankruptcy Appellate Panel (composed of Chapter 11 judges!). The appellate panel rendered a published decision[177] protecting Duck:

> The courts have recognized that "judicial immunity not only protects judges against suit from acts done within their jurisdiction, but also spreads outward to shield related public servants, including trustees in bankruptcy ...." ... This circuit has adopted a ... rationale stating that a trustee or an official acting under the authority of the bankruptcy judge is entitled to derived judicial immunity because he is performing an integral part of the judicial process. ... a trustee, who obtains court approval for actions under the supervision of the bankruptcy judge, is entitled to derived immunity. ... It is well settled that the trustee in bankruptcy is an officer of the appointing court. Courts other than the appointing court have no jurisdiction to entertain suits against the trustee, without leave from the appointing

---

[177] September 27, 1989.

court, for acts done in an official capacity and within his authority as an officer of the court. ... It is ... axiomatic that the Trustee, "as a trustee in bankruptcy [and] as an official acting under the authority of the bankruptcy judge, is entitled to derived judicial immunity because he is performing an integral part of the judicial process. ... Sound policy also mandates immunizing the trustee. The possibility that we would hold trustees personally liable for judgments rendered against them in their representative capacity would invariably lessen the vigor with which trustees pursue their obligations. Immunity is essential because, as Judge Learned Hand noted, "to submit all officials, the innocent as well as the guilty, to the burden of a trial and to the inevitable danger of its outcome, would dampen the ardor of all but the most resolute, or the most irresponsible, in the unflinching discharge of their duties. ... Accordingly, we hold that the trustee [Charles Duck], acting under the authority of the court, is entitled to derived judicial immunity.

The federal judges embraced Duck; called him one of their own, an officer of the court; and then held he could not be sued by the public that was swindled and destroy by Duck's criminal acts, made possible by the judicial corruption. What a system!

Duck (and others like him) financially ruined thousands of people who exercised the relief promised by Chapter 11. Instead of getting relief, this "officer of the court" misused the federal judiciary, with the aid and comfort of judges at all levels of the federal judiciary, including the U.S. Supreme Court. This same brotherhood holds that the trustee is immune from suit, and that the defrauded citizens have no remedy in law!

AGAIN PUTTING THE SUPREME COURT JUSTICES ON NOTICE

I sought relief from the justices of the United States Supreme Court for two years prior to Duck's exposure as a criminal in Chapter 11 proceedings, which others had done earlier, without obtaining relief. I filed several petitions for writ of certiorari with the U.S. Supreme Court, including one in November 1989. The Supreme Court Justices, who had supervisory responsibilities over lower federal courts, including the criminal acts of Charles Duck, repeatedly stonewalled my attempts to get relief available in law. In this November filing the Justices refused to accept the forty booklet-bound petitions, claiming the space between the lines on two last-page exhibits did not meet the criteria. (The space was less than provided by Rules of Court.) This was a minor deviation that is often accepted by the Court, especially by a pro se filing that is not held to the rigid requirements of those submitted by attorneys. Further, the all allegations of judicial corruption were so serious that the Justices of the Supreme Court had responsibility to act irregardless of how the message was conveyed.

The gravity of the allegations stated in the petition, the judicial subversive activities, the pattern of judicial misconduct in the Supreme Court's area of supervisory responsibilities, the obvious violations of criminal statutes by federal judges and people acting under color of federal law, invoked mandatory responsibilities of the justices.

JUSTICE DEPARTMENT STONEWALLING

The Justice Department used Duck in the scheme to seize my assets; they could not risk prosecuting Duck and having the air disaster scandal come to the surface. They could not risk having the seven years of persecution against me come to the surface. If it did, powerful people within the United States would be implicated. The entire judicial system rallied to protect their own corruption.

WASHINGTON PRESSURE TO BLOCK THE CHAPTER 11 JUDICIAL CORRUPTION

As the judicial investigation got closer to federal judges, Washington reduced the funding necessary to continue the investigations. The Justice Department fired U.S. Trustees who fingered the judges, including U.S. Trustee Kevin McCarthy of Indianapolis. McCarthy's investigation and prosecution of Chapter 11 corruption caused a federal Chapter 11 judge to be imprisoned. Assistant U.S. Trustee Gregg Eichler, who was responsible for uncovering part of the misconduct committed by Charles Duck, and whose continued investigation threatened to expose federal judges, the entire federal judiciary, and the Justice Department, was then fired as of January 24, 1990. In this manner, federal investigations into federal criminal activities against the public are blocked.

PROTECTION OF THE SCANDALOUS JUDICIAL RACKETEERING ACTIVITIES BY EVERY LEVEL OF THE FEDERAL JUDICIARY

The civil and constitutional violations associated with the seizure of my assets raised mandatory relief remedies when they were stated in federal appeals and petitions for relief. Commencing in January 1988, and continuing for the next two years, I filed over 20 petitions, appeals, requests for relief, with the United States Court of Appeals at San Francisco, and then with the United States Supreme Court. Every single request was denied, as the federal judges protected the judicial scandal. Typical of one response was the October 3, 1989 order by federal judge Eugene Lynch, which protected Duck. Judge

Lynch's order stated that my complaint against Duck, which raised the same wrongful acts in a civil action that the Justice Department raised in the criminal complaint, "raises fantastic and bizarre claims," and that Duck is "not required to answer the complaint."

The Justices of the U.S. Supreme Court were heavily implicated in this judicial scandal. They covered up for the FAA and NTSB corruption following my petitions for certiorari after the Ninth Circuit dismissed the actions. The Justices knew of the judicial corruption in their areas of supervisory responsibilities; they knew that thousands of people were being destroyed in the judicial scheme. Every time I filed a petition for certiorari with the Supreme Court relating to the misconduct, including that committed by Duck, the Supreme Court justices protected those committing the outrages, and refused to hear the petition. They did the same with my earlier petitions addressing the air disaster corruption. In both cases unsuspecting people paid the price for the Supreme Court's coverup.

The responsibilities of the U.S. Supreme Court justices to act arose from several areas, including their supervisory responsibilities over the lower federal courts. (Rules of the Supreme Court Rule 17.)

In early-1989, following several earlier petitions to the Supreme Court, I filed a motion for emergency relief from the criminal and constitutional violations committed by trustee Charles Duck and federal judges. The Supreme Court Justices protected the criminal acts in their areas of responsibilities:

The application for a stay in the above-entitled case [88-1452] has been presented to Justice O'Connor, who on March 23, 1989 endorsed thereon the following:

"Denied
Sandra D.O'Connor
3/23/89"

TWA wreckage on Staten Island, following UAL DC-8 ramming.

Stephen Baltz (R), who perished in the UAL DC-8 crash into
New York City, and one of many victimized in the continuing
air disaster corruption.

MORE CONGRESSIONAL COVERUP—or, what else is new.
Congress knew of this corruption, and acted to protect the
criminal acts, which are criminal acts of themselves. Besides
the frantic pleas to members of the Senate and House made by
thousands of people, I also made them aware of the corruption
in their area of Congressional oversight. Hundreds of letters
offering evidence, and making grave charges of hard-core

corruption related to a continuing series of air disasters, and warning of those that were to repeatedly follow. In 1988 I sent by certified mail to every Senator in the United States, and to most representatives, two petitions 18-pages in length, detailing the pattern of specific corrupt acts directly related to the air disasters; the misuse of government agencies to silence me; and making it obvious that hundreds and eventually thousands of others would experience the same brutal fate that others had experienced.

Despite these serious charges by a person who formerly held the most sensitive air safety position within the United States (United's crash-plagued programs), no person in any position of authority had the moral or legal right to ignore the charges. But they did do so. And with their criminal coverup, the deaths of many others were allowed to occur. Despite the gravity of the allegations, and the harm to people throughout the United States, not a single Senator or Representative answered.

VICTIMS OF THE CORRUPTION

During my several years of fighting with the bankruptcy club and federal courts, I came upon dozens of people victimized by Chapter 11 ring members. The stories were outrageous and sad. These outrages committed by people misusing the United States government could not happen if the news media met its obligations to expose government corruption for which they have been given extra-ordinary First Amendment protections.

Among the people I met were Bob and Virginia McCullough of Sunol, California, who lost considerable money to the Chapter 11 scheme. We, and several others, worked together to expose the vicious federal judicial corruption. Ginger wrote a seven-page letter to the Department of Justice, with copies to key members of Congress and government agencies,[178] describing part of the Chapter 11 corruption, part of which stated:

On August 15, 1989 Monica Spina-Forni, my husband and I, met with Assistant U.S. Attorney Mike Howard for almost four hours. Together we supplied him several large boxes full of documentation on several serious cases. Mr. Howard had an assistant present, whom he identified as a paralegal named Lynn Katz. Both of them listened intently and leafed through the files taking notes as they went. When we were through talking about the cases, Mr. Howard said that these

---

[178] Including California Senators Alan Cranston and Pete Wilson, and Representative Pete Stark.

were extremely serious cases and "the biggest civil and criminal racketeering cases I have seen in 22 years with the department." He picked up the phone and ordered the locks on his office door changed, and stated that he would have all the material copied and returned. He turned to Ms. Katz and told her that he wanted the material placed in the safe before closing. He then went on to say that most of the cases involved Bank of America and he told us that the first thing the bank would do was to "put several hundred attorneys against one or two attorneys from the justice department; then, if that fails they will begin a series of stalling tactics; and, if that is not successful, it could get violent."

He also showed us some very unsettling pictures he indicated were pictures of people that some of his adversaries thought were his witnesses. One picture was of a woman who had been burned alive; there was very little of her left, and it was horrifying to see. Another picture was of a black man whose brains had been spread out over a floor. But the third picture was absolutely sickening—a small boy, no more than eight years of age, lay on a bed clutching a teddy bear as his collection of baseball cards were scattered about the two of them. He could have been sleeping peacefully, but his throat had been split ear to ear and blood covered his bed clothes and the bedding. As we handed the pictures back, Mike Howard was telling us that he had to carry guns with him everywhere he went.

As we left, he shook our hand and told us that we could be assured that his office would pursue this, and that we would be hearing from him so he could set up a meeting with John Lyons, who was handling the criminal investigation of Charles Duck.

In later phone conversations he indicated that he would be addressing a letter to Monica Forni and to me, requesting that we gather as much information on Bank of America officials as we could, and that we continue to supply his office with information. The letters never came; the files were never copied, and we called to inquire about the delay.

When I called him at the end of the week and asked if the government was going to pursue any of the cases we had presented to him, he became very angry, and said that he was tired of people asking when the indictments on Charles Duck were going to come down. He said that he had not copied any of the material, and that the justice department was not going to do anything with any of it. ... The pictures he showed to us that day still haunt both my husband and myself. The little boy could have been one of our children. At this point, with Mr. Howard's sudden about face and antagonistic attitude, we are wondering if the whole scenario that day in his office was simply a veiled threat to silence our demands for justice.

Our family has endured economic starvation, crooked public servants, conflicted judges, blackmail, extortion, slavery to the bankruptcy system, the absolute denial of our civil rights and bomb threats phoned to our home.

Another person I met who had been swindled by the Chapter 11 club was Sandy Brick, who I learned to respect very highly. Sandy engaged in a public-spirited campaign for several years to expose this Chapter 11 judicial racket. Sandy, and her husband (who was 75 years old when I met them), lost their restaurant business in Northern California, lost their 7500 square-foot home, and lost everything they accumulated for their retirement.

They were induced by an attorney to file Chapter 11 to get extra time to pay a relatively minor restaurant improvement loan upon which the Bank of America was seeking to foreclose. The same attorney then jumped over to the other side, represented the trustee who stood to gain heavily by the liquidation of the estate the Brick's hired legal counsel to protect via the Chapter 11 proceedings.

Instead of relief, the pattern of the Chapter 11 judicial racketeers was to swoop down upon those duped into filing for the relief promised by Congress; their assets were unlawfully seized and systematically destroyed. The lawyers, the judge appointed trustees, the covert relationships with federal judges, made financial killings. It was a feast for the Chapter 11 club.

The Chapter 11 judicial gang acted like a pack of wild animals pouncing upon those people who had innocently wandered into their private territory—Chapter 11. The trustees milked the assets for everything they could before discarding the corpse of the estate. The bricks lost everything after being duped into exercising Congressional statutory relief.

Sandy became an advocate to expose the rampant judicial corruption. She tracked down chains of title to properties in which members of the Chapter 11 club had hidden interests. Sandy described the practice where federal judges divided the cases among the judge-appointed trustees, and the covert relationships in which the spoils would be divided.

Sandy took an interest in my case, and told of examining bank records and discovering that Duck had sequestered $400,000 of my funds into a secret bank account, and then submitted records to the court omitting these funds, as if they did not exist.

During one visit,[179] Sandy told me of the many times that she had been in Chapter 11 court proceedings, and saw elderly people, widows, leave the court, sobbing after the club seized their life's assets. Many of these people had only a partial financial problem when they exercised Chapter 11 remedies and need not have filed Chapter 11 to retain most of their assets. They were deceived by government-funded corruption.

Sandy worked to expose the Chapter 11 gang, without compensation, submitting her findings to U.S. Trustee Anthony Sousa, who had a paid staff of government employees doing very little if anything to prevent the corruption for which they were paid. In my case Sousa aided and abetted the actions taken against me, supporting the unlawful seizure, blocking my defenses, using his office to protect the criminals in Chapter 11 and in the air disaster scandal. He protected those who seized and looted my assets. He became an unindicted accomplice.

The Justice Department duplicated the same stonewalling tactics to cover up and not prosecute the Chapter 11 corruption as they used in the savings and loan, the HUD scandals, and the air disaster scandal. Justice Department spokesman David Runkel stated[180] that Attorney General Dick Thornburgh opposed congressional efforts to get him to name a special prosecutor to investigate HUD. In the Chapter 11 corruption they protected Duck and the judges who made Duck's conduct possible, for many years, and than when the lid couldn't be kept on Duck's massive embezzlement, the Justice Department attorneys charged him only with two relatively minor counts.

It would be difficult to find any private racketeering enterprise that has caused, or made possible, the harm inflicted upon the public, that the Justice Department coverup made possible.

PROTECTION OF BANKRUPTCY SCANDAL BY NEWS MEDIA, PARALLELING THEIR COVERUP OF THE AIR DISASTER CORRUPTION

When news articles did appear, the corruption was described as the worst corruption in the federal Chapter 11 system. Obviously Duck did not operate in a vacuum, and needed the protection of federal judges to commit his dirty work. The press made this clear, and then before the higher ups could be fingered, the press clamped the lid on the scandal. I notified over a dozen magazines and newspapers of the misconduct[181] two years before the Chapter 11 was exposed, and they kept it quiet. They continued to keep it quiet after a few papers

---

[179] October 28, 1989.

[180] On October 27, 1989; *Associated Press* October 29, 1989.

[181] During 1988 and 1989.

exposed the scandal as one of the nation's worst, and certainly one of the most arrogant. Just as in the air disaster scandal, the news media covered up, making possible the harm suffered by others. Reporter Linda Martin of the *San Francisco Examiner* spent over two months investigating the Chapter 11 corruption, interviewing many of those victimized by the "bankruptcy club," including Virginia McCullough and Sandy Brick (who offered her hard evidence of the judicial scandal). During the end of January 1990 Ms. Martin revealed to Mrs. McCullough that her paper was not going to print the story. In this manner the *Examiner* subjected their own readers to great harm that they could have prevented by exercising their First Amendment responsibilities to report government corruption.

CIRCLE THE JUDICIAL WAGONS

Preparing to protect themselves, the Ninth Circuit Court of Appeals rendered a judgment[182] in the midst of this judicial scandal, holding that irregardless of criminal conduct committed against the public, the public had no remedy against the judges, or anyone acting with the judges.

Earlier Supreme Court decisions held in *Stump v. Sparkman*,[183] that a judge can deliberately commit unlawful, unconstitutional, and corrupt acts upon citizens, can destroy personal and property rights, and be immune from damages. The self-serving decision held that the public had no remedy against judicial corruption. But Federal civil right statutes and constitutional rights to seek relief from government harms clearly do not provide federal judges immunity from civil and constitutional violations, corrupt, criminal or conspiratorial acts.

In *Stump v. Sparkman* the judge entered into a conspiracy and ordered a young girl permanently sterilized. The Supreme Court held that the girl had no remedy against the judge. The Supreme Court Justices held that the public's welfare requires that a judge be free to exercise his duties without fear of the consequences. That is a farce contrary to statutory law and constitutional rights. No where does it state a judge is immune from the consequences of his clearly unlawful, unconstitutional, or corrupt acts.

The public's welfare does not require protecting state or federal judges who make a mockery of their judicial office, who knowingly render unlawful or unconstitutional orders. Even the appellate remedy is often non-existing. Very few appeals are successful. In California the success rate is less then ten percent. Even if the appeal is successful, the judge committing

---

[182] *Ashelman v. Pope*, 793 F.2d 1072 (9th Cir. 1986).
[183] 435 U.S. at 362.

the outrages is held immune from the consequences of the harm they have inflicted upon others.

That is not what the Constitution says. It is not what the civil right statutes say. It is what the highly political judiciary says to protect themselves from public outrage.

By law, the U.S. Trustee had the responsibility to *prevent* corruption. He wasn't doing it. For two years I made the U.S. Trustee aware of the corruption that continued without letup. Yet, U.S. Trustee Sousa, if anything, made things worse. After Sousa dismissed Duck in July 1989, Sousa appointed attorney Jerome Robertson as trustee over my two estates, seeking authority in the unlawful order seizing my assets. That order seizing my assets was void, but the U.S. Trustee acted upon it as if it was a lawful order rendered under lawful conditions. The U.S. Trustee ignored the rampant fraud surrounding the property seizure and protected those committing the criminal acts.

Robertson immediately accelerated the harm done to my estates that Duck had started. Within a few months Robertson and his retained law firm of Murray and Murray had requested and obtained court approval to take over $250,000 from my assets for legal fees their defenses against what I argued were corrupt acts.

When the U.S. Trustee refused to prevent these continued acts of corruption I filed a law suit against him—and his boss, the Department of Justice, in the U.S. District Court, District of Columbia.[184] The judicial conspiracy protected itself. District of Columbia judge Stanley Sporkin dismissed the action on January 17, 1990, without a mandatory hearing, and despite the law barring dismissal when the complaint state federal cause of actions. Sporkin joined the conspiracy that was getting larger all the time, and he made possible the continued air disaster, Chapter 11, and other corruption by people acting under color of federal law.

HOLDING THAT JUDICIAL EMBEZZLEMENT AND CORRUPTION IS A DISCRETIONARY FUNCTION

I filed an administrative claim with the Administrative Office of the United States Courts, addressing the judicial misconduct (necessary before filing a law suit against the United States government under the Federal Tort Claims Act). Addressing the Chapter 11 racketeering activities, including those committed by Duck, they denied my claim on October 17, 1989. The denial stated the "claim may not be settled under

---

[184] *Stich v. Stanton; U.S. Trustee Anthony Sousa; Richard Thornburgh; United States of America.*

authority of the Federal Tort Claims Act because that act specifically excludes claims arising from the performance of a discretionary function."

Duck's embezzlement activities were a discretionary function? That letter, and Ninth Circuit decisions, held that a judge-appointed trustee is an officer of the court, and thus entitled to the purported immunity of judges. The entire Ninth Circuit was protecting its criminal enterprises.

These so-called officers of the court had misused their positions of trust, violating numerous statutory laws, constitutional protections, engaging in various criminal acts, and then held that the public had no claims against them.

Duck, who committed what had been described as the nation's worst Chapter 11 embezzlement affecting hundreds of people, was sentenced on January 18, 1990 by federal judge William Swarzer. Would you believe, Duck was ordered to pay only a $5,000 fine and sentenced to 27 months in the jail of his choice, which he selected as the federal correctional institute at Sheridan, Oregon. Duck moved his family to nearby Lake Oswego, to reduce the inconvenience upon himself.

U.S. Attorney Joseph Russoniello at San Francisco, resigned on April 1, 1990 to return to his former San Francisco law firm of Cooley, Godward, Castro, Huddleson and Tatum. This law firm represented the government, including Charles Duck, in previous actions filed against them by defrauded citizens. That same law firm was hired by the State of California in February 1990 to prosecute corruption in the savings and loan industry—the same industry that they represented during the savings and loan debacle.

This relationship appears to be *another* reason Russoniello refused to take any actions against Duck and the system for the past decade. It appears he was protecting the system of which his law firm was a part, and the firm that he would probably rejoin upon leaving government service; another form of the revolving door. Upon returning to private practice Russoniello headed a department to protect corporations and others against government regulators.

The replacement for the U.S. Attorney position at San Francisco would be recommended by none other than Senator Pete Wilson, who has been implicated in this scandal for the past ten years; and approved by the Justice Department in Washington.

In early 1990, to keep the lid on the scandal, Washington reduced the funding for the United States Trustee at San Francisco, and fired assistant U.S. Trustee Gregg Eichler on January 24, 1990. It was Eichler who exposed Duck, and who threatened to expose the judicial involvement in the racketeering activities that went right up to the Justices of the U.S. Supreme Court. In this way the judges and others were protected.

While all this is going on, federal Judge Edward Jellen charged me with criminal contempt for filing appeals and oppositions to the seizure of my assets that were part of this corruption. Denying me the right to testify, denying me a jury trial, he sentenced me to prison for objecting to the seizure of my assets. Federal judge Samuel Conti approved the prison sentence, and it was sent to U.S. Attorney Russoniello for prosecution. The government persecution never ended. The press, and Congress, kept the lid on every facet of this scandal.

Every attempt to get out of Chapter 11 failed. Normally, I should have been out of it within a few months. But to do so would make the assets available to me which I used to expose the air disaster corruption. By keeping me in Chapter 11, the attorneys could continue looting the assets until they were all gone. They could control any self-published book publishing exposing the government corruption. Three years after filing for Chapter 11 relief, I was still trapped. The criminal seizure of the assets of thousands of people then continued, as before.

VICTIMS OF A LITERAL CARTEL OF CORRUPTION

The Justice Department attorneys, federal judges, Senators and Representatives, the news media, were a literal cartel, engaging in a conspiracy of silence and persecution, to keep the lid on the awesome scandal of government-funded corruption. Stephen Baltz, the Bennett sisters, thousands of others, were victimized by the cartel of conspirators, in much the same way that you are threatened by this group.

These acts also destroyed my liberties, my privacy, the human rights "protected" by the laws and Constitution of the United States, for which the American public pays large sums of money to support the thugs that have made all of these outrages possible.

CHAPTER TWENTY SIX

Legal Brotherhood

In my many years of fighting the air safety and government corruption, I found the common denominator in the entire sordid mess was the legal fraternity. I wrote of this in the first two printings of the *Unfriendly Skies—an Aviation Watergate*, but did not really understand the significance of this until recently.

It was the legal fraternity within the FAA and NTSB that covered up for the hard-core air safety misconduct at United Airlines and within the FAA. It was the legal fraternity in the Justice Department that protected the scandal in the 1960s and up to this date, blocking *every single attempt* to obtain an investigation of the crash-related corruption. It was the legal fraternity within the Justice Department and the judicial brotherhood that dismissed the 1974, 1975, and 1980 actions filed against the FAA and NTSB. It was the legal fraternity, using the San Francisco law offices of Friedman, Sloan and Ross as a front, that filed the sham California action against me, and then suspended every state and federal protection that existed. It was the legal brotherhood who conspired together to send me to prison. And it was the legal brotherhood that stripped me of my life's assets.

At best, before becoming involved in this scandal, I found the legal fraternity to be a sleazy group. After becoming involved in the air safety scandal, I found myself at a loss for the proper words to described their lack of even the most basic ethics or honesty. Looking at the facts I uncovered, the legal fraternity appeared to be a secret fraternity, a literal fifth column, subverting the very Constitution that is the basis for our form of government.

Sabotage of my exposure activities commenced with the Denver attorney, J.E. Kuttler, whom I hired to represent me at the FAA air safety hearing in 1965. The Dènver attorney either sabotaged my exposure efforts from the very start, or was grossly incompetent. I'm convinced he sabotaged my case. Within thirty minutes of the start of the hearing I called a temporary halt and discharged Kuttler. In retrospect, and with knowledge of the abysmal level of integrity in the legal fraternity, it was realistic to expect that the attorney saw his future income opportunities higher by protecting United Airlines, the primary employer in Denver, than in a one-shot representation of a government employee.

The attorney-sabotage continued as I sought legal counsel to expose the FAA corruption. While residing in Oklahoma City I asked for help from attorney Clyde Watts to expose the FAA misconduct. He was a former attorney with the Department of Justice in Washington, and was presently defending General Walker, whom the federal government was trying to silence, and who had been placed into a federal detention facility on the argument that he had mental problems.

Watts felt that it was virtually impossible for me to succeed with the power of government against me. He was surprised the government hadn't made trumped-up psychiatric charges against me and had me locked up, or some other charges to destroy me. (That would come in later years.) Watts explained that it was an easy matter for United Airlines to cause government pressure to be exerted where most effective. They, like other vested interests, bought their power by donating large sums of money to political funds.

Watts advised me that he was going to Washington to argue General Walker's case to the Supreme Court, and while there he would check with his former associates in the Justice Department to find out what was going on.

When Watts returned to Oklahoma City he wouldn't talk to me. When I went to his office to pick up my papers, his associate greeted me, looked at me rather sadly, and wished me luck. Other attorneys advised that they would check into the matter and get back to me. They all then avoided me.

The questionable attorney misconduct surfaced time and time again. It surfaced when I sought to expose the NTSB coverup of the PSA San Diego drinking. Attorneys contacted me, presumably to help me force an NTSB investigation, and then simply used the information to extract more money out of PSA without bringing about an exposure of the NTSB misconduct.

This occurred when Los Angeles attorney Ned Good stated he would use my testimony against United Airlines in the litigation relating to the crash of the 727 into the Pacific Ocean after taking off from Los Angeles International Airport on January 18, 1969.

It was the attorneys at the U.S. Department of Justice and FBI whom I felt were behind the coverup after I tried to get help from other government agencies. They blocked every attempt I made to expose and correct the air safety corruption, from 1965 to the present date.

Attorney Ralph Nader and his associates knew of the crash-related corruption throughout this time frame. They kept the lid on the scandal, following the pattern of every other group related to the legal fraternity.

The attorneys in the ACLU repeatedly covered up, as they also protected those whose air safety corruption violated the civil and constitutional rights of those who perished. The ACLU knew of every aspect of the constitutional outrages committed against me. Not only did they refuse to prevent the outrages, but as described in an earlier chapter, they aggressively supported those committing the outrages which exceeded the simply act of coverup for the crimes committed. While subjecting the American public and others to the consequences of the civil, constitutional and criminal violations described throughout these pages, the ACLU collected large sums of money from the public to support their legal activities purportedly protecting civil and constitutional rights.

THE START OF THE CALIFORNIA JUDICIAL ATTACKS

It was the legal fraternity who acted as a front in the sham California action filed against me, that continues to this day, almost eight years after it commenced. The San Francisco law firm of Friedman, Sloan and Ross—active members of the ACLU—inflicted grave harms upon me by their gross violations of California and federal law. Indirectly, they made possible the brutal deaths and injuries of those harmed in air tragedies caused by misconduct I sought to correct.

In the first few months of the California action I hired several attorneys to defend me. Whether they were cooperating with the scheme, or typical of the incompetency and unreliability problems with California attorneys, I can only speculate. I had to appear in pro per status to raise the controlling California and federal laws prohibiting the California law suit. None raised the primary defenses in law. The attorneys I hired argued forty and fifty year-old California laws that had been long superseded, did not raise the federal defenses which superseded California law, and did not address the cause of action raised by the Friedman law firm. They either didn't know the law, or they feigned an ignorance of it.

My first attorney jeopardized my defenses by substituting a young attorney right out of law school to argue important matters of law at a critical hearing, contrary to our employment agreement. The substituted attorney knew nothing about the unusual issues arising in the bizarre action filed against me. I fired both attorneys.

I then hired an attorney who claimed he was a specialist in the area of law raised by the sham California action. He also argued case law forty years old that had been superseded by modern state and federal case law and controlling statutory law. The defense he used was on the edge of preposterous. I had to get rid of him. I hired another attorney, and his ignorance of the law was the worst of the three. He represented himself as an expert in the field, and in short order I discovered his ignorance surpassed any that I had yet seen. I had to repeatedly point out certain areas in law where he was wrong, and prepare briefs correcting his major errors. The Concord, California attorney agreed to argue the law that I researched, and agreed that he would not file any briefs without my prior examination. Then, without telling me, he submitted a brief that left out all the California and federal statutory and Supreme Court cases that barred the cause of action, and instead raised equitable defenses. Discretionary equitable defenses don't work with judges showing a pattern of lying and violation of mandatory statutory law.

When the California judges rendered the first unfavorable decision, I told the last attorney I had to file a notice of appeal. He stated the order couldn't be appealed. I again had to show him the law that clearly showed the order was appealable. He still refused to file the appeal, as he had to leave for New York, where he reportedly had a tryst with a French woman that he was courting. By that time I had to discharge him and substitute into pro per status so as to file the notice of appeal before the time ran out.

I must have contacted thirty attorneys during the next few years, seeking legal representation. Sometimes their knowledge of the law in the related area was a half century behind the times. Other times attorneys admitted that I faced a judicial gridlock, and that their legal practice would suffer if they defended me against the determined actions of the state judges.

As time went on, and my appeals and petitions for relief required enlarging on the earlier violations of law, it became obvious we had a major judicial scandal. The scandal became an open secret in the California legal fraternity.

When I decided it was time to exercise federal remedies for the massive civil and constitutional violations, I engaged Sacramento attorney James Reed, who taught civil and constitutional rights in the local law school. He wasn't much on California law relating to the underlying action filed against me by the Friedman law firm, but he used the law I researched on the matter, and got it into his federal briefs. It was necessary to sue state judges to obtain declaratory and injunctive relief, something very few attorneys will do, fearing judicial retaliation.

Reed finally named Solano County judges Dwight Ely and Michael McInnis as defendants, along with the Friedman law firm. Pressure must have been put on him, as he quickly filed an amended complaint removing the judges, over my objections. This was the first federal action, and was heard by federal judge Raul Ramirez, who quickly dismissed the action. Reed then changed residence and became county counsel at Mammoth Lakes, causing me to look for another attorney specializing in civil and constitutional rights.

I contacted in 1985 attorney John Moulds who specialized in civil and constitutional law. Moulds, you may remember, was the part-time magistrate who in 1987 sentenced me to prison for filing three federal actions addressing the air disaster corruption. After Moulds looked over my papers, he admitted the gravity of the violations, but then claimed he couldn't represent me in federal court because of his part-time magistrate position. He had known that earlier, and never raised the objection, until he recognized the judicial conspiracy.

ANOTHER IMPOSTER

I wasn't doing very well in finding attorneys by referral, or even on blind calls. I tried a different approach; I advertised in the San Francisco newspapers for an attorney. I received a telephone call from an attorney who stated he was Sid Saperstein with offices in San Francisco. I resided in Reno at that time, and Saperstein stated he would be in Reno the next day, and arranged to meet me at my place. At that time the Solano County bench warrant out for my arrest was still outstanding, and I wanted someone to get that matter settled.

Saperstein came to my Reno residence on January 23, 1987, and stated to me that he had connections in the courts, and would get the bench warrant lifted. He asked for money. I wrote him a check, and asked him for his calling card. He pulled out a hand-written card, stating he had changed offices and that his printed cards had not yet arrived. Sounded strange, but possible.

Several days later, Saperstein called, and stated that he had succeeded in getting the bench warrant lifted. This sounded fishy, as it normally requires a noticed hearing to have the matter heard. I asked him if he had the judge's order in front of him lifting the bench warrant, and he stated that he did. I asked him the name of the judge who signed the order. "Judge Schwartz," he replied. There was no Judge Schwartz in the Solano County courts. I asked Saperstein what court issued the order. "The Superior Court in San Francisco," he answered. The San Francisco courts had no authority over the order rendered by the Solano County courts. Something was obviously fishy.

I asked Saperstein to read off the exact wording on the order that he stated a few minutes earlier was right in front of him. He couldn't do this because there was no such order. He stated he would call me back shortly. That was the end of Saperstein. I never saw or heard from him again. I sent a certified letter to the address that he gave me as his office. The letter came back with a post office notation that the address didn't exist.

What apparently had happened, was that the Friedman law firm saw my advertisement for an attorney in the San Francisco legal paper, and got Saperstein to contact me for the purpose of giving me false assurance that it was safe to return to California. Than upon entering California Friedman would insure that I was arrested.

Following the scheme by Judge Schwartz and the Justice Department to put me in prison, described earlier, I obtained Sacramento attorney Joel Pegg to represent me against the California action and against the false contempt charge involving federal Judge Milton Schwartz and the Justice Department. Pegg has a prestigious looking office, and a charming picture of Rhonda Fleming on his desk, supposedly one of his clients. He looked impressive, and said the right words, and I felt confident that I could trust him. I paid Pegg a $20,000 retainer. It was urgent that he file several appeal briefs with the California Court of Appeals that were already due.

Pegg repeatedly put off filing the appeal briefs. I was appealing decisions that would overturn the past three years of illegal and unconstitutional orders by the California judges. Their timely filing was of the utmost importance, involving ten million dollars of property ownership. The California Court of Appeals had already given me a time extension, and the three judges, King, Low, and Hanning, were anxious to find some excuse to dismiss the appeal.

When the deadline for filing the appeal briefs was just a few days away, I forced Pegg to give me an answer about when he would file the appeal briefs. He responded, stating that he had requested a time-extension from the court, and the court granted him an extension. To be on the safe side I telephoned the Clerk of the Court of Appeals at San Francisco. The clerk advised me that no extension of time had been requested, and no time extension was granted. Pegg had lied to me. I wrote Pegg a letter and asked him for an explanation, which he refused to give me. He never answered.

I then had to file my own appeal briefs. They were well written and the law extensively researched and argued. But pro per litigants are almost always denied due process in California courts. This is probably true in most state courts. If the judges gave equal consideration to pro per litigants appearing without legal counsel, than any intelligent individual could argue the facts and the law against lawyers. If this condition became widely known the attorneys could not get away with their exorbitant fees and they would possibly become a thing of the past. Also, there is a "we" against "them" mentality in the legal and judicial brotherhood. "Them" are the public, and "we" are the fraternity of attorneys and judges.

The California Court of Appeal Justices[185] refused to consider the briefs. They fraudulently stated that the decisions being appealed were not appealable orders, repeating the misstatement of facts and law that kept the sham California action going for the past six years. I then sought relief from the judges of the California Supreme Court. By this time the California courts had become so deeply ensnared in the scheme that judges had to protect judges to keep the scandal from blowing sky-high.

Pegg was to seek removal of the lis pendens that halted my business operations and caused loss of valuable properties. He continually refused to do this, even when I presented him with the papers ready for court filing. His refusal to seek this basic relief caused to me seek relief in Chapter 11.

Pegg represented me in the defense against the criminal contempt charge. He refused to raise the hard-core defenses that would expose the Justice Department and federal judicial misconduct. Then just before start of trial Pegg notified Magistrate John Moulds that he wanted to withdraw from the case. By that time Pegg had my money, and the Chapter 11 seizure of my assets left me without funds to hire other legal counsel.

THE BANKRUPTCY SCENE

After I sought relief in Chapter 11, I obtained other legal counsel. I hired attorney Vernon Bradley of Sausalito, California, who was to represent me both in the California action and in the Chapter 11 proceedings. He in turn hired Las Vegas attorney Joshua Landish to handle the filing of the Chapter 11 papers in Las Vegas. Both Bradley and Landish agreed before I

---

[185] Judges Harry Low; Donald King; Zerne Haning.

hired them that they would seek relief from the federal judge in Chapter 11 from the illegal orders of the California judges. But then as soon as they became attorneys of record, they refused to file the necessary papers to obtain the relief.

I was present at the first hearing on the Chapter 11 cases, on September 11, 1987. The two attorneys made a passionate argument on my behalf, and although they failed to raise the civil and constitutional violations that forced me to seek Chapter 11 relief, they argued in my defense. They praised my management style that built up an estate from nothing to many millions of dollars within twenty years. They argued that the sham California action filed by the Friedman law firm was the cause of my seeking relief, and that if this action was eliminated there would be no reason for my seeking relief in Chapter 11. This was the hearing where federal Judge Robert Jones rendered an order abstaining from hearing the cases, refusing to accept jurisdiction, and ordering that the two cases would be dismissed in 60 days. This was not the full relief I wanted, but it removed the lis pendens and permitted me to pay off the mortgage loans that had come due.

These attorneys then sabotaged my defenses. Attorney Landish appeared at a hearing that took place on September 28, 1987, without my knowledge, in which a mortgage holder[186] sought to foreclose on the properties for which the mortgages had come due. Attorney Landish, whom I had hired specifically to protect my properties, then requested Judge Jones to vacate the earlier order providing me relief; to seize the business, home, and assets on both the personal and corporate Chapter 11 cases via appointment of a trustee; and then to liquidate the assets, leaving me penniless.

I would later learn that this is a common trick used by attorneys after they recommend to their clients that they seek Chapter 11 relief, and then act to strip their clients of all assets! In this manner the attorneys generate huge fees as the assets are plundered by the judge-appointed trustee, cooperating attorneys, and hidden interests in other corporations. Bank of America was famous for this since the 1930 depression days.

Landish kept notice of the seizure from me until after the ten-day period to appeal passed. I discharged Landish, but by that time he had done the damage. I did not learn what occurred at that hearing until several months later, after I obtained taped recordings of the court proceedings.

I hired other legal counsel, and the integrity problems continued. I hired attorney Raymond Goodman of Concord,

---

[186] Robil, Inc., and Superior Home Loans.

California, to represent me in the bankruptcy proceedings, and he too agreed to file briefs to remove the illegally appointed trustee. He didn't tell me that he had been suspended by the California State Bar, and that he would turn my Chapter 11 cases over to someone I had never seen. He turned my cases over to an associate, William Rubendall, who was a disaster. He failed to file opposition briefs, and refused to file the briefs to remove the illegally appointed trustee as was agreed before I paid the retainer. He refused to return phone calls. Contrary to my instructions, he notified Judge Jellen that my earlier appeals would be withdrawn. And much more.

I then retained attorney Robert Ayers of Walnut Creek, California, and paid him a retainer. After six weeks of failing to file the required briefs, he then stated he was not my attorney. But he kept the money I gave him. I even had trouble getting my files back.

SEIZING MY ASSETS AND THEN STRIPPING ME OF LEGAL COUNSEL

After attorney Pegg abandoned me, I asked for a public defender to defend me against the false imprisonment. Judge Raul Ramirez appointed assistant federal public defender Carl Larson, who was paid by, and was an employee of the Department of Justice, my main adversary for the past two decades in the air disaster scandal.

Larson refused to file a motion for stay pending appeal, which is a mandatory requirement to avoid incarceration during the appeal. Larson advised me to get ready for prison. Larson refused to acknowledge the numerous violations of law and Constitution involved in the charges against me.

Larson refused to obtain the hearing transcript or the records that were needed to prepare a defense. He refused to file any briefs on my behalf, arguing that he would give a verbal presentation. That was totally unacceptable. A written brief is required to address the dozens of case and statutory laws, the constitutional protections, the argument. A hearing is limited to a brief verbal argument, and is totally inadequate as the sole means of stating dozens of case laws, the holdings in the case law, and other complex issues. Larson was protecting his employer, the Justice Department, and the federal judges.

I discharged Larson, and requested another attorney. At first the federal judges would not appoint another attorney, and I had to present briefs in pro se status. Finally, after other requests, the federal judges appointed Clifford Tedmon, who duplicated the conduct of Larson. Again I discharged the attorney. They appointed another attorney, Sacramento attorney Brian Deamicis, who repeated the tactics. Finally, I discharged him, and filed my own briefs.

HOW WOULD THEY PROTECT AGAINST MALPRACTICE?

The serious malpractice and misconduct by these attorneys required disbarment, if the system of attorney discipline worked. It didn't work. I filed complaints with the California State Bar Association concerning Pegg and other attorneys. They protected the misconduct. I filed a complaint with the Nevada State Bar and the governor of Nevada concerning the misconduct of attorney Joshua Landish who sabotaged me and caused the loss of my ten million dollar estates. Both parties approved the conduct of Landish.

Attorneys that I knew stated that I probably could never find a Nevada attorney to file a malpractice action against Landish; the attorneys all protected each other. I contacted at least half a dozen California malpractice attorneys concerning the malpractice of California attorneys. None would take the case, even though several stated the attorney misconduct was very serious. I was gridlocked not only in the California and federal courts, but in the legal fraternity.

I sought to circumvent this block by filing my own legal malpractice actions. This avenue was blocked. The California judges dismissed each action before I could get anywhere. In one case, federal Judge Edward Jellen dismissed the state action, clearly in violation of my rights under law.

Eventually the California and federal judges settled on two quick responses to strip me of all defenses. They placed a frivolous label upon anything I filed, and then called me a vexatious litigant for seeking relief.

POWER OF LEGAL AND JUDICIAL BROTHERHOOD

In *With Justice For None*[188] the author attorney described the power of the legal and judicial fraternities, and that most judges are the lackeys of big-money interests. Mr. Spence spent much of his life representing insurance companies and government contractors, and then protecting the rights of people adversely affected by injustice, such as the case of Karen Silkwood against Kerr-McGee. He also sympathized with me when I sought his help in 1988—and refused to get involved.

In *A Feast For Lawyers*[189] the author describes the hacks, vultures and scoundrels in the legal fraternity, referring also to the judges, who feed on the public, in a mentality of "we against they." The "we" being the legal fraternity and the "they" being the public.

---

[188] *Times Books*, Gerry Spence.
[189] *Evans & Company*, by Sol Stein.

CHAPTER TWENTY SEVEN

Endemic Corruption

Reference is made in this chapter to other government and industry scandals in an attempt to show that corruption is endemic in the government of the United States, that the FAA and NTSB corruption are simple other examples. These interwoven examples of government corruption feed on each other. It is probable that if the corruption relating to the air disaster tragedies had been exposed and corrected, some of the other scandals such as the savings and loan, HUD, Abscam, and others, could not have flourished. The primary difference in other scandals and those within the FAA and NTSB are the forms in which the public pays.

LAME EXCUSES FOR ALLOWING OTHERS TO DIE

Members of the U.S. Senate and House, many of whom are members of the legal fraternity, were active in the criminal coverup of what is stated within these pages. My letters to members of Congress went into the hundreds over a period of years. Often, members of the Senate and House admitted the gravity of the allegations, and covered up in different tactics. Among the many implicated in the scandal included Senators William Proxmire, Robert Kennedy, the original Keating-Five from the savings and loan scandal, and others.

Without fail, those who expressed a strong interest in learning more about the scandal when I first contacted them, and who admitted the gravity of the charges, would suddenly back off. Something triggered the sudden reversal of interest. I suspect they contacted key officials at the Department of Justice who in some way or other caused them to back off and make excuses for not taking action. Never did they question the validity of my charges.

Something triggered their sudden change of attitude. Could they have been threatened by the Justice Department? Did they discover that one or more of their corporate contributors were involved, such as United Airlines? Did they discover that the scandal involved many of their own members? A government investigation would have brought the answers out, but as an author and air safety activist I did not have the subpoena power necessary to probe into *why* they committed the crimes of coverup. A major investigation into this scandal, if it could be conducted without being compromised by the many interests implicated in these multi-faceted scandals, would probably expose even bigger scandals, and certainly identify the triggering mechanism for so many to commit the crime of coverup that they knew made possible more tragedies.

PUBLIC HAS SHORT MEMORY

Many books have been written about the deeply ingrained misconduct by members of the House and Senate. But the misconduct continues, made possible by the public's indifference. The public reelects almost every Senator and Representative, resulting in a reelection rate for incumbents in the high ninety-percent range, even when the elected officials are associated with corruption. The public appears more interested in what their representatives can do for them.

In *Above the Law*,[190] author James Boyd described the influence-peddling and buying of votes in Congress. Vested interests pass money under the table—bribes—disguised as honorariums, speech-fees, loans that never come due, and other thinly disguised graft. In its book review the *Christian Science Monitor*[191] said: "Only the completely cynical can read Mr. Boyd's book without mounting distress."

The review described the indifference, or coverup, by the FBI, the Attorney General, and the live-and-let-live philosophy of Congress for their peers. The book review addressed the press coverup, stating "the press doesn't smell too sweet either. It rushed into the kitchen only after the kettle boiled over." Ironically, the Christian Science Monitor knew of my allegations from 1965 through 1988, and continued to keep the lid on the scandal. I contacted the *Monitor* in the 1960s, and then several times in the late 1980s. They expressed concern, and then silence. While covering up, the *Christian Science Monitor* editor-in-chief Earl Foell stated the Monitor organization has

---

[190] Authored by James Boyd and published in 1968.
[191] March 1, 1968. Christian Science Monitor.

a moral mission to support socially responsible journalism. (*Business Week* September 26, 1988.)

A *Washington Post* article dated September 4, 1969 stated that "Committees in Capital Run Like Swiss Banks." The article continued: "The devious ways that Congress used the "District of Columbia [for a] haven for committees that can be used by senators and congressmen to hide embarrassing contributions."

A three-page *U.S. News & World Report* article on November 10, 1969 was captioned, "Scandals in Congress: The Record." The article continued: "Activities of a staff member have put the office of the Speaker of the House high in the headlines. The result is one more entry in the record of scandals that have dogged the U.S. Congress for years."

Government corruption has been uncovered in almost every agency in the executive branch, as well as in Congress and in the federal judiciary. Why shouldn't the FAA and the NTSB be guilty of the same? Members of the Senate and House pressure high FAA officials to relax the safety requirements at certain airlines who contribute heavily to the Congressional members. Just as in the savings and loan scandal, pressure is put on the regulators-inspectors who seek to enforce the law.

A *New York Times* article[192] had the apt heading: "Everybody in D.C.'s Doing the Scandal Shuffle." The same basic articles appeared twenty years earlier. There is no change.

ABSCAM SCANDAL

Among the many Congressional scandals was Abscam. It broke in February 1980 when the FBI released for television video pictures of members of Congress[193] taking bribes from an FBI agent posing as an Arab Sheik. The intent of Abscam was to expose political corruption. A United States senator and seven members of the House of Representatives, as well as a number of private attorneys and state and local officials, were implicated as a result of the video-taped sting operation.

THE HUD SCANDAL

Following a long line of lurid headlines, some of which were quickly covered up, the 1980s went out with several major scandals. One of these shameful events cost the public billions of dollars in the federal Department of Housing and Urban Development (HUD), including corruption and political favorit-

---

[192] October 8, 1989, by R.W. Apple, Jr.

[193] Among those convicted in Abscam included Representatives John M. Murphy (New York); Michael J. Myers (Pennsylvania); Frank Thompson, Jr (New Jersey); Raymond F. Lederer (Pennsylvania); John Jenrette (South Carolina); Richard Kelly (Florida); and Senator Harrison A. Williams, Jr.

ism and kickbacks. Investigators reported finding graft, political kickbacks and fraud of monumental proportions. Large sums of public funds were siphoned off to politically connected developers and consultants, with part of the money going to members of Congress in various forms of bribes.

For years the HUD corruption was covered up. The Inspector General of HUD tried from the early 1980s to force corrective actions before the scandal broke in 1989, after it became difficult to hide several hundred billion dollars of losses that must be funded. High HUD officials, the press, Congress, kept the lid on the scandal, until the damage was so severe that it could no longer be contained.

The General Accounting Office (GAO) also tried to stop the corruption in the early 1980s, and they too were blocked. The Department of Justice knew about the corruption early in the game, and stonewalled corrective actions. Too many attorneys, developers, banks, and members of the Senate and House, received largess from the HUD corruption. Consultants with political connections reaped huge fees of as much as $400,000 for a few phone calls or visits to Secretary of HUD, Samuel Pierce.

Before resigning, California Congressman Tony Coelho admitted on May 14, 1989 that he received a $100,000 bond from a California savings and loan executive, to be paid by a $50,000 unreported loan from the same savings and loan. Apparently to halt the Congressional investigation into this and other shady practices, Coelho promptly resigned from his powerful seat in Congress. Much of the news media did not address Coelho's irregularities or dishonesty, but instead lamented the loss of a powerful Congressman who produced benefits for California interests. Little was said of the horrendous debt inflicted upon the public by the protection of corrupt practices. If it had been left to the constituents of Congressmen Jim Wright or Coelho, the benefits the constituents received outweighed the national harm caused by the corruption. New York Senator Alfonse D'Amato received huge campaign contributions from Puerto Rican developers. The developers received through the efforts of the Senator, a disproportionate number of projects.

California Representative Tom Lantos led a congressional investigation into the matter and called it "influence peddling of the tawdriest kind." Former Attorney General Mitchell received large sums for his connections. The *Wall Street Journal* called the corruption a "system of spoils and favoritism."

"The scandal at HUD is one of the most complex national scandals that we have seen in decades," said Representative

Tom Lantos, of San Mateo. "There is a degree of mismanagement, fraud, abuse, waste, influence-peddling that we have just barely begun to touch," he said. Representative Charles Schumer, a subcommittee member said: "Like picking up a large stone only to discover that bugs and slime have grown in the darkness. This investigation has exposed the corruption which flourished unchecked under Secretary Pierce's HUD."

Congress tried to block the HUD exposure by blocking confirmation of those government officials expressing an intent to expose the HUD scandal. After Jack Kemp took over HUD and stated his intent to prosecute those involved, Congress blocked confirmation of Kemp's management team; a common tactic used by members of the Senate and House to sequester scandals.

The two houses of Congress ignored warnings of the HUD and other scandals as they profited by protecting those committing the misconduct. The same happened in the FAA when I and other inspectors sought to force a particular airline to comply with the law. Members of the Senate and House puts pressure on upper FAA management, and the pressure comes down the line within the FAA, with everyone profiting who plays the game.

When the Department of Justice started an investigation into HUD, members of Congress then investigated the Justice Department, and threatened to cut back its funding. The Justice Department investigation stopped.

When the Chapter 11 corruption threatened to expose the powerful judicial involvement, the Justice Department fired the U.S. Trustee in Indianapolis, another one in the Washington, D.C. area, and assistant U.S. Trustee Gregg Eichler in the San Francisco office.

Referring to Representative Jim Wright's arrogant blocking of corrective actions to stop the HUD corruption, a *Wall Street Journal* editorial dated April 17, 1989 stated:

> What is most disturbing ... is the obvious pattern of so many violations extending over so many years. ... the brazenness is amazing. Obviously, Mr. Wright felt assured there was no prospect that he ever would be called to account for his actions. ... When Congress is so powerful it can intimidate the Justice Department from another Abscam case, who should be surprised at corruption?

Investigations showed that House speaker Jim Wright obstructed investigation of the HUD corruption, and accepted $145,000 in unreported gifts from savings and loan officials after blocking an investigation into their corrupt practices.

The House Committee investigating Wright's dealings with the HUD scandal quickly dropped the investigation after some House members reminded them that an investigation would implicate many other members of Congress. After pressuring Jim Wright to resign on the relatively minor charge of ethics violations, the HUD scandal then died down. The public still is left with the multi-billion dollar tab that must be paid.

JUSTICE DEPARTMENT STONEWALLING

Another Congressional committee, the House Judiciary Committee, requested on November 2, 1989 that the Department of Justice appoint an independent prosecutor to investigate the HUD scandal. Attorney General Richard Thornburgh resisted, accusing the committee of introducing partisan politics into the HUD investigations. Representative Charles Schumer of New York replied at a news conference:

> There's ample evidence of wrongdoing at HUD, but there's stonewalling at the top. And the only way to get to the bottom of the mess at HUD is through the appointment of an independent counsel. Instead of attacking us, the Attorney General should be focusing on making sure that high-ranking officials at HUD don't get away with breaking the law.

Representative Schum characterized the attorney general's objections as a "political response." My comment would be criminal coverup.

Congress quickly shifted the investigation away from HUD to avoid implicating other House members, and concentrated on trivia, calling it an investigation into ethics. In truth it was something akin to investigating the Mafia for parking violations. The investigators than held that the problem was solved and halted further investigations. The Pandora's box stayed closed.

The time-honored way that Congress stonewalls sensitive investigations is to reduce the funding to finance the investigations. This is occasionally done when the Department of Justice attempts to investigate Congressional misconduct. It is done by the Department of Justice to stonewall investigation of the Chapter 11 judicial corruption which the Justice Department uses in its bag of tricks. This was done to halt further FBI investigations of Congressional wrongdoings in Abscam. (As the FBI's continuing investigations became too threatening to members of Congress, they responded by dragging Justice Department officials in for gruelling oversight hearings that made it clear the budge for the Justice Department was in danger if the probes into Congressional wrongdoings did not cease.)

LIFE OF EASE FOR POLITICAL WHITE-COLLAR CRIMES THAT SADDLE THE PUBLIC WITH DEBT

What happened to those implicated in scandals? Congressman Jim Wright, for instance, whose activities cost the taxpayer several billion dollars in the HUD scandal, retired on $115,000 a year, receives $120,000 yearly office expense, has three paid staffers, $67,000 for stationery and telephone expenses, continued use of the franking privilege, and enjoys other benefits. His staff answers his downtown Fort Worth phones, "Speaker Wright's office." In addition, he has a rich book contract. Not too bad. Former Congressman Tony Coelho landed a million-dollar job on Wall Street.[194]

CONGRESSIONAL REWARDING OF THE MUTILATION OF A YOUNG WOMAN

The attention given by the press to Congressman Jim Wright's so-called ethics problems exposed a sordid episode which the press had covered up for years. During the investigation into Jim Wright, the *Fort Worth Star Telegram* focused attention on Wright's top legislative aide, John Mack. Before becoming a Congressional aide, Mack had been the manager of a furniture store when a young lady, Pamela Small, entered the store to look at some merchandise. Mack lured her into a back room, and then repeatedly hammered her head with a claw hammer, beating her skull into a bloody pulp, and exposing her brains. Mack broke one of her legs in the process, and finished by slitting her throat. Bleeding, and seemingly dead, Mack put the bleeding woman in the back of his car, and went to a movie! Miraculously, she survived.

The police apprehended Mack, and a court sentenced him to 15 years in prison. A woman also accused Mack of raping and manhandling her on a date in an earlier incident reported in suburban Fairfax County, Virginia. The police and the judge dismissed the charges.

CONGRESSIONAL MATERIAL?

Mack's conduct impressed House Speaker James Wright, who then used his Congressional influence with a Virginia judge and parole board, and obtained Mack's release from prison. Wright hired Mack for a Congressional staffing job, and eventually Mack became Wright's closest aide, and eventually, one of the most powerful staff members in the House of Representatives. Meanwhile, the poor woman who Mack had beaten nearly to death suffered serious financial problems and endured months of painful and intensive hospital care and

---

therapy. Mack didn't pay a cent to help his victim.

House Majority Whip Tony Coelho of California defended Mack, saying he owed nothing to the young woman. Coelho answered a reporter's questioning, "John Mack owed his debt to society, not to this young woman." Manipulating the system hardly meets the criteria of paying his debt to society or the young woman. Coelho was a business partner with Mack in a business venture. Coelho used his powerful Congressional committee assignment to get financially profitable speaking fees for Mack from interest groups in Coelho's district. Coelho, using his Congressional office and power, gave Mack the umbrella of respectability of the United States Congress.

The bribes that determines how Senators and Representatives use their office come in many forms. One that is little recognized are the Congressperson's back-home law offices. Special interest groups pay for their legislation by retaining these law firms, often in little towns far removed from Washington, with the expectation of getting results; which they get.

OTHER CONGRESSMEN, AND THE PRESS, APPROVED THIS CONDUCT, AND COVERED UP

Mack's sordid past was widely known in Washington by other members of Congress and the press. They all remained approvingly quiet. In January 1987 anonymous letters began circulating on Capital hill about Mack's crimes. The *Fort Worth Star Telegram* was the first to publish the story. Reporters from the *Washington Post* kept the lid on the matter. But one reporter accidentally broke the story, evading the censorship. The congressional reporters for the *Washington Post* called the Mack story a "non-story." (They also kept the lid on the air disaster corruption described within these pages; could that also be a non-story?) Finally, *Washington Post* ombudsman Richard Harwood, reported that the story "had been ignored—is suppressed too strong a word?—for more than two years by leading journalists in the congressional press galleries." When public attention focused on the matter, other papers followed.

Even after the *Post* published the Mack story, the national networks refused to publicize it, protecting Wright and the many other interests who would be embarrassed by an exposure. A *Wall Street Journal* editorial on May 16, 1989 stated that Barbara Cohen, chief of the CBS Washington bureau, said she wouldn't want to broadcast the story because it would cast "a shadow" on House Speaker Wright. Could this "shadow" on members of Congress be the reason the news media covered up for the air disaster scandal, and willingly sacrificed lives?

Barbara Walters and Linda Ellerbee covered up for the FAA corruption when they saw the Supreme Court petition for writ of certiorari that I had filed in 1976. They contacted me, and then quickly quashed the story. Reporters from major news services routinely check all court records for filings and orders, and knew of each of my highly sensitive filings over the years. They kept the lid on the scandal, knowing that it would continue to flourish.

The Washington press establishment viewed Congress as a group of corrupt hacks, until Vietnam and Watergate soiled the image of the presidency. Congress became, in the eyes of the Washington press corp, the White Knight. *Washington Post* ombudsman Harwood stated that "the press came to understand and tolerate some of [Congress's] frailties." Some newspapers reported their refusal to print the Mack crime on the basis they did not wish it to unfairly link Congressman's Wrights fight against the charges of ethics violations.

The press coverup was reported in a *New York Times* article released on May 26, 1989, describing the attempt to get the *Wall Street Journal*'s explanation for the coverup: "Jeff Birnbaum, who was The [Wall Street] Journal Reporter on Capitol Hill, declined to be interviewed." Even Mr. Wright's press secretary, Mr. Wilson Morris, who once worked at the Washington Post, expressed surprise that when the *Fort Worth Star-Telegram* revealed the Mack story most newspapers kept the lid on it.

Washington Post officials explained that it was unethical to publish such a damaging exposure of Mr. Mack after what they considered successful rehabilitation. Rehabilitation? He never paid for his crime. His victim suffered terrible physical, mental, and financial trauma. Congressman Wright and other members of Congress rewarded the brutal criminal with a position of prestige and high pay. Mack became the most powerful aide in Congress, influencing legislation that affects the entire nation. He became part of the bribe network. It is frightening to think that Jim Wright was second in line to the presidency, assisted by likes of Mack.

In a perverse manner, this book might be a tribute to the art of coverup by the nation's press. Without their duplicitous coverup there would probably not have been a Paris DC-10 or Japan Airlines 747 disaster, or many of the others described within these pages. The endemic government corruption would probably not have blossomed to its present stage if the press had exposed it early in the game.

THE FDA SCANDAL

As the HUD and other scandals surfaced, there also surfaced the FDA corruption. The Food and Drug Administration regulates 25 percent of the nation's consumer economy, and affects the entire nation. Evidence surfaced that FDA officials engaged in corruption, bribery, illegal gratuities, associated with generic-drug makers. Generic pharmaceutical companies admitted bribing FDA officials, submitting falsified data, and other wrongful acts. Just like FAA officials, the FDA officials treated the industry that it regulated as partners.

The scandal surfaced when the House Energy and Commerce Committee commenced an investigation following a complaint from Roy McKnight of Pittsburgh-based Mylan Laboratories Inc. By creating an atmosphere of embracing the generic-drug industry as a partner rather than an adversary, the FDA created an atmosphere of lawlessness, said Sidney Wolfe, head of the Public Citizen Health Research Group. "It isn't surprising that the generic companies pulled these shenanigans."

REQUESTING INVESTIGATION OF ITS OWN OFFICIALS

FDA internal regulations prevent the approval of a new generic drug if inspectors find manufacturing problems at the drug company's plant. Officials within the FDA plant inspection department refused to provide inspection reports to other FDA officials reviewing new-drug applications. This prevented the FDA from meeting its official responsibilities. The FDA's new-drug department had to resort to the Freedom of Information Act to get copies of the FDA's plant inspection reports from its own agency! This unheard-of withholding of information by one part of a government agency from another part of the same agency prevented the agency from accomplishing its lawful functions. When the documents were finally obtained, much of the needed information was blanked out.

COMMON KNOWLEDGE, BUT NO ONE COMPLAINED

Fear of retaliation kept companies who knew of the FDA corruption from complaining. Clark Research & Development Inc., filed a lawsuit accusing the FDA of losing documents and pursuing a "pattern of harassment" after Clark complained that FDA officials allowed a competitor to make misleading claims.

The impetus for the FDA corruption came from companies scrambling to be the first to win FDA approval for their products as patents expired. High stakes were involved. The first company to get FDA approval, and get their product on the market, were often the ones who captured a lucrative share of the market by undercutting the brand-name product.

Middle management at the FDA commenced receiving reports as early as December 1985 that drug reviewers favored one company over others in return for bribes. FDA officials based drug approval on bribes—either sex, money, or other perks. There was a tip that a woman executive from a drug company exchanged sex with a FDA drug reviewer, and then got quick approval of the company's product. No one investigated the tip.

Two small generic-drug makers[194] had a phenomenal success in obtaining quick FDA drug approval. They received a stunning 77 drug approvals in 1986, almost twice as many as any other company, including those much larger.

DRUG APPROVALS BASED ON BRIBES

"We screwed you on this one, so we'll take care of you on the next one," FDA officials stated to H. Lawrence Fox, an attorney for Barr Laboratories, Inc. Fox testified before a Congressional committee, showing the passing out of drug approvals based upon bribes. They sounded like crooked judges and attorneys, making favorable decisions based on quotas and not on the merits of the case.

Bribery and favoritism caused the disappearance and destruction of documents submitted by companies for drug-approvals. A Congressional investigative panel embarrassed the FDA by producing the original copy of a generic-drug application that a former FDA branch chief, Charles Chang, had torn in half and thrown in the trash. Chang pleaded guilty in a Baltimore federal court to two counts of interstate travel in aid of racketeering.

The FDA official accepted a paid, round-the-world trip costing over $3,000, and computer equipment worth $8,000, from American Therapeutics Inc., a generic drug maker based in Bohemia, New York. In return, the FDA official sped the company's application through the approval process, and held back competitor's applications.

The Congressional investigations showed major drug companies submitted falsified data, filled generic drug test samples with brand-name products, claiming the products as their own, and winning FDA approval.

THE GREAT GRAPE CATCH—or, the power of government intimidation of industry

As news media attention escalated on the FDA internal corruption, a sudden occurrence shifted public attention in March 1989 to another matter: the great grape catch. The FDA allegedly received a tip that a shipment of grapes from Chile contained cyanide. In a scene from a school-play, a hoard of FDA officials converged on a particular pier in Philadelphia, went to a particular group of boxes containing millions of grapes, found *two* grapes with two small needle-size holes in them, allegedly laced with cyanide. The FDA issued a warning that consumers not eat any Chilean fruit. This act cost Chile over $300 million, and cost commercial interests in the United States many millions as well. Consumers paid more for fruit.

---

194 Par Pharmaceutical Inc., and its Quad Pharmaceuticals Inc. subsidiary.

Everyone lost, for what could very well have been a diversionary tactic to get the public's mind off the FDA corruption.

An in-depth investigative article by the *Wall Street Journal* on November 16, 1989 described what may actually have happened, and stated that inconsistencies and implausibilities of the FDA's actions cast "serious doubt on the FDA's miracle find." FDA officials went to a pier in Philadelphia after receiving a vague tip that grapes from Chile were sabotaged with cyanide. Out of dozens of ships containing huge shipments of fruit from Chile, the FDA officials singled out the Almeria Star from an armada of fruit-laden freighters. They went to a row of crates containing an estimated 280 million grapes, and plucked two grapes that allegedly contained cyanide injected into them before the ship left Chile.

The *Wall Street Journal* article described the incongruities in the FDA's story. The FDA stated that the cyanide was injected into the two grapes before the grapes left Chile, over two weeks earlier. The *Journal* article stated that many people believed FDA officials fabricated the grape scare. Some speculated it was fabricated to show the Pinochet government the power of United States economic sanctions. (Could the power to take economic sanctions against the news media and others explain the news blackout on the scandals within these pages?) Senator Jesse Helms of North Carolina stated "I don't believe it happened in Chile. [this is] the most bizarre episode I have ever seen."

ADVANCE WARNINGS

Attorney Ricardo Claro of Chile stated that George Jones, until recently the deputy chief of mission at the U.S. Embassy in Santiago, asked Mr. Claro over lunch in early 1988 what the Chilean reaction might be to a United States ban on fruit from Chile. A year later the hypothetical happened.

The pier superintendent in Philadelphia, John Hamilton, described the events when the FDA officials came to the docks looking for the cyanide-laced grapes. "All of a sudden, I saw an army of Guys. They never told us what they were looking for, but it was obvious they knew where to look."

Out of millions of grapes, the FDA officials found two, each with a tiny needle hole, through which the cyanide was allegedly injected. But subsequent laboratory tests conducted by FDA and Chilean laboratories showed that grapes change color about two days after injection with cyanide. The two grapes picked by the FDA officials did not have any color change. Further, tests also showed that cyanide dissipates rapidly into the air as a gas, and leave an ugly, unappetizing blemish. The tested cyanide-laced grapes shriveled and darkened within two weeks. There were no blemishes on the two grapes picked by the FDA officials. University of California researchers at Davis, California, believed the two grapes became contaminated *after* the FDA officials seized the fruit.

In the background of FDA and other government intrigue, the real truth can only be speculated. Before we talk about controlling south-of-the-border politics, let's look at cleaning up our own!

200 TO 600 BILLION DOLLAR DEBT TO PAY SAVINGS AND LOAN CORRUPTION LOSSES——compliments of your Congress and Department of Justice

Just as in the HUD corruption, government investigators advised Congress of widespread and serious corruption in the savings and loan industry and the government agencies regulating them. Instead of investigating, members of the House and Senate put pressure on the regulators, blocking an investigation. In return, those engaged in industry corruption gave substantial sums——sometimes demanded——to members of the Senate and House. Outright crooks were stealing huge sums of money from the public, either indirectly via government insured savings and loan deposits, or through worthless uninsured securities.

Corrupt savings and loan officials and closely aligned developers, consultants, and others, siphoned off huge sums of money through savings and loans that made shady transactions. Money was loaned, and lost, on overpriced raw land and development projects. Congress and key government officials, on the take, participated in, or blocked corrective actions, causing taxpayers to be saddled with a debt now estimated to be from 200 to 600 *billion* dollars, an amount far exceeding America's cost of fighting World War II!

Many, including the news media, kept the corruption covered up, until in 1989 the corruption required infusion of massive sums of money. The problem couldn't be hidden any longer, although Congress tried to do so. The corruption would still be going on today——and probably covered up——except that the taxpayer had to come up with the money to pay for the corruption. The staggering debt could trigger a 1930-type depression, especially if foreign money is withdrawn that is now used to bankroll the huge American indebtedness, much of which is caused by the rampant corruption.

One of the worst examples of savings and loan fraud occurred at Lincoln Savings and Loan and its parent corporation, American Continental Corporation (ACC), owned by its chairman Charles Keating. Keating managed to stave off federal regulators by a pattern of bribing members of the U.S. Senate and House, California regulators and politicians, and paying huge salaries to government regulators to become his employees. It was a Ponzi scheme in reverse, wherein the huge payoffs for various forms of bribes and continued looting of the insured deposits caused the destruction of the fragile house of cards.

MORE CONGRESSIONAL CORRUPTION

The most-publicized members of the U.S. Senate who made possible the huge losses to the tax-payers, especially at Lincoln Savings and Loan, were known as the Keating-Five. These included Senators Alan Cranston (California, and senior member of House Banking Committee), Dennis DeConcini (Arizona); John McCain (Arizona); John Glenn (Ohio); Don Riegle (Michigan). These Senators received approximately $1.5 million in what some would call bribes. After receiving the funds the Senators pressured regulators against taking corrective actions to halt the corruption.

These names were familiar to me. Each of them blocked the exposure of the scandals described in these pages. It is understandable that those engaged in the savings and loan corruption couldn't expose corruption involving other subjects.

In 1986 the Keating-Five applied pressure upon Washington regulators to halt government investigators from taking actions against Keating's Lincoln Savings and Loan. After the Keating-Five received huge financial donations from Keating, regulatory responsibility for Lincoln Savings and Loan was removed from San Francisco—where corrective actions was imminent—to Washington, where no action was taken.

This 1986 Congressional obstruction increased the costs to the taxpayers by an estimated two *billion* dollars, solely involving Lincoln Savings and Loan, and far in excess of *two hundred billion* dollars or more for the entire industry. The taxpayers also must pay for the bribes paid to United States lawmakers and officials, their namesakes in California, and to the former government officials who became high salaried employees of Lincoln.

To the very end, Congress sought to cover up. In June 1989, Congress quietly rejected a request by President Bush for 36.8 million dollars to hire investigators to accelerate the investigation and prosecution of corrupt savings and loan officials. Congress did the same with the Chapter 11 judicial corruption, Abscam, and others. Its a routine employed to defuse exposure of government corruption.

Among those members of Congress trying to expose this awesome scandal was Representative Jim Leach of Iowa, who told a panel of journalists in May of 1989 that "You have the opportunity to hold your Legislative Branch accountable, and perhaps bring it down." The same applies to the air disaster scandal. If the news media had exposed the corruption, the underlying causes for many of our worst air tragedies could have been corrected and prevented. But this was not to be.

MANY BLOCKED THE EXPOSURE OF THE CORRUPTION

A California banking investigator, Richard Newsom, testified that he went to the FBI in July of 1988 after he found explosive evidence of wrongdoings. He testified he had found that the parent company of Lincoln Savings and Loan funneled over $800,000 to Senator Alan Cranston, and that "the stuff was too hot." The FBI and Department of Justice used the power of their office to protect the guilty by doing nothing. In this way they protected the many lawyers and powerful government officials involved in the scheme.

The Justice Department attorneys did the same with the Chapter 11 corruption that financially destroyed thousands of people who exercised the relief promised by Congress—and used as a carrot by the "bankruptcy club."

Referring to the coverup by the government regulatory agency that permitted the corruption to continue, Representative Jim Leach of Iowa stated, "This Bank Board did the opposite of making timely warnings. It tried to put people to sleep while a fire was raging."

The same members of the senate and house that obstructed earlier corrective actions were now fighting to retain the head of the regulatory agency who caused the biggest financial debacle in the nation's history. Senator Cranston and Representative Donald Riegle fought hard to retain Danny Wall as head of the new agency addressing the massive savings and loan fiasco without a confirmation hearing. In this way Wall would not be subject to questioning concerning the debacle that unfolded while he held the responsibility to take corrective actions. Simultaneously, [195]Lincoln President Charles Keating paid $839,000 to various Cranston-supported election committees to reelect Cranston.[196] The five senators receiving the huge payments claimed they were only helping constituents—for a price!

It was Wall who protected Lincoln Savings and Loan from the San Francisco regulatory board intent on shutting down the corruption-plagued institution. Wall removed Lincoln Savings and Loan from the regulators who had uncovered the corruption. In an unprecedented action, he transferred regulatory jurisdiction of Lincoln to Washington. No action was taken on the uncovered misconduct, which continued. This delay increased

---

[195] Charlie Keating was chairman of American Continental Corporation, a major land developer in Arizona. American Continental acquired Lincoln Savings & Loan Association of Irvine, California. Keating became its chief executive officer. Lincoln was then used as a private bank for Keating's own investments, many of them highly questionable.

[196] *San Francisco Examiner*, October 8, 1989.

the loss to the public by an estimated $2 billion.

ADMITTING TO PAYING FOR INFLUENCE

Keating admitted giving over five million dollars in political contributions to influence members of the U.S. House and the Senate, and state politicians in California and Arizona. Cranston and the four other Senators than blocked the regulators from shutting down the corruption riddled Lincoln Savings and Loan. Keating wasn't hesitant about the effects he expected when he spent the money belonging to the taxpayers and uninsured bondholders, as he told the press: "One question, among many raised in recent weeks, had to do with whether my financial support in any way influenced several political figures to take up my cause. I want to say in the most forceful way I can: I certainly hope so."[197]

Cranston obstructed the actions of the regulators who sought to prevent others from losing money, such as those elderly and retired people who invested in the uninsured bonds issued by Keating's enterprises. This obstructive action interrupted the regulatory process, delaying the government takeover of Lincoln Savings and Loan, as it continued selling worthless uninsured securities to the public.

Even Alan Greenspan, then a private consultant, and later chairman of the Federal Reserve Board, sent a letter seeking to block corrective actions, claiming Lincoln was in good financial shape and had good lending practices. This was preposterous. Lincoln's primary assets were grossly inflated desert land. Lincoln had a practice of lending money to closely related investors or their own real estate enterprises, often without any credit check and without collateral.

Despite the huge losses that would be paid by the public, Keating paid himself and his family members over $34 million in the three years before its demise, even though losses during this time were destroying the company. The public paid for this largess.

Representative Henry Gonzalez of Texas, the pseudo-champion for air safety, initially played the system as he sought to protect Texas banks in the HUD scandal. Gonzalez used his post as chairman of the House Banking Committee to benefit the banks in his hometown, obstructing an investigation into questionable banking practices. Gonzalez pushed an amendment to protect Frost National Bank of San Antonio, and other insured banks it owns, from the Federal Deposit Insurance Corporation.

---

[197] *New York Times* November 9, 1989.

As the savings and loan scandal shot out from under the news blackout, Representative Gonzalez, now head of the House committee[198] with oversight responsibilities for the savings and loan industry under the Office of Thrift Supervision (OTS),[199] focused heavy attention on the savings and loan corruption. This diverted attention from Gonzalez's role in the HUD scandal.

The investigations uncovered horror stories of corruption in government agencies. The investigators trying to blow the whistle on the rampant corruption testified to the House Banking Committee in October 1989 that Washington officials repeatedly overruled or restricted their investigation of corruption-riddled Lincoln Savings and Loan.

Only the names are changed. The mechanics of the savings and loan scandal have parallels in the air disaster scandal. Except, it has been easier to hide the deadly consequences of the corruption within these pages then it was to hide two-hundred-plus billion dollars of losses. In the savings and loan corruption, the public faces depression-like economic conditions. In the air safety corruption, the public is threatened with injury or death; some have died; and other deaths will surely follow.

CALIFORNIA COVERUP

California, with its rampant judicial and governmental corruption, played a key role in the savings and loan corruption, just as they played a role in the air disaster coverup via the sham California action against me.

Numerous California officials and friends of California governor George Deukmejian became involved in the scandal. Another Keating enterprise, TCS, made political contributions totaling $48,000 to Deukmejian's campaigns. Keating paid over $189,000 to Deukmejian, in addition to the nearly one million given to California Senator Cranston's interests. Everyone, it seemed, was at the taxpayers' money trough. Over 23,000 investors purchased $250 million in uninsured bonds (most of them thought they were government insured) after California regulators approved their sales, knowing the corporation was insolvent. Thousands of elderly people lost their life's savings in this way, losing their sole means of financial support.

California officials got on the gravy train. California's top regulator, Lawrence Taggart, was shown as the highest paid executive in a company owned by scandal-plagued Lincoln

---

[198] Gonzalez moved up to the chairmanship of the House Banking Committee in 1989 after his predecessor, Fernand St. Germain (Rhode Island) lost his re-election bid because of investigations into his cozy deals with savings and loan lobbyists.

[199] Successor agency to the Federal Home Loan Bank Board (FHLBB).

Savings and Loan. Taggart rendered a decision that protected Lincoln, three days before a confidential federal order was to be released, preventing the very thing that Taggart approved for Lincoln. Another Lincoln subsidiary, Vernon Savings and Loan, reportedly gave Taggart a $686,547 unsecured loan.

Barbara Thomas, a former SEC commissioner, reportedly called the SEC to act as a character witness for Mr. Keating during the SEC's investigation. Representative Henry Gonzalez, chairman of the Banking Committee, said his staff's investigation showed that Ms. Thomas received a $250,000 loan from Mr. Keating with unusual payback provisions.

The auditing firm handling Lincoln Savings and Loan accounting for submission to the government was Arthur Young & Company, and primarily handled by Jack Atchison. Atchison sent several letters to three senators saying that Lincoln was a sound institution, and that federal regulators were harassing Lincoln executives. Atchison then left his employment with the accounting firm and went to work for Lincoln at a salary exceeding $900,000 a year. There is no justification for such a salary.

In November 1984, Taggart—who was still California savings and loan commissioner—became a director of TCS, and rendered official decisions that caused thousands of investors to lose their life's savings. On December 7, 1984, Taggart gave Lincoln approval to move almost a billion dollars to its subsidiaries (three days before a crucial deadline that nobody was supposed to know about besides highest-level federal regulators). Records showed Taggart was already hired by TCS at that time. On January 1, 1985, Taggart left the California position regulating savings and loans, to work full-time as TCS's highest salaried executive. Additionally, he was to receive half of the after-tax profits earned by the consulting department he headed, and other perks. Three weeks later, Lincoln bought $2.89 million worth of TCS common stock.[200]

A California Department of corporations lawyer-regulator issued a strong early warning about uninsured bonds sold in Lincoln's offices. California officials kept this warning quiet, making possible the sale of worthless bonds to thousands of California investors.

California politics made the Lincoln bebacle possible. The California General Services Department (and the California Department of Savings and Loan) obstructed the investigation of Lincoln's corrupt practices, and rendered administrative

---

[200] TCS was losing $70,000 a month and was basically insolvent, paying $2.89 million for a 24 percent ownership of a company with less than $100,000 of solvency.

decisions that made possible the loss of almost a quarter billion dollars in savings of the elderly, all subsequently lost to the corruption and to political contributions or bribes.

California politics also made part of the expanding air disaster scandal possible. I notified the governor, the attorney general, and numerous state legislatures of the California judicial corruption to silence my exposure activities. They all covered up, making the corruption possible.

California officials denied state examiners and legislative investigators access to the records, stating that there was high danger of asbestos contamination where the boxes were stored. The building owner denied there was any danger:[201] "They [the records] could have been picked up any time in the last 200 days. They knew there was no problem [of asbestos]."

Assemblywoman Delaine Eastin of the California House Banking Committee stated that subpoenas would be necessary in the Lincoln case to get response from the California Department of Corporations and the California Department of Savings and Loan, who blocked the investigations. Departments under Governor Deukmejian refused to turn over the records.

The California Department of Savings and Loan finally got access to seven boxes of documents pertaining to Lincoln on November 1, 1989 that had been blocked by the California department of General Services.

California and Arizona committees conducted interim hearings dealing mostly in relative trivia. The committees avoided exposing powerful state politicians that made the scandal possible. California Assemblyman Patrick Nolan received large financial contributions from Keating, after Nolan sponsored legislation removing investment restrictions on state-chartered institutions.

Attorney Joseph Cotchett of Burlingame, California, representing many of the elderly who were swindled in the Lincoln bonds, described the obstruction to exposure by California officials, "And now we have reached the 1,000th coincidence in this case."

Both United States Senators from California received money from Keating, who expected the money to be followed by blockage of corrective actions. Senator Pete Wilson also received Keating's largess, reportedly in excess of $75,000. Reports appearing in the San Francisco papers in 1990 showed Wilson receiving large financial contributions, starting within two months of his election to the U.S. Senate.

---

[201] *San Francisco Chronicle* November 1, 1989.

FRAUD WAS PERVASIVE

The Federal Deposit Insurance Corporation prepared a 1989 report, repeating statements made in past years, that they had found evidence of criminal fraud and abuse at almost half the failed Savings and Loan institutions.

Federal Deposit Insurance Corporation's chairman, L. William Seidman described the hopelessness of recovering the huge losses. He warned that the amount of money recovered from any people found guilty of self-dealing and other insider abuses would be small. "The money is long gone, spent," Mr. Sidman said. "We cannot expect any substantial recovery from criminal abuse."

SOME OF THE VICTIMS

Part of the money to pay bribes to U.S. Senators and Representatives came from the life's savings of many elderly retired people after California and federal officials blocked the closure of Lincoln Savings and Loan. The bonds, issued by now-bankrupt American Continental Corporation, owned by Keating, were literally valueless when they were issued, and known to be valueless (except to those kept in the dark by government officials and the press). Lincoln relied upon fictitious net-worth in over-valued desert land to justify the bonds.

Many widows, retired persons, elderly, testified before a House Banking Committee on November 14, 1989, that they lost their entire life's savings, blaming California Senator Alan Cranston (and other members of Congress) for their losses. Many invested their life's savings in the over $300 million in junk bonds (unaware they were uninsured) after Cranston and other members of Congress blocked the actions of government inspectors and regulators. Many of those who made this great financial debacle possible were also those who covered up for the air disaster corruption, and made possible many of the deaths described within these pages. Fortunately for these members of the Senate and House, the American public is easy to swindle, both of their money, and of their lives.

THE PENTAGON SCANDAL

Pentagon fraud and bribery was another scandal that surfaced in the mid-1980s. U.S. Attorney Henry Hudson charged the smaller parties with crimes, but let the big ones off the hook. An *Aviation Week & Space Technology* article on April 3, 1989 described the pattern of corruption:

> The pattern of corruption that has emerged from the Ill Wind cases involves classic influence peddling. Government employees received bribes in return for providing consultants with early notice of upcoming contracts and for helping them devise strategies for winning those contracts. The consultants convinced contractors to hire them based on their access to an inside source.

A bribed government employee like Berlin could use his influence to determine which firms would be eligible for a contract and, in some cases, could help determine the winner by inserting specific criteria in a service's acquisition plan, favoring one contractor over another. Berlin did this for Teledyne and Hazeltine. The corrupt official also could provide confidential bidding information so a favored contractor could submit a superior best and final offer to win an award.

RETIREMENT FUND AND OTHER SCANDALS NEXT

The next big scandal may be the retirement fund scandal, in which private pension plans lack the funds to pay workers' pensions. "Pension disaster is looming," was a headline on an *Associated Press* story of November 14, 1989. The article stated that "Fraud and mismanagement could wipe out the retirement nest eggs of millions of working Americans in private pension programs and saddle taxpayers with a multibillion-dollar bailout, according to government officials and agency documents." The article stated that the Labor Department Inspector General's office warned that the fraud and mismanagement could dwarf the recent savings and loan financial debacle.

The report stated that many of the unfunded pension plans are not insured by the government, and that those retirees will often get nothing. The report stated that only some of the 107,000 private pension plans are covered by the government's Pension Benefit Guaranty Corporation (PBGC) insurance.

Director of the Pension Rights Center, a public interest group, stated in the article that "It's astonishing how much of the money is being stolen." The article referred to some $14 million that had been stolen from two union locals.

The Pension Benefit Guaranty Corporation protects the pension benefits of the 30 million Americans in programs which come under the federal program. Many don't. If the pension funds are guaranteed by the government, and are unfunded, hundreds of billions of dollars may be the debt heaped upon the taxpayer. More than $1.6 *trillion* in pension funds are potentially at risk because of poor regulations and refusal to enforce federal law, according to the report of the Labor Department's inspector general, J. Brian Hyland.[202]

One of the schemes in the leveraged buy-outs involved the corporate raiders seizing the cash in the pension funds and replacing the cash with junk-bonds, many of which became worthless in 1990.

---

[202] Stated on June 2, 1989 and reported the following day by *Associated Press*.

Those pension funds that are not guaranteed by the government, and which are or will be without money, will leave still more of the American public suffering the consequences of government misconduct, most of which involves the legal fraternity.

Hyland urged Congress to immediately investigate potential abuses and shortfalls of federal pension laws. Hyland said that existing laws and regulations allow employers and pension-fund managers to hide abuses from the government, and that understaffing at the Labor Department leaves the government little chance to catch offenders.

The more direct losses are those in which the pension funds are not guaranteed by the government. When these people retire, there are no funds. In this manner other segments of the American public pay for the government corruption that they ignored for many years.

Pan American Airlines's pension fund, for instance, is grossly underfunded. In one instance involving LTV Corporation, government lawyers stated[203] in a Supreme Court case that the taxpayers were liable for "an open-ended source of industry bailouts" which would probably spark a financial crisis similar to the one facing the government's insurance program for the savings and loan industry.

While it was an Inspector General that exposed years earlier the savings and loan corruption, which Congress kept under wraps, the Inspector Generals in the Department of Transportation and Department of Justice did the opposite; they kept the lid on the scandals.

With the February 1990 collapse of the junk-bond market, more losses were heaped upon the public. Many of the assets held by the savings and loans were junk bonds. Many of the corporate raiders looted the cash in the pension funds and replaced the cash with annuities, backed in many cases by junk-bonds. The pension fund disaster may be next. Every participant, especially the law firms, in the scheme reaped financial rewards, taken from the backs of the American public.

AVIATION-RELATED BRIBES

Bribing of government officials exists in the aviation field. Lockheed, Douglas, and other aircraft manufacturers have repeatedly been identified with paying bribes to incur orders for their product (and possibly to approve elimination of design safeguards).

Lockheed was accused, and admitted bribing foreign government officials to induce them to buy military and commercial

---

[203] *The Recorder* October 31, 1989.

aircraft. In one instance Lockheed officials resigned after the Lockheed was charged.[204] These corporate officials admitted sanctioning bribes in excess of 22 million dollars to European and Japanese officials. Lockheed pleaded guilty to secret payoffs[205] to Japanese government and business officials to promote the sale of Lockheed L-1011 aircraft. To promote the sale of Boeing 747s to Middle East Airlines, Boeing paid bribes in excess of three million dollars.[206] Northrop Corporation is suspected of bribing Korean officials in a fictitious hotel project that served as a conduit for bribes.[207] American Airlines agreed to pay a civil penalty for making illegal political contributions.[208]

Bribes to Japanese politicians and firms to obtain sales of aircraft were described in an *Air Line Pilot* article of July 1979, adding that "government auditors could not account for $3.4 million that Boeing and McDonnell Douglas paid.

Boeing agreed to plead guilty[209] to felony charges of illegally obtaining classified Pentagon documents, hiring Richard Fowler to illegally obtain the documents from insiders in the Pentagon. The defense department investigators stated they were looking at a number of other major defense companies suspected of trafficking in secret government documents. The Boeing investigation was pursued independent of the massive Pentagon bribery and influence-peddling probe code-named "Operation Ill Wind."

Fowler was convicted by an Alexandria, Virginia, jury on December 7, 1989, on 39 felony counts related to unlawful acquisition and distribution of Pentagon papers. Boeing pleaded guilty the month earlier to receiving unauthorized Navy documents, following the government's "Ill Wind" procurement fraud investigation. Many believe Boeing got off with a slap on the wrist as many Boeing executives were directly involved with the unauthorized handling of military planning material. Loral Corporation, a major defense-electronics contractor, pleaded guilty on December 8, 1989 to federal charges of fraud and obtaining inside information on defense contracts. The defense contractor unlawfully obtained the military documents by paying over half a million dollars to William Galvin.[210]

---

[204] Dan Haughton and Lockheed President Carl Lotchian resigned. February 13, 1976.
[205] *San Francisco Chronicle* June 2, 1979.
[206] *Wall Street Journal* April 16, 1979.
[207] *Wall Street Journal*, October 27, 1989.
[208] *Wall Street Journal* May 2, 1975.
[209] *New York Times* November 7, 1989.
[210] *San Francisco Chronicle* December 9, 1989.

Mass grave funeral services for Paris DC-10 victims.

I frequently heard inspectors describe money or perks received by FAA officials. I often wondered if this was one of the reasons United Airlines and Congress could block the inspectors' safety activities. One wonder's if bribes also played a part in the FAA's refusal to act on such glaring aircraft design defects as the DC-10, Beech V-tail Bonanza, and other defective aviation products.

CORRUPTION EVERYWHERE

Even a household name such as Beechnut committed fraud when it sold a sugar and water concoction as "100 percent pure apple juice" for over five years, starting before 1977. This deception on little babies and little children went ignored by government investigators for years. Not until a detective from the Processed Apple Institute informed Beech-Nut of a law suit, did Beech-Nut stop the deception. Eventually the government was forced to intervene. Former Beech-Nut executive John Lavery was convicted of conspiracy and mail fraud selling corn syrup to babies and children as pure apple juice. When Lavery appealed the conviction, the Court of Appeals stated: "The evidence was ample to permit the jury to infer that Lavery conspired with the suppliers to perpetrate a fraud on the public through the distribution of the adulterated juice."

Corruption exists in the kind of music played on the radio stations via Music-Payola, the catchy term used for bribes to radio stations to play records. This scandal first came to light in the 1970s, and persisted, despite federal criminal laws prohibiting the practice. The Justice Department's Organized Crime Strike Force charged four people with violating the federal payola laws by paying over $300,000 in bribes to radio station executives in Southern and Western states between 1980 and 1986.

POWERFUL PUBLISHING CONGLOMERATES, VESTED INTERESTS IN AVIATION-RELATED INDUSTRIES, AND COVERUP

Many of the book publishing houses are controlled by a relatively small number of conglomerates, and exert vast control over what books get published. The news media has large intertwining interests throughout our society, and an exposure of the vast corruption within these pages would adversely affect almost every publisher and newspaper conglomerate.

Control of the news media is a charge of long standing. My only knowledge of this is the hard-core coverup I encountered by the news media commencing in 1965, and continuing through the publication date of this book. Obviously, the air safety corruption and the thousands of related deaths would not have happened if the news media met their responsibilities and reported the allegations of FAA and NTSB misconduct. Many papers, such as the *Wall Street Journal*, have conducted excellent investigations into public-interest related subjects, and printed an exposure that acted to protect the public.

But for reasons that I can only speculate, these same newspapers have all covered up the multi-faceted scandals described within these pages. In doing so, they knowingly sacrificed the lives that would be lost. In Chapter 11 judicial proceedings, their coverup permitted thousands of people to be financially destroyed.

Could it be that the news media has close interconnecting ownership interests with airlines, and they do not want to jeopardize these financial interests? They certainly protect the judicial branch as was so clearly shown in the air disaster and Chapter 11 corruption. Their readers were sacrificed for reasons that can only be speculated.

NBC News in Washington covered up for much of this scandal, commencing in late 1977 when Alan Goldstein and then Linda Ellerbee contacted me after reading the U.S. Supreme Court's refusal to vacate the lower court's dismissal of my action against the FAA. Not knowing of previous NBC contacts and coverup, they appeared very interested in what I told them. They asked for further details, which I sent. That was the end of that. NBC had repeatedly distorted the news in midair collisions between small planes and airliners, and covered up for the misconduct that I described within these pages.

NBC news, and the other news services and major newspapers, examine federal complaints filed in the U.S. District Court at Washington, where several of my complaints were filed. They knew of the scandal all along.

During an appearance on Larry King's television program on June 28, 1989, the author of *Senatorial Privilege*, Leo Demoore, described the coverup he witnessed while a reporter on Kennedy's Chappaquiddick accident. He described the coverup by the press of the more sensitive and sordid parts of the scandal. Demoore claimed that although public attention forced news coverage, most if not all the papers omitted damaging facts, and distorted what they did state. He stated that the press protected Kennedy as much as possible under the lurid circumstances. The press didn't want to hear anything that reflected any worst than necessary on Kennedy's image. Demoore described the muzzling of the press, and even of the publishing houses.

Demoore had a firm contract with *Random House* to publish the book, which they had already accepted in 1985. Suddenly, *Random House* refused to go ahead with the book, claiming they were dissatisfied with the contents, even though they had already expressed complimentary approval of the first half. Demoore felt that unknown people pressured Random house not to publish the book.

Random House was also one of the publishers that had tentatively agreed to publish my first printing of the *Unfriendly Skies*, and then suddenly refused to do so.

COVERUP BY THE PUBLISHING INDUSTRY?

When I finished the first manuscript of *The Unfriendly Skies* in the late 1970s, I queried many publishers, several of whom requested to see a copy. Several publishers expressed interest in publishing the manuscript, but each one suddenly cancelled at the last minute. When Ballantine Publishing Company returned the manuscript after showing a strong initial interest, they accidentally left an interoffice memorandum in the returned manuscript. One of the editors referred to the manuscript as a blockbuster.

It was as if the material was too sensitive. No one wanted to touch it. Even when I became a self-publisher, a California book printer refused to print the book, fearing law suits. The next printing that came out in 1980 was even more sensitive than the first, and I didn't even bother to look for a publisher; I self published. The second printing had the benefit of excellent book reviews by top reviewers, including the American Library Association and other influential book reviewers. The second printing also had the benefit of hundreds of talk show appearances which publishing houses take into consideration in determining the marketability of the book and the author. Still, no publisher would touch me or the book.

In 1988 I sent over thirty query letters to publishing houses to determine their interest in publishing the highly sensitive third printing. By that time the extent of the air disaster and superimposed government scandal was no secret to the news media. Not a single publisher expressed an interest in even looking at the manuscript. That was odd. In the mid-1960s when I offered the then-primitive manuscript to publishers, at least one out of three wanted to read it. In the late 1980s, when the public's interest was peaked due to the many airline crashes and air safety problems, no one was interested in my book. My credentials to write such a book exceeded those of most any other known author.

At this same time, a three-page *Time* magazine article in 1989 described the demand for authors and non-fiction books, and the high bids to get public-interest material. The air safety crisis was a constant topic in the news and on talk shows. My manuscript was the only insider book on the subject, and unlike any other air safety book. (Incidentally, the high bidding for authors collapsed toward the end of 1989 as many publishers over-extended their financial resources with high prices for author's whose books did not sell.)

Strangely, many in the news media refused to accept prepaid advertising for my book. I sent prepaid advertisements to various newspapers after the first printing came out in 1978. These were tasteful, unoffensive advertisements, that simply contained the title of the book, the price, reviewer's comments, and the address at which it could be ordered direct. It couldn't possibly offend anyone—except those implicated in the misconduct and coverup.

The newspapers that rejected the book advertisements included the supermarket tabloids that are not exactly the pillars of authenticity, including the *Globe, Enquirer, Weekly World News,* and others. I couldn't understand how these papers could reject my pre-paid ads when they contained such preposterous articles. Some of these tabloids featured such preposterous headlines as: "Docs Deliver Baby Frozen 600 years," or, "Five Year Old Girl Delivers Baby". A *Weekly World News* article contained the bizarre headline: "GIRL GIVES BIRTH TO BABOON'S BABY! Healthy newborn has an ape's body—and a human brain!" A February 6, 1990 headline in the tabloid *Sun* contained the bizarre "Girl, 6, Gives Birth to a 22-LB Baby." The reason for the rejections certainly couldn't be on an offensive basis, and must have been related to a desire to limit the exposure of the highly sensitive book.

Even the *Wall Street Journal* refused to accept my advertisements, and refused to give me a reason when I asked. The *Airline Pilot Magazine*, which routinely carries classified ads for aviation related books, refused to accept the advertisements. By that time, the news media was already heavily involved in the coverup.

SOME IN THE PUBLISHING INDUSTRY PAID WITH THEIR LIVES FOR THE COVERUP

Among the members of the press and publishing industry who knew of the air safety corruption, and whose silence made possible its continuation, were *Playboy* officials. I offered *Playboy* my manuscript in the mid-1970s, and described the air safety and government corruption. They didn't accept the manuscript. Several years later several *Playboy* officials perished in the Chicago DC-10 tragedy from problems that their publicity could have corrected.

After the Chicago tragedy, *Playboy* published a nineteen-page air safety article that complained of the status of air safety. But the article covered up for the hard-core safety misconduct that must be addressed before any meaningful corrective actions can be taken. The article was entitled, "Airline Safety, a special report," and stated in part:

> The closer you look at airline travel, the more it looks like a game of angels and great good luck, rather than skill and know-how and high technology. ... based on the same statistical manipulations, it was safer to walk the tightrope than fly his planes and it was also safer to repair your roof then to take a bath. ... Statistics can devil the hell out of you if you let them, but you pay your money and you take your chances, and in this game, undelivered goods are nonreturnable.

Even the Air Line Pilots Association, who refused to accept advertisements for the book promoting air safety, lost a former president, Clarence Sayen, in the United 727 crash into Lake Michigan. Their own pilot members were victims of the corruption, and they still wouldn't expose the misconduct, apparently preferring to sacrifice their own members rather than blow the whistle on this sordid scandal. ALPA repeatedly blocked my efforts to improve the safety problem that killed its former president, and other safety problems that killed many of their pilots and thousands of other people.

KNOWINGLY DUPLICATING MY TITLE AND DISTRACTING ATTENTION FROM MY AIR SAFETY MESSAGE

One of the publishing houses to whom I offered my nearly-completed manuscript in 1988 was *Bantam-Doubleday*. I described the highly sensitive material and the coverups, and stated my intention to be a self-publisher if I could not find a large publishing house to take it. *Doubleday* responded they were not interested in the subject matter. You can imagine my surprise when I saw the title of *my* book, *Unfriendly Skies*, heavily promoted on the *Today Show* nearly a year later, on April 26, 1989. Instead of showing me as the author, it showed the authors as an airline pilot identified as Captain X, and writer Reynolds Dodson.

Doubleday knew my book existed. They knew that I spent years promoting it as a public service to expose government corruption, and that its publication was to generate public interest in bringing a halt to the ongoing air tragedies. *Doubleday* published the book using the same name, promoted it as an exposé, and then filled it with pablum, implying air safety is in excellent shape. Their tactics covered up for the misconduct, and acted to obstruct corrective actions. It acted to negate my message, and contributed to the corruption described within these pages.

Doubleday heavily promoted their book, expanding money far beyond that justified by its contents. The publisher implied that the contents were highly sensitive, an exposé, and for that reason the pilot's name was withheld. Captain X appeared on television via computerized composites, so that his identity was unknown. The stated reason was that the contents of the book were so explosive that he couldn't reveal who he was.

It was a snow job to deceive the public. The book didn't contain a single documented or specifically identified occurrence throughout its pages. It was one of the most poorly written books that I had ever seen relating to aviation, and must have been a rush-job.

The duplication of a title that was being promoted by an air safety activist for the last decade, periodically updated, was a blatant misrepresentation. It was the publisher's means of deceiving the public. Possibly it was intended to divert attention from my next printing of the same name. And if it was, these tactics made possible the continuation of the air safety misconduct that threatens everyone who flies, and made possible some of the subsequent air tragedies.

There was nothing of any sensitivity in the book to warrant any pseudo author, except four-letter words. The book dealt heavily on the dating habits of flight attendants, and ramblings by a pilot with limited experience.

The so-called Captain X was scheduled to appear on the Larry King show on May 1, 1989. Several hours before Captain X was to appear, I talked to Pat Piper, an associate producer on the Larry King show, and reminded him that they knew *I* was the author of the *Unfriendly Skies*, and that *Doubleday* copied my title. I felt King should address this important matter during the show. Piper stated that he read *Doubleday*'s *Unfriendly Skies*, and there wasn't anything to it. He stated he didn't know why Captain X was asked to appear.

During Captain X's appearance that night, King didn't ask Captain X why he copied my title. King did ask him why all the secrecy for a book that was rather bland, and portrayed air safety as being in good shape, contrary to the considerable publicity given to the book's promotion. Captain X had the politician's knack for avoiding a difficult question.

I requested an explanation from *Doubleday* on May 10, 1989 as to why they copied the title of my book. Their law firm replied that they had a right to duplicate any title they wanted. A major publishing house does not duplicate the title of another book that is being actively promoted. It is my strong belief that there is much more to this than meets the eye, and that the duplicated title was in some way intended to defuse the gravity of what my upcoming book could be expected to expose.

The *Air Line Pilot* magazine, who years earlier refused to even carry my book advertisements, gave Doubleday's version a glowing review.[211] By lauding *Doubleday's* version that covered up for serious safety problems that adversely affected their own pilot members, the union harmed their own members. The article stated that the book tells it like it is. But the book described air safety as in good shape, contrary to earlier *Air Line Pilot* magazine articles written by their technical staff that is noted for its good in-depth articles. The article stated in part:

> There's just a pilot's and copilot's seat. Some 600 functions have been eliminated from the control panels. On the wall to the right, where the engineer was sitting, there's a box with some shelves. Behind that, there's a wardrobe closet. How simple it is! It's not much worse than ... a sports car dashboard! You've got some computer-terminal screens, and they have some weird-looking graphics on them, but other than that it doesn't seem all that complicated, and you have dreams (foolish dreams!) that you might be able to fly this bugger.
>
> In a chapter entitled "The High But Not Necessarily Mighty," the authors discuss "built-in risk factors" like the "noise pollution factor," the "bird factor," and "the airline versus the fork-tail doctor killers." The latter refers to those general aviation aircraft like the Piper Cherokees and Seminoles flying down in "Indian County," many of them, the author claims, owned by rich doctors or movie producers. These aircraft menace his skies, especially in Southern California.

Following this book review there was a multi-page article describing an interview with Captain X, and describing the mechanics of how *Doubleday* came to duplicate the title. The so-called Captain X described how he was approached by writer Reynolds Dodson, who asked Captain X to contribute to the book. Captain X then described sitting in his backyard and relating "war stories I've told a hundred times before—both to fellow pilots and to friends and relatives."

EXPOSE MATERIAL?
One of the so-called exposé stories was of the captain correcting a landing by a copilot, an event that is as routine as getting up in the morning. Captain X stated a few weeks later

---

[211] July 1989 *Air Line Pilot.*

he received some typewritten pages putting in print his back-yard description of the rough-landing story. "For me, reading those pages was a revelation," Captain X stated. The article continued: "I've got problems. My company won't want to come within 10 miles of a story about a copilot who almost broke one of its airplanes."

This embarrassing naivete was evident throughout the book. There wasn't anything in the book implying an exposé. *Doubleday* must have conned this pilot into contributing to the book, and paid him handsomely for cooperating.

Captain X continued his description of how *Doubleday* arranged for his participation. His first-person writing suddenly took the position of a third person:

> He [co-author to Captain X] sent the first chapter, plus an outline, to his agent. His agent in turn sent it to 15 differ-ent publishers, and 13 expressed interest in it. Within days, Ren was calling excitedly. Three of the publishers had gone into auction, and the winning bid had been quite consider-able. [no legitimate publishers would have gone into auction on such a bland book, when other books far more creditable were on the market.]
>
> I am not always the most patient guy, and a couple of times we almost came to blows over whether a pilot would "shout" or "speak" during the throes of a thunderstorm and whether the emotions that a pilot feels would be fear or hostility. [big deal!]
>
> Now a mini-bureaucracy sprang up, and suddenly I was confronting a new group of personalities. ... When the time came for me to sit down with Doubleday's executives—who still didn't know who I was: as far as they knew I was "Cap-tain X," and to this very day, that is all they know me by—I suddenly found myself sitting in a high-rise conference room staring at a bunch of women who, to my middle-aged eyes, looked like fresh-scrubbed flight attendants.

Captain X described *Doubleday*'s statements that book sales depended on media exposure and advertising, as much as the contents of the book. In this case, far more depended on hype than on contents. *Doubleday* then arranged for Captain X to be coached to prepare him for radio and television appearances. Despite the bland nature of the contents, Doubleday obtained appearances for Captain X on national network shows such as the *Today Show*, *Larry King*, and others (who had repeatedly refused to interview me).

A Los Angeles newspaper review[212] summarized the contents of what *Doubleday* called an exposé:

> Captain X said the worst is over. ... Air travel is actually safer than ever. ... as far as Captain X is concerned, the future is bright for aviation.

This surely wasn't an expose. What were *Doubleday*'s motives? If it was to divert attention from the exposé in my book with the same name, it only takes street-smarts to know that they are sacrificing lives in the process.

Possibly one of the most unusual book reviews that was ever written, and good for some laughs, despite the dangerous consequences of *Doubleday's* tactics, was that which appeared in *Flight Training* magazine on October 1989 which actually advised the readers not to buy the book:

> This is a bad book. ... I suspect Captain "X" elected anonymity after reading what he dictated, and some residue of both ego and pride required that he divorce himself from it. ... This is a book that simply mocks maturity and professionalism. ... Beware! This is not the way it is. The incidents he reports, and which he allowed to happen (and from which he extricated the airplane) bespeak an impaired captain, unable to recognize acceptable aircraft performance. They are not the compliments to himself that he solicits.

DEADLY FALLOUT FROM DOUBLEDAY'S DECEPTION

Doubleday played a dangerous game that knowingly obstructed exposure of the air safety scandal. *Doubleday* knew that I used the title as a springboard to reach the public, trying to motivate them to act. They also knew that anything diverting attention from the serious hard-core problems would continue the crashes caused or made possible by the misconduct.

During a radio appearance with host Anthony Hilder in Anchorage on July 19, 1989, Hilder mistakenly introduced me as Captain X of the *Unfriendly Skies*. Hilder stated that he had seen *Doubleday's* version of my title stacked on the floor of the local book stores, and assumed that it was my book, and that I was Captain X. He recommended the new book to his listeners.

After a few minutes of host comments I was able to say, "Anthony, I'm not Captain X." After I explained *Doubleday's* deception, Hilder became angry that he had been duped. Hilder stated *that* explained the reason that he received complaints

---

[212] Los Angeles *Herald Examiner* May 10, 1989.

from those who read the *Doubleday* book, who stated there was nothing to the book.

Hilder then recommended to his listeners that they return the books they bought, on the basis of misrepresentation. Callers, including an attorney, stressed the need to sue Doubleday. I didn't have the opportunity to describe that the federal judiciary had me gridlocked, and barred me from filing any federal law suits.

The amount of money spent by *Doubleday* to promote the book can be speculated by the reports I received that piles of the book were in bookstores all over the country. Hundreds of thousands of dollars must have been spent on flooding the bookstores with these books.

MANIPULATING WHAT THE PUBLIC READS OR HEARS

Manipulating the news was described in a *Harper* magazine article dated July 1989, explaining in part why I encountered the news gridlock. The article stated how politicians leak the "news" to favored reporters, who then reciprocate by rarely reporting unfavorable articles. The article described the government oligarchy in which power vests in a few persons, doling out "news." *Harper* stated: "By their subjugation of the press, the political powers in America have conferred on themselves the greatest of political blessings—Gyges' ring of invisibility."

The article detailed how some of the most momentous stories of our times never get reported. It described the fear of offending government officials who are the source of a majority of the news stories. The reporters, and their papers, do not want to lose the benefit of these government news sources.

The release of news by powerful Washington figures is described as a soup kitchen, where reporters go to get many of their articles. The article described how self-serving politicians bully and threaten employees of news gathering agencies not to print a story.

The *Harper* article described how the CIA's domestic spying under the transparent guise of "counterintelligence" was kept from the public by the press for at least ten years. The article described how the *Associated Press* fired a reporter that printed the true side of a particular story that was fabricated by Assistant Secretary of Defense Arthur Sylvester. The true story infuriated Sylvester, who then called the reporter's boss at the AP. The news service fired the reporter. Sylvester was reported to be "the master of the soup kitchen at the time."

Several days after Nixon's reelection, White House aide Charles Colson, in charge of handing out news releases and intimidating the press, was infuriated when CBS viewers heard Walter Cronkite describe in detail the high-level campaign of political sabotage and espionage. Colson called William Paley, board chairman of CBS, and warned him that if they did not stop the second program, CBS would be stripped of the licenses to operate its five lucrative television stations. CBS watered down the next show, but not enough to please Colson. Colson again called Paley, and threatened to use the White House's power to ruin CBS on Wall Street and Madison Avenue. "We'll break your network," Colson warned. CBS kept these threats, and the significance of them, from the American public, compounding the harm inflicted upon the public.

A January 15, 1990 *Newsweek* article stated that "while the White House press corps waited to be spoon-fed instructions on the best "visuals," scandals in housing programs and savings and loan regulation went unreported." The article continued,

> No administration really wants reporters snooping through the Agriculture Department or other places they can break new ground; better to have them hanging around the White House briefing room, waiting for handouts. It's this system, rather than any particular handler or press secretary, that conditions and corrodes Washington coverage. That's why it's up to reporters to redefine the concept of news so that it relies more on what they find, and less on what the president—or his press secretary—would have them believe.

Occasionally the system goes out of whack, such as in Watergate. For weeks, most newspapers kept the lid on the relatively minor scandal (compared to that described in these pages), until public interest reached the point where the press could not ignore the drum-beating of the *Washington Post*.

In *The CIA and the Cult Of Intelligence*, the authors describe the pressure and threats upon newspaper and book publishers not to publish matters adversely reflecting upon the CIA or other government agencies. The book describes the planting of moles in the news media, including radio and television networks. The authors describe the pressure put on others not to report government misconduct, and makes them think coverup is in the national interest. (Could this be a key reason for the press coverup in this scandal?)

NEWS DISTORTION

In an in-depth investigative report that is as true today as the day it was published on July 25, 1967, the *Wall Street Journal* described the news distortion and coverup in an article entitled: "*Ethics & the Press*, Conflicts of Interest, Pressures Still Distort Some Papers' Coverage." The in-depth article described how "Advertisers and outside work of Newsmen color stories" and halt investigations. The article stated in part:

In Boston and Chicago, newspaper investigations into suspected hanky-panky suddenly are aborted. In one case, a
subject of inquiry turns out to be a stockholder of the paper
and friend of the publisher. In the other, the investigation
threatens to embarrass a politician who could help the paper
in a building project.

In Denver, the advertising staff of a big daily wrestles
with an arithmetic problem. A big advertiser has been
promised news stories and pictures amounting to 25 percent
of the ad space it buys; the paper already has run hundreds
of column inches of glowing prose but is still not close to
the promises allotment of "news" and now is running out of
nice things to say.

SHORT-CHANGED READERS

All this hardly enhances the image of objectivity and fierce
independence the U.S. press tries so hard to project. Yet
talks with scores of reporters, editors, publishers, public
relations men and others reveal that practices endangering—and often subverting—newspaper integrity are more
common than the man on the street might dream. Result: The
buyer who expects a dime's worth of truth every time he
picks up his paper often is short-changed.

All newspapers, including this one, [how very true!] must
cope with the blandishments and pressures of special interests who seek distortion or omission of the truth. ... on some
papers the trouble starts at the top; it is the publisher
himself who lays down news policies designed to aid one
group or attack another.

It is plain, however, that a sizable minority [or is it
majority] of newspapers still are putty in the hands of their
advertisers, that they allow personal as well as business
considerations to favor the news to a marked degree, ... that
they tolerate staff practices hardly conducive to editorial
independence and objectivity. ... blackouts of news involving
newspapers are quite common; hardly a working journalist
could deny that one of the gravest weaknesses in coverage
exhibited by the American press is its coverage of itself. ...
another grave fault of a good many papers: Favoritism
toward business in general and advertisers in particular. ...
the paper itself, by actual policy or common practice, dis-
torts the news to suit advertisers or literally hands over
news space to them. ... Everyone in newspapering pays lip
service to the ideal that a paper's news columns should not
be for sale, ...a staffer is "on the take" ...

The *Wall Street Journal* article also described the news distortion of virtually every media in the United States, caused by pressures from vested interest groups. The Federal Communications Commission charged NBC-TV with falsely presenting the facts associated with general aviation and airline problems in midair collisions. The FAA charged the NBC staff with twisting and distorting its coverage of the midair collisions, favoring the airlines by distorting the facts. The FAA ordered NBC to take "appropriate steps to achieve fairness" in the coverage of air saety and cease distorting the facts against the general aviation pilots and in favor of the airlines.

PRESSURE ON ADVERTISERS TO REMAIN SILENT

Following a series of Delta Air Line incidents in mid-1987, Delta put financial pressure on the news media who reported the many near-crashes of Delta's aircraft. Delta threatened to cancel valued advertising accounts with the newspapers and radio stations making these reports. An *Associated Press* article dated August 13, 1987 described Delta's threats to cancel large blocks of advertising. Delta responded by stating there was a "misunderstanding." What else could they say.

With yearly advertising budgets for a single airline approaching one hundred million dollars, a newspaper must be careful not to offend a particular airline, or the **entire** airline industry. Federal Express dropped its ads on ABC prime-time television network after a critical report on ABC's 20/20. The program[217] said Federal Express mishandled Government and military documents and packages. The program also accused their employees of drug use, shipping of illegal narcotics and opening packages that they suspected contained drugs. President Frederick Smith of Federal Express wrote on July 14, 1989 that the company was cancelling its prime-time advertising with the exception of commercials scheduled for the ABC telecast of the World Series and Monday Night Football. Federal Express spent over $40 million a year on advertising according to the Standard Director of Advertisers, an industry publication. In another letter, President Smith wrote that this cancellation would cost ABC "in excess of $100 million." Its easy to understand how the news media hesitates to print anything that would dissatisfy that valuable customer.

Air Transport World of March 1970 described the value of airline advertising: "airlines are a major source of ad revenue." Airlines such as Delta run full-page ads in the *Wall Street Journal*, and rarely run articles highly detrimental to the airlines' interests.

---

217 *New York Times*, October 18, 1989 report of July 7, 1989 show.

THE ADVERTISING DOLLAR MAKES SMALL
PLANES FLY BACKWARDS

The multi-million dollar advertising revenues may explain the uncanny ability of small planes to fly backwards, or catching up and ramming into a jetliner traveling at twice their speed. The news media had attributed this remarkable feat to small planes and their pilots in numerous midair collisions. In the PSA San Diego midair collision, the airliner actually rammed the small plane from the rear. But the news media reported that the small plane crashed into the jet. In the Cerritos midair collision, the DC-9 jet, flying in a northerly direction, rammed into the side of the small plane that was on an easterly heading. The news media reported the small plane crashed into the jetliner. A *Time* article of September 15, 1986 showed the east-bound small plane on a southerly heading so as to place the blame on the general aviation pilot.

Most newspapers wouldn't print anything about the reported all-night crew partying in the PSA San Diego crash, or the many other wrongdoings described within these pages.

The amount of financial leverage that airlines exert over the news media is enormous. United Airlines, for instance, in the mid-eighties, normally spent about $70 million annually in advertising, with occasional increases above that when the situation warrants. (Bruce Horovitz/Marketing, *Los Angeles Times*, October 13, 1987) The *Wall Street Journal* often carried full-page or near-full-page airline advertisements in 1989, constituting big-bucks in their advertising income.

In February 1988 an eighty-two year old friend of mine, Graydon Milton, concerned about what was being done to me, asked a reporter friend on the San Francisco Chronicle to look into the matter and write a story about it. I told Graydon that the Chronicle already knew about the scandal and had kept a lid on it. However, I met with two reporters[214] who responded to Graydon's request. I gave them documents supporting my allegations, and made reference to federal law suits that provided additional support.

When Graydon later called his reporter friends they stated they did not write an article because I refused to give them supporting material. I gave them large amounts of material, and withheld nothing. They lied.

PRIMARY EXPOSURE MEDIUM—Talk show hosts

The *local* radio and television shows, however, were not reluctant to have me appear. Some hosts were especially effective at alerting the public to the serious threats affecting

---

[214] Jeff Palline and Bill Wallace.

air safety. With them, I could get into the hard-core misconduct that caused and made possible some of the world's worst air tragedies. Some were not mentally geared to pry that deeply, and with them, I stayed within the framework where they felt comfortable, and still managed to get a partial message across.

Censorship occasionally arose. Many radio stations are affiliated with newspapers, and it was the newspapers that presented the greatest obstacle to exposing this national scandal. The first time I stated on a talk show that there appeared to be a newspaper coverup of the scandal in 1988, on radio station WERE in Cleveland, Ohio, with host Joel Rose, the show abruptly ended fifteen minutes early. In addition, two subsequently scheduled shows for the next week on nearby stations were suddenly cancelled.

On another show the producer called me several hours before the show was to start, and said the host was sick. But the plan wasn't too well coordinated, as I was later called about two minutes before I would normally be on the air, and advised the show would go on in a few minutes, indicating the host was indeed in the station, and not sick. When I replied, "I thought the show was cancelled," the caller checked, and then advised that it had been cancelled. Host Michael Jackson cancelled my appearance hours before I was to appear. As the government and judicial scandal worsened in the late 1980s, these cancellations increased in frequency, even though the stations that did not cancel often times went out of their way to state the seriousness of, and the interest in, the matters we discussed.

"You can't Say Anything Against United Airlines"!

The radio and television networks, recipients of large airline advertising revenue far exceeding 300 million dollars annually, said very little about the hard-core air safety problems. I was to appear on NBC's *Tomorrow* Show, and given a date to appear. The precise time for me to appear would be given before noon of the next day. During this initial conversation the producer stated that I could not say anything against United Airlines because NBC had a very profitable advertising account with United. I replied that I would concentrate my attention on the misconduct within the two government air safety agencies.

The producers must have reconsidered, and didn't want to risk offending United. I was never called back, and a replacement appeared in my place.

CHALLENGER DISASTER

Coverup of a serious safety problem preceded the Challenger disaster, which carried seven people to their death, including school teacher Christa McAuliffe. Those who had the technical competency to know, wanted the launch scrubbed, because of serious safety problems caused by the cold weather conditions.[215] But to do so would cost money, and delay the launch. Also, President Reagan had planned a television appearance that evening, using the Challenger launch to convey a theme in his State of the Union message. Management personnel, sensitive to political and other pressures, overruled the technical personnel, and approved the launch. Tragedy followed, as forewarned.

DEATH OF GOVERNMENT INVESTIGATOR TO COVER UP FOR SCANDAL GOING INTO THE WHITE HOUSE

Government investigators who blow the whistle on government corruption face all types of dangers. Federal inspector Henry Marshall, an employee of the Agricultural Stabilization and Conservation Service, was found dead in June of 1961 on a farm in Texas. Marshall was known to have evidence of a multimillion-dollar commodity fraud linked to an LBJ political agent, and Lyndon Johnson himself. Alongside Marshall's body was the .22 caliber rifle that had fired the fatal bullets. The Texas authorities ruled Marshall's death a suicide, even though the position of the wounds would be difficult to self-inflict with the long-barrel rifle found alongside his body.

An AP article prepared by the *Dallas Times Herald*,[216] stated that convicted swindler Billy Sol Estes secretly testified before a grand jury empaneled at Franklin, Texas relating to the Marshall death. Estes testified that he was present when Lyndon Johnson and two other men discussed having Marshall killed. Estes testified that Marshall knew too much about illegal manipulation of cotton allotments, and that Johnson gave the order to have Marshall slain. Estes identified the two men as Clifton Carter and Malcolm Wallace. Carter was once Johnson's top political operative in Texas and later his White House liaison to the Democratic National Committee. Wallace was a

---

[215] Infrared temperature-sensing instruments showed abnormal "cold spots" on the lower part of the right-hand booster, which later failed during launch. The Thiokol engineers were adamant that the launch be delayed. They felt that the O-rings lost some of their resiliency and ability to seat tightly in their grooves, when their temperatures fall below 50 degrees. The O-ring temperatures had fallen to 30 degrees, far below the safe limit. Despite the engineer's protest, NASA officials went ahead with the launch, with fatal results. The company later fired the inspectors who exposed the defects in the Challenger launching.

[216] March 24, 1984 article appearing in *Sacramento Bee*, prepared by the *Dallas Times Herald*.

former University of Texas student body president and con-victed murderer—and friend of Lyndon Johnson.

The Marshall killing and its relationship to Lyndon Johnson had been the subject of intense gossip and rumor in Texas political circles for years. Estes, who had aged since Marshall was killed, agreed to testify about the Marshall killing at the urging of U.S. Marshal Clint Peoples of Dallas. Peoples had pursued the case for more than two decades.

Other testimony in the grand jury hearings brought out that Johnson approved the killing out of fear that Marshall would give Attorney General Robert F. Kennedy evidence about cotton allotments that would incriminate LBJ. Robert Kennedy was known to have had no respect for the Texas politician.

The deaths of other key parties to the alleged murder con-spiracy prevented further grand jury investigation. Former President Lyndon Johnson died January 22, 1973 on his ranch near Austin, Texas. Wallace died in a car accident in 1971, and Carter died September 22, 1971. The grand jury didn't reach any decision on who killed Marshall, but held that he was killed.

The actions taken to silence me shows the extent to which people in control of our government will go to keep scandals from the public.

There is no limit to what corrupt government officials will do. It isn't any secret that the Kennedy White House discussed the political assassinations of foreign leaders. When leaders of the United States can actually entertain such a thought, is there any doubt that the crimes described in these pages exist?

"You're going to get killed!"

When FAA inspectors warn another inspector they risk getting killed for reporting internal government corruption, the public might get the impression that FAA inspectors are not going to report safety problems! "You're going to get killed," warned more than one FAA employee, as I tried to expose the FAA corruption. If other inspectors felt that getting killed for reporting safety problems was a possibility, obviously they would not be reporting the same problems.

The web of intrigue under these breakdowns of checks and balances and massive government corruption is such that no one is free to speak up. If an honest Senator or Representative sought to expose the FBI and Department of Justice miscon-duct, the Justice Department could promptly destroy that person. They could do this by charging them with a grey-area crime, or simply leaking to the press that an investigation was underway. The same goes for an FAA air safety inspector. I saw FAA inspectors harassed for reporting safety violations and problems. Many were made to suffer financially from doing their highly sensitive jobs in the hotbed of FAA corruption.

TEXAS POLITICS AND THE U.S. SUPREME COURT

President Lyndon Johnson relief upon voter fraud to get into the U.S. Senate, which was described in the 1964 publication of *A Texan Looks At Johnson* and the 1990 *Means of Ascent* by Robert Caro, published by Knopf. When Johnson discovered that Texas governor Coke Stevenson had received 112 votes more then he did, Johnson arranged for a recanvass and an additional 202 votes in a district he controlled. When the matter was taken to the federal district court and the court issued an injunction barring Johnson from claiming victory, and setting a hearing to address the voter fraud, Johnson obtained the assistance of influential attorney Abe Fortas to protect the voter fraud. To circumvent the unfavorable evidence being presented in the U.S. District Court in Texas, Fortas (who was later appointed to the U.S. Supreme Court) presented the matter to Supreme Court Justice Hugo Black. Black ruled in Johnson's favor, without allowing the evidence of voter fraud to be presented. Johnson later rewarded Fortas as he helped Fortas get onto the U.S. Supreme Court, a position from which he later resigned because of his judicial misconduct.

The sordid state of Texas politics, the corruption that goes all the way to the White House, within the Congress, and within the Supreme Court, are described in many books. Nothing stated within these pages should be shocking to a serious student of dirty American politics and government. This is the only known book that associates the misconduct with the deaths of American and foreign citizens, including the little children who are no match for this gang of thugs.

HARASSMENT OF NUCLEAR PLANT INSPECTORS

Harassment of company inspectors at a nuclear plant under construction by Brown & Root, Inc., was described in a *Wall Street Journal* article dated November 7, 1984. The *Journal* reported that the plant, Comanche Peak, was riddled with poor workmanship. When quality-control inspectors refused to pass defective work, the companies fired the inspectors. The company claimed the fired inspectors did not follow orders. The Nuclear Regulatory Commission conducted an inquiry to determine whether harassment and intimidation of these and other inspectors compromised the plant's safety. Dozens of inspectors around the country complained of pressure to ignore defects, which otherwise would be costly to the companies. The inquiry found the company fired inspectors who adhered to quality control standards required by federal regulations (similar to harassment of FAA inspectors).

The *Wall Street Journal* article described the actual physical threats against inspectors at the Zimmer plant of Cincinnati Gas & Electric Company in Moscow, Ohio. Inspectors were doused with water and with fire extinguisher fluids during inspections. Ultimately, the quality of the plant was in such doubt that the plant converted from nuclear energy to coal. At a nuclear plant built by four utility companies near Bay City, Texas, the Nuclear Regulatory Commission threatened to halt the project in 1980 after it found that supervisors consistently overruled quality-control inspectors in favor of construction workers.

KAREN SILKWOOD

A movie and a book were written about the Karen Silkwood episode. Silkwood met her death while driving to a meeting to show a *New York Times'* reporter documentary evidence that Kerr-McGee lacked adequate safety measures and quality controls in a plutonium recycling plant where she was employed. I have no evidence in this matter, and simply raise it as intriguing speculation.

AIRLINE MAINTENANCE INSPECTORS ARE PRESSURED TO LIE

Many newspaper reports described falsified approval of maintenance work at airlines, without the work having been done or inspected. Pilots and mechanics at Eastern Airlines repeatedly reported this problem, which the FAA stated did not exist. Company officials reportedly pressured inspectors to sign off on work that was not done, or not inspected. Some inspectors and management officials resigned, rather than be a part to it. A former Eastern management official, Paul Kilpatrick, stated to me[222] that he resigned his position, giving up 24 years seniority, when management officials wanted him to sign off for work that was never done. Many of the Eastern Airlines pilots complained about pressure from top management to fly aircraft that had numerous system malfunctions, and which were dangerous. Despite many similar reports, the FAA gave Eastern a clean bill of health following the inspection.

Douglas Aircraft Company at Long Beach falsified records preceding the Paris DC-10 crash, making possible the 346 deaths at Paris. The falsified records indicated the company made modifications that had life-or-death consequences, when the modifications had not been made.

In 1985 the FBI investigated an alleged cover-up of violations by the FAA at Continental Airlines. FAA Western Region officials deleted significant portions of a safety report prepared by FAA inspectors from a final version sent to Washington. The leader of the FAA inspection team, Harry Langdon, found significant problems with Continental's pilot checkout

---

[222] May 1989.

and training procedures. He reported: "It shows either a lack of understanding of federal aviation regulations or a disregard for them. Continental does not, in our opinion, presently meet certification standards" The report also criticized FAA officials at Western Region headquarters in Los Angeles, stating that they were "remiss in condoning the situation." Nothing has changed since I and other inspectors made similar reports over the past thirty years.

Just as the NTSB politically sensitive Board will sequester evidence uncovered by its air safety investigators, the FAA deleted the sensitive parts of the FAA investigation of Continental Airlines. The final inspection report prepared by FAA management officials in Los Angeles deleted the inspection team's three pages of violations and criticisms.

Langdon wrote that the changes showed "a lack of integrity and the abuse of authority."

INTO THE WHITE HOUSE ITSELF

While Ronald Reagan was president, I notified his office of the scandal, giving details of the misconduct, and reminding the President of the consequences of coverup. No response. In 1988, while Vice-President George Bush campaigned for president, he promised to get tough with criminals, which I took to include those within government. After Bush became president, and continued to articulate his concern for government ethics and crime, I made him aware of the worsening scandal, sending him a May 1989 letter and attachments describing the criminal misconduct shown within these pages. The White House advised me the matter was turned over to the Department of Justice (who had committed many of the corrupt acts I described).

Bush was head of the CIA in 1976 and 1977, while much of the air disaster coverup was going on. In an earlier chapter, The Imposters, I described the mysterious men who met with Edith Armstrong, trying to discover what we knew about the scandal, asking if we suspected the CIA was involved. They were fishing to discover how much I suspected. Possibly the CIA *was* involved in the coverup, and possibly this continued while Bush was head of the covert organization. It would be natural to continue the coverup when he became president.

From 1965 until this book was published in 1989, I sent out hundreds of letters and petitions to members of Congress, notices to the news media, and others. I identified specific air tragedies, with specific hard-core misconduct, offering hard evidence to support my allegations. My credentials, and the gruesome consequences if my allegations were correct, made an investigation mandatory. Despite the consequences of coverup, despite the repeated air tragedies obviously related to the misconduct I charged to exist, not a single person, group, news media, or check and balance, made any effort to publicize my allegations, or bring about an investigation.

CONGRESSIONAL PRESSURE TO KEEP QUIET

In his book, *Blind Trust*, author John Nance described the pressure from Senator Henry Jackson following the Air Florida crash at Washington National Airport. Following the crash, one of Air Florida's captains, Jim Marquis, discovered for the first time the dangerous pitch-up problem with the Boeing 737 caused by contamination on the wing leading edge. Boeing and the airlines knew of this problem for several years, and gave it very little attention, despite the need for the pilots to know of its existence, and how to prevent fatal consequences.

Nance describes how Marquis obtained records from Boeing Aircraft Company showing that they knew this problem existed. Marquis sought to get publicity through the news media (lots of luck!), and to force the NTSB to change the primary blame for the Air Florida crash to Boeing's dangerous pitch-up problem.

Boeing was sufficiently concerned about bad publicity that they reportedly sought help from Senator Henry Jackson. Jackson is reported to have personally called Marquis at the motel room in Seattle where Marquis was staying. The Senator tried to dissuade Marquis from continuing the exposure of Boeing's wing problem, advising that he was concerned about the loss of business to his Washington constituents if Marquis' continued his exposure activities. The Senator tried to intimidate Marquis by asking if he was on some kind of vendetta against Boeing, and warned him that his actions threatened to shut down 737 operations all over the world.

This was, of course, not true. The European operators already knew of the wing problems and addressed the matter by increasing the takeoff speeds approximately 15 knots when there was any danger of leading edge wing contamination. If Boeing and or the FAA had required the Boeing 737 operators to add the 15 knots of extra speed under these conditions, the problem would have greatly diminished. However, to admit the problem existed, and increase the runway requirements or reduce takeoff gross weight, occasionally reduces revenue. The FAA chose to ignore the problem and take a calculated risk. The danger is not impressed upon the pilots, and the extra takeoff airspeed does not become an FAA requirement. The problem is thus "solved!"

SIMULTANEOUS WRITINGS ON TRAGEDIES, AND COVERUP

The press repeatedly write articles on the sufferings arising from air disasters. Then they cover up for the misconduct causing the crashes, becoming a contributing cause to subsequent air tragedies and deaths. Some of the best researched articles on the human sufferings associated with air tragedies can be found in the *Wall Street Journal*. Their investigative reporters often present a well-researched documentary. But they carefully omit the corruption that causes or makes them possible.

From 1965 through 1988, I repeatedly made the *Wall Street Journal* aware of the corruption causing and permitting the air tragedies to occur. They covered up. And once their coverup played a contributing role in subsequent crashes, the *Journal* *had* to continue the coverup to protect their own involvement that made the crashes possible. As the cause-and-effect repeated itself and left no question of the relationship, these same powerful newspapers were forced to continue the secrecy. Their responsibilities as a free press to report the government and industry corruption has been colored by their own duplicity of silence.

An article in *Aviation Week & Space Technology* on May 1, 1989 stated:

> ATA President Blasts U.S. Government's Failure to Reform Aviation Agency. The article stated "The U.S. government has failed inexcusably to respond to reforms recommended by the Aviation Safety Commission a year ago, according to Robert J. Aaronson, the new head of the Air Transport Assn.

The basis for these charges is a fraction of the actual misconduct. No one can blow the whistle on anyone else, without implicating themselves, or vested and protected interests.

Despite the continuation of the misconduct and the resulting air tragedies. The *New York Times* and the *Wall Street Journal* kept the lid on all aspects of the scandal. The Portland papers kept the lid on the United DC-8 crash into Portland. The San Diego newspapers, and San Diego Mayor Pete Wilson—later, U.S. Senator Wilson—kept the lid on the PSA San Diego scandal. The Salt Lake City newspapers kept the lid on the United Salt Lake City scandal. All of these papers, including the *Wall Street Journal*, carry large aviation-related advertisements.

An editorial in the *San Francisco Chronicle* on May 1, 1989 entitled **Aviation Safety,** lamented the decline in air safety. Its answer? Remove the FAA from under the Department of Transportation and make it an independent agency. But the FAA was an independent agency when I was an FAA air safety investigator, uncovering scandals that had world-wide tragedy relationships! The FAA should be separate, but the main problem is exposing the corruption, taking firm actions to address the criminal misconduct by specific FAA people, those within the

NTSB, the Department of Justice, federal judges, members of Congress, that engaged in criminal coverup. That will never come about, until the public gets off their duffs and force it to happen.

In 1988 I sent over 20 certified letters to the nation's largest newspapers, making them aware of the multi-faceted scandal, and the serious judicial corruption taken to silence me. Any aspect of this was a scandal worthy of major news reporting. Not a single newspaper responded to my mailings.

HYPOCRITICAL HAND-WRINGING BY THE PRESS

Almost every year there are demands to do something about the air safety problems. In the 1960s and 1970s the demands occurred every few years. The same occurred in the 1980s, with the demands escalating toward the later 1980s.

PUBLIC POSTURING

Wonders never cease. A conference was held in Washington on October 6, 7, 1988, entitled, "How to prevent, Investigate, and Litigate Aircraft Disasters." And who were some of the speakers on air safety? Donald Madole, who was listed as managing partner of one of the nation's largest aviation crash litigation law firms. Congressman James Oberstar, chairman of the House Investigations and Oversight Subcommittee of Public Works and Transportation—responsible for aviation safety, who repeatedly refused to respond to my serious air safety allegations. Richard Witkin, Transportation Editor for the New York Times, was present, representing the paper that had kept the lid on the scandal since 1965.

What did they have in common? Donald Madole was an attorney with the Federal Aviation Administration when my predecessor on the United Airlines assignment went to Washington seeking help, and told Madole about the criminal activities at the FAA and United Airlines. Madole was in a higher position of responsibility when I contacted him several years later. I made similar complaints, now reinforced with the knowledge of additional resulting air tragedies that his previous coverup helped create. Both Harrell and I had highly sensitive positions on the United Airlines program that was riddled with corruption. We both had hard evidence to support our allegations. Madole was head, at that time, of the Bureau of Safety of the Civil Aeronautic Board—the predecessor of the National Transportation Safety Board, responsible for investigating air safety problems. If Madole had responded to the desperate pleas of my predecessor, and myself, the dozens of airline crashes and deaths, and the hundreds if not thousands of deaths arising in those crashes, would very probably not have happened.

THE NADER GROUP

Ralph Nader's aviation group also kept the lid on the scandal. When I had firmly identified the extreme gravity of the air disaster corruption in the mid 1960s, I contacted the Nader group for assistance, asking them to help with an exposure to prevent more air tragedies needlessly occurring. Nader representative Reuben Robertson traveled from Washington to discuss the matters with me. He admitted the gravity of the allegations, and left. Nothing was done by him or the Nader group to address the crash-causing misconduct. Robertson later accepted a position with one of my adversaries, the CAB.

After going through the revolving door syndrome, Robertson and the Nader group filed a federal law suit under the Freedom of Information Act[223] against the FAA in the District of Columbia.[224] The complaint sought information on safety problems discovered during the FAA Washington inspection team investigations. The FAA refused to release the information, holding it to be confidential. The federal judges upheld the FAA's position, and refused to require the information relating to air safety violations to be released to the public. In 1988 I again contacted the Nader group concerning the worsening problems. They wouldn't even answer.

THE ACLU

The ACLU gets large financial donations from the public on the argument that they protect civil and constitutional rights. While some of their stated motives and actions are meritorious, there are many who question whether their goals enhance the quality of life or cause great harm, arguing that the ACLU protects subversives and criminals. I notified the ACLU of the attacks upon my civil and constitutional rights. The first contact occurred in 1965, and continued through 1988. No help was offered. During a 1988 Reno talk show, the ACLU upheld the right to imprison citizens who report government misconduct when a federal judge's self-serving and unlawful injunctive order bars the person from reporting the wrongful government conduct. This subject was discussed in an earlier chapter. The Friedman law firm that commenced the judicial action that served as the basis for judicial persecution for the last eight years was heavily involved in ACLU activities. Further, the corrupt acts taken by those identified within these pages also violated the civil and constitutional rights of those who perished.

---

[223] Title 5 Section 552.

[224] *Robertson, III, et al., v. Butterfield, Administrator, Federal Aviation Administration, et al.,* C.A. No. 72-2186.

MORE ARROGANCE OF THOSE IN CONTROL OF GOVERNMENT

Members of Congress proposed legislation in mid-1989 to shoot down private aircraft and private citizens, and then make those doing the shooting immune from the consequences. Various government agencies proposed shooting down private aircraft that did not respond to signals from an intercepting aircraft. The senate voted to authorize the Customs Service and other federal agencies in August 1989 to fire upon small planes that do not respond to interception. Entire families can be wiped out by gunfire in this manner.

The United States government held in 1989 that it has the moral and legal right to sneak into a foreign country and use force to seize a foreign citizen and return him to the United States for allegedly violating laws in the United States. The abducted person would be in a hostile environment, without funds to hire legal counsel, and with legal counsel usually protecting the government's position. It can be safely presumed that if a foreign country, such as Iran or Libya, felt that a United States citizen violated one of their laws, that they would not be given the same legal right to sneak into the United States and seize one of our citizens by force.

We trust young kids in the United States Navy to blindly send missiles against an unknown target on airways heavily traveled by commercial aircraft, shooting down an Iranian jet near Basra, killing over 200 people. We seize vessels in international waters to inspect for drugs that may not be illegal in the foreign country. We blockage foreign countries to stop flow of drugs, intruding upon the sovereignty of foreign governments. We force foreign countries to accept our form of government, including presumably the government conduct described within these pages!

ONE-SIDED JUSTICE TO PROTECT GOVERNMENT CORRUPTION

In the late 1980s numerous people were charged by the Justice Department with crimes, sent to prison, and their families destroyed. What were these "crimes"? Typical were the charges filed again Robert McFarland; he was charged with four misdemeanor criminal charges for withholding information from congressional committees probing support for the Nicaraguan rebels. He was sentenced by District of Columbia chief judge Aubrey Robinson, Jr. who was simultaneously sequestering evidence of the air disaster and judicial scandal by dismissing my highly sensitive law suits.[225] In 1989 the Justice Department

---

[225] 86-2523; 87-2214.

charged a young lady, Lisa Jones, with a crime, and a federal judge sentenced her to prison, for not remembering details on one of her stock-broker transactions. Compare these "crimes" with the judicial, Congressional, and air safety crimes described within these pages. Who caused the greatest harm to the public?

PART OF THE PROBLEM—THE REVOLVING DOOR SYNDROME

Part of the reason for influence peddling and corruption arises from the revolving door syndrome. It is seen in many scandals, including   HUD, the savings and loan, Defense Department, and in air safety. Ignoring regulatory violations by government employees seeking employment with industry is an accepted fact of life.[226]

The revolving door problems were described in *This World* on June 2, 1985. It stated in part:

> ... a quality control officer nearing the end of a military career was likely to keep his mouth shut if he spotted a problem with a company that might offer him a job after retirement. ... People are frequently looking for the next job, and you're going to do things that make that next job easier to get. ... a Department of Defense attorney ... acknowledged that there was "a lot of concern" about the issue at the department. ... [a company] comes around and offers him a job at $50,000 to $75,000 per year. If he stands up and makes a fuss about high cost and poor quality, [the company won't] come to him when he retires.

---

[226] NTSB chairman Webster Todd became director of ALPA's department of engineering and air safety; FAA Administrator Butterfield became employed by IASCO, an aviation concern near San Francisco; FAA Administrator Najeebe Halaby became president of Pan American World Airways; FAA chief counsel Bert Goodwin became director of regulatory affairs at ALPA headquarters in Washington; FAA Administrator John Shaffer became a director at Beech Aircraft Corporation; FAA official John Baker became head of the Aircraft Owners and Pilots Association; Don Madole left the NTSB's Bureau of Aviation Safety to become a partner in a key law firm; NTSB Board member Hogue went with Airline Passengers Association; the bankruptcy judge who ruled favorable for Continental Airlines then left the bench and joined the law firm representing Continental; Robert Remley, a former FAA official who ruled favorably in a 1984 safety audit of Continental (despite contrary inspector reports), went with Continental; Those going to Texas Air Corporation included Richard Hirst as Vice President, who was a former attorney with the CAB; Clark Onstad, Vice President and Chief Lobbyist, who was former Chief Counsel with the FAA; Dewey Roark, General Counsel, who was formerly Special Counsel for regulations in the FAA; those government officials going with Eastern Airlines: John Keyser, Vice President for Regulatory Compliance at Eastern, and former FAA attorney and official (with whom I worked in the FAA in the early 1960s); Phillip Bakes as President and Chief Executive Officer at Eastern Airlines, was former Chief Counsel of CAB, was former counsel to Congressional committee which wrote Airline Deregulation law.

A *Wall Street Journal* investigative reporting article on January 4, 1989 addressed the revolving door problem:

> **Competition to Hire Officials Leaving Government Is Fiercest for Pair of Lawyers From Trade Office.** [Describing the high financial rewards received by government employees going with the industry they formerly regulated and giving as examples two government employees going with industry] it is reliably understood that they each will be paid upwards of $300,000 a year to launch an international trade practice at [a major law firm]."

Another front page *Wall Street Journal* article on January 31, 1989 described the rewards received by employees involved in the savings and mess loan: "Revolving Door—S&L Mess Isn't All Bad, At Least for Lawyers Who Were Regulators." The article described an attorney who left government to join a law firm and started at triple and more of what the government paid.

I described the hard-core safety misconduct to Don Madole, a high government safety official, the corruption that caused several recent air tragedies. Madole protected United Airlines, the FAA, the NTSB, and who knows who else. Madole left government service and reportedly became a multi-millionaire, and a partner in the law firm with whom he associated[1] and later became a partner.

Former Reagan aide Michael Deaver parlayed his government contacts after leaving government service, and was sent to prison for not waiting the required 12 months before using his contacts. Deaver became a symbol of the "sleaze factor" because of his effort to build a lobbying practice based on his access to the White House. But this was peanuts compared to the hard crimes committed by those prosecuting Deaver and sentencing him to prison.

Speaking of those departing government officials at the Bank Board that helped bring about the Savings and Loan fiasco, Representative Jim Leach stated "My impression is that they'll all go out and earn a million dollars. The revolving door at the Bank Board makes the problems at the Pentagon look like peanuts."[2]

The Wall Street Journal described the speaking appearances before industry groups by government officials, seeking clients after their departure from government or for employment positions. These government officials act to protect their future benefactors.

The Revolving Door problem was addressed by *Newsweek* on February 6, 1989, making reference to middle and high level officials with the Federal Trade Commission who triple their former government salaries upon going with those they formerly regulated. The practice of cashing in their government contacts and knowledge, and working against the public interest, was described.

The *Newsweek* article described examples of the profitable revolving door syndrome. John Norris, former deputy commissioner, Food and Drug Administration, went from a government salary of $75,500 to an estimated $360,000 salary. Gene Lucero, who supervised enforcement of Superfund and hazardous-waste laws against private companies, went from $75,000 to an estimated $190,000. Robert Paul general counsel for the Federal Trade Commission, went from $78,000 to an estimated $240,000. The list goes on and on.

Former Texas Senator John Towers left the Senate in 1985 after serving as chairman of the Senate Armed Services Committee, joined a high-powered consulting firm whose chief clients were major defense contractors, and was paid over $750,000 for his advice to contractors following a very short period of work.

Department of Transportation Secretary James Burnley left government to join a prominent Washington law firm under suspicious circumstances. He was reported to be actively negotiating to join the law firm at the same time he issued an important ruling in favor of Eastern Airlines, one of the law firm's major clients in the transportation field. In December 1988, before leaving his government position, Burnley took the unusual step of personally handling a request by the Air Line Pilots Association that the department investigate Eastern's "continuing fitness" as a carrier in view of its continuing financial troubles. Such matters are usually dealt with at the assistant-secretary level. A week after Burnley intervened personally, Burnley rejected the petition in a strongly worded order saying it "borders on abuse of the department's processes." At the same time, Burnley was negotiating to join the law firm of Shaw, Pittman, Potts & Trowbridge, which represented Eastern Airlines and another Texas Air subsidiary, Continental Airlines.

The Air Line Pilots Association accused Burnley of a conflict-of-interest, accusing Burning of seeking employment with two law firms having close ties to Eastern Airlines at the same time he denied ALPA's petition for a fitness examination of the airline.

President George Bush made ethics his first "priority" when he entered the White House. I sent Bush an eight page petition to conduct an immediate investigation into the air safety/air disaster scandal and the superimposed government, Justice Department, and judicial scandal. He turned the matter over to the Justice Department, one of those listed in the petition as being deeply involved in the misconduct.

Benevolence toward industry by the regulators who plan to become employed after leaving government service by those they are regulating is an accepted fact of life. NTSB chairman Webster Todd became director of ALPA's department of engineering and air safety; FAA Administrator Butterfield became employed by IASCO, an aviation concern near San Francisco; FAA Administrator Halaby became president of Pan American World Airways; FAA chief counsel Bert Goodwin became director of regulatory affairs at ALPA headquarters in Washington; FAA Administrator Shaffer became a director at Beech Aircraft Corporation; FAA official John Baker became head of the Aircraft Owners and Pilots Association; Don Madole left the NTSB's Bureau of Aviation Safety to become a partner in a key law firm; NTSB Board member Hogue went with Airline Passengers Association; the list goes on and on. It is one of several reasons for the hesitancy of government safety officials in the FAA and NTSB to force compliance with the federal safety laws.

In 1989 Samuel Skinner was the Secretary of the U.S. Department of Transportation, which had considerable influence over the FAA's safety activities. This important office has been made into a position dictated by political considerations, despite the literal life and death effect upon the nation's air safety activities. In 1977 the Federal Drug Administration requested Samuel Skinner, while he was a U.S. Attorney, another political post, to conduct a grand jury investigation into allegedly fraudulent tests conducted by Searle Pharmaceutical, which were used to obtain approval for the artificial sweetener, aspartame, or commercially known as Nutra Sweet or Equal. The FDA discovered that numerous early tests with the artificial sweetener resulted in tumors and deaths of laboratory animals.

Skinner withdrew from the case several months later. He was interviewing for a job with the law firm of Sidley & Austin, who was defending Searle in that very investigation. The case was then assigned to assistant U.S. Attorney William Conlon. Upon being offered a job by the same law firm defending Searle, he withdrew from the case. The case was then assigned to assistant U.S. Attorney Thomas Sullivan, who took no action on the investigation into the allegedly fraudulent tests, and finally the five-year statute of limitations expired.

Under Searle's president, former U.S. Congressman and Ford Administration Secretary of Defense Donald Rumsfield, the FDA then approved aspartame for human consumption in 1981. Between the years 1979 to 1982, four additional FDA officials who helped approve aspartame went onto the payrolls of industries linked to NutraSweet.

AIRLINE PASSENGER ASSOCIATION

The International Airline Passengers Association (IAPA)[227] earns its revenues from airline passengers, purporting to protect their interests in the air. But the IAPA kept the lid on the scandal for years, making possible the continuation of practices that killed some of their members. IAPA obtained considerable news media publicity with their knee-jerk reactions to safety problems, but usually their shots fall far away from the problem. In an early press release[228] they blamed the pilot of a Braniff Lockheed Electra for the crash of the plane, citing his failure to use another route of flight. The plane was in the clear, between towering buildups, an acceptable procedure. The crash actually occurred due to a design flaw; the engine and wing ripped off in flight.

IAPA called for grounding the DC-10s in 1989 after United's Sioux City crash. But after Douglas announced that within two years it was installing a one-way check valve in one of the hydraulic lines, the IAPA expressed satisfaction that the problem was solved. The problem wasn't solved. The IAPA is a profitable group that makes a lot of noise but avoids confronting the dirty issues that are the real problems.

I kept them informed of the corruption that threatened their members and that killed some of them, and would continue to do so. In the 1960s I notified them, and again in 1989. They continued the coverup. In 1989 they wouldn't even respond to my letters.

AIRLINES SACRIFICE SAFETY FOR MONEY

The willingness of airlines to sacrifice safety has existed for years. The airlines know the dangers of outward-opening cargo doors; the absence of backups for flight controls; the dangers of no fire extinguishing agents in the cargo compartments. Airlines sought to make one of the emergency exists on the 747 inoperative, to save pennies. They knew that in emergency evacuations, lives may be lost by closing off an emergency exit. The airlines know that eliminating the flight engineer increases dangers. They know the dangers of the early Boeing 737s when there is wing contamination, and fail to require speed adjustments to offset the problem.

The airlines even opposed legislation requiring a medical kit on board the aircraft to handle heart attacks, asthma, and diabetes emergencies. I noticed in 1951, when I first started

---

[227] Originally called Airline Passengers Association (APA), located in Dallas, Texas.
[228] May 29, 1968 *Fort Worth Star-Telegram*.

flying for the airlines, that the on-board medical kit consisted of nothing more than Band-Aids and Iodine, meaningless for anything other than a slight cut. Numerous inflight emergencies occur where a meaningful first aid kit can mean the difference between life or death. The Air Transport Association (ATA) opposed the legislation requiring the same medical kit required by most foreign airlines. The ATA argued in a statement released on September 15, 1985 that most domestic flights can land within minutes of an on-board emergency to rush injured or ill passengers to hospitals trained to handle medical emergencies. That is not so.

The truth is that there are many emergencies where the person perishes before a plane can descend from cruising altitude, make an approach and land, and unload the person suffering an acute emergency attack. Representative Norman Mineta, chairman of the House aviation subcommittee, acknowledged the airlines resisted these safety improvements.[229]

Year after year the perils of air travel are lamented. In 1985 a congressional panel investigating air safety stated that air travel was less safe; this was the third scathing criticism of the FAA in less than a month. A month earlier another congressional study said investigators found disturbing gaps in the FAA's airline inspection program. A week later, an internal Transportation Department report found that the FAA had been slow in devising safety regulations and that they enforce them inconsistently. Similar reports were made for the 30 years before those reports. Nothing changes.

LACK OF INTEGRITY AT AIR-CRASH TRIALS

The level of integrity at court trials is of the level expected from the legal fraternity. Many professional expert witnesses are nothing more than witness "brokers," whose testimony is shaped by the employing law firm. They often get a percentage of the damage award, insuring a biased, false testimony, and further traumatizing of the aviation environment. Expert witnesses often have impressive *sounding* credentials that are often meaningless, with the expert witness knowing very little about the subject.

The participants at crash investigations have an ax to grind. Some seek to hide anything that implicates themselves. Lawyers representing the next-of-kin in the United Sioux City crash obtained a court order barring General Electric from testing the General Electric engine that led to the crash. The attorneys argued that the testing should be done by an independent

---

[229] *Aviation Week & Space Technology*, October 7, 1985.

laboratory.[230] The best performer, or the best liar, is believed by the unsophisticated jury.

WHISTLE-BLOWER LEGISLATION

This saga of corruption shows the urgent need for legislation protecting (and encouraging) government whistle-blowing. Past legislation was rendered valueless by placing people in charge of the program who gutted it. In 1978 the Civil Service Reform Act created the office of Special Counsel (OSC) for the purpose of protecting whistleblowers from reprisals, and to prosecute those who retaliate. President Reagan gutted the office by appointing Alex Kozinski to head the OSC, who openly violated the intent and the specifics of the legislation. Nearly half of the office personnel and seventy percent of the attorneys and investigators at the OSC either resigned or were fired. During that time over 7000 federal employees sought assistance from the OSC. Only two cases were filed by the OSC, and these were limited to job reinstatement.

The OSC failed to meet its congressional mandate," said Senator Levin on February 5, 1987, when he introduced the Whistleblower Protection Act of 1987. "It has not protected employees who have been the victims of unfair personnel practices, and its failure to do so is a reason why federal employees remain afraid to blow the whistle." Congresswoman Patricia Schroeder of Colorado introduced legislation in 1987, known as the Contractor Whistleblower Protection Act. She stated: "We urge [whistleblowers] to come forward; we hail them as the salvation of our budget trauma, and we promise them their place in haven. But we let them be eaten alive." She should know. I described the details of this scandal and the actions taken against my whistle-blowing air activities. She was plenty of talk, but no action. Representative Barbara Boxer of California promoted the legislation. None of them responded to my communications.

The Cavello Foundation in Cambridge, Massachusetts, who assists whistle-blowers, wouldn't act. I contacted the Government Accountability Project in Washington on June 30, 1988 and gave them sufficient evidence to show the gravity of the misconduct. GAP staff associate Carina Campobasso expressed concern when I talk to her on the phone, but her subsequent letter stated there was a case-freeze in effect which prevented them from taking on new cases. These lawyer-related groups wouldn't touch the matter.

The need for whistle-blower protection couldn't be more tragically demonstrated than the record of deaths and injuries

---

[230] *Aviation Week & Space Technology*, October 23, 1989.

suffered by thousands of people due to the misconduct within these pages. A classic example for the need of whistle-blower legislation was the Challenger blowup on January 28, 1986, in which seven astronauts were killed, including school teacher Christa McAuliffe. Following highly-sensitive testimony given by engineers from Morton Thiokol (who designed and manufactured the Challenger's solid rocket booster), the engineers were transferred, harassed, and terminated. *Multinational Monitor* stated in its May 1987 issue the consequences of blowing the whistle on the Challenger disaster:

> Because of the growing reaction to OSC inaction, hostility to its intended mission, and ineffectiveness, Senators Carl Levin, D-Mich., Charles Grassley, R-Iowa, and David Pryor, D-Arkansas, and Representatives Schroeder and Frank Horton, R-N.Y., have spearheaded new reform efforts. These reforms would clarify the role of the Special Counsel as a protector of whistleblowers, not protector of "the merit system."

The engineers opposed the launching because of their concern about the cold weather's effect on the O-ring seals. They testified that on the eve of the launch, they argued with their own superiors and NASA officials to postpone the launch, without success.

JUSTICE DEPARTMENT DIRTY POLITICS

The Justice Department is the highest security office in the United States, entrusted to enforce the laws and constitution of the United States. However, its lawful intent has been corrupted by the mentality of attorneys, making it one of the most corrupt agencies in the executive branch of government. Numerous Attorney Generals have been associated with corruption and at least one, John Mitchell, went to prison. It misuses its awesome powers to destroy citizens. It works in close harmony with federal judges, many of whom are former Justice Department attorneys. Federal judges who oppose the Justice Department in key cases are punished, and sometimes charged with crimes by the same Justice Department, and impeached, on relatively minor issues.

The Justice Department has misused the IRS, the Chapter 11 bankruptcy code, and other legislation, to destroy citizens they seek to punish. For years the Justice Department has blocked every effort to expose and correct this awesome air disaster scandal, willingly sacrificing lives to bring about their coverup. It is safe to say that the Justice Department has contributed to several thousand deaths in air tragedies that have their roots in the government-funded corruption and coverup. Some might argue that the obstruction of justice by the Justice Department attorneys, in the air disaster scandal, indirectly killed more innocent citizens than organized crime.

The politics of the Justice Department shows its hands in many way. When the investigative activities of the U.S. Attorney in Philadelphia threatened too many politicians involved in political corruption President Carter reportedly pressured the Justice Department to remove U.S. Attorney Martson from office, and in that manner take the pressure off the political corruption.

Speaking before the Washington National Press Club on January 25, 1978, Martson stated: "If a single Congressman can remove his home-town prosecutor who's actively investigating public officials, with a single call to the President—if that can happen, and that's what did happen—our federal criminal-justice system won't work. No amount of rhetoric will ever convince the bagmen and the fixers that they can't pull strings in Washington, because they're sure that strings got pulled in Washington."

The Justice Department—under the United States Attor-ney—investigated President Carter and his political friend, Attorney General Griffin Bell, for possible obstruction of jus-tice. Is it any wonder the Justice Department cleared their boss of any wrongdoings?

The Justice Department attorneys, working with California and federal judges, forced me to seek protection in Chapter 11, and then seized my life's assets without a hearing. These actions violated numerous constitutional rights to a hearing, to defend; violated constitutional property rights and due process; violated statutory and case law. It was outright judicial fraud, openly committed, with no fear that any single check and balance within the United States would intervene. The signifi-cance of this raw and brutal power was frightening to me, and should be for anyone else in these United States. Directly and indirectly, this naked criminal misuse of judicial and Justice Department power by the legal brotherhood continued to affect and result in brutal air tragedies.

Under these endemic government corruption conditions, that which is stated within these pages no longer is hard to believe. With me, they first obstructed my government air safety duties. Then, when I left government service and used my own funds to correct the air safety problems, they misused government power to silence me. They violated civil, constitutional and criminal protections, and then denied me the right to defend. When I exercised the right to defend, they charged me with a crime. They seized my life's assets, denying me the right to object or appeal. Rights of a free country were denied to me.

CHAPTER TWENTY EIGHT

Crashes Amidst Corruption

Let's look at some crashes occurring during the late 1980s that had a direct or indirect relationship to the government corruption. It isn't a pretty picture.

We've addressed brutal air tragedies that had their roots in the misconduct and coverup, including the big ones such as the Paris DC-10 crash and its 346 deaths, and the Japan Airlines 747 crash with its 520 deaths. There were others, of course. Let's look at a few not yet described which occurred while the attorneys in the Department of Justice and federal judges were persecuting me and trying to silence my exposure activities. They and their government-funded corruption made many of the brutal crashes possible.

HAWAIIAN NIGHTMARE—747 style

The public had not yet forgotten the exploding Aloha Boeing 737 when another mishap occurred over the Hawaiian Islands. It had close parallels to the Paris DC-10 cargo door disaster. Once again the dangers of outward-opening cargo doors took their toll.

United flight 811, a Boeing 747, departed Honolulu Airport shortly after midnight on February 24, 1989, enroute to Auckland, New Zealand. About 100 miles south of Honolulu, as the aircraft climbed through 22,000 feet altitude, passengers in the forward cabin heard a buzzing sound, like an electric motor, and a hissing sound in the forward part of the aircraft. Pressurized cabin air was escaping to the outside.

The passengers didn't have long to wait before the source of the sound revealed itself. Sounding like a gun going off by a person's ear, an explosive sound ripped through the huge 747 aircraft, immediately followed by the vapor cloud accompanying aircraft depressurization. A large section of the right fuselage ripped away from the aircraft as the inside pressure exploded outward, destroying a large ten foot by twenty foot segment of the fuselage. Attached to this disintegrating section was a large section of the aircraft skin, a section of cabin floor, nine passenger seats—and nine passengers.

Most of the disintegrating and separating aircraft and its pathetic human cargo shot from the aircraft and fell 22,000 feet to the surface of the Pacific ocean. One or more passengers were sucked into the number three engine, and parts of them expelled out the rear of the engine. There is only one other known instance in commercial aviation where passengers were ingested into the engines, and that was the United Airlines DC-8 that crashed into New York City.

ON THE FLIGHT DECK

Immediately upon hearing the explosion and seeing the telltale signs of an explosive decompression, Captain David Cronin and the crew followed standard procedures which included immediately donning oxygen masks to keep from passing out. The captain put the engines in idle-thrust position, extended the wing spoilers, and started an emergency descent to lower altitude so as to assure an adequate oxygen supply to the crew and passengers.

During the descent the crew found they couldn't get any oxygen out of the oxygen masks. Unknown to them, the explosive disintegration of the section near the forward cargo door had ripped out the oxygen lines, preventing the crew and the passengers from obtaining oxygen. Fortunately they were not at higher altitude where the crew would have been unconscious within seconds. Had they been, the aircraft would probably have plunged toward the ocean in an out-of-control condition, with the crew unconscious.

The aircraft shook badly and yawed to one side. During the emergency descent the number three engine started to disintegrate and stopped rotating, due to structural damage caused by the ingested bodies and aircraft debris. The flight engineer's panel lit up with numerous warning lights, taxing his skills and taking his full attention. Fortunately this was not a 747-400 in which the flight engineer position was eliminated.

During the emergency descent the flight engineer ran back into the cabin to survey the damage. The first thing he encountered was the huge hole in the side of the aircraft. Through the hole he saw fire coming from the number four engine. He rushed back to the cockpit and shut down that engine and the fuel supply at the fuel tank.

The crew dumped fuel to lighten the weight for landing. It was necessary to reduce the weight so as to continue flying on only two available engines. Approaching Honolulu Airport the crew made a high-speed approach to compensate for the higher minimum control speed with two engines out on one side. A higher speed was also required due to the crew's inability to get landing flaps. Fortunately, Honolulu Airport had long runways, and the aircraft was able to stop before reaching the end, despite the nearly 200 miles-per-hour approach speed.

Everyone on board could be thankful they had an experienced captain on board. Unfortunately his experience would soon be wasted. The captain was 59 years of age, and the FAA required him to retire from part 121 airline operations at the age of sixty.

HORROR STORIES

Back in the terminal, the surviving passengers who sat near the structural disintegration had horrifying stories to tell. "All of a sudden the people sitting next to us just disappeared," said Paul Holtz, of Sydney, Australia. "It was a hell of an experience, everything flashed before your eyes," said Dr. Kennedy, traveling home from a ski vacation in Aspen, Colorado. "All I could think about," said Roger White, a 23-year-old radio broadcaster from Newcastle, Australia, "were shark bites. I just put my head down and waited." The thoughts of those who perished we will, of course, never know.

In a *National Law Journal* of March 13, 1989, staff reporter Andrew Blum wrote of his interview with several attorneys who had clients that were on this United 747: "It's one of the most gruesome cases I've ever heard of," said one attorney. "My client told me he witnessed people being sucked out of the plane, ingested into the engine, and spit out the rear!"

One of the ejected passengers was 27-year old Lee Campbell. During that same night his mother in New Zealand awoke shortly before dawn and had a strange sense of foreboding and saw what she later described as a clear vision of her son before her. Her husband sought to calm her anxiety, "Lee's alright." They went back to sleep. A few hours later United called with the bad news.

THE CAUSE

It was a close repeat of the Paris DC-10 tragedy, except that this plane was lucky. The right forward outward-opening cargo door opened in flight when the ten locking cams unlocked. This allowed the tons of air pressure inside the aircraft to force open the huge door. The door ripped off when it reached the end of its upward arc. The lack of adequate fuselage strength in that area caused huge sections of the aircraft fuselage to rip loose with the door.

United Air Line Boeing 747 cargo door mishap.

Was this mishap preventable?

The direct cause of this tragedy was a serious safety problem that the FAA, the NTSB, Boeing, and United, knew existed. They all knew the dangers of outward-opening cargo doors. Two years earlier, in March 1987, shortly after takeoff from London, while passing through 20,000 feet, a forward cargo door partly opened on a Pan American 747 when eight of the ten door latches failed. Fortunately, two of the latches held, permitting the huge cargo door to open only slightly, and bleed off the pressure before the door fully failed. If all latches had failed simultaneously, the depressurization would have been of an explosive nature rather than a fast leak, and the plane possibly could have been lost.

Any outward-opening cargo door presents an extreme danger to the aircraft if it opens in flight, as experienced in the American Airlines DC-10 Windsor mishap and the Paris DC-10 crash. The only reason that the outward-opening door exists is to save money. Offsetting this saving, everyone is threatened by possible opening doors. And some will occasionally pay with their lives. These dangers and occasional deaths are an accepted byproduct by the airlines and the aircraft manufacturer.

A plug-type door that eliminates this risk costs slightly more (and even this added cost is debatable). In the few times that the entire cargo compartment space is filled, the outward-opening door permits placing cargo behind the door, something that could not be done with the safer inward-opening door.

The fact that Pan Am experienced an opening cargo door that could easily have duplicated the Paris DC-10 cargo door tragedy required immediate corrective action. As in the Paris DC-10 crash, the FAA, the manufacturer, and the airlines, did virtually nothing. The FAA refused to issue an AD until almost a year later. Even then, the FAA issued notice of a *proposed* AD.[226] The cargo door problem was an emergency situation that required an immediate emergency AD. The FAA's proposed AD did not take effect until July 1, 1988, almost a year and a half later. And even then, when the AD took effect, the airlines had a year and a half to install a steel plate that *may or may not* prevent the cargo door from opening. The AD stated in part:

> [The directive was] "prompted by a lower lobe [locking cam] forward cargo door with damaged lock sectors that partially opened in flight." ... This condition, if not corrected, could result in the opening of a lower lobe cargo door in flight, which could result in rapid depressurization of the airplane."

---

[226] Federal Register, February 1988.

The AD required inspection of the cargo door and locking mechanism for "broken, bent or otherwise damaged" parts, and gave the airlines five months to *look* for the damage that could have been done within 24 hours. The AD required repeated inspections of the door mechanism if the door electrical closing system didn't work, and the door had to be manually closed. The installation of the reinforcing plate did not have to be installed for another year and a half, even though a mechanic could have installed it in a matter of hours, such as during an overnight layover. During this long lead time tens of thousands of passengers and crewmembers were subject to a fate similar to the Paris DC-10 victims.

This check of the cargo door following manual closure is done by the baggage handlers, while standing on a high platform, possibly at night, and sometimes during windy and raining conditions. This subjective analysis that has a life-or-death consequence is delegated to employees who are not mechanically skilled, often don't know what they are looking for, and don't know the consequences if they make a judgmental mistake. The baggage handlers was given the responsibility to check on a design defect, and if his judgment was wrong, many could die.

A SIMPLE TASK TO SAVE HUNDREDS OF LIVES—not accomplished

The cargo door that blew off the United 747 had repeated locking problems when using the electrical system. The baggage handler had to manually close the door, requiring a check of the locking mechanism. But United officials did not tell the people closing the doors that a check had to be made, and these checks were not made. For an additional six weeks after this Honolulu tragedy, United failed to check the cargo doors after manual closing. (United officials did not pass this information to those closing the doors.)

Compounding these problems, United used power tools to manually close the cargo doors, a technique specifically prohibited by the Boeing maintenance manuals. The technique was prohibited to protect against damage to the door locking mechanism.

On this aircraft, United Airlines had not installed the steel plate, despite the gravity of the problem. Eight months after the AD took effect (almost a year after the proposed fix was announced), only six of United's thirty-one Boeing 747s had the steel plate installed. By contrast, TWA had installed the steel plates on all 20 of its 747s, and Pan Am had done so on all 38 of them. United testified at the NTSB hearing that it would have required taking the plane out of service for ten hours (overnight repairs could have been made) and cost $3,027.

WHEN WILL THE NEXT CARGO DOOR EXPLODE OPEN?

At this time two *known* cargo door openings have occurred. Either one could have duplicated the Paris DC-10 holocaust. Others will probably follow. In the Pan Am instance, luck prevented a catastrophe. In the United 747 instance, luck prevented losing the entire aircraft and its occupants.

The NTSB issued a report on this incident on August 23, 1989. It stated that even with the reinforcing metal plate other "unpredictable failures" could occur, such as malfunctions of the manual or electrical door-drive units, which could force open a locked latch. The report stated that the FAA should issue a directive covering all transport aircraft. The directive should require installation of positive indications to ground and flight personnel to enable them to determine that the latch cams and locks are physically in place. This requirement was in the federal regulations when the aircraft was designed, and violated by the FAA and the manufacturer.

However, even with this requirement fulfilled, the lives of hundreds of people are still dependent upon the subjective analysis by the baggage handler, or whomever makes the visual check of the complex locking mechanism. Further, out-of-adjustment locking mechanisms, expansion of the door frame, spurious electrical signal causing the locks to unlock in flight, could cause failure of the door locking mechanism. The NTSB report recognized this when it added that the FAA require failsafe design for non-plug cargo doors on present and future aircraft to account for conceivable human errors as well as malfunctions. The only way that this requirement can be met is with plug-type doors, retro-fitting all outward-opening cargo doors with plug-type doors. There is no other safe alternative.

THE ACTUAL CAUSE OF THE DOOR OPENING IS STILL NOT KNOWN

To this date, the actual cause of the Pan Am and United door-openings is unknown. In a follow-up report, the NTSB stated that the plate probably would not prevent another similar incident, and stated that the cause of the cargo door openings were unknown. Whatever caused those doors to open can still occur, possibly on your next flight.

UNRECOGNIZED DANGERS OF OXYGEN DEPRIVATION

Everyone was lucky that the plane wasn't at a higher altitude when the cargo door ripped off. The crew had no oxygen because the oxygen system lines were ripped out by the structural disintegration. The crew would have passed out within seconds if the plane had been at a much higher altitude, and everyone would have been lost with the plane.

Oxygen deprivation, even for a minute or so, can cause brain damage that may not be immediately detected. It is possible that brain damage could have occurred to many people on flights experiencing high-altitude depressurization, symptoms of which may not occur until a year or more after the incident. However, in this United 747 incident, the shot time at 22,000 feet would probably not result in brain-damage.

A typical example of brain damage occurred when a Lockheed C5-A aircraft lost pressurization after a cargo door failed, and an explosive decompression occurred. Before the aircraft could get to lower altitude, over 150 persons suffered permanent neurological disorders from brain dysfunctions.[227] U.S. District Court Judge Louis Oberdorfer of Washington called the case "one of the most protracted, costly and unpleasant litigations in the history of this district."

On any aircraft depressurization this danger exists. If the oxygen mask doors do not open, or if the passengers do not pull on the string attached to the mask that opens the oxygen valve, oxygen deprivation damage can occur.

NEWS MANAGEMENT

After the explosive cargo door opening, United Airlines management issued orders forbidding any of their employees from talking to reporters or anyone else. Did they have something to hide? Did United have maintenance problems they didn't want anyone to discover?

In a subsequent *San Francisco Chronicle* article dated March 8, 1989, United Airlines mechanics complained about the poor quality of the maintenance training, and about the many employees doing mechanic work who didn't know what they were doing. The article stated that "Mechanics at the United Airlines maintenance base in Oakland charge that their training is woefully inadequate, and that the quality of the work done at the base may ultimately suffer."

"We're going too fast," said J.R. Heier, the chief machinists' union officer at the base. "There are too many new hires, too many inexperienced foremen and not enough experienced mechanics to offer training." The article continued: "The union's complaints highlight an issue that is causing concern throughout the airline industry." The union said that a new, three-hour sheet-metal class and more on-the-job training has helped. (Three hours? How about three years!)

An *Associated Press* release on March 1, 1989 stated "United has refused to allow [Captain] Cronin and the other 17 crewmembers of Flight 811 to talk publicly about the flight." Oakland/San Francisco channel 2 television reported on February

---

[227] Law suits filed in the U.S. District Court, District of Columbia, *Friends For All Children v. Lockheed*, No. 76-0544. Also *Maupoint v. Lockheed*, No. 76-0544-68.

24, 1989 that a United Airlines security guard had halted their efforts to talk to a United employee, by ordering the employee to leave. United Airlines provided the press access to the crew at a San Francisco press conference held on March 3, 1989 that appeared to be orchestrated to take the heat off United Airlines. The crew praised United Airlines' maintenance. However, the crew had no knowledge of these incomplete maintenance requirements that had not been done; therefore, how could they praise the maintenance?

Tragic as was this 747 cargo door opening, it was sheer luck that it wasn't another major disaster. For everyone but the nine ejected passengers, statistically this was a safe flight!

SIOUX CITY DC-10—Payment For Design Compromises

One of the nation's most publicized crashes occurred on July 19, 1989. United Airlines Flight 332, a DC-10, departed Denver for Chicago, and was cruising at 37,000 feet when it happened. The crew and passengers heard a loud explosion at the rear of the aircraft, followed by shaking of the DC-10. A jet engine had exploded, and when it did, one of the most-feared emergencies occurred.

The flight deck crew immediately donned their oxygen masks and started an emergency descent. Captain Al Haynes moved the control wheel to counteract the right turn, and sought to control the descent. He found the controls had no effect upon the aircraft.

Simultaneously, most of the warning lights on the engineer and pilot's control panels illuminated. It was fortunate that flight had an engineer to handle many of the compound emergencies, rather than the new DC-11s that have no engineer position. The crew had lots of problems. The engineer reported loss of all hydraulic pressures and quantities, explaining why the aircraft did not respond to the pilot's movement of the yoke or rudder pedals. These cockpit controls move hydraulic valves at various points in the aircraft near the respective control surfaces, which ports hydraulic fluid to actuating cylinders. These cylinders move the elevators, the rudders, the ailerons and the horizontal stabilizer. (In addition to the spoilers and the nose-wheel steering.)

There was no emergency procedure listed for total hydraulic failure. The theory was that this multiple hydraulic failure would never happen, even though multiple hydraulic failures had repeatedly happened. The crew now faced a dangerous design

problem that the FAA, the manufacturer, and the airline, fore-
saw would occasionally happen, when they compromised on
design safety requirements. Now the loss of control again occurred due to saving a relatively small amount of money. It had
happened to American Airlines over Windsor; it happened to the
DC-10 near Paris where 346 people lost their lives; it happened
to a Japan Airlines Boeing 747 near Tokyo where 520 people lost
their lives.

Luckily, in the cabin was a dead-heading DC-10 flight instructor, Dennis Fitch, whose instructing experience gave him
skills not taught in the normal training of pilots. His experience in handling the DC-10 during training flights, with its
multiple simulated-emergencies, became life-saving—for some.

Fitch rushed onto the flight deck to provide assistance. As
the aircraft descended in a right turn, with the nose of the
aircraft porpoising up and down and the wings wallowing from
side to side, Fitch manipulated the power levers to provide
partial pitch control. Advancing the two wing-mounted engines
raised the nose, and retarding the power caused the nose to
lower. Pitch control, however, was marginal, but it was the only
game in town.

EXTREME UP TO FRIGHTENING DOWN PITCH

The aircraft went from an extreme nose-up to an extreme
nose-down attitude. There was always the danger that the nose
would pitch down and continue downward, as in the Paris DC-
10 crash, followed by the aircraft diving into the ground at high
speed. Because of structural deformity in the tail section, the
pilots couldn't make left turns, compounded by a tendency to
turn right.

Airlines provide no training for this type of emergency. If
they did, they would admit their irresponsibility in purchasing
a plane with a dangerous design defect. The airlines would risk
the dangers of either the crew or passengers refusing to fly in
an unsafe aircraft. The airlines, the FAA, and the manufacturer, took the position that the loss of all three hydraulic
systems would never occur. They recite figures showing that
statistically the loss of all three hydraulic systems will only
happen on a certain number of flights, although multiple hydraulic system failures frequently occur. The passengers didn't
know any better. Most of the crews didn't realize the dangers,
or choose to take their chances.

Shortly after the emergency started, Captain Haynes radioed to air traffic control that an engine had failed, and that
the plane had lost all hydraulic pressure. He advised that he
was diverting to Sioux City, Iowa. The crew sought help by

making radio contact with United's maintenance base at San Francisco. Instead of help, the maintenance base kept asking the crew for clarification, refusing to recognize the fact that the aircraft had experienced total hydraulic failure.

Air traffic control gave radar vectors to position Flight 232 for landing at Sioux City. The crew dumped fuel during descent so as to lower the landing weight, which in turn permitted a lower landing speed. Because of the marginal control over the aircraft, and the need to lose altitude over Sioux City, wide turns were necessary to get into position for landing.

The loss of hydraulic pressure prevented extending the landing flaps, requiring a higher approach speed to prevent a stall. The crippled DC-10 approached Sioux City Airport at speeds exceeding 200 miles per hour, partly because of the absence of flaps, and partly because engine thrust had to be maintained to keep the nose from dropping. The crew manually lowered the landing gear by free-falling.

During the last wide turn it became obvious the aircraft could not circle into position for landing on the intended north-westerly runway, 31. The crew decided to land straight ahead on the short inactive southwest runway 24, where the rescue vehicles were lined up. They quickly repositioned as the DC-10 approached. Even if the crew had pitch control, the fast approach speed would have required two or three times the 6700 foot runway length that existed. If all went well, a survivable crash was a possibility.

The DC-10 went through a series of pitch-up and pitch-down porpoising as it approached the airport. Fortunately, as the aircraft reached the airport the DC-10 was in a momentary horizontal pitch-attitude. Approaching the runway, the captain shouted to Fitch, "Ease the power back, ease the power back!" Fitch said, "We'll lose it if we do." As the runway approached, Fitch had to pull off the engine power to avoid overflying the runway. And when he did, the nose and right wing dropped. "God!" shouted one of the crewmembers, and then the right wing hit the ground.

The huge, fast-moving plane cart-wheeled, bursting into a huge fireball and breaking up into five major pieces and millions of little pieces. The flight station ripped loose from the aircraft and eventually tumbled to an inverted position, as did most of the other aircraft segments. Some passengers were trapped in a section of the aircraft that turned into a fireball, and didn't have any chance of survival. Some passengers found themselves suspended in their seats upside down. Many perished. Among the survivors were those who quickly unfastened their seat belts and ran from the aircraft sections that had not yet burst into flames.

Observing the huge fireball from a hovering helicopter, Dr. David Greco, a medical team leader, feared that no one could have survived the crash. He expected the worse as the helicopter landed near the crash scene. He later stated:

It wasn't real. We expected everyone to be dead, and then, when we touched down, we saw all these people walking towards us from the corn field. We thought, "this is wonderful, a miracle." But as soon as I turned around, I saw heads squashed like pumpkins.

"She had no feet!"

Typical of what others found at the crash scene was Charles Martz of Castle Pines, Colorado. He said the scene "looked like a battlefield. Bodies were strewn all over the place. Bodies had burns, their clothing burned off, stripped off." Martz stated, "This one gal I just remember seeing had no feet and she was still breathing a little bit and moaning, but what could you do?"

Of the 296 passengers and crew, 112 died. Miraculously, 184 people survived; a credit to the ingenuity of the flight instructor and crew. Some would be permanently crippled. Doctors at the local hospitals were warned that crash victims faced a long recovery. "Everybody who survived that crash is going to have a lot of potential for problems to overcome," said Larry Foster, medical director of the burn unit at St. Luke's Regional Medical Center. "We're talking about many, many months of initial care and then years of rehabilitation, if the patient survives," he said.

Survivor Joseph Trombello of Vernon Hills, Illinois, won't forget the horror. He saw the wingtip hit the ground and waited for death as the plane turned over and over again. Partly trapped by debris, he managed to extricate himself and escape. He saw a woman passenger with a piece of metal protruding from her forehead. He staggered by human body parts scattered throughout the area. *Two days after the crash*, his attorney filed a law suit against United, McDonnell Douglas Corp. and the General Electric Co., for the physical and psychological injuries he sustained during his ordeal. The FAA was not named, although the crash would not have happened if the internal FAA misconduct had not permitted design safeguards to be violated.

Before the crash, as Flight 232 approached Sioux City a young woman with blonde hair cried. Flight attendant Susan White later stated, "She was sobbing and saying, 'I have to get to Chicago, I have a husband and two young children waiting for me' she said." Susan hugged the woman and told her to prey. The mother was one of the 112 people killed. Susan then stumbled from the burning and disintegrated DC-10. She was further shocked as she passed the bloodied half of a body; a woman without a foot; and a field of dismembered bodies.

Susan recalled thinking after hearing the explosion and learning of the loss of hydraulic systems, "Oh, my God, I'm going to die." She rushed into the toilet, weeping, and praying that she would live. She thought of calling her family on the air-phone and saying goodbye to them.

After pulling herself together she assisted with crash preparations. Flight attendant Del Castillo said afterwards, "A mother [who lost her baby] came up to me and said, 'You said everything would be all right.'"

DETAILS OF THE SYSTEM FAILURES

The General Electric CF-6 engine mounted in the tail section had exploded and destroyed all three hydraulic systems. With the approval (or collusion) of the FAA, Douglas eliminated the formerly required hard-backups[228] for controlling the aircraft. They relied solely on the three hydraulic systems, which have always had multiple failures, and always will. Luck keeps all three systems from failing on the same flight.

These people died needlessly. Just to save a relatively small amount of money, the FAA Western Region officials that I fought during the Denver grievance hearing were simultaneously eliminating the mandatory regulatory requirement for a hard-backup that was recognized for years. Lockheed didn't go along with the reduction in safety. They installed in the Lockheed 1011 four hydraulic systems instead of Douglas's three; an electric motor to reposition the horizontal stabilizer in the event the four hydraulic systems go out; and in the event there was also an electrical failure, Lockheed provided a hand-crank to position the horizontal stabilizer. Hard backups existed on the DC-8, DC-9, Boeing 737, the Constellation, and other aircraft.

OTHER MISSING SAFEGUARDS

Additional design safeguards should have included protective shrouds around hydraulic lines that are especially susceptible to damage from disintegrating jet engines, and especially in the DC-10 tail-mounted engine. The need for this protection was obvious for years. In the early 1970s, numerous engine disintegrations occurred,[229] with catastrophic damage to fuel and hydraulic lines. In 1972 the NTSB recommended that the FAA issue an AD requiring a protective shroud around the fuel and hydraulic lines near the rear-mounted fuselage engine.

---

[228] Electric motor or hand crank for the horizontal stabilizer and the direct cable control over the aerodynamically assisted trim tabs on the flight controls were eliminated.

[229] Including Overseas National Airline DC-10 during takeoff from JFK Airport at New York City; Air Florida DC-10 takeoff from Miami.

This recommendation addressed the mandatory regulatory requirement already existing. The FAA Western Region ignored this NTSB recommendation, just as they ignored the regulatory requirement.

THE CAUSE OF THE CRASH IS SOLVED, OR SO THEY SAY

After the crash, McDonnell Douglas Corporation announced on September 15, 1989 that the problem causing the Sioux City crash could be solved by installing a hydraulic fuse-valve[230] in the number three hydraulic line at the rear of the aircraft. FAA Administrator James Busey stated, "It's a solid step forward in insuring that there will be no repetition" of the Sioux City crash.

Fuse valves are important, and the FAA should have required them at different segments of the hundreds of feet of hydraulic lines on the DC-10 and other aircraft. After the American Airlines Chicago DC-10 crash occurred, the need for the fuse valves throughout the DC-10 hydraulic systems were obvious, and ignored.

Another incident showing the need for fuse valves occurred when an engine disintegrated on an Air Florida DC-10 on September 22, 1981. This engine disintegration ruptured two of the three hydraulic systems. The entire aircraft was threatened with loss of control, and the wing leading edge slats retracted—just as they did in the Chicago DC-10 crash. A fuse-valve was then put in, but only to prevent a slat retraction. The FAA and Douglas ignored the many other areas needing similar protections, and especially the rear of the aircraft in the vicinity of the fuselage engine.

The so-called cure following the Sioux City crash was *eventual* installation of a fuse-valve in a section of the number three hydraulic system going to the various flight controls at the rear of the aircraft. If the number three hydraulic line fails downstream of the horizontal stabilizer hydraulic actuator (which is slightly ahead of the actuators for the elevators), there will be partial pitch control via the horizontal stabilizer. But does it solve the serious problem?

If a hydraulic failure occurs anywhere else in the hundreds of feet of hydraulic lines, that partial fix will be valueless. This so-called fuse-valve fix requires that the hydraulic line failure occur in a short length of the hundreds of feet of hydraulic lines, in order to be effective. If the hydraulic lines fail ahead of the hydraulic actuator for the horizontal stabilizer, than total loss of the aircraft controls again exists.

---

[230] Hydraulic fuses are fast-acting valves that sense a sudden drop in hydraulic line pressure, and shuts off the main hydraulic system to the hydraulic line break downstream of the "fuse" valve.

TWO YEARS TO DO WHAT COULD BE DONE OVERNIGHT

Compounding the problem, Douglas stated the fuse-valves would not be available and installed for another two years. (July 1990 to get the valves and another year to install them.) Fuse-valves were in production, and could have been installed within a few days.

McDonnell Douglas Corporation testified at the NTSB hearing that simulator tests show that getting the aircraft on the ground depended on making ground contact when the aircraft was on the short horizontal segment of the roller-coaster-like cycles. The tests showed that as the plane descended below 150 feet above the ground aerodynamic changes occur because of the ground effect, and the nose pitches downward, making a crash-landing inevitable.

The only acceptable fix for this design defect is to retro-fit all aircraft with a hard backup system (electrically driven or crank type for the horizontal stabilizer—and preferably both). Until then, anyone who flies on aircraft relying solely on hydraulics are taking a gamble with their lives.

Victim of ignored safety problem.

HIT AND RUN AT LA GUARDIA

The headline on a *Newsweek* article dated October 2, 1989 described a bizarre crash that rivaled the Japan Airlines DC-8 crash into Tokyo Bay (where the captain fled from the scene of the crash and hid out for several days). The article was entitled **Hit and Run at La Guardia.** It described the crash of a U.S. Airlines Boeing 737-400 during takeoff from La Guardia Airport in New York on September 20, 1989:

> Both [pilots] quickly disappeared after the accident and remained unavailable to investigators for more than 36 hours, precluding any reliable tests for drug use. They eventually showed up to submit to urine tests and to talk to NTSB investigators, ...

The almost-new Boeing 737 took off on Runway 31, just before midnight, into weather conditions of 500 feet overcast and light to moderate rain and fog. The captain, who had very little experience in the 737, allowed the copilot to make the takeoff. But the copilot had even less experience; he had never flown a 737 in passenger operation, at heavier weights occurring in line operation. He had, in fact, just finished very limited training.[236] The decision was poor judgment on the captain's part.

Numerous errors followed. Before it was over, two women would be crushed in their seats and perish as the rear aircraft section fell into the water at the end of the runway.

For unexplained reasons, the rudder trim tab was set at full-left deflection; this setting turned the nose-wheel sideways to the takeoff path. There had been several reports of the electrically driven rudder trim tab moving to full-extreme position instead of remaining in the centered position, due to either switch-sticking or other problems.

Shortly after setting the auto-throttles in the automatic-throttle setting,[237] the copilot hit the auto-throttle disconnect

---

[236] The NTSB reported that the pilot had just 33 hours as captain and only 133 hours overall in a DC-9. The copilot had never flown a commercial trip before, and had finished his limited training five weeks earlier.

[237] The Boeing 737-400 had a computerized power setting system, in which the power levers are manually advanced by the pilots to approximately 60-70% of N_1 (engine fan speed). As the engines stabilizes at that setting, the pilot pushes a button on the front of the power levers called a "toga" switch, that automatically sets the engine power setting to the preset N_1 settings.

switch on the side of the power levers in error, disconnecting the automatic power system. The captain then manually advanced the power levers to the power setting for takeoff, and continued the takeoff. As the airspeed increased, the full-left rudder trim caused the plane to veer increasingly to the left. The fully-offset rudder trim positioned the nose-wheel at an angle relative to the movement of the aircraft, and caused scrubbing of the tire and rumbling sounds.

The increasing pull of the aircraft to the left, and the increasing sound of the scuffing nose-wheel tires caused the captain to reject the takeoff. But the aircraft speed was already beyond the V1 reject speed, and there was inadequate runway length remaining to stop the aircraft, especially on the wet runway. The plane ran off the end of the runway and onto a fragile walkway connecting concrete piers on which approach lights were mounted. The aircraft broke into three main sections, with the aft section sinking into the water.

If the walkway had not been there guiding the nose wheel onto the first of several heavy concrete piers, the entire aircraft would have been submerged in the East River that ran along the end of the runway, with probable heavy loss of life. The tide swept some of the aircraft's occupants down the East River, where they were later rescued.

Seats that ripped loose from the floor trapped four women at the back of the aircraft. Two of them died in their seats. Rescuers swam through the water to them, shining their flashlights upon the women. Fire Lt. Al Warta spotted one woman "hopelessly trapped" under debris, her face only inches from the rising water. Lt. Warta said he heard another woman's voice. Shining his light toward the sound, he saw the woman's hand waving from a mass of debris. "She reached down and grabbed my hand and squeezed it," She pleaded: "Please don't leave me here."

The pilots helped in the rescue operations, and then left the scene of the crash, before they could be questioned, preventing drug and alcohol tests.[238] They remained hidden, available only to the pilots' union and the airline. When they finally made themselves available to the NTSB accident investigators almost two days later, the captain was interviewed, holding a blanket over his head, to avoid having his picture on television and in the newspapers. The scene compounded the weird nature of this crash.

FAA Administrator James Busey suspended the licenses of

---

[238] Similar to the captain of the Exxon Valdez.

the pilots, stating: "For these two pilots to have been sequestered for more than 36 hours after an accident that took two
lives [and injured many], and to do so without explanation, is
highly questionable.

LEAVING THE SCENE AND REFUSING TO SUBMIT TO TESTS, AND THIS IS COOPERATION?

The pilots union said in a statement[239] that "there was nothing unusual in the crew's performance; no Federal rules were
broken, and the crew cooperated completely with the investigation." The only known aircraft accident in history where the
crew left the scene (except the captain on the JAL DC-8 crash
at Tokyo), and this head of ALPA thinks it is not unusual, and
thinks that the crew cooperated!

Long after alcohol could be detected in their urine, both
pilots showed up 36 hours later, and agreed to a urine test.
Both pilots refused to submit to a blood test, which can detect
drug usage for longer periods.[240]

The crew's conduct caused the New York Queens County
District Attorney to request the grand jury to conduct an investigation, an unprecedented local reaction. ALPA President
Henry Duffy stated the grand jury investigation threatened to
undermine future airline-crash inquiries, stating: "Never has
anyone talked about criminal penalties in airline safety before."
Never before had a flight crew left the scene of an accident in
this manner.

Duffy talked air safety out of one corner of his mouth,
while encouraging irresponsible actions by the pilots out the
other side. The union encouraged pilots not to submit to long-
recognized responsibilities to remain at the crash scene, be
interrogated, and submit blood and urine samples. The conduct
of the crew, which the pilots' union president approved, opened
the crew to suspicions of their own making. The pilots were
justifiably under suspicion as much as a motorist who leaves the
scene of an accident.

In a subsequent *Air Line Pilot* magazine article published in
October 1989 Duffy supported the crew's conduct:

> We all recognize that the pilots involved need time to re-
> cover and regain composure so they can offer rational an-
> swers to NTSB or other authorities. We also know that
> responding to questions under any other conditions will
> generally result in giving erroneous answers. ... Others have
> better begin to understand this reasoning, because we will

---

[239] *New York Times*, September 23, 1989.
[240] *Aviation Week & Space Technology*, October 2, 1989.

never relinquish our union's right to represent our pilots in a manner that best protects us. If that means withholding post-accident voluntary statements, that is what we will do.

It is standard practice following an accident for the pilot to immediately report the facts to the nearest FAA or NTSB office, and for the flight deck crew members to submit a written report within ten days. This requirement is shown in the Federal Aviation Regulations, the company operating manual, and Part 830 of the National Transportation Safety Board regulations. In accidents that I had investigated, the flight crew always remained at the scene until they reported the facts of the crash to the airline and the FAA. Part 830.5 says that the operator of an aircraft shall immediately ... notify the nearest National Transportation Safety Board field office.

NTSB SUPPORTING OBSTRUCTION OF INVESTIGATION

NTSB spokesman Ted Lopatkiewicz said that it was not unusual for the NTSB crash investigators not to know the whereabouts of the crew. That is hogwash. Officials of the NTSB Board said that despite the harsh criticism of the pilots by the FAA, it was not unusual for pilots to turn to their union for counsel immediately after a crash, and not to talk to investigators for a day or so.[236]

These same NTSB officials knew that it was standard practice for a crew to make themselves immediately available for questioning, and for drug and alcohol tests. They knew that legal counsel is not permitted at accident investigation hearings (so as to increase the probability that the true facts of a crash can be obtained).

A *Wall Street Journal* article of January 12, 1990 stated that U.S. Air pilots had themselves complained about the adequacy of the training more than a year prior to the La Guardia crash. Not until a Washington investigation team made an inspection after the crash did the problems get reported. The Washington investigation team found what I found at United Airlines years earlier, that the airline check pilots rarely failed pilots for mistakes made during training, saving the airline money.

Former NTSB safety board member, Patricia Goldman, now a U.S. Air official, defended the airline, stating its training procedures were "studied and studied and approved all the way through" by the FAA. She added that the FAA sent US Air letters of commendation and a plague for the airline's purported safety operations.

---

[236] *New York Times*, September 23, 1989.

CHAPTER TWENTY NINE

FIGHTING BACK

MAN WITHOUT A COUNTRY

In the fictional story written by Edward Everett Hale, *The Man Without A County*, the fictional Philip Nolan was stripped of his constitutional rights and protections. An army colonel acting as a military court, sentenced him to banishment from the United States, and imprisoned him for life on a naval vessel.[242] The suspension of my civil and constitutional rights—in the effort to silence me—was perhaps even worse than that suffered by Nolan.

I lost every relevant right and protection under the laws and Constitution of the United States, and of the State of California. I was viciously persecuted by those paid and entrusted to uphold the law. I was stripped of my life's assets, my ability to earn income—and my ability to expose the sordid government-funded misconduct that played a key role in many air tragedies.

---

[242] The fictional Philip Nolan, an army officer, was tried with numerous other officers for cooperating with the unauthorized military exploits of military commander Aaron Burr. Before sentencing, each officer was asked to make a statement. Nolan, tired of the military life and dirty politics, stated: "Damn the United States! I wish I may never hear of the United States again." The military officer acting as judge (fictional Colonel Morgan) ordered Nolan placed on a U.S. Navy ship, never to see or set foot on the United States again, or to hear the words, "United States." Constitutional freedoms and protections were ignored during this fictional novel. The officers in charge of him during fifty years knew him as "the man without a country."

Each time a major violation of protected rights occurred, I exercised the remedies provided by law, and sought relief. Each time I did, federal judges dismissed my actions without a hearing or trial, in gross violations of constitutional due process and equal protection, and in gross violations of specific statutory and case law. Every time I sought relief from terminal destruction of my personal and property rights, federal judges called me a frivolous and vexatious litigant for objecting to the outrages committed by the litany of attorneys from the Justice Department, and federal judges. Then, the previous frivolous and vexatious decisions were used to dismiss every subsequent action seeking relief. The federal judges had a racketeering enterprise going that was endemic throughout the federal judiciary.

Even though judicially gridlocked, I continued seeking relief, never sure that maybe somewhere some federal judge had enough integrity to do what he was paid to do. Also, I wanted to leave a record, so that when I was no longer around on this earth, someone, somewhere, might have the courage and responsibility to investigate and expose the rampant government corruption that was overthrowing our form of government.

Federal law provides that any person in the United States can file a federal law suit seeking declaratory judgment to establish his personal and property rights under federal law and under the federal Constitution. Federal law provides that a person can file a law suit seeking injunctive relief to halt actions taken under color of state or federal law that violate federally protected rights. Federal law provides that law suits can be filed seeking damages against others who violated these federally protected rights.[238]

---

[238] Federal statutes Title 28 U.S.C. Sections 1331, 1343, 2201, 2202; Title 18 U.S.C. Sections 1961 and 1962, the RICO Act; directly under the U.S. Constitution, including the First, Fifth and Fourteenth Amendments; as a *Biven's* claim; and Title 42 U.S.C. Sections 1983, 1985, 1986;

Title 28 U.S.C. § 1343. Civil rights and elective franchise.

(a) The district courts shall have original jurisdiction of any civil action authorized by law to be commenced by any person:

(1) To recover damages for injury to the person or property, or because of the deprivation of any right or privilege of a citizen of the United States, by any act done in furtherance of any conspiracy mentioned in section 1985 of Title 42;

(2) To recover damages from any person who fails to prevent or to aid in preventing any wrongs mentioned in section 1985 of Title 42 which he had knowledge were about to occur and power to prevent;

(3) To redress the deprivation, under color of any State law, statute, ordinance, regulation, custom or usage, of any right, privilege or immunity secured by the Constitution of the United States or by any Act of Congress providing for equal rights of citizens or of all persons within the jurisdiction of the United States;

(4) To recover damages or to secure equitable or other relief under any Act of Congress providing for the protection of civil rights, including the right to vote.

Every action I filed contained numerous federal causes of action involving violations of rights protected under the Constitution and laws of the United States. Any one of these violated rights invoked mandatory federal court jurisdiction. But the judicial gridlock was everywhere. First it was the California judges that gridlocked me. Then it was the federal judges who stonewalled every attempt to seek relief via federal lawsuits. It was enlightening to see the extent of the judicial corruption that crossed from state to federal courts. Every judge that became involved committed judicial corruption with no signs whatsoever of concern for the people that would suffer from their judicial corruption.

IMAGINATIVE USE OF LAW TO CIRCUMVENT JUDICIAL GRIDLOCK AND EXPOSE CRIMINAL ACTS

Realizing that I may never recover from the persecution, I sought to put on notice those who had responsibilities to prevent the outrages, and who misused their office in criminal activities. I filed several law suits with this in mind.

Two law suits were filed against members of the U.S. Senate and House.[239] The primary basis for these suits was that they knew of the violations of my civil and constitutional rights; knew of the violations of the civil and constitutional rights of those who perished in air tragedies based upon unlawful acts; they knew of the criminal acts that others (and they themselves) inflicted upon me and others who were harmed. They had the same (and greater) lawful responsibility as any other citizen holding the power to prevent and report such acts. They incurred liability of the federal government under the Federal Tort Claims Act for their criminal and wrongful actions. Ironically, the Keating-Five were among those that I sued.

Another purpose of the law suits was to put into a judicial record their position as to the coverup of the air disaster misconduct and the other misconduct described within these pages.

In response to the filing of these actions, the Senate legal counsel filed a motion to dismiss my complaint on February 27, 1989. The motion to dismiss *admitted* that the defendant Senators and Representatives knew of my allegations; knew of the alleged consequences in air tragedies and the harms inflicted

---

239 In U.S. District Court in District of Columbia: No. 89-0170 SS. *Stich v. [Senators] Edward Kennedy, Strom Thurmond, Ernest Hollings, Albert Gore, Pete Wilson; [Representatives] Joseph Biden, Jack Brooks, John Conyers, Peter Rodino, Harley Staggers, and Henry Gonzalez*; In District Court at Reno: *Stich v. U.S. Senator Alan Cranston from California, and U.S. Representatives George Miller, Fortney Stark, Norman Mineta, Don Edwards, and Daniel Lundgren*, No. 89-85. February 10, 1989. U.S. District Court at Reno, Nevada, under the provisions of Title 28 U.S.C. Sections 1331, and 1343, and Title 42 U.S.C. Sections 1983, 1985, 1986.

upon me; did not deny the relationship between the misconduct and the deaths in the air tragedies I listed or the Chapter 11 corruption; and that they failed to take any actions to prevent the wrongful acts. Under federal pleading practice, any allegation in the complaint that is not denied is deemed admitted as true.[245] The defendants admitted the truth of my allegations relating to the air safety and government corruption, and their causative and permissive effect upon many of the air tragedies I listed.

After these admissions, they then had the gall to argue that they were immune from the consequences of their acts, under the Speech or Debate Clause of the United States Constitution. To put this response in perspective, picture an air disaster scene in which the crash and deaths were related to misconduct that they could have prevented, and they had the gall to admit the misconduct, implied their ability to prevent the consequences, and then argue they were immune from liability for their coverup.

This response has serious implications. No longer could these members of the Senate and House argue they did not know of my allegations or of the corruption related to a series of continuing air tragedies. All they could now argue was that regardless of their inactions—which made possible many of the deaths described within these pages—they could not be sued.

The defendants' motion to dismiss stated in part:

(1) This suit is barred by the Speech or Debate Clause, Art. I, sec. 6, cl. 1, of the Constitution, and (2) the complaint fails to state a claim upon which relief can be granted." In other words, the response admitted my allegations, but denied that they had any legal responsibility, because of an alleged constitutional immunity.

I opposed the motion to dismiss by stating case law showing that the Speech or Debate Clause only related to actions taken on the floor of the Senate and House relating to passage or non-passage of legislation. I recited case law[246] that held the clause did not protect illegal or unconstitutional conduct. I also

---

[245] Federal Rule of Civil Procedure 8(d):

(d) **Effect of Failure to Deny.** Averments in a pleading to which a responsive pleading is required, other than those as to the amount of damages, are admitted when not denied in the responsive pleading. Averments in a pleading to which no responsive pleading is required or permitted shall be taken as denied or avoided.

[246] *Miller v. Transamerican Press,* 709 F.2d 524 (9th Cir. 1983); *Kilbourn v. Thompson,* 103 U.S. 168, 204 (1881); *Eastland v. United States Servicemen's Fund* 421 U.S. 491, 502. (1975).

argued law prohibiting dismissal of law suits that state federal causes of action, and that the allegations in the complaint must be accepted as true for the purpose of opposing dismissals.

In addition to seeking dismissal before the matter could go to trial, the defendant Senators and Representatives requested that the judge remove all evidence from the court records that the law suit was ever filed. The intent of this motion was to protect the Senators and Representatives from consequences at a later date if the judicial records were examined by an inquisitive investigative reporter. In this way there would not be any evidence a law suit had been filed; the charges and responses would remain unknown.

But there is no law permitting removal of evidence of the filing of an action. These are public records, protected by the public's right to know. Their destruction would violate federal law. Further, federal law, including Rule of Civil Procedure 60, permits a party to file a motion, years later, to reinstate an action. This right, however, becomes valueless if the record is destroyed.

Even though I raised federal causes of action which under federal rules of court, case law, statutory law, constitutional due process, prevented dismissal, U.S. District judge Stanley Sporkin rendered an order on May 8, 1989 granting the motion to dismiss, and to destroy all evidence of the filing:

> On consideration of the motion of defendants to dismiss plaintiff's amended complaint, the entire record, and this court's opinion in this case, it is ORDERED that the defendants' motion be and hereby is granted and the amended complaint is dismissed with prejudice.

I immediately filed a notice of appeal of that order. (Appeal No. 89-00170.) The Senators and Representatives then filed a motion with the Court of Appeals requesting that my appeal be dismissed without allowing me to present appeal briefs. The Court of Appeals judges promptly came to their rescue, and granted the request. A copy of part of the Court of Appeals order follows:

United States Court of Appeals
For the District of Columbia

No. 89-5163

Rodney F. Stich
Appellant
v.
Edward Kennedy, et al.,
Appellees

On Appeal From the United States District Court
For the District of Columbia

Motion of Senate Appellees For Summary Affirmance

The six Senators named as defendants in this action, Edward M. Kennedy, Strom Thurmond, Ernest F. Hollings, Albert Gore, Jr., Pete Wilson, and Joseph R. Biden, Jr., move for summary affirmance of the district court's order of May 8, 1989 (Tab A), dismissing the amended complaint in this case with prejudice.

STATEMENT

The plaintiff has had a longstanding grievance against the Federal Aviation Administration ("FAA") and the National Transportation Safety Board ("NTSB"), which he has pursued through substantial prior litigation.[247] In this lawsuit plaintiff alleges a "conspiracy" between the FAA and United Airlines "to violate federal air safety requirements, and obstruct government inspectors reporting and correction of the air safety felonies and misconduct which made possible the major air safety misconduct and numerous fatal crashes." Complaint, par. 9, at 5. He asserts that the "misconduct" of the NTSB "played a causative role in several other major airline disasters." *Id.*, at

---

[247] The plaintiff has sued both agencies several times. *See Complaint*, 16, at 7; *Stich v. United States, et al.*, 554 F.2d 1070 (9th Cir.)(table), *cert. denied*, 434 U.S. 920 (1977); *Stich v. National Transportation Safety Board*, 685 F.2d 446 (9th Cir.)(table), *cert. denied* 459 U.S. 861 (1982); *Stich v. United States Department of Justice, et al.*, No. 86-2523 (D.D.C. March 27, 1987)(1987 WESTLAW 9237), *aff'd*, No. 87-5262 (D.C. Cir. Feb. 4, 1988)(dismissing claims against the FAA and NTSB and also the United States Department of Justice, United States District Judge Milton L. Schwartz, California Superior Court Judge William Jensen, and United States Supreme Court Clerk Joseph F. Spaniol, Jr.).

5. His grievances extend to members of the California, *id.*, Par. 18, at 8, and federal judiciaries, *id.*, par 22-26, at 9-12.

Plaintiff alleges that the congressional defendants[248] "have responsibilities and the power to prevent and aid in the prevention, of violations of these rights and privileges which were inflicted against plaintiff." *Id.*, par 6, at 3. He states that he "notified members of the Senate and the House of the constitutional violations, and submitted petitions under the First Amendment and other safeguards for relief." *Id.*, § 27, at 12. He asserts that "defendants misused their positions of trust and power, refusing to provide the relief to prevent the violation of rights and privileges suffered by plaintiff," *id.*, par 34, at 14, and that the defendants "actually joined the conspiracy by remaining silent," *id.*, par 36, at 14.[249]

In a Memorandum Opinion filed on March 29, 1989 (Tab B), the district court dismissed plaintiff's complaint with prejudice. The court first held that the suit was barred by the Speech or Debate Clause, Article I, section 6, clause 1, of the Constitution, because "[t]he acts and omissions complained of by the plaintiff clearly fall within the legitimate legislative sphere protected by the Speech or Debate Clause." Memorandum Opinion at 3. The court also held that the action failed to state a claim under the First Amendment upon which relief can be granted under Fed.R.Civ.P. 12(b)(6), because "[w]hile the plaintiff's right to petition Congress is guaranteed by the First Amendment, a member of Congress is not required to 'listen or respond to individuals' communications on public issues.' *Minnesota State Board for Community Colleges v. Knight*, 465 U.S. 271, 285 (1984)." Memorandum Opinion at 3.

Shortly before the court's dismissal of the action, plaintiff filed a "first amended complaint." Like the original complaint, the amended complaint alleged a conspiracy between the airline industry and the government's air safety regulatory bodies, Amended Complaint, par 3, at 3, and asserted that, notwithstanding his notification to the congressional defendants, *id.*, par 35, at 17, they failed to act to prevent the violations, *id, par 4, at 4, and "actually joined the conspiracy by remaining silent,"* id., par 42, at 19. On April 6, 1989, plaintiff moved to alter or amend the order dismissing his first complaint, pursuant to Fed.R.Civ.P. 59(e), and on May 8, 1989, the court reaffirmed

---

[248] In addition to the six Senate defendants, plaintiff named as defendants in this action five present or former Members of the House of Representatives: Jack Brooks, John Conyers, Jr., Peter W. Rodino, Jr., Harley Staggers, Jr., and Henry B. Gonzalez.

[249] Plaintiff has also filed a substantially identical action in the District of Nevada against Senator Alan Cranston and several other present or former Members of the House. A motion to dismiss that complaint is currently pending. *Stich v. Cranston, et al.*, CV-N-89-85-ECR.

its earlier judgment and dismissed the amended complaint with prejudice. Plaintiff filed a timely notice of appeal from the district court's May 8, 1989 order on May 19, 1989.

****

The Court of Appeals identified the very serious issues raised in my complaint. They recognized the heavy loss of life associated with air tragedies that at least suggest a relationship between the misconduct and the crashes. They recognized that there had never been an examination of my allegations, and that my constitutional and statutory right to due process had been repeatedly violated. They too recognized that the very least that could be done—that should be done—was to request appointment of a special prosecutor on the basis of government misconduct (as in Watergate and other investigations of government officials). It is the function of the United States Court of Appeals in the District of Columbia to make such appointment.

The federal judges arrogantly dismissed the highly sensitive political scandal, knowing that they were sacrificing more people to death. Each of the wrongful judicial dismissals following the 1974, 1975, and 1980 law suits against the FAA and NTSB were followed by more crashes directly related to the misconduct, and followed by crashes that were probably related. None of the judges showed a single iota of concern. Their only concern was protecting the system of corrupt attorneys and judges in the Justice Department and closely aligned federal judiciary.

ADDRESSING THE CRIMINAL COVERUP BY THE NEWS MEDIA

I used the same federal statutes and case law to address the news media coverup that constituted criminal acts leading to air tragedies. Commencing in 1965, the *Wall Street Journal*, the *Washington Post*, the *New York Times*, and others, knew of the corruption which they could have prevented by giving it publicity in any manner that they saw fit. I filed a federal action in the United States District Court at San Jose, California,[245] naming these newspapers as defendants, along with the *San Francisco Chronicle* who became implicated at a later date. The filing of this law suit also put on record the allegations against the defendant news media, and their response. This law suit was assigned to Judge Robert Aguilar.

---

[245] Number C 89 20262 WAI.

Shortly thereafter the Justice Department charged Aguilar with using his office as a racketeering enterprise to obstruct justice. The specific acts that Aguilar allegedly committed were peanuts compared to the crimes committed by the Justice Department attorneys who charged Aguilar, and federal judges Stanley Wiegel, Samuel Conti, and Robert Peckham who testified against Aguilar. Aguilar had rendered decisions unfavorable to the Justice Department and it appeared the Justice Department was retaliating. The law suit against the newspapers that threatened to blow the lid on the entire scandal were then removed from Aguilar and assigned to another judge.

The *Wall Street Journal* and its managing editor, Norman Pearlstein, filed the first reply, on June 15, 1989, requesting that the federal complaint be dismissed. They responded as did members of Congress, that they knew of the charges; they did not dispute the relationship between the misconduct and the consequences; but that they were immune from liability, based upon the First Amendment. They argued that they did not have to print what any person requests them to print. But I wasn't requesting the news media to print what I wanted printed. I expected them to exercise their ability to aid in the prevention of the civil and constitutional and RICO violations, the criminal acts, and the related air tragedies.

Even though the law suits against them were newsworthy, and raised grave issues of national concern, none of these newspapers, nor the news services, nor any other newspaper, printed a single word about it.

The *Wall Street Journal* and Pearlstein argued, in effect, that they should be allowed to obstruct justice and cover up for crimes. They impliedly argued that the liberal First Amendment freedoms given to the press, so that they would be free to report government misconduct, should now protect them for coverup of government corruption. The responsibility of the news media under the First Amendment was articulated in a Supreme Court decision relating to the Pentagon Papers and the *New York Times* publication of their content. Supreme Court Justice Hugo Black stated:

Only a free and unrestrained press can effectively expose deception in government. And paramount among the responsibilities of a free press is the *duty* to prevent any part of the Government from deceiving the people ... The New York Times, the Washington Post and other newspapers should be commended for serving the purpose that the Founding Fathers saw so clearly. In revealing the workings of government ... the newspapers did precisely that which the founders hoped and trusted they would do.

The district judge dismissed the complaint against the newspapers, without a hearing, and despite the fact that numerous federal causes of action were states, and that criminal misconduct was shown that would have tragic consequences if not acted upon.

I didn't appeal the complaint as I accomplished the primary goal of making a judicial record of the news media's complicity and their responses. Despite the news worthiness of the law suit against these papers, none of them printed anything about the precedent-setting law suit and the serious implications in air tragedies.

CULPABILITY OF SUPREME COURT JUSTICES

The same laws that I relied upon to sue members of the Senate and House also applied to the Justices of the United States Supreme Court. The Justices had covered up for the pattern of criminal behavior by federal judges, the Chapter 11 judges, private trustees such as embezzler Charles Duck, all of whom were officers of the court over which the Justices had supervisory responsibilities.[246] Like a police chief protecting rampant criminal behavior of their police officers committed against citizens, the Supreme Court Justices protected the criminal behavior of those over whom they had responsibilities. The Justices were just as guilty of criminal acts, or more so, for such crimes as misprision of felonies, coverup, accessory after the fact, conspiracy.

Since the Supreme Court justices had the responsibility to prevent the commission of these corrupt acts, and refused to act, and aided and abetted the acts, I filed a law suit against them in the U.S. District Court in the District of Columbia.[247] I named each of the Justices as defendants.[248] Since they were employees of the U.S. government, acting under color of federal law, I also named the Government of the United States as a defendant. This was probably the first time in history that

---

[246] Rule 17.1(a) of the U.S. Supreme Court. Responsibility to intervene exists when a lower court "has so far departed from the accepted and usual course of judicial proceedings, or so far sanctioned such a departure by a lower court, as to call for an exercise of this Court's power of supervision.

[247] Filed February 17, 1989, No. 89-0470 SS; amended complaint filed March 14, 1989.

[248] William Rehnquist; Antonin Scalla; Sandra O'Connor; Anthony Kennedy; Thurgood Marshall; William Brennan; John Stevens; Bryon White; Henry Blackmun.

Supreme Court justices were sued for civil, constitutional, and RICO violations. The allegations made in the complaint could be easily verified by any newspaper. The allegations were serious. Every major news service monitors the filing of complaints in the federal court in the District of Columbia. Each of them kept the lid on the scandal, to the detriment of their readers.

The arguments raised in the complaint were based on solid facts and law. It was, however, bizarre that a person was forced to resort to that unusual act in seeking justice and relief from persecution.

REFUSING TO RESPOND

Federal law provides for service by certified mail. If the defendants don't respond by returning acknowledgement of the service, personal service is then required, and the defendants must pay for such service. Despite their position as Supreme Court Justices, they refused to return the acknowledgement. I then had the Supreme Court justices personally served, which was done on June 17, 1989.

I filed a 28-page amended complaint on March 14, 1989 which stated in part:

This suit addresses the wrongful acts and omissions by the defendants, relating to (a) an ongoing, air safety/air disaster scandal, and related air tragedies; (b) upon which has been superimposed a government and judicial scandal of coverup; (c) government and judicial scheme misusing government powers to destroy plaintiff's freedoms, liberties, property rights, privacy, in an effort to halt his exposure activities.

Defendants knew of these wrongdoings, and participated in them. The defendants also had the power to prevent them and refused to do so, aiding and abetting those committing the violations. Defendants knew that plaintiff would suffer great and irreparable harm from massive violations of rights and privileges under the laws and constitution of the United States and of the State of California; and knew that by such refusal to act, the misconduct causing and permitting the prior loss of life in fraud-related air tragedies would continue, with continuing loss of life. The defendants willingly sacrificed the lives that were lost, protecting their own vested interests, their own coverup, and the guilty parties involved in what has become the world's worst air-safety-air-disaster scandal, upon which has been superimposed the nation's worst government and judicial scandal.

Defendants are liable to plaintiff as a result of their wrongful acts. (Title 28 U.S.C. § 1343 and 42 U.S.C. § 1986.) Self-proclaimed qualified judicial immunity does not deprive a citizen of the United States of the rights and privileges under the laws and Constitution of these United States, including the right to redress of the harms suffered from judicial misconduct. The federal government has incurred a liability from defendants' wrongful acts.

It is argued that the many persons who perished, and who suffered in airline tragedies caused and made possible by the misconduct of federal officials, have a cause of action against defendants, and against the federal government.

The specifics in subsequent pages of the complaint related to knowledge by the Justices of the air disaster and government corruption; the repeated violations of civil and constitutional rights in the sham California action; the coverup and extension of the civil and constitutional violations by Ninth Circuit judges; the false imprisonment for exercising constitutionally protected rights; the Chapter 11 racketeering activities; the seizure of my multi-million dollar assets without any hearing, without cause, and under corrupt conditions.

The Assistant U.S. Attorney filed Defendant's Motion To Dismiss on August 17, 1989, admitting knowledge of all the allegations; failing to deny their truthfulness or the resulting harm to others and myself. The motion claimed that the defendants "enjoy[ed] absolute immunity from plaintiff's claims."

The motion to dismiss was riddled with false statements of fact and law, and trivial matters, which surprised me. I thought the Justices would respond at least on a higher level, rather than what could be expected of a shyster attorney in a small state court. Their answer lowered the Justices' integrity and conduct to that which the California and federal judges inflicted upon me. The justices argued that the complaint should be dismissed because "Rule 8 (a) ... requires that a complaint be a short and plain statement" and then argued that the complaint was too long.

The complaint described the brutal deaths of several thousand people in fraud related air tragedies, and the Justices of the Supreme Court wanted the complaint dismissed, without addressing these serious issues, on—would you believe—the argument that too many wrongdoings were charged!

The complaint was long because of the great number of specific acts described in the complaint. Further, if the allegations had not been specific, the complaint risked being thrown out for not being sufficiently specific.

After arguing that the complaint was too long (there is no limit to the number of pages in a federal complaint), the Justices then argued that the allegations were not specific enough! The Justices argued that the complaint did not "state facts with particularity in his complaint that demonstrate who did what to whom and why." The complaint stated very clearly what the Supreme Court Justices had done.

The Justices made the usual statement used by the legal fraternity when a pro se complaint is filed, that the "allegations are imprecise, unclear." It is questionable how a shorter complaint could have made the allegations more clear. Further, a complaint does not have to *prove* the allegations, but make reference to them so the defendants know the nature of the alleged wrongful acts.

The Justices argued that the complaint stated "unbelievable allegations." Every fact stated had support, more than required under federal pleading practice. The Chapter 11 corruption was specific, and to many unbelievable. The prison sentence as punishment for exposing government corruption was unbelievable, but obviously true. The total suspension of due process by federal judges was unbelievable, but true. The air disaster corruption, and the obstruction of justice by the Justice Department and federal judges were unbelievable, but true.

The Justices sought to have the action dismissed by making reference to the California action, referring to it as a matrimonial action. The very fact that I was in the seventh year of a so-called matrimonial action, when five divorce judgments showed me as divorced, raised serious federal causes of action. The California action was riddled with a pattern of civil and constitutional violations that were major federal causes of action, raising federal court jurisdiction. That response showed the Justices were fully aware of the outrages in that sham California action.

The Justices argued that the statute of limitations prevented law suits against them, but never stated how the *ongoing* wrongful acts could have imposed a statute of limitations defense.

The justices then argued that the allegations were already adjudicated and dismissed by other federal courts. To that date there has never been a single law suit that was ever litigated and adjudicated. The complaint made it clear that federal judges over whom the Justices had supervisory and other responsibilities had repeatedly dismissed every law suit in clear violation of statutory and constitutional rights. Further, the Justices were never named in any law suit, so obviously the matters could not have been adjudicated.

The Supreme Court Justices argued:

The nine Justices of the Supreme Court are entitled to absolute judicial immunity from plaintiff's claims. A judge

will not be deprived of immunity because the action he took
was ... done maliciously, or was in excess of his authority.

The criminal statutes, such as misprision of a felony, Civil Right
statutes, do not state a judge is immune when he violates their
clearly stated provisions. Under a *Bivens* claim, the rights and
protections of the Civil Rights Act that relate to wrongful acts
taken under color of state law extends to federal actors. The
Constitution of the United States provides for redress of
wrongdoings by government actors, and says nothing about
judges being immune. The Justices were contradicting their own
decision in *Pulliam v. Allen* 466 U.S. 522 (1984). The Supreme
Court held:

> ... there is little support in the common law for a rule of
> judicial immunity that prevents injunctive relief against a
> judge. There is even less support for a conclusion that Con-
> gress intended to limit the injunctive relief available under
> § 1983 in a way that would prevent federal injunctive relief
> against a state judge. In *Pierson v. Ray*, 386 US 547, 18 L
> Ed 2d 288, 87 S Ct 1213 (1967), the Court found no indica-
> tion of affirmative congressional intent to insulate judges
> from the reach of the remedy Congress provided in § 1983.
> [N]othing in the legislative history of § 1983 or in this
> Court's subsequent interpretations of that statute supports
> a conclusion that Congress intended to insulate judges from
> prospective collateral injunctive relief.
>
> Congress enacted § 1983 and its predecessor, § 2 of the
> Civil Rights Act of 1866, 14 Stat 27, to provide an inde-
> pendent avenue for protection of federal constitutional
> rights. The remedy was considered necessary because "state
> courts were being used to harass and injure individuals,
> either because the state courts were powerless to stop
> deprivations or were in league with those who were bent
> upon abrogation of federally protected rights." *Mitchum v
> Foster*, 407 US 225, 240, ... every member of Congress who
> spoke to the issue assumed that judges would be liable under
> § 1983).
>
> Subsequent interpretations of the Civil Rights Acts by
> this Court acknowledge Congress' intent to reach unconsti-
> tutional actions by all state actors, including judges. ...
> Judicial immunity is no bar to the aware of attorney's fees
> under 42 U.S.C. § 1988.

The primary importance of this law suit against the Justices of
the United States Supreme Court is that it now puts them
firmly on notice of the serious air disaster, Justice Department,

and federal judicial corruption; its relationship to thousands of airline crash deaths; its relationship to the Chapter 11 judicial racketeering activities; and much more. It makes the highest court of the land implicated in the tragedies that follow, and makes the United States liable for the deaths and the harms that follow the coverup by the Justice of the Supreme Court. It also establishes that the nation's highest court knowingly and arrogantly engages in criminal and wrongful acts, including deception, fraud, and obstruction of justice.

District of Columbia judge Stanley Sporkin came to the Justices rescue; he rendered a *sua sponte* dismissal on January 17, 1990. Under federal law a law suit cannot be dismissed without a hearing; cannot be dismissed if a federal cause of action is stated in the complaint. My complaint stated numerous federal causes of action. I was stonewalled again, showing the extent of the federal judicial corruption, and showing the awesome power of this one branch of government that makes it one of the gravest threats that ever confronted our nation.

IMPLIED ADMISSION OF GUILT IN AIR TRAGEDIES, BUT HOLDING THEMSELVES IMMUNE FROM MORAL AND LEGAL LIABILITIES

All of the defendants (members of Congress, news media, Justices of the U.S. Supreme Court) raised the same argument. They admitted knowing of the charges; they did not question the relationship between the wrongdoings, the criminal acts, and the dreadful consequences. Their position was that they could cover up, make possible the consequences experienced by the victims, and be immune from the consequences!

Some of the next of kin may have a little trouble digesting that outrageous position. Each of the Justices joined the conspiracy that made possible the deaths of little children and others in fraud-related air tragedies, none of the victims being any match for these thugs criminalizing key institutions in the United States. Apparently this is the form of government that they seek to force upon other nations, as they intrude into the internal affairs of other countries.

INTO THE WHITE HOUSE ITSELF

While Ronald Reagan was president, I notified the office of the President of the misconduct described in these pages. No response. In 1988, while Vice-President George Bush was campaigning for the presidency, he promised to get tough with criminals. I assumed he included those within government. After Bush became president, and continued to articulate his concern for government ethics and crime, I made him aware of the worsening scandal. I sent him a May 1989 certified letter and attachments describing the criminal acts within the government air safety agencies, the Justice Department, and the federal judiciary. The White House responded by advising me the matter was turned over to the Department of Justice, even though I charged the Justice Department with committing many of the criminal acts. So much for that.

Bush was head of the CIA in 1976 and 1977 while much of the coverup was going on. The dirty tricks of the CIA perpetrated upon foreign citizens and citizens of the United States are no secret. Bush was involved in the CIA drug-protection schemes, while Noriega was on the CIA payroll, and a part of the CIA's dirty tricks. Bush was head of the CIA while CIA involvement was suggested in an earlier chapter (The Imposters). It would be somewhat natural for Bush to continue the coverup after he became president.

After Bush became president he acted to protect the rampant misconduct, while he simultaneously encouraged the public to comply with the law.

Bush was a Naval Aviator in the Pacific during World War II, flying single-engine TBF aircraft. I was also a Naval Aviator in the Pacific, flying four-engine Liberators and Privateers. From this experience Bush surely recognized the consequences of air safety violations even though sophisticated air safety matters were not part of that type of flying.

When Bush became a junior senator from Texas in the United States Senate he led a group of junior senators purportedly pushing for ethics in the Congress. The *National Observer* stated of Bush:

A little-noted event that took place on the floor of the House of Representatives early last week, two days before the House voted to bar Adam Clayton Powell from his seat in the 90th Congress. ... With the House chamber nearly empty, freshman Republicans spent an hour philosophizing about Congressional ethics. The seminar of sorts had been organized by a young congressman from Houston, George Bush, 43, ... The discussion was remarkable in that Mr. Bush had quietly convinced his rookie colleagues of an almost revolutionary proposition. Although freshmen are traditionally expected to sit back unobtrusively while learning from their elders on matters of legislation and procedure, he contended, the question of ethics is another matter entirely.

"True, we lack experience in the House," he told his young colleagues, "but we bring to this problem a fresh look. We feel totally uninhibited by tradition in this sensitive [Congressional ethics] area, because we think we heard the unmistakable clear voice of the people saying on Nov. 8, 'Go there and do something to restore respect for the

House.'" Their proposal is so starry-eyed in its idealism that it looks as if it could have come out of a political-science class on good government. ... Mr. Powell's [denial of his House seat and] fate was decided by an Ivy League Texan and a freshman philosophy class.

Bush seems to have forgotten his idealism, as he joined the scheme that would continue the terrible consequences of cover-up.

This weird scandal took me into uncharted waters. My imaginative use of the law was proper, but bizarre that the conditions existed that made the unorthodox law suits necessary. I filed a law suit against Bush on the basis of his coverup, violating the same laws as were violated by any other government official. The law suit seeking relief was filed in the U.S. District Court, District of Columbia, No. 89-1908. The law suit was filed under authority of federal law,[249] and assigned to Judge Stanley Sporkin.

The preliminary statement in the 69-page First Amended Complaint stated in part:

PRELIMINARY STATEMENT

1. This lawsuit addresses (a) graft, corruption, and conspiracies related to a series of ongoing air tragedies; (b) government and judicial misconduct misusing facilities of the United States government to silence plaintiff's reporting, exposure, and correction of the air disaster, government, and judicial corruption; (c) subversion of our form of government, and of the laws and constitution of the United States of America. It addresses the rampant Ninth Circuit judicial corruption in the bankruptcy and district courts, and the subversive corruption of the federal courts. It addresses the rampant air safety corruption and involvement in dozens of great air tragedies. It addresses corruption in all three branches of government, of unprecedented gravity and consequences.

The complaint was served by certified mail on July 14, 1989, in accordance with federal rules of court. Bush refused to return the acknowledgment of service. I then had to effect personal service, which occurred on October 21, 1989.

---

[249] Title 28 U.S.C. §§ 1331, 1343, 1346(b), 2201, 2202; 18 U.S.C. §§ 1961, 1963; 42 U.S.C. §§ 1983; 1985; 1986; Bivens claim; First, Fifth & Fourteenth Amendments to the U.S. Constitution.

In the meantime, while Bush was avoiding addressing the national scandal, the persecution by the Justice Department, the Chapter 11 judges, the U.S. Trustee, continued. Airline crashes with their roots in the misconduct continued to occur. The federal judges continued their abuse of thousands of Americans, stripping them of their life's assets in the Chapter 11 racketeering activities.

Before Bush answered this complaint, he issued more of his PR. On December 2, 1989, Bush stated to the press that "nothing is more important than freedom." George, I could use a little of that!

Bush never answered my complaint. Judge Sporkin made another *sua sponte* dismissal on January 17, 1990, that violated numerous rules of court, statutory and case law, constitutional due process. What else is new! I then filed a notice of appeal on February 5, 1990.

MORE BAD NEWS

Shortly before Christmas 1989, on December 5, the Ninth Circuit Court of Appeals at San Francisco turned down my appeal of the prison sentence rendered by federal Judge Raul Ramirez. The three judges, Browning, Kozinski, and Rymer, turned down my appeal without addressing a single one of the many defenses that I raised.

I had challenged the judgment sentencing me to prison, on the basis that (a) the judge lacked authority to send me to prison for refusing to commit the crime of coverup; (b) for seeking relief from the civil and constitutional violations inflicted upon me in the sham California action; (c) the right of a whistleblower to expose government crimes; (d) establish the right of a party to exercise rights under the Constitution and laws of the United States; (e) and other issues.

Without addressing the defenses, the appeal decision simply stated (except for routine reference to the filing of the appeal): "The judgment is affirmed."

PETITION FOR CLEMENCY

Seeking to avoid prison, I mailed on December 14, 1989 to President George Bush by certified mail a petition reading: "Petition for Executive Clemency To the President of the United States." It was a five-page petition with approximately 70 pages of exhibits showing my defenses against the sham prison sentence. The petition stated in part:

Petitioner Rodney F. Stich, an air safety activist, and former government air safety investigator, and citizen of the United States, petitions the President of the United States (a) for executive clemency relating to a prison sentence. (U.S. District Court, E.D. Cal. CR 87-124) The sentence was imposed upon petitioner by federal judge Raul Ramirez, as punishment for filing federal actions seeking to halt the continue pattern of air tragedies arising from deeply entrenched air safety corruption in government; and, the imposition of a prison sentence for filing a federal action seeking relief from the government-funded persecution, as the U.S. Department of Justice and federal judges conspired to block petitioner's exposure activities of the air disaster corruption, and related coverup by the Justice Department and federal judges. The prison sentence was imposed by those who petitioner identified with coverup, that made possible the deaths of several thousand people in air tragedies tainted with corruption by the Federal Aviation Administration (FAA) and National Transportation Safety Board (NTSB).

In response to that petition for clemency to the president that reminds us of the need for law and order, of the quality of life in the United States, of the due process that we enjoy that other citizens of other countries do not, my petition was denied on January 23, 1990.

They were closing in on me.

ADDRESSING THE CHAPTER 11 JUDICIAL CORRUPTION

There were other law suits seeking to stop the total loss of my assets. I filed a law suit against the United States Trustee Anthony Sousa, the Director of the trustee program, Anthony Stanton, against the Department of Justice who misused the U.S. Trustee and Chapter 11 program against me, and against the U.S. Government for funding the Chapter 11 corruption. The law suit was filed in the U.S. District Court, District of Columbia on October 27, 1989, No. 89-2974, and was once again assigned to Judge Sporkin.

Some of the allegations raised in the complaint included corruption charged against private trustee Charles Duck. (Duck had been charged earlier with embezzlement by the Department of Justice, who charged him with the two minor counts even though he committed the country's worst Chapter 11 embezzlement.)

I sought relief from Duck's criminal acts, the missing funds, and the destruction of my assets. Each law suit sought relief from those judges who had protected the judicial misconduct for years. Judge Sporkin protected Duck and the others by unlawfully dismissing my law suit on January 17, 1990. Sporkin was aiding and abetting the conspiracy while simultaneously violating the laws he was paid to protect.

The news services and major newspapers continued to cover up for the widening scandal. In this manner they were covering up for their own part in the escalating crimes against me and against our country and its citizens.

While these law suits were filed and fought, the air tragedies continued to occur. The press, Congress, others, refused to look behind the scenes at the causes of these tragedies. To do so would blow the lid on the western world's worst air disaster, government, and judicial scandal.

SUING UNITED AIRLINES

I filed a federal law suit against United Airlines and the Federal Aviation Administration (U.S. District Court, Reno, No. 88-554), charging them with taking part in the conspiracy. On procedural matters the federal judges dismissed the action, despite the grave allegations in the complaint which under law must be accepted as true at that stage of the proceedings. The complaint served to inform the judge of criminal acts associated with over 1,000 deaths in United Airline crashes, invoking mandatory responsibility under criminal statutes for the federal judge to insure that the charges are investigated. Instead, he covered up.

CLOSING IN FOR THE FINAL KILL

In early 1990 these adversaries were closing in for the kill. The California Court of Appeals and Supreme Court refused to provide any relief from the unlawful orders rendered. Every level of the federal judiciary, up to and including the Justices of the U.S. Supreme Court, protected Duck and the others who lawlessly seized my assets, and protected the expanding air disaster scandal. The Supreme Court refused to halt the incarceration for exposing the government misconduct. My assets were just about gone. My age was working against me. My coronary heart surgery was limiting my ability to continue the fight. The press solidified its news blackout.

SEARCH FOR HELP, ALL IN VAIN

All my fighting seems to have been in vain. The initial persecution commenced to halt my government air safety activities. Their pressure forced me to leave government service. Then, when I made a new life for myself, and used my assets to strive to bring about corrective actions for the ongoing air disaster slaughter, the power of the United States government, wielded by the attorneys in the Justice Department and federal judges, finished me off. The eight years of steady persecution was unrivaled in any western government operating under a system of laws and Constitution. Abscam, HUD, savings and loan, and other scandals, would probably never have happened if the mid-1960 coverup had instead, exposed the government corruption.

Wing-damage resulting from midair collision.

United's DC-10 crash at Sioux City caused by elimination of
hard backup for flight controls.

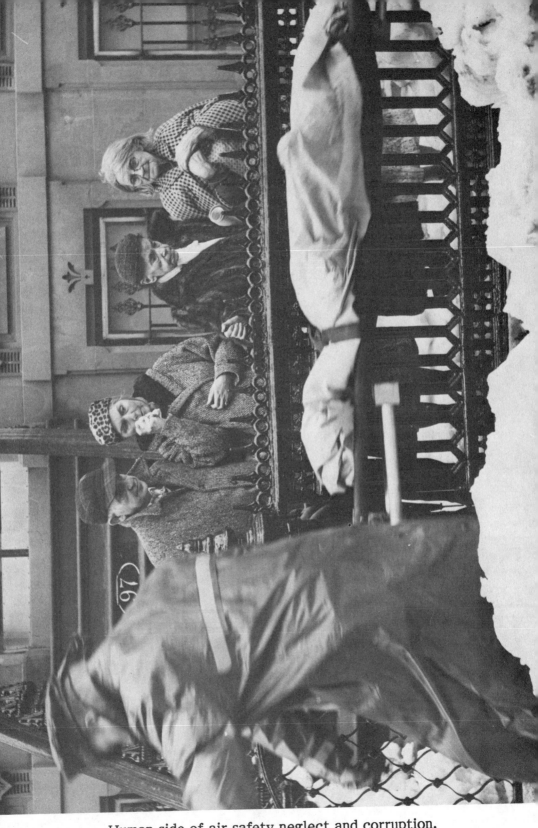

Human side of air safety neglect and corruption.

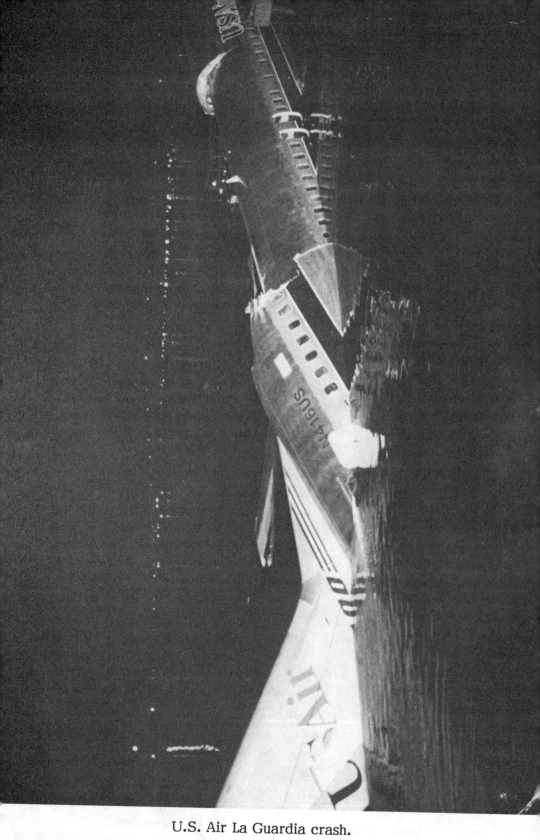

U.S. Air La Guardia crash.

CHAPTER THIRTY

GRIM OUTLOOK

MEASURING AIR SAFETY

When the many safety problems are examined, the future of air safety looks bad. This scenario doesn't arise from looking at statistics that measure the number of deaths, but rather, from recognition of the rampant safety problems and the corruption of the two government air safety agencies.

The amazing part is that hundreds of near-tragedies avoid becoming actual tragedies by the slimmest of margins. Air safety is in far worst condition than fatality figures suggest. Statistics are misleading. They measure the number of deaths under various conditions. Fatality statistics do not necessarily measure the status of air safety or the number of uncorrected safety problems. They often provide favorable figures when many near-crashes or actual crashes result in few fatalities. When a plane crashes and everyone miraculously survives, or hits power lines and narrowly averts crashing, the statistics show these flights as safe. Those who survived the United 747 cargo door opening over Hawaii, or who survived the United DC-10 tragedy at Sioux City, show up on accident statistics to support safety-of-flight arguments; they weren't killed. Even the brain-dead survivor of the Delta 1011 crash at Dallas supports the safety-of-flight statistics. Obviously, the figures are misleading.

Further, how can be argue that air safety is in good shape, when hundreds of people perish from air safety problems that knowingly existed.

MANY OF THE CRASHES DESCRIBED WITHIN THESE PAGES ARE NO ACCIDENT

The definition of an accident is an occurrence by chance or not expected. It is an occurrence that could not have been foreseen by the exercise of reasonable prudence. It is an occurrence which happens unexpectedly from the uncontrollable operations of nature alone, and without human participation. Very few of the crashes described within these pages were unanticipated. Some were the end result of hard-core misconduct that caused or permitted to occur design problems, training related problems, maintenance problems, or operational problems.

The crashes that have occurred, and many that have yet to occur, are symbols of the air safety problems within the United States. The public is unaware of the part that misconduct plays in some of the most brutal air disasters. The savings and loan, HUD, FDA, Defense Department, Abscam, and other scandals are duplicated in the government air safety agencies. In both, the public is used as a literal feed-trough. In one form of scandal the public pay with indebtedness and corrupt government. In the air safety scandal, the public pays with unnecessary dangers and with their lives.

If this book had been written as fiction, many would not have believed it. Horrendous as the scandals are, there are far more duplicity and intrigue behind the scenes than what has already been exposed.

PROPHETIC FORECASTS

During the FAA safety grievance hearing I described the corruption and deaths that had already happened, and warned what would happen. And these warnings were prophetic statements of what was obvious. In the first printing of the *Unfriendly Skies*, in 1978, I made comments in the last chapter that time has proven correct. A few of the comments follows:

The scandal is now so serious, and involves so many, that correction can only come from outside of government. That means you, the unorganized citizen, must step in, and this is highly unlikely. No one within government can risk taking corrective actions involving any of the participants as any one of the many who are involved could threaten to blow the whistle on everyone else. It is virtually impossible to have the provisions of law respond in a situation of this magnitude. The Executive Branch of government is going to cover up so as to protect itself from very serious criminal charges. The Congress is going to cover up to protect its criminal participation in all this. And the Judicial Branch——

acting piously above the law——is going to go to any length to protect its own involvement in this protective scheme.

The most common bond linking so many together in this government and air safety scandal is the legal fraternity. No other force in our society today can so adversely affect our lives, can block our constitutional and statutory safeguards. They are the ones who can openly prostitute the laws, knowing that they interpret the law, prosecute or not prosecute for such violations, and in their capacities as judges, punish or not punish for such violations. The lawyers control the courts; they control and man the Department of Justice investigative and prosecuting functions. Attorneys occupy more Congressional seats than any other profession, and Congress controls the selection of federal judges from the legal fraternity.

These pages reveal a virtual "government Mafia" in which a massive conspiracy exists to protect the perpetrators of a vicious air safety hoax that considers lives expendable. It seeks to protect the perpetrators and those in all three branches of government guilty of criminal coverup. Arrogant bureaucrats who should be in prison are protected at a cost in human life, potentially yours.

Watergate was child's play——involving a foolish coverup of two-bit bugging, common political skullduggery. High government officials including the United States Attorney General received prison sentences for a relatively minor coverup. They were prosecuted by the Department of Justice and Congress, and sentenced to prison by the federal courts. Many of these same individuals who appeared so pious and respectful of the law in judging and prosecuting the watergate defendants actively participated in a criminal coverup that would knowingly cause great loss of life.

The consequences of the Watergate coverup were minor. The consequences of this air safety coverup were and still are horrendous. The scandal described with these pages exists at this very moment. The Paris DC-10 crash was an especially horrible consequence of long-standing FAA misconduct, but there will be more of the same as government corruption adversely affects air safety.

The FAA's coverup of this safety problem goes to the heart of the fact that it is presently unfit to manage the nation's air safety activities. The question of wilful misconduct as it pertains to crashes resulting from this coverup also enters the picture. Some personnel in key positions should be charged with criminal activities that led to the deaths of innocent air travelers. But this won't happen.

Respected business men are prosecuted by the Justice Department and have had their personal and business lives ruined, ending up in prison, for often unintentional violations of some obscure law, such as price fixing, when they did not even know such an act was occurring. Yet, the Justice Department engages in this criminal coverup knowing that death is a resulting byproduct, showing its contempt for the lives of our citizens.

****

Its been twelve years since those comments were made. What has happened since then? Those who engaged in the corruption, either directly or in the criminal duplicity of silence, are on a roll. The corruption continues. The FAA and NTSB conduct continues as before. The NTSB continues to falsify official crash reports, partly to protect themselves. The Justice Department attorneys continue their coverup and persecution to protect their earlier misconduct and keep the prior lines of conduct going. The news media continues their coverup. Senators and Representatives continue their duplicitous coverup.

The gravity of the charges and exposures in the 1978 book was articulated by numerous book reviewers. A few samples: *American Library Association Booklist* stated, "Unfriendly Skies is a record of scandal, disaster, and heartbreak that demands an accounting from the highest levels of the industry and government." *Professional Pilot* magazine wrote, "May make Watergate look like kid stuff." *Manchester Guardian* publisher Ed Loeb wrote, "A fine book." *Bookviews* stated, "He charges a cover-up of such proportions even the mass media don't want to touch the story, and I must say, makes a good case." *Book Review*'s Jan Frazer said, "In this shocking book, Rodney Stich presents impressive evidence to show that a virtual government Mafia does indeed exist. Larry Rumley of *Seattle Times Magazine* wrote, "The Unfriendly Skies is a shocking report ... the facts he cites are devastating, indicating dereliction of duty and responsibility by airlines and the federal authority supposedly checking on them."

Many members of the U.S. Senate and House admitted the gravity of the allegations. Federal judges admitted the gravity of the charges. They then engaged in coverup, knowingly sacrificing the lives that continued to be lost.

Everything stated in the 1978 *Unfriendly Skies* has worsened. Nothing has changed for the better, and everything stated then, applies now. The public—crewmembers and passengers alike—have paid the price for this corruption that riddles our government and our institutions, especially those with legal fraternity involvement.

FURTHER SUPPORT FOR THE CHARGES

The truthfulness of what is stated in these pages is supported by hard facts, evidence in government records, letters, resulting crashes, and what I personally uncovered:

1. The government air safety reports and testimony introduced into the FAA air safety grievance hearing at Denver, and the FAA's coverup reaction to that evidence.

2. The NTSB repeated coverups of the misconduct for the last two decades and longer, which is shown by letters and legal briefs. Their repeated coverups are obvious and documented in letters and court filings. There is no possible excuse for failure to investigate, unless they were already a part of the coverup misconduct.

3. Admission by numerous members of the United States Senate and House of the seriousness of my charges.

4. Admission by Assistant U.S. Attorney George Stoll at San Francisco, who admitted the gravity of the charges in the law suit against the NTSB, and his recommendations to Washington superiors to support my federal action.

5. Admissions by federal judges Schnacke and the three judges of the Ninth Circuit Court of Appeals (Anthony Kennedy, Choy, Ferguson), shown in the judicial records of the 1974 law suit against the FAA, admitting the gravity of my charges.

6. Admissions by federal judges Wiegel and the three judges of the Ninth Circuit Court of Appeals (Browning, Sneed, Schroeder), shown in the judicial records of the 1980 law suit against the NTSB, admitting the gravity of my charges.

7. Admission by federal judge Milton Schwartz in a 1986 law suit describing the wrongful acts, that they were serious. (No. 86-210 MLS.)

8. Admission of knowledge of the charges, admission of their truthfulness, by defendants in federal actions. (Senators Kennedy, Cranston, Biden, Thurmond, Hollings, Gore, Wilson; and Representatives Gonzalez, Conyers, Rodino, Staggers); the news media; the Supreme Court justices; President Bush. All admitted knowledge of my charges; None denied their truthfulness. They simply held that they were immune from the consequences of their (coverup and) refusal to act.

9. The proof in the numerous air tragedies, some directly identifiable with specific misconduct, and some impliedly related.

10. My vast aviation experience lending credibility to the specific charges.

11. Opportunity to know of the problems raised in these pages. As a government air safety investigator, assigned to the at-that-time most crash-plagued airline, and within the FAA

section where corruption was rampant, gave me the opportunity to discover the wrongdoings stated in these pages.

12. Pattern of obstruction to the exposure by the Department of Justice, the FBI, Congress, making possible some of the most brutal forms of death inflicted upon thousands.

13. Absence of denial of my allegations. No one denied the truthfulness of my allegations. No one could; I had the hard-evidence.

OPPORTUNITY TO DENY THE ALLEGATIONS

Many people had the opportunity to deny these allegations. I requested United Airlines several times by letter (1978 through 1981) to respond to my charges. They refused to do so. Sacramento television station KMUV wrote to United, and asked them to respond and appear on a show with me. Writing for United Airlines President Dick Ferris, public relations director Marden Leaver refused to answer the specific questions. His January 22, 1979 answer simply stated that the book contained many errors, without identifying what they were.

Pacific Southwest Airlines (PSA) was asked to comment on the charges relating to the all-night crew partying related to the San Diego disaster. PSA refused to respond to the allegations.

Editor Norman Pearlstein of the *Wall Street Journal* refused to respond to my letter of February 22, 1988 accusing the *Journal* of covering up for the misconduct. In the law suit against the newspaper they admitted knowing of my charges; they did not deny their truthfulness. They simply argued that irregardless of the consequences of their acts they were immune under the First Amendment to the Constitution. Of course, coverup for a crime is not protected by any constitutional amendment.

WHY THE COVERUP?

The internal FAA coverup was to protect its own, and causing a breakdown in the internal checks and balances. At this late stage the only concern is to continue the coverup, so as to prevent exposing what has become a far worse scandal of corruption.

The reason for the *initial* NTSB coverup can only be speculated. Either the Department of Justice instructed the NTSB to cover up; the internal politics caused it to cover up as a normal reaction; or pressure from the White House did it. *After* the NTSB covered up initially, making the subsequent crashes possible, the NTSB had to continue coverup, which it must do to this day. For that reason the NTSB can never function as intended by law. It can't blow the whistle on FAA misconduct, except very guardedly on relatively minor oversights. It can't blow the whistle on itself.

The Justice Department attorneys covered up as an in- grained habit. Extending the dismal level of ethics in the legal fraternity to the Justice Department, it is easy to understand that the Justice Department protected the FAA at the expense of human life when I first brought the corruption to their atten- tion. Then, after the series of air tragedies made possible by the criminal coverup, the Justice Department attorneys had another reason to continued the cover up, regardless of the price paid by others.

The news media must continue the coverup because of its involvement in the scandal.

WHO PAYS FOR THIS, AND HOW?

Most of the 1,000 or more people who perished in United Airline crashes probably would not have perished if the known causes of the crashes had been acted upon instead of becoming the subject of criminal activities. Certainly the 346 deaths in the Paris DC-10 crash, the 520 in the Japan Airlines 747 crash, the 112 in the United Sioux City crash, would not have occur- red, if the FAA Western Region officials had not eliminated the design safeguards.

SHOULD THE GUILTY GO FREE?

Should the guilty parties that engaged in the earlier miscon- duct go scot free because criminal coverup by the Department of Justice kept their wrongful acts from being prosecuted? Some talk show hosts have implied this should occur as some of the misconduct occurred some years ago. But the conspiracy and misconduct continues, and under law, the original conspira- tors are as guilty as those who later join or expanded the con- spiracy.

Those within the FAA and NTSB, the Department of Justice, who committed the wrongful acts should be prosecuted. Federal judges and members of the U.S. Senate and House should be prosecuted and impeached. Those who have retired should be prosecuted and their retirement pay should be terminated. Those who are attorneys should be disbarred.

CONSIDERABLE GOVERNMENT CORRUPTION COULD HAVE BEEN PREVENTED IF MORAL AND LEGAL RESPONSIBILITIES HAD BEEN MET IN THE MID-1960S

Would there have been the nation's worst financial debacle, the savings and loan corruption, HUD, Abscam, if those who had a responsibility to act in the mid-1960s when I brought govern- ment corruption to their attention had acted to expose it? Would there be the 346 deaths in the Paris DC-10 crash; the 520 deaths in the Japan Airlines 747 crash; the 112 deaths in the Sioux City DC-10 crash; and the many others, and those yet to occur, if the news media, members of Congress, others, had not engaged in a coverup that aided and abetted the crimes? Of course not. And exposure of this misconduct would have probably stopped many of the other major scandals that followed, and continues to this date.

Corruption leads to more corruption, and it would be difficult to find a more classic example than within these pages. Duplicitous coverup within the FAA, and then the NTSB, led to more and more coverup. Federal judges then had to cover up. Then, they had to misuse the judicial branch to attack a single citizen, trying to silence him. All that they accomplished was a worsening of the government scandal.

PEOPLE HAVE SAID IT IS IMPOSSIBLE TO AROUSE THE AMERICAN PUBLIC TO GOVERNMENT CORRUPTION

Many people stated to me that my exposure activities will never correct the rampant problems. They say the public is too apathetic, too indolent, too engrossed in their ball-game sports trivia, to take the actions necessary to correct these problems. They say the American public resembles ducks, capable only of following what the news media dangles before them. When the issues are no longer raised in the press, the public forgets them. The important thing in their lives are the opiate qualities of sports, with no concern for important issues, it has been said.

People can die, can be swindled of their life's assets, the nation's greatest financial debacle inflicted upon them, and the public won't respond. The cries of pain from the dying in air tragedies, the cries of those left behind, are ignored by the public. Those impoverished in the Chapter 11 judicial racketeering activities are ignored.

Those who say the public will never respond may be right. At the start of the 1990s, I had been on over 1500 radio and television appearances, describing the corruption and price paid by people who were no match for the thugs described herein. Callers expressed concern, and then did nothing. Either the public can't understand, or they don't care.

We are lulled into thinking that the laws and Constitution are protectors of human rights. The liberty and justice babble is fed to the public. We think justice is working when several federal judges are charged with crimes and impeached. Their transgressions are often far less than other judges that are promoted in the federal judiciary, with the help of the Justice Department.

This saga of corruption is ongoing, and the crashes, the deaths, the government abuses, will be the same or worse next year. Additional books can be written about it, if there is anyone around to write it. The government intrigue and corruption described within these pages is only the tip of the iceberg, and the full story is undoubtedly far more brutal.

The manner in which you and the public reacts to these exposures will determine the fate of many people. The public has it within their power to destroy the cancerous government corruption described within these pages, and which have destructive influences throughout our society. Remember, what happened to the people shown in these pages, and what has yet to happen to others, could happen to you, or your loved ones.

WHAT CAN THE READER AND THE PUBLIC DO?

Here are steps you can take to help:

1. Send certified letters to each of your U.S. Senators and Representatives. Demand that they immediately request the Department of Justice and the U.S. Court of Appeals in the District of Columbia to appoint several special prosecutors, to investigate the charges; that they convene a Congressional investigation, open to the public, and include representatives of those who perished in some of the related air tragedies; that they request of the Government Accounting Office (GAO) an investigation into my allegations; that they request the inspector generals of the Department of Justice and the Department of Transportation to conduct an investigation into the misconduct in their departments; that an investigative body of reliable investigators investigate judicial misconduct, and exclude attorneys to assure a degree of honesty. Expect to be stonewalled, and don't let them do that to you. Keep the pressure on.

2. Demand of your Senators copies of the two petitions that I sent to them by certified mail in 1988, and request an honest response as to why they failed to make an open investigation. Again, expect a deceptive answer, and act accordingly.

3. If you had a prior claim against an airline or the government as a result of an airline crash, try to find an attorney who will file a claim, or reopen the prior law suit, on the basis of the government fraud, which tolls the running of the statute of limitations. Even if settlement of prior law suits occurred, fraud permits reopening of the case, or filing actions against parties who were not formerly shown as defendants. The legal and judicial brotherhood have blocked every attempt to expose this scandal; finding legal representation will be difficult. This would change if publicity is given to the scandals.

4. Demand that the Attorney General of the United States appoint several special prosecutors (independent counsel) to investigate all aspects of this scandal, including the matters stated in these pages, and in my various federal law suits. Since the Attorney General is deeply implicated in this scandal, along with the Department of Justice and the Federal Bureau of Investigation, this will be difficult, unless forced by members of the U.S. Senate and House.

5. Demand that the Inspector General of the Department of Justice conduct an investigation of the Justice Department misconduct described within these pages, and that he issue a detailed report addressing each matter described in these pages and in the various law suits that I filed in federal court.

6. Demand that the Inspector General of the Department of Transportation conduct an investigation into the FAA and NTSB misconduct alleged within these pages, and issue a report addressing each alleged wrongdoing within these pages and in the federal law suits that I filed..

6. Make repeated phone calls to your radio talk shows and keep the subject alive. Ask them to have me appear as a guest to describe the details of this scandal. A series of appearances could be scheduled to get into the many facets of this multi-faceted scandal.

7. File complaints with the Chairman of the National Transportation Safety Board in Washington, demanding that he investigate the allegations made in these pages and various law suits, and to reopen the airline crashes affected by my allegations. The Federal Aviation Act provides for the public to file a complaint with the FAA and the NTSB, demanding that an investigation be made of any violation of federal air safety laws. Such complaint could be made by anyone reading this book, or having knowledge of FAA wrongdoings. Direct your complaint to the chairman of the NTSB and to the FAA Administrator, with copies to your local talk-show host and newspapers.

8. If the NTSB refuses to do so, file a mandamus action under Title 28 United States Code Section 1361 against the NTSB, forcing them to reopen the accident investigations.

9. Write to the federal and state grand juries where any of the misconduct occurred, demanding a criminal investigation into the wrongdoings. This investigation would be of federal judges, California judges, U.S. Attorneys, and others. Remember that anyone who aids a conspiracy becomes a part of it, and has the legal and moral liabilities of every other person in the conspiracy, whether that person knows of the full details of the misconduct or not. The State of California, arguably, is liable for those deaths occurring after its judges and officials became a part of the conspiracy to silence my exposure of the air disaster misconduct. Their actions have blocked exposure and corrective actions since the 1982 sham law suit was filed against me, and every protection in law was openly violated, in a state judicial pattern.

10. Don't reelect the same Senators and Representatives. Every Senator in the United States knew of this scandal and engaged in one form or another of coverup.

11. Request your Senators and Representatives to pass a statute providing for personal financial liability of federal and state judges when they knowingly violate statutory law, clear and settled case law, or clear constitutional rights and protections, and cause a person to suffer financial or personal harms. Further, that the respective federal and state governments be held financially liable for the harms committed by those judges (and others acting on their behalf) who act under color of state or federal laws.

POWERFUL PEOPLE ARE AT RISK

Many powerful figures in government, the integrity of many government and non-government institutions, will fall, if these scandals are vigorously pursued by the public. Those include the two government air safety agencies, the FAA and NTSB; the Department of Justice, including its head, the U.S. Attorney General, and the FBI; other government agencies such as the GAO; members of the U.S. Senate and House; many federal judges in the Ninth Circuit at San Francisco and the District of Columbia, and the Justices of the U.S. Supreme Court; the legal fraternity.

Impeachment, criminal prosecution, removal from office, prison, should be the fate of those directly and indirectly involved in the air disaster, government, and judicial scandal.

DON'T TAKE IT ANYMORE

Hopefully, there will be more people like those in the fictional story, Network, who wouldn't take it any longer. Almost any member of the public who is sufficiently persistent can help break this pattern of corruption and scandal. The public has been taken, and played for fools, long enough.

Its now up to you and others like you. You can either exercise some initiative, or sit back and watch the consequences. Everyone who remains silent helps continue these outrages, and are a contributing cause to subsequent air tragedies and other outrages inflicted upon the public. Since my warnings in 1963, many have died. Since I went public in 1978 with the first printing of the Unfriendly Skies, many more have died from the effects of the corruption. In the coming years many more will die. Many more will be swindled in the federal judicial scandal in Chapter 11 proceedings. Many will be swindled in other government-funded scandals as in the savings and loan scandal. None of these great harms and great scandals could have occurred without the coverup by the press, the great numbers of checks and balances, or the indifference of the public.

What you and many others do, or don't do, will affect the lives of many people.